THE ORIGINS OF WESTERN LAW
from Athens to the Code Napoleon

THE ORIGINS OF WESTERN LAW
from Athens to the Code Napoleon

Volume **II**

JOHN E. ECKLUND

CONSTANCE CRYER ECKLUND
Editor

TALBOT
PUBLISHING
Clark, New Jersey

ISBN 978-1-61619-371-3 Set
ISBN 978-1-61619-372-0 Vol. I
ISBN 978-1-61619-373-7 Vol. II

Copyright © 2014 Constance Cryer Ecklund

TALBOT PUBLISHING
AN IMPRINT OF
THE LAWBOOK EXCHANGE, LTD.
33 Terminal Avenue
Clark, New Jersey 07066-1321

*Please see our website for a selection of our other publications
and fine facsimile reprints of classic works of legal history:*
www.lawbookexchange.com

Library of Congress Cataloging-in-Publication Data

Ecklund, John E., 1916-2000, author.
 The origins of western law from Athens to the Code Napoleon / by John E. Ecklund, Treasurer,
Yale University ; Constance Cryer Ecklund, editor. --
Lawbook Exchange ed.
     pages cm
 Includes bibliographical references and index.
 ISBN 978-1-61619-371-3 (hardcover : alk. paper) -- ISBN 1-61619-371-9 (hardcover : alk. paper)
 1. Law--Europe--History. 2. Law, Ancient. 3. Law, Medieval. I. Ecklund, Constance Cryer, editor. II. Title.
 KJ147.E25 2013
 340.5'3--dc23
                                                                                    2013034551

Printed in the United States of America on acid-free paper

Contents

Volume II

Part 11
Humanistic Study of Roman Law in a Time of Scientific Expansion
Petrarch, His Successors, Montaigne — 503

- Western Europe in the Modern Age to the *Code Napoleon* — 504
  - Humanism — 504
    - Petrarch — 504
    - After Petrarch — 515
    - Montaigne and the Revival of Skepticism — 542

Part 12
Reformation and Counter Reformation
Individual Conscience and the Response of Church and Crown — 571

- Reformation — 572
  - Introduction — 572
  - The Condition of the Church — 575
  - Reformation; Erasmus — 575
  - Luther — 577
  - Calvin — 583
  - The Catholic Reformation — 591
  - Effects of the Reformation on Canon Law and the Universities — 605

Part 13
The New Hinge Period
Geographical Expansion, Capitalism, Scientific Revolution — 611

- Rise of the Merchants and Middle Class; The New World; Capitalism — 612
- The Seventeenth Century and the Scientific Revolution — 620
  - Introduction — 620
  - Copernicus — 623
  - Stevinus — 628
  - Galileo; Kepler — 629
  - Newton — 634

Part 14
The Seventeenth Century's Encounter with Natural Law
Grotius, Descartes, Hobbes, Pufendorf — 641

    The Mood of the Seventeenth Century — 642
    Secular Natural Law
        The First Period — 643
      Grotius — 643
      Descartes — 663
      Hobbes — 673
      Pufendorf — 685

Part 15
The Expansion of Secular Natural Law in the Seventeenth and Eighteenth Centuries
Louis XIV and Pascal — 715

    The Progress of Secular Natural Law — 716
      Overview — 716
      Louis XIV: *Legislator and Legal Educator* — 717
      Life of Domat — 743

Part 16
The Second Period of Secular Natural Law
Daguesseau and Pothier — 765

    The Progress of Secular Natural Law — 766
      Henri-François Daguesseau — 766
      Pothier — 813

Part 17
Montesquieu
The Sociological Case for Governance by Secular Natural Law — 839

    Montesquieu — 840
      Introduction — 840
      Early Life — 841
      Les lettres persanes — 845
      Travels, 1721–1731 — 847
      The History of the Romans — 850
      De l'Esprit des lois — 852
      Death of Montesquieu — 873

PART 18
Beliefs and Institutions in Enlightenment, Revolution, and Empire — 877

- The Enlightenment — 878
  - Introduction — 878
  - The *Philosophes* — 881
  - The Physiocrats — 888
  - The *Avocats* — 892
  - The Universities — 897
  - Revolution — 900

PART 19
The Nineteenth Century Intersection of Re-emergence *Antiquity, Empire, and Advocacy* — 925

- Portalis and the *Code Napoleon* — 926
  - Introduction — 926
  - Young Portalis — 930
  - Portalis at the Bar — 932
  - Portalis in the Revolution and Its Aftermath — 936
  - The Philosophy of Portalis — 939
  - The *Concordat* of 1801 Between France and the Pope — 944
  - Portalis and the Code Napoleon — 951

Bibliography — 975
Index — 995

The Origins of Western Law from Athens to the Code Napoleon

Volume II

Petrarch
Courtesy of Yale University Art Gallery, Everett V. Meeks, B.A. 1901, Fund

PART 11

Humanistic Study of Roman Law in a Time of Scientific Expansion
Petrarch, His Successors, Montaigne

WESTERN EUROPE IN THE MODERN AGE TO THE *CODE NAPOLEON*

Humanism

Petrarch

Introduction

In any historic pattern, beginnings and endings have blurred borders. This means the decision to leave the Middle Ages with Ockham will not please everyone any more than the decision to begin our medieval chronicle with the end of Roman government. But the chronological smudge is inescapable. Augustine, who was long pervasive in later neoclassical thinking, was a Roman; and scholasticism as the academic method of the medieval universities continued long after Ockham died in 1347. When professors in northern Europe met the Humanism of Italy in the 1490s, their universities were still bogged down in scholasticism; encountering the *via moderna*, these scholars capitalized on the new, secular window on the world, the better to gain back enrollments dwindling with the old, lagging religious studies. Nevertheless, the controversy between Realism and Nominalism, so pervasive in the fourteenth century, would continue fiercely in the German universities from 1470 to 1520; it is said that on Ockham's English home turf, Oxford and Cambridge remained scholastic preserves until the Reformation.

Perhaps less contention will greet history's new chapter. *Petrarch: The First Modern Scholar and Man of Letters*, Robinson entitles his book, well aware that the man whose work marked the new era was in his dates of 1304–1374 a contemporary of both Ockham and Bartolus. Bergin, the distinguished Petrarch biographer, wrote (Bergin, *Petrarch, Twayne's World Authors Series,* 17) that even if all centuries are in some respects transitional, some are more so than others, and the term "transitional" applies to the fourteenth century "more than to any other." We should be wary of the term, understanding that far from a rapid change in tone, it is better defined as a lengthy series of modulations to a new key. This occurred in part because the second half of the century brought through war and plague such acute political, economic, and social decline that the innovative departures in thought sponsored by Bartolus, Ockham, and now Petrarch were slowed in their spread. The movement of Petrarch was probably the most held back; it did effect a penetration into Italian universities in the 1350s, but professors there appeared less than eager to encourage it. Traveling forth in search of more fruitful soil for his work, Petrarch found the same bleak scene elsewhere. The Paris of 1361 presented itself in fire and ruin, with many of its splendors reduced to ashes after English depredations of the Hundred Years' War. There were neither crowds of students nor a pulsing academic life. Even Oxford could show off not much more than a lethargic indolence. Two centuries seem a long time, but Petrarch would have to wait that long until his challenge to the human intellect that it walk through the rich heritage of antiquity, fostered a new way to study law. When that opening did occur, it led to triumph in the brilliant French juristic work of the sixteenth century.

Petrarch's delayed but dazzling achievement is again a fine case in point for those chroniclers who see history as largely influenced by the surprise appearance of extraordinary minds. One can argue, although with misgivings as one contemplates the energy and genius of the man and his amazing output in a short life, that if Bartolus had not done what he did when he did it, someone else would have. The reason is actually quite simple: the continent could not continue any longer the deification of Roman law for its current use without a more comprehensive interpretation to fit actual, contemporary facts. Likewise, one can argue, although again with similar misgivings, that the condemnations of Bishop Tempier in 1277 made it likely that someone would find a way to reject Aquinas's Realist road to truth and to present, instead, a Nominalism like that of Ockham—congenial to scientific study and yet protected against the disapproval of orthodoxy by a fierce affirmation of the sovereignty of God and revelation. But with Petrarch, no obvious external rationale presents a good case. Lawyers since around 1080 had been pouring over classical literature of the law as preserved by Justinian, all the time in acute need of an historical perspective which would enable them to see the anachronisms they were perpetrating. Roman historical development having been laid aside in favor of an eternally valid system of law, it was time to reassert roots and update historic vision, by again studying the language and institutions of the source. Coming out of nowhere, as it were, to play this long overdue role of literary detective, Petrarch unerringly made his mark by doing what no one else before seemed able to conceive *or* achieve: an historic sweep of over two hundred years of literary reportage.

Humanism has long been referred to as the revival of learning—hardly a credit to a legal profession which had already resuscitated it in the eleventh century. The fact that lawyers lost the revival attribution can be blamed on no one but themselves, for they not only failed to broaden their intellectual base into the 1300s but then showed themselves unable to expand upon Petrarch's revelations in any significant way until into the 1500s. The fact that there were some Paduan lawyers who before Petrarch contributed to classical resurrection in the making of their *florilegia*—the elegantly bound collectives of ancient anecdotes and wisdom—was not, for a critic like Gilmore (Gilmore, 63), enough to overcome both their general diffidence and their refusal of fame. Even Bergin makes no mention of law, as he proposes (Bergin, 182) it was due almost solely to Petrarch's inspiration that his contemporaries and successors read the classics with a new illumination. History's markers thus remain Justinian's *Digest* at the end of the eleventh century, the rediscovered Aristotle of the twelfth and thirteenth centuries, and now Humanism. This third thrust by the ancient world would be the last great one upon the minds of posterity. A landmark moment in time which shifted the course of thought in the intellectual world, *studia humanitas* with its emphasis on literature, languages, and history, left aside the total scholastic absorption in philosophy, theology, and science. Conceptually founded by Ockham, now released by Petrarch's ideated, modern form, this historic overview of the past in order to renew the present, left Petrarch the first who could look back at the medieval as being "Dark Ages" and, in his understanding he could do better, go from reverence to the pejorative epithet of "Gothic."

Life of Petrarch

With Petrarch our usual quixotic quest for elusive biographical detail ends. He was a man at pains to leave us scrupulously written autobiographical information, particularly in his *Letters to Posterity*, the title of which alone shows us that we have here no true son of the Middle Ages. Baptized Francesco, he tells us he was always called Checco and carefully paints the portrait from the dramatic birth at dawn on Monday 20 July 1304 in Arezzo. The town lay in fairly close proximity to the Florentine farm from which his father, Petracco dell'Incisa, a notary and a Guelph of the papal party, had been expelled along with his friend Dante. The father had a penchant for Cicero and not a little vanity for himself. Finding a grey hair on his head when a little past fifty, he filled his house with lamentations so loud that they roused the neighborhood (J.H. Robinson *Petrarch, the First Modern Scholar and Man of Letters,* 77). In search of legal business, the father and family were at Pisa in 1311, at Avignon about 1312 where the pope lived in his "Babylonian Captivity," and for four years in Carpentras. It was in this small Provençal town where little Checco went to school and, it is told, (Bergin, 37), at once "found delight in his studies." As he became as well rounded as the fruits for which the town is famous, he developed a fondness for Latin so intense that his schoolmaster, Convenevale, averred that he had before him his best pupil in sixty years. The father was evidently content enough to remain in his French surroundings and in 1316 sent Francesco, then twelve, to Montpellier for studies in civil law. The boy remained there four years. From 1321 to 1326 his legal courses were taken at Bologna—disrupted for over a year when the whole university went into exile at Imola to protest the punishment of student leaders in a riot, and with another break of nearly a year when Petrarch remained at Avignon. Like so many artistic and literary people before and since, it would seem the youth did not feel any grief at these interruptions in his legal work. When in April 1326 news of his father's death reached him, he at once abandoned the law, never to return.

Petrarch was surely one of the profession's most famous "drop-outs." His ultimate influence on law was no doubt much greater for having left it than it would have been had he stayed in the field—even, one supposes, if he had attempted once in advocacy to push legal study toward a Humanist approach. Possessing attitudes toward the law which were at heart unflattering, as a cynical lawyer he never would have attracted the audience he did achieve as a fervent classical scholar and as a lyric poet of the vernacular. In his fame it was this audience for his literature that made the difference. His own account of his legal study and the decision to quit it is candid and as revealing of a rebellious young person as it is of a profession in need of repair:

I heard the whole body of the civil law, and would, as many thought, have distinguished myself later, had I but continued my studies. I gave up the subject altogether, however, so soon as it was no longer necessary to consult the wishes of my parents. My reason was that, although the dignity of the law, which is doubtless very great, and especially the numerous references it contains to Roman antiquity, did not fail to delight me, I felt it to be habitually degraded by those who practice it. It went against me painfully to acquire an art which I would not practice dishonestly, and could hardly hope to exercise otherwise. Had I made the latter attempt, my scrupulousness would doubtless have been ascribed to simplicity. (J. H. Robinson, 66).

A lawyer is likely to see this reasoning, as well as Petrarch's later assertion that he preferred solitude, as fairly flimsy. Surely there was room even amidst the growing pains of the late medieval legal profession for a man of integrity; and a loner with no zest for advocacy could, had he the inclination and the ability, have tried to become, like Bartolus, an academic jurist whose university appointment brought good income and a respected ivory tower status. Petrarch, however, scorned academicians, too, saying that the motives of scholastic philosophers were as venal as those of law professors; this position frankly rings as hollow as his reason for the scholastic attempts to understand the world with logical rigor. The crankiness went so far as the writing of an ode to Rome without a single mention of her jurists. Reluctant or incapable of seeing law as Rome's greatest bequest, Petrarch's whole later life is evidence of a distaste for the precision of detail and the exhaustive search for facts that the legal profession demands. His happiness at Montpellier probably rested more on those non-legal studies thought to have been added to the curriculum in order to retain the interest of the restless young students; looking back in acerbic old age, he would dismiss these university years as "'not so much spent as totally wasted'" (J.H. Robinson 82).

When at last freed from parental control and possessed of a modest inheritance, a grown-up Checco changed into *Petrarco*, hence the English "Petrarch." The name change went along with an updated lifestyle appropriate to a well-dressed young fop in the busy, rich society of papal Avignon. Then one day, as he tells us in his *Letters to Posterity*, there occurred an epiphanic moment regarded by Bergin (Bergin, 41) as "the high-water mark of the medieval tradition": the first view of the desperately loved but unattainable Laura. Never could he forget the thrill or the where and when—"'in the year of our Lord 1327, upon the sixth day of April, at the first hour, in the church of Santa Clara in Avignon.'" The young beauty whose married name remains enigmatic—was it de Sade, de Neves, or something else—at once blotted out any lingering legal statutes for the rule of courtly love. Henceforth, it would be she who occupied life and thought and inspired the superb vernacular of love lyrics saturated in classicism, the *Canzoniere*, or "Rhymes." This exquisite product of a master poet and technician is still read and admired and is Petrarch's only major work for modern readers. However, it was not the Rhymes that were to make Petrarch important in law, but rather his work in Latin with the ancient classics. And to reach that plateau he had to cope first with more major life change.

The romantic crisis almost at once became compounded by the practical shock of a disappearing income. One possible cause beyond elegance of modish apparel includes fraud by the trustees under the paternal will; it has been dryly observed that the son's desultory seven years under law professors in Montpellier and Bologna were obviously an insufficient trusteeship to enable him to protect his estate. In any case, with no wish to work for money Petrarch therefore had to seek out a willing patron. He chose law's colleague, the Church, took the tonsure, entered minor orders, and went under the protection of the wealthy and powerful young bishop, Giacomo Colonna, whom he had met at Bologna. Continued need to find ecclesiastical patronage would of necessity become the essential problem of his life, since with lucrative sales of literary work awaiting the invention of printing nearly 200 years later, elegant rhymes produced no income. What patronage did guarantee was the common medieval arrangement: Petrarch the one-time lawyer, along with help from his agreeable personality, could enjoy a good receipt of steady money from Church benefices. He never accepted any remuneration connected to regular duties but was often the favorite of some wealthy and prominent man whose support he willingly accepted.

Having cheerfully moved into venality to solve the problem of food, clothing, and shelter, Petrarch could throw himself with six hours' sleep and without reserve into study of the classics. He devoured everything of the ancients he could find except Roman law and Greek works which to his shame and dismay he could not read in the original. With his usual penchant for negative criticism Petrarch's passion for books preserved only in the monasteries caused him to condemn the monks for failing to save more; he inveighed also against the errors of their ignorant copyists upon whom the scholars of his age now were forced to rely. Truculence had its positive side, however, for it stimulated a keen interest to fill in the gaps by discovering unknown classics. The Petrarch library ranked among the largest in Europe, and it included one of his best finds: the 1345 Verona codex containing the letters of Cicero to Atticus, Brutus, and Quintus. Petrarch could also show his guests all the great Latin poets except Lucretius. Though spotty in Latin prose—Tacitus was missing and some of Quintilian, whom he admired—he had an excellent collection of the historians. Seneca he owned complete and most of the best known works of Cicero; his book with copies of Cicero's letters was so big it had to stand on the floor. In the fairly narrow holdings of the Christian Fathers, Ambrose, Jerome, and Augustine were the prominent chosen. Medieval writers were very scarce. Reflecting his lack of confidence in Greek, Petrarch owned in translation a little Plato, a little Aristotle, and the Jewish historian Josephus, called in the first century the "Grecian Livy." There also were translations of Homer that he and Boccaccio had had made for them by a Greek. Such cross-over attempts were now much needed, since the twelfth century translators, having omitted Greek literary works, thereby had generally aggravated disdain for "belles lettres."

In a carefully prepared legal instrument which with notarial flair the attorney *manqué* drafted using current chancery style rather than classical Latin, Petrarch prepared a conditional offer of contract. He would bequeath all his splendid collection to St. Mark's in Venice if without delay the Venetian state could help by offering a fine building to house both author and his books. Venice accepted, hailing Petrarch as one of the unique glories in his time, if not in all history. On this, Petrarch's final legal exam, he seemed to have succeeded brilliantly. And yet, did he forget to cross the t's and dot the i's? Venice received only a few books at his death.

Petrarch's Works

It was Petrarch's opinion that his unfinished historical epic, *Africa*, intended to be the Aeneid of Italy, was his greatest work. It certainly has an intriguing personal note, for in its second century BCE hero, Scipio Africanus, the recalcitrant law student chose a celebrated evader of the law. However, the character of rebel outsider was not the current literary mode, and when *Africa* was finally published late in the fourteenth century, the reaction was negative and has continued to be so. Conversely, the highly esteemed *De viris illustribus*, the lives of twenty-three illustrious men of Rome, has the reputation of "'a stupendous achievement' " and "'the finest of modern histories,'" a work that "'must have kindled an intense interest in historical research fatal to its continued use as a text-book'" (Bergin, 116). The autocratic Caesar is the apogee of the famous twenty-three, among whom, we note, stands not a single jurist. When he reached the medieval, no figure, not even Charlemagne nor any of the saints, would garner the "illustrious" epithet.

Having attempted an historic panorama via highly selective biography, Petrarch then turned to but did not complete his *Rerum memorandarum*, an anecdotal illustration of the seven virtues, again from lives of the great. In failing to complete this moralized universal history, he may have thought a better outlet for the materials in mind would be in letters—the category we call "personal commentary." The letters—some prose, some metrical, many discursive, all attractive in their informal yet polished composition—are a high point in the work. Petrarch classified them, edited them continuously, and when he published them it was with the certainty of a wide and appreciative audience. They are of a highly diverse subject matter, set in form from very brief pieces to little books. Nearly each is full of classical allusions, though in Latin they have a modern feel, and today's reader senses in them that Petrarch is a friend he can understand.

Politics

The Petrarch public life was of a peculiar character. As much based on his literary fame as it was supported by his attractive personality, it creates the impression he charmed everyone wherever he went. An example is the most glamorous event in his literary life: being crowned Italy's poet laureate. Believing that such a designation had been regularly given to the supreme poet in antiquity, he had long burned with ambition to be the subject of a renewal of the practice. The honor came both because he had some claim to it and also because he had connived to get it, as he confessed later in an indirect way. On the first of September 1340 he received simultaneously two laureation offers, one from the Chancellor of the

University of Paris and one from the Roman Senate. Pretending at first to hesitate, he soon chose the accolade of Rome, the legitimate home of the antiquity to which he had devoted his life. Continuing his charade of modest diffidence, he insisted on being examined before the coronation, choosing as interlocutor King Robert of Naples. After spending nearly a month in friendly discourse and free meals with the monarch the candidate was pronounced worthy. It was then on to Rome where, in the palace of the Senate on the Capitoline hill, after a stirring acceptance address on poetry, little Checco made the family proud by being crowned with laurel and made *ex officio* a Roman citizen. Europe took the unusual combination of crown and tonsured head seriously and turned the indifferent lawyer almost overnight into the reigning intellect of his day. Though he had obtained the award because of the people he knew rather than because of the work he had done, in time the honor would be justified by magnificent poetry and solid scholarship, certainly not only the best of his age but an important pioneering step into the future. He had been highly acceptable wherever he wanted to go even before this honor; now Petrarch was in demand everywhere. He could publicly petition the pope to return the papacy from France to Rome and get in response not a cold rebuff but another canonry— pleasantly, one without regular duties. When in 1343 his patron Cardinal Colonna sought the release from a Naples jail of certain protégés who had rebelled there, the papal intervention was given through Petrarch as ambassador. Despite an unsuccessful political mission, the fine reward was not withheld: another canonry and deanery, both sinecures.

Realistically, it must be said that Petrarch lacked the stuff of statesmen and politicians. For him public activity was attractively appropriate only because Cicero had done it; he knew himself enough to understand his personality had no talent either for detail or the shrewd appraisal of the human nature of life's other players (J.H. Robinson, 329). His greatest failure in public affairs was his connection with Cola di Rienzo. This son of an innkeeper and a washerwoman, who represented the desperate social situation in which after generations of aristocratic misrule the lower classes of Rome found themselves, managed to receive an education which, as with Petrarch, instilled reverence for the memory of ancient Rome. Yet in 1347 after a careful coup, Cola surprisingly made himself master of Rome as Tribune of what was considered the same Roman Empire begun by Augustus. As the admirer of Caesar and Scipio, Petrarch was thrilled. He hailed Cola in two letters and then in an eclogue, broke with the Colonna family (whose Roman branch came out in opposition to Cola), and started for Rome. The new tribune's actions at the beginning were hopeful, but he had soon alienated both papacy and nobility by giving in to dictatorial megalomania. Disabused, Petrarch, in a letter from Genoa, rebuked Cola not only for his failure to restore old Rome, but also for his damage to the Petrarch reputation.

After giving up on Cola, Petrarch next shifted his hopes for Rome's political salvation to the Holy Roman Emperor, Charles IV. The times were difficult, compounded by the arrival of the plague from Sicily. Illness swept away the iconic and unattainable Laura as well as many of Petrarch's closest friends; Petrarch himself sheltered from the chaos in Parma and then Provence, for he had far more hard-nosed ambition than any romantic poet's death wish to join the beloved. Making known he was interested in winning the red hat of a cardinal brought merely the offer of a papal secretaryship. He cleverly arranged his own rejection by writing back in a limpid Latin repellant to practitioners of the florid style of the papal bureaucracy. Nevertheless, in June 1351, the papal commission of cardinals, appointed to draft a new constitution for Rome, did make a point of consulting him; and at last, the law lessons Petrarch once brushed off had become a help in professional advancement. Playing the jurist role on a very grand scale, Petrarch brought forth a plan in which he urged that power should be returned to the people at the exclusion, at least for a time, of the barons. With the political bit in his teeth, he wrote for Francesco di Carrara, son of his old friend then in power in Padua, a little work about the best form of government. The text was already pre-Machiavellian, yet its cleverness impressed the political players very little.

Old habits now took over the ambitious old man. Having failed to move forward his populist master scheme, Petrarch seemed content to fall back into self-absorption, responding little to the forces around him pressing for better government. This period of his life dismayed his friends, inspired as they had been by the ringing appeals for liberty he had written over the years. Uncharacteristically, they felt, he accepted the offer of residence and patronage made by the dictator of Milan, Archbishop Giovanni Visconti. How could Petrarch, a Florentine, and thus from Italy's only republic, go over to the enemy? To answer that question they would have again needed the astute analysis of the nineteenth century Milanese, Stendhal, with his complex nexus of church and state, altruism and cynicism. Petrarch claimed that he merely visited as a guest, not a servant, and that his decision was without political significance; yet during his years in Milan he was regularly available for whatever point of assistance, ambassadorial or oratorical, which Giovanni wanted. The early legal training could still be dredged up for a flourish of usefulness, but in its utilization the aging ambassador, like the desultory youth, was never very successful. Seeing and entrancing the great, Petrarch like Stendhal found in Milan much leisure and some solitude, and he avoided the barbs he would have attracted in closer contact with the Florentines. It is pertinent in Petrarch's defense that the dictatorship of Milan was far less discouraging as a center of caste and courtly ceremony than the French monarchies. The strong, self-made personality of Visconti attracted many able men, and Petrarch surely enjoyed their company until on the eve of his seventieth birthday, reading his Virgil, he gathered his laurel leaves for passage to Paradise.

Religion and Scholasticism

Bergin wryly suggests (Bergin, 98) that Petrarch, when he finally knocked at St. Peter's gates, may actually have been embarrassed that it was the pagan Virgil he read last and not the saintly Augustine who had once subdued his mind on the summit of Avignon's Mt. Ventoux. Petrarch's orientation on the ultimate questions had been throughout his life Christian, though of a sophisticated kind, always unwilling to grant any supernatural explanation to phenomena. Orthodox in opinion, the one-time friar could on occasion even display, at least for public view, a misogynist attitude toward women. His official line held up sex to be disgusting; and in his *Secret* he constructed a conversation with his favorite, Augustine, in which the sinner turned saint rebuked him for coveting women and fame. Obviously, the eternal longing for Laura combined with a stern monkish mask for the public translated into a complicated individual who, despite protestations in writing, indulged his carnal passion sufficiently to father two illegitimate children.

Petrarch the historian, knowing that the Fathers of the early Church were citizens of the Roman Empire as well as Christian authors, tended to see them all as one source. In fact, the Fathers were his second most important area of reading. Still, he theoretically faced the same problem as Aquinas did: how does one reconcile the pagans and the Fathers? In point of fact, though, he seems to have been little aware of the quandary and made no frontal attack upon it. Instead, in his *On His Own Ignorance and That of Many* he rejected the scholastic approach altogether and that included marking Aristotle in blistering language:

> I am confident, beyond a doubt, that he was in error all his life, not only as regards small matters...but in the most weighty questions where his supreme interests were involved. And though he has said much of happiness...I dare assert, let my critics exclaim what they may, that he was so completely ignorant of true happiness that the opinions on this matter of any pious old woman, or devout fisherman, shepherd or farmer, would, if not so fine-spun, be more to the point than his (J.H. Robinson, 39).

Having reduced scholasticism to a "'vast heap of rubbish'" with "'not a single grain of gold'" (Lyte, *A History of the University of Oxford from the Earliest Times to the Year 1530*, 381), he showed no interest in the problem of Nominalism and Realism (J.H. Robinson, 37). In his rejection of Aristotle, he rejected Aquinas, and with Aquinas out went the Averroists. This almost cavalier dismissal of medieval philosophy indicated an inconsistency and a lack of depth. In Bergin's opinion Petrarch was "constitutionally incapable of handling the grand design," be it in his narrative works or personal life. How, then, did this mind of mood rather than a message (Bergin, 152; 36) reconcile Christianity with the pagan writers? It was not difficult. Making no attempt at the absolutes sought by Aquinas, Petrarch opted for the Augustinian way; he was certain that if Plato could return to life or had foreseen the future he would have been a Christian. So, too, would have Cicero, whom Petrarch admired above all others. Humanism led not to seclusion but to those familial and social actions for which nature equipped man. Yet Petrarch liked to promote the classical writers who had advocated a moral life almost perfectly consistent with an ascetic Christianity; for him Ancients and Fathers could be woven together seamlessly through their urging renunciation of material goods. In each constituency he discovered freeing of the mind from passion and turning to the purity of a contemplative life.

It would be the art of the sermon which made Petrarch immediately popular all over Europe; and for the 200 years up to Erasmus, Humanists would accept his promotion of a brotherly compatibility between the classical and the Christian. This represented a turn away from medieval scholastic dialectic to a more modern conversation between individuals (Gilmore, 158), and it proved a felicitous transfer from Abelard's terse *Sic et non* to an economy of easier, more flexible dialogue.

Petrarch's History and the Law

Bartolus and Petrarch had each dealt with the literary remains of ancient Rome—Petrarch with Cicero and the historians (as well as the poets and Fathers), and Bartolus with the jurists preserved by Justinian. Petrarch saw Rome as something far distant in the past; Bartolus saw Rome as a current authority. Petrarch's attitude, however, led to a re-evaluation of ancient history, revision less important for the fourteenth century than for beyond. As citizens of the fifteenth century began to make their way across the bridge of thought whose span from medieval to modern rested on its recently constructed Petrarch/Ockham pillars, it would be Petrarch's signage which led them forward.

Even without Christianity the age of Livy—a fascinatingly separate, different way of life—seemed to Petrarch better than his own (Gilmore, 6), for from its great men one could pick up all the philosophy necessary. There was just one elite requirement: antiquity's materials needed good arrangement and eloquent expression. The better the rhetoric, the greater the content. Insistence on Ciceronian Latin was obviously a blow to progress in the vernacular; but it also set back the Latin, too, because Cicero's vocabulary, unlike that of medieval Latin, did not include words for the things and concepts that had emerged since the last century before Christ. It was the launching of yet another modern idea, long to be held, that a good classical style is necessary for political and diplomatic success. With this emphasis on style came a shift to the concept, later especially popular with Americans, that a great orator is necessarily a great statesman. From training in rhetoric to preparation in statecraft would suggest a mere step toward changing education into a powerfully expansive experience; when this idea made the Atlantic crossing it helped promote the foundation concept of service to "church and civil state" written into so many early American university charters.

In 1340 a young man from Genoa wrote the laureate for advice about law as a career. Petrarch was blunt about what it took: "'The greater part of our legists…care nothing for knowing about the origins of law and about the founders of jurisprudence…and it never occurs to them that the knowledge of arts and of the origins of literature would be of the greatest practical use for their very profession'" (Gilmore, 30). Here was yet another new process, this one for modern lawyers. If they and others were to return to the ancient sources themselves they needed training in discovery of the myriad mistakes of translators and copyists; they also required more precise understanding of the author's meaning by intense study of the grammar and philology of the ancient languages. The Petrarchean way made no attempt to embrace the whole of jurisprudence, but it was adding an innovative element. After Petrarch there would be the further necessity of historicizing legal science—actually comparing ancient sources for the light each could shed upon the other. Passion for the ancients and for what exactly they had said created the role of the man of letters—the scholar outside the university—and gave it honor (Bergin, 191). Now it reinvented the law school graduate as evidentiary expert, careful of precedence, of detail, and case comparisons. When the dust was blown off them, history and the ancient literary texts shone with the refurbished pomp and circumstance Bartolists had sorely needed to illuminate the Roman law.

It is not surprising that Petrarchians began their innovating with harsh words for their often shallow legal colleagues, conservatively holding onto the historic rules they knew should be known. As attorneys headed into practical careers, they had been graduated from universities where scholastic training tended to resist learning for learning's sake (Rudy, *The Universities of Europe, 1100-1914: A History,* 40). Even though individual university jurists were able to muster infectious enthusiasm when giving lectures with something new to say, these were men as faculties weighed down into the Bartolist position that Roman law continued to be in effect. University chancellors made sure that Humanist masters had to settle for temporary jobs and low pay, while they, the law professors with life appointment, received higher salaries. However, when the academic lawyers at last took up the historical methods of the Latin scholars, they were able forthrightly to carry the work forward from enthusiastic efforts to careful system. The Humanists failed to make this final step and legal opinion took its revenge by telling everyone—as Machiavelli put it in the sixteenth century—that early Humanists had simply failed in persuading anyone to learn from the ancient models.

In courts and palaces, the big houses of the wealthy bourgeoisie, and later in private academies not regulated by the Church, later Humanists would have to content themselves with employment as secretaries, house tutors, readers, court poets, historiographers, public orators and companions. Princes were given the ego enjoyment of receiving from members of their retinue panegyrics addressed to their royal person in prestigious Ciceronian Latin. Such luxuries depended on economic revival, and it was the fifteenth century's taste for luxury and for buildings to house libraries that accelerated the movement; finally entering the universities, Humanism lived at ease in the expensive buildings of the new colleges. Here, again, France would be favored ahead of England since, recovering from war about 1450, she could enjoy relative peace, economic recovery, and a burgeoning population until wars of religion after 1560 once more brought her to her knees. Fifteenth century Italian universities, too, could boast their chairs of Greek, poetry, and eloquence. They had been established from the period of glory in the 1430s, when urban wealth, fed by the ancient tradition of magnates required to dwell in town, joined together for a substantial homogeneity in Tuscan and Lombard society to aid vigorously the Humanistic spread. Then French armies invaded Italy in 1494. By the end of the first decade of the sixteenth century, the Humanistic exhilaration would have gone out of Petrarch's homeland, now destined to be long under the foreign heels of France or the Hapsburgs.

After Petrarch

The two earliest Petrarchian successors important in the study of law were both from republican Florence. Both came from outside the university and the legal profession, and both today are less well known than their own inheritors. The one Florentine effort came from Marsilio Ficino (1433–1499), known initially as the translator of Plato, but who went on to have a far greater impact through his own later influences. In his Academy students were stimulated by the Humanistic Christian philosophy of Erasmus (1466–1536)—the last such Petrarchian intellectual effort in Europe. Had that heritage been imbued with the energy to prevail, it might have saved the unity of the Church, her huge property, and possibly the canon law as an international system supplementing royal, customary, and commercial law. Instead the strong yearning for piety which produced it was picked up for Christian cataclysm by Martin Luther (1483–1546), fiercely reacting to the degeneracy of the papacy, especially in the person of the clever but imperious Rodrigo Lanzal y Borgia, Alexander VI (1492–1503). From Luther the Ficino heritage would then separate into deep but disparate channels: one for the lawyer "pope of Geneva" John Calvin (1509–1564); the other for the military mystic and Catholic theologian, Ignatius de Loyola (1491–1556), founder of the Society of Jesus (1534). These particular developments and the deep political, economic, and social forces lined up behind such hard and brilliant antagonists will be the subject of a later section on the Reformation.

The other important thinker in the lineage was the philologist Lorenzo Valla (1406–1457) whose work would lead to brilliant applications we shall shortly examine—from the contemporary Polizano to the sixteenth century French law professor Cujas. Cujas would become the culminator of legal Humanism and thereafter sole possessor of the field until succeeded in the nineteenth century revival of legal history by the German professor Friedrich von Savigny (1779–1861). By founding a school of jurisprudential philosophy based on historical work in law, it was given to Savigny to accomplish what Cujas did not. When we conclude discussion of legal Humanism by examining Cujas, we shall meet as well the sixteenth century appropriator of his work—Charles Dumoulin—and find him, not surprisingly, better understood as a successor of Bartolus than of Arezzo's native son writing his letters to posterity.

Valla

Lorenzo Valla can be said to be the man who more than any other picked up the tradition left by Petrarch and used it to give Humanist law teachers of the sixteenth century both historical method and accurate and elegant Latin. Like Petrarch, Valla would be unable to do this in his lifetime, for that was filled by fierce controversies with inimical law professors in which they were almost always to prevail. Vicariously living through Quintilian, the Roman Valla spent much of his real life just trying to remain in Rome. His repeated, sharp literary threats against the weaknesses of the Church made the city dangerous for him until almost the end of his life. Valla's was a period when law student bodies, professional appointments, salaries, and prestige were all incrementally increasing in devotion to the Bartolist tradition Valla despised. In spite of the opposition, though, Valla's treatise, *De Elegantiis Latinae Linguae*, written probably in Naples sometime after 1435, went on to become a standard text in the schools for most of the sixteenth century. Highly admired by Erasmus who published an epitome of it, the treatise was printed nearly sixty times between 1471 and 1536. In his *Elegantiis* Valla looked with gimlet eye at Latin grammar and the rules of Latin style and rhetoric, careful to do honor to his beloved guide's analysis and inductive reasoning while patiently seeking out true meaning and actual intent. The difference was that the pupil's quest would center on message not mood, essence not ornament.

The senior Valla had been in advocacy and served the consistory of the papal curia. If he had ever intended to groom son Lorenzo for legal work, that wish was cut off by his death when the boy was only thirteen. Fortunately an uncle, who worked as a papal secretary, supervised the boy in the papal cloisters, providing him an excellent education in both Latin and Greek. At twenty-five Lorenzo was ordained and tried to get his own apostolic secretaryship. Unsuccessful, he went on to Pavia as professor of eloquence.

Bartolism was currently reigning over the law faculty, and the medieval Latin of the law professors offended the ears of linguistic purist Valla. Since literary offense was something Valla throughout his life took pains never to tolerate, he immediately was embroiled in one of those bitter controversies that developed wherever he went; such disputes fit for the temper of his age gave full scope for exhibition of his skill in the rhetorical invective so admired by fellow Humanists. Valla minced no words. Bartolus, Baldus, Accursius, and company were all geese, mere quacking barn fowl successors to the quietly elegant swans of jurisprudence: Sulpicius, the Scaevolas, the Pauls, and the Ulpians. The brutal comment set off actual riots between arts and law students, and Valla, conveniently also escaping the plague which dispersed the university at about the same time, found it discreet to seek employment elsewhere.

It is peculiar that the precise occasion for the riot does not appear to have been any major legal work but rather a pamphlet by Valla attacking Bartolus's book on heraldry. Thus a confrontation that should have resulted in re-examination of the sources of Roman law both by Humanists and advocates brought sound, fury, but little enlightenment to the lawyers who, in dudgeon, closed their minds against the possibility of learning anything from this unpleasantly brash young man. For his part, Valla did not abandon the duel between the geese and the swans. In his philological research he consulted the *Digest* and "tried to uncover the words of the classical jurists whose work had been distorted by the compilers of the *Digest*" (O.F. Robinson, *An Introduction to European Legal History,* 287). What was Justinian's he rejected, shifting his interest from the maxims with their potential for vagueness to an effort at precision in the meaning of terms.

Now followed wanderings from university to university as Valla tried out his ideas. After Milan and Genoa, it would be in Florence that Valla finally attracted the notice of Alphonso, King of Naples. For some years he would play the role of courtier, providing a Humanist dimension for the Neopolitan court in the form of translations of Greek literature. It was not all esoteric savoir-faire, however, for Valla wrote another heavy legal thrust, this time against the constitutional law of the Church as embedded in the canon. Daring in idea, the attack fell short in critique of Church method. However, since the political climate of the patronal court was against Rome's temporal power, there was much anger when Eugenius IV claimed the right to dispose of Alphonso's Neopolitan realm as a lapsed fief. Valla knew he had to find a special way to lead the charge, and he succeeded brilliantly. Directing his critical eye at the Donation of Constantine, he produced *De falso credita and ementita Constantini donatione declamatio* of 1439—an exposé of the old supportive text as an absolute forgery.

Petrarch would certainly have beamed with pride at the Humanistic detective work. By carefully applying the learning of the *Elegantiis* to the language of the Donation, Valla was able to demonstrate through linguistic evidence that it could never have been composed in the age of Constantine. To this he added arguments based on historical evidence (omission of the document by Gratian, coinage), mixing into the whole a liberal dose of invective against the political pretensions of holy fathers. He wrote without timidity: "'I attack not only the dead but the living'" (Sellery, 200). But it was his philology and use of "hard" historical evidence like the coins which created a permanent contribution in handling the *Donation* problem.

Valla had a rival in the attack. His name was Reginald Pecock (1395–1460), and in a book written approximately ten years later this Oxonian from Wales is considered to have made a very persuasive case without, apparently, knowing anything of the Valla work. It has been argued by Sellery that except in the skills where Valla excelled, this scholastic in the Aquinas tradition did a better job in pronouncing the "Donation" to be a forgery. As Sellery writes (Sellery, 213): "The scholastic discipline, with its training in evidence and its disputations, so similar to the analysis of the decisions of the courts in a legal brief, was no mean preparation for the task presented by the 'Donation.'" Pecock was also the more modern, for he wrote in vernacular English.

We can feel, though, closer to Valla, probably because in personal life and professional work this Humanist comes across as highly "human." Though a cleric like Pecock, and concerned he remain eligible for church office by remaining unmarried, Valla fathered three children whom he openly acknowledged. What he could not openly acknowledge were a heart and head which saw many myths in the Church, such as the theory that the Apostle's Creed was neatly composed in seriation pieces by the twelve disciples. He was fearless in ridiculing the Latin of the Vulgate and even accused Augustine of heresy. He attacked the laxity of monks, condemned as inadequate the nearly sacred categories of Aristotle along with that sage's physics and morals, and even parted company with Humanists by exalting Quintilian's Latin above Cicero's (Sellery, 199). In the early dialogue, *De Voluptate*, his contrast between Stoics and Epicureans shows open preference for the latter's support of the human right to indulge freely natural appetites. It has been said that he was a vain and jealous person, but behind the cantankerous and sensual polemicist there is a bold critic as well as an acute scholar. In the end he would realize his ambition. When Eugenius IV died, Nicholas V invited Valla to Rome as a papal secretary and Dean of St. John of the Lateran, an occasion hailed as "the triumph of Humanism over orthodoxy and tradition." We have already noted admiration by Erasmus. But far more triumphant was the Valla march toward Reformation, his influence referred to unhesitatingly by Cardinal Bellarmine as "'praecursor Lutheri'" (*Encyclopedia Britannica*, xx, 86a).

Parenthesis for a Printer

About 80 years after the death of Petrarch and a little before the death of Valla, the learned world was changed forever by an obscure man printing on a press in Strasbourg. For this man, Johann Gutenberg (1398–1468), it is here worth pausing in the legal progression, just as Victor Hugo did when he stepped out of the melodrama in *Notre Dame de Paris* to describe printing's fabulous saga. However profound the influence Humanism and the Reformation were now going to have on legal science, neither intellectual movement would have imparted its precious heritage without Gutenberg's marvelous invention. The noisy simplicity of movable metal blocks, one piece for each letter, integer, and sign, permitted all the intellectual ferment of the questing brain to be written out that it might bear witness to what men and women had wrought. Infinitely more people could henceforth share in recorded facts and ideas: Durant (Durant, *The Renaissance*, 317), calculating about a half-century ago, put a medieval book at a cost of $160–$200 (a great bible could reach $10,000), while in contrast, at the end of the fifteenth century, Aldus Manutius at his publishing-printing business in Venice was producing the whole of ancient Greek literature in small, handy printed volumes at about $2.00 each.

The Chinese very early had made blocks for printing, one for each page; but this awkward method and the difficult Chinese script were not conducive to free development of ideas. Whether Europeans in the middle of the fifteenth century were inspired by the Orient is unknown, but they did understand the several relevant processes now combining to permit the movable type: casting of metal by goldsmiths; stamping of book covers by bookbinders and of cloth by weavers; the recognition by painters of the superiority of oil paints; and the development of powerful presses by vintners and paper makers. It was these paper makers who contributed the essential medium suitable for printing; unlike the lamb and calf skin vellum and the parchment skin of other animals, their breathtaking fiber and rag material was neither too expensive nor limited in supply.

Building on earlier German breakthroughs, Gutenberg was making his movable metal type and using it successfully before 1454, probably as early as 1445. A bible of 1456, although possibly not crafted by Gutenberg himself, is the first great achievement of his technique. To create it he borrowed large sums from one Johann Fust, sometimes spelled with more symbolic overlay as Faust. In an early version of publish or perish, when Gutenberg in spite of good progress with his idea did not repay, Fust, pre-Mephistophelean and pre-Machiavellian, took back the tools and with them created his own successful publishing and printing business. Thus denied his livelihood, Gutenberg the publisher sadly did indeed, perish...poor. Ironically, some 400 years later in America, Mark Twain relived the Gutenberg curse when he,

The Printing Press
*Courtesy of the Library of Congress,
Prints and Photographs Division, LC-USZ62-104445*

too, impoverished himself, this time trying to finance the development of a machine that would set Gutenberg's type automatically.

    Through the new process early printers began organizing Humanist scholars to edit and disseminate manuscripts, thereby pushing ahead the scholarship which had made the technology relevant. By such work authors could make a living with their pens, although in these early days of no royalties, few achieved success. The press of the Venetian Aldus Manutius was the most successful, able for a time to boast Erasmus as resident editor. Manutius worked night and day through strikes, war, and untrammeled literary piracy until his health was ruined; he, like Gutenberg, died exhausted and poor. The firm with its famous italic font carried on until 1597. In Switzerland the Froben press furthered the cause of Christian Humanism, while in Paris French printers were close behind. In only a generation the printing art had spread all over, as out of the dirty, shopworn boxes of metal letters the brilliant new concept of Europe had been born.

    The social, political, and economic effects of printing as a means of communicating ideas to many people can hardly be exaggerated. Populations, reoriented from the local outlook of the long Middle Ages, were exposed to fresh ideas which now could pour in from everywhere. The shortest items, or "broadsides"—works of keen aim with men and institutions squarely in their sights—were able to move minds against prejudice and vituperation and to manipulate public opinion on any topic whatever. By the time Martin Luther took the stage, harnessing his intellectual energy to the driving force of print, he was enabled to conduct the first really large scale propaganda campaign appealing to a general readership (*Dictionary of the History of Ideas,* Vol. I, 190a). Luther had arrived with revolution in his heart and at the tip of his pen at just the right time. Printing virtually rendered impossible the total suppression of heretical books although, realizing the dangerous loophole, the Church put her repressive law of the Index to first use in 1559.

As men could now more readily have a sense of their history, this history moulded and shaped politics far beyond Humanistic queries. Editors, more than ever in demand, could now count on an accurate text to be reproduced perfectly in any number of copies; the copies being identical, precise citation and cross-referencing page by page, and line by line, was simple. At the same time, the work of learned men who needed books not intended for broad markets was also revolutionized. Before printing any index to a manuscript book would have generally been the work of the user and thus set up in his own style. However, now, as indices were needed for a large audience, there appeared more abstract analyses and more critical appraisals of texts. For example, when by 1480 the famous glosses surrounding legal texts had been proudly reproduced in printing, their inferiority to footnotes became glaringly apparent. There was no turning back as the printed book became a crucial instrument of learning. In less than a hundred years the world had been presented with its first systematic general bibliography, Gesner's 1545 *Bibliotheca Universalis*.

Because of Gutenberg's blocks, legal studies began to enjoy and profit from the great increase in the institutional holdings of law libraries. Our eponymous hero, the lawyer, could enjoy in his office the same texts as the judge in chambers. On the university podium any law professor could assign pages to be read rather than give laborious lecture dictation. Many more of his students could come to class prepared to hear about ideas of origin, meaning, effect, and merit while leaving multiple unmentioned topics for the leisure of private reading. Cheaper and more plentiful books meant for these students a far more level playing field, allowing the shoemaker's son a better chance at the bar when competing against the son of a lord. In England the number of printed legal books was second only to religion, and law must have ranked at least that high on the continent.

As we bring our parenthesis to a close, we should also summon sympathy for the copyists who, now thrown out of work, bitterly denounced the new method. We can just sense the jealousy of many an erudite scholar who saw the presses and had to realize here lay the popularity to attract the thousands to the most vapid ideas. Such popularity increased daily through the many improvements made in typography; by the end of the fifteenth century less dense Roman and Italic type faces were replacing the old block letters except in Germany and except in conservative brahminist works, notably legal texts (*New Cambridge Modern History,* 366). Foreshadowing in this step one the similarity of complaint for today's communicative era of television and internet, people bemoaned the important loss of attentiveness and memory that used to be required for painstaking scholarship before printing came along. Lawyers and other academics noted how this ease in presentation ultimately meant loss of power for a centuries-old domination by the learned world. As the eighteenth century began, a bourgeois readership, noses in books and common sense encouraged, was denying scholars the thinker's lofty seat. Prominent in this bourgeois class, of course, were the practicing lawyers.

Taking as a whole this range of widely disseminated printed material, it is not too much to say that although the French king had destroyed the temporal power of the greatest medieval institution, the Church universal, it was Gutenberg rather than any monarch in silken glory, who, in his weariness and poverty, fingers singed by hot molds and stained by ink, was to administer the major, final blow. As the technological tool brought to the modern world, printing's blocks would put legal philosophy in the hands of any who wished to read it. Power-seeking monarchs especially smiled to see those same blocks carry on them the verbal weaponry to pulverize much of the mortar holding together Peter's rock.

Poliziano

Returning now to the intellectual succession after Valla, we are met with uncertainty in designating a pupil of his as the next literary man important to law. Admitting this as a fairly impossible task, the one who will get our notice next is Angelo Poliziano (1454–1494), born three years before Valla's death. His family of modest circumstances claimed their surname from Monte Polizano, and in commenting on this high birthplace no less a figure than Erasmus attested to the "miraculous" appropriateness of an "Angelo" descending among mortals, beatific in his spirit and in his writings.

In realistic terms Poliziano was a professor in the faculty of arts, a churchman whose daily life was supported by a priory and canonry as well as long residence in the palace of the "Magnificent" de'Medici, Lorenzo. Lorenzo ruled as leading statesman of his day and builder of a power system in which Naples, Milan, and Florence balanced Venice and the papacy. Here was a prince *de facto*, a banker, and an avid collector of ancient literary manuscripts. Poliziano, as the in-house Humanist, was a worthy protégé. He had been well educated in Florence in both Latin and Greek and had studied Plato and Aristotle; he did not begin as a lawyer, but later studies to support his ecclesiastical role included Hebrew and canon law. His precocity as a boy had been so remarkable that, soon after commencing a youthful translation of Homer into Latin, he had leaped suddenly to fame with his vernacular stanzas in honor of Giuliano de'Medici, verses which were still being read in the nineteenth century. Word had it he composed them at fourteen, a fact some still refuse to believe. They were enough, however, to bring Poliziano the princely notice, and he could soon be found enlarging his reputation as tutor for the sons of Lorenzo, one of whom would later rule Florence while the other ruled the Church as Leo X. It was from Leo that the former tutor received a papal commission to translate Herodotus. Poliziano also wrote a well-received history of the Medici, and at twenty-nine he was named professor of Greek and Latin in the University. His pleasing manner drew large numbers of students even to heavy-going civil law lectures in the Justinian Pandicts. In addition, Poliziano became in effect Lorenzo's personal librarian, caring for holdings which for long were the richest in Europe.

Angelo Poliziano, 1454-1494, Humanist
Courtesy of National Gallery of Art, Washington

Here Poliziano could immerse himself in ancient literature, teaching philosophy while making his elegant stylistic corrections of manuscripts known to Europe through his popular *Miscellany*. One thing he did not cultivate was theology; and it is hinted that his taste for the holy books, and even his breviary, lacked warmth and devotion to the cause. In all this the Angelic One is not far distant from the worldly Valla, including participating in his share of literary quarrels.

However, in work in the law, where he continued the attack on Glossators and post-Glossators, Poliziano outdistanced Valla. He extended his source materials for linguistic studies by studying intently great works of past jurisprudence. The *Paraphrasis*, his published update of an early Greek edition by Theophilus of the *Institutes of Justinian*, stands as one of the first, if not the first, Humanist publication in law. Grammatical and philological studies were acquiring great prestige, and it was Poliziano who made the initial study of the Florentine manuscript of the *Digest* from a philosophical and historical point of view. Encouragement for this lengthy critical study of Justinian came from Poliziano's hopes it could serve as a basis for a proposed re-edition of the original. In efforts to get at the earliest sources Poliziano included important study of surviving fragments from the ancient Roman jurists and the Theodosian code, works older than Justinian's compilations.

It has been suggested that such groundbreaking study of Roman law materials by new intellectuals followed for all practical purpose from the failure of lawyers to take up the Humanist approach after attacks like those of Valla (Gilmore, 32). This may be true, but it is also true that the Roman law materials were a rich source for philological study. Humanists should and probably would have explored them whether or not lawyers did so. In any case, Poliziano's hard work in effect transformed a unique document, the accidental preservation of which had itself turned upside down the jurisprudence of Europe. It must not be forgotten that until Poliziano, the *Digest* had been mainly an archaeological artifact, kept under guard and brought out only on ceremonial occasions. After Poliziano, though, there could be no doubt it had become one of law's major historical documents.

Thus one can say that although the work of Lorenzo Valla had been significant, Angelo Poliziano, the first thorough and systematic scholar-examiner, was the one with whom modern textual criticism begins (*New Cambridge Modern History,* Vol. I, 99). Such studies were able to elicit special interest among lawyers who lived in an age when fascination with the law was reflected in learned society. Lorenzo and Angelo became so enmeshed in their legal passion that they together made a trip to the University of Pisa just to hear a debate between Giasone del Maino, a lawyer of Milan, and Bartolommeo Sozzini, professor of law at Siena. Sozzini had challenged del Maino on the interpretation of Roman legal texts; it was said that the grasping ambition to be first in figuring out the antique origins had led each debater to aid his cause by forgery. How one wishes to have been privy to the gossip exchanged by Angelo and Lorenzo on the long ride home.

Budé

When the new ways of Humanism were at last applied by actual legal professionals to the study of Roman law, it would be done in France where economic recovery was powerfully reflected in flourishing universities. However, it was not just economics that brought Italian Humanism across the border. North of the Alps there had already been much intensive study of ancient literature by thinkers like Erasmus who were interested primarily in theology and the welfare of the Church. Humanists had been leaving these topics alone until the idea dawned on them that an in-depth return to the study of original Church texts might yield the basis for ecclesiastical reform, thereby responding to the fifteenth century's steady growth of piety. This idea probably reached France from the Platonic Academy in Florence via the Frenchman Jacques Lefèvre d'Étaples (1450–1536), and discussion of it belongs in the discussion of the Reformation. It is reasonable to conclude that when this innovation came to a France where scholasticism had decided to let down the bars for Humanism's entry, the freedom encouraged lawyers to apply intensive study of ancient texts to the jurisprudence preserved by Justinian.

Another current, even more direct in its pertinence to law, does, however, here bear upon the Petrarchian succession. In the chronological hinge between fourteenth and fifteenth centuries, about the time of the death of Petrarch, there were contacts between French and Italian intellectuals at the papal court in Avignon. This was especially true during the Great Schism from about 1378–1415. As priest-delegates who had been trained at the University of Paris discussed with their Italian counterparts, they were told about Petrarch and his intellectual heritage. The good news encouraged profound sociological change as literary and aesthetic minds now sought the leisure, tranquility, and freedom through wealth that could facilitate entertaining such humanistic interests. France began to follow Italy by changing the work ethic from that of a fairly ascetic teaching style—fiercely independent in the pursuit of truth, meeting classes in modest schoolrooms, and living in simplicity—to the comfortable, often beautiful college building, sheltering art, books, and ease of an elitist lifestyle.

Among the Frenchmen touched by this early Humanism were Clémanges, de Montreuil, Gautier, and Col; but the spread of their interest was hampered by the declaration of the final stages of the Hundred Years' War. It was not until after 1450 that the new scholarship of Italy began to attract the French professoriat which, except for a small group, had until then been quite satisfied with rigorous scholasticism. The intellectual changeover was slowed considerably by the fact that as late as the last quarter of the fifteenth century, academic minds from the University of Paris were still struggling between Realism and Nominalism, even though Humanist influence had been felt for some time in the arts faculty. Only when the University's leading enthusiast for the cause, Robert Gaguin (1433–1501), became Law School dean, did the Paris law faculty take to being called the cradle of French Humanism. Gaguin would find an invaluable colleague in the University librarian who, with a newly installed printing press, at once started production of the classical and Humanist texts. Greek was put into the Paris curriculum in 1476 and regularly taught after 1508.

As is often the case, war brought its own rough boost into modernity. When Charles VIII invaded Italy—an anachronistic French exercise in the dying art of chivalry rather than a necessity of statesmanship—Frenchmen found themselves face to face with Renaissance Italians. At first it would not appear a remarkable encounter for imitation, since the young and middle aged Italian intelligentsia were angry, anxious men taking refuge from conflict and arid research in the mental antidote of excessive Ciceronian purity. The French, though, using the obvious Humanist enthusiasm for ancient legal sources and for Hellenic rationality, would from that initiation launch their own updated, vigorous effort at "a legal science in the true sense" (*Continental Legal History,* Vol. I, 150). Convinced of the validity in a secular approach to ancient studies oriented toward law, French jurists were before long outdistancing their Italian colleagues as they turned Humanistic legal study into their own important phenomenon (O.F. Robinson, 280).

Guillaume Budé (1467–1540), born in Paris, would be first in the big race. His father was a lawyer and court official, and it was expected young Guillaume would begin his education in Paris, then move to Orléans for serious law study. In yet one more example of initial legal defection for the usual reasons, the adolescent was repelled by the rigorous teaching and attracted to sensual pleasures; not until he was twenty-three or twenty-four would he abandon dissipation and recommit to academics. His interest in learning having been aroused, however, he devoted himself to the original ancient texts with such constant and fierce intensity that he fell ill, beginning the torment of headaches he would suffer the rest of his life. Budé's specializations were eclectic—theology, architecture, mathematics—but his great fascination was jurisprudence. For him law stood as the most impressive of Roman monuments (O.F. Robinson, 289), but one so sadly defaced by medieval

Portrait of Guillaume Budé
Courtesy of The Bridgeman Art Library

interpretations that it cried out for accurate texts. He found it unbelievable that pure wisdom could be studied in forms so mangled by the negligence of time. Wanting only to know it all first hand, he plunged into Greek, acquiring the profound knowledge of it that guaranteed his fame as one of the most learned men of his century.

Budé began his published life with translations of Plutarch and a letter of St. Basil. Soon he had switched over to law, annotating the *Digest* in twenty-five books whose first printed edition appeared in 1508. Naturally, he attacked the faulty medieval "interpretations," as he gave his version of Roman law the full contextual treatment, complete with social and linguistic changes which had affected the source. Traditional legal scholarship had looked at the *Digest* as a single, coherent system written at one time. Any problems were vagaries to be forcibly reconciled. The seminal Florentine manuscript itself had not yet been published, but aware both of the interpolations of Tribonian and the errors of some Roman historians, Budé now broke with the past and used the notes and commentary of Poliziano on the Florentine as a basis of his presentation (O.F. Robinson, 289). Even contradictions were set into a framework of historical development. Readers understood at once that this French lawyer had come at old materials from the exciting new Humanistic angle, and they couldn't help but admire how thoroughly conversant he appeared with what could then be known about ancient civilization and language. Fully launched into the new science, Budé took time off to publish in 1514 a book called *De Esse*, an amazing, reliable, scholarly account of the Roman monetary system. Petrarch would have been proud.

Literary fame brought the expected learned quarrels and professional jealousies, including a tiff with the great Erasmus himself. But the strong words did no harm; for, as Erasmus admitted, he might refuse to be reconciled with Budé, yet nonetheless, never could cease for an instant to love him (*Biographie Universelle*, Vol. VI, 226). How the scholar had supported himself before achieving this stature is not known, although the early dissipation suggests family resources. Now, however, more than one patron sought to take care of Budé's needs. It is significant that lawyer Budé chose the secular court and not the Church, unlike both Valla and Poliziano who remained churchmen and professors. Budé made the craftier choice, for Louis XII named him royal secretary and sent him on a mission to Rome, while Francis I, promoting him to Master of Requests (a judicial post) as well as Master of the Royal Library, also gave him important ambassadorial tasks. Large favor at court was sufficient to enable Budé to persuade Francis into founding the Collège de France and approving the creation of the splendid library at Fontainebleau. Such unusually strong royal support probably was not hurt by Budé's view that magistrates had no proprietary right in the *merum imperium*. He reached this policy more from a gut feeling than a particularly well worked out political theory. Although he did acknowledge he relied more on Lothair than Azo, he was unable to find any positive contributions from Roman history to aid in the old puzzle of the right to command (Gilmore, 47).

Budé should probably be judged more Humanist that jurist, for his approach ultimately remained essentially philological. He unquestioningly advanced secular legal studies by his approach to Justinian, yet he took other paths, too; promoting the study of ancient ecclesiastical sources, Budé the scholar brought aid to the pietists as they attempted to return to a true Christian way. The Budé candle, lit so ardently for law and research, burned too brightly, it would seem. He turned into a grumpy old pedant, one who complained that the liberality of his monarch, the good wishes of Paris, (the city fathers named him Mercantile Provost), and the time-consuming affection of his wife, his numerous children, and his friends would all end by making him a dull ignoramus. Could they not they all understand that the only thing he had ever wanted was to apply himself wholly to study? And so cantankerousness bred canards, among the most famous being an account of the day a fire started in the Budé house. The scholar, it was said, was naturally immersed in work when a servant rushed all aflutter into his *cabinet* to announce the flames. The master's chill response: "'Tell my wife you know I do not involve myself in the household'" (*Biographie Universelle*, Vol. VI, 226).

Budé tried for retirement at the death of Louis XII. At first, it seemed private life was his to take, but then Francis issued his royal command for royal mission. This time, however, Budé's restless self found final liberation. Falling ill, he declined rapidly and by 1540 lay dead. Dumoulin called him "'*doctrinarum omnium* *splendor,'" while for Scaliger law had lost "'the greatest Greek in Europe, a phoenix who will not be reborn from his cinders'" (*Biographie Universelle,* Vol. VI, 226).

Alciato

Budé had a secular rather than an ecclesiastical career and devoted most of his scholarship to jurisprudence in the Humanist style; yet because he was not a professor at a university, he therefore was not himself the beginner of the new way in the faculties of law. That role fell to another Milanese, Andrea Alciato, (often written *Alciati*), whose adult fame began at Avignon. The major consequences of his work among the universities occurred on adopted French soil, notably at Bourges, which became the liveliest academic enterprise in law of the sixteenth century.

The Alciato family was well-off, the mother a noble and the father a merchant and a city councilor of Milan. For the son born in the year 1492 when conquest of New World riches filled the European imagination, easy family circumstances did not produce indifference to material matters. From boyhood to death in 1550 Alciato remained exceptionally sensitive to income; his repeated moves from one law professorship to another were propelled less by civil unrest and plague than a restless quest for the highest salary—a saga he once suggested would make a fine book topic (*Great Jurists of the World*, 76). Admittedly, to love of money was added vanity, making the reader of his life predisposed to dislike him as a person. His work, though, is another matter and duly commands admiration.

Alciato began to study law in the old Lombard capital of Pavia. Here he was fortunate to attend the classes of Jason del Magno who taught there from 1467 to 1519 and brought Pavia greater fame than Bologna. Smith (118) calls del Magno the last of the old school, that is, he lectured far more on the gloss and commentary than on the text; but he also had the new Humanism's definite taste for classical literature, and that impelled his eager young pupil of broad smile and magnetic eyes to aim for innovation of the highest caliber. As he went about acquiring an especially broad literary culture in both Latin and Greek, Alciato became the author of a comedy, poems, and even a book on dueling. Like Budé he always felt the wider the range of a lawyer's knowledge, the more he could help explicate the interrelationship of jurisprudence to other sciences. Nor was Alciato bashful about accepting praise for being a lawyer in the best Humanist rhetorical tradition; he was his greatest admirer, delighted with his pure writing style, elegance in speech, and charismatic personality he saw standing back at him from his mirror.

In 1511 Alciato left Pavia for study at Bologna. By 1515 he had published notes on the last three books of the *Code* of Justinian and had restored Greek passages in the *Digest*; in 1516 at only twenty-four he had achieved a doctorate of both civil and canon law. For a young man it admittedly was such remarkable work that the twenty-six year old, along with a few jests made behind his back about long, large ears, began hearing other, more flattering whisperings which used the term genius. At the very least, he was innovative. Alciato had already decided, on the basis of the intensive study of Justinian's *Institutes*, that the old way of teaching was futile

Alciato
From Sir John MacDonell and Edward Manson, *Great Jurists of the World* (1914). Reprint 1997
Courtesy of The Lawbook Exchange

given that new knowledge of ancient literature made a clear call for an equally new jurisprudence in the Petrarchian mode. In the year he took his degree he published six books of *Paradoxa*—short, pointed chapters that depart sharply from Bartolist practice by moving the citations from the text to the margin. In the end, though, his publications would fall well short of all the youthful enthusiasm for large-scale action on change. *Paradoxa* they remained—hard-fought parts without a polished whole, foreshadowings of a life's work unable to reach any comprehensive synthesis.

By 1518, after some years as a lawyer, the now famous author stopped private practice altogether, opting instead for the greater comfort and prestige of a lucrative law professorship in Avignon. Here Alciato met Budé, and now classroom and scholarly successes were enormous. Zasius (1461–1534), an older, eminent jurist working out of Switzerland and Germany, was so struck by the *Paradoxa* that he wrote at once to Boniface Auerbach (1475–1562), another Swiss, destined himself to be a friend of Erasmus and a distinguished professor of law. In his letter Zasius hailed Alciato for his prodigies in reforming legal study of Roman law, and Auerbach at once packed his bag for the effervescent Avignon scene, there to continue his studies with the great Humanist lawyer. Sitting in packed auditoriums with as many as 800 young and mature men of promise and achievement, Auerbach would have heard a professor who made dazzling use of a briefcase full of intellectual subjects: the history and grammar of ancient language; the history of Roman institutions; the restoration of texts; and the exposure of errors made by the Glossators and Commentators. Alciato would be accused (O.F. Robinson, 296–297) of his own importation into the Roman texts of new corruptions alongside the important corrections. His aim was high, even though he confessed that the chances of ever really getting to the true center of early Roman legal history were poor.

The canny law professor soon began to doubt that his teaching fees were being correctly accounted for, and he returned briefly to the Milanese bar; still on the money trail, promises of even better conditions in 1527 lured him back to Avignon for two years. From there it was on to Bourges for four—John Calvin sat among his students—after which Pavia for another four, then Bologna for what he believed would be his final four. The Bolognese students, however, with no built-in enthusiasm for Humanism, were cranky and disrespectful, causing Alciato soon to retreat to Ferrara. He died in 1550, still a lawyer and professor, disappointed in his strong expectations for receiving a red hat from the Pope. At least peregrinations had led to perquisites. When the ever-gracious Francis I had convinced Alciato to settle in Bourges, acceptance came easily, because Alciato had aroused so much jealousy at Avignon he deemed it prudent to leave. There was also the offer of benefices and a delightfully high salary, doubled in the second year. However, in 1553 the duke of Milan retrieved Alciato back to Italy by strong-arm outpointing of France's monarch: in addition to offers of presents, honors and salary the duke added the strong-arm threat of confiscation of the family property if Alciato did not move. Setting aside such brutish tactics, even the early twenty-first century's "star" professor system cannot outshine the out-of-proportion stipends, concessions in regard to class hours, monopoly of subject matter, and ceremonial precedence Alciato and fellow law professors enjoyed. Pomp, snobbery, and incessant bickering may have been the inevitable consequences (Gilmore, 66–67); but Alciato, actually quite flattered at becoming the butt of such famous satirists as Rabelais (1494?–1553), did not mind at all that his rich rewards for legal exercise netted him the epithet of "old mastiff."

Alciato's interest in the work of the Bartolists is illustrated by the several chapters his *Paradoxa* devoted to the great public law problem of the *imperium*. Far more polished than Budé's brief summation, the Alciato Chapter VI on the medieval dispute between Lothair and Azo became famous in the sixteenth century. He progressed with the discussion in his later *Commentarii in Digesta*, a work which enjoyed several editions over many years. Discussed at length by Gilmore, the fundamental Alciato objective is the same as that of Bartolus: to accommodate the law to the current facts of state power. The fundamental limitation is also the same: explanation has to be in terms of Roman law. Although Alciato accepted generally the gradations of *imperium* proposed by Bartolus and others, he saw them as "small utility" (Gilmore, 48–57; 56) and addressed mainly the problem of the theory of tenure. In his resolution of the Azo/Lothair debate he declared that Lothair was right in saying that only the prince had *merum imperium* in *ius proprium*, and that the function of "founding" law was a special function not included in it. *Merum imperium* became essentially high criminal jurisdiction only, even though in fact,

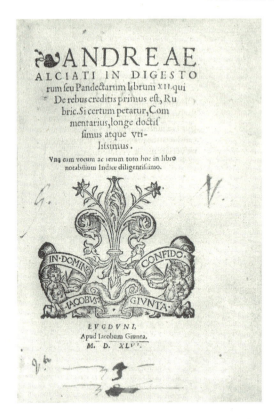

From Andrea Alciati, *In Digestorum Seu Pandectarum Librum.*
Lyons: Apud Iacobum Giunta, 1546
Courtesy of The Lawbook Exchange

however, the *praesides provinciarum* in ancient law, and dukes, heads of universities, bishops, and magistrates in Alciato's time all seemed to have it. It remained to distinguish between the unitary possession of *imperium* by the highest power and the exercise of it by delegates. Alciato declared that the delegates had only the right to administer the power, and that they had it not of the prince who appointed them but of "the law," i.e., the fundamental legal system of the land. Thus, for example, the power of the magistrate might survive the death of the king. It was here at the heart of power's realm that the ambitious Alciato had taken a far bigger step than simply bringing legal Humanism to his appreciative law students. With a little help from his beloved Roman legal history, he has made certain that all were working down a surprising new path that one day would lead lawyers to conquer the highest realms of presidential power.

Cujas and Company

The basic term, "*studio humanitas*," the Roman expression used by Cicero and others for literary education, was still in academic use in Petrarch's day. At that time it included the secular learning comprised by grammar, rhetoric, poetry, history, and moral philosophy. It remained independent of areas not part of this track: theology, metaphysics, natural philosophy, medicine, mathematics, and law. As the new Petrarchian interest in ancient classical literature developed and reached the Italian universities, professors and students of rhetoric were called in Italian *umanista* and in Latin *Humanista*; the earliest lexical examples so far found are from near the end of the fifteenth century, long after Petrarch. Soon the term was denoting all students of classical learning, or, as they were called, readers of *litterae humaniores*. The abstract noun, "Humanism," would not be first used until appearing as *Humanismus* in early nineteenth century Germany. Using the term as we have to talk about Petrarch and his successors, although convenient, admittedly falls into anachronism—the very sin Petrarch sought to avoid. Still, for our purposes "Humanism," in referencing the new way Petrarch studied classical literature, remains the most convenient word for considering the spread of the movement to law, because there its influences in philology, grammar, and history were paramount. This should not eclipse a broader use of "Humanism," equating it with the whole range of the Renaissance and many subsequent movements in thought and action. The old Symonds (Symonds, *The Revival of Learning*, 52) definition is still pertinent three centuries after he wrote it: "[The] essence of Humanism consisted in a new and vital perception of the dignity of man as a rational being, apart from theological determinations, and in the further perception that classical literature alone displayed it in the plenitude of intellectual and moral freedom."

In the study and teaching practiced by Alciato we see a practitioner as well as a teacher and scholar who embraced in his work both attention to the ancient Roman texts and concern for societal improvement. These strides forward in practical legal Humanism diminish when the classical ethos further proceeds in French universities toward its sixteenth century apogee. There, its focus is almost exclusively on the ancient texts set in an historical approach, and the very real needs of practitioners for more than a theoretical preparation are neglected. However, the leader of this French school, the remarkable scholar Jacques Cujas (1522–1590) whose name we already briefly mentioned in beginning our view along the Petrarchian ligneage, will now take the old Italian way, the *mos italicus*, before submerging it into the *mos gallicus*. It is Cujas who introduces an elegant, stylistic Humanism to train historians not advocates. But, in a century when France leads Europe in jurisprudence, it is Cujas whom many of his contemporaries readily hail as the greatest in French law.

Cujas stands on the same platform as Alciato, persuading law faculties to set aside the awkward and constrictive Bartolist technique that had been forcing thousand-year-old texts to apply to present day Europe. Like Petrarch, Cujas's approach studies Roman law within the context of its past, expanding it into a humanities program in Roman legal history which triumphs at French universities of the middle 1500s. For this triumph Cujas is nothing less than one of the principle founders if not *the* founder of the modern, scientific, historical method and of today's sociological school of jurisprudence. If the broad world of modern learning owes the university to the lawyer Irnerius, it owes its historical method in considerable part to the lawyer Cujas who, as the most outstanding of the legal Humanists, recognizes that Roman law developed diachronically and was not an

Jacques Cujas
From Sir John MacDonell and Edward Manson,
Great Jurists of the World (1914). Reprint 1997
Courtesy of The Lawbook Exchange

inevitable universal system laid down once and for all on seven hills in Italy. Although today's constantly increasing clarity of view of antique civilizations has outmoded many of the conclusions of Cujas, much of his work remains sound today, especially this advantage of perceiving that the ancient Roman law was not static but rather a system in living evolution.

Some words of caution. The Cujas apogee is also an end. Because his Humanistic studies in what the texts meant to the Romans themselves are overwhelmingly persuasive, they and other texts by jurisconsults of the 1500s gain an exclusivity of usage complete enough to bring the pure legal Humanism movement to a substantial halt, not again to revive importantly until German scholars begin to dissect the *Digest* after 1870. The Cujas field of victory lies in the modern universities rather than the modern courts, which obviously do not suspend the daily decision of legal questions before them in order to debate cases considered by some Roman jurisconsults. Studying Cujas alerts us that those who, like him, lit the Humanistic flame will now be found only on law's back stage. Ironically, Humanists are not going to be the ones known for changing lawyers' minds, even though we have come to understand they are fairly seen as having begun the scientific study of law in the modern world.

The preface to Cujas is, of necessity, his milieu—sixteenth century courts and bar where it was still the books on Roman law of the Glossators and Commentators which continued to control, along with the usual material on feudalism, customs, royal ordinances, canon law, and commercial urban statutes. In the South, Roman law was in effect just because it was the custom. On the other hand, in the North of about 1500, coming across the centuries in a slow rise from the fall of Rome, the Roman law which lawyers learned in the universities was lavishly cited. The question arose whether Roman law was indeed the common law of the North, the law from which the customs derogated and which, therefore, should be narrowly construed.

This was, according to Guy Coquille (1523–1603), the view of Lizet, First President of the Parliament of Paris. Lizet's successor, de Thou, declared instead that customs and royal statutes were the common law. Roman law was merely written reason. The sixteenth century universities, as originator venues of the rise of the Roman legal vision, were poised to concentrate on ancient, historical Roman law and repudiate the medieval Roman variation. Had their teaching been fully effective in practice, there would have been little Roman law for Lizet to apply. As it turned out, in this time of change and ambivalent feelings toward that change, practiced law increasingly reflected the economic necessities of the middle class, accelerating movement away from medieval forms to that later brand of Roman law made practical by the Commentators and now exalted by the universities. What had happened was that the main analytical device of the legists—the *imperium* of absolute monarchy—was being replicated downward as bourgeois power, be it for for the proprietor of a business or the father of a family. Practitioners of necessity separated themselves from what appeared to be the more esoteric Humanist characteristics of Cujas and the universities, yet since they all continued to begin their careers in the academy, once in advocacy they were not ashamed to pick up a Cujas point here and there when it would help (Ellul, Vol. IV, 40).

Even as Cujas enjoyed triumph, it was becoming acutely plain that the law defined by old sources, so lacking in uniformity as to people and place, was unsatisfactory. Today Cujas himself is still part of that realm of the unsatisfactory, eclipsed by an earlier law colleague, Charles Dumoulin (1500–1566), a legal Humanist learned in the Roman statutes, Dumoulin had assimilated and published on the custom of Paris when Cujas was a mere seventeen. Although he was less an academic than Cujas and did not confine himself to legal topics, his work had continued on other jurisdictions of France. Ambitious was the Demoulin agenda's watchword: a uniform private code, set under public law and based on royal sovereignty. With little success as an advocate, his subsequent career of writing and consulting brought upon Dumoulin the regularly bestowed accolades of "French Papinian" and "Prince of Jurists." Ego and fearlessness were immense, especially in his unflagging opposition to feudalism. Plunging somewhat too hotly into the Reformation controversy as a Protestant, he was compelled for a time to take refuge in Germany where he taught law. French Papinian he may have been, but he would never be a professor of law in his own country.

Once, across the Rhine, Dumoulin experienced first hand the important South/North contrast in Roman law interpretation. One infers that many court officers, lawyers, and litigants had grown fond of the customs as defenses against a potential growth of royal influence. In Germany, where centralized monarchy was almost non-existent and not feared, local princes and their local court officials and lawyers, all trained in Roman law at the universities, wanted to attract litigants to their courts. They found that the way to do it was to offer "learned law," that is, adoption in civil cases of the superior Romano-canonical procedures. This meant, first of all, acceptance of Roman substantive law as being the common law in effect unless contradicted by a custom forcefully proved and defended. Second, there was insistence that the best learning be applied to the decision of cases by sending pleadings and written evidence in a package to a law faculty. The faculty would consider the cases after which they returned draft decrees. Litigants liked this approach. Even though it meant delays and expense, it did lead to uniformity by promoting the wholesale "reception" of Roman law and serving as a definite stimulus to the law faculties. Again, such a reception, while clearly a witness to the general tendency toward homogeneity, was made easier without a strong central ruler pushing to unify customs which were probably of about the same diversity as in France (O.F. Robinson, 311–312).

The Dumoulin way, whereby Roman law was enlightened by Roman history combined with other legal sources administered by the courts, became an effort to create a national practice. This broad and practical endeavor, under one who remained a private scholar with an office practice, had already begun when legal Humanism reached Cujas on his university plateau. Gradually Dumoulin's approach to juridical study began to reduce the prestige of Justinian, the mastery of whose legendary books alone no longer put a lawyer in the front rank (*New Cambridge Modern History,* Vol. I, 448). Born twenty-two years before Cujas, Dumoulin would be the hardy pioneer, the miller who found the water and set up the wheel. It awaited Cujas, however, to learn how to turn the mill into a bread making enterprise. The struggle for a unified French national private law could not have proceeded as it did without the man in the black hat, and the expanded legal perspective offered by the Humanists working along side him. His story and theirs created the powerful stimuli to useful judicial review of the *imperium*.

Cujas was born *Cujaus* but he had soon changed the spelling to the one which he thought sounded better; fame encouraged him to give a patrician dignity by also adding a *de* before the *Cujas*. His father was a simple fuller in Toulouse whose manual trade offered the child little worldly advantage. Fortunately, the son enjoyed auspicious endowments: a happy disposition, an insatiable appetite for learning, freedom from ambition for power, and a birthplace in the southern land of Roman law. Who first encouraged him in study is unknown, but having to teach himself Latin and Greek, he did it so well that he attracted the attention of the jurist Arnaud de Ferrier who began the young man's formal legal instruction. Cujas, the student and then the scholar, would cherish a life-long affection for his mentor. Ferrier, an Alciato admirer, must have begun his protégé's orientation through history, rhetoric, philosophy, ethics, and poetry. Ancient languages and philosophy would have rounded out the Humanist base, with law introduced as the finishing touch.

It is not surprising that this disadvantaged youth chose the career widely regarded as the best avenue to fame and fortune. What is unique is the extreme ardor with which he pursued the law and how promptly he progressed in transferring Humanistic penchants into well-paid service. In Toulouse, while as yet without academic appointment or charge, he successfully gave public lectures on the *Institutes* of Justinian, a performance impressive enough to engage him by a prominent family as tutor. In 1554 when Cujas was thirty-two, a chair in law at the University became vacant. Tradition has it that three times the Cujas name was put forward, only to be rebuffed by the Toulouse governors who chose instead Forcadel, an inferior strongly supported by the local Bartolist faction. The city fathers soon came to regret their misstep; for when Cujas the same year accepted a chair at nearby Cahors, he drew many students from Toulouse with him. In almost no time Cahors could claim they had their star professor, and Cujas was soon being encouraged by the Duchesse de Béri, daughter of Francis I, who with her advisor, De l'Hôpital, was bent on building up the university at Bourges.

Unexpectedly, the Cahors appointment soon proved an uncomfortable disappointment. Violent verbal attacks characteristic among scholars were no less prevalent in the 1500s; and when the jurist Duaren, already in residence, jealously targeted Cujas, the star retreated to a prestigious chair at Valence. Occasionally he replied to denigration in kind, but seldom did he initiate academic assaults. Sensitive to criticism, he never forgave the Troyes jurist Edmond Mérille for compiling a list of his supposedly inconsistent statements. He did try out the post at Bourges, but in 1567 political troubles there forced Cujas back to Valence.

He was now attracting crowds of students from all over Europe, and the frequent moves only increased the draw. He kept on his restless wanderings, refusing along the way appointments at Avignon and Bologna (the latter communicated by Gregory XIII himself), abandoning Valence in favor of a year at Turin, during which he looked for manuscripts and tried to borrow the Florentine. Cujas seems not to have enjoyed the desired close relationship with this manuscript of the *Digest*. Undoubtedly he had been aided by its publication in 1553, but during the 1558 Italian visit he was never able to peruse the original. 1575 found him back in Bourges for good, except for a year in the capital for which the government suspended the ancient prohibition against the teaching of civil law at the University of Paris. Paris would always work hard to claim him as her own, and even today the modern tourist can stroll along Rue Cujas on the way to the law library near the Panthéon, the entrance of which is adorned by a statue of the great man. (Many were the times this author walked the same street on his way to daily library research.)

Fortune smiled less benevolently on the Cujas private life. First came the premature deaths of his wife and a promising son. In old age, still eager for a male heir, he married a young woman, Gabrielle Hervé du Chatelier, daughter of a royal official. The only issue of this marriage was Suzanne, an excessively amorous woman of multiple liaisons who squandered her father's fortune and in a pathetic and miserable old age depended for bread on the charity of her father's friends.

In the classroom Cujas could not tolerate interruption; even an unnecessary noise would cause him to walk out at once. Seldom did he invite a student voice to break the monologue and sustain a thesis in class; any permitted to do so knew it was a signal honor. The Cujas practice was not to read his lectures or even come armed with notes; he prepared by meditating on the several points he wanted to make. It has been asserted that his "delivery was hasty, his voice uneven and his pronunciation indistinct" (*Continental Legal History*, Vol. I, 257), but if so these defects certainly did not alienate his devoted students. He avoided dictation, enjoying instead the exciting new wave of printed books—cheaper, more plentiful, more accurate, or at least all the same. His students took their notes assiduously and carefully compared their records after class; this produced a copy so complete that some of their work found its way into print. Cujas was not quick in retort, and he had contempt for rhetorical flourish (*Great Jurists of the World* 94). His forte, rather, was classroom content, served up in a lucid style which was both exact and penetrating. He parried all student demands for legal opinion by referring the inquirer back into his lecture notes. Many considered that no one in Europe equaled Cujas in the art of clarifying the obscure. The explicating was perhaps the more compelling because of his highly unique physicality: short and stout, with a black (later white) beard of enormous length, and a curious, legendary sweat, which like that of Alexander the Great, had, it was said, an agreeable odor (*Biographie Universelle,* Vol IX, 537). Devoted in an avuncular way to his students, he often invited them to his table, even as regular boarders, and made his library available to them all. He took them on excursions to the country and lent them money when in distress. In gratitude they always accompanied him in procession to his lectures and his house. The reputation of the Cujas largesse and brilliance was such that in German universities the mere mention of his name caused the class to rise and doff their hats.

It was in his extensive library that Cujas took his delight; he was always on the hunt for old manuscripts and had over 500 in his possession. Studying, he would lie on his ample stomach on the floor, surrounded by texts and manuscripts; deep in thought, he was known to drag himself, *à plat ventre*, from one pile of books to another (*Continental Legal History*, Vol. I, 257). All teacher and scholar, his longing that tranquillity frame the complex study of Budé, Montaigne, and Descartes came into conflict with a turbulent century; several of his shifts from one university to another were motivated by escape from civil commotion or quarrels of the Reformation. In these religious disputes Cujas tried to take no part; practicing an outward Catholicism acceptable to authority, he kept his private counsel on the religious struggle. For him the study of law should consist of its ancient history *before* Christianity. He is believed, like Erasmus and Montaigne, to have been a man who lived for toleration while indulging in a mild form of skepticism (*Great Jurists of the World,* 93).

It was his publications rather then his lectures which had the broader influence in giving Cujas his place in legal history. From the practicing lawyer we have a collection of sixty consultations; from the historian there are writings on feudal and on canon law. Both demonstrate great familiarity with customs and royal ordinances as well as judgments and orders of the *Parlements*. Writing in fine Latin with an extreme conciseness sometimes hard to read, Cujas nevertheless brought an exceptional elegance to his rational sequences. Like Alciato he did not attempt to conclude the study of Roman law by producing a definitive comprehensive treatise. Probably he realized his age was not ready for that. Rather, with a profound and controlled erudition he prepared a base for such a treatise by studying one problem after another and publishing a series of commentaries on the ancient sources. The Cujas matrix was not the Justinianic texts but their original form under the Republic and the Principate. It was a stratum difficult to present, requiring that Cujas first utilize reconstructions from Justinian's books, moving from them to the then known fragments surviving from ancient time, and then attempting to put back together the books cut up by Tribonian for Justinian. We have also his posthumous Commentaries on Papinian, as well as other writings, mainly the substance of his lectures in which Cujas sought to reestablish the classic models like Paul, Ulpian, Modestinus, Marcellus, Julian, Scaevola, and others. In his *Observationes et emendationes*, an intervallic work of forty intended volumes appearing from 1556 on, Cujas presented—although with little order—a harvest of textual restorations, conjectures, corrections, and interpretations. He rediscovered the long forgotten texts, hailed by Romanists as incomparable in importance: the *Lex Dei*; the *Lex Romana Burgundiorum*; the Theodosian *Code*; the *Basilica*, or Greek digest of Justinian; and commentaries. In this crucial work of legal archeology Cujas boldly adjusted the old method of discussing a particular book in the style of the Glossators and Commentators. He scorned their lack of historic principle and felt especially severe toward the Commentators for being either silent, verbose, or diffuse in their reactions (*Great Jurists of the World,* 98).

The Cujas approach collated all the sources available to him in respect of each text. The 1585 edition of the Justinian *Institutes* is based on just such a rigorous textual compilation, imparting to the book an added prestige of veracity which would cause many later writers to arrange their treatises in the same order. Where Cujas did not strike out for new ground was in defending the doubtful order of topics in the *Digest*. He did, on the contrary, call on grammar as a primary humanistic weapon. In an early form of deconstruction Cujas, as Valla had done before, discovered many interpolations wrongly introduced, he felt, by Tribonian's commission. Not until the 1920s would it be concluded that Tribonian had, in fact, been placed in the untenable position of having to work with post-classical sources which already included far more serious add and pad sections than he personally ever introduced. In fact, looking back we see that in general Cujas and fellow Humanists were too hard on the old jurisconsult. It was rather the post-classical age, preceding Tribonian's sixth century reverence for the classical, that, cavalierly treating juristic literature like cookbooks (Schulz, 143), already had done the damage.

The two questions for Cujas always were: what did the ancient author write about the ancient problem before him? and what did he mean by what he wrote? Then, because he could not care less what solution an ancient author might be suggesting for a sixteenth century legal problem facing a sixteenth century jurisconsult, Cujas was freed to proceed at will with a radical, modern departure. The Cujas passion for historicity, of course, could not compel that the study of Roman law in universities, courts, and consultations of jurisconsults, be henceforth limited solely to a past tense. However, these modern venues, aided by the Cujas penchant for historicism, now had a better approach to understanding. Their discovery—what we today can envisage as history's determinant DNA—showed that in the contextual study of Roman law administered under the Republic and the Principate, even if the number of past legal problems to present were limited, analysis of that past could always disclose a predisposing structure of definition and rules. To accept this predisposition opens the solution of problems, even if one does not purport to apply directly an ancient Roman text.

Let us look at how this worked in the all-important question of command. Under feudalism the imperial authority had been clouded; public authority was seen as the private property of the vassal. In the sixteenth century the matter was still cloudy because the crown, having long before proclaimed the irremovability of magistrates, was now actually selling offices and accepting their heritability. As jurists in the Bartolist tradition tried theoretically to explain this trend, they would usually reject as abuses what they could not account for, and they would diligently remain noncommittal at the *Digest* title *De iurisdictiones*, particularly Ulpian's statements about the *merum* and *mixtum imperium* (Justinian, *The Digest of Justinian*, II, 1, 3) made in comment on the quaestorship.

Many had been the successive juristic flounderings over these words of Ulpian and the imaginative constructions lawyers then had hung from them. Here was opportunity become necessity for Cujas, and he did not neglect the challenge. In Book XXI, Chapter XXX of his *Observationes et emendationes* he published a commentary of definition. The *questor*, he wrote, did possess the *mixtum imperium*, but this cannot be traced back to holding the *merum imperium*. There is not, as had been claimed, a pure and simple Bartolist *iurisdictio* existing as a third form of power, because it is the *imperium—mixtum*, or attached to it—which alone makes it effective. In other words, *iurisdictio* and *mixtum imperium* are one. *Merum imperium*, on the other hand, does not, like *mixtum imperium*, inhere in magistracy; it rather is granted by special law, either to a private citizen or a magistrate, and it contracts a sword's power for the punishment of wrongs. Only one without *merum imperium* can, in serious crimes, wield the power to take the life of the accused. This solution by Cujas, adumbrated in part by Govea, Douaren, and Charondas (the latter a pupil of Cujas), was a year later restated by the jurist Hotman. Cujas, however, would leave the matter as it stood in the *Observationes*. He neither attempted to discern the implications of his interpretation for a contemporary political theory of magistracy nor did he attack exhaustively the constructions of the Bartolists, notably their position that the power to make law is the first characteristic of the *merum imperium* (Gilmore, 91).

Pupillorum patrocinium (1564)
*Courtesy of the Rare Book Collection,
Lillian Goldman Law Library, Yale Law School*

Perhaps the aging Cujas was too tired for rebuttal, but he now began to have camp followers who were energized for answering the questions the old warrior had raised. Political writer and magistrate Jean Bodin (1530–1596), in publications between 1559 and 1576, equated *imperium* with sovereignty. Bodin, whose monarch was to be hedged by the check of an estates general, like Bartolus made a hierarchical triage of power: the highest form is the power to create "the highest magistrates and the definition of the office of each"; making laws comes second; declaring war is third; final appellate jurisdiction fourth; and in fifth place, above the non-discretionary punishment required by the law, lies the discretionary power of life and death (Gilmore, 96).

It was the jurist Charles Loyseau (1566–1627), also seeking a rationale of the French constitution, who was next obliged to take account in his publications in 1608 and 1610 of the Cujas *imperium* and the ancient Roman constitution. He quoted the Cujas model with approval; and it might be supposed that such approbation would have led to Loyseau's abandonment of the *Digest* as a source for his own constitutional theory. Lawyers, however, hesitate to take daring leaps away from old books, and Loyseau was no exception. Usage of actual Roman law having been denied him by Cujas, he resorted to its medievalized forms, in other words, those distinctions left in heritage from Bartolus: 1) ownership as apart from possession; 2) power of an office is differentiated from the office; 3) both are separated from the person holding that office. Like Bodin, core values and the changing social ethos broke through the Loyseau concepts, disclosing a desire for a government which could be stable and effective but also fair. The achievement of this ideal was a royal sovereignty suitably limited by offices with which the sovereign could not tamper at will. Excitingly, Roman law was at last nearing a watershed where, as Gilmore writes in his conclusion (Gilmore, 117, 131), it could be used to moderate absolutism, as well as to support it. To understand this is to understand why the strong role of Roman law in France is due much less to the negative idea—that it in fact favored royal despotism—than to the heritage of an entire French bar academically trained in its philosophy (*New Cambridge Modern History,* Vol. I, 442).

Unfortunately, the components of constitutional practice which Loyseau wanted to try to harmonize in workable theory were now complicated, beyond those distinctions faced by Bodin, by the royal imprimatur having been accorded to those heritable offices. Loyseau concluded that although in Rome, as the great Cujas had said, officers possessed *merum imperium* only by special concession for each case, now it was an administrative necessity in France that they have it by virtue of their office. In feudal law this had been the domain of a property right; but it was no longer so in the seventeenth century. This change did not mean the king could arbitrarily deprive one of the *merum imperium*. But would officers who had no property right in the power of the office itself, nevertheless have the right once in the office? "No" in Rome, but "yes" in France, said Loyseau, since Louis XI had made officers irremovable from their offices. However, he concluded, this property in the office could not in theory be an absolute property, one which was alienable and heritable. That such offices were in fact alienable and heritable had to be seen as an abuse that ought to be abated (Gilmore, 120).

Neither Cujas nor his cohort had succeeded in coping with the pressing problem of procedure in creating new offices. Nor did they deal with the sanctions—which were to be as dramatic as revolution—needed to enforce theory. Finally, they did not account for the origin of theory. In other words, not yet had legal philosophizing made any illuminating proposal of a concession by the people to the crown, or of a social compact among the people themselves. In retrospect, brilliant as they were, the legal writers of sixteenth century France had on the whole been deficient in their failure to use their work as a basis for needed progress in the philosophy of law. Cujas was what historians of a recent age would call "scientific": he reported what he could learn with his eyes open. He did not attempt to fit what he saw into a system he could envisage by contemplating the facts with his eyes closed. Nor did he try to systematize the observed facts in a comprehensive, logically ordered, epitome of Roman law forms. He must have known something of Plato and

Aristotle, but sources do not tell us that he was either a Realist or a Nominalist or that he read Ockham or Aquinas.

We might add that Cujas, despite his open-eyed gaze, was not alone in such holding back from seeing the bigger picture. The same frustrating gaps obtained in the work of his academic colleagues at Bourges. Francois Baudouin (1520–1573) was content to curb the historical method to the study of Roman law. The civilist François Douaren (1509–1559) simply expounded upon Alciati. Hugues Doneau (1527–1591), an outright enemy of Cujas, prescient enough to escape the massacre of Saint Bartholomew did, however, start along a promising road where Roman law appeared as more than important history. His intelligent proposal was that the Romans be studied as offering a foundation of principles and structure for a truly systematic modern code inspired by the order of the *Institutes*. François Hotman, practicing and lecturing in Paris, followed Cujas, but to a drastic Humanism that accepted ancient literature only as an irrelevant pastime. Hotman's Roman law truly was an artifact of archeology which could have no authority in France. Rather, for Hotman the origin of Gallic legality lay deep within the unwritten law of the Franks. Thus Hotman approved the 1539 decision of Francis I that French courts should use the vernacular in all civil cases, with French law studied "in and of itself" as a system of education (Gilmore, 7).

Gaps and lapses aside, however, it is easy to see from Cujas and his post-Humanist colleagues that after about 1550, men of the law generally had begun to realize something very important: their knowledge matched or surpassed that of the ancients and their progress no longer needed to depend on imitation. In such awakening to a new era these busy practitioners showed awareness that one can manifest at least a philosophical attitude, if not a system, without writing a book of philosophy. When invited to discuss the Reformation Cujas would decline to do so with an academician's testy wondering what on earth that movement could matter to studying the edict of the praetor? This was more than an ivory tower riposte; indeed it might be regarded as a milestone in the Renaissance. In effect pre-modern Cujas was saying what many post-modernists were to profess, namely, that the lessons of antiquity are *not* to be drawn in as relevant to the problems of the present. His century had known a divorce of theology and jurisprudence and a beginning of "scientific," secular law. It was not a question of reconciling the ideas of the ancient jurists with the Church in turmoil and under attack, nor was there need to study that equilibrium between ancient philosophy and Christianity achieved by Aquinas (M. Villey, *Philosophie*, Vol. I, 132).

We have already mentioned that the work of Valla, Budé, and Alciato resulted in two currents. Current one: the pure Roman history of Cujas, a narrow research potential he would nearly exhaust—a vast subject crying out for the energies of jurists such as Dumoulin. Current two: the recognition of how Humanized Roman law could unify and simplify the complex local law which the French courts had to administer. The former, already in decline, stopped advancing with Cujas and his contemporaries, and, as we have noted, would not resonate again until the last quarter of the nineteenth century. However, there was really another current, as well, one whose negative activities cried out for a Molière to bring them around. The legal

Humanism and "pure" Roman tradition as carried on by Cujas showed academe a high level of scholarship, but the interest stimulated by Valla, Poliziano, Budé, and Alciato produced in the same university faculties, a group of pedantic *avocats savants* who concentrated so narrowly on grammar and philology that they compromised the historical method itself. Contrary to Cujas, their ferocious attacks upon the Glossators and Commentators were often made without benefit of having even studied them, while their instruction was at times nearly a farce.

A good portrait of this legal extremism can be found in Auerbach, that eager Swiss student of Zasius and Alciato we not long ago found picking up all the new ideas he could in Avignon. The sad result was that as he began his tenure as professor of law at the University of Basel, he insisted almost exclusively on being querulous: Was not all Humanism being carried much too far? How could one not bemoan the fact that basic, equally historic works of Glossators and Commentators were now going to suffer their own sad, historic neglect? Ultimately, it was this excess of third current Auerbachs which perhaps helped the most to pull down the importance level of the Petrarchan ligneage represented by Cujas and company. These smaller minds unfortunately succeeded to such effect that one is left today with the disparaging view of the *Cambridge Modern History* (*New Cambridge Modern History,* Vol. I, 17) that the work of the period 1520–1559 was merely "interesting second rate stuff." Even the eminent Romanist Schulz (Schulz, 141) pronounced the work of the legal Humanists to be "relatively immature." It is more measured and indeed more accurate to conclude that the best scholars of each age accomplish what they can with what they have. With this more moderate view it becomes clear that particularly in law the Renaissance daringly applied a new way of looking at antiquity, and that it was no other than the legal Humanists who "could invent jurisprudence, the critical examination of different ideals in law" (O.F. Robinson, 285).

Montaigne and the Revival of Skepticism

Introduction

The new bourgeois readers of the sixteenth century—the class from which came most of the lawyers—were finding Aristotle too philosophical and difficult, too encrusted with heavy scholastic glosses comparable to those worn by the Corpus Juris Civilis. Their reading went more toward Plato, where they were encouraged in their secular thoughts of an ideal system of law without religion. They also turned happily to their favorite Latin authors like Cicero and Seneca whose ideas from the Roman Hellenistic age set aside politics to give pride of place to concentration on personal life and individualism. These new readers in antiquity found Stoicism, especially Christian neo-Stoicism, made a similar appeal to the self; Epicureanism in its Christian form also supported individualism by suggesting that morality—more human, less god—meant more personal pleasure. With such influences from the past resurfacing in the changing present these entrepreneurs of the towns became what today we would call free wheelers, not enwebbed in the complex social, juridical, and economic status of a manor, but urban creatures, aspiring to live as free actors. They were open to a new vision centered on the study of self, open to begin preparing for a philosophy whose intuition would be the revolutionary "I think, therefore I am," or deduction of the existence of God from analysis of human nature. This was Nominalism with spirit strong enough to relegate Realism to the back burner while showcasing Ockhamist show-me skepticism as part of the conceptual foundation of Humanism.

It is fortunate that the fast-flowing stream of Humanist thought begun by Petrarch did not, as far as law is concerned, share the Cujas exhaustion when it came to encouraging future scientific legal history. Petrarch had been essentially a moralist seeking his example in ancient literature. Now in the second half of the sixteenth century arose one especially worthy of Petrarch's legacy and especially compatible with the individualistic readers who were searching as he did for moral guidance in the new proliferation of ancient texts. This legatee would be French and he, too, would be a lawyer and a judge. Humanist in the sense of attention to the Greek and Roman classics, he lacked the scientized technique of history being promoted by his contemporary, Cujas. Not a scholar, dominated by a taste for hard fact and common sense, he went from youthful study of the eternal verities of the Stoics to a mature man's sophisticated doubt when he encountered ancient skepticism. The whole gamut was set into a single book which he entitled, modestly, *Essais*—a quiet work but one from a prodigious mind still well known and still read with relish.

It seems more than speculation to assign Michel de Montaigne (1533–1592) as a pupil of Cujas. The classical approach was enjoying ubiquity in the French law faculties by around 1550, and Cujas lecturing in Toulouse without appointment between 1547 and 1554 is an appropriate timeframe. Yet, even if Montaigne had been one of those forced into rapt attention in the Cujas classroom, the teacher had little effect upon this student. When one day he became counselor to the *Bordeaux Parlement* the essay writer sought answer for a life question far broader, and shall we say far more human, than the Toulouse fuller's son had ever posed. Montaigne's query was nothing less crucial than how can a mortal best live the short life given here on earth? Although a faithful Roman Catholic, the iconoclastic Montaigne impatiently set aside, and in his book barely noticed, the answer of Christ's way which so confidently had been given for over a thousand years. He provided instead his own response, and it turned out to be one more appropriate for this world than preparation for the next.

The secular solution was arrived at by way of a brilliant presentation of the case for Skepticism, arousing an interest and creating a challenge the progress of which Montaigne would ultimately be unable to control. He concluded with results which would have startled any other thinker looking outward from the middle of the sixteenth century and staggered any but the most libertine of the seventeenth. Here were answers which eroded thought structures to the point of reducing certainty and denying epistemological systems a firm foundation for grappling with man and his world. This result had profound consequences in legal thought. Once more, ideas originating essentially outside the domain of either legal scholarship or legal practice entered the domain of these legal thinkers and pushed them into new channels. No estimate of Humanism in relation to law can be complete without reference to the life and work of a man who found his answers while sitting at a plain wood worktable or fighting back kidney pain on the stone toilet seat of a tiny, turreted library.

Montaigne's Education

An appreciation of the circumstances and events of Montaigne's life is made easy by the writer's unique autobiographical outpouring, amounting to 1,269 pages of essays in the recent Screech translation into English. Personal circumstances were conducive to such self-portraiture. Family fortune determined that Montaigne would be highly educated and that at thirty-eight, as a well-to-do noble, he might retire to his chateau and wholly devote himself for long stretches to reading and reflection about life and his place in it. Current events were challenging, and as parliamentary judge at Bordeaux for thirteen years he saw a great deal; even in retirement his devotion to public service provided a continuing close view of French life and manners. A spectator of and occasional player in the convulsions during the religious civil wars that began with the St. Bartholomew's massacre in 1572 and dominated the Bordeaux region for the rest of his life, Montaigne experienced in an acute form the antithetical reaction toward society in violent transition.

The paternal side of the family, the Eyquem, were of old French origin, and they had for centuries lived around Bordeaux. The grandfather was a successful merchant, building on the fortune made by his father, the first Eyquem to make a splendid career in commercial affairs. Like nearly all successful bourgeois, it was a family which aspired to use money for attaining higher social rank. They were delighted that situated on land they purchased about thirty miles east of Bordeaux came the handsome estate called Montaigne, a fief held under the Bordeaux Archbishop. Father Pierre would continue the familial ascent; deserting trade, he became a soldier and elected officeholder and embellished the simple yet elegant chateau and grounds. When Montaigne *fils* took over after Pierre's death, the estate seems to have won over social climbing. Dropping the family name of Eyquem, letters were signed simply *Montaigne*.

During Pierre's Italian campaigns he found himself deeply impressed by classical Italian learning, which to him meant Latin, if not Greek. As rock hard a character as his first name implied, the ambitious soldier was determined that his own personal Italian souvenir should be no less than knowledge of just how these Humanistic skills should be taught back home. Probably no one before or since has imparted a Latin formation so successfully, but it did mean baby Michel had to start crawling in full education mode. It is hard to overcome our own skepticism that this progeny, born after eleven months *en ventre sa mère*, ever was a baby. Even as we see him held over the baptismal font, we realize this, too, was a teaching class, for Pierre, here determined to instill some Christian humility in the infant's heart, had specifically placed the baby in the arms of poor farmers from the parish. Michel was next sent off to a peasant wet nurse in the village of Papessus. Pierre said it was to save his exhausted wife the trouble of early child-rearing stress, but later Michel thanked God for nurse's milk which instilled in him excellent health, and equanimity. He would need both for, still very young, he was returned to the chateau where the rest of the strict paternal regimen awaited implementation. For this, the third of his six children, the father had been planning, either a profession in the Church, or public service by way of the bar. Now, with choice made of the latter, Montaigne was started on a lawyer's academic education. As destiny would have it, at Pierre's death, Michel, as the eldest surviving son, did inherit the title and estate and become something of a military man.

A highly paid German Latin tutor, Horstanus, and two Latin-speaking assistants had been engaged for the small boy on law's long road. Without grammar book, precept, whip or tears, (Frame, *Montaigne: A Biography,* 40) young Montaigne began oral and then written communication in Latin. Papa Pierre firmly enforced exclusion of French, although it meant he and his wife had to learn a little Latin themselves to talk to their son. When at a precocious six their Michel went off to the Collège de Guyenne in Bordeaux, his use of only Latin made the professors terrified to address him, so much did his fluency shame theirs. Servants and others were equally put off but had to bulk up their vocabulary. Years later, some ordinary tools were still known in the neighborhood by Latin names, and even an elderly Michel discovered that in any great emotion it was Latin which always came first to his lips (P. Villey, *Les sources & l'évolution des essais de Montaigne,* 288).

Only with Greek did Pierre fail. He had intended Michel to learn as a game the challenging declensions of that language, but the entertainment tactic made the regimen too diluted. (Later, in maturity, Michel again tried Greek for a time but once more gave it up.) Greek planned as a game was, like Latin, a deliberate tough regimen, but the prescriptions were, in truth, given by a doting father who, already putting down a path for Rousseau to follow centuries later, believed in gentleness in education. When twice Michel did feel the rod, it was only "softly." Each morning the father arranged that his son be awakened quietly by dulcet music played by a man assigned to that duty. Despite the fact that the little brain was being crammed linguistically, Pierre was convinced that the shock of awakening with a start from the profound slumber of childhood would trouble the tender intellect.

What Michel's mother thought of all this Latin and early morning melody, and how much she was able to say to her little Latin-speaking lawyer-to-be we do not know. The revelatory autobiographical *essai* was not for her, and in the 1,269 pages, she is mentioned only twice amidst much space given to admiration of the father. Her family on her father's side, the Lopez de Villanueva ("Villeneuve" in French), were Spanish Jews in Aragon. Some had converted to Christianity under pressure, several burned at the stake after sentence by the Inquisition. One, condemned in 1486, managed to escape to Provence while another settled in Bordeaux around 1510; and as this latter branch produced wealthy merchants and, later, magistrates and public figures, they like the *de Eyquem* dropped their original family name of Lopez, or Louppes, in favor of the noble *de Villeneuve*. Bertrand de Villeneuve, a

Christian, married Honorette du Puy of Christian French ancestry; it was their daughter, Antoinette, all her life a devout Catholic, who was Michel de Montaigne's mother. The surviving clues well documented by Frame (Frame, 21–28)—wary more than outgoing, strict, hard-working, thrifty, acquisitive—suggest a strong-minded manager of her household. She was bitter that her husband failed to invest part of her dowry for her benefit as had been stipulated in the marriage contract; and she was bitter, too, that on his death she had to give up her job at Montaigne to a son who, uninterested in performing it well, was content merely not to slip backwards. Historians have cautiously weighed the role in Montaigne's mind and temperament of the maternal figure; capable as she was, there could always be felt an undercurrent of tension between son and mother. Frame's conclusion: the Eyquem side helped grow deep French Gascon roots; the Lopez connection helped make Montaigne a citizen of the world. What is clear is that the toleration he endorsed all his life had its base close to a home inextricably part of Catholicism, Judaism, and Protestantism.

Young Michel tended to be "sluggish, slow, inattentive"; even at five he had never been seen to play vigorously. He hated school discipline and he would always claim to have poor memory. His family feared he would grow up into a sophisticated nobody, despite obvious maturity beyond his years. Biographers have concluded that after leaving the college at thirteen he spent the next eight to eleven years studying, probably at the well reputed University of Toulouse where Michel's uncle had attended. Madame Montaigne had come from that city, and revisiting his relatives meant exposure to people active in the law. The Humanistic faculty was generally sympathetic to the new ideas of Calvin, which brought Michel into the center of Reformation talk. The students were sharply divided, and controversy and dissidence spilled from all the religious posturing into academic procedures. Rabelais reported, as only his sharp tongue could, that the students "'burned their regents alive like kippered herring.'" And why would they not, given the strict regimen. One of Michel's law companions, Henri de Mesmes, described the adolescents' ascetic days and nights (Frame, 40–41, 44–45). Up at four (seven in winter and six in summer would have been the norm), the students prayed, then began work at five with flickering candlesticks lighting the gloss of the day. For five hours they listened to the gloss being read and discussed by teachers like fiery young Arnaud du Ferrier, patron, it will be recalled, of Cujas; this is the time when Montaigne, who is considered not to have begun his career as a judge until 1554, may well have attended such presentations. At ten students reviewed notes, ate a meal, and then read literary classics to relax before going back to the teachers at one in the afternoon for four more hours. After an hour of putting all the day's notes in order and checking citations, there would be a light supper at six, followed by more reading in Greek or Latin for relaxation. Only on Sunday after mass and vespers were there the frivolities of music and walks.

Did the rather languid Montaigne ever really immerse himself in this draconian routine? It is hard to have confidence that he did. *Essais* that include much on education in general, as well as careful description of childhood experiences at the Collège in Bordeaux never mention study at Toulouse. Given that mention is made of any self-taught preparatory law study, it seems highly likely that he had done the necessary work toward his *license* before entering the magistracy at a precocious twenty-one. Required for membership in the bar, the *license* was obligatory also for *Parlement*, along with an examination there on the law. However, it is well known that in this period of academic decline universities sometimes in effect sold their *license*; and, moreover, the king could if he chose simply waive requirements for judicial office, especially for one whose family had money and standing in society. Frame (Frame, 46) believes that the under-aged Montaigne probably received such dispensation to take a seat in the Cour des Aides of Périgueux in 1553 before ascending to the Bordeaux councillorship in 1557. Despite taking on judicature without experience as an *avocat*, Montaigne worked on in law for over thirteen years, perhaps as many as sixteen. He may not have mentioned the *license* or how he reached *Parlement*, but he was alert to legal procedure, flaws and all, and shared with the lay public a rather jaundiced view of the entire profession:

> When our Courts of Parliament have to admit magistrates, some examine only their learning: others make also a practical assay of their ability by giving them a case to judge. The latter seem to me to have the better procedure, and even though both of those are necessary and both are needed together, nevertheless the talent for knowledge is less to be prized than that for judging. Judgment can do without knowledge; but not knowledge without judgment. It is what that Greek verse says: 'what use is knowledge if there is no understanding?' Would to God for the good of French justice that those Societies [courts of justice]…should prove to be as well furnished with understanding and integrity as they still are without knowledge! 'We are taught for the schoolroom, not for life. (Montaigne, I. 25; 158).

Venality of Office and the High Robe

The comparative ease with which a youth like Montaigne could access a judicial career was due to the system known as venality of offices. Inspired perhaps by the permanent status of a feudal vassal, offices, distinguished from the temporary appointments of commissioners, were created on a permanent basis by *ordonnance* of the king. Filled by a *lettre de provision*, the office did not expire with the death or resignation of the incumbent. In theory it was the king who held power to discharge and appoint; but the far-reaching ambition in bearing office title, realized over a long period of time, went way beyond life tenure to the right to designate a successor, the power to sell that right, and ultimately the recognition of the right to office as an asset of the incumbency estate.

Beginning in the 1300s and continuing in spite of a string of *ordonnances* which interdicted the practice, office holders step by step were permitted *de facto* what the king occasionally tried to deny *de jure*. The reason for the discrepancy was quite simply that between denunciations the king tolerated everything. Appointees themselves could name successors and make them pay dearly for the nomination; they could hold several offices and appoint delegates from whom they demanded payment; they were required to make a security deposit with the king and then recover it (with an addition) from their successors; and they were expressly permitted to resign the office into the hands of the king (imitating papal ecclesiastical practice) with nomination of a successor who paid the office holder. By the end of the fourteenth century the power of venality was well established, as was a record of failure from desperate reformist *Parlements* which had even tried to demand of new members a kind of clean hands oath testifying that they had paid nothing.

As late as 1566 there were *ordonnances* written against venality, but they remained mere declarations without any attempt to apply them (Ellul, Vol. IV, 59). The system, as it finally evolved, can be understood in effect as a tax imposed by the king in advance on the income of office holders, thus set free in a fee system to make as much money as they could. The fee, like direct taxes, was farmed by the king for immediate revenue. Four strong factors mitigated against change. First, affluent bourgeois merchants had the wealth to pay for prominent offices. Second, because a royal *ordonnance* of 1467 decreed that revocation occurred only in case of forfeiture, it was well established that these offices were appointments for life. Third, offices had taken on an attractively stable value as investments. Office holders had pressed for the firm heritability necessary to establish sound value, and by a series of complex technical steps, it had been fully established by 1581 that payment of a new tax would get the desired privilege. Fourth, in this byzantine patronage situation the crown decided the best way out of something it could not change was to profit from it as well. Louis XII sold offices in 1499 to cover a deficit; Francis I both put through regulation for this practice and created a bureau to administer it. The monarch made sure payment was required to him from any successor in case of sale of the office; the king relinquished only part of such profit to the resigning incumbent. Under this system, since a sale within forty days of death was void, the office then completely escheated to the king.

This evolution of offices was accompanied by social, economic, and political developments of great importance. As the French bourgeoisie grew in wealth and political power it achieved, at least at the level of the courts of *Parlement*, incontestable noble status with all its privileges. This social rise occurred whether or not title was added by buying land whose fief-ownership carried with it a title. Actually, the old nobility of the land were often excluded from office for lack of movable wealth. The exciting accrual of power became the domain of those active and intelligent young men who could begin at the bottom of the bourgeoisie, ascend as merchants until as financiers they took high financial office, even rising to king's minister. They, then, in turn, would watch their own sons with law degrees push the stakes ever upward—positioned in the highest courts of the land with the enviable opportunity of becoming Chancellor of France. The ruling class was in effect, in a revolutionary process of transformation and self-renewal. As early as the fifteenth century there had been a noticeable decline in the number of ecclesiastics in office; and while nobles, as office holders, were still numerous a century later, the majority already were bourgeois. Many of these held law degrees.

Thus the sixteenth century bore witness to ecclesiastics almost disappearing from office, while the number of nobles declined precipitously as many found themselves economically ruined. The bourgeoisie, on the other hand, dominated in the comforting knowledge they held the technical expertise in finance and law that the king required. What is more, they possessed the money to buy the offices that the king had to fill. Soon those at the top of the judicial administration began to be seen and see themselves as a new social class with terminology to match. They were the "high robe," wearing the "long robe" of judges and lawyers; they thus looked distinct from the old aristocrats of the "sword" who wore the "short robe" which more readily accommodated that weapon.

To the three ancient estates of church, nobility, and people, Montaigne now himself bore witness to this newly powerful echelon of the men who dealt in lawsuits. In the higher reaches of this fourth estate a man might even become through law a noble entitled to nobility's privileges, including exemption from certain taxes. The king frequently did the granting of this status, but with many high offices it came with automatic ease. Whereas older aristocracy elevated by birth was still required to prove the status of fathers to the third or fourth male generation, by the eighteenth century, bourgeois *robe* lawyers would with few exceptions be required to do nothing in justifying status except live nobly. That meant not working for money in an occupation. A heavy factor in the drift to Revolution, the "high robe" by then would have become a powerful, entrenched political class, held in check by Louis XIV but rampant after the Sun had set.

As the highest court of French justice, the *Parlement*, theoretically one, in actuality acted in the latter part of the sixteenth century by means of separate groups. These entities functioned in each of eight leading cities like Bordeaux, with Paris as oldest and strongest. The "high robe," being centered in the *Parlements*, held political as well as judicial function; in addition to the adjudication of disputes, theirs was the function of "registering" the king's legislation, essential to promulgation. Through the centuries the *Parlement* tended to claim that registry was in its discretion, while the crown downgraded registry to a mere ministerial duty, required only for informing the lower courts. If *Parlement* remonstrated against a royal decree, the king himself could then come to *Parlement*, take his place in a procedure called *lit de justice*, and require immediate obedience.

It was a case of a class leading a culture, and it was the lawyers who served as the outstanding leaders in the class. Although the circumstances are different, one is reminded of those two other historic intellectual leadership intervals for lawyers: the intellectual and moral standard bearing of the Roman jurisconsults, and the revival of Roman law by Irnerius that created the universities. Now the leaders were outside the universities, although an unusually high number, nevertheless, were academically trained lawyers who at the *Parlement* level easily infiltrated the old nobility by marriage and association. Even Montaigne the impartial judge saw the benefit in harvesting connections made in that milieu.

A lawyer today may well regard this mercenary system as an outrageous blot on French history. Many contemporary Frenchmen thought so, too. Some like Coquille blamed it on bad influence brought back from the fifteenth century Italian campaigns. Yet, although its defects were serious, the system did encourage into action active and intelligent people by a route that may have been the only way the

Old Régime could have done it. Instead of disastrous results, the administration was, in consequence, rather independent of royal power and could oppose it on behalf of collective interests. Moreover, it was generally independent of improper political influence from outside the government. As for justice, given that the body of law had profound need of unification and simplification, it tended to be as equitable as might be allowed. Superb legal work was done at least outside the universities, and the law faculties, too, were to rise in quality when Louis XIV made needed reforms toward the end of the next century. On the whole the high robe maintained loyalty to the king, for they knew well the value of their offices depended on the success of royal authority. A sort of strange bedfellow alliance developed between the crown and this professional bourgeoisie which the monarch used to try to control intractable men among those of the sword. In recompense of that alliance, office-holders were not financially disappointed. The seat of a councillor in the *Paris Parlement* worth 6,000 pounds in 1522 was worth 60,000 in 1580. Between 1593 and 1633 the price of offices rose by a factor of five or six, while wages went up 20% and the cost of living about 50%. Even merchants may not have done so well (Ellul, Vol. IV, 63). The king, too, added to his purse: sixteenth century Francis I raised 900,000 pounds on venality, while between 1600 and 1633 the crown took in, although irregularly, amounts from 625,000 pounds to 37,000,000 pounds.

The system, however, exhibited one fault more glaring than the rest. Needy kings created so many offices that the number tripled in the sixteenth century alone. Where one office would suffice, the king invented places for a group; in some posts two men were appointed to be alternated at six month intervals. The king even threatened established institutions with their own clouds of additional functionaries, thus forcing them into the bizarre expediency of buying blocks of offices for the sole purpose of preventing them from being filled. An Anglo-American observer today is surprised by the number of judges in a French court. Montaigne always thought there were too many and complained that "'the whole disorder of justice comes from the infinite number of officers that are put into it…[and from] the bad order of their election and…everything…venal…'" (Frame, 55).

Montaigne's Judicial Career; La Boétie

When Montaigne was at twenty-one introduced to bureaucratic monetary juggling, it was the same year when royal decree created a new Cour des Aides to help raise money. This court was located at Périgueux not far from Bordeaux, and its task was overseeing affairs for Guyenne, Auvergne, and Poitou. As a court having jurisdiction over cases concerned with taxes, levies, customs duties, etc., it effectively curtailed the jurisdiction of the Cour des Aides of Paris and Montpellier. The king farmed out the new offices to the mayor and consuls of Périgueux for 50,000 crowns; they then resold them to the local gentry, including Montaigne's uncle Pierre Eyquem, who probably transferred to the nephew his position as one of the eleven councillors. Protests by the losing courts and by the *Parlement* of Bordeaux would lead to the suppression of the new court in 1557. Its jurisdiction was henceforth given over to the *Parlement of Bordeaux* whose personnel could henceforth function without examination as a separate unit within the *Parlement*. Among these bureaucrats was Montaigne, now twenty-four, taking his seat among several relatives who were also judges. Here he served until 1570. Of the details of his judicial career Montaigne himself gives no direct account, and the surviving records offer only scanty reports. One sighting at twenty-eight shows him chosen to speak for the Périgueux group against the continued slights of the other councillors. At thirty he is accused with others of having shown partiality to the *grand sénéchal* of Guyenne—an appointee of Protestant King Henri de Navarre.

If Montaigne's life in the law remains vague, we, however, have many details about the judicial system in which he professionally functioned. The general course of civil procedure during the Ancien Régime called for the lawyer, or *avocat*, of the plaintiff, or *demandeur*, to arrange for the summoning of the defendant, or *défendeur*. He then presented the court a writing setting forth the ground of the demand and the legal arguments supporting it. The lawyer also included a formal conclusion stating the judgment sought. The *défendeur* replied with a similar paper, less the conclusion. Thereafter, the merits were discussed orally before the judge by the *avocats*, at which time the judge was concerned to see that the *dossier* was complete, including documents stating the facts. The case was then referred to one of the *conseillers*—councillors, that is to say, judges; he would then draft a report. Here could be found in writing the nature of the demand, the facts admitted and disputed, the points of law arising from them, the evidence supporting the disputed facts, and the legal arguments brought forward. This councillor might or might not add his own opinion, before sending his report to the other councillors (or the relevant bench in the case of the *Parlement*) who deliberated in private and then announced judgment without publication of separate opinions.

In the *Parlement* of Paris, and probably in the other *parlements* also, the duty of the report was performed by the *avocat général*, who, having completed a review of the case, called a pleading, then presented it orally (with the attorneys of the parties being also heard), together with his view of the considerations involved. He ended with a formal conclusion and, in technical language, made a proposed judgment. English procedure of the time aimed at the exchange of allegations (pleadings) by counsel for the parties until a single issue, determinative of the case, was arrived at. Only then was the evidence heard for the first time and all at once, with surprise a constant factor. In contrast the old French system seems more "scientific" and less hazardous: it was a judge who took command to assure full presentation of the case.

From La Boétie, a fellow *conseiller* and close friend of Montaigne, twenty-two reports survive, suggesting what was probably the fact—that Montaigne, in spite of his intellectual ability, did not assume a heavy burden as one of the leaders of the *Parlement* of Bordeaux. Yet it is fair to assume that he did not shirk the work, either; the historian de Thou accorded both La Boétie and Montaigne the honorific name of *assessor dignissimus*, or most worthy magistrate. Reports by Montaigne on five separate cases survive; all are terse, impersonal, and, except for one of them, short. In Frame's (Frame, 56) copy of a case example it appears that although the document is in Montaigne's hand and he is designated as reporter, the words are instead the judgment of the *Parlement* and not the actual Montaigne report. The prose merely recites that the various relevant writings have been seen, without presenting or discussing them; it is signed by the President of the panel—Montaigne's signature as reporter appended below—in behalf of the ten named *conseillers* who participated. The judgment reinstates on appeal the decision of an ordinary judge which had been reversed by the *Presidial* in September 1560. The ground of action does not appear.

It seems reasonable to infer that Montaigne was familiar with the legal literature: the *Corpus Juris Civilis*, Accursius, Bartolus, the royal ordonnances, the *coûtumes* of Bordeaux and Périgueux, and other necessary sources, with Roman law serving as the common law in this particular jurisdiction. Again one wonders about Montaigne the man. Did he like all these legal linkages from the past? Was he delighted in close study of them? Did he possess that *sine qua non* of successful legal work: taste for the meticulous and orderly preparation of facts and law in a detail without which fertility of mind and penetrating, convincing expression are crippled? Again, the answer touches off the skeptical chord, one to which was tuned the eminent colleague lawyer and man of letters, Étienne Pasquier (1529–1615): "'No man cared less for chicanery and legal technicality than he; for his profession he was entirely indifferent.'" Still, he obviously found other ways to enjoy the law. Who can forget Montaigne's arch defense of the male sexual member with mock, formal advocacy? Who does not sense the exhilaration when he criticizes his peers' ceremony, pedantry, and hypocrisy, noting how one magistrate provided 200 quotations in a single opinion, or how another, having just scripted the sentence against an adulterer, tore off a scrap from the same paper for his own amorous *billet-doux* to the wife of a colleague (Frame, 58–59).

Montaigne would always take seriously the importance of an efficient and equitable administration of justice, and his passionate strictures against the deficiencies of the French system were numerous and telling. He felt deeply that laws had burdened France with more of them than all the rest of the world together. The essential for Montaigne was a laudable universal ideal: justice administered by "men of virtue, learning, and integrity" (Frame, 61–62). The contrary was true. Judges enjoyed far too much discretion; and swayed by moods—sometimes easy-going, sometimes harsh—the justice they dispensed sorely frightened the people they were chosen to serve. Where laws should be rare, simple, accurate, and general, their legal language had become so unintelligible that the more study and interpretation were made of them the more were needed. Since confessions were usually induced by fraud and penalties, almost always cruel, plain death, thought Montaigne, would be better. On the whole, he concluded bitterly, the law is imbecilic and full of grievous contradiction and error. Men of affairs, however, wisely did not disregard the Perigueux jurist as a mere carper. When in 1584 Henry of Navarre consulted him about a plan for judicial reform, Montaigne was ready with many positive ideas, the chief one being opposition to the pernicious class system of different law for different social hierarchies. He thought it better to have several judges for each case rather than one, and he was against limiting the number of lawyers, while at the same time, hoping justice might someday cost less.

Important as were Montaigne's judicial lessons, they unexpectedly were less significant for the future of the philosophy of law and legal education than the intellectual and moral effect of his legendary friendship for Étienne de La Boétie. It was this extraordinary personal bond which moved Montaigne in the direction of a Humanistic devotion to the ancient classics as a major source. In turn this influenced his decision to devote himself wholly to philosophy, and despite the usual denial of being a titular philosopher, it helped hold Montaigne to thinking large thoughts once he had begun. One may doubt whether he would have become an influential skeptic had he not first become with La Boétie a devoted Stoic.

La Boétie was nearly three years older. Frame describes him (Frame, 69) as an excellent writer, already an influential negotiator in the *Parlement*, a man whose idealism, discipline, and self-confidence gave him an aura of trust. He was the son of a distinguished civil servant. His mother was the sister of a President of the *Bordeaux Parlement*. Orphaned at ten he was brought up by his namesake, a curate who helped him get his *license* in law at Orléans in 1553. He was twenty-four when in 1554 he purchased, or someone purchased for him, the councillorship held by Guillaume de Lur in the *Bordeaux Parlement*. The crown waived his lack of required age in view of his precocious ability. Like Montaigne, La Boétie, too, married a *Parlement* president's sister, this one sister to a bishop as well, and widow of Jean, Sieur d'Arsac. An accomplished Humanist and man of letters, a poet in French and Latin, La Boétie tried to quiet the Reformation by proposing Catholic changes he thought the Protestants could and should accept as part of their return to Mother Church. His *Discourse on Voluntary Servitude*, probably written while a student in the law faculty at Orléans and later revised, was well known as an argument against dictatorship. Its formidable erudition and persuasion led to its 1942 translation for republication in England and America, one more powerful contributor from the literary arsenal then ranged against the Axis powers.

Neither could say what drew one another together. Perhaps it was the fact that neither had a brother—each man called the other *frère*. They met formally at a great feast in Bordeaux in 1559, but Montaigne received already spent more than a year in *Parlement* with La Boétie, each having had reports about the other. At their actual introduction Montaigne wrote that "'we found ourselves so taken with each other, so well acquainted, so bound together, that from that time on nothing was so close to us as each other.'" Probably what struck Montaigne most about one he referred to as "'a soul of ancient mark.'" was the feeling he now knew the embodiment of a living hero of old, a man whose very conduct revived ancient wisdom's credo: love of liberty, hatred of tyranny. Together the friends tried to achieve the equivalent of one of the famous friendships of antiquity. They never tired of discoursing on philosophy, and though both were young and in full health the central subject was the mature Stoic's dilemma of how to die properly. The subject turned out to be more poignantly practical than they knew. Only about four years after they met La Boétie became ill and in a few days died. Montaigne was at his bedside, and Montaigne's name was among his last words. The friendship did not end, for, more poet than politician, Montaigne felt its beauty even more in absence: "'We filled and extended our possession of life better by separating: he lived, he enjoyed, he saw for me, and I for him, as fully as if he had been there. One part of us remained idle when we were together; (now) we were fused into one. Separation in space made the conjunction of our wills richer'" (Frame, 69, 80). On his deathbed La Boétie had encouraged Montaigne to imitate him, to play the same role, to love antique wisdom, to practice truly their studies and philosophy, to prove whether all the talk had been from the mouth or from the heart (P. Villey, 44). Although Montaigne was strong and lusty and may even have experienced a licentious period to erase his sadness at the loss, he was also level-headed, and a full and lively conscience soon pointed him down the road to follow. La Boétie, the eternal presence, was not to be disappointed, and for that the legal profession is the richer.

Translation of the Book of Raymond Sebond

Sometime between 1538 and 1546 Pierre Eyquem de Montaigne, who admired the company of learned men, had offered a few days entertainment at Montaigne to the Toulouse scholar Pierre Bunel. At parting Bunel gave his host a book by the Spaniard, Raymund de Sabunde—frenchified to Raymond Sebond—who had over a hundred years earlier taught medicine, theology, and philosophy at Toulouse. At his death there in 1436, he had left *Theologia Naturalis*, a manuscript in a strange linguistic combination of Spanish and Latin which he had written in the 1420s or early 1430s. This *Book of Creatures*, or *Natural Theology* was published in 1484 to great acclaim in Holland and Germany, and after 1509 it could be found in France as well.

The book's timing could not have been better. Protestantism had begun its Gallic advance, and the Catholic faith of many was ending or weakening. This laxism included a brother and one of Michel's sisters who would become no less than the Protestant mother of a Catholic saint. Bunel, a Humanist tempted but not yet convinced, thought the book would be helpful. Pierre misplaced his gift for a time under a pile of papers, then found it and asked his son to translate it into French. Beginning his assignment around 1565 Michel struggled here and there but gave it enough of a good try that the father took the big book of about a thousand pages and had it printed.

Although Sebond had been initially placed on the Papal Index of 1558–1559, the work except for its Preface had been free to circulate after 1564. The French version must have aroused the interest of many, for the text had an attractive thesis which was not excessively hard to understand. Sebond loftily claimed he would teach a reader in a few months—infallibly—all that was needed to know about the nature of God, humankind, and the relation between them. God, he said, had given us two books: the book of the Universal Order of Things, or Nature, and the Book of the Bible. The former was given first, composed of a multitude of creatures which are its "letters," humanity being the "capital letter." Joining the creatures, like joining letters, created clauses and sentences, and this form of writing made a science. But men and women, blinded as they were, could not read this science, and God, therefore, had helped by placing in their hands Holy Scripture. This is not so good as Nature's Book, the study of which turns no one into a heretic. Scripture, on the other hand, requires a clerk to read it and, unlike the Book of Nature, it can be corrupted, effaced, and falsely interpreted. Nevertheless, Scripture's strength lies in being derived like Nature from God. Fully in accord with Nature, it does not contradict it. It is also the only way most of humanity can have access to the Word, for only one enlightened by God and cleansed of original sin can see and read the Book of Nature. This, writes Sebond, explains why the great pagan philosophers of antiquity were closed off from grasping completely its importance; they gleaned merely partial comprehension, while at the same time, ego led them to draw their other sciences and knowledge from it. Sebond self-confidently concludes that in his book the reader of this new day will find that Sebond, the discerning author, can engender true understanding both from his orderly combinations and enlightened clarifications.

Frame (Frame, 107) believes that in translating, Montaigne, probably with one eye warily on the Vatican, watered down Sebond's Prologue claims. The changes reveal that in the course of the work Montaigne must have developed doubts about Sebond's convictions of necessity and infallibility while at the same recognizing the value of having an alternative to rabid Protestant or atheistic proclamation. What Montaigne did not lose sight of were Sebond's words about Nature. In them the grown man would recall vividly how as a small boy he had been literally gang-pressed into Education's service; it was time to turn instead to Nature and the freedom of a free-thinking program. So Judge Michel de Montaigne adjusted his wig and gave his ruling: simply let a child read the book of the world. In centuries yet to come, this revolutionary conclusion would be presented as innovative by rebellious compatriots Jean-Jacques Rousseau and André Gide.

Marriage and Retirement

In 1565 at thirty-two Montaigne married twenty-year-old Françoise de La Chassaigne (1544–1625), member of a distinguished Catholic family from Bordeaux. Her grandfather and father both served as Presidents of the *Parlement*, and her humanistically inclined brother was a translator of Seneca. Françoise was said to be beautiful, pious, and a good hostess; she would give Montaigne six girls of whom only one, Léonore, survived infancy. Pierre pinned his hopes on a dynasty and gave his son at the wedding one-quarter of the income of the estate of Montaigne, less the chateau and other buildings. But Montaigne being a very reluctant house-holder, was poor in practical affairs, unable even to remember the names of his servants. Legal training did not prevent his being daunted by mathematics, and he professed willingness to do anything to avoid reading a contract. Never would he even look at his title deeds, and indifferent in budgeting, a poor negotiator, fearful of litigation, he was known for being positively grumpy about augmenting his estate. If the master showed unfamiliarity with the simplest techniques of farming, ignorant even that yeast makes bread rise, the mistress possessed the needed talent for running the household with the order and cleanliness her husband required. Unfortunately, Françoise seemed to lack the virtue of economy, and Montaigne therefore had to be involved in domestic matters more than he liked. Frame thinks (Frame, 97, 99) the marriage probably was an even mix of satisfaction and frustration, and that Montaigne was faithful although doubtlessly disappointed that his life's companion, with neither the interest nor the ability to read the *Essais*, could not participate in the great adventure of his life. The *Essais* never mention her name (Leake, *Concordance des essais de Montaigne,* Vol. I, 551), and when he writes about wives in general he is normally fairly bitter; the one tender spot occurs when after a close brush with death and only semi-conscious after a fall while riding, he thinks to order a new horse for Françoise.

The beloved father died in 1568 while Michel was in Paris attending to the publication of his Sebond translation. In a will drafted in 1561 Pierre, now ever more doubtful about his heir as an estate manager, had named Michel the official head of the family but given management of the property to Michel's mother. The final paternal will of 1567 put more trust in the son, but just how much remained unclear. A couple of months after Pierre's death mother and son had to make a formal testamentary agreement to clarify their uncertain legal status. For Antoinette came support from the estate "with the same authority and in just the same way as she had been during life"—meaning "no superintendence and mastery other than honorary and material" (Frame, 34–35). For Michel came freedom for whatever occupation he might choose without concern for earning income beyond estate superintendence. Contentedly returning to *Parlement* in 1569 after its long vacation, the young husband sought promotion to one of the two higher chambers. This was denied; he had a close relative in each. The crown might have again granted a dispensation, but, surprisingly, Montaigne did not ask for one. Instead, he made some money, selling his parliamentary position in 1570, while ceremonially making formal resignation of his councillorship into the hands of the king. Nudged, perhaps, by the ever-present fraternal spirit of La Boétie, Montaigne finally was ready to do what law needed and what he really wanted:

> In the year of Christ 1571, a the age of thirty-eight, on the last day of February, anniversary of his birth, Michel de Montaigne, long weary of the servitude of the court and of public employments, while still entire, retired to the bosom of the learned Virgins [the Muses], where in calm and freedom from all cares he will spend what little remains of his life now more than half run out. If the fates permit he will complete this abode, this sweet ancestral retreat; and he has consecrated it to his freedom, tranquility, and leisure. (Montaigne quoted by Frame, 115).

The "sweet ancestral retreat" perches on the crest of a little hill. Visiting today, one finds Montaigne's spirit well-served by modern managerial talents that sell tourists an attractively bottled estate wine. The old buildings sit in the shape of a square about fifty yards on a side surrounding a courtyard; at the southeast corner stands a tower with the entrance gate under it. Upstairs in the tower on the third floor is a round room, formerly a wardrobe, and here Montaigne had arranged the study, with his beloved library of about 1,000 volumes on shelves around the wall in a half circle. A little sitting room still adjoins with its unassuming fireplace. We are told how the first floor was the chapel, the second Montaigne's bedroom and dressing room, and how the famous inhabitant was to find the tower ideal for his purposes although drafty in winter. And yes, there is still the unforgiving tiny stone hole where the Stoic with kidney problems had to deal with his body's special, painful

Ceiling joists in the library of Michel de Montaigne
Courtesy of The Bridgeman Art Library

kind of challenge. We gaze reflectively upon his table and chair, looking up to admire on the wall the many declarations painted in Latin followed by some fifty quotations from ancient authors placed on bottom surfaces of the writing studio's ceiling joists.

Here, for some twenty-one years, subject to interruptions for two, two-year terms as Mayor of Bordeaux, for a long trip to Italy, for a role in negotiations between the crown and Henry of Navarre, for some military service in the religious wars, and, after 1577–1578, for those terrible bouts with illness, Montaigne reflected and wrote mainly about himself. Frame describes (Frame, 63–65) that *moi*, short and thickset, with a sturdy build good for horseback. The rosy face, plump but not full, was marked by a broad round forehead, clear soft eyes, a moderate nose, small ears and mouth, good teeth, and a thick chestnut beard. He wore black and white like his father but liked adornment and affected a theatrical, aristocratic carelessness—he might deliberately put a shoe, shirt, or cloak on wrong. He was very energetic, ate greedily and with his fingers rather than the new forks and spoons, talked loudly, walked quickly, seldom listened to the whole sermon, thought best when pacing in his tower, or in bed, at table, or on his mount. Unlike his father, he was not agile or adroit at all, had a bad voice for singing, never learned to play an instrument, was poor at most athletics, had very bad penmanship, and read aloud poorly. In an age especially aware of the body, all who knew him marveled at his being impeccably odor-free. It was a lesson Montaigne could have and probably should have shared with the monarch, always a garlic man.

The Essais

Reading and reflection in his tower achieved for Montaigne an impressive philosophy of life. He was not academic or systematic, but, especially in his defense of Sebond, he discovered that ancient doubt could serve as centerpiece of a method—one buttressed by conversational observations about natural law and positive law, consistent with skepticism, and generally nominalistic in disposition. Man and presentation blended into one as Montaigne presents his thought to us in the innovative new form of the *essai* (from the verb "to try," *essayer*). With no overall plan to control or conclude, Montaigne reacted to what interested him at the moment; the flexible, fresh recording of a passage or an event in his life aroused the meditations. Each *essai* was written regardless of the nature of the last one and no doubt seldom with any clear idea of the next. Montaigne once described his work as picking bouquets to which words added only the string to tie them together (Montaigne, P. Villey, ed., *Les essais de Michel de Montaigne,* 295ff).

Montaigne keenly believed that by study of a single human life, he as a Nominalist had a privileged glimpse of those universals which tell the truth about us all. Autobiography, in essay form, accents a process where nothing need be trapped in stultifying rigidity – not thought, not structure, not style, and especially, not personhood. The twenty–first century sensibility can, far more than Montaigne's contemporaries, empathize with the *essai's* tentative nature, its tantalizing lack of closure. Our Freud-conditioned eye and mind find appeal in that open hole undercutting the phallic tower, the doubtful male in a dominatrix female household. Today's reader cannot help but wonder whether it all worked subliminally to help Montaigne cast off in the *essai* structure the leftover stone weight of Pierre d' Eyquem and of Aristotle, those Humanistic All-Father believers in integrity through completeness. An *essai* certainly suggests a pre-feminist construct, one which is open-ended, flexible, autobiographically essentialist. And living far from the madding crowd, almost maddeningly inconclusive, and maidenly emotional with La Boétie, this Montaigne *persona,* questioning "Who am I?" tempts us to another question. Borrowing the title Gilbert and Gubar gave to their feminist study of patriarchal subversion and control, does the flexible *essai* preference make Montaigne the first truly liberated madwoman in the attic?

At the end of his twenty years of meditation and writing Montaigne had produced and published 107 *essais*. Some were very short, some long, and the one that most interests us, the *Apology*, very long. First publication was in 1580: ninety-four *essais* arranged in two books. By 1588 he had published a third book of thirteen additional *essais* and a new edition of the first two books increased by about 600 items. He considered these to be literally "additions," since it was his intention to change nothing even if in 1588 he would not have written what he published in 1580. At his death in 1592 he was preparing a third edition with more additions, written on a copy of the 1588 edition in unbound sheets; there were no new *essais*. This version was published in 1595, appropriately by a female disciple, the brilliant Marie le Jars de Gournay, who would go on to write her own book on the equality of the sexes.

Michel Eyquem de Montaigne
Courtesy of The Bridgeman Art Library

In 1922 Villey found it impossible to arrange in chronological order the contents of the last two editions; the first, on the other hand, yielded considerably to his analysis. For Villey the work bore the imprint of three philosophical stages. Around 1572 Montaigne's thought is rather stiff and taut, he demonstrates still the stoicism that he had promised La Boétie on his deathbed. By 1576 Montaigne has passed through an intellectual crisis—the Sebond period—concluding that it is Skepticism, not Stoicism, which is the way to understanding. By 1578 or 1579 he has extracted himself from this absorbing influence of Skepticism and is forming the amalgam of his personal philosophy, adumbrating the second edition of 1588 which will include his third book. Because it is the doubtful period which influences Montaigne's philosophy of law, we should therefore now review Skepticism's ancient origin in a little more detail, finding some justification in the fact even Montaigne made his readers wait several hundreds of pages before broaching the topic.

The Revival of Skepticism
Looking Back at the Ancients

Realists beget Nominalists. Our earlier meeting with the Socratic Plato's and Aristotle's unchanging universals brought the realization that when many are certain something is true, others will be provoked to question and deny. When the fourth century BCE reign of Alexander the Great meant the day of the city-state was gone, the human drama was entangled into a much larger cosmopolitan whole. Since the civic act in this new whole was ill-defined by that whole, a citizen began naturally to see himself as a questing individual in need of personal guidance for moral values. Where dogmatic knowledge had ruled over conduct, now ethics increased their importance in relation to ontology. But fresh metaphysical speculation was not attempted; to the extent they needed metaphysics the new thinkers, resorting elsewhere than to Socrates, Plato, and Aristotle, by this reversion came up with their own philosophies for individualism: Stoicism, Epicureanism, and Skepticism. Such concentration on the practical was particularly encouraged after the Roman conquest of Greece emphasized standards for life. It was this aspect that appealed to Humanist Montaigne.

Stoicism, it will be recalled, began with Zeno, a Cypriot whom we met in Athens, studying and teaching philosophy from about 300 BCE. For forty years he paced up and down among those painted colonnades of the Stoa Poecile, lecturing on a philosophy given form by Chrysippus (280–206 BCE) who rejected the doctrines of the universal held by Plato and Aristotle. In Zeno only the individual existed; knowledge consisted of particular objects which, through sense perception, made an impression on the soul. Against Nominalism, without a worry for consistency, the Stoics maintained a Rationalism that taught of general ideas antecedent to experience, virtually innate and known through the mind. This rational aspect became the more influential, and Stoicism took for itself an attitude of personal devotion to the Divine Principle. People could grasp how the beauty of Nature proved the existence of the prime principle of thought in the Universe: God, arranger of all for the good of all, a force material like fire, finer than the dross of the world, and in which lie the active seed forms of all things. The Stoic staunchly saw all that man did as determined; freedom was assenting to it. No act could be evil, but rather the intent of the actor, out of harmony with right reason. Seneca thus maintained Stoic philosophy as an ethical science of conduct. Knowing how to die, the goal stressed by La Boétie, was but a small feature of a complex body of thought in which the cardinal virtues of moral insight, courage, self-control or temperance, and justice kept duty fulfilled in the right spirit. Through the wisdom Stoics imparted, passions and affections—that domain of the unnatural—could be purged by self-conquest and independence from externals.

At about the same time as Zeno began to pace and lecture, Epicurus had set up school in his garden at Athens. As building up the complexity of our conception of Stoicism means laying aside our limited, modern concept of "stoic" impassivity and toughness, still more must our culinary materialistic sense of "epicurean" be banished in considering Epicureanism. When we met Epicurus earlier, we saw, in fact, a very simple man, content with little, a pre-Candide in full cultivation, a placid spirit who probably accepted—stoically—the consignment of his immense library to Vesuvian ash. The hedonist's dolce vita exaggerates Epicureans' sense knowledge. Far from revels or sensations of the moment, the adepts of Epicurus sought the long view of pleasure that could endure for a lifetime. Such serenity of soul and health of body was mainly absence of pain rather than positive satisfaction and was reached through the quiet intellectuality of pleasant contemplation. Law always wrote an Epicurean's bottom line, since with prudence being the way to measure pleasure and pain, a society carefully and legally governed would alone be a conduit for the nirvana of calm.

In their quest of tranquility for the soul, both Stoics and Epicureans subordinated theoretical precision to daily practicality as they attempted to pin down answers through new, positive knowledge. Then came Pyrrho whose goal of tranquility became a denial of the possibility of knowledge. Pyrrho was with Alexander's army in India, studied there, and spent the rest of his life at Elis in Asia Minor expanding his "half-Hindu" philosophy. Here we have a guru who wrote no books but was fortunate in the bookishness of his pupil, Timon (c. 320–230 BCE). It is through him and his series of satires that we can listen in on Pyrrhic opinions. We learn Pyrrho had a broad band of tolerance, feeling comfortable with the Democritean atomism in regard to sense-knowledge (objects give off atoms which are images), with the relativism of the Sophists, and with the Cyrenaic/Epicurean counsel that practical conduct has to be based on subjective sensations. He had reached the decision that human reason could never know the inner substance of things but merely how they appeared to be. Because these appearances manifested themselves differently to different people, it was impossible to know whether a person were right, since equal grounds existed for every assertion and its denial. Succinctly put, no one could be certain of anything. Since most of humankind is compelled to take part in practical life, the wise were those who followed accepted custom and law without any delusion that they were true or right. Pyrrho taught that merely by withholding judgment on everything, one might be allowed to realize happiness. Pyrrho seems himself to have done rather well with this philosophy which did not hold its breath: living contentedly until ninety, he received special tax exemption from Elis and died covered with honors.

Pyrrho's phlegmatic approach, diametrically opposed to Plato's, exercised so much attraction that it found a niche at the Academy where its attack on metaphysics was eagerly carried forward by other thinkers. There was Arcesilaus (315–241 BCE), who flatly said he was certain of nothing, not even of that uncertainty; and Carneades (214–129 BCE) denying any criterion of truth, any sense-perception of guidance, who came up with a flat nothing both for a God and for the Universe. Living out his credo as an ambassador from Athens in 155 BCE, Carneades could argue one day in defense of justice and the next day hold up justice as but an impractical dream. On the third day an annoyed Cato sent him home as a danger to public morals. Carneades, however, on the road to Montaigne's final phase, also had seen an exit out of nihilism. He realized it was impossible to suspend judgment completely and that, by maintaining a middle-of-the-road pragmatism, one could follow a theory of probabilities which as a practical matter allowed a *modus vivendi* within the customs of the time.

Pyrrho and the Academy Skeptics were known to Montaigne mainly because of the c. 250 CE work of the Greek, Sextus Empiricus. Still looking for the evanescent tranquility of mind, Sextus had written, about 500 years after Pyrrho's lectures, an account of their powerfully seductive doubt. Sextus lived up to his name in being an empirical physician rather than a Dogmatist or Methodist, the other ancient schools of medical practice. Along with ill bodies he explored the syllogism, arguing that when we say "all men are mortal" we have already announced the Nominalist conclusion that "Socrates is mortal" since the observation of all men as to their mortality must include the individual. Implicitly, (and fortunately for his patients), Sextus knew he had rejected Aristotle who, perceiving the essence that was universal human nature, did not try for the impossible examination of all people. The Realist's universal premise of mortality, founded on the nature of man, did not, and could not, reach assumption of the unicity conclusion.

Sextus was the last ancient Pyrrhonian. Quietly dormant in manuscript form, his work lay apparently unstudied by any notable writer for about 1300 years. Then, in 1562, Henri Estienne published the first edition of the original Greek text followed in 1567 by a Latin translation. The ancient book could now encounter in Montaigne the notable mind for which it had been waiting. Its ideas were revived, and skepticism has been a mood in philosophy ever since. Once more, from near its final end at the dawn of the medieval age the ancient world had come forward to challenge and affect later thinking, this time the intellectual enquiry of the early modern era. Unlike the academic discovery of the *Digest of Justinian* and the appearance of the "new Aristotle," it seemed purposefully to have skipped over the whole medieval period for the far more person-oriented moment of Renaissance.

The Skepticism of Montaigne

1576. The lawyer in the tower had been reflecting and writing for five years. The Stoicism with which he began in obedience to La Boétie had weakened; but he had not yet taken up another approach with confidence. Then he found Estienne's Sextus, whom he must have not merely read but studied with rapt attention. Montaigne did not favor us with a diary but the evidence is impressive. In that year, once before his forty-third birthday at the end of February and once again after it, he ordered to be struck two medals to commemorate the coming of Pyrrho into his reflections. Each bore Montaigne's name, the date "1576," his coat of arms, a pair of scales in balance, and the Pyrrhonian motto, "I abstain." The famous Montaigne variation, "Que scay-je?"—"What do I know?"—had been born from this theme, and along with sixteen other Pyrrhonian maxims, it was added to the verbose long beams of the library.

Frame questions (Frame, 175–176) the sincerity of Montaigne's skepticism, suggesting that he had been playing at being a non-judgmental Pyrrhonist in the *Apology* only as a clever tactic to confound Protestant dogmatism. Where Pyrrhonists refuse to judge, Judge Montaigne judges. Screech, as well, notes (Montaigne, M. A. Screech, trans., *The complete essays,* xli) that, taking the *Essais* as a whole, since skepticism "makes the running" only in the "Apology," it suggests a "shield of last resort ever ready in reserve to use against those who sought to oppose his Church's infallibility by a rival one." On the other hand Villey sees the medals as marking a major event, a commemoration of the exhilaration felt by Montaigne in coming upon Pyrrho via Sextus. Montaigne borrows from Sextus almost thirty times in the *Apology*, and he praises the wisdom of the Skeptics above all other philosophers. Villey therefore sees the study of Sextus as the principal intellectual crisis of Montaigne's life, symbolized by the posed scales and the "What do I know?" motto.

Unlike any other of the *essais*, the *Apology*, so far as can be ascertained, was a direct response to the power of royal, and, in its case, a commandingly feminist, command. Marguerite of Valois had read Montaigne's translation in 1576 with much comfort. Sometime during the period 1578–1579 she asked if Montaigne would himself write something in defense of the author he had translated. A powerful patroness, Marguerite was Princess of France and daughter of Henry II by Catherine de Medicis. Her youthful beauty and learning competed against an infamous reputation for loose conduct. She had married in 1572 Montaigne's personal friend Henry of Bourbon, King of Navarre, the future Henry IV, after ending a previous affair with Navarre's archenemy, the very Catholic Duke of Guise. The wedding had been held on the very eve of the Guise-instigated St. Bartholomew's Day massacre. Not unexpectedly, the twelfth *essai* of Book Two—the most important of all the *Essais*—is in its nature closely involved with these serious rifts which had led to civil war in France.

Montaigne, nourished by his advances into the ancient learning to which he and La Boétie had dedicated themselves, gave pride of place in his *apologia* for Sebond the devastating argument for skepticism which still reverberates in contemporary thought. Using resources of his experience and library he turned over and over religion's great crisis. Had the Protestants brought new truth or only a new falsehood? Either of the choices was precipitating the most cataclysmic heresy the Church had yet to face, and the result was turning into both another schism between Catholics and a whole collection of alternative churches. Sebond's apologist in the tower room, although a loyal Catholic, much preferred toleration to controversy and calm to the neighborhood bombardments. His argumentation clearly left aside all the theological artillery provided by the Jesuits and the Council of Trent in the form of the militant positions, as if Montaigne, sharing at last in some measure the yearning of Pyrrho for tranquility, purposefully refrained from overtly vigorous presentation of Catholic rectitude. Instead, with Pyrrho's help, he composed a devastating indirect attack on the Protestants. We hear his voice: How do you know you are right? We hear his answer: In fact, it is not possible for you to know you are right. Still Montaigne clearly knew there was risk in what he was doing, and he cautioned his royal patroness that what he was giving her was a two-edged sword. In other words, here was the skepticism of Pyrrho applied with as much force to the Catholicism of Sebond as to the Protestantism of Luther and Calvin. In the end that was not Montaigne's worry, because, like the empirical doctor Sextus, his Rx had put his own philosophy in place, and could accept current customs without risking destructive, suicidal probes as to their ultimate truth.

Montaigne and Natural Law

Even this much of Montaigne's Sebond argument would touch legal history, moving inexorably, forcefully through later prestigious minds who influenced or engaged in thought about law. Among that roll call would be the names of Bacon,

Descartes, Pascal, Diderot, and Rousseau. In some of the other *essais*, future influence widened by promoting a stand on natural law bold enough to expand the practices even into his own day.

To try to summarize what Montaigne wrote on any question presents problems. He suffers more or less in the translation of his sixteenth century French, all the while benefiting more than a little from the punctuation, spelling, and paragraphing his editors and translators have provided. It is inevitable, though, that any explicator or summarizer—a "graduate," Montaigne would sarcastically call him—trying to present the inconclusiveness of an *essai* in logical form, must bear the burden of Montaigne's admonition not to pin down his willed ambiguities too much.

Nevertheless, for the seeker of a law of life Montaigne did have a response: there is something that truly exists without change, which has never been born nor will never end. That ontological being could only be God. Montaigne had begun his response with the senses, without which man cannot exercise his rationality. Even readily embracing all of them, the judge, who here largely followed Pyrrho via Sextus, doubted if he here moved in a realm of reason, or cogitated on a base of true data. When at length he reached a point where he knew he must consider perception, he resigned himself then and there to mere impression, sensual deception, and the ignorance of the tenuous, shifting nature of the objects the senses confusedly apprehend. He concluded: "The unreliability of our senses renders unreliable everything which they put forward.... We can see every day that the senses have mastery over our reason, forcing it to receive impressions which it knows to be false..." (Montaigne-Screech, 681; 669). Then Montaigne did what he had to do, what all politicians love to do: he left it to his successors in the next century, notably the group in Paris who in the 1620s rallied around Mersenne, to find a practical life path through this labyrinth of the sensuous. In the end he had found that no Reason can be established except by another Reason. The *que sais-je?* of all cogitation is that we cannot help but retreat into an infinity as devilish as trying to understand a book and finding there are more books on books than on anything else.

As an individual living long before individualism, diversity, and heterogeneity reigned as social and political strengths, Montaigne confessed complete diversity really made him uncomfortable. He would not struggle for universals as he grew older but not an inch wiser. However, when even his law degree had to be consigned to the *que sais-je?* docket, this did not and would never mean that Montaigne the philosopher was anything but committed to his profession's quest for natural law. He saw it was quite believable that rules of nature exist, lost through the distorting power of our ego, our reason, our habits, and those bothersome senses. It is near the very beginning of the *Essais* where Montaigne, standing on the threshold of being an eighteenth century constitutionalist, judges all men to be of the same species and, in varying degrees, all furnished with the same conceptual tools and instruments of discernment. Gathering his Humanistic credo to him like a soldier's shield, he begins the legal battle with a winning tactic: finding the way back to trust in Nature and her wise laws of conscience and honor. This natural law—the glorious *conscience* which invalidates positive law—supplies us, and the *Essais*, with a teleological, paternal competitor for life's open-ended, hybrid, unstable condition.

Montaigne and Positive Law

Montaigne was in a position to see first hand a lot of legislation, judicial law making, and religious and moral caveats. And he did not like what he saw. As a magistrate with the philosopher's yearning that truth present the same face everywhere, Montaigne realized that the world's variety in law and custom meant two men could never judge identically about anything. Improper extraneous matters were always getting into the result; there were, as well, the personal idiosyncrasies of the judge, and all the undue influence of personality vibrating from the involved parties. Even a devoted lawmaker, candidly observed Montaigne, had to make law through the nuisance haze of everyday life—with its foot problems, digestive vagaries, and meteorological realities.

Added to these stumbling blocks, he complained, there was that perennial superabundance of statutes. The variation of human action being limitless, to have even 100,000 categories covered by 100,000 laws was as useless as trying to cover infinity. Written in a legalese which ordinary Frenchmen could not even read, these statutes were uncertain and capricious. Were one to invoke Bartolus, Baldus, or Tribonian as authorities, even their accepted wisdom appeared fractured because of multiple interpretations. Add on Ulpian and the result was more in doubt, thanks to points indwelling hidden corners which the gloss never reached. To describe this chaotic image Montaigne imagined the scenario of a crowd of peasants, rushing into his chamber to tell him that, stabbed in the woods, a man lay begging for water and help. All have run away fearing to be found near the victim and charged with the crime, but now the poor wretches have neither the skill nor the money needed to prove their lack of complicity. What, wondered Montaigne, could he have advised to prevent the innocent among them from being punished? He remembered being in one court, a murder sentence having been settled and determined if not pronounced, where officials of a nearby lower tribunal announced that some prisoners held by them had actually confessed to the murder and thereby thrown an undeniable new light on the facts. The higher court refused to vacate the judgment; they feared to set a precedent for stays of execution, and once sentence had been passed they considered that they had no power to change.

Montaigne was equally sour on positive law's purveyors: "You give your lawyer a simple statement of your case; he replies, hesitantly, doubtfully.... But if you offer him a good fee to get stuck into it and all worked up about it, does he not begin to take a real interest and, once his will is inflamed, do not his arguments and forensic skills become inflamed as well?" In prose as evocative as would be Daumier's caustic engravings, Montaigne painted the portrait of contradictory, obscure attorneys, their every syllable so weighed, every species of conjunction so parsed, that they ended up entangled and bogged down in an infinitude of grammatical functions and tiny sub-clauses. No wonder, the historical Humanist acidly concluded, that "[w]hen King Ferdinand sent colonies of immigrants to the Indies he made the wise stipulation that no one should be included who had studied jurisprudence, lest lawsuits should pollute in the New World..." (Montaigne, 638, 1209).

Roused against the folly of the law, knowing he could not change it, Montaigne the magistrate suggested stunningly extreme, revolutionary solutions: "Our French laws, by their chaotic deformity, contribute not a little to the confused way they are applied and the corrupt way in which they are executed. The fact that their authority is so vague and inconsistent to some extent justifies our disobeying them and our faulty interpretation, application, and enforcement of them." The magistrate's rebellious anger then spilled over into equally liberal sympathy for the criminal: "[N]ever, if I can help it, will I submit to be judged by any man on a capital charge, during which my life or honor depend more on the skill and care of my *avocat* than on my innocence." "How frequently have I done myself an evident injustice so as to avoid the risk of receiving a worse one from the judges after years of agony and of vile and base machinations which are more hostile to my nature than the rack or pyre" (Montaigne-Screech,1216–1217; 1215; 1151).

Was this more rhetoric than revolution? Perhaps so. Basically conservative, Montaigne was living his own philosophic synthesis that refined the Stoic, the Skeptic, and the Rebel, into the constitutionalist, the moralist, and the legalist. When he did settle his bearings and find his pure judicial heart he came up with the simplest and purest of solutions: we must live by the rule. "I never break the law," he said, "I maintain that we ought to live by authority of the law…." He had noticed that the humanity seeking protection was after liberty, too: "That is the way humans proceed. We let the laws and precepts go their way: we take another…" (Montaigne-Screech, 1182; 1093; 1119). But Montaigne knew the limit, and in the end when rhetoric ended and reality took hold he opted over and over for actions within the legal compact.

Montaigne and the Scientific Revolution

Montaigne continued his Humanistic admiration for ancient literature, but it was not as a scholar applying the new scientific approach to old texts. No tower could have kept a mind so curious from the big changes: printing, the Protestant and Catholic Reformations, geographical discovery, the rise of the merchants and the middle class, secular Natural Law. But Montaigne was indirectly fighting a rearguard action with his corrosive skepticism. Whatever he learned about the principal roots of the Scientific Revolution, he, despite the stimulus of medieval scientific work and the Humanistic imperative to correct the errors of the ancients, denigrated them and failed to perceive their significance, even though as a group, scientists adopted the principles and general attitude of the Skeptics as a starting point.

The principle work of Copernicus (1473–1543) had been published ten years after the birth of Montaigne, yet philosophic reluctance to credit even the brilliance of a mind capable of rearranging the celestial orbs suggests the unprogressive stance to which doubt was leading. Tycho Brahe (1541–1601) recorded his groundbreaking astronomical observations in Montaigne's lifetime also. Although their fruit did not ripen until Kepler (1571–1630), using them, published in 1609 and 1619—considerably after Montaigne's death in 1592—the Brahe equations should have attracted the legal mind through revelations that the universe was a structure governed by mathematical law. Galileo (1564–1642), the discoverer of the experimental method of science, had in 1588, during Montaigne's lifetime, published on the center of gravity in solids. Again, to be fair to Montaigne in his indifference, Galileo's public support of Copernicus and Kepler and his great fame did not come until, post-Montaigne, he built his telescope in 1609. Montaigne could have known about Simon Stevins (1548–1620), who experimented with the cannonball that in 1586 demolished Aristotle's rule that heavier bodies fall faster; this alone, in the mind of both a legalist and mathematician, might have produced a glimpse of the quantitative, deducible character of the universe.

But Montaigne was no mathematician and had no such horizon. He denigrated geometry to a class alongside the Reason which his skeptical brain told him was unreliable. His education had been pure Pierre Eyquem: Latin and Greek. Along with confession of other practical blind spots, the son would write:

> I cannot reckon.... I can see...that these writings of mine are no more than the ravings of a man who has never done more than taste the outer crust of knowledge.... For, in brief, I do know that there is such a thing as medicine and jurisprudence; that there are four parts to mathematics: and I know more or less what they cover. (Perhaps I do also know how the sciences in general claim to serve us in our lives.) But what I have definitely not done is delve deeply into them... My game bag is made for history rather, or poetry, which I love...
> (Montaigne-Screech, 163–164)

When Peletier, the poet and mathematician, visited at the Château de Montaigne our judge decided his guest had revealed the very folly of man with all his talk of conic hyperbola and asymptotic lines (Montaigne-Screech, 644). In the long run Montaigne's bottom line of intellectual ferment was not, then, mathematics, but rather those wonderful laws of Nature which shone as a beacon. Occasionally even overly sophisticated civilized man could discern them, but—and he had seen this first hand when meeting two Brazilian cannibals in Rouen—in primitive societies it held full sway. Let us just say that for the counselor, unwavering in his legal allegiances, the Scientific Revolution had basically turned out to be a case lost on weakness of advocacy and proof.

It is here that we today can see on the firmly planted heroic feet these various lumps of clay, deteriorating into a muddy blot as the flood of science rises. For a nobleman at ease in his tower while others run his estate, a safe suspension of judgment on everything may be possible, but it is a pose that holds back life's serious actors and thinkers. When a scientific hypothesis so far resists dislodging by experiment that it is called a law, it permits its logical implications to be drawn and tested by experiment until in their turn new laws emerge. Montaigne missed this exciting turn on the road to legal sophistication.

It is ironic that Montaigne, the believer in natural law and follower of positive law, was unable to enter and link his professional theories to the exploding universe of scientific theorems. A Pyrrho long ago might well have declined to accept them also, but for the Renaissance men of discovery who were seeking to make life better,

Title page of the first edition of *Essais* by Michel de Montaigne
Courtesy of The Bridgeman Art Library

these laws were true and to suspend judgment on them only a spur to others in continuance of the quest. Those ambitious in practical affairs saw advancement resting on the growth of such theoretical knowledge, knowledge which lay behind all practice. Thinkers had begun to suspect that their age at long last was surpassing the intellectual grid which had controlled so long; the economic changes, discoveries of new land, inventions—all undermined the ancients, and it was the rise of science more than anything else which was separating the modern world irrevocably from preceding eras. Men like Louis Le Roy (published 1594), the lawyer Étienne Pasquier (1529–1615), and others led this mood toward the idea of progress against Humanists like Montaigne whose uniformitarianist stand was just that: the world stays the same, it does not progress, it does not decline (*Dictionary of the History of Ideas*, Vol. IV, 150b). It was an attitude to retard science, and for victory science had to overcome it. Since the next great movement in legal philosophy—secular natural law—was to be stimulated by the Scientific Revolution, Montaigne's stand tended in this additional way to delay that, too, despite his trying in later life simply to strike for equilibration between beloved antiquity and perceived novelty.

After Montaigne

Montaigne left behind many manuscript additions to the *Essais*. His wife and daughter enlisted the services of Pierre de Brach who prepared a new edition sent to Mlle de Gournay in Paris. De Gournay arranged for publication, and this edition of 1595 was followed by many more printings. The Stoic maxims were greeted by the public with approval, as in the case of earlier editions, but the personal revelations of Book III which charm our age and which must have been deemed essential by the confessional Montaigne, were viewed as verging on dotage. However, the *Apology for Raymond Sebond* was given new prominence when Pierre Charron (1541–1603), a successful orthodox preacher and friend of Montaigne, published in 1601 his major work, *Of Wisdom*. For a time read as widely as the *Essais*, the Charron work was a kind of analytical, didactic version of the *Apology*. Charron probably felt he had upgraded his friend, being, as Frame writes (Frame, 310, 313), critical less of Montaigne's disorderly presentation that wasted philosophical weapons needed to support the Counter Reformation. Charron turned Montaigne's light charm into earnest disputation, thereby highlighting the very risk in the use of the two-edged rapier of skeptical argument which Montaigne had earlier explained to patroness Marguerite. The seventeenth century would be unwilling to take on either the Montaigne risk or the Charron propaganda. Charron's book went on the Index in 1605, the *Essais* in 1676, and the rest of the century undertook to cope on its own with the sharp issues already put on trial and judged on a Périgord hill.

The bones of the man who tried so long and so hard have today found their repose in a sarcophagus in the entrance hall of the building housing Faculties of Theology, Science, and Letters at the University of Bordeaux. On it rests his statue, recumbent in full armor. Irony continues to surround the great mind into eternity, for although the epitaphs in Latin and Greek were probably composed by a lawyer, Jean de Saint-Martin of Bordeaux, neither he nor his judicial colleagues even bothered to proffer honor to Montaigne, the legal professional who had so far surpassed them all.

Martin Luther
Courtesy of National Gallery of Art, Washington

PART 12

Reformation and Counter Reformation
*Individual Conscience and the Response
of Church and Crown*

Reformation

Introduction

Humanism, including the legal antiquarianism discussed in the preceding chapter, certainly made its mark on European development, but it was the religious revolutions of the sixteenth century which turned the world toward modern thought. From the beginning of the fourteenth century the possibility of ending the idea of a Church universal which could exercise unrestricted temporal power had already become reality. Although Rome would try to renew its grip on Catholic hegemony at the Council of Trent (1545–1563), large areas of Europe slipped from the spiritual grip as many European princes, inspired by the blows of the French king against Boniface VIII, in effect took the pope's place by electing for Protestantism as a state religion. In France the king, while remaining Catholic, was already well advanced in wielding for himself papal jurisdiction over the French Church. Despite both widespread support for Rome by lawyers and the vision of most Europeans that Catholic Emperor Charles V was the last chance for peace in Christendom, the idea that there could be a comprehensive secular government in which a medieval Roman emperor supported a pontiff (or tried to dominate him) finally ended.

Upon reaching this crucial point, Charles V was unwilling to take the final bow. He had long seen himself as a second Charlemagne and actively maintained the legal principle of dynastic family units holding nearly all of Europe except England and France under at least nominal rule. But Charles, even from a Spain at her height, could not mount enough power to roll back the Protestants and make his claims a reality. Interestingly, on the Protestant side the great religious power changes were equally unproductive of any new systematic philosophy of law. Luther was no legal scholar and criticized philosophical speculation in the theological domain (Copleston, Vol. IV, 103). The sixteenth century, therefore, was pronounced by Russell (Russell, 493) to have been largely barren of progress in any ordered epistemology. However, we are about to find exceptions among the Dominicans and Jesuits whose initiatives portended large differences. These changes would enter the very structure of law—its courts, its practice, and its academic faculties.

Earlier discussion of the medieval Church showed her unable to cope with the consequences of her success. It will be recalled how at the end of the eleventh century Cluniac dominance, the work of Gregory VII and later of the Cistercian order provided imaginative responses to the demand for better religion. As the thirteenth century began, the leadership of Innocent III, coupled with Dominican and Franciscan education of and preaching to the rising towns, meant a fairly adequate Church response to continued demands for improved piety. On the other hand, fourteenth century opposition to papal absolutism and opulence took sharper tones which could vacillate from democratic to violent, as illustrated by Marsilius of Padua, Ockham, and by populist fervor in uprisings led by Wat Tyler in England (1381). By the sixteenth century the wealthy self-made and self-confident burghers, increasingly sophisticated and being more frequently educated than their fathers, found stimulation by readings in the new mass-produced books. It was this intellectually curious group which knew they needed more satisfaction from religion, and, as we have previously mentioned, craved more confidence in their personal salvation and afterlife in heaven.

The Church response was again to create yet another brilliant new order of priests: the Jesuits under Loyola. This time the reaction would come too late; probably even a timely reciprocity would have been insufficient. For government had also continued to evolve, often at a quicker pace, pushing ahead its pattern of royal nation-states. Greedy and ambitious, some of the hungry monarchs had seized the opportunity in one stroke to rid themselves of papal political interference and, in the Cathar heresy, to grab valuable Church land and buildings to allay, at least temporarily, their chronic shortage of cash. Here lay the difference between earlier attempts at improvement and a 16th century intensity for reform. Now secular men moving dramatically had sufficient momentum to make change effective with the force which could finally expel papal and imperial power. Admittedly, the theological ideas of Luther, reconciled with God, can be seen as no more radical than those of Abelard and Aquinas—momentous concepts which the Church had already contemplated without breaking up. Yet in the Reformation the consolidation of national states had been proceeding so vigorously that the outward splendor of Charles V was in reality too weak to hold back these tides of a new time.

Reformation's cataclysmic consequences, it should be noted, were intended by none of its leaders (O.F. Robinson, 310). These were lawyers who hoped that winning their extraordinary case would capture all secular government, but do it with no arms brandished. By the end of the sixteenth century, however, no thinker of the new way had found that peace. All were battle scarred, and heroic failure had imbued each with an aura both tragically ancient and admirably modern. Many German states and all of Scandinavia would be Lutheran; most of the remaining German states and Spain and Italy remained Catholic; England would have her own national church on generally Lutheran and Calvinistic theological principles but with some Catholic organization extant when not forcibly driven out. Strong reform congregations followed the vigorous leadership of Calvin; while France, where Catholic royal power was slow in its response to Geneva's predicator, would be rent nearly in two.

While the national state and its armies ended the old concepts of a Christendom to unite Europe, there grew ever stronger the Nominalists' credo of each human's importance and dignity. It was the birth of the stunning idea that persons should be generally free to worship and do as they pleased. This liberal ideal finally became countenanced when rulers practiced at last a modern statecraft in which security did not depend on uniformity. General revolt against authoritarianism led also to the equally advanced understanding that religious protection and guarantee of safety could exist actually in a greater degree through toleration. The ramifications of such remarkable concepts illumined the revolutionary theory of a contract between ruler and people—some of whom might talk divine right when the throne was occupied by one of their own, but who could just as well turn to democratic processes of dislodgment for breach of that contract. Controversial proposals like these, although far less religious in character than the old faith, took on aspects of belief, aspects important to have in order to manifest new religion. Thinkers like Niebuhr and Weber have underscored how the Reformation's new burst of freedom, by shattering the medieval power structure, paved the way for pluralistic national democracies and, quite possibly, capitalism (Rudy, 76). A framework of tolerance and individualism helped the continuing plight of numerous religious congregations, many of whom wanted to rise from minority status to become themselves the one true state religion. Like the Calvinists in Holland, England, and America it was frequently and notably these minority congregations who, seeking secular control but failing to get it, made inadvertently the inestimable contributions needed by a world about to turn new age.

The Humanists had looked back, when through printing's keyhole they became reacquainted with Church fathers as well as ancient pagans. Their gaze of amazement in turn opened the eyes of the reform leaders who, thinking there had been a decline from an ideal, started their own review of early Christianity and found in its simplicity a model for change. Rather than any religious promoter, it would be such scholars and later, in the seventeenth century, their colleagues the scientists, who began the undermining of dogmatic theology. It is important to note that the Reformation leaders were not responding to new intellectual thrusts like those of the re-discovered *Digest*, the *new* Aristotle, and the Ciceronian Petrarch; rather they were grappling in ill humor and high dissatisfaction with the current theology and administration of the Roman Church. After all, the Reformation should be seen, as was suggested above, not as the collapse of religion but rather as a great age of revived interest in religion. Princes had now an attractive choice between competing faiths, for they had been given new flexibility to establish, under princely control, the religion they preferred.

There were equally remarkable patterns of change which stimulated intellectual study and reflection about belief. An individual's freedom of choice became equally exercisable by moving from state to state, if not by moving from congregation to congregation. There was a particularly great increase of interest in the Bible; personal study shifted emphasis to the Old Testament which many Protestants found in some degree substituted for the canon law books burned by Luther. The trend in secularization inevitably interfered with the medieval Church monopoly on training ecclesiastics whose careers we have long followed as they brought to the bureaucracies of government reading and writing skills and the inestimable ability to think abstractly. As the Catholic pontificate lost its hold on many universities and no Protestant equivalent arose to replace them, higher education became more and more secular in faculties and students. As those secular graduates grew up to be the new government staffs, there was created a ripple effect. The old canon law faculties in Protestant states were summarily disbanded. The English chancellors were no longer ecclesiastics. Discipline, instilled by church government, diminished, as did the accuracy once encouraged by scholasticism (Russell, 493). An accidental but no less central effect in the longer run was the conferring of autonomy on philosophy as an academic discipline (*Encyclopedia of Philosophy*, Vol. VII, 101a). At last freed from the domination of the theology faculties, the doctrine of Luther shattered the old Aquinas synthesis of Aristotle and Christianity. In that hermeneutic shattering many have heard the fall of pennies from Heaven, tracing to the Protestant work ethic the seeds of capitalism's surge.

The Condition of the Church

By the sixteenth century the Catholic Church had long worn a papal crown of remote indifference under which the personae of her rulers ran a sinful gamut. "It is doubtful," indicts Butterfield (*Dictionary of the History of Ideas*, Vol. I, 388a), "whether the directors of the Catholic system took even the minimum measures that were required to maintain their guidance over religious life or ensure the survival of the system as a whole." Too much had been left to a lower clergy often hardly able to understand their own religion, wholly unqualified to stand up to attacks upon it, and required to deliver an effective preaching which they could not deliver. From this clerical weakness had grown paganism and popular superstition among ignorant parishes. To become or to remain devout, these were audiences who depended for salvation on an overtly theatrical *deus ex machina* approach, the mechanically operated awe of painted images and saintly relics provided in God's house. There were always here and there the continued swellings of intelligent piety and reform, together with educational improvements arising from below, but no man of genius and vision directed intellectualism down from the top.

Over the centuries the Church had amassed great wealth in productive lands, and the papal states were still the extensive domain of the pontiff. Unfortunately, time had so encumbered this fortune with benefice grants, lucrative arrangements with lay officials, and imprudent management that, by the 1500s the bureaucracies of pope, archbishops, and bishops were in constant financial crises. A complex system of taxation had been, as we have said, much frustrated by royal power. Venal devices short of taxation had been overused: offices were sold for profit, and when they brought large prices, new offices were created that they might be sold for greater profit. In particular, the prelates in Rome were absorbed in the great project of building the new St. Peter's. The cash bleed proved so acute that these men had been resorting to the old practice of granting indulgence toward sin in return for offerings of money. The picture was obviously not very attractive. Where Catholicism's central power began the century of its peril in an energetic and active posture, it soon became clear that energy for the wrong activities meant it was open for chastisement.

Reformation; Erasmus

As an umbrella rubric, Reformation covers three movements: the Humanistic "philosophy of Christ," the Protestant Reformation, and the Catholic Counter-Reformation. Although Humanism is customarily considered as part of the Renaissance, it is logical and useful to consider its luminous Christianized response as part of the reformative pattern. Paradoxically this response was prepared through rather unsavory circumstances.

It began with a priest's illegitimate son, orphaned early, cajoled into a monastery by guardians who had apparently stolen his money. Rebelling against the religious life thus thrust upon him, the youth displayed such talent for learning that it became his escape route back into the secular world as secretary to the bishop of Cambrai. Thus began the career of Desiderius Erasmus of Rotterdam (1466? –1536), perhaps the greatest of the Humanists, already an accomplished Latinist and an admirer of Valla's elegance. The adolescent spent some time at the University of Paris listening to the disputes between Thomists and Scotists ("Ancients") on the one side and Ockhamists ("Moderns") on the other. Erasmus found it all to be ill-directed hot air since in the initial debate both camps shared common detestation of the Humanists. When all three camps decided to unify in 1482, it must have been quite a vindication for their confident teenage critic. We next find the restless student in 1499 England, charmed by the custom of kissing girls, but also encouraged to higher aspirations by John Colet, soon to be Dean of St. Paul's, and the young Thomas More, already familiar in law circles. Still impecunious and without a formal teacher, Erasmus spent much of his time gaining proficiency in Greek.

Erasmus of Rotterdam
Courtesy of National Gallery of Art, Washington

It would be a visit to Italy, where with his customary blasé approach he felt the scholars had nothing to teach him, which again lit enough inner fire that Erasmus once more set to work to show what he could do. By 1516 he had edited Jerome and was offering a brilliant new edition of the Greek New Testament accompanied by notes and a Latin translation. His fame, however, had already been set in 1509 when he had written quickly, as part of a lifetime of prodigious literary output, a book called *The Praise of Folly*. Dedicated to his friend More, with illustrations by Holbein, the book's heroine sings her own praises while satirically covering the waterfront of human life, its classes, and its professions. Some of the most acerbic invective went straight against current excesses in indulgences, worship of saints and the Virgin, and fierce disputes about the Trinity, monks, and popes. Erasmus concluded with the serious Pauline suggestion that true religion is but a form of Folly, a Christian simplicity that springs from the guileless heart, rather than the perverted head. Yet, Erasmus was no rationally systematic philosopher. He disliked the determinism of Luther no less than the rigors of scholasticism, and he shunned the medieval wish to create a new, single church universal.

Erasmus believed that any purification of Catholicism would require one make the eternal return to primitive roots. In this revival of literary sources, "philosophy of Christ," dogma and institutionality were minimized in sublimation to the sacred teacher of virtue. Erasmus hoped this vague ethical program might correct abuse and avoid the disruption of Christendom, but it was decisively rejected at the Council of Trent. All Erasmus's books were placed on the first Index of 1559 even though the rather phlegmatic author had neither tried to start a movement nor be an activist. He was not a populist and claimed no reform leadership; all he had hoped for were good religious texts that in clarifying the Bible's meaning would end the controversies and maybe the misuses. However, the excesses continued, culminating as Pope Leo X, known for colorful fund-raising techniques that sold cardinal's hats and memberships into the "Knights of St. Peter," proclaimed a flamboyant public indulgence sale. It was the spark which, having found tinder in the mind of Erasmus, now began in the mind of Martin Luther the fire which would permanently divide the Church.

Luther

Martin Luther (1482–1546) was made, one could say, for his extraordinary role in history. With men less resolute and less profoundly devout to lead the revolt against abuses, the Church might have embraced sufficient reform early enough to survive intact. The early Fathers had, we know, ignored Tertullian and contentedly accepted pagan literature as the basis of schooling. However, the challenges posed by Abelard and even Aquinas, as well as the revivalist ethics of Erasmus, had grown beyond interesting to influential; and with a great leader, the forces of change finally had the momentum to overturn centuries.

The circumstances of Luther's youth were vital to his character. Born a peasant, the short, stocky man retained always the directness, ruse, and stubbornness of a child of the *terroir*—fond of colloquial wisdom, accepting of a degree of superstition, and conservative in religion. His father, Hans, inheriting no land, was a miner who by hard work became the owner of six foundries. He and his equally industrious wife sensed the strength of mind behind the charm of their curly haired boy and sent him to school along with their dreams: he would become a jurist, he would, naturally, marry well, and what a support would he be to them in old age. The Luthers lived in Erfurt, and as it had a university with a renowned law faculty, they proudly saw their Martin enter in 1501 to take an M.A. and then study law. Second in a class of fifteen, having been given by proud parents his very own expensive copy of the *Corpus Juris*, he easily achieved the dual course objectives: fluency in spoken Latin, still the language of all law and learning, and the mental agility of scholasticism encouraged by the legal profession. Erfurt had not yet "gone Humanistic" and regarded Aristotle's physics as God's thoughts. The faculty felt nervous about Aquinas, looked at nearly everything through the perspective of Ockham, and in the arts course better prepared boys in church music than for the law. Although he did not attend the Humanist lectures, Martin looked upon this movement as the forerunner of a great new religion, cleansed through protestation and strong against attack. He carefully read the Latin authors and learned enough Greek to facilitate the careful working out of a theology.

Martin had been at law study for two months when on a hot day in July 1505, returning to school after a visit home, he was knocked to the ground by a great flash of summer lightning. Like Paul or Pascal, he was at once illumined with a vision of the whole Christian drama of salvation: the hope of heaven, the fear of hell. In a sudden but deeply grounded decision, the law student implored St. Anne, patroness of miners, to help him become a monk. The exceptionally intense young man had always shown extraordinary sensitivity as well as sudden oscillations between joy and despair. On that uplifting July day he had actually only just emerged from six somber months of depression, perhaps brought on by too much reading of the day's best seller manuals on the art of dying. There was thus a framework for the turn toward a cloistered life. Monastic mission, far from being a cenobitic retreat from action, would be but an early opportunity to exhibit in a different form the law student's capacity for work. In the inspired adult that assiduity would create arguments for Christian testimony both prodigious and brilliant. Considering himself bound by the legalism of his oath, the youth presented himself, although reluctantly as he said later, to the monastery of the reformed Augustinian friars. When he made the entry promises as a novice, his father was outraged by loss of this jurist intended to prop up his old age. Martin's final vows were, however, taken in contentment, and he would wear the cowl for nineteen years.

During the first dozen years Luther lived an intensely introspective religious life, seeking to know God through his own syllogistic exercises. However, two major crises would compel exceptional study and reflection and lead him to the theology which would shake the world. Crisis one came when saying his first mass. While he recited the introductory portion, he became, as he wrote later, almost struck dumb with fright. Bainton imagines the scene: "The terror of the Holy, the horrors of Infinitude, smote him like a new lightning bolt, and only through a fearful restraint could he hold himself at the altar to the end." The fear was primarily of an all-powerful deity, the same One who hid within the malevolent storm cloud over Sinai, the God before whom Moses had veiled his face. Luther was, in a very real sense, putting himself on trial. For the defense, he realized that if a person could be in harmony with this awesome God, he could find a longed-for peace. For the prosecution, he laid against his case a fear complicated by an overwhelming recognition of personal unworthiness. In an appeal for support from his father, who had attended on this important occasion, Luther recalled how he had been called to the cloistered life by none other than heavenly thunder. Shrewd old Hans demonstrated the son was not just a block off an old chip, as he probed expertly in reply the weak spot of medieval religion. "'God grant,' he grumbled, 'that it was not an apparition of the Devil'" (Bainton, *The Reformation of the Sixteenth Century* 30, 32). Luther could not parry the point, and his inner anguish grew even more.

Thus was made the decision to undertake a colossal effort at achieving inner peace that would assure salvation and close the door on hell. As a monk, Luther was free from distraction, in position to devote all his time to his goal and to take full advantage of every help offered by the Church. Fasts, vigils, prayers in numbers and length beyond the rule's stringent requirement, rejection even of the few blankets permitted, utter poverty—all these he embraced in passionate deprivation only to realize that however he might strive, imperfection remained. At this time Luther was sent on a trip to Rome, one of only three travels in his life. It gave him an opportunity to perform at the source as many as he could of the multitude of pious acts available. Sadly, he found the whole process greatly disappointing. His confessor turned out to be incompetent. After climbing Pilate's stairs on hands and knees to the very place where Christ had stood, with a Pater Noster for each stair and a kiss for good measure, the ecclesiastic with a *Corpus Juris* next to his Bible rose at the top with nothing but uncertainty as to whether he had, by this exemplary exercise, accessed in his behalf any of the saintly jury above.

Returning to the monastery, Luther was transferred to Wittenberg, a village of a little over 2,000 yet boasting a university newly founded by the doting elector, Frederick the Wise. Here the intense trainee faced crisis two. In addition to all other practices prescribed by the Church and his Order for a holy life, Luther had been resorting with fierce attention to the sacrament of penance after confession, knowing that to repent sins in this energetic posture surely guaranteed forgiveness. He thus performed the rite with immense care, on occasion consecrating as much as six hours to an avowal that so wearied his priest he was commanded in the name of God to take hope, cease, and desist. At this point, however, hope met the stone wall of a technical problem not resolved by the canon lawyers. If one granted that the sins confessed were those that were forgiven, Luther, ever the legalist, reasoned that a person could also sin and forget that sinful commission. Worse still, a person could sin without ever knowing sin had been done. Advocacy understood the abysmal conclusion: no human, being, by nature, after all, corrupt, could ever confront Christ at the Last Judgment free of sin. The lawyerly part of Luther's brain announced to the devout heart that this case was definitely closed. The penitential system had turned out to be an inevitable, complete failure (Bainton, 41). Recalling the moment later, Luther would avow that love for his Maker turned to hatred. He had reached the bleakest of crossroads where Ockham's God, the God of absolute power who could even require man to hate Him, loomed as a God easy to fear, hard to love, and impossible to serve.

As he saw the young monk being drawn into this spiritual black hole, the wise vicar of the Order, groping for a solution, told his tortured brother to enter the university at Wittenberg, take the degree of Doctor of Theology, and then fill the chair of Bible studies that the vicar had held. The only way he could cure himself would be to cure others (Bainton, 45). Luther complied. On 1 August 1513 he began to lecture on the Psalter. By 1515 he had reached Romans and in 1516–1517, Galatians. The vicar proved to be right. In study, quietly, without dramatic meteorology or inner tribunals that had brought him to the cowl and then to the panic of the first mass, Luther found his way.

In the 22nd Psalm Luther read the words of David later recited by Christ on the Cross: "My God, my God, why hast thou forsaken me?" Reflecting on this question, Luther finally perceived that the desolation into which he had plunged had been suffered also by Jesus. He began to glimpse the ultimate problem of all theology for which philosophy is unequal and reason cannot penetrate: understanding the inequity of human life on earth and the personhood of a "God [who] hides his power in weakness, his wisdom in folly, his goodness in severity, his justice in sins, his mercy in anger" (Bainton, 48). Luther was convinced at last that God is neither malicious nor capricious. Nevertheless, like all men prone to self-flagellation and a legal track of thought, he was still suspicious of the legal correctness of grace. If God is just how can He forgive a sinner? Justice is justice, not leniency. Here, however, Luther was able to find his solution in that special form of Roman adjudication: Paul's epistle about law and judgment sent to the Romans. Luther perceived that his fellow convert had wrestled with the same problem with which he, Luther, was wrestling. "The just shall live by faith" (*Bible, Revised Standard Version,* Rom 1:17) was the Pauline command which Luther decided he could interpret by using a technique from the Humanistic books he had studied. In Greek, Paul's *justice* might mean a sentence for crime, but it also might have the connotation of *justification*. Luther perceived that justification meant faith, faith that God sent Christ to save humankind. This faith was not achieved by one's own effort, but a gift freely given by God.

That the free will offering of faith comes from an intellectual exercise was to be an article of credo crucial to Protestantism. It accorded with the bourgeois desire for education and for self-reliance. Moreover, it was individualistic; each person, internally, aided only by Christian fellowship, had to achieve a state in which God might grant the great gift. One read the book, pondered, and made interpretation. Such a nominalistic emphasis on the individual signified how Luther's own experience thus had become normative. His life, as Bainton writes (Bainton, 49), was henceforth his theology.

From this Pauline study, with its driving forces of Ockhamism and Humanism, emerged the philosophy which, unintentionally for the most part, set liberty and augmented individualism and toleration as cornerstones of lasting new philosophies

Traffic in Indulgences
Courtesy of National Gallery of Art, Washington

of law in the centuries ahead. But for 1517 inner turmoil and its resolution had first to explode society. The occasion for final rupture was the old problem of the indulgence of sin; let each person decide it was efficacious to make the crawl up Pilate's steps.

The science of indulgences, as long ago as the crusades, had never been fully worked out by the canon lawyers. The attraction to the faithful was clearly reduction of time in purgatory, not only for the immediate penitent but for relatives living and deceased (in the case of the deceased the purchaser did not have to be contrite) and others designated by him. The Church could not know the time of the Second Coming and the Last Judgment, but under canon law she felicitously found herself able to calculate precisely the number of years of reduction of purgatory achieved by a given pious act. This time was available, because taking its lead from the 1230 work of English theologian Alexander of Hales, the papacy had proclaimed the merits of the saints, the Virgin, and Christ to be a treasury of merit. For example, viewing of the 19,013 holy relics amassed by Frederick in his Castle Church in Wittenberg was worth 1,902,202 years and 270 days. Dipping liberally into such a rich trove of awards, one could confirm for the faithful the mighty Vicar who had the power of the keys to bind and to loose. Three times in sermons, Luther however, had by 1516 already criticized the indulgences granted in Wittenberg under Frederick's auspices each year on All Saints' Day. The pope, he proclaimed, cannot deliver souls from purgatory. No one but God can know that contrition and confession are worthy.

These pulpit topics were now to come alive before Luther in a most venal form. Albert of Brandenburg, a Hohenzollern not yet old enough to be a bishop, already held two sees. He aspired to a third one, currently vacant—that of Gutenberg's Mainz—for here he could reign as archbishop and primate of Germany. The required installation fee was 10,000 ducats. On account of deaths, it had already been paid by the diocese twice in ten years; the people could not afford another, especially since to overcome Albert's irregular primacy over three sees at once would take even more than paying the hefty fee. Albert turned to the bankers of the house of Fugger who enjoyed a monopoly on collection of papal accounts in Germany. They replied that the Holy Father demanded 12,000 ducats be provided in honor of the twelve apostles; Albert offered 7,000 in recognition of the seven deadly sins; Fugger offered to compromise at

10,000, although not, comments Bainton (Bainton, 57), "for the ten commandments." The papacy thereupon granted Albert power to dispense for eight years the indulgence promulgated on 15 March 1517 with its *raison d'être* being to raise funds to complete the new St. Peter's. Half the revenue raised by Albert could be used for his needs, but the other half was earmarked for the building campaign.

Although indulgence was already offered for the benefit of Wittenberg and vendors were forbidden from entering Saxony, they did reach the parishioners of the pastoral professor Martin Luther. Among them was the experienced Dominican, John Tetzel, making no mention of paying off the Fuggers as he offered the St. Peter's indulgence for full remission of sins, restoration of the innocence of baptism, and elimination of purgatory. Princes and bishops were being put down for an offering of twenty-five florins, abbots and barons for twenty, bourgeois for three, others one, and the very poor for prayers and fasting. Semiotics of the setting were dramatic and effective. The red cross of Indulgence Pardoner, emblazoned with the papal arms, had been set up strategically in the center of the town. The papal bull of indulgence lay prominently elevated on a cushion; near it stood a table for writing the indulgences and a chest for the contributions. Under the cross the pardoner preached his fiery sermon the better to retain the faithful while straining for their money.

For Martin Luther this represented the hypocrisy of pure carnival masked in religious finery; when his eager parishioners brought him their letters of indulgence for official attestation, he adamantly refused. What is more, taking a step the future would regard as the beginning of the Reformation, he put his entire legal training to the service of passionate, yet careful protest and in 1517 drafted in Latin ninety-five theses of objection to indulgences. There was not one he was not ready to debate, he declared, and posted a printed copy on the church door at the dramatic day-lit hour of noon on All Hallows Eve. The timing was perfect, with the town already jammed for the annual indulgence regularly granted by the Castle Church on, appropriately, All Saints' Day. As might be expected from a lawyer born again in the flash of lightning and reputed to speak like thunder, the theses were not the usual abstract, technically worded debate topics. Daring and straightforward, they attacked both Albert's instructions for the St. Peter's indulgence and Tetzel's sermon. Luther firmly objected to raising money for the shrine for Peter and Paul; he denied Rome's power over purgatory, and above all he stressed that sinners were being cruelly deluded. The theses at once became the talk of literate and illiterate Germany, and the sale of indulgences precipitously declined.

A furious Leo X tried to get Luther to recant, but each effort pushed the rebel a little further toward defiance of papal authority. Finally, Luther was summoned to the Holy City. Leo no doubt would have had him burned except that Frederick, the elector of Saxony, seems to have perceived that in Luther he had not only a problem but also an asset. On 18 December 1518 he wrote Leo's legate, Cardinal Cajetan, that he would neither send Luther to Rome nor banish him; the theses had been presented as one man's challenge, but now the gauntlet thrown was Empire's.

Before Luther's death Protestant Reformation would produce the hitherto unthinkable spectacle of separated Christian churches following Luther's new theology and denying any legal connection with the papacy and its hierarchy. With their subsequent history we need not concern ourselves in detail except to reiterate that one of the wonders of history had occurred: a single man—through genius, vernacular German, and the printing revolution—had gathered economic, political, religious, moral, and intellectual conditions "into a rebellion transforming a continent" (Durant, *The Reformation*, 415). Luther's incomplete thought and the stormy development of it during his lifetime left a tension: Christians were encouraged to study the Bible themselves and thus learn the essentials of the faith, while at the same time Luther increasingly set limits to what they, by such study, might be permitted to believe. In the end he left his followers in large doubt as to his stand on important theological issues. This resulted in two German Lutheran groups, united in one government and discipline by force of civil authority without attempting to compel a single doctrine and liturgy. Although Luther promulgated no systematic statement of his position on the relation of church and state, there can be no doubt that this method of solving the theological split conformed to his attitude. His strong belief, which would lead to glorification of the state and its class system, confirmed *jus episcopale* as belonging in the last resort to the secular authorities. Along with the opportunity to seize the Church's wealth this was one of the gifts his Reformation made to monarchs, whom Luther expected to listen to him and more or less to substitute the Old Testament for the rejected books of Roman Catholic canon law.

Luther's attitude toward a strong but purely secular state was obviously attractive to the German princes. It pleased them to find that the former power of the Catholic bishop to appoint consistorial courts through which Rome managed the affairs of the diocese, was to be given by Lutherans to the civil authorities. Such power re-allocation contributed to the settlement reflected in the Peace of Augsburg (1555). Like the Emperors Constantine, Justinian, and Charlemagne, each prince was now freed to settle doctrinal issues; and each would henceforth decide for himself whether to be Lutheran or Catholic, bringing along all subjects to follow his lead. England's rulers were mainly Protestant, but for a brief time, Catholic; the French rulers were mainly Catholic, although for a very brief time, Protestant. Protestant congregations existed in France at all times. Henceforth the general attitude of the German Lutheran churches spread onward to Scandinavia. Sweden under King Gustavus Vasa (1496–1560), and a Denmark which in 1536 was impelled by peasants and burghers supporting King Christian III, both made Lutheranism the state religion. Although not strong in America until fairly late, the Evangelical Lutheran Church organized its General Synod in 1820 (it split in 1867), and the Synodical Conference of North America was set up in 1872.

Calvin

When it came to the systematization of the new faith and in the organization of it into a new church government, Erfurt's legendary attorney now needed another legal partner in the Protestant firm. In a case where lawyer helped lawyer the

Lutheran contribution to the development of crucial legal issues—individualism, liberty, tolerance—was achieved in very large part when his main theological ideas were accepted by Frenchman John Calvin. Going farther than his model, this colleague used them as a basis for promoting establishment of tough theocracies. Fiercely attempted in many places—notably, in England, Scotland and New England—the Calvin religious unit of governance opposed the state by attempting, albeit unsuccessfully, to *be* the state. Under Calvin's personal direction, these societal organizations reached their highest point in the Geneva of the latter half of the sixteenth century.

Born in 1509, Calvin was the son of Gérard Cauvin, or Calvin, a Picard canon lawyer and notary from the cathedral town of Noyon. Gérard, a papal appointee, held several county and episcopal offices including secretary to the bishop. He had married Jeanne le Franc, an innkeeper's daughter from Cambrai whose personal life has unfortunately disappeared behind the towering biography of her second son. Noyon was at that time a near theocracy in which both secular and religious life were dominated by the bishop; not surprisingly, Gérard and Jeanne intended that John should have an ecclesiastical career. In keeping with the day's accelerated professional pace, the twelve-year-old was given a chaplaincy at the cathedral in Noyon. After taking the tonsure, his duties were, as was the custom, carried out by older ordained men who received a part of the stipend of the benefice. In 1523, to escape the plague, young John accompanied the noble family in which he was being educated to the Collège de la Marche of the University of Paris. Later he transferred to the strict Collège de Montaigu where more than sixty years earlier Erasmus had studied; John's 1528 departure coincided with Ignatius Loyola's entrance—one of history's more stunning crossings of important destinies.

Calvin had received some training in dialectics and scholastic philosophy, speedily outdoing fellow students in his studies. Remarkably, they showed no jealousy but rather became quite devoted to their bookish classmate; their loyalty testifies to a compelling character which throughout life could attract friends and supporters. The canons at Noyon were so pleased with their young chaplain that a year before graduation, they added to his duties the curacy of St. Martin de Marteville which he exchanged in a couple of years for Pont l'Évêque. Already having held two benefices at an age most men were still in training, his ecclesiastical career seemed well started. Gérard, however, wanted higher financial prospects for his son and sent word unexpectedly to the Montaigu graduate that he was now to go to Orléans and enroll in the faculty of law. Parental control was then something different from what it is now; John not only at once did as directed but, pleased with law's monetary lure, was highly content to do so. It did not take much exposure before the ambitious son gave his opinion that "'law, not philosophy or literature, [is] the outstanding intellectual achievement of mankind, the molding of man's anarchic impulses to order and peace'" (Durant, *The Reformation,* 459). He would go on to Bourges in furtherance of his training, arriving there in 1529 to study under the great Alciato.

Calvin's legal studies were to be one of the profound influences in his life. Yet, although in time he would become one of the world's great law-givers, Calvin never formally took up practice. Having earned his law degree in 1531, he returned to Paris, turning now to a different field as he began voracious study of the classical literature so favored by the ever more popular Humanists. At age twenty-three he published, in the polished Latin of which he had become a master, an essay on Seneca's *De clementia*, an ironic choice considering that the idea of Mercy is not one suggested by strict Calvinism.

It was only a year later, just when the law graduate gave every semblance of complete dedication to his new Humanistic enthusiasm, that a second decisive influence occurred in his career. Some sermons by Luther had reached France, and many Parisian circles were buzzing with talk about the bold German. As Calvin read he was stirred by Luther's audacity. When his friend Nicholas Cop was appointed rector of the University, Calvin is believed to have helped draft the inaugural address which began with the philosophy of Erasmus, continued with Luther's salvation by faith and, in the *De clementia* vein, concluded with a plea for tolerance. The Sorbonne erupted against the pride of Noyon, and *Parlement* began heresy proceedings. Cop at once fled to Protestant Basle, and Calvin prudently retreated to Angoulême. There, probably in the library of one Louis de Tillet, the twenty-six year old began and in 1536 completed and published at Basle an orderly and comprehensive statement in Latin of the theology, constitution, and administration of a new Christian religion. The book, mostly Lutheran in theology, was entitled *Institutes of the Christian Religion*, probably in imitation of Justinian.

The work bore also the imprint of ideas held by the Swiss reformer Ulrich Zwingli and the German Martin Bucer. Calvin felt comfortable with their views on the Last Supper and the Divine will; for he was here moving toward a break with advocate mentor, Luther, who, he felt, put too much of the real Christ into the divine elements. At intervals throughout his life Calvin would revise the *Institutes*, although never in any fundamental way. The final version reached 1,118 pages. Impact of the 1541 French version would be prodigious, an influence the more remarkable when one appreciates that it was at heart a coordinated French restatement and systemization of received German doctrines. However, even though not conceived as theologically revolutionary, the method of its application in the churches produced just that: a boldly changed belief system. Once again a lawyer's book, its first edition sold out in a year, having become the unifying foundation of a great Protestant movement. Directed by Calvin himself from Geneva, this second wave of so-called Reformed Churches would take possession of the minds of millions all over Western Europe and North America. Among them would be John Staples, preaching the new message for fifty years in the little town of Canterbury in far off Connecticut, while proudly watching his son, Seth Perkins Staples, initiate the academic teaching of law in the new world of united states.

In its Calvinization, Lutheran theology had been so refined that its clarifications had developed it into something quite un-Lutheran in polity. The French lawyer's idea was enormous: a man of religion should guide the state. How Hildebrand would have envied this Protestant "pope" at Geneva, stiff and strong in faith, stern and steadfast in opposing civil power. Calvinism's new creed had left behind the comforting Lutheran confidence that the individual could interpret the Bible for himself. Paul was still the role model of choice, only instead of Romans the epistle for Calvin was Ephesians 1, verses 3–7: "God...has chosen us...before the foundation of the world, that we should be holy and without blame...having predestinated us unto the adoption of children by Jesus Christ to Himself, according to the good pleasure of his will." Here stood the God of absolute power—Ockham's God—who by a choice not based on man's vices and virtues had simply, breathtakingly, decided long before creation which individuals were to be saved and which damned. Calvin realized that the essential, if subordinate, question became whether God might change the decision as to an individual. Ockham would surely have said 'yes.' Calvin had to decide whether the answer was 'never.'

It had been Augustine who long ago considered this very problem. His early writings left room for human free will to influence one's final fate, but later thoughts brought him close to a consistent determinism. Here lay a problem for theologians: if God is good, how can he predestine so many to damnation? Luther the lawyer and Augustinian monk was oriented toward the great architect of God's city. Lawyer and Humanist Calvin had also sympathetically studied Augustine, but he knew the problem was compounded by the stern belief, also held by Luther, that because of Adam's fall, all men are sinful from birth and with no escape will remain lapsed on the very day of Judgment. At epochs when men were satisfied that the sacraments brought salvation, the subject could be more one of academic speculation than real theological terror. But Luther had concluded that the sacraments alone were insufficient, and therefore he and the century after him had to confront the issue *ab initio* in the most direct and intense manner. Luther was driven toward the wages of sin by the conclusion that prelapsarian humanity, irrevocably corrupt, has no chance of arriving free of taint at the final trumpet. Admitting what Erasmus could not bear to believe, Luther went as far as a God who sometimes could damn those who did not deserve it.

Luther's mind, not strongly systematic, did not require him to dwell starkly on the logical, grim implications. The mind of Calvin, on the other hand—more legally inclined and less passionate about philosophical speculation—was devoted to comprehensive, yes or no paradigm building. The all-important guidepost predestination had to be developed and set in place as intricately as Calvin could craft its form. To put it bluntly, in Adam the free will/good works experiment had failed, and Calvin wanted to convince us of how our lapsed progenitor had forfeited free will and by his sin "merited," one might say, predestination. As in all cases of trial, there were to be dark corners in salvation: everything rested in the hands of the Judge whose purpose was that some would be saved, some would be damned. Here was a rigor mortis so unyielding that with no Purgatory there could not even be room for prayers offered the dead.

Calvin's followers never stopped talking about their charismatic but controversial leader. Long after his death in 1564 their intense discussions returned over and over to the predestination question. They would think they had settled it at Dort in the year 1618–1619, but the eighteenth and nineteenth centuries, appealing to minds influenced by science, only increased the doctrinal rigor. Russell remarked (Russell, 523) that predestination startlingly, paradoxically, reduced Church power since salvation no longer depended on priestly intervention. Yet, in another way, it sustained that power, since its tight communal web denied complete individual freedom to strike out for the chosen land alone. Why did this depressing, even frightening concept—one repellant to reason, Calvin himself admitted—win converts to the Reformed churches? It is probable that the corollary of predestination which held that those who studied the Word in fellowship, confessed faith, lived an exemplary life, and participated in baptism and the eucharist, could and did receive a conviction that they (and their children, too, said Calvin) were among the elect. Such assurance of inclusion among the chosen few, comparable to the similar belief that has sustained Jews in their terrible difficulties, gave Reformists strength in adversity and pride in prosperity. They knew the comfort of election which, unlike one in a political system, could not be revoked from error. It should be noted that a more material boost for Calvinism's conversion rate was the helpful combination of feeling chosen and being comfortable in Geneva during Calvin's lifetime and for sometime thereafter. Paradoxically, when adversity later struck in France, England, and elsewhere in Europe, this negative condition which would drive many to the New World was turned into its own kind of election as early theocracies metamorphosed into the successful democracy of the American constitutional republic. It is common to view France's revolutionary manifesto of the Rights of Man as taking life blood from the new United States. One must not overlook that the French Reformation protestation had already taken its early part in forging America's 1776, before returning home for France's 1789.

John Calvin
*Courtesy of the Library of Congress,
Prints and Photographs Division, LC-USZ62-72002*

On 4 May 1534 Calvin resigned his posts at Noyon and Pont l'Évêque. Committed irrevocably to the religious system of his *Institutes*, he had become a legend in more than one land. The spring of 1536 found him determined to move off the pedestal and devote the rest of his life to study. His health had become precarious enough to help dictate the change; he suffered from headaches, asthma, dyspepsia, stone, gout, and fever, and continued to do so to the end of his life. His diet, though abstemious, when combined with sleep deprivation must have been quite wrong, or at least so betokens the likeness in oil hanging in the library of the University at Geneva; the thinly bearded face is that of an ascetic, with intense eyes that pierce and an unhealthy looking, sallow skin. Short like Luther, he was the thin one in Reformation's duo but with a tenacity and mental strength that matched him to his stocky German legal partner.

Calvin decided to start his studious phase in Basle but did return briefly to France for a farewell visit. War issues making travel difficult, his trip back to Basle took him on a roundabout route through Geneva. It would be a felicitous hostelry, since far from being just a summer stopover, this worldly canton on the banks of the Léman was about to become predestination's austerely legendary capital. In the Middle Ages the city had fallen under the rule, secular and spiritual, of its Catholic bishop, chosen by the chapter of the cathedral. By the fifteenth century, however, the nearby Dukes of Savoy, having wrested control of the chapter, directed the choice of its bishops.

The once excellent government had gone into decline, forcing the leading families to organize a Council of Sixty with four Syndics as executive officers. Their church-state mix was unique: the Council made city ordinances, regulated morals, and even issued excommunications. The princely bishop minted the coins and led the army. By 1520 Geneva was a busy town of about 20,000, in a sense an echo of antiquity's *polis* whose goal-oriented citizenry were to seek and find earthly satisfaction by sharing a social fabric. The city leaders were businessmen who controlled an expanded Great Council that then chose a Small Council of twenty-five. Council members opposed duke and bishop and for all intents and purposes were Geneva's real rulers. Anger and belligerency grew, and to settle the power question the clergy supported the duke. The Great Council declared for the reformed faith, and two months before Calvin arrived Council members seized jurisdiction both secular and ecclesiastical. Their religious leader, William Farel, a fiery apostle of reform, saw in Calvin the man to consolidate Protestant victory. It would be Farel who persuaded the Frenchman to stay and accept appointment as a minister.

By acquiescing, Calvin chose what would be home for the rest of his life except for a brief period between 1538 and 1541 when factions opposed to him forced his temporary withdrawal to Strasbourg. In 1539, taking advantage of this exile across the Rhine, Sadoleto, a Catholic Humanist, penned his *Epistle to the Genevese*, urging the town's reacceptance of the Roman Church. This aroused Calvin to reply with a brilliant Protestant *apologia*. His words could not fail to impress a Council, now dismayed by the ineffective preaching of the successors to Farel and by the resulting civic corruption and general moral laxity. Fearing a return to the regal bishop, they and Farel begged Calvin to come back as sole spiritual leader. Calvin long demurred, then agreed at least to visit, encouraged, perhaps, by the beloved wife whom he had married a year earlier. Overwhelmed by petitions and honors of the Genevans, the couple stayed.

Now in a very strong position, the prophet proceeded to build his theocracy. The ministry consisted of pastors, teachers, lay elders, and deacons; the pastors as the "Venerable Company" governed the church and trained future ministers. The French lawyer turned dictator ruled that the real law of a state is the Bible; when the ministers interpret it, the civil government must enforce it as interpreted. It would be an oligarchical government which, although there were no church prisons, sought protection for members of the church congregations by building in aspects of a police state. By will and character, if not by fiat, Calvin thus put divine law on top of existing town statutes, urban customs, and Germanic mores. Ministers, exercising authority over the life of all citizens, worked through the tight control mechanism of a Consistory or Presbytery chosen by a Council of five pastors. These members for life were aided by twelve lay elders elected annually and, therefore, less influential. The entire body defined the religious worship and moral conduct of every inhabitant and, to make sure of compliance, arranged that each home receive annual visitation by both a minister and an elder. Under powers reminiscent of the Catholic Inquisition, the Consistory could summon anyone for examination, issue public reprovals, excommunicate from the Church, and expect the Council to banish the excommunicated forthwith from the city.

For over twenty-five years, working twelve to eighteen hours a day and preaching several times a week, Calvin functioned as Geneva's titulary spirit. He honed his *Institutes*, wrote Bible commentaries, corresponded with followers all over Europe, taught theology to future ministers, superintended churches and schools, advised the councils, and regulated public behavior and church liturgy. A new church code, *Ordonnances écclesiastiques*, was approved by the Great Council of 1542, and its essential features are still followed by Reformed and Presbyterian Churches.

Calvin's fame and the lure of his policies for the reform minded attracted many new citizens to the Christian Commonwealth of Geneva. These added followers strengthened Calvin's hand and ultimately made Geneva a highly cosmopolitan if highly regulated city in which every citizen could be found attending church on Sunday. No separate creeds were permitted, since sects represented weakness. When Calvin looked out at the Catholicism of his fathers, his steely eyes saw it as a creed both heretical and clearly punishable by death. Between 1542 and 1564 fifty-eight devout Christians, torture having been applied to win confessions from the obdurate, met that very punishment. To this number add fourteen alleged witches burned in one year, plus the Spanish theologian Servetus, who, having escaped the French Inquisition by acting on a tip from Calvin, chose Geneva as an escape only to meet the pyre there.

In matters of a personal behavior code Calvin started at the top. Ministers could marry but not hunt, gamble, feast, engage in commerce, or attend secular amusements. Their flock were also forbidden to gamble, play cards, swear, get drunk, frequent taverns, dance, sing bawdy songs, give plays, be extravagant in living or immodest in dress, or name children after saints (the Old Testament was preferred for names). Law seemed to define everything—color and quantity of clothing, number of dishes at a meal, permissible books. To speak disrespectfully of such patterns of comportment was as forbidden as criticizing Calvin or any of the other ministers. A Protestant resident from Italy contentedly wrote his touristic *wish you were here* note back home by saying: "'There are no organs here, no voice of bells, no showy songs, no burning candles or lamps [in the churches] no relics, pictures, statues, canopies or splendid robes, no farces or cold ceremonies. The churches are quite free from idolatry'" (Durant, *The Reformation*, 476). He could have added that strict class distinctions, too, were considered natural and were preserved, although poor relief existed and was carefully administered. Genevan economics cut across social hierarchies and wrote a bottom line of sobriety, diligence, frugality, and thrift. Calvin permitted reasonable interest on loans, but he fixed prices for food, clothing, and health services; merchants who cheated were fined. Luther's promotion of an agrarian economy downgraded the cash flow mercantilism of a burgeoning Europe. Urbanist that he was, Calvin chose an economic policy compatible with the wishes of a highly active sector of businessmen, and in this favorable economic climate Geneva could establish a municipal bank to watch out for local industries.

Luther had advised the achievement of faith by hearing and studying the Word; he had even advocated compulsory education enforced by state sanctions. Both Luther and Calvin appreciated how full participation in religion now required more of the very education that had brought to the bourgeois the mobility to demand reform. As part of civic growth, schools and an academy were established; Calvin himself scoured Europe for the best teachers. The Academy, founded in 1539 as a seminary for ministers, was prestigious enough later to extend its scope. Such educational reform enriched Reformation. Aided by Humanism in its genesis, Luther and Calvin promoted the *via moderna*, and although they bore a heavy debt to Ockham's sovereign God (Rudy, 51; 53), they generally frowned on scholasticism. Going as far back as its eleventh century beginnings, legal science had been slow in coming to Switzerland. Under theocratic Calvinism, law could not make inroads at the University of Basel since the great attorney leader disapproved of litigation, either taught or practiced. After all, why litigate if there were only one way? It would not be until fairly late in the sixteenth century when one could study in the theocracy under distinguished Humanist jurists.

Geneva ministers trained under Calvin spread over Europe; the new religion appeared in France in 1541, and there was a Calvinist church in Paris in 1555. In as short a time as eleven years Calvin's Geneva sent 161 men of strict theology into France, many to die for their faith, confidently singing psalms at the stake. Calvin was so amazed by the speed and extent of the spread of his message that at a certain moment he felt obliged to counsel caution in the rate of expansion. In Calvinism, the Reformation had metamorphosed into religion whose core was deep within the ethics of private life. Being less aesthetic, the commanding sovereignty of a Calvinist God stressed more than the ineffable beauties of grace, as faith found itself bonded to a heightened demand for the strictest human obedience. Church meant bureaucracy—a congregation of believers who governed through assemblies and elected pastors, all of whom, like the churches, were equal, and none of whom had immunity from taxes or was endowed by a benefice of land. Each congregation could readily sense its importance; they accepted only one fundamental creed, and when occasional variations were allowed, it was only after decision by the congregants *inter se*. Paradoxically, having broken the power of sacerdotalism, Calvin at the same time continued the dominance of religion over daily affairs. The result was a hybrid: a democratized congregationalism, yet a medieval emphasis on religion with no secular control.

From the tenacious and intense labors of this legal licentiate had come a faith of apocalyptic contrasts: unconditional election and draconian disapproval. Said Pius IV: "'The strength of that heretic consisted in this, that money never had the slightest charm for him. If I had such servants my dominion would extend from sea to sea'" (Durant, *The Reformation*, 477). Physically and philosophically, the antithesis of his equally brilliant compatriot—iconoclastic curate, physician, and writer François Rabelais (Langer, 414b)—the dour minister would outlive the irrepressible Humanist by eleven years. Who can say who died with more confidence in the next destination?

The Catholic Reformation

Spain

We turn now from the two great Protestant movements to the Catholic interpretation of reform. Although usually referred to as the Counter-Reformation, one is not incorrect to leave off the first word since in chronology, it may well be regarded as having preceded the Protestants. Many Catholics, other than men like Luther and Calvin who carried their concern to the point of separation from the Catholic hierarchy, were well aware of the need for change. Outstanding among them were their Spanish Catholic majesties Ferdinand (1452–1516) and Isabella (1451–1504). They had married as astute and unsentimental adolescent diplomats, he at seventeen and she eighteen, and already at that young age had perceived the possibilities for a united Spain. Ferdinand would bring to the nuptial chamber Sicily and Aragon, while his bride provided Castile. Ironically, as anti-Semitic as they would soon demonstrate themselves to be, they forever had to carry as an engagement souvenir the fact that it was an affluent and highly capable Jewish lawyer whose loan of 20,000 *sueldos* permitted their wedding.

The two were cousins, but the groom's father and the archbishop of Barcelona forged the papal bull needed to make the union legal; only later was a valid bull obtained. The groom appeared cold and aloof. He was inclined neither toward fidelity nor luxury, but did have talent in foreign affairs and statecraft. Isabella emerges as one of the jewels of history: incomparably beautiful (or so her court thought), the educated patroness of poets, philosophers, and priests, and totally devoted to the faith. Frank, direct, incorruptible, she was also tender and loyal. Her generosity in charity is well documented as is her bravery and steadfastness in war and policy. Opulent and splendid in public, she preferred simplicity in private. But although dedicated to legal ideals of justice and order, the jewel was darkened by the bloodstained flaw which became legend: she was harsh and cruel in the suppression of heresy. She, no less than Ferdinand, aimed to achieve in Spain a considerable reform of Church and monasteries; yet it is obvious that, unlike Protestantism, this effort at change utilized terrible violence in bringing about Spanish hegemony.

Historic irony imbues Spain's prejudiced march into secular glorification. For every event of barbarism came great achievements in architecture, sculpture, painting, literature, scholarship. On one side clamor religion's tortured, hapless victims; on the other, lies open a complete edition of the Bible in the original languages with Greek and Latin translations included. Juristically, Ferdinand's pressure obtained from the Pope power over appointments to ecclesiastical offices, achieving a unity that was the foundation for Spain's role as the leading force in Europe in the sixteenth century. It meant that, together with Portugal, Spain henceforth placed the Americas from Mexico southward under the rule of European civil law. This phenomenal rise of national power would, in conjunction with the remarkable fervor of the Catholic Reformation, arouse in Spanish professors trained by the Jesuits a notable development in thinking about law as they raised the central question of whether there were limits on the monarch's power. Such inherently revolutionary thinking made the age a bridge between medieval thought and the new way of the seventeenth and eighteenth centuries (Pound, *Juris*, Vol. I, 479–480). In addition, complex new law grew out of the monarch's colonialism which forced decisions on how to deal with the natives in the lands to which Columbus and later explorers sailed.

Thus, successful as they were, no political conquests and no secular strides could mask the theological blot bred by law turned into rules for religious intolerance. Cohesion was built on attacking, despoiling, exterminating. Catholics fell victim when regarded as doubtful supporters of the regime; the Jews and Moors if allowed their lives were brutally expelled. As law had been the guiding path for Luther and Calvin, the Spanish monarchs appealed to the Church to supply the statutes and the means for such reform that impoverished the national talent pool as it brought chaos to a citizenry. Inquisition usually never itself condemned to the stake, but by turning the offender over—"relaxing" they euphemistically called it—to the secular arm, the Holy Office prepared the pyres of *auto da fé* while keeping apart from the killing. Thus did legalized extermination grotesquely lead the way to enhanced royal power.

Italy

Rome's interests in the state of the Church rose several notches as soon as Luther's challenges were published in Milan and Venice. The official papal awareness was more than matched by the countless faithful who for many years had been consolidating a policy for no change and fervor for retaining the Roman rite. Yet converts could be found as high in rank as Renée, daughter of Louis XII and Princess of Ferrara, or as low as the peasant tending his master's flocks. Some of the neophytes accepted Luther, others Calvin, but whichever detour from the straight road they took was enough for the pope by 1530 to decry wide evidence of heresy's vitality in Catholicism's Italian heart.

The ebullient burst of free expression from Renaissance Italy, where exuberant liberalism at times reached near anarchy, found itself sharply curtailed as that country went under the yoke of heavy Catholic reform espoused by Charles V and conquering Spain. Writers like Russell (Russell, 522) have gone as far as seeing the Protestant reform movements as a rebellion of less civilized nations against Italy. Artists and scholars like Petrarch who had converted Catholicism to art and were supported by Catholic benefices saw their popularity and their pay threatened by the new ideas from Switzerland, Germany, and France. If there had to be change, it was thought, let it at least not demolish the Church.

However, that there had to be reform was increasingly evident, not only to relapsed Humanists, but to Mother Church as well. To increase revenues canonists had led the institution to excesses barely justified by legal rationales which in themselves proved deeply insufficient in morality. At least one mind saw the error and told it aloud. This man was Paul III (reigned 1534–1549) who early in his pontificate received from the jurist Caccia a treatise on reform. The Caccia report, fearlessly and with startling clarity, laid out Catholic abuses. Vision, however, came too late. As soon as Luther read the treatise he translated it into German, publishing it not as a basis of the reunion and rebirth of ancient credos but as a justification of the final break with Rome.

Yet improvement had definitely taken up residence inside the Italian Church. Shocked by Caccia, Paul III in 1542 revived the concept of an Italian Inquisition. In 1555 his successor Paul IV instituted a flagellant's text of don'ts by unequivocally presenting a long list of transgressions and transgressors: absentee monks; officials living away from the cloister on monastic revenue; bishops and abbots whose actual occupations were secular; plural benefices; excessive fees charged by the Curia; simony; fees for confirmation as archbishop (the very problem that had led to the events that set Luther on fire); usury; worldly lusts; and on and on into the catalogue of decadence. When in 1559 Paul established the Index as the first censorship, he gave full motion to the inquisitory apparatus that seventeen years earlier Paul III had resurrected.

The Council of Trent

Italy's reconciliative yet anti-Humanistic moves could not hope to draw back Protestant deserters who required more than matches to light fires of improvement. Paul III in 1535 and 1536 had already unsuccessfully sounded out leading Protestants on the need for the more direct step of a general Council. In 1541 his legate, Cardinal Contorini, actually negotiated agreement on several problems of dogma before having to return to Rome empty handed when the question of real presence in the Eucharist produced the same deadlock it produced between Luther and Calvin. Undeterred, in 1542 Paul III made his first actual summons for a Council to be convened at Trent; although near papal territory, this Austrian venue was a neutral site. The king of France, busy with war, would not approve. In 1545, with France and Spain at peace, Paul III renewed his call; this time both Francis I and Charles V cooperated, and the Nineteenth Ecumenical Council of the Christian Church began active sessions. The appellation of ecumenical was hardly appropriate, since the Protestants were not there and the Italian bishops had a majority. Paul was represented by three cardinals, astutely reinforced by two Jesuits whose erudition and energy clearly dominated the meeting. All the legates evidently had decided that since Protestant sectarianism had gone too far to be reversed, they should start going just as far themselves. So on the table they ostentatiously and proudly spoke their beliefs: a reaffirmation of the whole Nicene creed, the equal authority of Church tradition and scripture, the sole power of the Church to interpret the Bible, and the definitive status of Jerome's Vulgate. The *Summa Theologica* of Aquinas, that definition of orthodox theology, was given pride of place above all but the Bible and the canonist decretals. Full opposition to the Calvinists and Lutherans was capped by strong statements for freedom of the will and importance of good works.

Despite the papal panache, little was achieved in reform of Church administration. The Holy Father wanted sole control, whereas the Emperor wanted the Council to consider reopening the power question. Paul III craftily proposed to move the Council to Bologna, presumably to increase the desired papal control; but the Spanish and imperial prelates refused, and the Council broke up as the Italian bishops went on alone to Bologna, their departure expedited by the plague's sudden appearance in Trent. In 1551 a new pontiff, Julius III, reconvened the council again in the Austrian city, this time with Protestants invited and given safe conduct. The Protestants—minus the French—boldly justified their name. They demanded that everything decided upon so far be annulled and that before proceeding further the Council affirm the principles of the Councils of Constance and Basel which established the very authority of Councils over popes. Julius III refused these demands, while nearby renewed military operations by the elector of Saxony caused the councillors to end Trent II by, again, precipitously making their exit. The Protestants dropped any further interest in the Council.

Paul IV decided not to try to accomplish anything through council, but in 1562 Trent III was convened by Pius IV (1559–1565). Although no Protestants were present, protest certainly still hung in the air. Some of the nations represented stood up to confront the papacy once more, this time with a long list of precise demands: equality among bishops, communion for the people in wine, as well as bread, clerical marriage, the vernacular mass. In this fourth Pius, however, the rebels would meet their match, for he had honed his diplomatic astuteness with vibrant presentation made on the legal turf. Though from an obscure family, he was a graduate of both Bologna and Pavia and had practiced for some years before entering the service of the Church. He cleverly avoided both yielding to the demands and falling out with their authors. The result was a rapid resolution of remaining business; the Council was able to dissolve in 1563 and in 1564 Rome could confirm its decisions. After a delay the hierarchies of France and Spain accepted despite their reservations, allowing the worldly and affable Pius to give himself over to pontifical ease and the embellishment of Rome.

Trent III truly stood as an achievement of important change. From it came seminaries for better training of clergy. Sexually suggestive Church art was now curbed, and while the concepts of purgatory, indulgences, and the special status of saints were all retained, abuse of them had been forbidden. Trent III gave the signal that now Protestantism had a worthy competitor; and when all the delegates had gone home the doctrine and government of the Church, henceforth no longer the Church universal but rather the Roman Catholic Church, had been fixed for the succeeding 450 years. To this day Catholicism in doctrine and government follows the Trent III model. Even the current dismay and debate over priestly celibacy and scandals of sexual misconduct trace their legal context back to Trent's strict interdiction of clerical marriage and concubinage.

Loyola

The reforms decreed in Rome and confirmed after Trent III by Pius IV were to depend in considerable part upon the organization of new religious leadership. It was obvious that changes, no matter how needed or imaginative, had failed to attack the great problem of hierarchization: the top can reform, but at the lower level, if there is lack of aptitude for the service, it risks bringing any changes to dilution, if not negation. Given the continued low qualifications of parish clergy, an ignorant priest could be no better at explaining Trent than at explaining the sermon of Tetzel the indulgence seller who had aroused Luther to protest. More than ever before, Rome needed a different breed of erudite and dedicated men interacting with the faithful. Providentially, this need would be answered by a Spaniard of the faith. The innovative cohort came too late to reconcile or control Calvin and Luther, but it has been credited with avoiding the loss of half the faithful not already in Luther's camp. Its creation had considerable ramifications for legal history because, producing a revival in education, this upgrade in turn led to professors who now renewed once more the philosophical dialogue about political science and natural law.

The new order began with the energetic personality and deep intellectuality of one Inigo Lopez de Recalde (1491–1556). This son of Beltran, lord of Onaz and Loyola, was born to fairly high nobility from the Basque country. In the castle study young Inigo, or Ignatius, had soon mastered the rudiments of reading and writing and was sent away at seven to serve as page and prepare for a military career at the court of Ferdinand and Isabella. The professional choice had a marked influence upon the nature of the order he was to found, for it pitted battle tactics of the soldier against the lawyerly work of Calvin and the theology of the legal drop-out Luther. As has so often been the case with history's saints, for a long time the youth put religion a low second to the shining gleam of armament. Until twenty-six one could find the young soldier doing his part in the service of the Duke of Nagera, while enjoying the usual diversions of womanizing, gambling, and fighting. He did, however, demonstrate exceptional talent in a courageous and prudent leadership of the men he commanded. On 19 May 1521 he was struck in the leg by a cannon ball and severely wounded. His French captors released him to his home where he went through a long, difficult convalescence. Twice his leg had to be reset, but despite the excruciating pain Loyola, to everyone's amazement, clenched his fists and uttered no sound.

During recuperation, his diversion was reading the only two books in the meager castle library: a life of Christ and a volume on the miracles of the saints. Bored at first, he began after a while to be extremely interested in his reading material; thoughts leaped in bizarre, baroque alternation between Jesus and Queen Isabella, the object since fourteen of his courtly yet unattainable love. Soon he began to re-orient his ideal, imagining that the noblest war would be to fight against the infidels at Jerusalem. With the Lady out of reach he could instead be the chivalrous Christian soldier, marching onward and accomplishing great deeds for Mary and for God. This was a mental and spiritual crisis which, although not as in Luther's case primarily driven by any sense of sin, did cause Loyola increasing concern about his intense psychological stress. Then, one night as he lay awake, he reported having seen a likeness of the Virgin and her Son. Immediately were felt such waves of total loathing for his former life, especially the carnal passions, that he would after that day never again yield. Many more would be the visions, but all were basically steps in defining a rigorous personal regimen. Loyola sought to practice all the austerities of the saints and bore witness by making a pilgrimage to Jerusalem.

Away to the North, Luther was in full protest with no inkling a holy *miles gloriosus* was readying to do battle against his Reformation cohort of legalisms. Recovered from his wounds, Loyola began preparation for the fray by pilgrimage to the Benedictine Abbey at Montserrato. There he confessed his past transgressions and read the *Spiritual Exercises* of the former abbot, Cisneros (d. 1510). From them he probably formed the idea of writing down his own spiritual experiences as a guide for others. Completed later, Loyola's *Spiritual Exercises* would become a basic drill manual for his novitiates and himself. We marvel as he leaves the abbey, giving away all his arms and clothes, even his mule. Arriving at Manresa, he there undertook months of fasting and self-flagellation, praying as much as seven hours a day. He soon had become filthy and emaciated; frequent illnesses brought thoughts of suicide. But others began to petition this holy indigent for advice, and their interest aroused his energies. As he himself groped toward the vocation of his own life, he returned to good grooming that he might become more acceptable and set about in earnest to try to influence his dévotés for good. With financial help he finally reached Jerusalem only to be told there by the Franciscans, whose presence was tolerated by the Muslims, that he should turn around and leave. Threatened with excommunication if he remained, he left the city of his dreams and arrived at Venice in January 1524.

It had taken a long time, but finally Loyola was realizing that to achieve anything substantial, devotion needed to be fortified by education. Already thirty-three, the late-blooming pupil found a lady of rank willing to supply funds and a schoolmaster willing to teach Latin; after two years he was ready and entered the university at Alcalá as a philosophy student. He shared with friends his *Spiritual Exercises* as well as some instructions in doctrine which he had been writing. These, his peculiar dress and his intense mode of life brought inquiry, then denunciation, and finally imprisonment by the Inquisition, but Loyola was acquitted on condition that he study four more years before again attempting any teaching. When he resumed academics it was at the University of Salamanca, this time with some companions. Soon all of them had been put in prison by the Inquisition, but Loyola was again released on a similar condition of more studious regimen. Neither he nor his group of friends had yet thought of founding an order.

Loyola now decided France could offer him more freedom to pursue his objectives. He walked to Paris, arriving in February 1528 to join there the 12,000–15,000 university students whose academic institution—far from being an island of tolerance—had condemned both Erasmus and Luther and, soon after Loyola arrived, had burned Louis de Berquin for attacking the clergy and advocating that the people read their Bible in French. For two years Loyola attended academic Humanistic lectures, always attracting new companions to whom he gave the *Spiritual Exercises*. His actions brought upon him the usual inquisitory interdiction to speak at all on spiritual matters; and as usual he persevered. Then, on the Feast of the Assumption, 15 August 1534, he and six others made a set of formal vows. They would live in poverty and chastity, go on pilgrimage—to Jerusalem if possible, otherwise to Rome—and they would place themselves at papal disposal for any purpose. The pilgrimage to Jerusalem proved to be impossible, so part of the group including Loyola went to Rome, arriving in October 1537. Loyola at once began teaching those who would hear him but now added to his pedagogy a newly displayed talent for organization; he founded institutions for fallen women, for orphans, and for catechetical instruction. It remained the idea of a religious society which clearly filled his heart and mind, and on 27 September 1540 Paul III, the convenor of Trent I, recognized the little "Company of Jesus." "Company" was a military term, and Loyola, become its General in 1541, undertook now to complete his *Spiritual Exercises* and to prepare constitutions for his Order.

General Loyola comes to us in portraiture as one of olive complexion, his face emaciated by austerities. A large forehead, small but brilliant eyes, and high bald head were strikingly set upon yet again one of history's short of stature giants; despite a mere five feet two inches, this commander carried himself so well that hardly anyone noticed a slight limp. Naturally impetuous and enthusiastic, Loyola had by this time made famous the gripping self-control he had displaced as the youth who secretly wanted to surpass everyone about him. That personal ambition brought firmly under the stricture of prudence, now manifested itself in commanding his equally obedient militia in Christ. Loyola would remain the rest of his life in Rome, directing the Society from a small bare room, coping with popes and writing thousands of letters which all testified to a keen insight. Charisma there was in abundance, too, for by 1565 the Order had swelled to 3,500 members living in 130 houses in eighteen provinces or countries.

Loyola's Christian army—"Clerks Regular of the Society of Jesus," as they were officially called—was no contemplative group bent only on personal salvation and prayer for the world but lived under the equivalent of military law and camp discipline. They became informally the "Jesuits" in 1552, an actually hostile epithet coined by Calvin and the *Parlement of Paris*, but which Loyola's men both accepted

Ignatius de Loyola
Courtesy of The Bridgeman Art Library

and turned into positive self-promotion. All other monastic orders had sung the offices in choir in a fixed cloister atmosphere; from this the Jesuits were excused and did their devotions separately and privately. Where all the other orders were more or less constitutional monarchies with a democratized spirit, the Jesuits were all under their General, the Order's only elected official. His was office held for life, and his power, like that of any commander, was practically autonomous. A small group of permanent advisors did meet with him regularly, but he did not have to take their advice. Obedience was everything, expostulated in detail when Loyola drafted his famous letter to the Jesuits at Coimbra. A superior was to be followed literally and without question regardless of his character, wisdom, or piety. Any individual intellect had to be sacrificed to this leader, although if his command offended conscience, one could consult with two or three members of discretion and then abide by their decision. Loyalty—the word resonated with the precise personal inference—had to be unquestioned, and no member could accept any dignity of office that would make him independent of the Society. As a community in the social fabric, Jesuits worked full time in worldly contact with ordinary people to reform the evils that had brought revolt against Rome. No peculiarity of dress or rule was to impede acceptance by the laity. No member was to have a home, for each man was a cosmopolitan, able to travel forth at any time. Loyola considered the old monastics as cadres of infantry—stationed at a place—whereas his Jesuits were light horse scouts and skirmishers ready for quick deployment anywhere. Since that "anywhere" meant far-flung missions, mastery of foreign languages was an essential part of the quick-order drill that allowed members to take up work effectively on any foreign assignment.

The Jesuits approved of the Inquisition but did not take part in it. Rather, they decided that the contest against Protestantism would be won indirectly, by controlling, as far as possible, the education of young men. At first concerned to educate only their own members, the Jesuits became for centuries the best schoolmasters in Europe, training under their approach a large part of the social elite. Thousands of lawyers were among them. Said Francis Bacon of their highly reputed schools: "'Such as they are, would that they were ours'" (Durant, *The Reformation*, 915). His evaluation was correct, for at this time, schools generally, in spite of some notable and successful Humanistic experiments which had influenced the new Order, were pedantic adherents to obsolete methods. Jesuits, on the other hand, were innovators, both in systems and instructional materials. They mingled firmness and gentleness in a quality education which for a long time was free of charge. At Loyola's death he could count a hundred Jesuit secondary schools and universities, all busily editing classical texts to eliminate what they thought was undesirable, all recalling that the General always insisted upon a single, clear doctrine with no dissent. "Let us all think the same way," was the command, and where the Church was undecided Loyola made the choice. As a result Jesuit education fell short in forming character and independent judgment but was excellent in imparting information and developing skills. In addition, the Jesuits were indefatigable preachers, tended the sick even in times of plague, and being educated and of good manners proved to be the favorite confessors of women and nobles, and ultimately of kings. From high nobility's holy beggar had come the sophisticated religious of the world who believed that Jesus could better be served by more prudence and less piety than more piety and less prudence.

Chosen with care and schooled intensively from as young as fourteen, trainees began with a solitary retreat for the *Spiritual Exercises*. Next came their long novitiate of two years of prayer and asceticism during which time weaknesses were noted and the will tested. If approved, the novice made a vow of poverty, chastity, and obedience and became a scholastic, that is, a university undergraduate committed to five years studying the arts. Then he taught in Jesuit schools for five or six years while continuing his own studies. When at last he stood forward, it was to renew the triple vow of poverty, chastity, and obedience, while adding on a pledge for care in the education of boys. At twenty-eight or thirty came a four to six year course in theology, followed by ordination between thirty-four and thirty-six. Vows included also a promise not to change the Society's constitution as to poverty, not to accept office outside the Society unless required by obedience, to denounce violations by others, and to hear the advice of the General if elected a Bishop. The member was now a "professed of the three vows." A few at about forty-five made to the pope their fourth vow of obedience to support the missions. From these elite few came the Society's chief officers. Loyola told his secretary that he looked at prospective candidates, less for purely natural goodness than for firmness of character and acumen for business, being of the opinion that only they were fit for executive roles.

The Jesuits were a formidable association which on the whole served the Church well in doing what could be done to roll back the Protestant tide. Ultimately, though, as an organization they failed. Their greatest humiliation came on 21 July 1773 when they were suppressed altogether by Clement XIV, an action not to be revoked until 1814. There had been a noticeable lack of truly great intellects after Loyola and his close friend and fellow saint Xavier; no Aquinas, Anselm, Bacon, or Richelieu came to the fore while they trained and then lost Pascal, Descartes, and later, their critical alumnus, Voltaire. Corporate interests of the Society were always put first in an attempt to master the Church rather than cooperate with it. Remarkable cohesion aroused hostility, both Catholic and Protestant, as well as a corporate concentration on the rich and influential. Jesuits flocked to courts and centers of power, and their higher-ranking men especially took sides (too often the losing side) in politics. In amassing for the Society impressive social connections and great wealth, the soldiers finally became, like the ill-fated Knights Templar, involved in undertakings which failed to honor their own principles. Behind the better known name of Guy Fawkes were Jesuits acting as accessories in the English Gunpowder Plot. Nevertheless, they produced able men among the highly educated professors in their universities; Mariana and Suarez—about to enter our story—were among the best. Leaders of the "Second" or "Neo" Scholastics who were read by Grotius, Descartes, and others, these Jesuitic academics dominated thought of the universities for two centuries.

Paralleling the individualism, toleration, and liberty which surprisingly grew from the labors of Luther and Calvin, speculations of all persuasions on politics and law were one of the unexpected results of the work of the visionary, but practical Loyola. Jesuitical legal ramifications make us recall Montaigne who rebelled against a direct defense of the Church which marked the style of militant Catholic reformers and sought instead to defend that same Church by his revival of the Ancients' Skepticism. Doubt thus was conjoined to conviction for individual believers seeking to undermine the possibility of faith in any of the Protestant pretensions. Risk was definitely now on the table, and it stirred questions in many minds—about the parent faith itself and about the need to brave both Inquisition and Index.

Suarez

Francisco Suarez (1548–1617) was the younger son of a wealthy lawyer of Granada. At sixteen he came under the influence of the Jesuit John Ramirez who convinced the boy to join the Society. Copleston implies (Copleston, Vol. III, 353) that Suarez had already studied canon law at Salamanca; but, perhaps because of poor health, he failed his first examinations in the Order. Appealing the decision, he failed again but persisted and was finally admitted at a lower rank. Even in the first few months of his philosophical studies he showed little promise and thought of accepting a lesser role, but encouraged by a sympathetic superior he continued forward. Within a few years the unprepossessing neophyte had transformed into an outstanding student

Francisco Suarez
*Courtesy of the Library of Congress,
Prints and Photographs Division, LC-DIG-hec-13754*

and changed his area of specialization to theology. Suarez would hold professorships at Segovia, Valladolid, Rome, Alcalá, and at Evora, his doctoral alma mater. Although his life remained plain and unassuming—the whole of it devoted to lecturing, study, and writing—his collected works in the Paris edition of 1856–1878 fill twenty-eight volumes. The sickly and mediocre student had become a superlative: the greatest of the Jesuit intellectuals and the greatest scholastic after Aquinas. It was Suarez who capped the eminence of the Anselm tradition. At the time of his death he enjoyed such an extraordinary reputation that his intellectual heritage took flight, to continue in importance both at Catholic and Protestant universities. Students and faculty alike came to appreciate that, although the theological and metaphysical contributions of Suarez were widely read and influenced minds as demanding as Descartes, Wolff, and Leibniz, it was his work as a philosophical jurist that could be defined as remarkable. Reflecting the early study of law and surpassing as it did the medieval scope of scholastic legal philosophy, this foray into legal philosophy was inevitably leading forward to elaboration of wide-reaching political theory.

The neo-scholasticism of Suarez was not the only Renaissance thought whose inspiration came from medieval scholastics. The Dominicans had initiated an intellectual revival in Spain starting in the late fifteenth century and continuing into the sixteenth. Spain, however, was touched less by renaissance and reformation than the other major states of Western Europe. Her revival, keenly analyzed by Copleston (Copleston, Vol. III, 335–355), did not become sapped by the aridities into which fourteenth century Nominalism led most of the universities outside her borders. Among the early leaders of Spanish resurgence were the Dominican Cajetan (1468–1534), Francis of Vitoria (1480–1546), and Dominic Soto (1494–1560). By the 1500s the Jesuits, bent on the theological and philosophical education of their own men as well as others, necessarily made a strong entry on the scene. Toletus (1532–1596), a pupil of Soto; de Fonseca (1548–1599); and Vasquez (c.1551–1604) were leaders among them. There were to be rocks along the road forward, since it was not long before Dominicans and Jesuits fell into spirited controversy, their differences focused on the relation between divine grace and human free will. A special Congregation at Rome (1598–1607) examined the question; and since in theological dispute a judge could decide not to decide yet bid the parties to be quiet nevertheless, it was adjudged that even though both opinions were permissible the Jesuits had to stop calling the Dominicans "Calvinists" and the Dominicans were to desist in calling the Jesuits "Pelagians."

The new Jesuit Scholastics like Suarez were not lost in the clouds. They were aware of contemporary developments of which the rise of nation-states and the decline of medieval unity were the most drastic. Thus, they bent their minds to working out a political theory to fit the changing world, one which in their Jesuitical hands necessarily had to give the pope a suitable role. They refused to honor the extreme papal position of direct power over monarchs, but they would not have been Catholic if they had not accorded him an indirect power. Man's end is salvation; and since it was the pope who knew how to go about attaining it, the secular sovereigns had to take his advice when their action put them in the realm of soteriology. Similarly did the Congregation shrink from honoring the monarchy's ancient claim that sovereignty came directly from God, proclaiming instead the modern view that it came from the people. This was so daring a position that James I of England burned a book written by Suarez in which such bold interpretation was carried forward.

The major Suarez work in philosophy was the *Disputationes metaphysicae* (1597). He considered it an indispensable foundation, presumably because theology—particularly the Thomist base on which he proposed to build—required human reason. The broad horizon envisaged by Suarez was reached by a road map of cognition: being, unity, individuation, universals, distinctions, truth and falsity, good and evil, causes and effects, infinite and finite being, God's existence and his essence and attributes, and substance. But far from being collections of building blocks these epistemological centers of the *Disputationes* cogently brought Scholastic controversies together in a complete and coherent structuring. Here was the first work on philosophy which was an independent treatise rather than a commentary on Aristotle. It was obvious Suarez had abandoned the order of Aristotle's *Metaphysics* in favor of his own dispute structure; divided into a sectional pattern, a table showed readers how to find Aristotle's topics in the new orientation.

Two good illustrations of the Suarez method are his treatment of God's existence and his approach to universals. God's existence was to be proved not physically but metaphysically. Suarez believed that by reaching this divine truth which could be known by reason apart from revelation, one would reach the essence of law. The physical argument had been made by Aristotle: everything that moves is moved by another, hence there has to be an unmoved mover. For Suarez this principle was only probable, and in any case, as we have just said, God's existence as an immaterial, uncreated substance could not, in the Suarez system, be established by argument from physics. It instead had to come from metaphysics, and Suarez himself pronounced, as a metaphysical principle, that everything which was produced was produced by another. This did not reflect a circular production in which A was produced by B which was produced by C which was produced by A, nor could there be an infinite non-circular series. There had to be an unproduced producer. But was it one or many? Revelation could admit only one God. God equated with unicity, said Suarez, because "'the beauty of the whole universe and of all things which are in it, their marvelous connection and order, sufficiently show that there is one first being by which all things are governed and from which they derive their origin'" (Copleston, Vol. III, 363). That is to say, what has been produced displays a unity of planning that could come only from a single, unproduced producer. Suarez then reasoned that the ultimate origin of law had to be God and that the ultimate essence of law was its glorious participation in God's single great cosmic order.

Having shown that human reason proved the existence of the Great Lawyer God, it was necessary to know how man's reason worked. This involved Suarez in the epistemological question of universals: were the thoughts of the mind valid, true reflections of the world outside the mind? Up to and including Suarez, man's medieval method of constructing them was, let us say, three parts logical reflection with eyes closed and other senses subdued, and one part peering at individuals with all senses active. With the same gimlet eye as the legendary General of his Order, Suarez stared at this baggage of old learning heaped before him. Eternal "forms" (including mathematics) of external things, themselves always in flux, had become, as it were, hardened into philosophers' rune stones. In the soul at birth, on a voyage from another existence, they were the only reality; and the acquisition of knowledge through their petrine essences was like recuperation of souvenirs in the trip's baggage. Suarez knew Plato's enormous prestige had been confronted by Aristotle who, undaunted, began to tinker with Plato's approach. Principles inseparable from the physical world came to be thought of separately from the world; the souvenirs took on a life of their own outside the baggage, where the mind could sort them out. Suarez next approached Augustine, who skipped Aristotle for Plato, and from the Suarez pen came a Greek transformed into a Christian by saying that the forms which are interiorly known by the mind are put there by the divine illumination of God. But Suarez also saw Augustine questioned by Aquinas, that student of the "new" Aristotle who, rejecting the Platonic idea that immutable universals are the only realities and exist outside the mind, decided rather that the only realities in the world were individuals. Aquinas did not abandon the universal concepts—undoubtedly formed in the mind—all those souvenirs lying around outside the baggage. But the Thomist valorization of sense experience by which personhood is perceived in thought forced Suarez, too, into recognizing the phenomenon of individualism.

Suarez's last baggage would belong to William of Ockham, escaping the risks imposed on the reconciling of Aristotle and Christianity by positing a terrible God of power so utterly absolute that it was sufficient even to cause men to hate God. Providential but not bound by any system, Ockham's God had created man never to know whether a phenomenon reflects a universal or divine whimsy. In this bewildering metaphysical world of individuals, but no universals, there were no souvenirs for Ockham; the reminiscences could be constructed in the mind, but they remained only words without existence or operation outside it. Suarez opted for placing these philosophical problems before his reader without any theological given. He would promote individuals; the passive intellect could abstract universals, but only after the active intellect had knowledge of these individuals in the real world. Suarez seems finally to have chosen to pick up Ockham's bags; and, by insisting that every individual was a unique essence, he helped open the way for the new scientific method which Ockham's emphasis on the individual had prepared.

However, in his legal philosophy the Jesuit, like Grotius after him, edged toward Plato as he tended away from the Aristotelian and Thomistic empirical study of the ways of mankind as the basis of law. When he promoted his metaphysics as the necessary firm foundation for theology, he opened a door to regard it also as a foundation for law in God's earthly domain. Thus, in his preface to the *Tractatus de legibus* a theologian's eyes contemplate God, seeing Him, and in Him, man's end; this sacred teleology leads to concern with how to reach salvation, along a road marked by free acts and moral rectitude. Law, the rule of human acts without which moral rectitude languishes, makes Suarez list many concrete legal questions, among which are some potent eighteenth century ammunition: for example, what happens when custom has progressed into statute? Is it ever possible to lift the requirement of royal revocation and permit licit disobedience?

The place of Suarez in the historical development of legal thought is above all controlled by his ideas on natural law. Here he would reject Ockham's view on God's power, so awesome it blankets natural law, too. For Suarez the "commands and prohibitions of God in respect of the natural law presuppose the intrinsic righteousness of the acts commanded and the intrinsic wickedness of the prohibited acts." Thus God cannot "command man to hate him" and God cannot "dispense...[with]...any of the [Ten] Commandments." Divine volition is predicated on moral qualities inherent in certain acts. God, too, has a nature and, having it, "God is not the arbitrary author of the natural law, for He commands some acts because they are intrinsically good and prohibits other acts because they are intrinsically evil. Stunningly simple and breathtakingly modern—with God left on the other side of the courtroom door—the Suarez conclusion was that "the natural law, taken simply in itself, reveals what is intrinsically good and evil, *without any explicit reference to God...*" (Copleston, Vol. III, 390; 384–385). True, Suarez felt that Aquinas's definition of law put too much emphasis on reason, but he fell into Thomistic step by holding natural law to be discovered by man, despite its reflecting Eternal Law. It is ironic that Suarez the devout Jesuit theologian should, following Aquinas, the Angelic Doctor, have powerfully helped open the way to the Enlightenment's separation of theology and law by underlining the unity of the philosophical and the legal. But as we promised, there was a tip of the philosophical hat to Plato: although man can discover natural law, he cannot, of course, change it. The Suarez legal foray had in the end been a trip into the real existence of universals—more than Suarez seems to have admitted in his metaphysics.

We can now see why James I caused Suarez in book form to be put to the flames. The Spaniard was clearly well aware of the disposition of the kings of France, Spain, and England to boast of absolute authority and to claim it as a divine right. Yet, boldly foreshadowing the societal contract theories of the seventeenth and eighteenth centuries, he was also adamant that these rulers should be subject to restraints, the prime one, being the immutable natural law. Transgress that and the people have a right to resist, a right that flows directly from the origin of the ruler's power. Moreover, although individuals may only defend themselves against the ruler, the whole community may rise against a legitimate but tyrannical monarch. As a good Jesuit pledged to papal service, Suarez recognized Rome was shorn by secularism of direct temporal power, but he accorded her role, indispensable for a Catholic believer: a pontiff-judge of secular acts and omissions in their effect upon the soteriological endgame of seeing God in salvation.

Thus did this quiet soldier from the Order leading Catholics in reformation, a devout scholar in universities insulated by Spanish royal power and inquisition both from Calvin and Luther and from the extremes of the Italian Renaissance and Humanism, nevertheless boldly reach out over the Pyrenees. From the flow of his ideas—probably without his conscious intention—came a basic contribution transforming thinking and teaching about law. Here was a non-canonist philosophy which bowed to God in the introduction, then in its unfolding suggested a way law in the human mind could set in motion democracies of a future as yet unborn.

Effects of the Reformation on Canon Law and the Universities

Gratian's twelfth century *Decretum*, that unofficial but influential compilation of canon law, had achieved wide public acceptance as the basic academic text prescribed by the Faculty of Decrees for the degree of *Doctore decretorum*. After Gratian, papal decisions were carefully collected as supplements to the *Decretum*, while the *Decretum* professors, or *decretists*, continued to make their glosses and commentaries. These later decrees, called decretals, were sent on by Rome to the University of Bologna; the ones collected by order of Gregory IX in 1234 were intended to supersede everything since Gratian. The later decretals, of course, also attracted commentary by their own professors of expertise, now called *decretalists*, who provided less gloss and more abstract statements of the law in their *Summae*.

Popes continued to send a stream of decretals to academe, but they now specified insertion in the collection of Gregory IX, for it had become and continued into the twentieth century as a major monument in canon law. In time the new decrees became official enlargements rather than mere insertions. There was the *Liber Sextus* added to Gregory's five volumes, then the *Clementines* of 1311. When these were supplemented by two further collections—private but comprised of authentic documents—the *Corpus juris canonici*, as the whole was informally called, was in about 1500 considered a closed code source. It was this body of the law that Luther attacked and that Calvin sought to displace.

The German princes and free cities had installed canon law at the end of the fifteenth century to avoid losing business to ecclesiastical courts. As one state and free city after another, chiefly in Germany and Scandinavia, embraced Lutheranism and rejected the authority of the papacy, one might have expected that this canon law would be entirely abrogated. As a practical matter, though, this proved impossible to do and not even desired by the reformers. Although secular authority in Lutheran princedoms and free cities displaced papal authority as the authority behind canon law, the rules of Romano-canonical procedure continued generally to be followed nearly everywhere on the continent in both ecclesiastical and lay courts. It was a system fully accepted by the same Humanists who looked scornfully at the Glossators and Commentators. Nor were the seventeenth and eighteenth century natural lawyers to express any major objection on religious grounds (O.F. Robinson 182; 320). It is not surprising, then, that as the difficult century wound down, codification remained the Roman remedy for any vagaries of the canon law. The Bolognese Gregory XIII (1572–1585) made his bid for legal reform in between his more successful work sessions on the calendar year. Then, between 1580 and 1582 an official text of the *Corpus juris canonici* appeared, while Clement VIII produced the collection of scattered decretals he called *Liber Septimus*. Yet Rome's reformation into nearly absolute papal monarchy still had to make a last reach. In spite of continuous development from the days of the Council of Trent, infallibility could not flower until 1870, and it would be no sooner than 1904 when at last Rome announced the master plan for a codex. When this could at last emerge from the horrors of world war as the bulky *Codex juris canonici*, effective in 1918, Gratian must have affirmatively nodded his twelfth century hoary locks while Luther and Calvin interrupted with many a sharp lawyerly objection.

The course of substantive canon law was far less smooth. Political passion can burn brightly in universities, and both in Protestant countries on the continent and in England the faculties of canon law were simply dissolved and instruction in that specialization ceased. In addition, the ecclesiastical courts in these Protestant states were dissolved, and the Church property that had supported so many canon lawyers entered under state appropriation. A large source of legal careers thus abruptly ended, and with it, the flow into the universities of students who wanted such careers. The religious wars brought grief to many jurists. There were those like Dumoulin who was Protestant and had to flee; others like Cujas followed the practical path of Henry IV, doing at least outwardly what the Church demanded while, in Cujas's particular case, at the same time saying that the religious struggle had nothing to do with Humanistic study of Roman law. Although the Jesuits became important in French education, they did not confer degrees in law, leaving that to faculties of the universities who continued on with their old work. As the great challenge to the development of French law in the sixteenth century—the writing of the customs—went forward (Imbert, *Histoire du droit privé,* 53), much of it was done by scholars who were not professors.

The general effects of war, political controversy, expulsion of the Roman Catholic churches and other disturbances meant chaos for the universities. With their considerable lack of funds and cohesion came the obvious: shrinking student bodies and declining pay for all professors. There was true agony in having to choose sides. Many had little passion for either, and the choice became especially excruciating in places where Protestant and Catholic authority alternated. As active local secular authorities displaced the distant and generally lenient papacy, academic independence lost ground. Statesmen were pleased to decide that universities existed for the purpose of supporting their state policies, rather than promoting learning for its own sake. Although this latter phenomenon actually lifted the social status of the universities, their academic quality was so greatly depressed that, certain periods of brilliance in law on the continent excepted, they were to lie almost moribund until the 1800s. It became clear that any major intellectual advances of the seventeenth century were going to have to take place outside academic centers. Badly organized, misdirected by powerful bureaucratic interests, these struggling universities could offer only an uninspired scholastic curriculum, one which did not cover the traditional scope of human knowledge, let alone treat those new subjects arising on every side. Calls frequently came from warring denominations seeking learned men to lead them, but paltry choice within the university milieu meant an equally frequent inability to respond. On the positive side, however, the great theological controversy which for the first time gave individuals choice in religion, itself encouraged thought and study even if the university were not always the venue of choice for either. This intellectuality now actually tended to be liberated by schism, since the need to reconcile new learning to old theology could no longer by controlled by weakened ecclesiastical authorities.

Fortunately, in this awkward period of intellectual division, law continued to attract the bourgeoisie and some nobles, especially because in the sixteenth century, as in far earlier times, law was always useful in estate management. Increasingly, one member of a well-off family would be chosen to leave home and become a legal expert; when at last he returned fully trained—often from Bourges or Geneva—the rest of the family immediately put him to work at their continuous and acrimonious litigation (*New Cambridge Modern History,* Vol. II, 415). In general the Reformation, tending to produce its across-the-board divorce of religion and law, was finally turning the legal profession away from its old contingent of ecclesiastics and toward an entirely secular profession. These new men, separating faith and law, ethical duty and positive statute, liberated the civil regimen from its traditionally hierarchical premises; this, in turn, helped build nation-states which themselves manifested the same secular intellectual tendency. Needless to say, the clergy of the ancient Church were angrily opposed to all these moves away from the altar. They could see they were losing a lucrative field of legal business, and they vociferously challenged any claims that the study of Roman law and legal science shared any compatibility with Christianity (*Continental Legal History*, Vol. I, 383). Even the Inquisition became suspicious of civilian lawyers, causing some to stay away from secular legal studies. All in all, when one recalls the lofty pedestal canon lawyers had erected for themselves, such combative attitudes of a fading Catholic clergy are hardly surprising.

As a practical matter, canon law, although it might need amendment to suit Protestant thinking, had to survive. The voluminous provisions for Church administration and churchmen could be displaced by new rules for Protestant churches and clergy, thus giving rise to Protestant ecclesiastical law as a new subject—and offering, one might add, far less red meat for the legal profession than the old canon law. But there were still the Church's ubiquitous rules for marriage, testamentary succession, and the poor. They had been everywhere recognized by secular authorities, already highly sensitive to the incursions of Church courts in all matters of sin—defamation, usury, sexual offenses, perjury, breach of faith in contract. These ubiquitous legal structures, so much a part of daily social life, had to be maintained in a university's curriculum, even if taught by secular faculties expanding that curriculum by the addition of Roman law (O.F. Robinson, 320; 307). The result was that the lay courts began to assume the jurisdiction formerly exercised by the Church courts while at the same time, like the professors, continuing to consult the old books. A larger number of younger jurists took the Protestant rather than the Catholic road, yet the profession in general upheld the validity of the canon law, except for those parts which Protestant ministers successfully condemned as in conflict with the Bible (*Continental Legal History*, Vol. I, 382).

The French king had already achieved substantial control of the Church at the expense of the pope; the Pragmatic Sanction of Bourges (1438) and the Concordat of Boulogne (1516) were important steps in this process. France's royals especially opposed Protestantism because the Catholic Church, under the policy of *Gallicanisme*, had become an indispensable source of income for the royal treasury (Ellul, Vol. IV, 38). Since in France the Protestant triage happened to favor Calvinism rather than Lutheranism, Calvin's theocracy with ministers of religion dominating policy-making had certainly no chance of pleasing a French king. Yet, ironically, although at the opposite end of the social spectrum from the monarch, Calvin had made no headway among French peasants either; he had definitely drawn many supporters from the nobility itself. Indeed, at one time 40 to 50 percent of the aristocracy was Calvinist. Named Huguenots, perhaps after a Genevan leader, they and the bourgeois capitalist and artisan class, including, of course, many lawyers, comprised a population of much power. Not merely a religious sect, but a political party, their next menacing transformation was an armed force bent on civil war to control government. The inevitable ensuing religious conflicts occupied the years 1562–1598; and the violence reached large enough scope to be divided by historians into eight separate wars. Each was marked by the paradox of Protestant forces, superb in noble cavalry, but weak in infantry, tending to lose while at the same time demanding and receiving concessions (Langer, 411–413). At the end of the eighth war, the royal Valois line ended as Protestant Henry of Navarre, whom we met in discussion of Montaigne, became Henry IV (1589), the first Bourbon.

Henry ironically would disappoint the Protestant power dream. He had escaped death in 1572 during the St. Bartholomew massacre by feigning a return to Catholicism, but now in 1593 he fully embraced French royal policy by publicly becoming a Catholic. His *Paris vaut bien une messe,* (Paris is worth attending Mass,) recognized that it was the faction of mostly Catholic advocates of strong royal power to which he owed his top spot. Henry was at heart ecumenical and tried to find some peaceful compromises. His greatest attempt was granting the Protestants the famous Edict of Nantes (1598), with equal political rights and a large, though not complete, measure of freedom to exercise their religion. It proved an uneasy right, for the Huguenots would not abandon their ambition to control the government. Looking ahead to 1685 and the Edict's equally infamous revocation by Louis XIV, more than 50,000 Protestant families, including many able industrialists, artisans, and thinkers, whose combined mental capacity might well have delayed the Revolution, would finally choose to leave or were deported from France. Having appeared to bring calm to the religious strife through a modern policy of tolerance, the monarchy snatched its own defeat from victory. As Protestantism ultimately exploded into mass social and political protest, it was the sun king who guaranteed that the resplendant crown of Catholic divine right would in The French Revolution become nothing more than the gloomy old hat of an *ancien régime* without a royal head to wear it.

Isaac Newton
Courtesy of National Gallery of Art, Washington.

PART 13

The New Hinge Period
*Geographical Expansion, Capitalism,
Scientific Revolution*

Rise of the Merchants and Middle Class; The New World; Capitalism

The important transformation in thought introduced in the early fourteenth century had created a great "hinge" time in history whose changes infused with a practical bent the work of Ockham, the Nominalist; Petrarch, the Humanist; and Bartolus, the academic jurist. Now came another important "hinge" period, this one around the beginning of the seventeenth century. Like the early 1300s these were years when later expert partisans would hail the genius of changing the way men thought about society. Our study concentrates on a trio chosen from the multiplicity of these stunning thinkers. First we shall meet Grotius, the initial leading light in the new natural law—versatile as a scholar and jurist but longing to show off his talents as a statesman. Next will come Hobbes, the mathematician turned philosopher. For him the challenge lies in creating a new kind of complete thought system which, although he is not a jurist, includes the philosophy of law; his epistemology will be based on ideas that achieve large currency later as the Nominalist "positive law" movement in legal philosophy. Finally, there will be Pufendorf, another academic jurist who begins with the work of Grotius and then brings forth a specialization in detailed natural law which reaches its apogee in the grandeur of the *Code Napoleon*.

Since natural law will be the central theme in the remainder of this book, it is first necessary to speak of two important movements that fully inform its unique character. The first is economic and social: in the modern age's accelerated rise of the bourgeois middle class—lawyers among them—wholesale merchants and statesmen lead the way in identifying increased state power as responsible to their own welfare and needs. The second, greater even than the first in decisive and continuing impact upon the society of which law is a part, is the scientific revolution, brightening salons and laboratories in an already gilded age. During such triumph of invention and daring, the world turned upside down will be righted again and illumined by Galileo's formulation of the scientific method. Inquiring minds will be introduced to the world as machine, then progress to the completion of such understanding in the physics notes of Newton.

The story of the rise of the merchants has been somewhat clouded by a natural tendency to see it as only the consequence of the daring overseas discoveries achieved around the end of the fifteenth century. The new heroes were the navigators, brilliantly plotting oceans of discovery for their wooden ships while profiting enormously from new technology. In their cabins were spread out improved maps; on deck their men steered the vessels under guidance of the twelfth century's innovative magnetic compass. Latitudinal estimating had been updated by cleverly using the angle of the sun. The very vessels themselves had borrowed efficient rigging changes from the Arabs and boasted powerful gunpowder cannon for use on board. These finds brought new overseas trade, not so much because the European export/import professionals were astute (the Arabs and Chinese had been better), but because naval superiority forced their business as inevitable (Langer, 25).

We can add to our long list of accidents of history that the first European state to use the innovative navigation aids in discovering new coasts was the small, poor, and backward kingdom of Portugal. When their navigators in 1415 crossed the Strait of Gibraltar, the feat aroused the interest of one of the pivotal characters in history, Prince Henry the Navigator, the right man at the right time and place. The son of Portugal's John I, Henry became the director of a school dedicated to geographical discovery; his goal was not so much making money from exploration as it was finding a mythical Christian kingdom on the east flank of the Muslim world. Even before he died, his countrymen saw the opportunity for gain, first in yellow gold and then in the infamous "black gold" of slaves brought back from the west coast of Africa. When in 1497 the Portuguese da Gama reached the west coast of India—a central Arab trading location—financial aid from profit-hungry merchants, shippers, and bankers in Genoa, Florence, and the Netherlands promoted ever more overseas voyages of discovery.

Exploration depended on many variables, the first being how much appetite a monarch had for the adventure. In 1492 the Portuguese crown turned down a remarkable personality, Christopher Columbus. Indomitable in persistent pursuit of his conviction Columbus instead gained to his cause Portuguese-born Isabella the Catholic of Spain ready to play the conquest game. The next requirement was to work with meteorology. Gradations of temperature cause motions of air, and the mechanics of these motions on a rotating earth create fair winds for any westbound sailing vessel from Spain taking a southerly route in the North Atlantic toward the Caribbean; the winds operate for eastbound vessels by a more northerly route sailing easterly home to Spain, while the Gulf Stream does the job of moving a vessel to the beginning of this eastbound route. Columbus, an accomplished navigator, discovered these particular routes, mostly by luck, and made passages to and fro which were fast sailing even by today's standards. For our purposes it makes no difference that Columbus thought he had found islands ("Indies") south of China and Japan. What is crucial is that as a result of the Spanish sponsorship and the early follow-up of Portugal, Central and South America became permanently Hispanic, thus falling under Roman influence in law and the Roman Catholic Church in religion.

For about a century, the Spanish and Portuguese kingdoms, united in 1580, had this New World to themselves. The Dutch, English, and French—destined to control everything north of Mexico—could not force even the weakened Spaniards out of the southern area, alone considered desirable because of its gold, silver, spices, and sugar. The Spanish strength came from having devised a successful strategy: centers of activity were settled inland in the mountains, while trade was concentrated with coastal defense in only three ports: Cartagena, Portobelo, and Vera Cruz. Defenses of the flotillas to and from Spain (two west and one east each year) made privateering too risky to attract much investment by the north Europeans (Langer, 37). Except for scattered successes in the eighteenth century, they had to settle for the "good for nothing" North that could sustain only "bread colonies."

Colonization in the South had prospered, at least for the Spanish though not for the natives, and Mexico City with a population in 1550 of 100,000 was larger than any urban center in Spain. Yet in the long run, the Spanish crown, forgetful that bullion is an advantage only if used to advantage, rode its enormous inflow of colonial gold and silver not to prosperity, but to the financing of war which ended in defeat and poverty. When northern states sailed much later into these discovery channels, they became discouraged because Spain and Portugal seemed already to have the best places. Yet they were to be also impressed that their capital available for maritime activity could bring in good returns from older areas. By the later sixteenth century, the northern leaders had both a capital surplus for their New World visits and a war with Spain in Europe to stimulate such national efforts in America.

The French followed the Dutch who, having displaced the Portuguese in the East Indies, had prospered without, however, making any lasting progress in South America. Their limited progress in North America ended when they lost control to the English in 1664. French attempts in Florida and the Carolinas fell to Spanish opposition; but Frenchmen achieved three permanent North American venues for continental civil law: in Quebec; in an eighteenth century spread to Louisiana after English pressure exiled Acadians; and in a bid to control all of Canada and all of the later United States west of the Mississippi. Intrepid explorers of the waterways, New France's Quebec was the first French colony anywhere, although for long term success intrepidity could not override wrong method. Many of the French people who continued to come to Canada, even after the hope of gold and silver vanished, still came for financial profit; their dreams were mainly of lucrative fur trading but they also tried for fortunes in fish and cut timber. Ultimately, they would discover these items had lost their appeal back home and the great riches were not to be.

The New France government was in form and largely in fact under absolute monarchical control; the authoritarian procedures of Louis XIV and his minister Colbert were aided by dedicated Jesuits who even in the forests of North America never lost their organization or principles of absolute authority. Colonists were, in effect, royal wards, enervated to a substantial extent by awaiting largesse and receiving instead a plethora of rules. We have seen how Huguenots, who would undoubtedly have committed to the faraway country by seeking a permanent new life there and trying hard to realize the full potential of the new land, were rigidly excluded by a king wedded to Catholicism. It made little difference that Louis was in church politics more Gallican than Roman. As for the indigenous people who hunted rather than cultivated land, they were comparatively few and quite poor. They could not, like the more numerous and culturally advanced natives harnessed by the Spaniards, be converted to labor gangs, and few embraced even the gentler yoke of Christianity. The strength of New France thus lay in the Jesuits, the army, and a few French peasants who lived on the shore of the St. Lawrence. The rambunctious body of fur traders, who seldom obeyed royal regulations, joined the mix as doubtful contributors.

Generally efficient, but weighed down by such motley and rather puny structures at hand, French troops were in the end insufficient to hold their monarch's enormous territory against the English, arriving next in the colonial line. These settlements generally flourished; and their population, unlike Quebec, multiplied despite the fact they *had* settled, with little opposition except from the Dutch, that "good for nothing" area from Maine to Georgia. In efforts geographically very different from Spain, Holland, and France, the initial 1607 English settlement in Virginia was a struggle between staying alive or being killed. Next was the turn of rocky Massachusetts which saw a great wave of English immigrants rapidly colonize around the Bay and then push up the coast in the 1620s and 1630s. It was of crucial importance to the future of America that this surge occurred when the British government was wholly preoccupied with the titanic constitutional struggle at home that culminated in civil war. Finally in 1689 the victory of the landed gentry and merchants over a crown, forced that crown to abandon its dream of absolute power by divine right.

The first British settlers were nearly all dissenters from the established Church of England, determined not upon a quick profit and return, but upon a permanent new life in what they regarded as a New England. Thus would grow the Calvinist theocracies organized as self-governing church congregations without nobility. These facts meant that for long the home government had no colonial policy at all, while the colonists were probably better educated, more politically conscious, and therefore, better qualified than anyone in Europe to fend for and govern themselves. They already understood crucial legal principles: law and politics conjoined for the welfare of a middle class; social need put before arbitrary confiscation or taxation of property; participation by the ruled in making their laws; no restraint of liberty except for violation of law; all malfeasance deserving of an early trial when charged (Langer, 60).

Unwittingly, the English situation was moving the social unit a little closer to the ancient Greek propagation of independent city-states. Growth in English America brought not only more Calvinists, but notable variations both in legal organization and religion, so that the mother country's religious uniformity, to say nothing of "Englishness," could not be enforced upon an Atlantic coast already something of a "melting pot" by 1700. Significantly, on the legal front there was no overall colonial administration. Nor was there any uniform policy toward the sparse indigenous Americans who moved West or stayed East in clusters, making local arrangements to their general disadvantage. On the other hand, the spirit of government subordinate to law and based on the participation of the middle class was general, and all moved under English common law.

This wholly uncoordinated, yet promising, activity of the European powers and the colonial people laid the early groundwork for the vision, then the reality of today's interdependent world community. What is more, as Langer shows (Langer, 43; 61–62), the seventeenth century "literally changed the face of the earth" through an ecological revolution which increased commerce and contributed to rising mercantile strength. Population curves of animal and vegetable life were redistributed in a geographical shift that continues to this day. Coffee migrated from the Near East to Java and South America; American Indian corn, pumpkins and potatoes, tomatoes and string beans found themselves crossing the ocean to Europe; while wheat, rye, oats, and rice took up residence in the New World, along with a shopping list of horses, donkeys, mules, oxen, pigs, goats, cows, sheep, and domestic fowl. The Western hemisphere would be the great gainer of all this migration. The fact that the route to America was relatively short meant high value/low volume ladings of bullion and spices now became feasible, as did shipment to Europe of the bulkiest cargoes: fish, furs, tobacco, rice, cotton, cocoa, coffee, indigo, sugar, timber, and cattle.

There was a basic disconnect inherent in the burgeoning trade flow. Merchants dealing with this flood of opportunity from the heightened commerce hardly could handle their windfall. The home monarchies, as we know, were without clairvoyance as to the stunning colonial promise. Initially, governments did manage to demonstrate their innate grasping ability by keeping the royal eye open on what was coming in and going out of ports, attempting to make certain that any commerce be fit for or, if needed, jammed into the context of kingly need. The royal bottom line was always self-survival through survival of the motherland. Such survival did utilize economics as weaponry of choice. But armed conflict's catechism—the weak will be absorbed by the strong— was ingrained in states whose troops were ready and able to wage war as an effective adjunct to exports and imports. This meant, in the period of colonization, spending half the revenues on maintenance of an effective professional standing army with infantry, trained in intricate maneuvers, preceded and supported by artillery. Such an army was very expensive—a state had to pay in gold and silver—and government policy had to be primed to turning imports into revenue for arms.

The solution to commercial enthusiasm and royal necessity was a royal policy advocated by writers and practiced by statesmen. Called "mercantilism," its elegant design could ironically enhance and protect a nation's supply of gold and silver by crude fiat: carry on foreign trade solely with those places where the outlay of specie for imports is exceeded by the receipts for exports, and forbid it elsewhere. From this economic philosophy would grow complex new legal controls: on the use of ships and ports, on structures taxing imports and exports, on embargoes, on the discouragement of colonial manufacturing, and on the award of monopolies. Canny statesmen in the pay of grasping rulers perceived clearly the cruel factoring of goods versus slaves. Areas where coffee, teas, furs, sugar, tobacco, and Negro labor were available made for a goal more viable than direct attempts to get gold bullion by mining, capture of mines, or outright theft. Unfortunately, the places of supply were sites least suited for settlement, and sophisticated devices were needed to bring these *bread colonies* into the mercantilist system. Some merchants gained, others knew loss, while the brutally worked labor force always suffered.

There were always merchants ready to support any policy which would produce a stand-up profit for some on the bent backs of the many. Seventeenth and eighteenth century writers, statesman, and men of the law reasoned that labor added value to raw materials and, therefore, to their price in gold and silver: the more work, the more value. So hours were set long and wages were set low because, it was said by the policy makers, higher wages meant more workers would spend their free time loafing or purchasing luxuries, the importation of which would drain the nation's gold and silver (II Langer *W Civ.* 118).

Mercantilism lasted until the end of the eighteenth century. It failed miserably for Spain; she could not produce enough manufactured goods to satisfy colonial demand, and her merchants diverted the colonial gold and silver to buy goods in other countries. The mercantilists failed miserably for France, too; as her strength was dissipated in continental wars, she lost her ambitious American empire to England. Ultimately even English mercantilism produced the tension of *no taxation without representation*, the first misstep toward loss of the American empire.

For 200 years after 1450 there had been a gradual increase in the population of Europe, interrupted at times by war and famine while constantly hampered by dismal figures from disease and childbirth mortality. Demographics had especially shifted fast forward after the catastrophic demoralization and depredations of the great plagues and the Hundred Years' War. It is doubtful whether in 1700 there were 20 percent more Frenchmen than in 1300, but by 1789 there were 45 percent more than in 1700. It was about the same elsewhere in the Western world. Capitalism traces back to these old beginnings, when new interest patterns of business were leading a national middle class to rise into an "age of the merchants" (Langer, 99). These were to be the men to reinvigorate legal philosophy and law. Where economic change since the Middle Ages had been slow, now population increase stimulated marketing, agricultural specialization, commercial farming, and manufactures. Paris, London, and Amsterdam became great metropolises after 1500 and, having to be supplied, provided the impetus for population centers arising near coal seams, ore discoveries, and places of falling water. Yet to 1700, with no matching improvements in farming methods, one-third of the best soil lay in pasture each year. The overseas discoveries before 1700 added little food beyond some cane and cod; even the imported South American potato was long considered by Europeans to be inedible.

Most estates had converted to fixed cash payments the old feudal dues once payable in service and in kind. Rulers had borrowed profligately to fight their wars and then inflated to pay back, while the flood of specie from the New World was itself enough for a price revolution. Worse still, from the end of the fifteenth century to 1600, the cost of living increased about six times, more than at any recorded time before or after, at least up to World War I. Many owners were ruined. It took astute planning and legal acrobatics to beat the peasants to the profits—enlarging the landlord's acres while reducing those of the tenancy, reconverting fixed payments to rent in kind. In Western Europe, at least, the peasants did not sink to serfdom as in the East; they could escape to the towns where, if they stayed, they found public courts in which were heard appeals for protection of legal status and rights. In these statutory struggles English landlords and yeomen did better than the French landlords, who belatedly grasped English strategies but too often joined the army for the debilitating religious wars or wielded too much judicial power vis-à-vis royal judges. French landlords may have made less money, but they aroused more hate; instead of buying out a tenant or succeeding in the enclosure of common land, they fought yearly legal battles with share-croppers over the division of the harvest and compulsory processing with the lord's equipment.

In manufacturing options, woolen cloth had long been the chief product of Europe; from before 1250 to as late as 1750 textiles were the major industry. Then, when printing became an important new profession, armaments grew with the technology, and there was increase in the use of coal as forests were depleted to make iron. The explosive advent of steam power would not come until after 1750; tools were still hand-operated and there were only glimpses of factories. Clearly, however, the demographic manufacturing shift from town to country meant capital was still required. With a good feeling for investment opportunity, ambitious wholesale merchants—not the landowners, producers, or retail distributors—saw clearly that the countryside offered proximity to raw materials, a freedom from stifling monopolistic restrictions of the urban guilds, lower taxes, cheaper food, and easy siting for new water mills. As these traders made their power moves, laborers, as usual, lost in the process; without the powers they enjoyed in the towns, their wages fell ever lower. Twenty-first century global economy is still writing much of the same scenario.

Mercantile law organized the great East Indian trading companies and, later, partnerships for the American trade. It structured the dominant woolen cloth markets of Europe as well as the financial markets at Antwerp, Amsterdam, and London; it was behind each push and success in production and distribution. This meant the men of capital were given a key position, assured by the character of the producing and distributing units, which were numerous, small, and widely scattered. As is the case today in many industries, if a producer's market was to be larger than local sales a coordinator was necessary, and a very important new legal device, the joint stock company, began to facilitate the enlarged trade. As compared with partnerships it had permanence.

Not dissolved by exchange or death, the company shares were easily transferred, the shareholders had limited liability, and management was centralized. The structure was a union of capital rather than men, and its rise or fall brought the new money economies into the modern world. However, without guarantee against loss any more than with partnerships, there came notorious failures. Collapsing stock companies in both England and France left shareholders with such grievous losses that, after about 1715, the use of the new form would be retarded by restrictive legislation. In this modern interpretation of resurrection and damnation, the great phenomenon of boom and crash had been born. Instead of clergy, new lawyers and newer lawyering were called upon to sort out the anguish.

Important as the joint-stock company was destined to be, even greater was the contribution to business efficiency, security, and growth of the system of notes and bills devised by the merchants and accepted by the jurists. Carrying large amounts of gold and silver coins from place to place was burdensome and hazardous, and even after the outpouring from the mines of Peru had been arduously portaged out by the Inca laborers, there were not enough coins to meet the needs of business. By a convenient new method a merchant could legally pay his supplier with the proceeds of the resale without using cash. The buyer, for example, could write an order directing his banker to pay the wholesaler, and the wholesaler could, by endorsement, transfer it to his supplier who could present it to his own banker for collection, a process which could further reduce transfers of cash by netting the mutual obligations of the bankers. Initially private bankers handled such transactions until supplanted by the great public banks of Amsterdam (1609), Hamburg (1619), Stockholm (1656), and England (1694). Bankers perceived that merchants could settle obligations with the bankers' written promises to pay gold to the merchants. Since these notes were never all presented at once, at least as long as the public believed in the solvency of the bank, more could be issued than the cash on hand.

As paper became cash, the wheels of commerce turned faster and faster. Merchants' exchanges or *bourses* at Antwerp (sixteenth century), Amsterdam (seventeenth century), and London (eighteenth century) became meeting places of buyers and sellers of commodities and finished goods, as well as the shares of the joint-stock companies. Unlike the medieval fairs these exchanges were continuous in fixed locations. They functioned, even were the goods to be found in other towns and villages or perhaps nonexistent, until the next harvest. Such venues of commercial activity led inevitably to the establishment of market prices, with the positive legal buttress of greater confidence that the price for any given transaction could be accepted as just.

Given the constantly lurking stress of failure, medieval producers and traders had sought to limit risks by being part of a group: caravans, convoys, guilds, trading towns, or leagues. Now, in the early modern period, there had grown many more kinds of hazard. Certainly a calamity to one party might have no effect on others, and some ventures, like a loan to a prudent government, might involve but little danger. At the other extreme, though, chances like a gamble on a violation of the monopoly of the East India Company involved a tightrope walk of economic peril, yet at the same time, greater reward for success. The new principle of diversification of exposure—spreading capital across the spectrum—was welcomed as allowing the investor in these tight situations more control over net risk.

Here, then, is the significance of the Merchant for the philosophy and growth of law: the modern enterprise systems cried out for a commercial class acting with personal initiative which could be trusted, verified, *and* developed into profitable industry. Medieval restrictions had grown acutely burdensome, but so also had the restrictions of mercantilism for those not favored with monopolies or other governmental favors. The result was that in large numbers the cadre of intelligent and energetic men, all hard at work amassing wealth and swelling in the self-confidence which is always the result of self-made riches, made economic freedom of the individual—liberated to assume risks and reap rewards where he willed—the keynote of commercial thought. God may have created, but He could no longer change. *Telos* had become telluric in a world of commercial Creation and metallic Grace. It was now time for writer-philosophers to make of it all human systems equally inevitable, eternal, and unchanging. Such systems would embody these qualities, not because they came from God above, but because they flowed from the natural law of man and his earth.

The Seventeenth Century and the Scientific Revolution

Introduction

The lawyers of Europe did not wake up on the morning of 1 January 1600 and peer out upon a world they perceived to be entirely different from the century into which they had been born. Although immense, the change in thought about to be wrought among the educated was going to be a gradual movement. Nevertheless, had one of these lawyers enjoying a New Year's Eve party the night before heard for the first time an explanation of the work of the Italian professor of mathematics, Galileo, and exclaimed in opening the shutters the next morning, "it *is* a different world," the amazement would have been a pardonable exaggeration. Although the physical world would have the same look as the one seen from a carriage on the way home from the party, the basis had been laid for an entirely new perception of it, and the end of this new century would bear striking differences from the beginning. In that progression, Galileo's method led to a parade of startling practical inventions, even to some actual transformation of the physical earth itself. It would bring soaring confidence in man's ability to improve his condition, such that a Condorcet in 1794 could see no limit on man's potential for progress (Copleston, Vol. IV, 54). It would cause many to view the seventeenth century as the decade of greatest change—even more than the previous hinge in the 1300s. And, unlike Irnerius in the eleventh century, the "new Aristotle" in the twelfth and thirteenth, and Petrarch in the sixteenth, this transformation was not a movement forced upon Christian Europe by new discovery and appreciation of ancient sources. True, it would get a little stimulation from uncovering conflicts in those sources, such as when the disparity between the qualitative physics of Aristotle and the mathematics of Archimedes was brought to light by intellectual labors. Encouragement for the optimistic new century came also from the general thought patterns learned from the Renaissance—from Humanism, Reformation, and even the rigorous logic of Scholasticism, especially the Nominalism credo of Ockham. Still, the drive and potency for change had an essentially contemporary orientation, energized by the excitement of craftsmen, artisans, and engineers empowered over nature to make life better here below.

This quest to find the best way to organize society by applying the promise of the latest in scientific method was the signal for a parallel explosive period of growth in law. Led by attorney Hugo Grotius—in this sense a second Irnerius—law would in the seventeenth century make a remarkable stride forward. Grotius's ambitious philosophical investigations had the advantage of playing out dramatically when set against the incipient new science of Being led by the moralist and mathematician Descartes. The idea of man's supremacy over nature through the rational route of science led onward to a social leveling movement; and in that movement people could actually understand it was time to review, if not the old sources, then the evergreen ideal of humans contracting together to create a government.

When we meet Grotius we shall find he was not an academic lawyer; it will be the nineteenth century before universities regain what had once been their habitual major role. The mission of the university appeared jelled into teaching approved learning, rather than discovering new truths. The reign of the "schoolmen" was over, and, in the meantime, their studies were being transformed for them by thinkers mainly outside academic walls. Such learned men, including many lawyers, now met in "academies" outside the universities to carry on programs of research, discussion, and publication that were inspired by the struggles and gains of mathematics. Physics was about to secede from natural philosophy, while philosophy joined hands with political theory and theology or found a felicitous replacement in history. Encouraged by experimental science to continue attempts at comprehensive systems including law, the new epistemologists would, in their very style, abandon the unyielding cadences of scholasticism for an easier prose.

As the old and comparatively blind adherence to authority risked abandonment, thinking people began the long and intense examination of all in life, rewriting the old, easier rationalizations. Having abandoned the scholastic idea that a proposition is true if the man offering it refutes all objections to it, and discovering one by one the ironclad laws regulating geometry and the uniform behavior of the phenomena of nature, the age of Moderns fighting back Ancients could achieve certainty at last. At this juncture the human mind appeared equal to laying down truths that even God of the clockwork universe could not change. This, in turn, forced a turnaround in the attitude of theology and philosophy. Ultimately, clockwork does not have a "final cause," that is, an ultimate human destiny for which alone it exists. In the universe of Pascal and Newton, man became a tiny thinking dot on one small sphere in an infinity of space.

What was therefore ending up as an Aquinas replacement was a universe morally indeterminate and non-providential. Not replaced, however, was bedrock belief that man as part of this universe and as the unique possessor of rationality could both exercise choice over his conduct, and deduce from his essential being universal and immutable rules of natural law to control it. Even though seventeenth century Europe was still a deeply religious place in which few would not be sincerely devoted to God, the principal theologies of Catholicism, Lutheranism, Calvinism, and Judaism, along with other belief systems, allowed men's minds to be stimulated by the necessity to decide what was true, and, having decided, to continue to think about it.

Science now was presenting to the orthodox, and especially to the Catholics, sharp challenges not unlike those introduced in the early Church by the problems of pagan education and the "new" Aristotle. This time, however, the Church lacked leaders who could stretch to embrace the new inevitability. Galileo would be condemned by the Inquisition. There were no clear thinkers who could see that science was only revealing mechanism, that God had, in fact, created this mechanism as a mathematical system distinct from the one the authors of Genesis thought He had created. Christianity had conquered antiquity, Aristotle, even

Islamic civilization by embracing as much of each as was possible. An exception might be found in England, where Puritans held that with traditional civilization on the brink of extinction, only through science could God vouchsafe to His new Adam the means to a new world. The major established religions, though, would falter for a long time, never achieving the degree of consensus produced by Aquinas. Indeed, Protestant scholasticism after Luther would put forward a biblical science competing with Copernicus. Thus, for many, hard science which attracted the learned because of its reassuring certainties, ironically, was causing new tortures of doubt. It was far from reassuring to think system and invention constituted part of one's duty to God.

For most, though, condemnation and fear were but feathers floating in the powerful stream of science. An unstoppable scientific method was rapidly going to replace old authorities, not only for those who could understand it, but for a multitude ready to believe without understanding. For this latter majority the frustration of having to test various hypotheses by experiment could not deter or affect their faith in the marvels of innovative structures. Because science proceeded in public as though in a fishbowl, the application of its new paradigms made dishonesty fortuitously hard to conceal. Science did little preaching, cried for no persecution of doubters, used no force or threats, and required no confession or penance (Langer, 150). Its errors, provoking new progress, only increased faith in it, as freedom to press on was seen to be more important than timid holding back out of fear.

Such an effort solely to disclose truth meant often that the researcher felt no responsibility for social or cultural consequences of stunning new concepts which were, in time, to appear overwhelming. In 1624 a submarine went two miles under water in the Thames. The theory of the steam engine was advanced. Navigators' new worlds forced mapmakers into a frenzy of updating. Any assemblage of great minds of the period even today causes the mind to bend under their weight. There is Descartes laying down the law of inertia, inventing analytical geometry, and coming up with a provisional computation to find truth through method. He also, alongside Gassendi, anticipated the molecular theory of heat, with Gassendi going on to measure the speed of sound. Torricelli studied atmospheric pressure and developed the mechanics of winds, while Mersenne defined the overtones of a sounding string. De Dominis analyzed refraction and reflection in rainbows, and Snell formulated the laws of refraction with precision. Gilbert explained terrestrial magnetism, then Jesuits Strada proposed a magnetic telegraphy, Caleo described electrical repulsion, and Kircher described a method of measuring magnetism.

The effect of these enormous gains, to state a banality, has been incredible. Who, sitting down at the wheel of his automobile in the twenty-first century, about to experience the utterly overwhelming pleasure of being able to go rapidly anywhere almost without effort, is inclined to doubt the men who discovered the laws of science that control his engine and program his on-board location system? Or, even more overwhelming, who can lose faith in a method of investigation that leads to a little device implanted in the skin that gives regularity to a heart that God had permitted to flutter? It is marvelous to think about improving life on earth whether or not we think less about life in heaven, and whether or not we are comfortable with the human genome or the human clone. No wonder that historians have hailed the scientific revolution of the seventeenth century as the era when the greatest names made the greatest advances since the Greeks. The sobering discovery that man's morality might sag in consequence of science was to come later.

By the twentieth century most would say that the efforts of the four preceding centuries to give law the form of this brilliantly elegant science invariably failed. Overwhelmed by the science of nature, lawyers would give up making comprehensive systems, as they, henceforth, put effort into concentrating on the cases at hand. Jurisprudence thus had lost much of the rich cross-fertilization gleaned from philosophy, and rhetoric would in time simply collapse. Especially in the latter part of the 1900s, as the possibility emerged that the irresponsibility often spawned in the scientific effort of disclosing truth had no place in acceptable guidance systems like law, the scientific legalism begun in the 1600s became even less attractive. Although one can say that mathematics is the handmaid of science, logic has not been the equivalent for philosophy. Writers like Cairns (Cairns, 3, 10) underscore that the mathematical method cannot bring to jurisprudence the possibility of discovery it imparts to mathematics. They reemphasize how logic studies logic, not its application, and that mathematics forms a complete mental system with no direct reference to the outside world. Law, too, is a mental system, but its base is personality in the human world. What the critique of the seventeenth century comes down to is that attempts to put together a science of nature and the human social order ran up against the implications of the clockwork universe; such attempts at fixed system could not handle the idea of living things in a continuous process of evolution. Clearly these earlier times needed a Darwin but had none.

The tendency toward realism, universals, and natural law which appeared long ago in the character of Antigone combating the opposite tendency toward nominalism, individualism, and the positive law of her opponent Creon was now furthered as both sides sought to apply the methodology of science in new versions of the ancient Greek dualism. Once more the battle lines were ranged under the old flags of the philosopher-generals: Plato, Aristotle, Augustine, Aquinas, the Second Scholastics and their supporters, opposing the Sophists, Boethius, Roscelin, Ockham and their camp. The new recruits lined up under impressive new commanders: Grotius, Descartes, Pufendorf and their colleagues in the Antigone forces; while Bacon, Hobbes, Hume and their cadre marched more to the drum of Creon. These fresh minds and their successors in the eighteenth century will much engage our attention as they influence jurists. However, first we must spend some more time with the methodology of science, since, while the divided lawyers parried at each other, the scientists back in their quiet labs were building principles that were to serve brilliantly to refurbish the structural framework of law's dwelling.

Copernicus

Galileo's work, not merely for astronomy but in the general development of the experimental scientific method for physics, built the foundation of the seventeenth century's scientific revolution. This man from Pisa, forging systems of daring experimentation, worked against an intellectual atmosphere whose time was obstructed by the Catholic counter-reformation and the Protestant absorption with literal Biblical interpretation. But time had opened an aperture to mental adventure because of experimentation led by Copernicus in the preceding century. Both the Italian and the Pole confronted motion, courageously presenting their ideas in opposition to fundamentally erroneous theories prevailing from antiquity to the seventeenth century. There were many other important doors opening onto advancement—for example, the microscopic dissection of bodies at rest. Motion, however, had the strong suit: it was apparent everywhere to the naked eye.

The pre-Socratic and Aristotelian explanation laid it down that motion was of two kinds, terrestrial and celestial; in both, however, the natural state was rest rather than continuous displacement, and there was no motion without a push or a natural return to the natural place. The most noble motion was circular; in an overwhelming drama seen every day, heavenly bodies were embedded in invisible spheres that rotated about the earth as their center. Sphere one was for the moon, the fixed stars resided in sphere eight, and the ninth, called *primum mobile*, turned the whole system from East to West every twenty-four hours. The terrestrial world consisted of four concentric spheres: fire, air, water, and earth. All things were mixes of these four, and each of the four sought rest in its sphere. Air and fire having levity moved up; water and earth having gravity moved down. All other motion was unnatural and stopped as soon as the push from the external body that started it stopped. The earth, at rest, filled the harmonious center, appropriately so, thought the Church as it harmonized this celestial architecture with its own systematized Christianity (Langer, 122–124).

Among the learned the astronomical part of this system was a "quiet scientific scandal" (Langer, 125). Even from the second century when Claudius Ptolemy's *Almagest* had proclaimed geocentric theory with force and learning, ever more complex adjustments had had to be offered, piece by piece, sphere by sphere, to explain the inconsistencies between the theory and what was observed by looking upward, both as to the position and the magnitude of the heavenly bodies. There were problems also as to the motion of things on earth. Why, for instance, did a battlefield projectile go a long way laterally, without the continuous push of a man behind a two-wheeled cart? Sixteenth century minds knew astronomical alternatives had been suggested in ancient times. Philolaus the Pythagorean in the fifth century BCE held that earth and the planets moved around Hestia, a central fire visible only from unknown parts of the earth; Hicetas of Syracuse proposed in the same century rotation of the earth, while Aristarchus of Samos in the third century BCE had brashly suggested the revolution of the earth around the sun—a theory to be promoted when Tycho Brahe proposed his elegant movement of planets around the sun, and sun circling the earth. But Claudius Ptolemy's second century restatement of the geocentric theory had come with too much force and learning to be easily challenged.

It was in the first half of the sixteenth century that Ptolemy finally met a master, and, once again, it was a master who had trained in law. His birth in 1473 took place

Nicolas Copernicus
Courtesy of The Bridgeman Art Library

in West Prussia, then part of Poland. The Kopernick family named their son Mikolaj, Latinized into history as *Nicolaus Copernicus*. Son of a Polish copper dealer and a Prussian mother, he was left after the father died in 1483, to be brought up by his maternal uncle, Lucus Watzelrode, Bishop of Ermland. At eighteen he entered the University of Cracow to become a priest. Repelled by the scholasticism that had there suppressed humanistic influence, he persuaded the uncle to let him study in Italy. Nicolaus had evidently taken minor orders, and the pleased Bishop granted material support in the form of a canonry in the Cathedral of Frauenburg with leave of absence of three years to study. It was at the University of Bologna that between 1497 and 1500 Nicolaus took course work in mathematics, physics, and astronomy. Soon he had become well acquainted with the question of Ptolemy vs. Aristarchus, and at a mere twenty-seven he lectured on the subject in Rome. When next he reentered his canonry in 1500, the idea of making there a permanent residence was hardly in the young man's mind. Again he begged for leave to study, this time canon law and medicine. The law was good preparation, for Copernicus found himself in the middle of complex diplomatic maneuverings in administration of the large manors supporting the cathedral. His medical studies were less than his legal work, and he took his degree at Ferrara (1503) before returning to Frauenburg. Among other things, he now labored on economics for the King, and, in the problem of Polish currency, had the clarity of mind to state what would later be called Gresham's law: bad money drives out older, good money.

But it was astronomy that gripped this lawyer's mind. In the short intervals allowed between the dark clouds constantly generated by the Baltic Sea, he made his observations while envying Ptolemy the clear skies of Egypt. Using Ptolemy's data, he worked to disprove the Egyptian's theory and in so doing, achieved universal revolution. His uncle, perhaps sensing that in the stars his nephew was on the verge of celestial law which totally pulverized traditional thought in religion and legal philosophy as well, liberated his time for astronomy by bringing him into his household as secretary and physician. It would prove a great career move. By 1514 Copernicus was able to summarize his extraordinary conclusions in the pages of an unpublished *Little Commentary*. He wrote in part:

1. There is no one center of all the celestial circles or spheres.
2. The center of the earth is not the center of the universe, but only of gravity and of the lunar sphere.
3. All the spheres [planets] revolve about the sun as their mid-point, and therefore the sun is the center of the universe.
4. The ratio of the earth's distance from the sun to the height of the firmament [limit of space] is so much smaller than the ratio of the earth's radius to its distance from the sun that the distance from the earth to the sun is imperceptible in comparison with the height of the firmament (Durant, *The Reformation*, 858).

Paradoxically, it was the traditionalists, not the innovators, who listened first. Even Pope Leo X asked for a demonstration. Luther, however, thought he knew better, commenting: "'This fool wishes to reverse the entire scheme of astronomy; but sacred Scripture tells us that Joshua commanded the sun to stand still, not the earth.'" Calvin, not to be outdone, replied with a line from Psalm 93 verse 1—"'The world also is stabilized, that it cannot be moved'" —questioning, "'Who will venture to place the authority of Copernicus above that of the Holy Spirit?'" (Durant, *The Reformation*, 858). Copernicus had enough determination to finish his *Commentary* by 1530, and while he relaxed with a little diversion in politics, it furnished food for the thought of a young professor at Wittenberg. That professor, Georg Rheticus, visited Copernicus, studied the volumes accumulated by the old man, and was convinced. He persuaded Copernicus to permit publication in 1543—the year of his death—of the book of 1530. It was the same year that Andreas Vesalius at twenty-nine published what Sir William Osler said was the greatest medical work ever written, *On the Structure of the Human Body*, a large folio of 663 pages with 277 woodcuts of painstaking, elegant accuracy. Modern medicine began with this text, but, ironically, it could not save Copernicus who, receiving on May 24 the published new edition of his 1530 work, read the title page, smiled, and died in the same hour.

Rheticus's friend, the minister Andreas Osiander, had on his own added to Copernicus's book a cautionary preface, stating that the propositions of Copernicus were only hypotheses. This, and perhaps the dedication to Paul III, saved the book from objection by the Church until one Giordano Bruno, calling the heliocentric "hypothesis" a certainty, clearly pointed out the consequences for religion. In connection with the proceedings against Galileo the Copernican work was placed on the 1616 Index "until corrected"; that correction, the removal of nine sentences which stated that the theory was a fact, removed it from interdiction in 1620.

Copernicus seems to have combined a sincere Christianity with a brilliant attorney's genius for proving the case. Both penchants brought him to conclude that the multiple spheres and other geometrical gadgets of Ptolemy impugned the Creator. Surely God's mathematics were better than Ptolemy's; an earth rotating on its axis and revolving about the sun would vindicate God's virtuosity. Copernicus did cling to the old idea that circular motion is the more noble and, therefore, believed the orbits of the planets followed that divine route; when circularity could not be made to fit his observations, he was constrained to restore some of Ptolemy's eccentricities. But for the major challenge of the retrograde motion of the planets, (some seem to stop, go backwards, and then forward again) his summation would reveal the answer: this is only the apparent effect of changing lines of sight from earth as the solar system carries on its majestic clockwork operation within a single assemblage. The Copernican system was psychologically more complex than Euclid—it is easier to see that the sun moves than that the earth does—and it was quantitatively more difficult, having brought forward the dilemma of the physics of heavy, moving bodies.

If Copernicus envisaged the right system, he had nevertheless not discovered the laws of physics and mathematics that control it. He contented himself with denying the Aristotelian view that heavy bodies naturally rest and cannot rapidly move. However, his system remained deductively simpler, for, in contrast to his predecessors, with Copernicus one could more easily intellectualize and conceptualize the patterns presented. His scientific contribution was no less than radical. He rejected the old knowledge by denying that terrestrial and celestial physics are different, from here it was a short route to the theory that a super-heavy object like Earth moves. This shattering piece of news invited the inference that other phenomena in nature might occur in ways hitherto thought impossible (Langer, 130).

As a philosophical thinker of ideas, Copernicus persuaded most learned minds that the human position in the universe is neither privileged nor at the center. Foreshadowing Pascal who would soon so strikingly depict the human disproportion, Copernican humans were, henceforth, only little specks on one planet in a vast space, so vast that no one could conceive the enormity of its extension. But persuasion met doubt: how could God's Christian drama—creation, fall, redemption, judgment, and finally paradise or inferno—be universal were it constrained to unfold on an insignificant planet? Can God be God only for this paltry celestial body? It was an impossible conclusion, and in fact—and Pascal would appreciate this—Copernicus had actually enhanced God. To understand he had done that meant and means reading much of the Bible either as a manmade first attempt to probe God's creation or, if accepted as divinely inspired and literally true, then as something which can be read in large part only as allegory, the nature of which is revealed by reasoned science. In either case, the Copernican process had been set in motion, freeing both religious and secular man's mind for inquiry wherever inquiry might lead. Moving to a better knowledge of God or to a better knowledge of nature was a process which had been carried on by the ancients, had been constricted by early Christianity, haltingly restored by the universities and scholasticism, encouraged by the Renaissance and Humanism. Now it had been given a phenomenal shot into modernity by the unexpected concatenations of an old canon lawyer from snowy Poland.

Stevinus

The Dutch mathematician Simon Stevin, or Stevinus (1548–1620), as writers often call him, marked in his own right an important chapter of this history of science and technology. Here was another thinker who shunned the ivory tower to live as a practical person solving practical problems. An engineer, he joined the many trying to respond to the daily needs created by the discovery of new worlds—geographical, commercial, and intellectual; and as it turned out, a tower would help him solve a major problem. Beginning life as a merchant's clerk in Antwerp, by application of his mathematical talent Stevin attracted the notice of political leaders through whom he became an advisor to and later a public official under Prince Maurice of Orange, military chief of the United Provinces of the Netherlands during their struggle against Spain. Stevin, probably a secret Catholic, for that reason escaped the deadly conflict between Protestant sects. With many "firsts" to his credit, his greatest coup would be in mathematics when in 1586, writing a small pamphlet, he showed the immense importance of how to extend to daily use the method of decimals; he correctly predicted decimal coinage as well as the role of the mighty tenth in standard weights and measures.

Being mathematical, the Dutchman's work lay in deduction from axioms; he was, however, active also in the testing of hypotheses by experiment, and here we find his special role in the history of legal philosophy. Becker, the acute historian of the eighteenth century enlightenment, says that the subtle change of attitude which occurred in Stevin's consistent decision to undertake controlled experimentation is "'the most important intellectual event of modern times'" (Copleston, Vol. III, 280). It was Stevin who could proudly stand in the forefront of change from the rationalization of facts to the examination of facts. This single impulse would rapidly define modern history and modern science and have a seminal influence on fellow Dutchman Grotius, the first important jurist to be stimulated in a new direction by this scientific revolutionism of the seventeenth century. In the crucial year of 1586 Stevin published an account of an experiment to test the Aristotelian proposition that like objects fall at different speeds proportional to their weights. In a procedure Galileo is supposed to have repeated from Pisa's Tower, Stevin and Jan de Groot, Grotius's father, dropped from a height lead balls of different mass and observed their simultaneous arrival. When Stevin invented a combined pre-auto, pre-airplane, sail-powered land cart that outdid horses on the flat and windy Dutch terrain, it was Grotius who wrote a Latin ode for its maiden run.

Stevin would also demonstrate the resolution of forces, and that the downward pressure of a liquid in a vessel depends on its height and base and not on its shape;

further, he succeeded in showing how to measure that pressure at any point. He was as prescient in suggesting that tides are to be explained by the attraction of the moon as he was in urging princes to separate in bookkeeping their personal and public expenses. A mind of grand strategy, it was he who designed sluices in the Dutch dikes for defense. It would not only be Napoleon I indebted to these careful analyses which also laid it down that forts should be defended by artillery, rather than small arms and that, fortification should be taught in universities. How many more minds, writing the laws both of war and of peace, would bear their obligation to a clerk from Antwerp whose passion was the grandest strategy of all: the power of proof.

Galileo; Kepler

Although Grotius wrote his elegiac ode to the ingenious Stevin, he gave his laurels for scientific method to the greatest mind of all time: Galileo Galilei (1564–1642). Begin with skepticism, this great mind of Pisa believed. Then, by all means, start accumulating, as fellow contemporaries Descartes and Bacon recommended, each individual fact, those hard nuggets of knowledge that Bacon's remote predecessor Ockham had held to be the only reality. Because of Ockham's accent on immediate experience for obtaining actual knowledge, some had been attributing the scientific revolution to him. But Nominalist encouragement was far different from Galileo's intense method en route to Realism (Copleston, Vol., III, 154).

Utilizing inductive reasoning, Galileo first sought to discover the universals applicable to his beloved facts. However, he also wanted to make more rapid and spectacular advances by developing from these facts intuitive explanations, more universals, and ever more profound hypotheses. So, leaning hard on deductive reasoning, he proposed expanding outward from the hypotheses to arrive at new universals; these could then be tested by experiment with measurement devices invented for the purpose. To gauge accurately length, weight, time, and angle, and by use of them speed, volume, and density is nearly as old as recorded history. In Galileo's day new ways were invented to measure these quantities more accurately, and to them for the first time were added the measurement of temperature and pressure. Physics became the study of things that could be measured, thereby increasing the old tendency to regard mathematics as a central core of *a priori* knowledge—an abstract mental discipline of true generality, great exactness and certainty, and traditionally considered absolute (*Encyclopedia of Philosophy,* Vol. V, 192–193). Galileo had returned to raise the old science of motion to new reality, transforming physics and discerning a marvelous "book" of nature written in mathematical language whose letters were triangles, circles, and other geometrical figures.

Like the elegance of the DNA structure today, the Galilean mechanical universe astounded deep thinkers and confounded ordinary minds. It invigorated thousands to science, but especially enthralled jurist-philosophers who did not notice that scientific genius had forever separated physics—which, henceforth, dealt with what can be measured—from philosophy, which deals with what cannot be measured. Fundamentally important as this was, both to Galileo and the future, Galileo—perhaps because he knew he was on new ice that might be dangerous—did not meticulously set down his innovations in scientific journal form. They instead were to be extrapolated, if found at all. Absorbed in methodology and believing that he had shown man how to achieve certainty, the old genius himself spent time trying to develop mathematical proofs for physical laws of which he was already aware. Despite a multiplicity of closed arithmetical doors, his faith in the ultimate calculator never wavered; God had created the world as a mathematical system, and Biblical writers simply did not know it. The fact that God certainly had not revealed this exciting structure meant he was desirous that man discover the system by reason just as Aquinas had discovered natural law. In the climate of the Reformation and Counter-Reformation conservative faculties were initially outraged at all this hortative manipulating of God, for both Protestants and Catholics were centered on the literal reading of the Bible's earthbound drama of human history. Ultimately, though, people came to be convinced by Galileo and by his successors; after 1700 it would be the theologians who had to show that their Joshua fit Galileo's now secure science (Langer, 154).

Galileo's notoriety and expertise created to some extent an injustice toward Johann Kepler (1571–1630) whose head for mathematical science may have been greater than Galileo's. Tycho Brahe had taken Kepler as his assistant, passing on to him his massive records of observations, along with his position as astrologer to Emperor Rudolf II. Kepler used both (without instruments which he did not receive) to effect an intense study of the orbit of Mars. He discovered that it is an ellipse—not a circle as Copernicus supposed—and that the recorded observations of the other planets supported the same conclusion for them. Moreover, Kepler published in 1609 two laws. The first stated that each planet not only moves in an elliptical orbit with the sun as one focus, but moves faster when nearer the sun. The second proposed that a radius from sun to planet sweeps equal areas in equal times, and in that sense the speed of the planet is regular.

With the death of his imperial patron, Kepler, despite hands and vision impaired by smallpox suffered in his youth, went out to teach school. The students were treated to an extraordinary master, sold on heliocentrism and on the way to laws of gravity, Kepler turned fascination with the problem of computing the volume of the contents of a cask with curved sides into a published essay helpful in the discovery of calculus. He would also reflect ten years on the relation between the speed of a planet and the length of its orbit; after making a colossal number of computations, in 1619 a third Kepler law appeared: the square of a planet's year is proportional to the cube root of its mean distance from the sun. Kepler was thrilled, exclaiming: "'God has waited six thousand years for a discoverer!'" (Durant, *The Age of Reason Begins,* 599). Partial to mysticism—his mother would be accused of witchcraft—he went on to proclaim that each planet's speed is like a note in music, with the combined notes blending into a "harmony of the spheres" audible to the "soul" of the sun. Disturbed by the Thirty Years' War, he nevertheless continued to work at both astronomy and astrology until dying sick and poor at fifty-nine.

Although Kepler's impeccable scientific advances had some of their luster dulled by the whimsy of spherical melodies, he had revealed the universe as a structure governed by detailed mathematical law. In essence, Kepler had set up the basis of the Scientific Revolution. For our particular history, his belief in math's legal governance was especially fascinating in its extension, for Kepler presented all the universe as under law—the same law—thus making him the grand precursor of states united, Europe as union, and even galactic federations which so attract today's imaginings. Unfortunately, he never had the promoter's personality. Attention was sparse for his achievements, the details of which only a few could understand, in any case.

His concentration on astronomy seemed to have conspired to keep him from star power. Galileo, on the other hand, was brash as well as brilliant, wrote the best Italian prose of his time, studied intensively a broad range of physics as well as astronomy, and was your quintessentially cultured Renaissance man. He played the organ and the lute, liked to draw, and longed to "design a temple, carve a statue, paint a portrait, write poetry, compose music, and guide a ship." Occasionally, he could even manage to be modest: "'I have never met a man so ignorant that I could not learn something from him'" (Durant, *The Age of Reason Begins,* 600, 605). Born on the day, it is said, that Michelangelo died and Shakespeare was born, his family was of small fortune but high culture, his father being a mathematician and musician. As a small boy Galileo, like Leonardo, built ingenious toy machines. He was sent for his education to the monastery of Vallombrosa near Florence where he acquired good Latin and fair Greek. He went as far in orders as the novitiate but was unintentionally saved for science when his father, denying him the mathematics considered to be unremunerative, decided the son should become a physician and repair the family fortune. Toward that goal, the student at seventeen entered the freer academic atmosphere of the University of Pisa.

Already a skilled musician, the artistic Galileo was inclining toward the profession of painter when, in his first academic year while sitting bored in church his mind was diverted by a swinging lamp. Noting that the time of oscillation was constant as the range diminished, he by experiment discovered that the time varied with the length of a pendulum. Once home he made his own pendulum to synchronize with his pulse, thereby contributing a useful medical instrument, although he had never yet studied mathematics. About the same time he chanced to be an unseen listener at a lesson in geometry given by Ostilio Ricci to the pages of the Grand Duke of Tuscany. Attention now riveted and genius aroused, Galileo procured his own copy of Euclid and followed the lessons book in hand. After some private instruction by Ricci, he was granted his father's reluctant consent to abandon medicine for mathematics and science. Sadly, with no funds to continue the new studies, he finally had to withdraw from the university without a degree.

We next see him lecturing on Dante's *Inferno*, publishing his invention of the hydrostatic balance to measure relative weights of metals in an alloy, and attracting a patron for whom in 1588 he wrote a treatise on the center of gravity in solids. This brought him at twenty-five an appointment as lecturer at the University of Pisa and an opportunity to establish the first principles of dynamics, repeating from the

Leaning Tower the 1586 experiment of Stevin, and then demolishing the old Aristotelian motion science as to projectiles and elemental weight. Galileo's unstoppable brainstorming was depriving professors of their stock-in-trade and doing it without much tact. There must have been a collective sigh of relief as he resigned when the Marchese Guidubaldo persuaded the Venetian Senate to give him the chair of mathematics at Padua. It was an eighteen year appointment of both scope and cash: his salary went from 180 to 1,000 florins, and he attracted so many students from all over Europe that a hall to seat 2,000 had to be assigned to him. Like Kepler, Galileo was far more prolific than the usual student mentor, and protégés could look back in amazement at what their professor had been up to during their training: inventing the proportional compass and the thermometer; affirming that matter is indestructible; formulating the principles of the lever and pulley; establishing that the speed of falling bodies increases at a uniform rate; experimenting with inclined planes; arriving at the law of inertia—Newton's first law; reducing musical tones to wavelengths of air; and showing that pitch depends on the number of vibrations of a string. He also had been able to share how the properties of matter are those that can be measured and dealt with mathematically; he may have been forced to concede that sound, taste, odor, and color are only in the consciousness of the beholder, but he promised his classes that one day these factors, too, would be measurable.

Toward the end of his stay in Padua Galileo gave more and more time to astronomy. In a collegial letter to Kepler he praised his shy colleague and declared himself also to be a Copernican and in possession of many proofs he dared not publish for fear of ridicule. In public he mainly stuck to Ptolemy until his conviction could be supported—with the aid of his handmade telescope—and by irrefutable observations. The first practical telescope had probably been made in 1608 by an obscure optician in Holland named Lippershey; Galileo wrote that when in Venice in 1609 he had heard about a Belgian who had invented an instrument which made distant objects appear nearer and larger. Not to be outdone, the first night of his return to Padua from Venice he reflected at length on refraction, and the next day, by putting a convex lens at one end and a concave lens at the other of a lead tube, he had crafted his own telescopic instrument. All his time was now devoted to improving it, grinding and polishing lenses with skill and patience to increase its power. The first version magnified three diameters; his last thirty-three. Critics of Copernicus had said that if Venus revolved around the sun it should, like the moon, show phases; with his telescope Galileo saw them.

He used this success to persuade the Grand Duke to name him "First Mathematician of the University of Pisa and First Mathematician and Philosopher to the Grand Duke," henceforth earning a comfortable 1,000 florins with no more obligation to teach. It was as close to heaven on earth a professor who favored research and astronomy could get. Galileo's chosen title was "Philosopher" and he delighted in it. Holding as he did the opinion that the study of nature had gone to sleep with Aristotle, being a titled Philosopher gave Galileo the confidence that it was he who could revive that study. He boldly spoke of the Copernican hypothesis as proved and even more daringly wrote of the sun, situated in the center of the heavens while the earth revolves about it as it rotates on its axis. Going further, he urged that if a physical fact like this were confirmed by sight or experimentation, no Biblical passage could contradict it.

The philosopher had boldly, proudly peered over the edge of danger, his statements on sense, reason, and intellect taking him straight into mortal conflict in the midst of Catholic Reformation. In 1615, leaving his mistress and three children, the still confident Galileo gathered up his latest theories and left for Rome to persuade the high prelates. By 1616 Rome's answer was to summon him before the Inquisition. Here theory was crushed by the flat condemnation of heresy; it was impossible that the sun stood motionless at the center of the universe while the earth made a shocking celestial twirl of daily rotation. Galileo was sent home with angry words. There was no contrition, and in 1622, responding to a Jesuit attack on his view of daily rotation, he daringly published a defense for science which rejected all authority but observation, reason, and experiment. Pope Urban VIII at first actually enjoyed the feisty riposte and accepted its dedication to him, while the Jesuits fumed. Encouraged, Galileo again took the road to Rome, with the astounding ambition of converting the Pope to Copernicus. Urban gave him six interviews but would not lift the ban.

Galileo now determined to put all his energy into making a final response. It would be his chief work, a lawyer's final summation, as it were. He chose to frame it as a cleverly scholastic pro and con exposition of Copernicus in dialogue form.

The Astronomer Galileo
Courtesy of Yale University Art Gallery, Everett V. Meeks, B.A. 1901, Fund

At first the Pope allowed it the imprimatur, but on condition that the Copernican position be treated as a hypothesis. However, prodded by the Jesuits, Urban changed his mind and appointed a commission to decide what the official Church reaction should be. There was no hesitation. Galileo, it was found, had treated the Copernican position as fact and had misrepresented the book to the Holy Father. The Inquisition angrily imprisoned him in a palace for four examinations. At the outset Galileo tried to be clever by claiming he had presented the Copernican position only as an hypothesis. Even hypothesis, though, had come too close to life and death, and at the fourth examination the proud philosopher turned old man crumbled into the admission that the Ptolemaic position was, of course, true and incontestable. At sixty-eight, with many infirmities, Galileo simply wanted to go home even if it meant life-long house arrest.

It was not until 1992 that the Vatican reversed the Inquisition. However, the self-styled philosopher had erred in not properly applying that scientific method whose virtue he had himself established. His statement should, indeed, have been presented only as a hypothesis. Although canon layers were more than ready to mete out punishment for the Galilean failure, there could be no going back on the progress made by the use of mathematics. The stunning results possessed a certitude in strong contrast with rhetorical conclusions proposed in the verbal science of scholastic logic, where just stating a proposition allowed one to consider that proposition had been proved, if all arguments against it were refuted. Copernicus, Stevin, Kepler, and Galileo had all helped science inexorably build a stronger case, one which could not help but impress and change those lawyers who functioned outside the canon. Clearly, the brilliant saga of experimental science had made it understandable to the bright or even not-so-bright legal minds that the convincing method of these sons of Euclid—deduction from axioms expressed as verbal propositions supported by diagrams—should now next be tried in the law.

Newton

Before the quartet of Grotius, Hobbes, Descartes, and Pufendorf bring us into the fertile field of secular natural law which mathematical science had begun to render so exciting, a chronological fast forward to Isaac Newton (1642–1727) can leave us with that one mind who, sustaining Copernicus, finally brought together the progress of Kepler and Galileo. Newton's initiatives born of the new science would only late in the twentieth century become blunted by some loss of faith in progress. Yet even this blunting occurred in the midst of such continued remarkable achievements in the use of the scientific method that no mass desertion can be detected from faith in its efficacy for "hard" science.

Newton himself knew none of the doubts about earth/heaven dichotomy. For him deity was obviously a genius at mathematics whose divine expertise found reflection in the intricacies of nature which as God he could re-infuse with force by correcting problems as needed. What better way to understand religious truth than to pursue science? During his professorship at Oxford, Newton completed nothing less than discovering laws that enabled man to deal with any aspect of motion. Yet Newton said little about epistemological theory and its limitations, and the spread of his ideas occurred within the restrained circumference of lettered circles, rather than in academe. More cautious than Galileo, he could feel certainty about his views on light, but his conviction went only as far as how light rays appeared to the observer. So also as to the force of gravity; mathematical laws describing motion as affected by terrestrial pull could be discerned, but just what the force of gravity was remained unknown.

Newton's birth on Christmas Day in the year Galileo passed away was an astrologer's dream of felicitous conjunction. He was so small his mother thought he would fit in a quart mug, and so weak he was not expected to survive. His father had died a few months before, and when the child was two his mother remarried. This second husband also died when Isaac was a fourteen year old, leaving an uncle to act as the paternal surrogate. Newton had left his neighborhood schools at twelve for grammar school at Grantham. There he demonstrated little industry and stood low in his class, but when he repelled the attack of an older bully, his pluck made him head boy. Like Galileo, the student showed avid interest in making mechanical toys: wind-mills, water clocks, kites, dials. Farm work did not interest him. Seeing that he had an unusual mind but no future in agriculture, the uncle urged him at nineteen to enter Trinity College at Cambridge. The young collegian bought a book on astrology but could not understand it, bought a copy of Euclid as a door to astrology, but thought it trivial, and turned in desperation to the analytical geometry of Descartes. At last here was a writer to arouse his latent energy and brilliance. Newton was granted his B.A. at twenty-three and at twenty-seven was appointed to the University's prestigious Lucasian chair of mathematics, a post he held during thirty-four intense years. Using a simple prism purchased in 1666 at the Stourbridge Fair Newton began his cataclysmic work in optics by discovering nothing less than the sun's seven color spectrum. He also made a succession of lenses and corrected defects of the refracting telescope by constructing one with reflective properties and basing his new studies on the theoretical work already done by Mersenne and Gregory.

Even before this, probably in 1665, Newton had begun to think about the mathematics of acceleration and the method of calculus which he called "fluxions." He put the work on paper in 1665 and 1666 and described it in a letter to his teachers in 1669. Ever careful, he held back from publication until 1704. It was only a little later that Leibniz independently made the same discovery and reported it in a paper in 1671. Because his method of notation was better than Newton's it has survived.

In 1666 Newton made his great move into permanent legend. Beginning work on gravity, he soon could report that the force, so easy to observe on earth, extended all the way to the moon where, he estimated, it was sufficient to hold that celestial body in orbit. A legend propagated by Voltaire has it that these ideas occurred to him during a profound meditation after watching an apple fall from a tree. Newton extended gravitational pull to the planets and the sun and calculated that the force varied inversely with the square of a planet's distance from the sun. Of course, others earlier had presented similar thoughts, but Newton's achievement lay in applying the idea to all bodies in space, bound inextricably, as he believed, through gravitational forces. His working out of the mathematics of this force field showed results conformable to the astronomical observations of Kepler. Medieval thinkers had made of the universe a purpose-driven drama, still unfolding toward its certain end, but long ago fully written. Newtonian science made of it a machine long ago wound and, with no end discernible, fully operational in a celestial hum. As Langer describes it (Langer, 156–157), here one had a theory which did not prove that there is no supernatural, no purpose, no first cause. Rather, coming at it in an attack more revolutionary, it offered a rationalized explanation of nature where the supernatural was left out of the picture. Its simple certainty, astounding and startling, reduced the universe to the compelling unity and elegance of equation.

Newton had worked out his orbit calculations in detail in 1679. By 1684 they were redone and submitted to the Royal Society; three years later, published in Latin to huge acclaim, they could stand as Newton's master work: the *Philosophiae Naturalis Principia Mathematica*. Although his calculus method of fluxions had been of great help in the computations, Newton did not display it in the results. The Galilean syndrome persisted, and Newton felt everyone would be more comfortable with a framework from the ancients. Therefore, he presented his work on the model of Euclid's *Elements*, beginning with the statement of eight definitions and three "axioms or laws" of motion from which he could deduce theorems and corollaries. The Newtonian law triad reads:

I. Every body continues in its state of rest, or of uniform motion in a right [(i.e. straight)] line, unless it is compelled to change that state by forces impressed upon it.
II. The change of motion is proportional to the motive force impressed; and is made in the direction of the right line in which that force is impressed.
III. To every action there is always imposed an equal reaction; or, the mutual actions of two bodies upon each other are always equal, and directed to contrary parts' (*Encyclopedia of Philosophy,* Vol. V, 491b).

By Definition II "motion" may be replaced by "momentum," which is mass times velocity. Axiom II is therefore now usually condensed into "force equals mass times acceleration.

The axioms encouraged minds usually less mathematical than Newton's who were bent on establishing a mechanics of human society parallel to his mechanics of space. Their approach, too, was to begin with *a priori* axioms. It is therefore of interest here that from Newton's day to the present, controversy has raged among experts in the mechanics of motion as to what justification exists for accepting Newton's axioms. Kant thought them deducible from *a priori* principles of the permanence of substance, of causality, and of reciprocity; while others also have said that they are *a priori*. Against this some have argued, conversely, that the causes stated by Newton are not necessarily *a priori* correct. Many others have said that the axioms are empirical, that is, not *a priori* but summaries of past observations based on them. Against this it has been asserted that the first axiom refers to abstractions that cannot be observed, and that the necessary conditions for true inertial motion cannot be realized because of friction, or of the infinite reach of all external gravitational attractions.

There has also been controversy as to whether Newton was a true practitioner of the scientific method at all or only a disciple of Bacon who collected facts and then sought to present the only possible explanation of them. The confusion rests upon Newton's statement that he feigned no hypotheses; but this was merely a riposte to those who had complained the *Principia* was inadequate because, by merely stating how it acts, it offered no explanation either of what gravitation was or its cause. In fact, Newton in full consciousness *did* advance hypotheses, not only as to laws of mechanics for verification by experiment, but also as to his opinion, for example, of light.

Surprisingly, there is no controversy in portraying Newton as a rather poor teacher, yet an eminently colorful character. In descriptions of his daily routine compiled by the Durants (Durant, *The Age of Reason Begins,* 532) he appears as one who both sat little—walking about his room or his garden, stopping to record an idea—and ate little—forgetting some meals, begrudging time for food and sleep, neglecting to arrange his clothes and hair for appearances in the college hall. Sometimes he would awake in the morning only to remain for hours on top of the bed engrossed in thought, forgetting to dress at all, often leaving his visitors in order to write down an idea so as not to forget it. He then forgot the visitors. Although neglectful of private prayer, his habit was regularly to attend at the Anglican Church. It was his duty to lecture once a week and be available to students two hours a week. Unfortunately, so few could understand him that his secretary wrote that he, often being bereft of an audience, presented the classic "wall lecture."

The northern universities were still lagging badly in science; many were censored by the Roman Church and hence barred from the new ideas, and all, according to Lavine (Lavine, 87), were generally unimpressive and hostile. At least at the Royal Society Newton could enjoy a learned audience. Whether they enjoyed him is unsure given that from 1661 to 1692 he immersed himself in alchemical experiments and 100,000 useless words to prove that elements are variations of a basic substance. His theological writings, which reached a mass greater than his scientific works, included among them a commentary on the Apocalypse, another commentary on the Book of Daniel, and a study of the dimensions of Solomon's Temple as a guide to the heavens. Newton had obviously felt the Lutheran winds of rebellion, for he firmly believed that Antichrist was the Roman pope.

Newton would not himself, any more than Copernicus, Stevin, Kepler, or Galileo, try to apply his method of scientific laws to a philosophy or science of society. The sophisticated elaboration of mathematical models for sociological applications would await the computer age. Still, in the philosophic revival of the seventeenth century where are found earnest attempts to reason scientifically about being and about the jural relations of men, Newton would win wide acceptance. If God was a practical legalist, his servant actually showed a surprising capacity for juridical advocacy in the world of affairs. He was appointed to a committee of the University of Cambridge to debate prosecutorially the attempt of King James II to force award of a degree to a Benedictine monk. Twice he served as member for

Cambridge in Parliament. In 1693 the great machine of genius suffered a nervous breakdown, but he recovered. Friends obtained for him in 1695 the post of warden of the Mint, ostensibly to produce a new coinage, but also to get him away from his gloomy room and laboratory at Cambridge. Newton entered old age in triumph, showered with honors and six servants as befitted high place in London society. He was viewed as promising positive extension of the scientific method into results of startling certainty. Learned, non-mathematical promoters saw in such utilization what seemed—at least before Einstein and quantum theory—absolute finality in man's understanding of the greatest set of physical laws: the awesome, divine engineering of the solar system. Even though he remained reclusive and temperamental, famously unable to bear criticism of his work, the old man knew he stood on a very high pedestal. When he died in 1727 at eighty-five, to be laid to rest with greatest pomp in Westminster Hall, only the stars and planets seemed not to care.

Hugo Grotius
Courtesy of the Rare Book Collection, Lillian Goldman Law Library, Yale Law School

PART 14

The Seventeenth Century's
Encounter with Natural Law
Grotius, Descartes, Hobbes, Pufendorf

The Mood of the Seventeenth Century

The material heights of the seventeenth century's merchants and the mental heights of the intellectual world formed twin peaks. Yet their grandeur was but a tiny part of the population below, most of whom did not make large sums of money or write ground-breaking books. Enlightenment was coming, but it still had years to go during which the general impression of history would indicate that trouble and suffering were far more characteristic than peace and prosperity. There were frequent periods when very large numbers could not get enough to eat. In a climate which tended to be cold, wet, and too often unfavorable for agriculture, four-fifths of the population of Europe had to depend on cereals to stay alive. So high was the incidence of disease that one can speak of "chronic morbidity" in describing the undernourished population. The average man was a bare five feet three. Wealthier people tended to be taller, but Louis XIV exceeded the average by only an inch—presumably enough, when added to his high heels, to help make him look *grand*. As these too often hungry and sick multitudes surveyed their social scene, a constant topic must have been how the pressures of war and its aftermath made a few rich while interrupting trade for most. War so accentuated the problems of famine and disease that rebellion broke out in most states, particularly around the middle of the century. Europe's Thirty Years' War (1618–1648) remained the most damaging armed conflict until the twentieth century.

On the whole, people were both terrified of the constant wars and angered that about half of their revenues went toward preparing for and fighting in them. Yet all this did have another side. Inimical to nobles and clergy, the new nation-state served as the instrument of the commercial classes, a supreme example of individualism. War was accepted in the pursuit of commercial and territorial expansion as inevitable, glorious, even burnished by a kind of divine ordination. Only Erasmus declaimed against the trend. Yet statecraft made uneven progress, for whether bellicose or peaceful, the attempts of central governments to reform were strongly countered by noble magnates trying still to hold fast to their feudal exemptions and prerogatives as local governors. In yet another ambivalence, much of the medieval unquestioning belief in God not only continued but was actually strengthened by the competitive emotions unleashed by the Reformation. These religious issues festered as the central concern of the educated world, while the masses stubbornly persisted to cherish their Roman beliefs, as seen in vivid relief in New France's Jesuitical centers of piety at Quebec and Montreal.

On the whole, then, the seventeenth century hinge period needed to oil the various squeaks in the mechanism. Fine achievements in baroque music, art, and architecture were civilizing elements, although without much penetration far down the social scale. Troubles of all sorts—suffering from them, and questing for security to defend against them—set the tone for society's dominant mood. Only the more successful of the bourgeoisie were capable of expressing need forcefully, along with demands for freedom from old regulations which impeded opportunities to make money. These middle of the road interests were to impart a powerful stimulus to an influential quartet of philosophers all of whom now would try to come up with appropriately updated legal structures of facilitation and advancement for the growing pains of national state systems.

Lawyer with client, 1647
Courtesy of the Rare Book Collection, Lillian Goldman Law Library, Yale Law School

Secular Natural Law
The First Period

Grotius
Introduction

The first important legal scholar to attempt transfer of the scientific method to law was the Dutch jurist Huigh de Groot, better known by the Latin version he used as an author, Hugo Grotius. One can consider him even more broadly as the first important scholarly thinker applying the method of science to legal philosophy and the general study of man's governance. Moreover, since Grotius and his family were leading members of the middle class, we may also see him as the first important thinker bringing the bourgeois point of view to the field.

Grotius authored important books on poetry, drama, classical literature, history, theology, ecclesiastical government, and one on navigational science. But the central vehicle for the Grotius efforts was natural law, and his writings led to a new era. They became a springboard from which readers would depart from the medieval-based idea that there exists an *ab origine* law of eternal value, based on the commonality of human nature. The important new Grotius variant on the theme was that God cannot change natural law or human nature, nor would He, having completed revelation with the Creation. The time had come for humankind to till this fertile terrain and in that process do the extrapolating of custom and statutes—that is, "secular natural law." Such bold moves reflected an intellect that, ranging far beyond jurisprudence, seemed determined to proclaim to the world: "Groot" means "great." Including five major works on law, there are 120 titles under the illustrious name, each published several times, making a bibliography of 1,200 entries. Books by others about this father figure whose intellectual paternity ranged from international to natural law are legion.

Mathematics had been the base science that really impressed Grotius, but it neither provoked a detailed study, nor is much said about the degree of his talent in the field. However, it is well known that the scholarly societies or academies springing up in Rome, London, and Paris, as well as in several provincial towns included many lawyers captivated by general scientific ideas, especially the mathematical method, its prestige for philosophical reasoning now greatly enhanced by the general success of experimentation and theory. For them this world of numbers appeared to offer the most promising route to knowledge; and while by no means captivated enough actually to "do" mathematics, like the scientists, they were attracted to the possibilities revealed by observation of facts, induction, hypothesis, deduction, and experiment.

The specific study that appealed to the legal thinker was geometry, for like law, geometry is presented in words rather than algebraic equations. True, it relates to symbols drawn on paper and deals with abstractions which neither can be reproduced exactly on that paper nor exist in fact anywhere in nature. But this problem did not deter the legal scholars, perhaps because there was a certain comfort level with Euclidean concepts known and written out laboriously and continuously since ancient times. Now, too, there was the enhanced prestige this clearly *a priori* method held for society in transition: state true axioms, be led by reason to true deductions, and then reconstruct the real world. It would appear that the exciting transposition of geometry to law involved an intellectual process no more rigorous than these simplistic attitudes. Perhaps for this reason the movement's excitement and propulsion did not have a permanent future; leaders of new legal philosophies in the nineteenth and twentieth centuries would hold not only that the mathematical approach had failed, but that it could never have succeeded. Villey, for example, was adamant that the sciences of nature have nothing to say to the human social order. Nevertheless, natural law had the fundamental merit for its time of opening wide a door comparable to the experimental scientific approach. That door remains open in our own time as we study man as though and in fact in a test tube, leaving theology to the sectarians and metaphysics to the metaphysicians.

Whether it was general mathematics or precise geometric givens, the rationale of science boosted immeasurably the confidence of seventeenth century jurists in devising comprehensive, orderly statements of law. Universal and immutable in the form of code-like treatises, these writings would necessarily be right because their rules would be required by human nature. The concept fit easily the office of legal philosophy which encouraged law making, yet, seldom avowed this as its goal, claiming rather that it had sought and found the one complete truth. The broad sweep of the new process was not like the technique of eminent classical period Roman jurisconsults thought to have been encouraged by Stoic natural law. They had proceeded slowly case by case, concentrating intently on each factual situation as it came along. Yet this difference should not be exaggerated. After all, the new natural lawyers had been university trained in Roman law and, depending on their experience as official or practicing lawyers, were familiar also with customs, feudal prescriptions, town statutes, and mercantile regulations. Inevitably, the solutions which they deemed propelled by innovations in geometrical deduction still drew heavily on these older sources. One can even view their supposedly new direction as being offshoots from two well-known trees of legal knowledge: the Roman codices, as well as humanism's rules or life principles that moved toward the summation of social virtues.

How seventeenth century growth differed was that axioms, deemed to compel a narrow conclusion, in fact, were permitting the authors greater scope. They could propose at last bold resolutions of conflicting sources and reform defective solutions. The new natural law was exciting, for it stressed learning as the key to systematize the natural necessities of man. Ironically, as its adoption branched out into two kinds of responses, neither of them was to show a true understanding of the basic roots in scientific regimen. One response was what came to be called "Continental Rationalism." Thinkers in this group were those stressing mathematics; their effort lay in deducing new knowledge from the axiomatic a priori principles they were comparing to Euclidean definitions. Encouraged by Galileo, Grotius and secular natural lawyers belong to this group, realists led by the non-jurist Descartes as their supreme theoretical exponent. The other response was called "British Empiricism." Proponents of this second approach conceded that deduction from *a priori* principles, as in pure mathematics, *does* bring conclusions which have a certainty. However, denying that these conclusions give factual knowledge about the real world, the second group responders held, instead, that such conclusions were limited in their impact to relationships or linkages between ideas. For factual knowledge of the world the only road is observation using sense perception, and although induction from it will give knowledge about reality, such knowledge can be no more than probable. In blunt terms, any philosophical system which is certain, gives information about reality, and can be extended by deduction, is impossible (Copleston, Vol. IV, 25). Francis Bacon (1561–1626) belongs to this second tradition which, led to success by David Hume (1711–1776) as its champion, would plunge its roots deep into Nominalism and the positive law movement.

Life of Grotius

Grotius (1583–1645) was not only a phenomenon as an adult; to borrow a felicitous phrase from Dickens he was an "infant phenomenon" as well. His friend Heinsius said that "he was a man from the instant of birth and never had any childhood" (Vreeland, *Hugo Grotius, the Father of the Modern Science of International Law,* 15). Pattison wrote (*Encyclopedia Britannica,* Vol. X11: 6216) that "in the annals of precocious genius there is no greater prodigy on record." Newton was yet to come as a Christmas epiphany. Grotius, his mother thought, already was the Easter Sunday gift of Heaven to a desperate mankind. She constantly brought up the significance of the birth day, and Grotius reciprocated by always celebrating it on Easter, rather than its precise date of 10 April. He had more than Heaven's blessing, for his family's social, political, economic, and intellectual position could hardly have been better—and they knew it down to their Dutch shoes. When Grotius's proud great-grandmother, a Dutch de Groot, married in 1509 a Frenchman named Cornets, France was put in its place as Cornets, to get his fourteen-year-old bride, found himself obliged to agree that all children should be de Groots. Aware of the paternal family tree, Grotius's grandfather and father both made certain they married Dutch blood.

The Dutch had wanted a monarchy but could do no better than a loosely organized republic because, after victory against Spain, they were only able to agree on foreign monarchs, and none would take the job. This meant there were seven so-called "united" provinces and no effective constitution. However, in Grotius's youth the United Provinces were economically and culturally on the way up. Holland, where Grotius was born, was the largest and richest of them, with an affluence symbolized by Amsterdam, Rotterdam, Leyden, and the De Groot hometown, Delft. Grotius would be an ardent patriot all his life, a thoughtful philosopher, but with that jealous family arrogance which defended, sometimes loudly, the reputation of Dutch beer against French wine.

The discoveries of the New World and the East Indies in the late fifteenth and sixteenth centuries were the chief source of Dutch wealth. The Dutch had built such a unique maritime and financial economy supporting an oligarchy of wealth and influence, that only a few hundred of these bourgeois controlled all Holland. They were nearly a closed group, and penetration from without was difficult. Little Hugo's father, a leader among them, was a successful lawyer who held office as Burgomaster and Senator of Delft. The leading de Groots were not themselves merchants, but as members of the powerful middle class, they became indispensable commercial allies in law, education, and politics. Influenced by the constitutionalism favored by the Calvinists who, as compared with the monarchical Lutherans were generally in the minority in Europe, such vigorous burghers were ready to guarantee the Netherlands strong and stable government as it became a model for Europe.

Jan de Groot was a proud parent, always on the alert for brilliance in his son. He made sure to engage a tutor when Hugo was very young, and was thrilled that the pupil did not disappoint, but delighted in all study. Seeing himself, as he thought, in replica, Jan dressed the son in clothes identical to his own except for size, and, accompanied by this small self-replication, frequented the town drawing rooms where distinguished men were regularly entertained. The lad appeared to have every qualification. The adult society and weighty questions led him to gain the maturity which as early as eight permitted him to be his father's comforter when a sibling died; at twelve Hugo's cogent argument converted his Catholic mother to the reformed church. So eager was he to read voraciously at all hours that to save his eyes candles were forbidden; Hugo cleverly foiled the plot by electing to save his Sunday money and buy the candles secretly. Despite the studies, he kept a good physique by playing hard with the other boys among whom he was always popular. The only flaws in the petit paragon seemed to be that he showed no interest in art and exhibited very poor handwriting.

At age eleven, joining 136 others, Grotius entered the University of Leyden, founded in 1574 by William the Silent as a reward to the town for bravery in a Spanish siege. It was intended to be a Calvinist school, rivaling Catholic Louvain and Douai, but unlike a medieval university, which typically had substantial independence, it was state controlled. Hugo's father happened to be one of the three curators. There had been a recent hiring for which they and the city were busily digging deep into well-lined pockets to remunerate their great new star professor: Joseph Justus Scaliger, the foremost scholar of 1660 Europe, a wine-drinking Frenchman with a father boldly surnamed Julius Caesar. Leyden became at once the leading intellectual center in Holland, her citizenry certain that being one of the best in Europe meant they were the best. Understandably, the students of Leyden at that time were described as having more than their share of self-assurance.

Although his uncle was both Rector and Professor of Law, there is no evidence that Hugo, too, studied in the faculty of law at Leyden; but he did prepare under the faculty of arts, which was the necessary preliminary to law. He lived with the Professor of Theology and was frequently at the eminent Scaliger's house. Known since childhood for his ability to write good Latin verses, he would at fourteen pen lyrics dedicated to Henry IV of France. By graduation, to enthusiastic applause it is said (Knight, *The Life and Works of Hugo Grotius,* 30), he delivered public theses on "Mathematics, Philosophy, and Law" and, as the fourteen-year-old faced the world, he adopted for a personal motto time's inexorable march—*Ruit Hora*. It was to be a perfect definition of the man and his work: a pace so furious that it would exact the price of some errors.

Grotius had been told for so long that he was the hope and hero of his circle of family and friends, it is no surprise the adulation made the youthful graduate excessively talkative, even quite pushy. Still, there remained a naïve child behind the house of cards; for his assertive manner, his restless ambitious pride in his connections and ability, and his obvious pleasure at being in the society of distinguished people, all fell apart whenever he was asked what he was going to do when he "grew up." At last, trying to come forth with a grown up answer, he produced his own edition of school books written by the fifth century lawyer, Martianus Capella. Naturally, Jan de Groot at once set about arranging for its publication.

There would be an even greater ladder rung for adulthood. The leading United Provinces statesman, Johan Oldenbarneveldt, was chosen to head a Dutch mission to France. The goal was persuading Henry IV not to make separate peace with Spain which at this period held all the Spanish Netherlands, approximately the size of modern Belgium. Aware of the adolescent's laudatory poem to the French monarch, Oldenbarneveldt invited Grotius to accompany him along with Oldenbarneveldt's young son. Grotius, of course, accepted, hoping that in the course of the mission there would be the exciting opportunity to meet a King, his ministers, and many of the most distinguished men and women of France. Grotius especially wanted to be presented to the famous lawyer and historian de Thou, but de Thou was away from Paris at the time. The consolation prize was not too onerous—meeting the glamorous and voluptuous Gabrielle d'Estrées, the King's mistress, whose seductive portrait hangs in the Chateau of Azay-le-Rideau on the Loire. Despite an unsuccessful political mission, Grotius did have a life-changing royal job interview. It took place at a sunny garden party, where he and young Oldenbarneveldt were being brought forward to speak to Henry. As Grotius stepped forward, he was presented as the one his professors all destined to be more famous than Erasmus. The King, always equal to an occasion for a phrase, announced to the assembled company: "'Look you upon the marvel of Holland'" (Vreeland, 24). He then graciously offered Grotius a knighthood—declined—and a medallion with the King's portrait—accepted, along with a gold chain to hang it around his neck. The Prince de Condé, heir to the throne, was also there, and the monarch tactfully hailed him with equal panache as the miracle of France. The prince was about Grotius's age and he at once pressed the Dutch boy to become his private secretary. Grotius accepted on an honorary basis. Upon this miracle of dual miracles the spirit of Old Cornets must have been raising high his celestial glass of French wine.

The mission now departed France, leaving Grotius behind to stay on for the year. After probably reading law privately for some time, near the end of his stay he received the degree of Doctor of Laws from the University of Orléans, by now the best law faculty in France. It was honorary in the sense that Grotius had not studied at Orléans, but it evidently also included the *licence* which on the continent constituted admission to the bar. Orléans would have had no problem about granting the degree on that basis—even to one so young— since venality had been rife in the French universities and bureaucracy for some time. Admittedly, there is no clear evidence that Grotius bought his degree, but there is no doubt others did. Returning home to Holland, in mid-December 1599 a sixteen-year-old Grotius was admitted to the bar of the two highest Dutch courts. The ambitious father wasted no time placing his prodigy in the home of a well-regarded politician at the capital, and Grotius began the practice of law to instant success. Such progress by this mere boy may seem amazing to us, and as we look upon the engraving of him wearing his fine French medallion, we cannot help noticing that the somewhat smug adolescent must have thought so, too. It is a relief to find that in his Annals, written late in life, he could look back and describe this initial court experience lightly and with deprecating wit.

Despite success at the bar, Grotius affected some disdain for law practice, just because it tended to interfere with other studies close to his heart. His *tempus fugit* motto in mind, he wrote to Heinsius:

> You cannot think how the thankless court runs away with all my time…. This is very different from the University…. I have pulled myself out of the ruck of little lawyers, thanks to one or two causes which have succeeded well enough. But the reward bears no relation to the labor, and were it not that by jolts of this kind one has to struggle towards a position in the state, all this toil would be thrown away. What time wasted in writing opinions which might better be devoted to Philosophy, History, or Letters! (Lee, *Hugo Grotius,* 8)

He soon, however, had one matter that gave him plenty of scope for the philosophy, history, and letters. A Dutch East India Company ship had taken as prize a Portuguese vessel called the *Catharina*, claiming that it had interfered unlawfully with Dutch trade in the Far East. The Dutch court was asked to confirm the seizure, and this had roused to action the consciences of some of the Company's pacifist Mennonite stockholders. Equally strong misgivings were expressed in the capitals of other countries. The Company, an organization of merchants of vital importance to the Dutch commercial class, engaged the twenty-one year old Grotius in 1604 to write for publication a defense of the seizure. The propagandistic importance of such a defense of the legality of prize—a public opinion piece rather than a court brief—is obvious. The result was a substantial book on the law of booty: *De jure praedae*. Completed in 1606, the text is important for it shows an early stage of ideas later incorporated in Grotius's major work on rights of war and peace: *De jure belli ac pacis* (1625). Probably because the situation changed during the time of research and writing, only chapter XII, on freedom of the Seas—the *Mare Liberum*—was published. The rest languished, unknown, until 1864 when professors at Leyden found it in a bookseller's shop and edited it for publication four years later.

De jure pradae has been hailed by Dumbauld as a "triumph of the juristic art" and a "masterpiece of structural perfection" (*The Life and Legal Writings of Hugo Grotius* 29, 150). The opportunity to link sea booty, Dutch merchants, and the ways of science arose here because, as Grotius emphasized, the legal criteria as to capture of enemy goods *a fortiori* could not be found in the law of Holland or of Sumatra or Malacca, the states on either side of the strait of Singapore where the *Catharina* had been taken. Nor could they be discerned in written records of Roman law.

Retained for his legal expertise by the Company, it was with certainty that Grotius centered all on natural reason. It was to be his approach both in youth and maturity, although later Grotius would see in law more of an expression of human nature. The crucial second chapter, the famous *Dogmatica*, opened in an almost joyful confidence with the *prolegomena*, basic axioms divided into two groups: nine *regulae* outlining the sources of law, followed by thirteen *leges*, which are the first deductions from human nature. These laws of natural reason as summarized by Dumbauld (Dumbauld, 35) are as follows:

(1) It shall be lawful to protect life and ward off harmful things.
(2) It shall be lawful to procure and retain those things that are useful for living.
(3) Let no one do injury to another.
(4) Let no one take possession of that which is possessed by another.
(5) Wrongs done must be remedied.
(6) Benefits must be rewarded.
(7) Individual citizens shall not only not injure, but shall protect other citizens individually and collectively.
(8) Citizens shall not only not steal what belongs to another or to the public, but shall contribute to the community those things that are necessary for them.
(9) Let a citizen not execute his right against a citizen without a judicial judgment.
(10) The government must in all things act for the good of the republic.
(11) The republic must ratify whatever the government has done.
(12) Neither the republic nor a citizen may execute its right against another republic or its citizen without a judicial judgment.

(13) Let all laws be observed simultaneously where possible; where that cannot be done let the worthier law prevail.

When reading the Dumbauld summary, we do notice that none of these thirteen *leges* includes "A promisor should perform his promise," the basic axiom of later natural law writers. Probably Grotius found no contract argument in behalf of the Dutch fighting the *Catharina* case, but lacunae like this have encouraged those who give to Hobbes, not Grotius, the honor of being the first to apply the axiomatic method to jurisprudential writing (O.F. Robinson, 361). Nevertheless, the philosophical significance of the Grotius attempt to transfer Euclid and science into the field of human relations is important and innovative.

Political Career of Grotius

The Dutch East India job apparently contributed politically to the governmental position that Grotius coveted, because in 1607 he was appointed Advocate General of the Fisc for Holland, Zeeland, and Friesland at 1,000 guilders a year. The Advocate locally represented the Union's chief executive in litigation: police, prosecutors, revenue collectors, expenditures, and other similar matters. Grotius evidently did well at it, being appointed in 1613 Pensionary of Rotterdam with a 1,000 guilder a year increase. The Pensionary was a local official ostensibly under the Town Council but nevertheless able, if a talented personality, completely to dominate the group. In addition, the Pensionary was given a seat in the Dutch legislature, called the States. This important job was considered only one step away from Grand Pensionary, the position held by former mentor Oldenbarneveldt. At thirty, sitting in the States General of the United Provinces, the *Groot* had become a big man in Dutch public life.

The chief political issue of the time was a religious matter of high constitutional impact. The Protestant Reformation begun by Luther back in 1517 had long since lost its unity. The people of the Dutch Republic had mostly decided for the Reformed Church of John Calvin, but toleration for diversity left open the door to Catholics, Lutherans, Anabaptists and many other sects. Even among the Calvinists, themselves, there existed now a deep split. Most of them supported the orthodox state church which aimed at strict adherence, including some ministerial control of the civil power. A minority, following a leading minister named Arminius, admired the Church of England and wanted more ritual and a less exacting doctrinal discipline. The Arminians reflected humanistic and scientific tendencies and felt a broadminded repugnance to any puritanical idea of the total depravity of human nature. They remained doubtful about predestination without regard to merit, since, they felt, grace came only to those who strove to deserve it. The orthodox men favored strong central authority; the Arminians, a powerful minority in certain cities of Holland, wanted a central government that remained respectful of provincial rights. In addition, the struggle had its personal side. The military executive of the United Provinces, Prince Maurice of Nassau, son of the hero William of Orange, hated the Grand Pensionary, and the latter did not trust Maurice. The pendulum of power, which in Dutch history had tended to swing between the commercial oligarchy and the military representative of the House of Orange, moved toward the latter; while at the same time the danger from Spain, abated during Grotius's youth, increased again.

It was with the Arminians, Oldenbarneveldt, and the commercial oligarchy, that Grotius was allied. It had not been a political matter of weighing the two sides and making a decision. Grotius's deeply held political and ecclesiastical philosophy, his residence in Holland, his political debt to Oldenbarneveldt, and his connections with the merchants put him in this camp naturally. Nevertheless, because he had always taken an individual stance on church matters, the political linkages did create some theological reservations. These he used when he annotated, brilliantly and completely, both Old and New Testaments, bringing to his Biblical scholarship the modern method of scientific interpretation. It was not for brilliance that Grotius wrote but for the purpose of reducing Christian theology to the fewest simple fundamentals of the earliest Church in the hope that Protestants, and ultimately all Christians, could find unity through them.

Outside of the legal field Grotius also read widely in ancient literature, editing several items and producing original dramas and poetry in the ancient style. His goal here was to draw from antiquity—in the humanist manner begun so long before by Petrarch and crowned by Grotius's hero Erasmus—those lessons of morality offered by the wisest of the ancients. His words were thereby chosen to supplement the lessons of the Bible and the Church Fathers, and the vehicle was his long practiced Latin style praised as the equal of the classical past. There may also have been some of his own past. In the translation of a favorable Latin statement for the controversial preacher Johannes Wytenbogaert—used by Rembrandt on a 1635 etching—Grotius sounds a lot like the encomium from Henry IV years ago: "Behold The Hague, your Wtenbogaert [sic] comes home." It was such work which made Grotius a member of what is often called the "Republic of Letters," a camaraderie of European scholars cemented by the inspiration of one-on-one visits and by the constant flow of their personal correspondence. He remained one of a few of them who rejected the Humanistic prejudice against all things medieval. Instead he read carefully, among others, the works of Thomas Aquinas and the so-called "second scholastics," those Spanish Catholics of the sixteenth century, especially Suarez, the eminent Jesuit jurist.

Believing and pious, Grotius thought only political peace could bring religious unity, with the church serving as a chief means of the state to promote the morality of its citizenry. Unfortunately, he was never a proponent of religious toleration, stressing instead that there must be a state theology; however, he did feel that its tenets should be few and simple enough so that variations in beliefs could co-exist under its umbrella. Grotius set out his legal philosophy of church and state in *De imperio summarum potestatem circa sacra* (1647), a book he kept near at hand all his life, repeatedly touching it up, making it ready for press, but never publishing it—in his situation a prudent tactic. Like Erasmus, he rejected the repressive tradition of Pope Gregory VII—now represented in Protestant mode by Calvin, the "Pope of Geneva"—that in all things relevant to man's salvation officials of secular government should be controlled by the priests. Yet neither did Grotius follow the tradition of Constantine, Justinian, and Charlemagne, in which the secular ruler also played a sacerdotal role and was at once emperor and papal guide. Rather, the de Groot Dutch roots in flexible secularism seem to have grown into tolerating a republic and plainly putting state power under natural law.

As conflict between the Arminians and the orthodox Calvinists increased in passion, the Arminians resisted the central power, hoping to maintain their freedom in the large cities of Holland where they were strong. Their leader, as we have said, was Oldenbarneveldt, and Grotius, ever the faithful aide, drafted a stream of crucial legal documents in the dispute. The orthodox, however, proved fierce in defense of their theology and fierce in support of central power against the renewed danger from Spain, and they would give no ground. Finally, Prince Maurice sided with them, a move which sealed the fate of Oldenbarneveldt and Grotius. Maurice had more and better troops, and this soldiery, and most of the masses, stood with him against the oligarchs. Grotius, whose rather naïve persona did not put him at his best in positions of authority and interpersonal stress, found himself surprised by the violent course now taken by events. Both he and Oldenbarneveldt were arrested by the Prince who set up a special court to try them summarily without indictment, counsel, or witnesses. Even the court itself was illegal because the United Provinces did not have criminal jurisdiction; Holland alone could have tried lawfully. Both accused were convicted, Oldenbarneveldt was hanged, and Grotius was sentenced to life in prison with forfeiture of estate—an ironic bureaucratic turn of the law of prize against its famous author. In their haste, the court even forgot to put in the record the offense alleged. It was a full year later when they added the biting words of indictment: high treason.

Prison and Escape

Fourteenth century Loevestein Castle, sited for defense, is located on the peninsula formed by the confluence of the rivers Waal and Maas as they flow westward, about thirty miles east of Rotterdam. Water of fortification on three sides is complemented by walls six feet thick and a double moat on the fourth. The thirty-six-year old life-prisoner who arrived there in June 1619 is described by Vreeland (Vreeland, 120) as singularly handsome, his features finely chiseled, nose slightly aquiline, eyes blue and sparkling, with brown hair, a tall and well formed figure. He was active both in mind and body, had a prodigious memory, could read like the wind and was a facile and persuasive speaker. But more important than his own characteristics was the woman who accompanied him, his wife of eleven years, Maria van Reigersberg. She had been selected for Grotius by his always watchful father because of her fine connections to an oligarchical family of Zeeland. Among their children she would bear her husband three sons, fulfilling his wish for heritage under the family name. More than that, she now would show herself to be one more of those extraordinary women who helped change legal history, combining a deeply affectionate disposition with extraordinary moral courage and an ability to cope with disaster—qualities in which she fortuitously far surpassed her husband.

Grotius was given two rooms on the second floor of the jail; Maria was permitted to live with him on condition that she share his loss of liberty. It was far from an arduous existence, though, for Maria had enough money to support comfortably their life in the prison, and her husband had plenty of scholarly tranquility. He had a huge wooden top which he spun on the floor for diversion, but since one cannot spin a top all day—especially if pressured to change the face of law under a *Ruit Hora* motto—his main activity came from his books, many of which were transported in and out of the castle in a stout wooden chest provided by Maria. Grotius did research and wrote, studied law and moral philosophy, translated Greek and Latin tragedies into the original meter, and finished *De veritates religionis Christianae*, or *Truth of the Christian Religion*, later translated into eleven languages. He meant the book particularly for sailors, a kind of traveler's lectionary to help ward off pagan temptations and teach the reader how to find willing converts. However, it was also intended as a legalistic missionary code, the answer of legal philosophy to how one taught Christian truth above divisive sectarianism. The work was widely popular, gaining readership even in the eighteenth century, and it served as the classical manual in Protestant colleges. It was also in prison and mainly from memory that the important *Introduction to the Jurisprudence of Holland*, mentioned above, was finally completed, as well as an edition of Seneca.

While her husband filled the long passage of two summers and two winters, Maria chafed with the paucity of activity, commenting that darning socks was not really necessary for a man who mainly sat poring over his books. So she concentrated on something more practical. There was now fear of renewed war with Spain and of an increased guard presence at the castle. Maria convinced her husband this was the time to act on their long discussions about escape. Well aware she would have to concoct a bold plan, she soon centered her plotting on the great wooden book chest as well as on the source for such deliveries: the merchant Datzelaer's house in the nearby village of Gorcum, about two miles away. After two years the heavy container had gone in and out so many times, transporting the reading material to and from Grotius, that the guards no longer bothered to open it. One day Maria watched while Grotius in the privacy of their chamber climbed into the chest (said to have been two thumb-widths less than four feet in length) and by doubling up managed a tight fit inside with the lid shut. He practiced the uncomfortable position daily, lengthening his time with only the keyhole for air until he had reached two hours without injury.

The twentieth of March 1621 was the beginning of the annual fair, and Gorcum prepared for crowds of visiting strangers. One more might not be noticed. On the twenty-first Grotius's nine-year-old daughter—herself as prescient and crucial to the plot as Maria—suddenly announced: "'Father must go tomorrow'" (Vreeland, 134). Grotius thought it surely a sign from heaven, and as if to prove him correct, that evening the commander of the castle left for a couple of days to accept a promotion. Maria told the commander's wife, left in charge, that she had some Arminian books to be sent back to the owners. No doubt she thought the woman, an orthodox Calvinist, would see it as a pious duty to get the volumes out. On the twenty-second Grotius prayed for an hour and then got into the chest in underclothes and silk stockings, his head pillowed on the New Testament and held in place lest the chest be bumped too hard. The chest was locked. Maria gave the key to the maid, Elsje van Houvaningen, another female force who now surfaces into history for the few crucial hours she would accompany the chest. Maria went back to the big bed in the corner and drew the curtains. From inside she told an attendant that being indisposed this day her maid would take the chest. A couple of soldiers arrived and the plot was on.

Next ensued a series of cliffhangers to rival Harold Lloyd and which Vreeland (Vreeland, 136–148) recounts with obvious dramatic relish. One soldier complained: "Why is the chest so heavy?" to which Maria scornfully replied from inside the bed: "They are Arminian books," as though given extra weight by the devil. "The Arminian himself must be in it," was the soldier's retort as inspection was made on the chest exterior for air holes. Seeing there were none, down the stairs and through a mystic number of thirteen doors went the chest, the soldiers still frequently complaining of the weight. One said, "I will get a drill and bore a hole through him so the ---- runs out." But Elsje was up to this (or down to it). She pertly replied: "Then you will have to have a drill reaching from here to his room."

At the gate the soldiers asked the commander's wife if the chest should be opened. When she inquired what the Commander usually did in similar situations, they replied that he usually just let it pass by unopened. The wife waved it on, and the chest was carried to the boat for Gorcum. Maria was now watching, for once on board Elsje was to flutter a handkerchief if all were well, otherwise sit disconsolately with head in hands. An officer of the boat had sat down heavily on the chest and started to drum his heels. The vigilant maid, fearful that the weight would tighten the lid and reduce the air, warned that the chest had porcelain as well as books. The officer slowly stood up. Arrived at the dock in Gorcum, the chest was next put on a wheelbarrow to go down the gangway. Here the skipper's son made the excessively acute observation: "There is something living in the chest." Elsje, in another diversionary tactic, reached for a poetic height: "Yes, books have both life and spirit." At last the chest was wheeled to a rear door of the merchant's house and Elsje told Mme Datzelaer that Hugo Grotius was in the chest. The worthy housewife turned white. Her husband was informed and decided not to be an eyewitness; the escapee would have to be sequestered on the second floor.

Grotius had been in the chest the two hour limit, and in the crisis more forces were immediately needed. With the lid at last raised, the merchant's wife rushed to consult Kornelis van der Veer, a tailor friend. He passed the responsibility on to Jan Lambertzoon, a mason, who dressed Grotius in a mason's outfit, plaster smeared on his hands for a role similar to the one another Hugo—Victor—would use when, again backed up by a female mastermind, he escaped death by crossing into Belgium. It was eleven that morning when escapee and facilitator strolled openly through the crowded town, Grotius carrying one of Lambertzoon's measuring sticks. Once out of town, they walked vigorously for several hours, reached a ferry, and arrived at the village of Waalwyk where Grotius—his disguise had by now changed into that of an escaping bankrupt—got into a carriage with a friend. Assisted along the way by a sheriff who offered a horse and troops as escort, they drove all night to Antwerp which was then in Spanish territory. On March twenty-third at about 1 p.m.

the founder of the School of Natural Law was safe, and the hope of the world for a codified bill of rights on war and peace could be gratified.

Paris; The Natural Law Treatises

The exile—in fact an escaped convict—now had to decide what to do. Antwerp did not offer enough, even for a prominent citizen of the "Republic of Letters," and Grotius resolved to go on to Paris. As a famous Dutchman and French medallion holder, he was welcomed by King Louis XIII, who called him "The Just," granted him a pension, and took him and his Protestantism under royal protection. The French Treasury, however, was in bad shape, and the pension was not paid regularly. Maria's property (she had been released by the Dutch) was insufficient for the family to keep up appearances, even without a carriage. Certainly more income was needed. So Grotius began frequenting the Parisian courts where he could observe with critical eye the florid French *avocats*. He knew that for a Dutch Protestant obtaining a law practice in France would be impossible; nor did a university appointment seem feasible either; even if it were, the universities were in the doldrums. The Thirty Years' War and the bloody French religious civil strife were creators of many opportunities for soldiers, but Grotius did not choose to be one. After all, it had been his deep aversion to the horrors and consequences of armed conflict which brought him to *De jure belli ac pacis*. He kept hoping the Dutch would let him come back, but by 1631 it was clear that such hope was doomed.

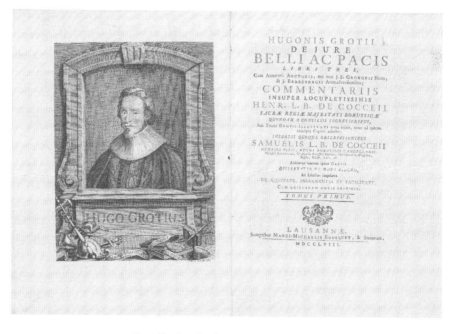

Hugo Grotius, *On the Law of War and Peace*
Courtesy of the Rare Book Collection,
Lillian Goldman Law Library, Yale Law School

Then after a four-year wait an attractive offer came: having longed for a government post, Sweden had decided to make the attorney of War and Peace her Ambassador to France. Work began propitiously, as that very year Grotius helped the Swedes negotiate a beneficial treaty modification providing for French support in the Thirty Years' War. Unfortunately, after that initial excitement, the job went on into ten years of mostly frustration and irritation until just near the end when Grotius did contribute influential background structures for the 1648 Treaty of Westphalia concluding in peace the thirty years of war. Perhaps it was the Grotius touch of equilibrium and pacifism which made this a treaty of opportunity for the new age of balanced power among sovereign states.

When final diplomatic recall to Sweden brought no new appointment and inexorable Time proved it *could* run faster than even the Marvel of Holland, left behind was a bitter man. Despite incredible success as an intellectual of letters and an international lawyer, Grotius felt that personal greatness, which for him consisted only in having accomplished some great act of statecraft, had forever eluded him. Death was obviously going to be his final posting. Standing in history's courtroom his last words pronounced on himself a harsh verdict: "'By undertaking many things I have accomplished nothing'" (Knight, 289). It would take History little time to overturn the judgment.

The Grotius Legacy

To measure how much Grotius actually did impact the philosophy of law, one must look again at the new learning. Paris, since the early twelfth century a leading intellectual center, was in Grotius's time both in the forefront and on the edge of the flowering of thought which under Louis XIV (1643–1715) would become *le grand siècle*. In 1621, living in a city where the learned knew science to be the big news, Grotius was a little ahead of Hobbes—who would spend eight months amidst scientific circles in Paris in 1636—and Descartes—who began active correspondence with both after 1637. This did not mean Grotius lacked for scientific contact, though, for we have seen that his family was close to Stevin and informed in the work of Copernicus, Kepler, and Galileo. Mersenne (1588–1648)—the French philosopher who wore the multiple hats of mathematician, theologian, and monk—had already settled in Paris in 1620 and was Parisian agent and defender of Descartes. We do not read that Grotius was in contact with this polymath, but living across the street from Mersenne's early mentor, the Prince de Condé, the Dutchman had many friends, mostly lawyers and literary people at the highest level. By frequenting distinguished salons he soon became part of the intellectual and political heart of France. So impressed was Richelieu with the foreign visitor, that upon taking power in 1626, the Cardinal offered Grotius a position in his private service. It was not to be. Political conditions were far too unstable. Grotius, always wary, could not accept the flattering offer.

In Paris of the early 1620s the Galilean scientific practicum shared much room with skepticism. This ancient and ubiquitous counter current in various ways and with various consequences still maintained that man cannot achieve reliable knowledge by his own efforts even though, if pushed into nuance, one does feel nothing can be known in an ultimate sense. Should not each of us believe in trying any way to gain a little imperfect knowledge of what can be observed, experienced, and judged? Montaigne, who ended up with divine grace as about all we can get, was widely read by men in the Mersenne circle, especially by Gassendi. But they could not be total converts. Sensitive as they were to the relentless, incontestable, startling march of science, the group was more confident in stressing the constructive aspect: push ahead with empirical study, and concentrate on the world of appearances rather than the futile quest for an elusive "true nature" of things. It was a variation on the *que sais-je* skepticism, a flexible encouragement of doubt about any deduction from axioms based on human nature. And in the end even this attitude would need to be overcome in any attempt to apply the methods of mathematics and experimental science to morality and law.

Although omitting civil and public law the *Introduction to the Jurisprudence of Holland* (1625), dealing with a developed, written legal system, follows generally the time-honored structure dictated by the Justinian *Institutes*. Initially intended merely for the private instruction of his son, when the text reached the public domain—and in fact until the Napoleonic codification of Dutch law in the early nineteenth century—it would stand as the Dutch Blackstone and the standard student text in the universities. Grotius begins with formalities less plainly reminiscent of geometry; his propositions, like the excerpts from Ulpian in the *Digest*, present a definition of "justice" no doubt devised to improve on Ulpian, and they end with Aristotle's legal categories. Similarly *Defense of the Lawful Government of Holland*, regarded by Grotius as his public law complement to the *Introduction*, refrains from fully taking the mathematical road. However, application of mathematics to legal philosophy already had appeared in the carefully crafted book on prize law.

Fourteenth century Ockhamism, experiencing renewal in the scientific seventeenth century, put everything under God's will. When carried to its edgy conclusion, this made everything in the natural world subject to the miraculous possibility of change of mind by God. But the idea that there are natural law principles discovered by man is a process separate from theology, even if since the creation of human nature these principles always have and always will exist as realities outside the mind of man. An intellect like Grotius refused to think that the lead balls of Jan de Groot and Simon Stevin, hitting the plank simultaneously on one day, could arrive on the plank at different times the next week. He believed firmly that far from being a matter of theology, the behavior of inert balls of lead—Grotius's scientized apple, if you will—was a clear signal for regulating the mores of sentient people of society, and for a review of godhead, too. By pressing forward with similar confidence to position fully axioms of human behavior as independent of God, Grotius was certain he need have no compunction about stating his principles and deducing a legal system from them. In a crucial alliance with Aristotle and Thomas Aquinas, he was laying it down that the essential of human nature was sociable man who, realizing his potential only by living in society, cannot do that without structures of behavior.

Grotius knew that Aristotle was a pagan, but he was rational, and, within the limits of his lack of knowledge of Christianity, he could also speak for natural law. As Grotius faced the old thirteenth century challenge whether to reject Aristotle as a heretic or to receive him as a wise man, the liberal Dutchman opted for wisdom. It was not an original decision, since that same thirteenth century, struggling with whether or not Christians should continue with the pagan educational system, had produced Aquinas, showing the Church how to take an open stance. Now Grotius had before him the Thomist matrix of legal sources. First came Eternal law, consisting of principles in the mind of God. Then there was Divine law, the corresponding positive law residing in the Bible which told as much about Eternal Law as God wished man to have in a set form. From this God, having made man rational, came the duty of exercising this rationality in order to deduce the controls made necessary by his sociability; Natural Law which, since God created human nature, was necessarily consistent with Eternal Law. Finally, Aquinas had traced the path of these permanent principles being moved out of eternity and into nature. As they were discovered by man, the positive law corresponding to Natural Law stood revealed, as Human Law, which although made by the will of man, had to remain consistent with natural reason.

Grotius saw man's sociality as innate. But he did not see it as a social goal post toward which humans were always propelled. Rather, he took the novel position that it was basically a weakness, in which social life as a requirement for survival fell back on achieving that survival through natural and then civil laws (Seidler, 18). As to where law came from, the *De Jure* showed Grotius inclined to think that law must be created by the exercise of a will, a divine one first, but a human focus being a very close second. Setting the concept of natural law and the method of mathematics into an attempted cohesive legal system, the *De Jure* brought the Grotius concepts forcefully to the attention of successor legal philosophers and started the so-called modern school of natural law, also called the Protestant school, despite its being essentially secular.

It is a peculiar feature of Grotius's work that his *Jurisprudence* treatise of 1625 has more often been seen as the reason international lawyers have built an altar to Grotius and to this day keep the flame lit; few of them probably have paid much attention to the great religious shift the work contained. The *Jurisprudence* treatise, more in the tradition of philosophical Realism than is Aquinas, admitted that an unchanging God created man once and for all with a certain nature, human nature. But like the *De Jure* it passed the legal baton to human beings who, by scientific study of human nature, must themselves deduce the ruling structures which have existed from Creation and are necessary for their welfare. Like godhead, human nature does not change; therefore, the rules for good governance do not change. They are secular not theological, and they are for all men and women.

Grotius, like Galileo with scientific law, patiently, clearly, proceeds to draw such natural principles as much as possible from physical facts, presenting human nature theory as essentially empirical: the sea may not be appropriated as property because one cannot plant boundary stones; war is permissible in a proper case because man has fists. Obviously, beyond empiricism the immutability of geometry proved hard to reach in detail, and some adjustments had to be made. There are, for example, natural laws that flow from a state of affairs which did not always exist in current form. Thus property is natural, yet before property there was community of goods. Courts are natural, yet before courts there was self-help (Lysen, *Hugo Grotius: Essays on His Life and Works,* 28). But even patience had to admit natural law is too complex to pin down. Grotius realized some natural laws order or forbid while others merely permit. The former cannot be opposed by positive law; the latter are at discretion. It is axiomatic that natural law is superior and cannot be modified by positive laws created by human will. Nevertheless, there are subtleties. By natural law obligations are to be performed, yet infants, for example, need not perform them for the rather inelegant reason that by positive law, the creditor has released infants in advance.

There is in today's European unification efforts a sense of the past which returns us directly to the hurdles Grotius had to jump. He understood nationalistic stresses but had to invent for them a positive spin as being the crucial secular impetus to surmounting problems and making natural law a successful legality. For his day, in a Europe split apart in the course of the Thirty Years' War, this meant trying to work from divisive secular anarchy, so harmful to the trade that nourished the Dutch commercial oligarchy. The attempt of Innocent III to unite Christendom under one pope with multiple feudal contracts was long gone, and any agreements of obligation by which emerging national states had once been fiefs of the kings of other states were all nearly subsumed by the theory of sovereignty. However, the 1625 natural law work was a strong effort to provide the needed theory for what was basically to be a new Europe. Grotius had set a high goal, one perhaps too ambitious for his time, but one especially sought after now, four centuries later. The key to his confidence was an attorney's practical recognition that, to control the balance of power among nations competing not only for economic advantage but separated by irreconcilable religious differences, one had to accept a willingness of response on the way to the possibility of peaceful agreement.

Violence, of course, can be internal as well as external; and Grotius made the bold decision to include the question of popular violence against the sovereign long before Enlightenment and Rousseau made it fashionable to express the origin of civil society in the context of a social contract. Raising the problem of whether the sovereign is subject to natural law, Grotius's affirmative was qualified by saying that the state, for "'the sake of public peace and order'" might "'resist that promiscuous right of resisting.'" Moreover, if the ruler were misled by fear or anger "'so as to deviate from the road that leads to tranquility,'" the people should bear it and be "'compensated by the alternative of better times.'" Yet, even public forbearance could not be expected in "'cases of extreme necessity'" felt by the people who "'first formed civil society, and from whom the rights of rulers are derived'" (Morris, *The Great Legal Philosophers; Selected Readings in Jurisprudence,* 90–91). In short, having resigned the whole power of government in the social contract to the form of government they preferred, a betrayed citizenry could not be expected to die rather than breach the rule of non-resistance.

Always sensitive to retaining the broad, multinational grasp of affairs, Grotius thus looked, unblinking, at civil strife and full scale war by keeping to his fundamental purpose: always reject the view that when arms are taken up law ceases. As one who would certainly have promoted national leagues and globalization as well as critiqued some of the responses to modern terrorism, he consistently believed in a "law of mankind," applicable whether the resort to arms were by a nation or by individuals in an unorganized territory. When Grotius understood the double provenance of this law of mankind, he always held firm to the usual dual outcomes: natural law, of course, and the positive law of nations—legal forms expressly written when made by nations in agreements or implied when established by custom. "Law of mankind" was conceived as analogous to the internal law of a state, except that the state's substantive law is supported by a system of positive procedural law giving to the state's tribunals a monopoly of violence in the enforcement of judgments. But mankind, even European mankind considered alone, was not a state; it had no government and, therefore, no positive law of procedure.

The concept of a world state had been offered by others, yet one cannot help sharing Gierke's view (Gierke, *Natural Law*, 86) that Grotius went farther than other thinkers in recognizing the possibility of something more than a mere confederation by contract. Period ideas of sovereignty precluded what, as a major proposal by statesmen, awaited the end of the World Wars. Nevertheless, as Grotius saw it, peace was the major part of the 1625 contributions. An unjust resort to violence in the form of war transgressed the law of mankind, requiring both discussion and legal intervention before violence might be used. As to who enters the judgment arena in Grotius's system, it is the state or individuals whose rights under the law of mankind have been infringed and who claim priority of jurisdiction. Their declaration of war is the precipitator of judgment, and their acts of war are the final execution on that judgment. Grotius, on the road to a World Court, Common Market, European Union, and United Nations, proudly saw *De jure belli ac pacis* as the first time anyone had provided a system of law to guide societal entry into nationhood.

In later centuries others would see the state as an abstract single entity subject to no law except that to which it consents. For the purpose of the law of humankind Grotius was ready to put both states and persons into the same category. The state is but an aggregate of individuals; because each individual has human nature, the state, too, thus is subject to the same natural law. Even the *ac pacis* part of his conflict text, its law of peace analyzing the rights which may not be impaired by violent action, looks in form similar to the presentation of the substantive internal law of a state as to rights and duties of individuals in respect of contracts, torts, and crimes (O.F. Robinson, 361). It was this peculiarity of the Grotius work that soon was to inspire a large number of legal academics led by Pufendorf to deduce from natural law principles an ideal system of internal law for a state.

The Grotian influence was aided by his conscientious effort at making his case through a large sample field. "'I profess, in all sincerity,' he wrote, 'that, as mathematicians consider their figures as abstracted from body, so did I, in treating of Rights, abstract my mind from every particular fact'" (Morris, 86). Yet he did not present only a system of abstract propositions, but offered his multitude of examples of personal actions that amounted in his view to obedience to the ubiquitous law of the species. It is not clear whether ancient Greece and Rome or the Bible were strong reminders of indebtedness to tradition or simply the "good old days" which offered the better examples. Perhaps he also did not fail to note that using ancient examples conveniently avoided the thicket of contemporary international controversies on which he understood he could never find agreement among his readers and, perhaps, ran the risk of incarceration again.

The essential fact is that Grotius evidently did not consider himself bound by traditional solutions, and this stance apart is the essence of the exciting new road he was following. Grotius constructed iconoclastic legal precepts, ultimately detaching them without qualm from theological natural law, from Roman law, from canon law, from customary law, and from town law. Universal and immutable were their claims, but once Grotius initiated them so brilliantly, the world would notice their utilitarianism allowed scope for the long sought actual use by actual society. This was radical. One day in Public law—first in America and then in France—it would sanction a new future. Indeed, McDougal suggested (McDougal, *International Law and the Grotian Heritage,* 166) in 1983 that Grotius was centuries ahead of his time in exploring essential social values for diverse nations and contributing the law of nature as his sesame to opening up legal inquiry for the millennium state.

As a result of the work of Grotius, mathematical attitudes were to permeate much legal thought and ironically continue long after his natural law had lost allegiance and positive law was king (O.F., Robinson 361). In his 1945 *Law Training in Continental Europe* Schweinburg looked to Western Europe and wrote as follows (Schweinburg, *Law Training in Continental Europe,* 47):

> To repeat the important point, the Continental jurist is dealing with law in an abstract manner; he is practicing and exploring a kind of legal mathematics, with principles, concepts and rendered decisions as elements in the place of figures and symbols. He does not study social phenomena, or their repercussion upon the mental machinery which purportedly directs them.

Gierke believes (Gierke, *Natural Law,* 55;71) that Grotius's success with posterity rested upon a fundamental assumption, one not invented by him and which he did not stress, but yet which was deeply shared by him and his successors. That assumption was the value of the individual. Left behind were the countless feudal groupings that had defined legal needs—weaker peoples under stronger, estates of nobles, clerics, bourgeois; a royal family, a noble family, a Church chapter or order, a military order, a guild, a trading league, an agricultural manor. After Grotius, there would be, in theory, only individuals and the sovereign state. We have frequently suggested sources of this fundamental, new individualism: the spirit of Humanism, the philosophy of Ockham, and recent and powerful choices forced on people by the Reformation. True, many sorts of intermediate groups between state and individuals continued to exist and had to exist; but from the Grotian system, based on the unique nature of personhood as the source of a natural law controlling positive law, came certain inevitable consequences.

First, human nature could be analyzed scientifically. For this kind of physical, psychological, and biologic study of people the age was not yet prepared. Even today lawyers must reach when faced with the breathtaking new ways in which science and ethics controversially co-opt Grotius's common right into the realm of intellectual property as diverse as DNA sequencing. The seventeenth century could, nevertheless, contemplate the separate person as a universal with rationality as the chief attribute, and this led to the innovative looking at humans as they were "in a state of nature," meaning as they were before organized society.

Second, there was only one way humankind in the state of nature could have passed into the phase of organized society: by contract. Grotius had studied social contracts in various works, among them his contemporary Joannes Althusius, but Althusius had built from groups rather than individuals (Gierke, *Natural Law*, 71). The secular early modern natural law theorists after Grotius, with his modern preference for the one, would concentrate on this state of nature, on the social contract, and on the implications of human nature as to the rules for a society created by contract. They would suggest many variations which came to penetrate the works of the philosophers, the legislative dispositions of the monarchies, the law faculties of the universities, and the officials, professors, and lawyers working on the modernization of continental law.

Finally, there is a consequence that need not have been inevitable, yet today in momentum seems to be. Standing as we do for the law of nations, a new anarchism ironically confronts us with its equal surge: the explosive perversion of personhood. Terrorist or warlord are natural law run amok, and in this headlong course to chaos, the rational social contract is being tossed aside for the irrational, anti-social cell. The noble Grotian individual plus state equation has run straight into this hard going, twisted and distorted by the very globalized mesh that was to be its glory. Grotius and personhood, Grotius and conflict resolution through the law of mankind, Grotius himself—all now stand on trial for life, as states and citizens are reduced by the same pulverizing, often single acts of chemical, biological, suicidal approaches to war.

In his day Grotius, philosophically on the side of Realism in his natural law theory, never lacked Nominalist dissenters. Antigone had her Creon, Plato his Sophists, Anselm his Roscelin, and Aquinas his Ockham. Grotius would soon encounter Hobbes, and he would serve as the next important philosopher to attack the new way. It would be seizure in order to destroy; and although Grotius's successors held the field for a couple of centuries, Hobbes had his followers, too, in a debate which continuing, even now, reveals Hobbes's lamp burning brighter than the flame of natural justice. Yet before Hobbes could mount his attack there would be another appreciation of Grotius—surprisingly again with French and Dutch foci. This time the beloved mathematical world turns bravely new world-mechanical, its hero demonstrating, yet again, the mindset of unicity.

Descartes

Introduction

René Descartes (1596–1650) wrote nothing significant about law. He never studied at a university. Neither was he a university professor. For him, erudition, organized religion and all the heritage of the past seemed trifles. He was, rather, an independent thinker who had resolved to obey the laws, be resolute in action, be faithful to his opinions once he had made up his mind, try to conquer himself, alter his desires rather than attempt to change the world, and be a spectator rather than an actor. To these considerable constraints he chose to add the most important. He would spend his whole life cultivating his reason in an effort to do what he considered no one so far had done: discover the truth about man within the universe and construct the system controlling them. What is more, he would effect these epistemological discoveries with certainty, setting aside the dialectical methods of the scholastics which he thought produced excess debate and opting instead for inescapable conclusions.

These conclusions and this certainty took the next step in the march of natural law. Although deeply influenced by the scientific revolution, the Cartesian progression went along unusual paths. He continued the time-honored tradition of working as a grand systematizer (Copleston, Vol. IV, 30), using metaphysics as his medium. His chosen orientation was Realism rather than Nominalism, and his preferred materials were the reflections of his mind, rather than the literature of the Humanists. The first leading metaphysician of the new science, Descartes structured a quaintly hermeneutic residence, divided like the body and soul into rooms for social activity and those forming a scientific laboratory. His treatises were written in a limpidly straightforward prose vernacular, because he hoped to reach a more general public than the esoterical technocratic professionals. One does not in his work discern with any clarity political motives born either of the aristocracy or the merchants and middle class, although he probably, by indirection, did more for the latter than the former.

Descartes began with individual consciousness then moved on to the existence and nature of God and the physical nature of man, animals, and matter. He did not present a system of morality for the relations of one man to another; such a system, of course, would have included the philosophy of law. Yet even though his work appeared too late to influence the juristic writings of Grotius, and Grotius does not appear to have affected Descartes's own studies, Cartesianism had its important legal input. The Frenchman's ideas infiltrated the orientation of English Nominalist and materialist Hobbes as he created his own important philosophy of law. And the German Pufendorf—he who first will deduce a complete legal system from natural law principles—clearly bears the marks of a fierce *cogito* encounter. Descartes's mechanistic explanation of man, animals, and the universe, even though not proposed by him in aid of natural law, still lent itself to natural law theories based on human nature. It did so by defining that nature as a common universal for all persons, a human thinking not as a group, but in the Grotian new math of One. Beyond that, Descartes set the stage for two centuries and more of continental rationalism in philosophy. Thinking and therefore Being made him a pillar of the modern ego and surely one of the most independent and original groundbreakers of any age. So dominant was he in his nation's philosophy, it has become a schoolchild's banality to affirm that to understand Cartesian ways of thinking means a eureka pathway to understanding everything French—and who knows? Perhaps to passing the dreaded baccalaureate exam.

Life of Descartes

René's father was of a family from Poitiers; moving later to Brittany, his purchase of a position in the *Parlement of Rennes* which entered him and his son into that *Noblesse de Robe*, so fateful in influencing French politics of the next century. Young René thus found himself part of one of the oldest and most respected families of the region, and in his early years he proudly wore the green velvet dress and sword of the French nobility. That his father was a lawyer put him in a legal atmosphere, but it did not attract him into jurisprudence. From 1604–1612 he studied at the Jesuit college of La Flèche founded by Henry IV, Grotius's early admirer. René liked his teachers, but among his subjects he took pleasure only in mathematics. Because of the excellence of his work he was among twenty-four students selected in 1610 to provide ceremonious welcome for the heart of the deceased royal patron as it found its final resting place at La Flèche. However, when he left La Flèche his mood had unexpectedly turned him against royal ceremonial, along with scholarship and academic prestige. To his family's amazement, headstrong René chose instead to practice horsemanship and fencing.

Completing this questionable professional preparation he went alone to Paris where he developed a passion for gambling, abetted, probably, by his passion for mathematics. Fortunately, Chance turned her wheel back toward the academic discipline, and Descartes retired for two years to a quiet house in the Faubourg St. Germain where his major focus was on exploring equations and studying geometry. In contrast to the group dialogism of the Ancients, such reflection in seclusion would continue to be his intellectual method throughout life. Unfortunately, this particular retreat was discovered by friends who pressed him to return to their entertainments. To escape them and frivolous temptations he joined in 1617 the army of Grotius's nemesis, Prince Maurice. The young man was already comfortably supported by his father and soon would be endowed with a fine maternal estate, conveniently entrusted for management to an abbé. Thus freed from material cares, soldier Descartes accepted his first and only pay in order to set it aside, keeping it through life as an amusing curiosity. There was peace in Holland, and despite the military career came ever more leisure to reflect and continue the study of mathematics and, now, music. In 1619, lured by the outbreak of war in Austria, Descartes volunteered in the Bavarian army. As usual, even there he found the ubiquitous room warmed by a cheerful stove and while off duty continued to meditate.

Then came 10 November. The day would be far different from most of the soldiery, for Descartes could claim that during his waking hours he was enthusiastically filled with the basis of a new scientific paradigm. That night he continued his unique parousia with extraordinary dreams. The next morning awoke a dedicated philosopher. From the feasibility of expressing modern algebra through the aid of coordinate axes used like lines in ancient geometry, the 1619 visions had brought Descartes awareness that mathematics was a life force, with powerful methods applicable to all knowledge. He had perceived human wisdom as one technique, and he had received revelation that there is only one kind of knowledge—certain knowledge—and ultimately only one science and one scientific method. To prove all this he knew he would need to build a perfect system using these ideas as a base (Copleston, Vol. IV, 70). But the challenge did not daunt him, for, being closer to pure numbers than Grotius, Descartes could make a tighter bond between mathematics and philosophy. Although he had read Montaigne and positioned extreme uncertainty at the center of his philosophy, he found doubt to be positive, performing reliably as a strong questing technique, or in modern terms as a philosophic search engine. He would remain impervious to the corrosive negativity of a skeptical nature throughout life. In fact, his true opponent in philosophy was not the give and take of Scholasticism but what he considered the dangerous search-and-destroy of Pyrrhonism.

René Descartes
Courtesy of National Gallery of Art, Washington

In spite of such serious dreams the twenties-something philosopher continued to lark about the world. Not until 1625 did he return to quiet seclusion, this time back in Paris's St. Germain. We may picture him there: a modest, distant yet kindly man, writes Copleston (Copelston, Vol. IV, 66), whose small stature was somewhat disproportionate to physical attributes of large head, projecting brow, big nose, eyes wide apart under prominent lids, and black hair descending almost to the eyebrows. He had a feeble voice and always dressed in black. It was said he held himself apart from others in aloof arrogance; his smile didn't help matters, being "one of gentlemanly scorn and contempt" (Lavine, 91). In conversation over a few glasses of wine he might have revealed that he was cynical about marriage and generally not amorous. Yet a few more glasses would have led to fond words about a mistress and a beloved daughter upon whose death at five he had wept with intense sadness. He was concerned for health, admitting in 1646 that staying well was the major aim of his studies. He liked to lie late in bed reflecting and writing, but he also insisted on plenty of sleep—at least ten undisturbed hours every night complemented by required periods of daily walking. When a friend offended against this sacrosanct routine by calling at eleven in the morning, an angry Descartes decided to move back to Holland. From 1629 until 1649 this became the pattern as he changed his residence twenty-four times, a restlessness usually attributed to escaping disturbances of his passionately philosophical repose. There is the *bon mot* implying that perhaps it was one of these importunate visitors who turned a little late night social life into the impetus for the famous "I think therefore I am." According to the joke, as the testy host spied his guest snatching at a premature sample of the hors d'oeuvres, he reprimanded him with "I think they're for 1 a.m."

These were the days of the most prosperous and brilliant period for the United Provinces. Not surprisingly, the doughty navigators, astute merchants, historical scholars, even the giants Grotius and Rembrandt—all seem to have been unworthy of the newcomer's solipsistic notice. Descartes wrote and thought while Mersenne, who had been a fellow student at La Flèche, busily served as his intellectual agent back in Paris. Soon the attention of Europe was riveted on Holland's famous pensive adoptee who remained on Dutch soil except for three short visits to France.

In 1649, Sweden's twenty-three year old Queen Christina urged an important philosopher-correspondent of hers named René Descartes to break the sacred routine and become a resident great mind at the Stockholm court. What the blue-stocking beauty in boots had in mind for her guest were a title and an estate; for herself she had concocted the scheme of private pre-dawn lessons in philosophy and a Cartesian code for establishing a Swedish academy of science. A vessel of the Royal navy bore the somewhat reluctant thinker to her majesty's cold and damp domain where soon he was nursing his Stockholm friend, Chanut, in an illness, while giving 5 a.m. lessons to the vigorous sovereign. It was all too much, and once again, as Grotius before him, a Christina protégé was to die from exposure to the rigors of the North. Eight years later the lethal Queen came to France, where forgetting her lessons in law and reason she arranged for the murder of her lover Monaldeschi at France's Fontainebleau castle.

Descartes observed the ritual of a Catholic; and Copleston, who ought to be able to detect a heretic, says (Copelston, Vol. IV, 173) he was definitely a Christian, but one who, in trying to keep faith and philosophy separate and abstain from theology as much as possible, could not satisfy the contemporary Catholic hierarchy that he was not an atheist. When news came of the result of the Church's prosecution of Galileo, Descartes suspended publication of his *Traité du monde*, feeling it imprudent to risk losing life when he could save himself without dishonor. Audacious in thought, he was no Martin Luther; and he softened some of his attacks on scholastic philosophy in the vain hope that the Jesuits, whom he respected and whose favor he always hoped to have, would use his works as text books. Although direct in the *cogito*, a Cartesian tendency was to hide behind oblique expression for unorthodox ideas. Unexpectedly, it is the man himself who would reveal this ambiguity of his personhood when he confessed: "'I wear a mask' " (Lavine, 88). His *cogito* may have brought him self-knowledge, but what knowledge, then, can we really count on about him?

We know that he had unlocked, he felt, the secret of the universe, but sadly, for us, he had no time to reveal specifically what that unlocking might teach about law. His starting point, both in a logical exposition of his thought and in the actual history of its development, had been mathematics, enriched by his own knowledge,

Queen Christina of Sweden
Courtesy of Yale University Art Gallery,
Gift of Mr. and Mrs. Samuel Duryee, B.A. 1917

by communication with his Paris friends, by trying—perhaps unsuccessfully—to understand the achievements of Galileo and others. Mathematics was certain because its fundamental ideas are clearly and distinctly perceived; they cannot be deceptions, but are eternal simple natures—no one invents the triangle, one simply rediscovers it. Descartes had not left mathematics with the comparatively shallow explorations of a philosopher qualified only to try to understand; were it only as the inventor of analytical geometry, published by him in his *Table des matières de la Géometrie* as appendant to his *Discours de la Méthode* of 1637, the name Descartes would occupy a distinguished place in scientific history. Yet, significantly, his analytical geometry was but an attachment to his epistemology; wanting certainty in philosophy, mathematics had been the only door possible. Many modern thinkers deny him the view beyond the door by stating that the plan was doomed to fail. Method leading to discovery in mathematics does not work in other fields where a single symbol cannot stand for a concept. Cairns (Cairns, 10–11), firmly believing legal speculation to be "remotely" pre-Euclidean, states the difficulty: mathematics goes from contemplation to manipulation. The law builds its great summary ideas in the reverse.

The Philosophy of Descartes

In diverging from the method of scholasticism which he saw as only a device for explaining what one already knows, Descartes counted with geometrical imperturbability on being led to the discovery of new truths. This was a flawed ideal, since it gives no place to experiment except, perhaps, to illustrate what is already known. Descartes could not, as is necessary in the true scientific method, confirm an hypothesis hazarded by observation of facts and thereby find new truth, or, at least an hypothesis not yet overturned by more experimentation. Admittedly, he did do significant work in optics, a science which had intrigued fourteenth century investigators into thinking light was the physical manifestation of reasoning that can unlock the secret of the universe. And here in his dissections Descartes did give some place to experiment. But his major thrust came in thinking that Euclid was insufficient for having failed to show how the first principles—the fundamental self-evident truths—are reached. Viewing the operation of the mind as consisting of intuition (seeing a proposition so "clearly and distinctly" that it cannot be doubted) followed by deduction (drawing all necessary inferences from such propositions) was not hard to posit, but the problem was how outside the laboratory to find rules to do this accurately and efficiently. Interestingly, it is Copleston, writing in the ligneage from Descartes's favored Jesuits, who gives (Copleston, Vol. IV, 72–83) one of the best analyses of how Descartes went forward.

Cartesian Method found the rules in "analysis" or "resolution" (divide the problem at hand into as many parts as possible, as in the study of a complex curve in geometry) and "synthesis" or "composition" (begin with the simplest part and ascend by deduction). Euclid had achieved explicit synthesis but not explicit analysis, and analysis was something Descartes loved, for it is discovery for which synthesis is its demonstration. With analysis Descartes found "simple natures."

Some are "material." For example, he saw a "body" as corporeal, having "extension" (taking up space) and "figure" (taking up space in a certain shape). "Figure" cannot be analyzed into further elements. It is "simple," a "clear and distinct idea." "Motion" is another such nature. There are also "spiritual" simple natures, such as "willing, thinking, doubting." Both the material and spiritual kinds have "existence, unity, duration." "Common notions" are simple natures which connect others; for example, "things which are the same as a third thing are the same as one another." These simple natures are used in deduction. Descartes appears here to have fallen into some confusion: are the simple natures non-existential like "triangle" or are they existential? Descartes's fundamental proposition is existential; but in the affairs of men non-existential ideas (one must exercise the care of an "ordinary reasonable man" or incur liability for harm he causes; the sum of the squares of the height of the ridge and its distance from the eave equals the square of the rafter) are always useful and sometimes crucial. The ideas of these simple natures are innate, not in the sense that we have them from birth, but that the mind produces them on the occasion of some experience. The experience, however, does not create them, nor are they accidents of the imagination.

Armed with his system, Descartes patiently and doggedly resolved to begin philosophy all over again. To achieve certainty he would supplement with the further technique of "methodic doubt." This meant he resolved upon an approach of suspended judgment, similar to British counterparts Francis Bacon, or later, Joseph Glanvill: do a cautionary inquiry and question everything. At the same time he decided to move beyond skepticism and seek a self-evident proposition the truth of which is absolutely undeniable. This proposition could then become a foundation for deduction.

The process appears to us as an old friend, for it has become part of the modern psyche; it appeals even to the youngest of a generation brought up on myths from Oz, Middle Earth, or far-off galaxies—fictions where the answer to the quest is present before the journey begins. So it was that Descartes found verity swelling within his very own mental doubt: "I think, therefore I am"—*Cogito ergo sum*. By thus starting with epistemology within the human consciousness of thought, he made an important innovation and a revolution in philosophy. *Cogito* was incontestable because the act of doubting it, which is thinking, confirmed it. Descartes considered that he had proved the existence of at least the thinking part of each human being; since even if God is deceptive and creates false sensations, or even if I am only dreaming, the individual must exist to have the sensation or the dream. Saint Augustine had had a similar idea, as Descartes knew, but he used it not as a fundamental but only to refute skepticism—"If I am deceived, I exist."

An idea can be clear without being distinct but not earn distinction without being clear. However, most ideas, unlike the *Cogito*, although clear and distinct, could be deception practiced by God as demon. Before advancing to deduction Descartes considered he had to face this problem. It would be a detour, but a logical one: rather than the application of the *Cogito* to material things, he, on the contrary, moved on to the proof of God. Perhaps this new destination came from having already demonstrated conclusively the efficacy of the "clear and distinct" standard which led to his *Cogito*. He probably felt he might as well immediately engage in this proof of divinity, realistic in accepting the fact that the order of discovery is not necessarily the best order for teaching (Copleston, Vol. IV, 111–112). So, again reminding us of a medieval thinker, Descartes proceeded to satisfy himself God exists and does not deceive. It was more an attempt to harmonize theology and philosophy than to separate them as Grotius had done, and it reminds us of Aquinas's efforts to equilibrate new science with old theology. Cartesian philosophical method, however, separated itself from theology. Although the form of reasoning differed from that of Anselm of Bec, it was based on the same propositions: God is perfect; this, like *Cogito*, is a privileged idea; it cannot be a mental fiction but is innate. Is it more fundamental than *Cogito*? Descartes thought not, since perfection excludes deception, and all clear and distinct ideas are true. Thus positioned, Descartes had met Grotian natural law which stays the same with or without God.

The next Cartesian move entered a shadowy area. He had requested that Mersenne send out his manuscript to a few friends. Among them, the Jansenist Antoine Arnauld responded by a piercing exposition of what he saw as specious Cartesian circularity: what is clearly and distinctly perceived is true because God exists yet we know God exists because indeed we do clearly and distinctly perceive it. Descartes tried to explain away the difficulty, but Arnauld did not like it and posterity has been loathe to accept the explanation. As Copleston says (Copleston, Vol. IV, 109), Descartes "might have been utilizing the divine veracity simply to assure himself that material things exist corresponding to our ideas of them"; he had not presupposed "the existence of material things when proving God's existence."

The only way to break out of this infamous circle was once again simply to push on. Descartes would admit awareness of his individual existence as an entity and he would admit awareness of God's existence as a spiritual being. Such acquiescence bought him time from critique and the felicity of a fundamental concept for his system: the separation of mind or soul from body. All things which we apprehend clearly and distinctly possibly exist; God could have created them. If we apprehend one thing clearly and distinctly apart from another, each is different and can have been created one without the other. The "Cogito" affirms only a thinking, unextended thing, yet at the same time I have a clear and distinct idea of body as an extended, unthinking thing. Ergo, my soul is distinct from my body and can exist without it. This does not prove the existence of my body, however; my power of changing position when I apply this power implies the existence of something corporeal, i.e., having extension without thinking. Further, I have the faculty of sense perception, be it passive or even involuntary, excluding thinking; when it inclines me very strongly to believe it comes from bodies other than my own, God would be deceitful if the idea so induced were false, i.e., produced by a cause other than a corporeal object. Hence such objects exist even if they are not exactly what sense perception suggests they are.

Substances—thinking or corporeal—are perceived only through their attributes. The principle attribute of a corporeal substance is extension—geometry which excludes motion and energy. Extension is essential; figure and quantity are not. At this point Descartes further separated the human soul—the thinking part, the body—only to encounter a considerable real difficulty since both are indubitably related. He again avoided the barrier, declaring to have found a physiological solution: the soul resides in the brain's pineal gland and there directs the motion of the body. Critics here pondered heatedly the problem connection linking these utterly different natures of soul and body. In response, some Cartesians resorted to fearless occasionalism: on the occasion when it is my will that my arm shall move, God moves it.

As for the "secondary qualities" like color, sound, taste, feel, Descartes proposed that they exist in us, not in the bodies outside of us. The extension of the bodies and the imperceptible motion of imperceptible particles in the bodies stimulate our sense organs, and this stimulation takes place on bodily surfaces through a process both mathematical and mechanical. At once Descartes knew he was in trouble, this time with the dogma from the Council of Trent which had proclaimed that the "accidents" (secondary qualities denoting bread and wine) in the Eucharist exist separately from the former bread and wine now Body and Blood. If the principal nature of bodies is extension, what then is space? Descartes answered, in effect, that there is none. It, too, is body with extension, as is what we call "vacuum." Because there is no vacuum, space empty of matter is impossible. Another impossibility? Divisible atoms; every particle has extension and is divisible, even if not by man.

The Cartesian universe where Time is an aspect of motion thus indefinitely extended itself. Bodies in the heavens were felt to possess the same matter as on earth. A body could be in motion and rest at the same time because motion is relative to another body; if two move together each is at rest relative to the other. God, the first cause of motion, has created a certain quantity of it, and it does not change, although it is transferred from body to body. Descartes here deduced from a metaphysical premise: God is perfect and, therefore, not inconstant, and it is God's constancy which itself implies laws of motion. There is no change in the motion of a thing except by agency of another thing; every moving body continues in a straight line (if it curves, it is encountering other bodies).

Now one can sense how the *Cogito* and the principles of method had been leading inexorably toward juristic drama. Given that there are rules for collision of bodies, a lead question for history's courtroom is: what are living bodies? Are they spiritual or corporeal? Descartes opted for corporeal, body's essence being extension. Animals have no thinking or feeling, although at times it may seem that they do because of their automatic reactions; however, they are like clockwork—the well-known Cartesian machines in motion. But so also is the human body—a machine whose systems—respiration, blood circulation—all are automatic; a living person is to a wound-up operating watch as a dead person is to a broken watch. It all poses the possibility for extraordinary legal extension. A trial lawyer might use a Cartesian corporeal motion defense for releasing clients glad that Descartes did not work out a moral—or legal—system. However, Descartes also believed the thinking faculty of the body or soul to be a "complete substance" as well as the corporeal body. Trying to resolve the relationship between body and soul Descartes again fell into a difficulty that no pineal gland concept could resolve, but here was left no doubt in his deistic conception: God had created the world and left it to carry on by itself—one could add, aided by lawyers.

Descartes found his first followers and supporters in the Dutch universities where professors defended him against Calvinist theologians. He had some influence in Germany, a little in England and Italy, although his works did go on the Roman Catholic Index in 1663. French minority Catholic movements like Jansenism were interested in him, but he never received the Jesuit approval he sought. The government and the universities—the latter at a low intellectual ebb—squarely rejected him. It was the fashionable and non-university, non-clerical, learned world of the salons and scientific academies of France which took him in warmly. By the next century his books were official texts in philosophy and were used even in some ecclesiastical seminaries. As a scientist his physics were found weak. Clearly a rejection of Aristotle, who in the early eighteenth century became an initial rival to Newton, they could not stand long against the *Principia*'s mathematical solutions. Nevertheless, as late as 1759 the French Academy of Science was still trying to harmonize the man who had sat pensively under a tree and the one who had pondered confidently next to a stove. To this day these English apples and Dutch oranges exercise us in their heady mix.

Cartesian philosophy in the development of natural law had as its essential foundation a belief in metaphysics. In this Descartes is closer to the Middle Ages than most of his contemporary thinkers, envisaging the metaphysical art as a firm rooting matrix for the tree of philosophy. As physics became the trunk growing out of this root, it branched into medicine, mechanics, and morality. Thus physics, rooted not primarily in observation of the physical world, but in deduction from first principles—that is, fundamental self-evident truths like the axioms of geometry—leads to morality not as a choice or an accident, but as laws dictated by physical science. Again, as Descartes did not live long enough to construct a rigorous moral code except as it came alive in his correspondence with friends, his significance for the law lies mainly in method, which indeed, is his chief claim to innovation.

In building this matrix of method Descartes, the solitary humanist, worked doubt far from the insecurity of modern psychoses into, instead, the equally modern exaltation of human capability. Cartesians post-Descartes would not need God to understand the world; the living and inanimate all existed and moved according to the same physical principles. The question of *final causes* could be left for theology, and theology was superfluous for physics. Descartes's forward thrusts at last did change to backward motion, as he himself, trying to reconcile what he could not know, had become the awkward combination of an extreme pre-Nietzcheanism struggling to coexist with a medieval's belief in God. No longer could any reticence, however, arrest the universalized spread of his heroic individualism—first into the French Enlightenment, then on to the French Revolution of 1789, and finally spilling over the world at large. Whenever there is a barricade, he still leaves his Panthéon tomb to stand high upon it with *Cogito*'s red flag, resolved that he can arrive at incontestable truth by rejecting every authority and every tradition and confidently, optimistically, consulting only his own individual reason. While courtroom lawyers wrestle with his analysis and synthesis in presenting their cases, they all must accept that the flag, this banner of reasonable doubt, is hanging prominently in the back of every jury room deliberation.

Hobbes

Introduction

While Descartes snatched the natural law of his rebellious *cogito* out of the jaws of doubt, ready to pass it on as the one intellectual heritage, another contemporary across the English Channel was also ready to propagate his concept of the thinking man's revolution (M. Villey, *Leçons*, Vol. I, 150) and transmit it to many a shore. It began with the Spanish Armada, which, said the mother of Thomas Hobbes, so frightened her she went into labor on 5 April 1588. It would be an occasion for the Malmesbury citizenry, made the more somber by the fact the calendar read Good Friday when Mrs. Hobbes finally gave birth. Hobbes later claimed that her trepidation and the dark wood of the cross melded into his personality; as he put it: "Fear and I were born twins" (*Encyclopedia of Philosophy*, Vol. IV, 30b).

Fortunately, the sickly and jaundiced youth did grow to be a man characterized by far more positive traits. Healthy, ruddy, tall, and erect, he lived temperately (although he confessed rather proudly to having been drunk a hundred times). He played tennis regularly even after seventy in spite of an increasing "palsy," was genial and courteous, and although subject to occasional outbursts of pique, to all he knew remained generous and loyal. Like Descartes, Hobbes was not a jurist. Like Descartes he never married but had an illegitimate daughter for whom he provided. And again, like Descartes, he had, at least in later life, little taste for extensive reading. He said that if he had read as much as other men he would know as little as they did. What he read, he read thoroughly, and what did not appeal to him he stated plainly; this list included Aristotle, theories of innate knowledge, learning by reading, universities, and teaching faculty. He described religion as a "'pill which it is better to swallow without chewing'" (Castell and Borchert, *An Introduction to Modern Philosophy: Examining the Human Condition*, 530). Despite a positive demeanor, fear, and probably hatred, also, of civil disorder was the dominant mood of his life. This personal logic always led to the aggrandizement of supreme power in the interest of order—usually a safe stand for the timorous. Nevertheless, few thinkers have followed more boldly the logic of their premises, and the brilliance of a studious mind led him through research, reflection, and writing to become the only thinker whose response to the scientific revolution was a complete philosophical system. In the course of that work, the Armada baby returned to an aquatic metaphor to produce *Leviathan*, considered one of literature's major political treatises.

It was natural law which led Hobbes to his conclusions on modern political theory. Ironically, though his innovative ideas were fertile, his method was calculated to destroy the natural law concept rather than sustain it, since absolute power concentrated in sovereign law-givers—whether a single person or several—

could not be reached by way of the natural principles and Grotian social contracts. Hobbes's thought constitutes, therefore, an immediate and powerful riposte to Grotius, to whom he actually seems to have paid scant attention, illustrating the common paradox of opposite trends gaining simultaneous power. Seidler (48) and others have recently suggested that in a broader sense Hobbes and Grotius, both of whom were skeptical, were not at philosophical odds. But by adroit manipulation and countering of natural law and social contract concepts, Hobbes, it is clear, did escape Grotian restrictions upon power. To these he united the motion mechanics of the scientific revolution and the geometry on which he thought it was based: if everything is motion, everything is matter, for it is matter that moves. The result was a Nominalist rather than Realist rationale, one that he deemed certain and inescapable for a reign of positive, rather than natural law. He garnered wide attention at once, and upon publication of his famous work, *Leviathan*, was covered with praise and attacked in hatred. Still, although it is certain that some of his reasoning influenced a few contemporary secular natural law thinkers, they and not Hobbes held dominance in legal philosophy and in much of continental legal education throughout the seventeenth and eighteenth centuries. Hobbes had to wait two more centuries for a larger share of acclaim except at German universities where it was common to find his books taught soon after publication.

Life of Hobbes

Englishman that he was, Hobbes had little proclivity for empiricism and experiment despite being employed for a time as Bacon's secretary. His greatest intellectual stimulation came in Paris, and his system, which is metaphysical and not juridical, fits well the continental mode. As a mathematician, he started late and did not rise to heights in that science; he knew enough, however, to be totally persuaded of the efficacy of the Euclidean method. It was the older Hobbes who took a lively interest in legal issues, jousting with the jurist Sir Edward Coke on how authority of the customary common law as expounded by judges had proved to be a shackle on sovereignty. Living on into great age, Hobbes remained active, a faithful apostle of positive statute law.

Hobbes's father served his parish as vicar. Illiterate and choleric, he quarreled so fiercely at the church door with another clergyman that he had to decamp. It fell then to an uncle, a flourishing glover, to attend to Hobbes's early education. The task would not be difficult, for Hobbes was precocious and throve on Latin and Greek; before fourteen he had translated Euripedes's *Medea* into Latin iambic verse. At fifteen he entered Oxford, steering clear of the popular accent on scholastic logic for studies in geographical and astronomical discovery. With Bachelor's degree in hand by 1608, he took up Petrarch's solution for getting the necessaries of life: accept the patronage of the wealthy. As tutor to the son of William Cavendish, Earl of Devonshire, he formed an almost lifelong connection with this prestigious family. The pupil was unusual: not only was he almost as old as his tutor but he was husband to a child bride he had married when twelve to please King James. Upon the restoration of Charles II, whom he also had tutored for a time in France, Hobbes received in the last twenty years of his life a handsome royal pension from a grateful and sentimental monarch who hung his old preceptor's portrait near his chamber.

Hobbes the tutor was more a congenial companion than a taskmaster; and enjoying much freedom to pursue his own intellectual interests, he made to the continent three trips which were to be crucial in the development of his ideas. On the 1610 "grand tour" Hobbes discovered that the scholasticism of Oxford was being neglected by the non-academic savants of Paris in favor of the inductive scientific methods of Galileo and the skepticism of Montaigne. The young man was at first baffled by the new science, but he formed the determination to widen his insular horizon, and following through with a plan to become a scholar, took up the ancient authors. It did not take him too long to complete a good translation of Thucydides, but he then held the book back for years until his dissatisfaction with the turmoil of the Petition of Right in 1628 caused him to release it for publication as a caveat against the risks in democracy. It was his first publication.

During the period before 1628 he had established through the Cavendish family a connection with Ben Jonson. In a mode foreshadowing Boswell, Hobbes decided to be a recorder of his own great man, and thus began accompanying his patron Francis Bacon on his walks. Despite his jotting down Bacon's eager "notions," and being engaged by the older man to put into Latin some of his "Essays," Hobbes rejected Bacon's inductive system. Perhaps he felt professional envy toward the *Novum Organum*. On a second continental visit in 1629–1631 Hobbes had another important encounter with the ancients as he began his study of Euclid and perhaps awakened to an interest in motion. It is said that when he accidentally opened Book One of the *Elements* to proposition 47, he exclaimed "'By God, this is impossible'" only to turn around and become so persuaded by the proof that he "'fell in love with geometry'" (Morris, 107). During another Devonshire engagement between 1631 and 1638 he enjoyed yet another lengthy continental visit, this time meeting Galileo in Italy in 1636. Finally, after eight months of daily conversation with the Mersenne circle in Paris during the winter of 1636–1637, Hobbes was ready to commit the rest of his life to philosophy.

Enthralled by the idea of natural motion as the key to everything, he now began to study it seriously, linking motility to the problem of what constituted sense. If bodies and their internal parts were at rest, he reasoned, or even in uniform motion, there could be no distinction of anything, no sense; diversity of motion had to be the cause of all things. This drove Hobbes back to the ground and modes of motion where he walked along with Euclid and Galileo during this initial phase of his understanding. But his perception soon became all-inclusive: geometry is motion—a line the motion of a point, a plane the motion of a line, and so forth. It would be this inclusive *so forth* which led Hobbes straight into law. A precise connection between mathematics and social science, to use the modern term, had been eluding him just as it had eluded Grotius in an age which had not put its mind to distinguishing mathematics, empirical science, and philosophy. As soon as he had returned to England in 1637, he enthusiastically put motion to work for a remarkable legalistic scheme of thought whose given—the behavior of inanimate bodies can be deduced from laws—overlapped with the behavior of human societies, which, as organizations

Thomas Hoobs (Thomas Hobbes)
Courtesy of National Gallery of Art, Washington

of bodies, can be deduced from their properties (Copleston, Vol. IV, 20–21, 291).

With civil war bringing a chaotic working situation to England, Hobbes found himself distracted by the cataclysmic political events. When Laud, the Archbishop of Canterbury, and his political ally the Earl of Strafford were sent to the Tower and beheaded—Charles himself would be executed a bare four years later—the royalist legal philosopher was greatly alarmed. In his papers were written drafts of his controversial political ideas, and he had already shown many manuscript copies to those in power. Fearing for his life, he left at once for exile in Paris where he found Mersenne's scientific circle, going strong ever since the abbé's arrival in Paris in 1620. All were pleased at their colleague's return. He was invited to comment on the *Meditations* of Descartes; but Descartes took umbrage at Hobbes's objections, a distance resulted, and the two thinkers never achieved any meaningful or understanding communication. It seems likely, nevertheless, that Hobbes had been influenced by Descartes, at least indirectly, and probably also by reading other Cartesian writings found in the possession of Mersenne. Hobbes would have considered his own system in place when in 1640 he made his remarks on the *Meditations*, and put out his *Elements of Law, Natural and Politic*; but it is probable that in the years 1629–1637 the Mersenne circle, with Descartes a part of it by correspondence, had made greater intellectual strides forward. It is likely Hobbes was the one to learn from the French intellectuals and, through them, be enabled to infuse his thoughts with dogmatic certitude.

In addition to Cartesian physics and Galilean dynamics, Hobbes must have heard from Mersenne's salon regulars about their work on Montaigne's skepticism. Theirs was an ongoing, constructive revisionism in which they urged that though man cannot know ultimate truths, he should do what he can with what he observes. Talk also surely flowed around the modern Epicureanism of Gassendi, another leader in the circle. Here Hobbes could have heard debate about ontological dichotomy: of humans once free, equal, and solitary, yet even *ab origine* at odds with each other in a state of war, chaos, and general insecurity. Gassendistes, even though not political scientists, were on a sympathetic wavelength for Hobbes's legal attentions, for they saw effective right and law as only conventional and not natural. Civil societies formed merely by contracts varying in time and place were nothing more than an escape. Hobbes no doubt also read similar ideas in the works of John Selden (1584–1654) the English legal counselor and scholar.

By 1640 it was time for new political theory. It would be a three part analysis, starting with a treatise called *De Corpore*, a systematic doctrine of Body explaining all physical phenomena in terms of motion. Next Hobbes would single out man from nature, and in a treatise, *De Homine*, present sensation and knowledge as bodily motion. Finally, continuing where Descartes had stopped, he would produce a crowning treatise, *De Cive*, showing how, in their role of citizen, humans having joined together as civil society could then go about its regulation. Hobbes's dream encompassed the whole—Body, Man, State. In his dream he could foresee achieving what no other of the philosophical and juridical responses to the scientific revolution and the mechanical world had: a universal construction of human knowledge to bring civilization and human beings both within nature's scientific structuralization and under social rules. Viewed from the beginning of the twenty-first century such intellectual audacity is staggering, and Hobbes staggered. The vast system would ultimately remain incomplete, natural law left without a corresponding system of private law and largely silent on Grotius's important groundbreaking attention to relations among national rulers. The anti-democratic Hobbes probably never saw any need for a special system of private regulation; rules of an untrammeled sovereign formed the legal structures citizens had to accept.

Interestingly, under the pressure of events the third treatise, *De Cive*, was handed out in private copies shared with eager colleagues and friends. When they favorably received the work Hobbes at first decided he could defer formal publication until the other two parts were completely done. Events, however, again overran his plans. Cromwell's hostile moves against the crown began in 1642. As the royalist cause went into its perilous decline after the Roundhead victorious battle at Marston Moor, Loyalists, including the young Charles II, streamed into Paris. It was against this dramatic backdrop, the *De Cive* was sent out for publication.

Almost at once Hobbes decided that he must try to influence events by taking a different tack. He would write a comprehensive, incisive, and easily read book in English for a wide audience, one in which a vivid and succinct prose style offered his theory of civil government as a practical guide to the solution of the current crisis.

True, the *De Cive* was a political how-to, but Hobbes had left out any foundation theory set in human nature. Until now pages on natural law had been included only in other still unpublished work. Setting himself a feverish pace, Hobbes finished the new project in 1650, and in 1651 the world met the impressive *Leviathan, or the Matter, Form, and Power of a Commonwealth, Ecclesiastical and Civil*.

The result was to be less a salvation for England than trouble for Hobbes. The book's strong secular spirit offended both English royalist émigrés and French Catholics, with the latter being stung by the added offence of an attack on the pope. Again Hobbes fled, this time back to London and the convenient haven of a Lord Protector. Hobbes's flexible *real politik* enabled him to accept with no problem his ostensible enemy now seen through the lens of political accommodation. At age sixty-four it was comforting to emerge from theoretical bookishness and embrace convenient *de facto* government capable of providing security needed to complete the great system.

By this time Hobbes knew that his trilogy would no longer appear unnoticed. *De Corpore* finally came out in 1655 and *De Homine* in 1658. *De Homine* unfortunately hardly fulfilled the great plan, being mainly a treatise on vision. Vision, in fact, seemed now just what Hobbes was lacking, for he did not see the time was not

Frontispiece to *Leviathan or the Matter, Forme and Power of a Common Wealth Ecclesiasticall and Civil*, 1651, by Thomas Hobbes
Courtesy of The Bridgeman Art Library

propitious for a tough approach to law. When the great plague and London fire frightened Parliament in 1666, that body resolved without delay it had better propitiate God by destroying those heretical writings which must have brought down such divine wrath. *Leviathan* was a named nemesis, and Hobbes, nearly eighty, hastily burned some compromising papers. At the same time, having quickly made a legal study of his situation, he tried to cover his flank by arguing that after the dissolution of the High Court of Commission there could be no prosecution of heresy, and that in any case he was within the Nicene Creed. The case was impossible to win, and Hobbes again was a name impossible to publish. Restraint by the censor held back his unfinished *Dialogue between a Philosopher and a Student of the Common Laws of England*. Five years before his death Coke had in 1628 completed his well known "Coke upon Littleton," or "First Institute," part one of his prestigious *Institutes of the Laws of England*. The Hobbes *Dialogue* offered sharp criticism of Coke's constitutional theory from a positive law standpoint, but this last big gun had no chance of being fired. Several humanistic pieces and a promise of something more sent off to his publisher would all come to an end in 1679 when illness and death arrived to celebrate the old rebel's ninety-second year.

Hobbes and Natural Law

To define the necessity of power Hobbes, an uncompromising materialist, worked far behind the Cartesian dual reality of body and spirit and instead chose for his subject every body or piece of matter of which we can have any knowledge. He did not spend in vain eight months with Mersenne in the shadow of Descartes, for he thoroughly rejected the Aristotelian teleological structure of all things having an ultimate essence or form toward which they are changing. Motion being the one thing that "really" takes place, and motion being only a moved body, it promotes the philosophy of "push from behind" (Langer, 157), the idea that everything that happens has its "necessity in things antecedent." Motion is not haphazard: "any effect at any time is produced by a necessary cause." As for thought, its close linkage to sense organs make it but an inner motive apparition. For it is by their motions that external objects "press" the appropriate sense organs; this pressure, carried inward by the nerves, causes a counter-pressure making the cause seem from without. It follows that "'that which is really within us in appetite or desire is nothing but motion…the appearance of that motion we call either pleasure or pain.'" When appetites and aversions to a thing alternate, we are in "deliberation," the last deliberation being "will" (Castell and Borchert, 532, 534).

In this inevitability Hobbes had crossed into determinism to regulate the machines which are living organisms. Having come to personhood in this way—Copleston (Copleston, Vol. V, 31) calls it "atomic individualism"—meant there would be no awkward transition to the defining Leviathan step: forcing creation of a sovereign wielding power as the only way for societal cohesion among individuals. Along the way to this strong executive force, Hobbes also picked up an extraordinary modern touchstone for circumstantial mitigation. Whenever contemporary legal defenses exonerate either tyrants or ordinary citizens on the basis of "push-from-behind" past problems or environments, it is Hobbes who directs the tough approach many find as uncompromising as any Leviathan.

"Atomic individualism" sets up a devastating attack upon Realism and the existence of universals. Hobbes, for example, presented truth and falsehood as being both totally dependent upon language to utter them, and, thus, only attributes of speech. This lack of moral, transcendent idealism still besets humankind and human courtrooms:

> Moral philosophy is nothing else but the science of what is good and evil in the conversation and society of mankind. Good and evil are names that signify our appetites and aversions; which, in different tempers, customs, and doctrines of men, are different....
>
> Every man calleth that which pleaseth him, *good*; and that which displeaseth him, *evil*. *Nor is there any such thing as absolute goodness considered without relation.* (underscoring supplied).
>
> Whatsoever is the object of any man's appetite or desire, that is which he for his part calleth good; and the object of his hate and aversion evil. For these words *good* and *evil* are ever used with relation to the person that useth them, there being nothing simply and absolutely so, nor any rule of good and evil to be taken from the nature of objects themselves; but from the man ... (Castell and Borchert, 535).

Hobbes does not shrink from the implication that man has no free will, nor from the equally inevitable concept that freedom can only be understood passively—not as freedom to will, but as freedom to do what is willed in us. He knew that this position would cause consternation among potential followers and that having set God aside he should nevertheless now return to Him; after all, if he denied necessity, he had denied and destroyed God. Hobbes now readied to draw the shocking yet inevitable conclusion for the world of legality. Since liberty and necessity are consistent, to make a law forbidding an action that an inevitable appetite causes in man is to alter the cause and therefore the appetite. Such law, once made, makes a questionable cause for justice itself. Why not then stress repentance, neither impossible nor foolish. If there is a cause that makes man go astray, he can regret it and have joy in the cause that made him "'return into the right way.'" And what is "the right way"? It is the law of the land, that law which the ruler or body having power to make law elected to make. "'What is it to say an act is good, but to say it is as I wish it, or as another wish it, or according to the law of the commonwealth?'" (Castell and Borchert, 536, 537)

In presenting his new right way in the case for positive law—the matrix meant to keep the collectivity together, the justice for mutual covenant over which watches a sovereign eye—Hobbes had effected the transition from "atomic individualism" to the construction of the State. There he had found a classless humanity. Although in this human maw all could not have the same quickness of mind and physical strength, the variations tended to offset one another with sufficient natural equality so that all people would seek to assure prolongation of life; if some sought pleasure too, they were naturally impelled to it by having a right to all things. The Hobbes portrayal was clearly foreshadowing the eighteenth century emphasis shift from natural law to natural right, here, the right to self-preservation (Friedman, 37). For Hobbes this right—the starting axiom—inevitably causes abandonment of the fierce and brutish state of nature for the ordered, contractual Commonwealth of Leviathan.

Remembering what he had observed in the Mersenne salon, Hobbes had been able to set aside any trepidation in a moralist's firm judgment: seeking preservation and pleasure leads human beings into competition, mistrust, resentment of slights, and quarrels. This is nothing less than war, for war is not only fighting, but the natural state's disposition for it. Hobbes denied the social instinct posited by Aristotle and continued by Grotius. Following Leviathan in the "twisting" sense of the word, he turned sociability 180 degrees into non-sociability. It at once brought him closer to Augustine's idea that sin is the origin of the state than Aquinas's acceptance of the sociability axiom of Aristotle (Copleston, Vol. V, 49). Hobbes observed that by carrying arms on a journey, locking doors at night, and guarding valuables all the time, men prove the veracity of his view of a profoundly anxious collectivity. Actually, Hobbes went on to nuance the immoral portrait. Passions, desires, and the harm they cause are not necessarily sin, since sin, a view consistent with a Hobbesian human—that material machine—is in disobedience only when his appetite for obedience is insufficiently stimulated by penalty. In other words, in positivist Hobbes's approach to innocent until proven guilty, the wrong is not wrong, until a law is made that forbids it.

On the other hand, because appetite for competition, mistrust, and glory is counterbalanced by will for survival and the comfort obtainable by hard work, people are always inclined toward peace. Reason shows this social balance occurs through the "Law of Nature"—not Grotian, but law in the sense of a dictate of prudence. The *Leviathan* presents a set of nineteen such dictates. "Law," being unable to claim the purple of eternal verity, is only the word of one wearing the purple of command. As for the sense of "prudence," it is not morality (that would be an inconsistency in Hobbes) but reason that leads to prudent feelings like self-preservation.

The very first Law of Nature is, in fact, in praise of that reason which impels seeking (a) peace and, when there is no peace, (b) self-defense. Although Hobbes makes clear that no words or signs should be understood as abandonment of the right of self-defense, the second law is that "'man be willing, when others are so too … as for peace and defence of himself he shall think it necessary, to lay down this right to all things; and be contented with so much liberty against other men, as he would allow other men against himself.'" This law leads Hobbes to an important and groundbreaking consideration of contract, the "'mutual transferring of right'"; if one promisor performs and trusts the other to perform later, then it becomes a "'pact or covenant'" leading to the third Law of Nature: "'men perform their covenant made.'" For Hobbes this is the whole of justice: if there is no covenant, no action is unjust. In the state of war there is always fear of non-performance, hence no valid covenants. To have them, there must be a commonwealth and a coercive power (Copleston, Vol. V, 36–38).

The Laws of Nature alone cannot coerce. In the plurality which confers all power and strength upon one individual or one assembly, pluralization thereby reduces all wills into one. Voiced plurality creates this one representative, this artificial person. It is the utilitarian act of reciprocal covenant as though each said: "'*I authorize and give up my right of governing myself to this man, or to this assembly of men, on this condition that thou give up thy right to him, and authorize all his actions in like manner.*'" This done, the multitude so united in one person, functions henceforth as Commonwealth, thus creating 'that great Leviathan ... that *mortal god*, to which we owe under the *immortal God*, our peace and defence'" (Copleston, Vol. V, 39) emphasis supplied). The resulting sovereign is made so by the device of a contract and given choice over the successor. Here is an absolute power comparable to the absolute monarch proposed by the sixteenth century's Jean Bodin or the ethics-free despot of Machiavelli. But in the writing of Hobbes, because it emerges for an England where the commercial class was strong and had a grip on the idea of popular power, there had to be a popular origin for this power.

Men of later times would look upon Hobbes's sovereign as the third-party beneficiary of the citizen contract and, therefore, legally enforceable. They would also take note of the major fact that Hobbes had made the first "modern" use of the social contract. Grotius had portrayed a government limited in law-making by necessary obedience to principles based on human nature. That, for Hobbes, implied insufficient power to guarantee order for the citizenry, and toward that compact guarantee he had conjured a power reminiscent of Job's seven-headed, serpentine beast with six long tongues of flame billowing from his back:

> Can you draw out Leviathan with a fish hook, or press down his tongue with a cord?
> Can you put a rope in his nose, or pierce his jaw with a hook?
> Will he make many supplications to you?
> Will he speak to you soft words?
> Will he make a covenant with you to take him for your servant forever?
> ***
> Will traders bargain over him?
> Will they divide him up among the merchants?
> ***
> Lay hands on him; think of the battle; you will not do it again!
> ***
> His heart is hard as a stone, hard as the nether millstone.
> ***
> He beholds everything that is high;
> He is king over all the sons of pride
>   (*Bible, Revised Standard Version*, Job 41. 1–8; 24; 34)

In the resolution to derive everything from motion by geometrical methods, Hobbes had set aside history and theology—except for God as the first mover. Thus, this Leviathan could not be completely Biblical, but rather lived the metaphoric life of power freed, like the laws of motion, from scriptural constraints. The Biblical point of similarity is that like God's mythic dragon the Hobbes sovereign is not a party to the covenant "of every man with every man." There cannot even be a breach of covenant by him; the exalted, undivided power Hobbes thinks he must have to quell violence precludes it. Moreover, Leviathan's existence does not begin in a separate covenant made among men after "every man" has covenanted with "every man" to create contractual society; the sovereign and society spring into existence together, and there is no moment of time without a sovereign who will enforce the covenant.

A crucial difference with the Old Testament Job is that Hobbes's Leviathan is not a God-made creature. This means Hobbes boldly transferred the metaphysician's cosmology of laws governing the universe to the politician's positive law cosmology governing the commonwealth. In subsequent ages, men have marveled at the giant bureaucracies which the modern Leviathans of nation states tend to become, and they have grieved over the difficulty of controlling these monsters so lacking in conscience. If the leader is an absolute monarch—and Hobbes who abhorred the separation of powers preferred this form to an assembly, whether oligarchical or democratic—it is clearly not because of holding any Divine Right. The sovereign's state is rather a device dictated by utility and necessity to curb the "centrifugal tendencies" of the atomic individuals and their "proneness to self-destructive mutual enmity and war" (Copleston, Vol. V, 41). The result is government which cannot be changed by the subjects, cannot be repudiated, cannot be alienated by the sovereign (though he can delegate certain authority to agencies that have no independent rights and no part of sovereignty), and cannot be forfeited.

Such absolutism, derived in the name of natural law to lead from chaos to contract, is an obviously extreme definition of the term. But the cohesion of Hobbesian society outweighs every other consideration. The sovereign's actions are a response to a need, not an injury to the subjects: the commonwealth action is the citizen's action. With no limits on this supreme judge and jury, subjection to sovereignty must be the first thing that sovereign and the universities teach. In this way alone they instill in all the notion that believing an individual citizen might judge of good and evil and have a conscience is a disease left over from the state of nature. It must be eliminated from the commonwealth. For Hobbes the Church, utterly subordinate to the state, is guilty of having tried to arrogate to itself the authority of the Roman Empire; but no less blameworthy are Protestants who claim for persons or groups a spiritual and temporal authority independent of the sovereign. Divine revelation is impossible as is any universal church; religion is national, and the sovereign has all authority spiritual and temporal over it. It is the sovereign who interprets Scripture, and if a part of Scripture is binding, it is because he says it shall be a law.

Were Hobbes and liberty inimical? He would not think so, pointing out that desires, or appetites, are the result of causes, and that when there is no external impediment to action in accordance with them, there is liberty. He would suggest, in addition, that if the external impediment appears to the uninformed to be positive law with a sanction, the sanction is instead serving to produce a desire to act in accordance with the law—another realm of liberty. The baseline for Hobbes was that obedience to laws made by a sovereign whose acts are the acts of the subjects is not a denial of liberty; any exemption from law means permission for terror and violence.

When waxing historical, legalist Hobbes viewed the celebrated freedom of antiquity's subjects as but a nostalgic misunderstanding of his time. Classical freedom, he felt, merely meant the freedom of the Athenian or Roman state, not the rights enjoyed by an individual Athenian or Roman. Here again, Hobbes equated liberty to the sovereign, not the subject. However—and it is a big however—the sovereign does not and cannot regulate everything. Although Leviathan permits no room for political parties or trade unions, the subjects are at liberty to buy and sell, contract, instruct children, choose their residences, their diet, and their trade.

Because the natural law covenant has been made to procure individuals' peace and protection, two cases legally leave an opening for the subject actually to resist the sovereign. It will be recalled that the first Law of Nature understands that no man by covenant has given up the right to save himself from injury and death. If the sovereign commands that a man kill or injure himself, cut off air or food, refrain from self-defense, confess crimes, or kill another, then, unless the purpose of Leviathan requires such killing, the subject may refuse. Here, however, Hobbes abruptly curtails any modern sense of liberation from tyranny since the citizen may be punished for any refusal. On the other hand, in the second case the mind which had leaned toward despotism does a remarkable turn toward revolutions and declarations of independence a century hence. Hobbes is forced to admit that if the sovereign relinquishes his sovereignty or, retaining it, cannot, in fact, provide protection, then subjects are absolved from duty to him. They then return to a state of nature where they may make another covenant.

Hobbes's position on the authority of the sovereign was such an extreme one that any foreshadowing deviations toward rebellion were themselves overshadowed by the obedience ethos for which history was inexorably making him famous. The Puritans, Huguenots, and other dissenters who feared despotism had no use for a philosopher in whom they saw an obsessive fixation upon preventing anarchy rather than granting liberty. After 1688 liberal minds who feared both sought a solution in the separation of powers. Both England in the Revolution of 1688 and France in the Revolution of 1789 would establish states able generally to keep order under constitutions more liberal, that is, more restrictive of the sovereign, than that generally proposed by Hobbes.

Nevertheless, Hobbes's broad conceptions—first, what he saw as the sole alternative to grubby individualistic anarchy in establishing strong state power and, second, that ability to envisage a when-in-the-course-of-human-events open door to establishing a different covenant—have generally been accepted by the world. Sadly, succeeding centuries have seen more than their share of leaders who egregiously and brutally pushed the darker side of Hobbesian natural law beyond limit. There would be many in the last two centuries who also especially accepted his ancillary conception of a sovereign ruling by positive law, law which he saw as supreme and not open to defiance as being subordinate to natural law. They would admire reflection of the extra-ethical sovereign preference. For accepting natural law as a philosophical conception that encouraged men to look at their current condition and reform jurisprudence in the light of it, meant positive law could also encourage progress. As the major Hobbesian inheritance, this positive law had a theoretical appeal by being more broad than natural law, which remained bound to the conception of human nature. It thus found expression in constitutions and statutes that recognized no limit except the will of the legislator and the political power to achieve obedience. By insisting upon the subjective basis of judgments of good and evil, Hobbes made as well the first comprehensive application to the field of law of the reworked Nominalism which would, in the twentieth century, be called "Legal Realism."

Pufendorf

Introduction

The progress of natural law had been lacking in any systematic success story. First, nationalism, commercialism, and the Reformation had brought along their own special requirement. The new, powerful sovereigns replacing the medieval ideals of Universal Church and Roman Empire needed a political rationale, and it was above all Grotius whose secular rules of justice, suggestive of universal structures, had brought legal clarity to guide an expanding, scientized world. Descartes had then glorified and automatized the power of reason which discerns the non-divine natural law matrix, while Hobbes's materialistic twists had reworked the Grotian concept into reformist positive law. Now it was to be Samuel Baron von Pufendorf (1632–1694) who at last gave to secular natural law the two foundations it needed to begin dominating the intellectual world of Europe: a major, comprehensive analysis; and, to supplement structure, a popular, condensed summary for teachers and students. This jurisprudential work on system and accessibility would climax the seventeenth century's natural law movement.

The Pufendorf books attracted a coterie of professors, salon regulars, scientific societies, and a few enlightened rulers. For them all it was through Pufendorf that came their introduction to natural law and natural rights. The Puritan revolution in England demonstrated the relevancy for such liberal concepts which soon would be providing both tinder and fuel for radical change—in the American colonies in 1776 and in France in 1789. Yet, although these ideas and these changes had important effects upon legal science, Pufendorf's early dominance of the natural law movement fell apart not long after the middle of the eighteenth century. In the turbulent coalescence of thoughts for a new, independent age, his impact, although considerable, was remarkably forgotten. For English readers it is only recently that the legal researchers in academe have begun turning back to him. Their alienation had largely come about when, having followed the old Leibniz denigration, critics like Krieger, author of the major study of Pufendorf in English, declined to take Pufendorf very seriously as a thinker and concluded that his "putatively creative" (Krieger, *The Politics of Discretion: Pufendorf and the Acceptance of Natural Law,* 2) contribution was more the provision of devices for theoretical compromise than successful theory. Ironically, just the very opposite is true. Pufendorf had done no less than to embrace in theoretical structure the whole reality of the law and politics of his time. In the process, he unknowingly, yet inevitably, embraced the outer spaces of law for a modern world.

Pufendorf's Life

Little is reported about Pufendorf's physical appearance and personal habits. It is said that he was severe, that he was lacking in vanity, and that he worked hard nearly all the time, even when living in royal courts where temptations to take it easy were rife. Krieger paints him (Krieger, 2) as a puzzling mix of courage and caution, arrogance and subservience, dignity and dependence.

Samuel was born the second son of a poor Lutheran pastor, himself a descendent of pastors, who lived in a small village in Saxony. Fortunately, while neighboring regions were ravaged in the Thirty Years' War, the village was left intact. Hostilities were only half over when Samuel came into the world, and their horrors deeply impressed him as a child. Though poor in property, Samuel's father had faith, character, and an education. Ambitious for his son to have them, too, he proposed enthusiastically that the offspring become another cleric. That pastor Samuel was not to be, but scholar he certainly became; and though as an adult he was essentially a secularizer in philosophy, his Lutheran faith from boyhood remained unshakable as he raised God to an important place in his thought. Like Hobbes, however, crucial for his legal orientation was standing back from his faith and refusing to base law on revelation or to place it second best to theology.

A local nobleman provided sufficient financial help for Samuel to attend the Prince's School at Grimma, forty miles to the north. For five years he absorbed a medieval curriculum supplemented by Lutheran training in Bible and catechism. To this were added personal excursions into Humanism, transformed later into wide familiarity with the literature of antiquity. In 1650 Samuel followed his brother Esias (1628–1689) to the University of Leipzig, where the older sibling was teaching as a lecturer. Here Samuel began with theology as his father desired, but he soon tired of both it and scholasticism and seems to have followed for the next six years whatever academic offerings interested him. Many students were equally eclectic, and were it Roman law, history, natural philosophy, finance, medicine, or political science—everything offered was pursued without a plan by the active and curious mind.

In 1656 Samuel moved for two years to the livelier University of Jena. Here Erhard Weigel, a professor of mathematics who also taught natural law, was brimming with the day's learning: Descartes, Galileo, Grotius, Hobbes. It was a critical maturation time for Samuel who studied under Weigel and even boarded in his house, a tall, remarkable structure with a deep shaft for stargazing. Weigel's ambitious astronomical work led him to envisage the Cartesian method applied to an elaboration of the natural law of Grotius and Hobbes, even of building with the new mathematical logic a comprehensive system to replace those produced by scholasticism. Esias, now in the Swedish diplomatic service, tried to shift his brother in the direction of politics, but Samuel had carefully made his own life plan. His career would be scholarship; his field of study, the ethical rules for successful social and political life; his method, rationalism; and his vehicle, natural law. Eager to begin this new, off-beat, intellectual journey in which he was apparently making more headway than his master while becoming more and more scornful of traditional academe, he began writing notes for a book and at first refused any further work toward a diploma. Weigel, however, persuaded him to take at least the master's degree. After all it was indispensable for the chosen university career.

Looking now for academic appointment, young Pufendorf turned down what he considered an unacceptable offer to join the faculty at the University of Halle. Then, when no invitation arrived from prestigious Leipzig, he fell back upon his brother's help and, feeling a bit ashamed of the demotion, received placement as tutor in the family of Peter Julius Coyet, Swedish minister to Copenhagen. Suddenly, Sweden, while talking peace with Denmark, renewed hostilities. The Danes cried foul and decided on a foul of their own in retaliation: they arrested the Swedish minister's family including Pufendorf, who suddenly found himself sentenced to eight months in a Copenhagen jail. Here was another Grotius come to Loevestein, for, like Grotius, Pufendorf was to make life-changing use of the loss of freedom. Without benefit of a masterful wife, a library, or of learned conversation he stayed out his term. Nevertheless, by doing so he gained the leisure needed for writing that book he had conceived at Jena. Once he had obtained his prison release, he rejoined the Coyet family at Leiden. Esias and some friends were so impressed by the book born in incarceration that they persuaded Pufendorf in 1660 to publish it. He had evidently thought of it only as a sample of what he could do—a kind of résumé bid for getting a job, once free. But the ambitiously titled *Elementa jurisprudentiae universalis* was impressive résumé material, especially from a twenty-eight year old ex-convict.

Pufendorf, like Hobbes, enjoyed considerable freedom as a tutor. He used the time to study classical philology at the University of Leiden; in addition, he edited and annotated a couple of ancient works and made the close acquaintance of two professors, one of them Grotius's son. Leiden was in the electorate territory of the Palatinate and strongly under the influence of its current incumbent, Karl Ludwig, who enjoyed bringing his royal power to bear through a rather undogmatic Calvinism: tolerant in religion but absolutist in civil government. The political connection to such a Hobbesian sovereign, supplemented by Pufendorf's astuteness in dedicating his *Elementa* to the Elector and in voluntarily writing a legal opinion defending the Prince's right to levy a certain tax, brought him in 1661 the offer of a Professorship in Roman law at the University of Heidelberg. Seidler, summarizer of Pufendorf's life, does not tell us whether Pufendorf's Jena degree had been conferred in actual ceremonial by the law school; one infers that, influenced by Weigel, he had studied under arts or philosophy faculty. In any case, Pufendorf brushed off queries into his credentials by stating airily he had "no desire to add yet another to the 999 existing commentaries on the *Corpus Juris*" (Pufendorf and Seidler, Pufendorf, Samuel Freiherr von, and Michael Seidler, *Samuel Pufendorf's on the Natural State of Men,* 7). Uppermost in his mind came the development and expansion of his own *Elementa*. As he refused the Heidelberg offer, though, Pufendorf with some cheekiness made a counter-offer: appointment instead to the law faculty as professor of politics. In Leiden the faculty on its part seems to have retained no great love for the ideas of their philology alumnus; but they probably took some heat from Karl Ludwig to prod their University senate to offer an associate professorship on the philosophy faculty in international law and philology. Pufendorf did accept this new field, even though at heart it actually was the Leiden law faculty to which he aspired and probably German constitutional law which he wanted to teach (Krieger. 20).

A law faculty was "the establishment" in juristic matters, and the fact that Leiden's professors had really not wanted him cut deeply with Pufendorf. In 1664 he himself changed his title to professor of "natural and international law" and later told everyone how he had held Europe's first chair of natural law. Before the titular change he had been passed over yet a second time by the law faculty, and he now burned his bridges by rewriting the two essays he had initially hoped would get him a law appointment. The revision was a bold one, for it changed a careful applicative approach into an unexpected broadside against the Holy Roman Empire and the guild of constitutional lawyers who faithfully defended imperial existence. Pufendorf reduced such partisanship to anachronisms that ought to disappear. The revised manuscript was published in 1667 at The Hague as the purported work of one Severinus de Monzambano, a traveling Italian nobleman. It was another instance in the long history of the law when an important reformulation of philosophy had arrived from outside the domain of legal faculties and practitioners. Seidler calls it an "aggressive, brilliant, and incisive" attack on what the book's author daringly regarded as a "freakish" institution (Seidler, 8). Not surprisingly, this idea of the Empire as incompatible with modern, sovereign states elicited an instant and angry response. Not only did the Pope condemn the book, but it was banned from universities. Still, in the end, Pufendorf proved not to have been so excessively rash, for even the hard-nosed Karl Ludwig liked the book and approved publication, although at The Hague rather than in Saxony. Pufendorf continued formally to deny authorship until the edition of 1684.

In the meantime Pufendorf prospered. His 1665 marriage to the well-to-do widow of a colleague brought him comfort and two loyal daughters. In his professorship, the lecturing on Grotius and his own new ideas proved popular with students, some of whom lived in the Pufendorf home where they listened in fascination as propositions were crafted for the provocative and exciting new intellectual wave. The proud Elector made Pufendorf a privy councillor and put him in charge of the education of his son. Heidelberg's textual holdings, although sacked in 1621 during the Thirty Years' War for the benefit of the Vatican (D'Irsay, *Histoire des universités françaises et étrangères des origines à nos jours,* 30), had been partially restored, and Pufendorf found pleasure in being able to rely on the "home library" to deepen and broaden his learning. Here he confidently went forward on the Grotian route of legal assimilation or, as he would have claimed, legal derivation of all law from natural law. His reputation spread, and in 1668 Charles XI of Sweden offered him a professorship at the new University of Lund, this time as fully accredited law faculty member holding a prestigious chair in natural and international law. His brother Esias had risen in the Swedish diplomatic corps; and Pufendorf, who had encountered many young Swedish notables in his classes, did enjoy seeing himself as a far-ranging humanist of that informally honorific "Republic of Letters." Still at odds with the law faculty at Heidelberg and tempted by the higher salary offered by the Swedes, he was content to accept the proffer and in 1670 began the teaching and writing that in all would lead to eighteen years of Swedish service—the most fruitful period of his career.

At Lund Pufendorf continued his research and writing on natural law, publishing in 1672 his eight-volume masterpiece, *De jure naturae et gentium*, to the praise of his friends and consternation of his enemies. Pufendorf was proud of the book's title, inclusive as it was of law between nations considered among themselves to be still in a natural state. He rapidly followed up the next year with a two-volume *Epitome*, or summary for law students: *De officio hominis et civis juxta legem naturalem* (*On the Duty of Man and Citizen According to Natural Law*). The change of title to the lengthier variation remains an unexplained mystery, given that the *Epitome* is a condensed form of the first work. Perhaps Pufendorf felt that as an educator as well as a legal philosopher his didactic message for youth should stress the ideal of duty. The longer title would impress; the shorter text would be accessible.

Because it was an essentially secular natural law which this devout Lutheran was putting forth, Pufendorf now began to face fierce and troublesome theological opposition. In advance preparation he had taken the prudent political point of view, dedicating his major work to Charles XI and the Epitome to Count Gustave Steinbach, Chancellor of the University. He had even gone beyond the normal protocol by previously obtaining publication approval from both men. Nevertheless, nothing could hold back Lutheran politics which pressed the attack. Pufendorf's confessor, Joshua Schwartz of the Lund theological faculty and Nicholas Beckmann, Professor of Roman law, both ostensibly jealous of Pufendorf's overflowing classes, had already demonstrated bad feelings soon after Pufendorf arrived at Lund. They now charged their colleague with "innovations" contrary to Lutheran orthodoxy, and far worse still, made the incredibly lurid allegation that Pufendorf had murdered his parents and raped his servant (Seidler, 56). Steinbach directed the University's defense; while Pufendorf, in a lengthy series of essays published as pamphlets, made devastating replies marked by satire, wit, and colorful, blunt language. His ripostes were collected and published as a book in 1686. The King finally had to silence Schwartz and Beckmann by official decree.

Pufendorf's research and writing now changed. Whether caused by intellectual development inspired by the essays as Krieger suggests (Krieger, 23–24) or by bitter controversies swirling about his professional position, Pufendorf stopped his exploration of natural law and turned to official political history. As the Danes laid long siege to Lund in 1676, Charles XI called his scholar back to Stockholm as privy councillor, secretary of state, and royal historiographer. Pufendorf had, in fact, earlier given some historical lectures at Lund, and there was thus an intellectual continuity between this former endeavor and the new assignment.

Having attempted the "juristic analysis of politics in terms of universal law and obligation" (Pufendorf-Tully, ed., *On the Duty of Man and Citizen According to*

Natural Law, xiv), he would now turn to past European diplomatic relations as seen through a long chronological perspective culminating in the Peace of Westphalia (1648). The scholarly challenge was again to be a Grotian project: Pufendorf encased law within a diplomatically flattering context: official histories commissioned by the reigning monarchs who now were to employ him. The men were all deeply concerned for the positive rationalization of their desires, as well as flattering lighting to illuminate their deeds and those done by their recent ancestors. To his credit and to their satisfaction, Pufendorf walked the tightrope, dexterously meeting the many bureaucratic challenges and restrictions.

Service to Charles XI ended in 1686 when Pufendorf next accepted a prestigious post in Berlin as royal historiographer to Frederick William. The Great Elector had been trying to bring the star law professor into Prussia's orbit for two years; Sweden was in decline, Prussia was ascending, and Frederick William is said to have had a wish list for mistresses and historians like those of the French Sun King, Louis XIV (*Biographie Universelle,* 286). Offer and acceptance, however, were not going to be quite enough to get Pufendorf to Berlin. He was at this time approaching in his historical writing the reign of his current mentor. Charles XI had a Swedish imperiousness clearly resembling Queen Christina's rapport with Descartes, and he strongly preferred to hold his philosopher in the Scandinavian snows with the idea that in the royal presence the historian might better, as Seidler writes (Seidler, 11), understand the royal merit. Only in 1688 did Charles relent and "loan" Pufendorf to Berlin for two years, keeping back the essentially completed manuscript lest it suffer change in Berlin and, more crucially, lest the writer not return.

Frederick William died shortly after Pufendorf arrived at the Berlin court, but since successor Frederick III added privy and judicial councillor to the titles of secretary and historiographer, Pufendorf, thus even more honored, seriously began on Prussian history. Life would as well grant him the leisure to examine church-state relations, and in response to Louis XIV's revocation of the Edict of Nantes in 1685, the visiting honoree attempted to extend natural law into the litigious realm of religious problems. But time was not to continue her generosity. When after the two-year loan period the idealistic jurist finally made a return to Sweden before going back to Berlin by sea, he could boast a "Von" before his name and royal permission to publish his Swedish history manuscript. He had, however, unfortunately joined Grotius and Descartes as a victim of ambition fatally fulfilled in northern weather. The cold sea voyage proved too much for the fatigued and aging scholar, and illness complicated by a poorly healed injury to his foot wrote his last chapter on 26 October 1694.

Pufendorf's Works and Style

Pufendorf left no direct descendants, but what he did give posterity were sixteen major works which broke new ground in natural law. His fundamental assumption had been similar to that of many scholars in the Middle Ages—Roman law *is* natural law. By starting with the state of nature Pufendorf freed himself from beginning with trite statements of legalisms, ancient or modern. Law, he would show, could be free to pick and choose.

We can divide his *œuvre* among three groups. The first and major group consists of the three books constituting his attempt at a comprehensive political, moral, and legal philosophy based on natural law. These works are the ones that concern us here. They are, rendering the Latin titles in English, *Elements of Universal Jurisprudence in Two Books* (1660); *On the Law of Nature and Nations in Eight Books* (1672; with second edition by Pufendorf, 1688); and *On the Duty of Man and Citizen according to Natural Law in Two Books* (1673). The student's condensation of *On the Law of Nature,* uncut, runs a hefty 1,367 pages in the Carnegie edition of 1934. To these three may be added *On the Natural State of Men* (1675), Pufendorf's final statement of his ideas concerning nature. For *On the Law of Nature* and *On the Duty of Man and Citizen* Krieger counted no less than thirty-five subsequent editions in the original Latin, thirty-nine in French, fourteen in English, and sporadic publication in German, Italian, and Russian.

The second group of Pufendorf's works flowed from the professorial farewell to university teaching in 1676 and entry upon new duties as royal historiographer. This historical work can be seen, as we have noted, as a second and competing approach to the subject of politics and law in the seventeenth century, and, as such, has been called a "prototype of Enlightenment encyclopedias of cooperative politics" (Pufendorf-Tully, xv). The third group—the smallest output—was the effort to define connections between religion and government. In a conceptual sense, Pufendorf's search for the external relations of states had here led him from natural law jurisprudence to history. His continued concern with understanding the base of internal relations of such polities also led from natural law to theology—or what he called church-state relations.

Once again, with its mix of abstract and technical expression, the professorial Latin style aroused little enthusiasm. H. F. d'Aguesseau (1688–1751), three times Chancellor of France and a distinguished lawyer who shall soon make his appearance, wrote for his son instructions as to the studies appropriate in the training of a magistrate. D'Aguesseau was brutally frank: might the son have more courage than a father who had never been able to finish reading Pufendorf. According to the Frenchman, only northern scholars thought highly of Pufendorf's hefty treatise. (Avril, a Paris doctor of law, kept this negative tradition alive, writing in 1903 (6) that it was actually a Frenchman—Jean Chretien of Bogneburg [1622–1672]—who first conceived a *Corpus Juris Naturae*.) D'Aguesseau much preferred Grotius and while conceding Pufendorf's profundity, faulted the scholastic, obscurantist writing style. Foreseeing that the young man might well be bored with the original, the father recommended Barbeyrac's 1706 translated abridgement, which, amusingly, the father did not seem to know was, in fact, Pufendorf's very own epitome. And so it went, with severe stylistic criticism continuing into the eighteenth and nineteenth centuries. It was said that Pufendorf, although judicious and methodical, lacked warmth and movement. Readers read but felt they could not see the point, so dry, hard, and cold was a writing style conceived like a proposition in mathematics. It took until 1922 when Wehberg brought in some fresh air by commenting

(Pufendorf-Tully, xiv)—as others would, too—that complaints against Pufendorf's style were tiresome exaggerations which themselves completely obscured the excellence of the Pufendorf content.

Influences on Pufendorf

It is a good thing that Gilbert and Sullivan never found their way to Pufendorf, what with his baronage, melodious name, and his studies of juristic affairs Roman, customary, town, and royal. They would have concentrated on the shallow question of whether or not Pufendorf's Jena degree may or may not have authorized him to practice law, and in their glee, imagining him to be an arrogant fraud, totally missed the profound depth of knowledge combined in his efforts. It is true that the fact he never did practice could account for the substantial omission of legal procedure in his natural law works. For him law meant substantive private law supplemented by the public law of political organizations. Insights of an able advocate into the ways procedure can often control the result in litigation—in spite of substantive law—played no part in his efforts. Yet, there is no reason why natural law should not have some application to procedure, and the problem he posed for himself involved reorienting its detailed development in statute and decision, thereby creating a new synthesis in thought about what public and private law should consist of in the years ahead.

The materials that had been put before him in his university education and that he continued to pursue intensively until arrival in Stockholm were science and its mental giants as presented by Weigel. The Pufendorf *cogito* was intellectually to reflect these influences—the Cartesian equality of the man-animal, the Grotian sociability and civil compact, the Hobbesian fear for self—then hone it by the very practical need to infuse the modest Pufendorf fortune with wealthy patronage. For Pufendorf, mind always was—disappointingly some would say—linked to money matters; and on that day when without cash or connections he made the decision to follow an intellectual career, he committed his thoughts to a life of dependency and royal patronage which would force legal ideas to open toward the ways and means of absolute power.

Since these several interests were to some extent actually or potentially in conflict, and since it was the character of Pufendorf to try to harmonize rather than to defy, the thought structure he created has not been able to satisfy scholars who look for rigorous internal philosophical consistency. Evidently, Weigel did not succeed in instilling in his student's mind either those strong, sharp thrusts of absolutism that distinguish Hobbes or the revolutionary outlook of Grotius. There was recoil from the mechanical world posited by Descartes, as well as from the materialism added to the French mechanics by Hobbes. To this idealism, however, Pufendorf would bring his own cynical sense of the practical based on experience in the world. In contrast to Descartes with his little joke of a framed pay voucher, Pufendorf's philosophy was heavy and blunt: in universities as in wars "'what comes first is money, what comes second is money, and what comes third is money.'" "'When one's subsistence is not provided for,' he concluded, 'one loses all desire to do anything.'" Pufendorf may have been an intellectual, but it was this bourgeois side that urged on sovereign central authority to ensure stable state power. Krieger goes so far as to propose that with the cynical Pufendorf it is principle that is malleable, while practical interests are written in stone. Was Pufendorf overwhelmed by too much variety in the field of morality? Was his logic for wisdom so weak that we must accept Krieger's metaphorical stricture (Krieger, 34–35; 245; 51) that "the owl of Minerva took flight in the morning"?

Some Philosophical Characteristics of Pufendorf

If Pufendorf's ideas were often inconsistent internally and straddled acrobatically the problem of natural versus positive law, his commitment to legal thought remains more complex than the evanescent loyalty of Krieger's owl. By leaving science to one side for concern with ethics, he had soon reached, via mentor Weigel, the idea that separates him from Grotius, Descartes, and Hobbes. Simply put, this was that moral concepts, tempering and securing an order and decorum in civilized states, are willed to, or imposed on men by other men or by God. In his *On the Law of Nature* (Pufendorf, Samuel Freiherr von, Introduction by Walter Simons, C.H. and W. A. Oldfather, trans., *De Jure Naturae Et Gentium Libri Octo,* 3–5) Pufendorf spoke of these concepts as being "certain modes…added to physical things or motions, by intelligent beings, primarily to direct and temper the freedom of the voluntary acts of man, and thereby to secure a certain orderliness and decorum in civil life." Pufendorf went on:

> Now the classification of natural things seems to have been sufficiently treated by those who have so far undertaken the consideration of that science, but it is perfectly clear that they have not been as much concerned with moral entities as the dignity of these requires…. It is the task of others to set forth all that in the way of concepts has been discovered…[as to]…the infinite variety of things. It is for us to observe, how…a specific kind of attribute has been given to things and their natural motions, from which there has arisen a certain propriety in the actions of men, and that outstanding seemliness and order which adorn the life of men. Now these attributes are called Moral Entities, because by them the morals and actions of men are judged and tempered….

Thus, physical entities are produced originally by creation, but moral entities in their stability and their variations are produced by "imposition." They "do not arise out of the intrinsic nature of the physical properties of things, but they are superadded, at the will of intelligent entities, to things already existent…." They cannot directly produce any physical motion nor do they change anything, but they "'make clear to men along what lines they should govern their liberty of action'" (Krieger, 74). "Moral entities, regarded as the analogy of substances, are termed moral persons. These are either individual men, or men united by a moral bond into one system…." But they are not physical men, they are "status," and one man can have more than one status at the same time. Otherwise regarded, they are "modes," which have quality (the way persons are "affected" in a certain manner) and quantity (the way they are "valued"). Moral entities, since they "owe their origin to imposition," from this obtain both their "stability" and their "variations"; and when such imposition "has ceased to operate," they disappear "just as a shadow disappears the instant light is extinguished." Since certain of these moral entities are imposed by God and others by the will of men, they can never "attain to the strength of a physical quality." A "person" can be imposed upon an individual, but he has not received a "permanent moral character" (Pufendorf-Tully, 6, 11, 16, 21).

The interesting idea of intrinsic norms originating in "imposition" sets Pufendorf apart from the ideas of Hobbes, more complicatedly mechanical and physical. Leviathan rulers were translated through the motions of external objects creating pressure which, carried inward from sense organs to nerves, caused pleasure or pain in alternation—first through deliberation, then will. Similarly Pufendorf has declined to follow Descartes's deistic view that living objects like inanimate objects move according to physical principles—body and soul separate, with the soul from its pineal gland base directing the mechanical motion of the body—so that God is not needed to understand the world once it is known that God does not deceive the senses.

Pufendorf assures his readers that his moral science is, like the geometry of Euclid, a matter of demonstrative certainty. He is undaunted by what he feels are Aristotle's erroneous ideas that "[t]hings noble and just, which are the subject of investigation in political science, exhibit so great a diversity and uncertainty that they are sometimes thought to have only a conventional, and not natural, existence ..." (Pufendorf-Tully, 22). Perhaps the value (size) of a moral entity cannot be measured with a ruler, but the quality of a moral entity is entirely different: it can be measured with scientific certainty.

Essentially metaphysical, Pufendorf promised results both universal and immutable. As he sought like Weigel for his personal axiom that all men would have to accept, he joined the intellectual throng and utterly renounced scholasticism as lacking the grace of Humanist scholarship. By classifying particulars rather than expanding knowledge, it led to polemics rather than agreement. Although Pufendorf ironically was a self-proclaimed Humanist, his new way to an axiom was not through intensive historical study in an effort to reconstruct the past. Moreover, he would not confine himself to deduction from his axiom. His tactic would be investigation and the prodigious recollection of nearly all writers (minus the Second Scholastics). In other words, Pufendorf decided on the highly modern, non-judgmental induction of natural law from human practices, grappling with what humans do as bearing heavily on what they ought to do.

Pufendorf, Grotius, and Hobbes on the Source of Law

Almost a theological "I am, therefore I am of necessity also with you," Pufendorf's axiom rested on the fact that to be safe, man in the weakness of his nature had to be sociable. While rejecting (with Grotius and Hobbes) Ulpian's idea that natural law is common to man and beast, Pufendorf did acknowledge man as a human animal. As he put it in his *Epitome* (Pufendorf-Tully):

> Man…is an animal with an intense concern for his own preservation, needy [when] by himself, incapable of protection without the help of his fellows, and very well fitted for the mutual provision of benefits. Equally, however, he is at the same time malicious, aggressive, easily provoked, and as willing as he is able to inflict harm on others. The conclusion is: in order to be safe, it is necessary for him to be sociable; that is to join forces with men like himself and so conduct himself toward them that they are not given even a plausible excuse for harming him, but rather become willing to preserve and promote his advantage…. [T]he laws of this sociality … are … natural laws … [and]…the <u>fundamental</u> <u>natural</u> <u>law</u> <u>is</u>: … <u>cultivate</u> <u>and</u> <u>preserve</u> <u>sociality</u> … [while] … all that … makes for sociality is understood to be prescribed by natural law. All that disturbs or violates sociality is understood as forbidden (Underscoring supplied).

Pufendorf would not shy away from contradicting and opposing both Grotius, the Realist, and Hobbes, the Nominalist, even though they were the two thinkers he cited most. Grotius, he noted with regret, had believed natural law to be the same without God once God has made determination of man's nature. But Pufendorf believed that what springs from man's reasoning from human nature cannot be law simply because law of necessity supposes a constant superior. The fact that some actions are good or evil because man's nature so requires does not mean morality can exist without law. Man has received his nature from God; the morality of actions must therefore come from the same source, and Pufendorf judges Grotius wrong to "refer the wickedness of some human actions to the class of things to which the power of God Himself does not extend." Still, Pufendorf's stance is not really so far from Grotius as he would have theological critics believe. Natural law—an ideal imposed on fact—may have been imposed by God, but God either created man's nature to be consistent with this natural law, or, having created man, God at least by implication had to set up the natural law appropriate to the creature He had created. Since, as Pufendorf assumed, "the world of nature and man remain constant, the law of nature, even though it was formed at the beginning at the pleasure of God, <u>remains</u> <u>fixed</u> <u>and</u> <u>unmoved</u>" (underscoring supplied) and "by this statement God is made the author of natural law." God is the great "imposer." But then, in one of his characteristic consistency shifts, Pufendorf draws back, reducing the place of religion in the very center of God-made natural law: "[T]here seems to us no more fitting and direct way to learn the law of nature than through careful consideration of the nature, condition, and desires of man himself…" (Pufendorf-Tully, 215; 30; 185; 205).

Perhaps because Grotius's *De jure praedae* had not yet been discovered, Pufendorf did not present Grotius as the thought bridge across which science had marched into seventeenth century law. That place he allocated by implication to Hobbes, although he nevertheless deemed Grotius to be the founder of modern natural law. Hobbes held a persistent attraction simply because, in applying methodological rigor, he had attempted a science of society along paradigms of mathematical science. But there were limits. Pufendorf showed no willingness to follow Hobbes's ideas about positive law. And, being accused fiercely by Leibniz and the Lutherans of holding discipleship to the English atheist, Pufendorf did admit Hobbes was seditious by holding that "what the legislator commands must be held *good*, and what he forbids, *evil*." Although moral entities owe their origin to imposition, "and for that reason are not in an absolute sense necessary, yet they have not arisen in such a loose and general manner, that scientific knowledge about them is on that account utterly uncertain." In addition, Hobbes would have it that heads of families in the state of nature acted like kings of the day, uncouth *paters* who violated no justice. Surely, pleaded Pufendorf, this is as wrong as it was unjust before states were formed not to honor pacts. No king, insisted Pufendorf (Pufendorf-Tully, 25–26; 1138–1139) with what we would consider the utmost in naïveté, is "so senseless as to enjoin something which is forbidden by the general laws of nature," for in the surety of natural principles of right there is "justice...before civil laws are defined."

Yet Pufendorf could not help demonstrating his own Hobbesian touch. "Knowledge of good and evil" does not "belong to individuals"; they are not permitted to pass judgment on the "aptitude of the means which a prince orders to be undertaken so as to secure the public good." Moreover, to hold that natural law meets "the full requirements of a science" we need not declare "that some things are noble and base of themselves without any imposition"; we should not define such actions as "natural laws," while those that "depend upon the will of a legislator, fall under the head of positive laws." For good and evil "are affections of human actions arising from conformity or non-conformity to...law, and law is the bidding of a superior" and that therefore they do not "exist before law, and without the imposition of a superior" (Pufendorf-Tully, 1139; 27).

Does such back-and-forth theory make Pufendorf a Realist or a Nominalist or just a clever attorney general? We must probably say the straddler paid visits to all camps. In seeming to rest all on God's power and will, he clings verbally—and scholastically—to Ockham, whom, it must be noted, he does not cite. The idea that the interaction of man and his environment changes the nature of man awaited Darwin in the nineteenth century. Pufendorf does agree with Grotius, however, that even if God can change the nature of the humans he created, he does not do so. Natural law has to be consistent with the intrinsic norms of that nature—good, firm and uniform, not dependent on the changeable opinions of men. As to universal principles, Pufendorf decides men lack freedom to choose. Not even Plato envisaged a natural law so universal and immutable that it would apply to every imaginable creature. Pufendorf thus does not clash with Grotius in the method (study of human nature) or in the result, (what, in general, natural law provides); his apparent Nominalism and positivism are in this sense inoperative, put aside so that Realism might produce results. By clouding his theory with the idea of "imposition" Pufendorf sought to avoid excessive offense to kings who find pleasure in the idea that their will takes effect as positive law and has a broad scope. He realized how practical politics lead rulers to give the Almighty some scope, too, and how pleased they are to have everyone believe that God wants obedience to royal law. No less pleased was Pufendorf, who, despite his inconsistent and wobbling stands, tried as well to avoid offending theologians who always wanted God to come first.

In prefacing his edition of the *Epitome*—which it will be remembered, is *On the Duty of Man and Citizen According to Natural Law*—Tully pointed out that an objective of the Grotian tradition of natural law thinkers—often presented as a seventeenth century Dutch/English trio by including philosopher Richard Cumberland and lawyer and statesman John Selden—was to conclude by working into natural law theory that the teleological basis of natural law—Aristotle, Aquinas, Catholic Reformation, and the Lutheran theologians—had been refuted once and for all by Galileo and the scientific revolution. Thus did the new natural lawyers attempt their hard sell of nature as atoms set in motion by God without purpose yet obedient to laws. Tully concludes (Pufendorf-Tully, xvii) that for Pufendorf to make strong insistence on "extrinsic imposition of moral concepts and laws by a superior onto an unordered realm of human movements" was not actually necessary in meeting such an objective. Noting that Grotius, whom Pufendorf took as founder, did not adopt it in his solution of Realism, Tully supports our conclusion that the dramatic "imposition" side of Pufendorf's acrobatic straddle was actually ineffectual, if not untenable, especially since struggling to emerge was a bombshell of civil rights.

Natural Law, Positive Law, and Theology

The mixed messages of the Pufendorf stance make fairly clear he did not want to be challenged as an opponent of either revelation or the positive laws of the state. Sensing religious differences as irreconcilable, Pufendorf knew the new scientific morality would definitely have to be independent of them to survive (Pufendorf-Tully xviii). The *Epitome* repeats the concept of a natural law inferred by right reason from the nature of men; civil structures as foundation of positive human laws equate to legislative imposition. As for the possibility that the latter will contradict the former, Pufendorf tries hard to reassure his reader that the silence of natural law on a subject covered by civil law in no way implies a conflict.

At the same time, all was definitely not felicity, and Pufendorf now seemed ready to speak for the "when" in the course of human events. The sovereign, superior to civil law, might find appropriate to conform to it when it applied. But the citizen was no doormat and for his part might claim that an unpopular civil law, set in an area contrary to natural law, could not be binding. For Pufendorf's royal patrons, and for Pufendorf, this posed a very delicate situation which the jurist could not confront squarely. Fortunately, no revolution loomed on his horizon, and he thus at first took a detour around it, as Krieger says (Krieger, 3) by pounding, bending, and snipping "the radical doctrines of the new natural law…until it became acceptable and respectable." A bit of elegant contortion and savvy accommodation thus at first seems to be the key to Pufendorf's legal sociability. However, unexpected and exciting eloquence fills those pages on which, with a pre-revolutionary idealism worthy of a Declaration of Independence, he proposes that the sovereign meets limits by agreement at the time his rulership is conferred and his manifold duties are set forth: to work at his job; to keep the people safe; to regulate by clear, written civil laws only as much as is necessary. Above all, the sovereign must not forbid by civil law what natural law does not, because contemplating behavior, a human being will deliberate more on the basis of natural reason than by knowledge of the civil law (Pufendorf-Tully, 152).

Although Hobbesian policy insists that will of the state translate will of the citizenry, Pufendorf rejects Hobbes's contention that a "state cannot do an injury to a citizen" merely because there is no pact between the two entities. Pufendorf's far different approach, utilizing a Grotian tack, opens wide the possibility of injury of state to citizen "since there exists between them a community of natural law." Consideration of such injuries is limited to extreme cases, as when the prince "abandons all care of the commonwealth," or "subverts basic laws." On the cusp of the Enlightenment, Pufendorf dramatically allows the daring surmise of a line beyond which the citizen need not bear such injuries without complaint and might even seek redress through force "in some cases." In his typical retreat style he shies away from any talk of outright rebellion, advising that even in case of a frightful injury it is better to fly, than take up arms. Nevertheless, one senses barricade material has made a powerful appearance. Citizens, says the Baron, without a blink or a retreat, cannot in the formation of a state give up God's sovereignty. They are not bound, after the state is created, by any command of a prince which violates a command of God (Pufendorf-Tully, 1103–1108, 1111).

And thus it was, that on some matters as to which natural law is indefinite, Pufendorf knew it was desirable that the civil law not define a duty since this latitude could permit good men to be seen acting justly without compulsion. Pufendorf left this large space of action within which natural law does not speak, yet within which, positive law can operate without making any authorial choice as to what that positive law should provide. The number of natural law rules remaining is, however, still very considerable, and twenty-first century natural law writers will condemn being forced to study such an overly detailed rule book. Pufendorf, never silent where natural law is silent, reviewed carefully the customs and the civil law, giving them, in Krieger's words, often a "radical, rational refounding" on the basis of his theory of human conduct. Any conflict tended to be dismissed by Pufendorf, holding fast to a discipline which united humankind through a common sense of duty (Krieger, 61–62, 68). In fact, Pufendorf's natural law system could never do without civil law. Nor could Pufendorf cease struggling to separate natural law from the ethical universe of theology. He did try to avoid trouble by admitting that what the Bible enjoins, but reason cannot encompass, had nothing to do with natural law. What is more, he determined that for external actions in this life, the greatest difference is that natural right is judged in the human court while moral theology confines the mind to God's chambers. But, nevertheless, in that human court of sociality, the very mainstay of natural law, Pufendorf heard equally clearly the Sermon on the Mount: love God and love your neighbor. Listening to both worldly and divine axioms Pufendorf's legal lyric ended up ready for the future when revolutionaries sang about their secularized natural law in settings as diverse as *Au clair de la lune* and *La Marseillaise*.

Pufendorf's Arrangement of Topics

The structure of *On the Law of Nature* and *On the Duty of Man* had been new. When the *Elementa* appeared as the first book on natural law, a strong structural emphasis reminiscent of Descartes and Wiegel (Krieger, 51) and a conscious imitation of Euclid organized the whole text under the headings of twenty-one *Definitions* and two *Axioms*. There was as well a formal if brief bow to Galileo in the five categories called *Observations*.

Structural reminiscences aside, the *Elementa*, too, was a book of departure. Its unusual composition in an exile jail without books meant quotations and citations were omitted and ideas scattered. But this outsider's iconoclastic creativity translated well a mind which wanted to found a new school of legal thought. Pufendorf aimed purposely at a cutting away from the traditional—from medieval volumes, from theology, history, and old authorities. For him, incorporating the best of the contemporary luminaries like Grotius, Descartes, and Hobbes was the beacon to illuminate the way by deduction from rational principle. His plan was clear: investigate concrete moral, legal, and social relations and institutions in a manner that would appeal to leaders and men of affairs. He recalled how Grotius in his major treatise of 1625 had abandoned the geometrical form of his youthful *De jure praedae* yet retained the geometrical reasoning. Pufendorf followed suit. Geometrical form of the *Elementa* had been laid aside by the time of his major treatise of 1672 and the 1673 *Epitome*. Both, however, kept an allegiance to the scientific method.

Every law student knew the Justinian *Institutes* structure, which, although arranged in four "books," conformed essentially to the classification "persons," "things," and "actions." It was a format which in Pufendorf's time was still favored by each European law faculty as the essence of preparation for the bar. The credentials were impeccable: origins in Gaius and usage by a myriad of writers after him, including Grotius put on a pedestal for his *Institutes of Dutch Law*. But Pufendorf, who was convinced he was drawing his water from a wider and deeper well by choosing the method of science rather than verbal logic, felt compelled to pour into different bottles. He would boldly ignore that most fundamental of continental distinctions: public law and private law. The *Institutes* had consisted mainly of private; Pufendorf intended to cover not only as much of that as he could derive from natural law, but also as much public law as was similarly derivable, along with aspects of ethics seldom or never reduced to this domain. Focusing on the whole duty of a citizen in a modern state—those responsibilities necessary for the sociality which alone could assure security and which shine forth from the *Epitome*'s title change to *De Officio Hominis*—Pufendorf conceived his work therefore as a list of duties. This seems overly simple to our modern minds, nourished by the complex, interlayered work on jural relations of the twentieth century's Wesley Newcomb Hohfeld, *Fundamental Legal Conceptions: As Applied in Judicial Reasoning and Other Legal Essays*, in which rights are supplemented by privileges, immunities, and "no-rights," each with its correlative "duty" correspondent to "right." Nevertheless, Pufendorf's "list of duties" did produce a broad succession of important topics: self-defense and necessity, protection of personality, duties of good faith, property (including succession), obligations, and family. Even in the miniscule space which five volumes of Pound devote to Pufendorf, that writer honors the seventeenth century plan of topics for its resemblance to nineteenth century treatises on the *Digest*.

Human Nature and the State of Nature; The Pufendorf Method

Human nature and its axiomatic, ancillary handmaiden, group theory, form a philosophic keystone Pufendorf could not induce from experience given mankind's visible works of divisiveness and inconstancy. Nor could he count on revelation by God, since the human condition was an imposed given. What was required was a universal moral science to deduce human nature by examining man in his natural state. Pufendorf's solution would be the first theory to present early modern bourgeois society this ideal environment against which to test existing conditions. Human essence in a state of nature is usually delineated as a neutral base with which classification must begin. Pufendorf, though—the prisoner once cut off from society—admitted that because such a state never actually existed before human intervention, save in modified and partial form, he would first have to envisage a tactical disengagement. Denying existence perhaps to avoid prickly theological involvement with the Garden of Eden, he proposed initially a "pure" abstraction of non-existence before human intervention. Next, he construed life as a "modified" abstraction, coming after families but before political, covenantal association of kinship units.

In applying natural law to current human conditions, Pufendorf had commenced with conditions—Roman law, the customs, modern statutes—and looked there for consensus. This, unfortunately, compromised his claim to have deduced natural law purely from axiom. He, in short, had laid down a universal with a circularity problem. Beginning with man and his institutions as they were in his time, his approach abstracted a universal concept of a generic human, then used the characteristics of this generic concept to deduce human behavior in the 1600s. From this circle he emerged believing that, although in the pure state the main characteristic and norm of man is liberty, in the modified state it is cultivation of sociability. One notes that where Grotius, following Aristotle and Aquinas, thought that sociability is innate, Pufendorf took it out of the innate into the necessary.

Krieger (Krieger, 80) makes his own *nota bene* that Pufendorf's human nature is not a self-evident proposition on the order of the Cartesian *cogito*. The relation of natural law to human nature is logical rather than metaphysical, a "hypothetical necessity" rather than an absolute. The mathematical analogy is evident. Man defines an abstraction, let us say a right triangle. He then deduces the Pythagorean theorem from the definition—an axiom. In nature there is no pure right triangle, yet the theorem aids a real life carpenter in natural situations that are similar to the abstraction. Putting it another way, it helps societal engineers build a working model of the economy. Pufendorf's abstract human had thereby been signed up for the job of laying out rules for actual, contemporary citizenry. His optimistic first version of what would become modernity's tragic Hollow Man was gradually yet positively Human with a void that law could fill with commitment and aspiration. Such definition of and response to needs of a changing society make it clear why to read Pufendorf is to hear law with a fresh voice. Authors like Krieger and Seidler discuss Pufendorf's central theory of sociability as in fact lying near the heart of a liberated "commercial" philosophy in which value assumptions emphasize freedom to succeed in a material economy.

Pufendorf's Attempt at a Complete Jurisprudence

It is Pufendorf's "fundamental natural law" of sociality, laid down *a priori*, which reveals both method and goal: find the axiomatic center upon which all men must agree however different their religions, nationalities, and characters, and from which they can deduce a detailed body of natural law. In some degree scientific, the method involves observing persons and inductively deriving a law as to their nature; nevertheless, his facts from causal experience bear the anecdotal imprint characteristic of the seventeenth century rather than rigorous analysis in laboratory style. One would expect that a truly scientific system of deduction from the nature of the human might lead to some results quite different from rationalizing the institutions of his time and place. The pseudonymous call of *Monzambano* for constitutional reform in Germany simply to make the facts fit theory was uncharacteristic; but Pufendorf, more than rationalizing contemporaneity, speaks as the author of books rich in information for any legislator trying to bring the civil law of his state up-to-date and into peaceful sociality. His call for imitation gratifyingly worked especially well with Frederick the Great, who modeled his new code for Prussia on Pufendorf's work.

Always deducing from the axiom of sociality, Pufendorf's Epitome carefully parses out natural law duties—to God, to oneself, to other men. Each category is limited by as much as deemed derivable by natural reason, recognizing that some of these natural laws are not legally actionable. Making his "reflection on the fabric of the universe" under the rubric of duties to God, Pufendorf entertains philosophical proofs for the Divine existence by presenting as bases the necessity of a first cause of motion. Obligation in worship is essential in appreciating religion as the "ultimate and strongest bond of human society" (Pufendorf-Tully, 39, 43). In considering responsibility to oneself, Pufendorf presents a compendium of paternal advice: the duty to care for mind and body, the need to be temperate, to exercise, to refrain from suicide, to work hard, to take risks for others, to be obedient, to defend one's person and property—here the paternal advice has quite a liberal note for an absolutist age—and to be alert when necessity creates an exception to law. Some of these categories are given with considerable detail, although much less than was afforded by the Roman and customary law of Pufendorf's time to those deemed "legal." Yet although all are good advice and probably were followed by the Roman jurisconsults in their personal lives as carefully as by any group in history, such inclusion in a law book of homilies on wisdom and the art of life would have been quite a surprise to the stiff-backed law giants of Rome.

Frontispiece portrait of Samuel von Pufendorf from
Pufendorf's Law of Nature and Nations, 1716
Courtesy of The Lawbook Exchange

The protocol of duties to other men occupies the remainder of the *Epitome's* first Book. Pufendorf's axioms are many, and included among these golden rules are educating oneself, making beneficial discoveries, not impeding anyone of benevolence, manufacturing available goods which can be offered without loss, not damaging beneficial societies facilities (such as road signs), winning reputation by practices both extraordinary and consistent with good sense, and showing gratitude for all benefits received (Pufendorf-Tully, 56, 61, 64). Here Pufendorf begins in his attempt to answer the Grotian call for a complete, or nearly complete, coverage of public and private law. One senses how he progresses only as far as he feels the legal universe can be deduced from natural law; at this barrier the attention shifts, finding the needed supplement in present and former positive law. The injunctions, combining legalism and evangelism, begin with the duty not to harm others, and this evokes rules for compensation, accessories to injuries, causation, conspiracy, negligence, and responsibility for acts by one's slaves and animals. Next comes the Abrahamic duty list in treating the other person—and here as elsewhere Pufendorf evinced a highly restrictive male orientation to personship. That other must be viewed as an equal, at least as an equal under law; one must not injure another's sense of self-esteem, one must serve others as one would receive this service, divide common property equally, avoid pride and signs of contempt, and accord due precedence. Third is consideration of duty to be useful to others. There is even a duty which any parent would appreciate: showing gratitude for all benefits received (Pufendorf-Tully 64).

The fourth duty brings Pufendorf into the actionable arena. If all the benefits which men might legitimately expect in a state of sociality are to be received, then necessity equally exists of making binding agreements and of having rules that cover such fulfillment. The main method by which such benefits can accrue is by contracts creating rights against another or others. In Pufendorf's system the enforcement of such contracts by means beyond God's sanctions is achieved by contractually forming a state.

Over the next centuries natural law thinking was increasingly to encourage the importance of such contract law, and Pufendorf would influence the provision of some of its rules. A step ahead of the Romans, he writes, for instance (Pufendorf-Tully, 66, 69), that when the parties intend an enforceable agreement it is "perfect" and enforceable; otherwise it is "imperfect." Other areas of contract terrain cover matters of expressing consent. Pufendorf looks into the capacity for mistake, fraud, force, impossibility, illegality, as well as promises which cause another to act, mutuality of consent, conditions, and agency. The forgoing duties he calls "absolute"; all others presuppose some human institution existing by agreement.

In addition this insinuation of a societal contract brings to discussion (Pufendorf-Tully, 76ff) two suppositionary duties: language-use and ownership of things, and the value of things. The natural law against deception clearly requires this language component if it is to be successful. One must agree on a certain vocabulary and disclose one's mind clearly, but only as to what another has a right to hear. Pufendorf, mindful of his many encounters with diplomats and sovereigns, privileges language shaping—to say something different from what one has in mind and withhold thereby a hurtful truth. He also considers what constitutes veracious speech and the different rules for oaths.

Discussion of the ownership of things covers wide terrain. There are allusions to the natural realm, not as an ecologist, but as a pragmatist who accepts the privilege to hunt and consume for sustenance despite pain caused to flora or fauna. There is the Humanist's stance, looking back at the time when the world's few inhabitants accepted possession as ownership, then, as demographics changed, accorded burgeoning populations new and complex property rights in things. God wills it, and men must consent at least tacitly. Ownership implies power to dispose of property at will and bar others unless they acquire a right by agreement. Limits upon it come from the civil power, and Pufendorf offers rules as to acquisition of titular ownership, profits from property, servitude, details as to transfer by operation of law and by the owner, succession at death, wills, gifts *inter vivos*, transfers by penalty and by prescription. He passes in equal detail to the economy of duties arising from ownership and then to consideration of problems of equality of value in exchanges, of money, and of effects of markets on values. Next he considers "contracts which presuppose value in things and the duties they involve" (Pufendorf-Tully, 97)—a subject which brings up more depth: loans for use, deposits, barter, sales, hires, loans for consumption, partnerships, bets, raffles, insurance, suretyship, and security. This legal panorama closes Book I with a magisterial dissolution of contract obligations: performance, compensation, release, breach of faith, changes in one's financial situation, passage of time, death, delegation, and interpretation.

The State of Nature and Human Institutions; The State

Book II of the 1673 *Epitome* brings Pufendorf to a third and major suppositionary duty—human government—as for the first time he faces duties to perform in the context of differing social positions. He evidently felt a preference to discuss "language-use" and the "ownership and value of things" before considering that state, yet was faced with a philosophical base which would seem to precede human institutions existing by agreement. As structured then, Book II deals with ideas familiar from Book I: men's natural state, duties of marriage, duties of parents and children, duties of masters of slaves and employees, and the reason for constituting the state. Under the last heading Pufendorf again ranges widely across public law: internal structure, sovereign power, forms of government, supremacy of civil authority, acquiring authority, duty of sovereigns, civil and criminal law, reputation, power of the sovereign over property, war and peace, treaties, and duties of citizens.

Pufendorf begins by saying that in his axiomatic social life man's state is either natural or adventitious. Marriage and the resulting relation of parent and child are expressly placed in the extrinsic category; we infer that being a master and being a ruler or citizen of a state are such also. In the natural state considered rationally man has a duty to worship the Creator, one of many acts divinely intended so that humans be set apart from animals. By the vehicle of imagination, Pufendorf leads us to consider a man in a natural state in which there were no support from any other man. Either because of his weakness he would die at once, or one can imagine and consider him in this natural state relating to other men. Because the others would be similar in nature there would be a common kinship preceding any agreement among them; with no common master, no one would be subject to another. Since this can be but a fiction, Pufendorf thereby concludes that in the natural state which actually exists, each person, in fact, is joined to others in special association, implying no more duty toward others in other groupings than to citizens of different countries or different states.

Arrival at this as his remarkable "in fact" *voilà*, the reader is jolted with the conclusion that never was the whole of humanity in the natural state. Even the children of Adam and Eve were under family authority, and it just happened that as people multiplied and certain of them wandered, the natural state emerged for some, while others went into family establishment. Membership in scattered families was little better, not so much because of poverty as lack of security. Further multiplication produced living close together, at first in small states and then in larger ones. Joining many of his fellow philosophers Pufendorf has come to a Hobbesian confession: although the liberty of a natural state might seem attractive, it is a bleak scene of eat or be eaten. When Vico (1668–1674) came to contrast the states of nature of Grotius, Hobbes, and Pufendorf, he could see them all with the eyes of Dante. In the first writer wandered a population of "solitary, weak and needy simpletons"; in the second, "licentious and violent men"; and in the third, a hapless set of "vagrants cast into the world without divine care or help" (Copleston, Vol. IV, 157).

However, to Pufendorf belongs the saving grace of legal procedure. He surmises that, with too much threat still existing, the new communities had resisted contentment with these simple associations and gone on to form complex states for the richer enjoyment of benefits in fellowship. Despite the surmise Pufendorf must continue along the road, realizing that any state cannot consist of men lacking subordination to any one of them, for a morass of humankind obtusely and stubbornly has the habit of defending the wrong options without indication of the only one who is right among many. Moreover, without compulsion a being is indolent. So Pufendorf brought forward his next *voilà*—a swift verbal, Hobbesian kick: the wills of the many must submit to the will of one man or one assembly whose will as to matters of security is to be taken as the will of all. Here lies the great juncture of the state, says Pufendorf (Pufendorf-Tully, 136), the moment human groups must accept two legal agreements and a legal decree. Agreement one: all must concur on becoming fellow citizens of a state; any who do not so agree are at once outside the compact. Next comes the decree: there will be majority fiat on the form of government to be instituted. Finally, there must be the second agreement (although here Pufendorf does not expressly say all must join in it): appointing the man or men on whom the government is conferred. The governor then will promise to provide security, and the governed will promise to obey. This duet of obligation triumphantly brings Pufendorf to the creation of a true state: moral man in composite and full format, with a name, rights, and property. When Pufendorf says "man" at this apogee he unfortunately means it; his state is male-created and male-run.

Succession, Wills, and Family

In the maintenance of the human body, needs both physical and cultural are met within the state construct by a proliferation of property, a material excess accepted by Pufendorf as the will of God and natural law that man should use things. Ownership began either as original in primary assertion or derivative through transfer from another. Pufendorf felt that after the introduction of property anything not taken in the earliest division went by convention to the first occupier; these derivative transfers were by act of the owner or by operation of statute. Such goods were not to be deemed abandoned, since Pufendorf—and, he believed, reason as well—suggested that they should devolve according to human feelings: first, on our descendants and next on our blood relations by degree of proximity. That goods pass on death in intestate succession was again in his eyes, emblematic of the preservation of compact tranquility and, therefore, natural law.

These dominant interests of peace required following common inclination and ignoring the personal feelings of the few who might favor an outsider. Hence occurred the natural law order of succession: children and grandchildren of both sexes, parents, brothers, and next of kin by blood. It fell to positive law to specify details and to a more enlightened time than Pufendorf's to include wives and sisters.

Where Grotius had written that the privilege of dividing things by will is assured by natural law, although the details of form are left to positive law, the Pufendorf approach lay in transfer by act of an owner. Natural law embraced only transfers *inter vivos* and those intended to take effect at death. Since such transfers were for positive law only, wills entered regulation in that domain.

Before going into the nature and origin of human government Pufendorf had paused—accompanying himself with his usual crushing humanistic back-up of sources—to consider matrimony, the kinship source of families and, therefore, of states. These he conceived as made up of lesser societies, either simple or associative. Of simple societies he delineated three: the husband, the father, and the master. God having made the sexes, implanted in them a mutual attraction so that they would "willingly and joyfully" have offspring. But natural law imposes beyond attraction a duty to marry and raise those offspring to preserve mankind. This duty overcame what Pufendorf saw, with a touch of the Rousseau to come, as the equally natural reluctance to undertake the trouble of having and raising them. Parenthood being a delight of nature, the unmarried mother is forbidden by natural law to avoid disgrace by killing her child, and, indeed ought to have been thinking about the matter before conceiving. On the other hand, natural law is not violated when the marriage produces few children rather than many, or when the wife is barren. However, a Pufendorf frown and a legal violation come when the parent indulges in obscene gratification, "for this lust disturbs the peace rather than knitting minds together" (Pufendorf-Tully, 839, 842). In need of today's DNA testing and woman's rights, Pufendorf appears understanding of a man, unsure of paternity, who will neither offer nor supply the labor and expense of childcare.

Whether a man has an obligation to marry or not was the next question, and Pufendorf reviewed many opinions. Certainly, he found it wrong to emasculate men against their will for, considering natural law alone, men are only obligated to enter into marriage when the conditions are favorable. Civil laws can require marriage in appropriate cases, though it is more mild in enforcement to use rewards or deprivation of advantages rather than positive penalties. Civil codes are the choice for legal specification whether a state office be better filled by an unmarried person; civil laws set the time and age for marriage or have the power to forbid certain union—for example, with a nobleman, a plebian, or a foreigner. And, with a prescient revolutionary foreshadowing that stepped forthrightly on many Church toes, the civil law was seen as capable of confining marriage vows to performance by a state officer.

Pufendorf completes his matrimonial sequence with the natural rights of both parties before and after marriage. His blend of natural and contract legalities leaves much uncertain and open to positive law: maternal versus paternal governance, parents and mature children in the home, rights and duties of children out of the home. There is the exciting, clear call for nuptial equality in the 1672 treatise: "By nature all individuals have equal rights." Also the faintest light of women's freedoms glints momentarily through the fog of sexual ambivalence. First the fog: the male surpasses the female in strength of body and mind. Then the light: this does not give him conjugal authority over her. This must come only "by her consent"—

here the glint for feminism—or by a "just war"—back to Andromache or even *Taming of the Shrew* phallocentrism. The first method Pufendorf promotes as better for wives, the second for handmaids. Fortunately, men who do marry women captured in "just war" and subsequently made into slaves usually lay aside the harshness of a master's authoritarianism. If the pact of marriage be only to give one another the service of the body, then no authority is conferred upon the one partner over the other. Tradition, however, usually governs: by nature the husband should court the wife, while she, in turn, should promise to admit no one other than him to her bed and to live in closeness to him (Pufendorf-Tully, 853, 855).

Pufendorf and Equality

The aspect of Pufendorf's work which was the most innovative and would have in the French Revolution's transformational century the greatest impact was his electric democratization credo of equality. The Middle Ages had tended to regard people not as individuals but as members knit into a group; each cadre of membership, from manor to monastery, had its law. Rudely was this system shaken by the rise of national power demanding centralization, uniformity, and bureaucratic service. Then with the humanism of the Renaissance came emphasis on this world and the capacity of the individual to make the most of it; by the Reformation breakup of the Church universal arose the necessity for each individual to seek within sectarian beliefs a personal understanding of the requirements for salvation. By the Scientific Revolution, the great challenges were set, questioning the earth-centrality and God-controlled providence of the old theology and quickening the pace of all the practical arts with which individuals could enhance their lot. No less than it now does in the twenty-first century, it was this last scientific whirlwind as the 1600s began which seemed to promise a method separate from religion in which individuals could rewrite the rules for living with one another in the modern state.

When Grotius stepped into this context, his offering of natural law promised the basis of rules for the individual. Then Descartes, declining to attempt such rules, broke through with an exciting idea of the individual human unit, a machine subject to strictures, each man the same as every other. Hobbes, passionate for peace at any price, defined the man-machines, but they now seemingly had lost their Cartesian souls and were controllable by laws which defined good and evil according to whatever the legislator chose. Finally, it had come down to Pufendorf's credo to empower the inevitable implication of Descartes and Hobbes: all humans, though different in strength of mind and body, stand as the same under natural law. With resolve to provide the rules for the equal human units that Descartes had left uncomposed, Pufendorf resolved upon the fundamentals of these rules—coming from God's determination of human nature, avoiding fallible legislators' dictates to suit their fancy. It was this modern outlook, expressed in the hesitancy to base any case on equal units as mere machines, that brought Pufendorf's democratization to the more advanced "moral entities" whose nature had been made by God.

Pufendorf's concept of such human nature thus was presented as a universal applied seamlessly to the unitizing man, each person equaling the other (Pufendorf-

Tully, 333). It was the beginning a new legal fiction of the Ordinary Reasonable Man, concealing the physical truth of idiosyncrasy, wearing the mask of sameness essential for the eighteenth century's shattering concept of equality before the law. Between Pufendorf's *On the Duty of Man and Citizen According to Natural Law* and the declaration of the National Assembly in 1789 *On the Rights of Man and Citizen* neither similarity nor difference is accidental. Similar they are, because for each, men are equal under law. Their difference arises because where Pufendorf emphasizes his concern that men shall do their duty to secure peace and sociality and thus achieve security, the National Assembly will be more concerned that each man shall have a legal dignity to be respected by law.

Living in an age when the power of princes was supreme and living out a career in which he was dependent upon these potentates, Pufendorf, courageously and as an article of faith, did not shrink from following his reason straight to individual parity. There he found and accepted an equality that, while denying divine kings as it denied social pariahs, also promoted national equality of states with each other. Thus in Book III of *On the Law of Nature* Pufendorf begins Chapter I with the strong impact of the subject of obligations, a rubric which in continental law includes the English law subjects of torts and well as contracts. On these pages two absolute duties of the love thy neighbor paradigm occur under natural law even before the formation of any human institution: "I. No one should hurt another; and II. If he has caused another a loss he should make it good." The dramatic intensity grows even greater in Chapter II, boldly entitled: "All men are accounted as naturally equal." The words (Pufendorf-Tully, 313, 330) are a memorable and eternally relevant civil rights manifesto:

> ...there is to be observed (in man), deep-seated in his soul, a most sensitive self-esteem; and if any one undertakes to impair this, he is rarely less and often more disturbed than if an injury were being offered his person and property.... [T]he word 'man' is felt to have a certain dignity... 'I am not a dog or a beast, but as much a man as you are.' ... [H]uman nature belongs equally to all men. ... Every man (by natural law) should esteem and treat another man as his equal by nature, or as much a man as he is himself.

A twenty-first century sensibility divines at once that Pufendorf is concerned with the profound, innovative concept of "the duties of natural right": "... [H]owever niggardly nature or fortune has been toward a man, he is not condemned on that score to share less fully than others in the benefits of the law.... [W]hatever law a man appeals to against another, he must under every circumstance admit against himself." Perhaps shivering a bit in the rarefied air any prophet feels on the mountain, Pufendorf again brings up the reinforcing troops, citing similarities to Phaedrus, Diodorus, Siculus, Quintilian, Seneca, Cumberland, Euripedes. Diversity helps him as well, via a statement by a Native American who, being brought from New France to see Charles IX, commented that the most striking thing he had seen in the capital was that the beggars did not attack the wealthy and seize their possessions (Pufendorf-Tully, 332–333).

Except for that inequality of power which of necessity resides in the head of a family, or in the head of a state and his delegates, it is just this sort of prejudiced dichotomy against which Pufendorf is writing, promoting "equality of right" deep within the common obligation of all men to cultivate a social life as an integral part of human nature. Do not all mortals find their origin in a common stock whether nobles or peasants? Are not all our bodies of the same substance, and conceived in the same manner? Does not that "portal," the womb, "usher the noble as well as the plebian into the divine light of day?" And does not "Death with foot impartial ... (as Horace says) ... knock at the poor man's cottage and at prince's palaces?" Are we not all alike subject to God's inscrutable power "to speed whom he pleases" and leave others as the "sport of fortune?" (Pufendorf-Tully, 334, 344).

Natural equality is the basis for contracts among men, and it is in Chapter IV of the same Book III that Pufendorf discusses the topic we touched on earlier: the necessity in sociality of making and keeping agreements. In contracting for services, until about the beginning of the twentieth century, freedom of an individual, whether princeling or laborer, was strongly protected in legal systems appropriate for a dominant middle class. Still, laborers had for some time wondered about the value of a power to negotiate a contract when penury made it necessary in the morning to take whatever terms were offered to get money for dinner in the evening. Even this Pufendorf seems to anticipate. Stating the legal issue from Robin Hood to entitlement, he considers the question whether necessity gives the poor man a right under natural law forcibly to take from the rich for the support of life, even though by natural law property is inviolable. Pufendorf's conclusion is a dose of more liberal natural law: the rich have a duty to aid the poor, and only if this duty has been made definite in positive law and enforced through its structures should there be a penalty for theft in distress.

Before we put Pufendorf on the soapbox amidst civil libertarians, listen to his comment on slavery—not established by nature but originating in acceptable contract as "goods for work." Listen, too, as he ponders the grant of life to the defeated enemy in return for a lifetime of servitude. No, it is not natural, but there is an appropriateness that positive law should countenance and regulate in process. More prescient is the manner in which Pufendorf consigns nobility to dwell outside the "natural" camp. Pufendorf, who rose by merit alone, believes the qualities associated with *noblesse* "come just as well from common birth," that the class is simply a status conferred by the sovereign using practical positive law so that a man nobly participate in military service to the state. Equally up to our date is his waiving any natural law requirement that a son must succeed to the office of his father (On LN 934, 936, 941, 1262, 1263, 1269).

In the end Pufendorf's advanced thoughts certainly did not attempt to ignite social strife by arousing the poor against the state or even by fomenting the bourgeoisie against the king and clergy; he worried, when all is said and done, within the stiff hierarchical and gender limitations of his time. Nevertheless, deep concern for order could not withstand his more passionate concern for freedom and his remarkable vision of equality. Modern, on the cusp of modern, or simply thoughtful, we must admit the bravely outward-looking ideas of a pastor's son to be vehicles ready and waiting for the sermons of Enlightenment's new law preachers. Born from a scientific revolution, such thoughts could only lead to a social cataclysm.

Pufendorf's Successors; Rise and Fall of His Reputation

In the late seventeenth century and the first part of the eighteenth Pufendorf's books had an immense popularity in Germany, at least among Protestants. Christian Thomasius (1655–1728), professor of natural law at Leipzig and later founder of the fine faculty of law at Halle, provided the official statement of the Pietist philosophy in religion. His was an eclectic, empirical, and rather unsystematic attitude which included tolerance and opposed Lutheranism; by 1720 his followers dominated in the faculties of nearly all the German universities, and to them he taught from his studies of natural law, carrying forward and completing the work of Pufendorf.

Christian Wolff (1679–1754) was another German philosopher of large influence whose study of Pufendorf also enhanced the influence of the latter's work. Wolff started his career as a mathematician the better to prepare his mind for scientific studies. After 1706 his career transformed into a professorship of law at Halle. Wolff lacked originality but was extremely systematic. During his middle years he lectured in philosophy and produced the eighteenth century's most coherent system until it collided with minds like Cassirer whose opinions consigned Wolff's attempt to failure. Wolff decided he had to begin anew from the essence and nature of man and make a code of natural law more complete than the Pufendorf model. Wolff's natural law, dominant in German universities until Kant, was purely rational and not dependent on God's will. In the seventeenth and much of the eighteenth centuries the French universities, dominated by their Most Catholic Bourbon majesties, would have none of him, while in England the near absence of academic effort in law left him known only to a few.

During most of the eighteenth century French universities did not read Pufendorf, since it was only after 1775 that natural law found its place as an academic subject. Nevertheless, outside of the law faculties, he and Grotius always stood for *the philosophy of law* in France's learned circles. Montesquieu, Locke, Diderot, and Rousseau all paid him serious attention. Here, they felt, would be appropriate and recommended reading for the enlightened monarchs; Diderot had no hesitation as he placed him strategically into his model university curriculum for Catherine II of Russia. The situation in England was similar, although Pufendorf's progress there was retarded by lack of a scholarly establishment in law. The earlier mentioned Jean Barbeyrac (1674–1744), professor of civil law and history at Lausanne and of public law at Groningen, translated Grotius's *De Jure Belli ac Pacis* and Cumberland's *De Legibus Naturae*, as well as Pufendorf's long and short treatises (1706). His fame rests on his preface and notes to Pufendorf's *On the Law of Nature*, an endeavor of wide circulation and important in the propagation of Pufendorf's thought. Together with the English translation by Kenet, Barbeyrac's French translation of Pufendorf crossed the Atlantic and entered American political literature. But it was Switzerland's Jean Jacques Burlamaqui (1694–1748), for fifteen years a University of Geneva professor of ethics and natural law and member of the Geneva Council, who with a simple and clear style put Pufendorf into more symmetrical and intelligible form in his *Principes du droit naturel* (1747) and *Principes du droit politique* (1751). A friend of Barbeyrac and a fellow Calvinist, Burlamaqui was read carefully by Blackstone and many Americans and preferred by the Encyclopedists. Even earlier, Gershom Carmichael (1672–1729) who taught ethics, jurisprudence, natural theology, and political economy, brought the new philosophy to Glasgow University, publishing in 1718 an annotated edition of Pufendorf's *Epitome*. Carmichael's notes to Pufendorf are linked to the formation of Adam Smith's ideas; Smith studied Carmichael's edition of the *Epitome* as a student under a Professor Hutcheson, Carmichael's immediate successor.

As scholarship gained stature during the eighteenth century's broadened interests, the Ulpian-Papinian dominance weakened just enough to open the door for Pufendorf, who was delighted at this sudden *entrée* onto the academic stage. Then, in the second half of the century, just when Pufendorf's strong, plain talk style seemed on its way to being transformed into the heady message of democratic rebellion, he begins to be lost from sight.

Recent studies of scholars like Haakonssen, Palladini, Hartung, Hochstrasser, Carr, and Seidler have begun to expand the meager Pufendorf bibliography and to propose answers for his success and previous eclipse. Seidler attributes Pufendorf's rise during his lifetime to his role, conjoined with others, in opposing the skeptics of the late sixteenth and seventeenth centuries, among them the tower sage of Bordeaux, Montaigne. His work answered the search of the Mersenne circle for moral as well as physical certainties to create a weapon against Montaigne's tempting denial of the possibility of universal and immutable guides to man's conduct. Recognizing Grotius as the first modern natural law thinker and Descartes as an anti-skeptical leader, Seidler and the others tend to include Hobbes also as a natural law thinker in opposition to enlightened skepticism. The recognition is generally reasonable, but the inclusion of Hobbes seems questionable, given his weak combat against doubt. Hobbes makes natural law, as he defined it, the basis of his rationale for seeking absolute government at any price to get order and security; but once his sovereign is in place, he has no more use for it. The positive laws of the sovereign, not moral certainties, define good and evil. The sovereign makes the laws at his pleasure.

To explain Pufendorf's relatively sudden disappearance from the briefcases of scholars and students, Seidler points to two new philosophers: the first is the devastating Nominalist and empirical skeptic David Hume (1711–1776) whose *Inquiry Concerning Human Understanding* was published in 1748. The second is Immanuel Kant (1724–1804) whose *Critique of Pure Reason* appeared in 1781. Although Kant replied to Hume's doubts, he was able to see reason's limits in a way that transcended doubt and dogmatism. Did Hume and Kant—and later Buhle (1802) and Standlin (1822)—make Grotius and his followers seem irrelevant? Or is Pufendorf, his ideas transformed into new institutions, one of those seminal thinkers who become anonymous when their thoughts progress stunningly from the innovative "what if..." to *fait accompli* banal? How often has success in infusing the universal intellect itself presaged failure in retaining a niche with fickle fame. To quote Georgio Tonelli's perceptive comment (*Encyclopedia of Philosophy*, Vol. VII,

343a) on Pufendorf disciple Wolff: "…[his doctrines] were so widely accepted that they began to appear trivial and he was thought of as a commonplace philosopher."

Pound and others who dismissed the originality of Grotius denied as well Pufendorf's deduction as mere restatement of Roman Law; Pufendorf, of course, would retort that this was precisely what he was trying to avoid; and revelatory of this attitude is the following statement from the preface to the 1688 edition of *On the Law of Nature and Nations*: "…everyone knows that most of the material in the books of the Roman Law concerns the subject of the Law of Nature and Nations…but there is interspersed with it much that is positive, and of application to the special nature of the Roman state" (Pufendorf-Tully, iii).

So today we shall await the research that remains needed to compare in detail *On the Law of Nature and Nations* with the *Digest*. Even without it, one can realize that Pufendorf invited lawmakers to a much broader frame of reference than the *Corpus Juris Civilis*. Whether the axiom of sociality—in fact, in logic, and in necessity born of Euclid—could lead with any clarity to conclusions on all the vast assemblage of rules in Pufendorf's treatise, let alone the conclusions drawn by him, is a question the nineteenth and twentieth century lawmakers answered uniformly in the negative. For a twenty-first century lawyer, however, there is hope that the great pages resonate as a seminal historic work, one of daring and prescience which, more than had ever been suspected, helped activate human rights while setting all lawmakers free.

Réparation faite à Louis XIV (Reparation Made to Louis XIV)
Courtesy of Yale University Art Gallery

Part 15

The Expansion of Secular Natural Law in the
Seventeenth and Eighteenth Centuries
Louis XIV and Pascal

The Progress of Secular Natural Law

Overview

As the Roman Church clashed with the Reformation, minds like that of Grotius decided the divine source of law had lost the power to unite humankind. Its earthly manifestation built on Peter's rock had been split, probably irrevocably, by the thesis/antithesis of faith in struggle. The old perception of authoritative unity about what the great Godhead required for salvation became lost, as contending parties struggled on through bloody physical combats of ever greater intensity. There grew a desperate need for a new theoretical foundation in ethics, what one might call a synthesized consequence of divergence on which all people might once again come together and resume with hope their earthly quest for order and tranquillity. Taking under one epistemological roof the powerful phenomenon of natural law was to prove the opening for secularizing that law. Unfortunately, the new theory did not escape the vice of the old base: although its ideas were presented as universal, the leading exponents so far—Grotius, Pufendorf, Wolff, Burlamaqui, and others—were Protestants; and in the universities of Catholic France, the new ideas were not even conceived as part of the curriculum.

We have, then, reached a point after which our legal story shifts, leaving the strongholds of Holland, Spain, and Germany, just as earlier it made the quantum leap from Italy. Some may be surprised that the English did not also make a move at this time, but we have already noted that but for exceptions like Bacon and Hobbes, a fairly low state of progress continued in regard to legal philosophy and academic law. Ironically, the still gaping void in viable ethics would be filled by France's dominance over Western Europe—in politics until 1763, in language, literature, and art until 1815. In 1660 the population of France was 20 million, while Spain and England counted only 5 million each, Italy 6 million, and the Dutch Republic 2 million. The Holy Roman Empire boastfully claimed 21 million, but these were citizens in over four hundred *sovereign* states, each with its own laws, government, army, and currency; none had over 2 million people and, being weak, in decade after decade some of these political entities fell to the French Bourbon kings. In contrast, Louis XIV was to bring unity for almost seventy-five years. He would live at the world power center, conferring laurel wreaths on geniuses from science and letters and creating the world's greatest military outreach.

When History's long, irregular, but relentless movement toward a centralized French nation state arrived at the stunning strength of the absolute Louis, it had only one more step before culmination in the almost equally grandiose absolute power which Napoleon, made Emperor in 1804, was going to exert over the nation. Both high points were occasions when a thorough change in the legal system made possible such exercise of central power. Under Napoleon it would be complete: reorganization of the courts and restatement of French law in codes. Unlike Napoleon, Louis XIV coped uneasily with ancient *Parlements*; his strongman's reach toward reducing them to submission effected incomplete but nevertheless immense change, and the Versailles enterprise of gilt and glory frightened and inspired half the world.

In this age of France accompanied by a crescendo of new legal discussion, two approaches gradually stood out enough that they were able to lead an unstoppable progression toward modern law. The first was the Enlightenment. Flourishing in the academies and salons outside the Church and universities before exploding into the mighty rebellion which overwhelmed both of them and the monarchy, the movement had a bluntly simple platform. Society, it was proposed, should dissolve the earthly institution of the Catholic God and, by banishing Him from any further consideration, free Frenchmen to appropriate as much of Protestant natural law as they wished. The second approach, rather than emanating from a broad intellectual movement, was instead the specific work of one man, Jean Domat, whose jurisprudence for the natural man will be the topic of greater detail in the next part of this book. Domat's interests had grown from a background combining devout Catholicism and Bible study, close contact with the Scientific Revolution, deep training in humanistic Roman Law, a career in the long robe of the bar during a period of progress in French law and legal education, and the generous personal support of the greatest Catholic monarch, Louis XIV. Not accidentally, to this top heavy curriculum vitae must be added Domat's close association with the French Catholic reform movement called Jansenism, which was, in doctrine though not in polity, not far from Calvinism. The Jesuit apostles of the Catholic Reformation, fiercely opposed by the Jansenists in religious interpretation and the practical care of souls, did not produce in the seventeenth and eighteenth centuries an important work in natural law. The Jansenistic way, which Domat shared with his close friend Blaise Pascal, at first may seem ill-placed in study of "Secular Natural Law"; however, at least by implication, it was a successful recognition of the inevitable worldliness of the new jurisprudence. Thus, with Pascal and then Domat, the long official reign of religion over law which had flourished ever since Constantine beheld the cross in the sky of 325 neared its close. What could never end, however, was the ethical cast and structural integrity that had framed modern legal thought's origins from the eleventh century papal revolution.

Louis XIV
Legislator and Legal Educator

The King and Colbert

As Louis XIV began his reign, conditions cried out for solonic remedy. There were an excessive number of judges and jurisdictions, to say nothing of uncertainties as to their powers. The legal world buzzed with a multiplicity of systems for procedural and substantive law. Each social class, each region, each town, and even each professional corporation had its own law. The long extant venality of judicial affairs accounts in considerable part for the former, while the fragmentation of power after the fall of Rome wrote the historic origin of the latter.

It would have been French farce were it not so serious a matter. Imagine an advocate preparing his case. He would be forced to consult the Royal Ordinances, the town charters, the jurisprudence of the *Parlements* and the courts local and royal, the books of jurists, the immense library of the canon law, and the countless sources he had been told at the university were essential. There was as well the annoying multiplicity of customs which had created an imbroglio of counsel that both lawyers and sovereign found especially offensive. Reduced to writing in the sixteenth century, the prose accounts were generic rather than quantitative and led to a seemingly endless parsing of behavioral acceptability. For instance, one single collection published in 1724 contained sixty "general" customary bodies of law and three hundred "special."

A comment offered earlier in this book bears repeating again: when one considers the endemic fragility of monarchical inheritance and the particular fragility of the Bourbon successions over many centuries, it is extraordinary that a royal family, in such crucial need, should have produced for law a successful crowned response. Ready and, he felt, able for the task of attacking and rationalizing legal chaos, the twenty-three year-old Louis celebrated the death of first minister Mazarin by declaring he, the monarch, would alone henceforth serve as *his own* first minister.

The remarkable grand gesture came from one only five feet five inches in height. But what the Sun King- to-be saw in his mirror was a figure strong and athletic, handsome, healthy, and proud of a prodigious appetite for food, women, and action. One-quarter French, one-half Spanish, and one-quarter Italian, his youth took heart from art and love. His was to be the longest recorded reign in European history, and he would astound France and Europe by his prodigious hunting, partying, and intrigues. At the same time he unfailingly worked hard every day, spending six to seven hours in meetings and more hours in his study. Intellectually, while not a scholar and with little taste for abstract reflection, Louis was quick to learn. He felt and showed interest politely, patiently, and astutely enough to pile up considerable success by a series of small moves (Olivier-Martin, *Histoire du droit français des origines à la révolution* 292). Moreover, he simply loved to rule. In his *Mémoires for the Instruction of the Dauphin* he wrote (Louis XIV, King of France, 1638-1715, Paul Sonnino, trans., *Mémoires for the Instruction of the Dauphin* 29–30):

> For you must not imagine, my son, that affairs of state are like those thorny and obscure recesses of the sciences that may perhaps have exasperated you, where the mind struggles painfully to rise beyond itself, most often for nothing.... [T]he function of kings consists primarily in using good sense, which always comes naturally and easily. Our work is sometimes less difficult than our amusements.... [N]o satisfaction can equal that of following each day the progress of glorious and lofty undertakings ... when one has planned it all himself.

As role model he chose his vigorous grandfather, Henry IV, believing through this example that monarchy was infinitely superior—who but a king can be free of the corrosion of self-interest—and learning from the model to feel immense pride in

France and its royal line. In 1662 the bold potentate went to the very center of the solar system in adopting the sun for his personal iconography. It did not bother him that he was no democrat. He felt an indulgent liking for the nobility in an immense regard for tradition—especially the tradition of *parlements* which he would reduce to substantial submission. His fondness for Christianity was paired with the politician's good sense which told him Catholicism taught subservience to the one of authority. Sainte-Beuve, writing in the nineteenth century with his usual cynical deprecation, cut down the royal grandeur but could not help but admire the Sun's bourgeois canniness: "'He had nothing more than good sense but he had a great deal of it'" (Durant, *The Age of Louis XIV*, 13).

Energy, intelligence, firmness, patience, and amiability—it was a personality profile certain to achieve results. Louis knew precisely what he wanted—internal order and legal stability—and he made sure to achieve both. Olivier-Martin, with the usual public safety anecdote writers are prone to recount as indicative of a strong government, reports that only after Louis XIV took control was it possible to go out at night in Paris without an armed escort, to encounter roads which were secure, and a countryside at peace. Louis knew who ruled. He forged an end to the tyrannical abuse of power by local village leaders, while suppressing undisciplined acts by lower royal agents. Foreign visitors were amazed at how institutions and infrastructure were made to work well because a king surveyed them personally to the least detail. For over fifty years Louis played his part—informed of everything, deciding everything, and making everyone obey.

The Ministers serving under Louis shared in the general admiring amazement and, believing they were under France's greatest king, redoubled their efforts to answer his demands. One of the best of the royal bureaucrats was the remarkable Jean Baptiste Colbert (1619–1683). He had been trained in a Jesuit college, then taken a banking and notary apprenticeship; he remained always the quintessential bourgeois. Son of a clothier and nephew of a rich merchant, Colbert never lost sight of the bottom line and hated confusion and incompetence. When he was not yet twenty, his uncle married the sister of the secretary of state for war, and the nephew's drive soon won him appointment as private secretary. From there his upward progress was relentless. By 1669 he was Minister of Navy, Colonies, Commerce, and the Palace, and Comptroller General of Finance, an office that brought into his fiscal dominion expenses in every major department except War; there power officially was held by his rival, Louvois, but Colbert made certain it was the Colbert voice everyone heard.

Richelieu, his predecessor under Louis XIII, had begun France's mercantile system. It would be Colbert, however, who found in Louis XIV the perfect associate for forging detailed state control of the French economy. Foremost in their minds was to make money. Colbert reduced imports to little but raw materials, getting them as far as possible at low prices from colonies run for export rather than for at-home manufacturing. Export from France of in-country manufactured goods, many from new industries, added more funds. To this end Colbert's favored internal manufactures boasted the latest in quality control, attention to weights and measures, and grants to monopolies; everyone was pushed toward productive work and given,

Jean-Baptiste Colbert
Courtesy of National Gallery of Art, Washington

if not the wages, then the means and milieu for such work. Colbert was glad to encourage liberty, but it consisted of freedom within an iron-fisted mechanism which through improved maritime transport, roads, and canals eliminated local impediments to internal commercial growth.

All this Louis XIV supported. His blind spot was lack of interest in the navy. This would prove a blundering move which sea-power nations like England privately cheered; and, as Napoleon would learn later, it marked an unfortunate lapse of the common sense Louis liked to counsel. In the latter half of his reign, two strong interests led the King into two other colossal policy errors: he reduced the French economy and people to near ruin to pay for wars motivated as much by thirst for glory as by necessities of state; and he allowed his other compulsion for a uniform orderliness, which he thought best for any monarchy, to cause him to attempt religious uniformity by revoking the Edict of Nantes in 1685. In vain did Colbert press for financial prudence in foreign policy; the King listened instead to the Marquis de Louvois—Michel le Tellier—his undersecretary of State for War, as well as, of course, to his own royal love of renown. When the Edict of Nantes was revoked, it drove out of France thousands of her most talented—men and women who were even forbidden emigration to New France where they would certainly have served French interest in the American course of events. There was no longer a

Colbert to demur, for he had died two years before. In 1684 Louis remarried, and fell much under the sway of the ultra pious Madame de Maintenon. As he lay on his deathbed he admitted to having loved Glory too much, but, fiercely Catholic, he did not repent the revocation of the Edict of Nantes. Ironically, such intransigence was perhaps his best legacy, for it bequeathed to the eighteenth century the strong reverse reaction for tolerance.

Louis must have realized that to succeed, mercantilism needed a good judicial system. Even his failed religious policy contributed to legal restructuring, and the King had time before his wars began in 1667 and in intervals between wars in 1668–1672, 1679–1684, and 1685 to devote himself to a major initiative in legal reform and education. The "*Mémoires*" reveal a wise juristic understanding:

> Justice, which was responsible for reforming all the rest, seemed itself to me as the most difficult to reform. An infinite number of things contributed to this: offices filled by chance and by money rather than by choice and merit; lack of experience among judges, even less learning; the ordinances of my predecessors on age and service circumvented almost everywhere; chicanery, established through long possession, fertile in schemes against the best laws…. [T]his excessive number of people delighting in trials…with no other concern than to prolong and multiply them…even my council…all too often confused them through an incredible number of conflicting decisions all given in my name as if coming from me, which made the disorder even more shameful (Louis XIV, 25–26).

Madame de Maintenon
Courtesy of National Gallery of Art, Washington

The King's Duty to Consult; The Chancellor

As Louis began his legal considerations, his biggest drawback was that he personally had no law training. In fact, in the civil disorder which followed the death of his father Louis XIII, the young monarch's complete education, and even sometimes his food and dress, were badly neglected. In childhood and adolescence he had scarcely been taught to read and write; most familiar historical facts and the commonplace of educated secular knowledge were unknown to him. But his mother trained him in Catholic catechism and in devotion, manners, honor, and chivalry. It was a program of comportment which, at least for a while, helped on the whole to render him serious and submissive. What he really liked, though, was others' submission to him. It was a fixed principle of French monarchy that although the king's power was absolute, under the doctrine of the *légistes* established by the end of the fifteenth and beginning of the sixteenth centuries, it remained subject by strong custom to the "fundamental laws of the monarchy" (Ellul, Vol. IV, 354). These required male succession to the crown, the inalienability of the domain, and, particularly, the duty to have *conseil* (advice) on every subject before acting.

The *conseil* syndrome promoted the concept of a king surrounded in his capital by a coterie of permanent councilors always present, ready to advise and act as agents for execution of royal commands. Although it was the King who nominated and rewarded this cabinet since the legal gentlemen of the long robe predominated there, it was they who could lay out what was just, and they who would remonstrate when they thought their monarch had acted unwisely (Ellul, Vol. III, 360). Everything Louis did found itself discussed, planned, and prepared in these elite power groups. A first minister would receive the council reports before presenting them to the king; but Louis XIV, when he began to function without a first minister, nevertheless still had such a full array of councilors below ministerial rank that their roles were actually expanded. They served as specialists *vis-à-vis* a king who was a generalist, and they themselves were aided in expertise by an array of technical bureaucrats beneath them. Nor were the men of the Ministries the only councilors. Provincial *Parlements* were in constant session, and there were the Estates General both of the realm and the provinces. The latter groups, however, were to be summoned by the king only when he required them, mainly to lobby for money when he saw no other way out. Louis XIV never saw a need to summon them.

The highest of royal councilors was the legal counsel. He bore the title of chancellor, and as the principal state personage in the seventeenth century he was the only survivor in actual power of the old medieval "great officers of the crown" (Ellul, Vol. IV, 163). He was no longer head of the royal chapel and was by this time never an ecclesiastic. Still, he had lost no other functions. In a throwback to Norman practice it was his seal rather than his signature which made effective all the monarch's acts (*Encyclopedia Britannica*, Vol. V, 833a). As a "great officer" he could not be removed. So independent was this attorney for Louis that, when the Sun set in death the law chancellor alone received exemption from wearing mourning. It is true that in the sixteenth century an excessively stubborn chancellor might be remanded to a special court which had the right to order capital punishment. In the seventeenth century the king had power to take back the seals—although not the office—and give them temporarily to a substitute commissioner.

It was the chancellor who prepared the ordinances, presided over the Privy Council and the Council on Finance, nominated to the Councils, determined the functions of the bureaus, and superintended all institutions of justice. After the seventeenth century his service expanded to duties as royal censor, a position the monarch hoped could lead the nation's intellectual activity and control its universities. As head of justice he was assisted by the king's *procureur général* (solicitor) who in turn controlled the royal *procureur* in each *Parlement* and locality; in these provincial venues he was also assisted by the king's *avocats* (barristers) who did the oral pleading. *Procureurs*, the "*gens du roi*" or the king's people, undertook law's written work and formed with the chancellor a unique aspect of the French legal system, one still reflected in modern French government. They met with the chancellor in a special room called the *parquet* where they could discuss positions to be taken. *Procureurs* decided among themselves how to share their duties in connection with pending litigation in the royal interest and whether or not the crown was a litigating party. When the advocates of the private parties in a suit over private right had finished, the king's man concluded by speaking for the king and in defense of the law. In this way a broad collaboration was established between the judges and the government. Even though the *gens du roi* did not sit with the judges in conference for decision unless invited, and the judges were not obliged to follow their advice, procurative influence was considerable. In time, like the great bulk of all other officers of justice, these men of the king simply purchased their offices and became irremovable objects, often of impediment.

The King and Private Law

The king's freedom was controlled beyond the necessity to consult, as well as beyond the various other ways, formal and informal, that his officials could influence his action. In regard to private law, for instance, he faced the custom, firm up to the fifteenth century, that private law lay outside the scope of royal legislation. Beaumanoir wrote that the king was permitted to intervene only for the "common profit," probably meaning what lay "common to all the realm" (Ourliac and Gazzaniga, *Histoire du droit privé français de l'an mil au code civil*, 166). The sixteenth century royal commissioners who drafted the customs in writing considered that while an ordinance expressed the will of the king, a custom existed by consent of those the customs ruled, a consent that had been given by long usage. After the drafting of a custom it existed through being published by the Estates General of the province, an act deemed by jurists to be a contract, or a quasi-contract, which the three social orders imposed on themselves and which the king had to respect even were he not a party. Hence, broad areas of the law of property and persons, family relations, and successions belonged to the customs, while areas like rules of procedure and proof, delicts and crimes, and the general police of the realm could be controlled by ordinances or other formal acts of the king. Since Roman law times, even in those areas where "written law" was only custom, the situation was not different. All the ordinances of the sixteenth century, usually given after request for them at a meeting of the Estates General, dealt with public law for reform of the state. Thus on the rare occasions when the king legislated on private law, rationale either claimed his action was not invasive, or rationale demonstrated how the king was required to act because of a special offense to justice or simply good policy in existing private law.

The Seventeenth Century Codes

It was 30 May 1665 when Louis shattered centuries of precedence, announcing to the Council his intention to reform the justice system. He would keep summer for the frivolities and entertainments of his court, but starting on 25 September, he held every fifteenth day a special council of justice. We are told (Gazzaniga, *Introduction historique au droit des obligations*, 54) that the King made Colbert the driving force, but that Colbert used his drive to keep Chancellor Lamoignon out while Louis ran the show. Naturally, the councils persisted in wrapping their bureaucratic web around the monarch. If ever the devil were in the details, it was in this time of the tightest protocol, with each of the many courts mired in ever-growing sets of regulations, while trying to conform to existing royal ordinances. All these legal shifts of some give and much take were complicated because the publications containing the ordinances lay in disarray of form and arrangement, procedure and topic. It was hard to find the relevant texts and, having found them, to ascertain which were still in force. Some previous jurists had tried to create order through subject classification, thereby overcoming the problem caused by so many ordinances covering a multiplicity of topics. It was the same juridical idea of a single set of laws for the whole realm which had been in favor since the sixteenth century, a practice which had produced what was called the unofficial "Code of Henry III." But little by little, as public demand for legal improvements increased, there had, even before Louis XIV, been an impetus for gathering together the relevant texts and proclaiming one long, inclusive ordinance for each subject—in other words, a new, official code. Records show at Orléans in 1560 the third Estate called for a restatement, a weeding out, and a procedural reform; at Blois in 1576 consolidation of royal legislation and customs was placed formally on the table before a commission of learned men appointed for the purpose.

The concept of official, top-down codification was tailor-made for an order-conscious absolutist who understood how a Protocol of Procedure for the realm would help everyone. Classicism's best bureaucracies were delighted to commence work as the royal call was now made for memoranda to be submitted from many sources, for commissioners to make drafts, and for commissions to call in advocates for counsel. The drafts were placed into discussion in the King's presence, thereafter to be revised by a mixed commission of councilors and members of *Parlements*. It was always the King, like Napoleon in 1804, who decided contested points. Finally, on 20 April 1667 to the stirring sound of fifes and tambours the new code was registered by the *Parlement of Paris*—an occasion, perhaps rare in history, when a work of legal craftsmanship called upon Muse Euterpe to give majesty to promulgation. The ruffles and flourishes were in order, however, for in the course of its work monarchy had displayed supple flexibility and prompt decision, and drafters had written with care and concision. Olivier-Martin (Olivier-Martin, 354) praises it as a "true code of procedure in 35 titles of perfect brevity and clarity," while Ourliac and Gazzaniga similarly comment (Gazzaniga, 167) that the "style and clarity are remarkable." The French code of procedure in force in 1948, when Olivier-Martin wrote, was to a great extent its offshoot. And Versailles's Hammurabi did not lose interest when his code was published; he at once put his hand to application.

With the systematic format under control Louis next set himself to further legislative work. Soon digests in multiple fields were flowing out in a continuous stream: the code of civil procedure led on to a code for waters and forests (1669); for criminal procedure (1670); for the Paris markets (1672). Next came a code for internal commerce (1673); several for government finance (1680, 1681, 1687); one for foreign commerce (1681); and another for slavery in the American colonial islands (1685). All have won scholarly praise for the quality of their draftsmanship and for the great care taken by Louis in obtaining the best expertise in each domain. He had astutely solicited comment by various craft and commercial organizations as well as the judges and counsels in principal places of business, then he had wisely sidestepped approval of the *Parlements*, which had little commercial expertise, going instead to experts on the royal Council of Justice. It was a proud moment. At last the diverse customs were in writing, and lawyers began to hope that in this form there lurked a foundation for an even broader, uniform private law. As booksellers put the codes together for publications, they stamped the backs of the elegant leather and gilt volumes *Code Louis* or *Code Louis XIV*, and these names of imprimatur were soon in popular use.

The *Code Louis* series was crucial to the progress of centralized national power, yet was always in considerable part dependent upon the effective and fair administration of the revised justice. Unfortunately, the codes' subject matter fell within the old tradition of forcing royal rulers to hesitate before actually legislating in the field of substantive private law. Thus the goal of unified procedures remained still far in the future, requiring not only time for further scholarly effort but also a revolution scattering power abruptly in 1789 at the expense of those men of law and affairs who thought they had created a firm foundation for the old way.

The King and his counsellors were ultimately forced to admit no code of private law came about merely by regal desire and a stroke of the regal pen. They came to understand how even the glorious constellations of leading scholarly lawyers could obfuscate enough so that the sun century would not be the greatest in French legal science. Louis, however, could be assured he had made an excellent step forward; from his reign on, French law, including the new codes, would be taught in the universities. At the same time, the scholarly law work of both academics and practitioners would be strengthened by improved teaching of Roman law.

The Reform of Law Teaching

The important reformist work done by Louis XIV had not involved the law faculties. Rather, the ambitious code drafting had fallen to a growing number of bright minds active in the legal profession either in government or in practice. Naturally, this meant the social rise of many of them who became as magistrates that special, powerful "nobility of the robe."

As they wrote the treatises on customary law and drafted the royal legislation, the newly strengthened magistracy was aiding the monarch's power every time they looked at the pages of their unified national legal system. Some of this seminal work was done by jurisconsults who were also professors, for whom the sixteenth century's code-dreamer, Charles Dumoulin, remained an outstanding role model. Most of seventeenth and eighteenth century legal science was situated in the Palais de Justice, in magistracy, and in practice, rather than in the universities. Most of the works which emerged were compilations, even though some under the influence of Humanism and natural law would rise to the level of new legal principle. All these lawyers, however, had been trained or approved after private study by university faculties in Roman law, for it was still the system which enjoyed the highest prestige. When finally Louis put his hand into controlling that academic training, he would be stimulated and aided by Le Tellier (1603–1685), now the current chancellor. This was not the Michel Le Tellier (1643–1719) who was to serve as the Jesuit confessor (1709) of the King. Chancellor and confessor were sadly united in name and in encouragement of the monarch throughout the Huguenot persecutions. In this they both ill served the interest of Louis, although Le Tellier the lawyer does deserve praise for supporting with Colbert the Edict of 1679 that reformed law teaching in France.

A consequence of the growth of royal power and the accompanying decline of the papacy had been change in the universities, who now knew they had to accept tight secular government control. The old medieval freedom in the scholarly search for the final philosophical-theological solution under more or less tolerant popes disappeared. Universities as trainers of royal bureaucrats had to please the bureaucracy awaiting the trainees; and their law schools, which continued to dominate among the faculties—although still second in formal standing to theology—were crucial to the preparation. We recall that well advanced by the end of the fifteenth century was a university milieu moving toward more aristocratic students, with faculty of more sophisticated ways, fine buildings reminiscent of great abbeys which were often provided for teaching and residences, and larger, finer libraries. But comfortable living and political control would not prevent and probably would contribute to a long period of decline; in the sixteenth century and the first half of the seventeenth law faculties of French universities, slow in accepting Renaissance scholarship, were stellar leaders of the downward spiral.

We already know the catalogue of decay: a recalcitrance toward scientific advances, countryman Descartes not studied until the 1700s, a Reformation fiercely resisted in civil war and by Catholic academics, natural law of the Grotius entourage unaccepted in law faculties until late in the eighteenth century. Universities remained stubbornly Aristotelian; their scholastic and Catholic faculties trained on the Gallican model taught Roman law more in the late medieval style of Bartolus than the humanistic style of Cujas. This mixed state of Parisian teaching methods degraded into far less favorable situations in the provinces where some schools had even stopped teaching the Roman ligneage altogether. Unbelievably, as late as 1624 it was decreed that expounding maxims contrary to the ancient authors should be punished by death. The Bourges and Valence law faculties had been strong for some time, as we have seen, but at the beginning of the seventeenth century, influenced by the papal presence, the best law faculty was at Avignon, then outside of France.

Putting aside the universities, though, the brilliant literary culture that had begun under Louis XIII (1601–1643) and flashed in the rays of his son, lead to acclamation for the seventeenth century as the intellectual sovereign of Europe. While the preceding century had followed the classical tradition of Greece and Rome with an often injudicious zeal, the Ancients were now handled "with so fine an insight, so sure a sense of proportion, and so instinctive an art of combining natural originality with the inspiration of classical tradition…as to have resulted in a success almost unparalleled in the whole history of literature" (*New Cambridge Modern History* Vol. V, 64). It is Montaigne who by influence rightly belongs here and not in his time; for, so avidly was he now read by the intelligentsia, most Catholic writers felt compelled to oppose him as though he were an actual living, breathing adversary. Classicism's moralistic concern with mankind's passage through earthly travails came in large measure from him. Descartes, on the other hand, supplied the perfect order and large horizon that Montaigne sometimes lacked or did not want; while Malesherbe's plain, clear, and concise language and stately cadences, both prose and poetry, taught the French to become a nation of declaimers, capable of transposing their Cartesian logic into trial peroration. A whole generation of writers—Molière, Racine, Corneille, Boileau, Bossuet, La Fontaine, La Bruyère, Pascal—began a hold on France's intellectual tradition which far into the twentieth century formed the matrix of multiple generations of young minds struggling through the entrance to university.

In spite of their provincialism, the law faculties, as the only official place of preparation for and admission to the bar, never lost their cachet of importance. A glimpse at the University of Paris, the premier of law training sites as Louis XIV began his reign, brings us the portrait of the "Faculty of Decrees," a title held for the official teaching of canon studies. This offering formally set Paris apart from other faculties teaching Roman law. *Parlement* had once made an exception for Cujas to teach Roman civil law, but in 1579 the Ordinance of Blois renewed the old 1219 prohibition against it made by Honorius III. Nevertheless, all was not going well. Except for the occasional comparative references, no faculty anywhere else taught the customs and the royal ordinances actually applied by the magistracy.

This decline in the quality of university law teaching was, ironically, not a reflection of any lack of interest in the legal profession, which continued to attract crowds of young men as litigation rose steadily in volume and interest. Complained jurisconsult François Hotman (1524–1590), successor to Cujas at Bourges, "'Everywhere in France today a class of men predominates whom some call lawyers … in every town where [a court] is located, nearly a third of the citizens and residents, attracted by the great rewards, have applied themselves to the practice and study of the art of verbal brawling'" (Bell, *Lawyers and Citizens: The Making of a Political Elite in Old Regime France,* vii). Some of these "brawlers" at the top had careful preparation overseen by their fathers, and there were devoted and intelligent tutors engaged by the high robe families. Ambitious young men from less favored circumstances, on the other hand, were often quite ready to accept shortcuts offered by faculties desperate for fees. By the days of Louis XIV, there were many of these "so-called lawyers," ready to plunge into the code after barely receiving their *licence.*

In 1500 one would have found in Paris only three Regent Professors of law. In 1533 François I, concerned about the quality of the law faculties, had required interrogation of candidates by two of his counselors before the professorship granted election. In 1534, when the crown fixed the number at six, Paris faculty became known as the *Collège sexviral* which for some twenty years did distinguished work until the wars set it back around 1550. In 1598 complaints that degrees were being granted for too little study, that the quality of the professors and their pay were both too low, and that their teaching and living quarters were poor, led again to blunt royal intervention. Well-drafted, detailed statutes were imposed by the royal government to control both faculty and students, a gesture of kingly crackdown after which the last traces of academic liberty disappeared. In 1600 *Parlement*, in a reform approved by Henry IV on the advice of his statesmen de Thou, Coquelay, and Mali, designated themselves watchdogs of surveillance over the faculty.

Troubles during the minority of Louis XIII intervened. There was a catastrophic enrollment drop and the professors, whose fixed salaries were already very low, found that the disappearing student fees cut hard into the small income source. To try and offset the monetary decline, each time a professor passed away or retired, the remaining incumbents immediately divided his income. No new successor faculty were elected. By 1651, as the thirteen-year-old Louis XIV chafed at the bit of his minority reign, a Professor Buisnes had outlasted all his colleagues to be sole Paris Regent, contentedly sitting on any income-draining plans to add more faculty. He and his family occupied nearly the whole of the law faculty's building on Rue St. Jean de Beauvois. Buisnes ignored the University's statutes as to duration of study for the degrees and examinations and even graduated some who never appeared in his lecture hall.

In the decline of matriculants curriculum narrowness undoubtedly played a role, but it must be recognized that the prohibition of the teaching of Roman civil law was not fully effective. A look at the statutes of 1598 confirms the study of Justinian's *Institutes* as the principal work of the first year. When *Parlement* in 1656 formalized practice, it was decreed that licensees in canon law at Paris should be allowed to take the oath as *avocats* after examination and proof of capacity in a public exhibition. Now with the faculty having been brought up to the full strength of six, all the regents were laymen and not ecclesiastics, and they were supplemented by private tutors in civil law. Since at the same time *Parlement* added twenty-four lawyers as "honorary doctors" to share the work, there was intense lobbying to keep at full strength the privileges of the *sexviral* regent faculty.

With the bleak horizon of a struggling educative branch, Louis XIV doubtlessly was inspired by Colbert. It was fortuitous that the great minister had learned much about law education in the course of his inquiry leading to the code of civil procedure. He personally possessed the skills to undertake building a more complex society and a more modern continental system. And so it was that eighteen years into the King's personal rule, there was produced the Edict of 1679, regarded by many as the most important legislation in the history of law teaching in France. It was another action illustrative of how neatly affairs could sometimes be handled in a monarchy nearly absolute and very bright. Jourdain describes the 1679 requirements as follows:

1. In every university with a faculty of law, including Paris, the faculties shall teach [Roman] civil law as well as canon law, and also the French law of the ordinances and customs.
2. No one else may give public lessons in civil and canon law.
3. The *licence* in civil and canon law shall be granted only after proof of three years assiduous study, examination, and public interrogation.
4. The oath of *avocat* shall be administered only to those who have the *licence*. Candidates for the judiciary shall also give proof of two years of attendance in court. Persons already admitted to the bar, without study, as some have been, must undertake prescribed studies.
5. The addition of professors of French law is authorized, but they will be nominated by the king and not be elected by the faculty as are the regent doctors in civil and canon law.
6. The professors and students are to obey detailed rules looking toward daily serious study of the law for three years (four for the doctorate), followed by meaningful examinations, public theses, and disputes before award of degrees. To take the oath as *avocat* the candidate must have proved also a detailed study of French law and have passed an examination and public interrogation.
(Jourdain, *Histoire de l'université de Paris au XVIIe et au XVIIIe siècle*, 474–481)

Here, then, in the proverbial "single stroke," the King had revolutionized legal academe. His intent first and foremost, was to lift the quality of the teaching of Roman and canon law, but he also clearly wanted to free the University of Paris to teach Roman law, as well as to revive it elsewhere where it had lapsed. Perhaps it was politically necessary not to require the Regent Doctors of Roman and canon law to teach French law. That subject would, henceforth, be added to all the faculties under the aegis of a royal professor for the third year—a chair organizationally somewhat separate from the professors of Roman and canon law. Unfortunately, despite such subtleties, Louis and his ministers left their revolution incomplete. Was it because royal finances were nearly always in a desperate condition? Were too many wars and too many rooms and gardens at Versailles the reasons that the Edict of 1679 did not think to correct the greatest weakness of the university faculties: lack of adequate, assured compensation independent of direct dependence on the number of students? Even in the absence of reform of remuneration, why should as vast a field as French law have to struggle along with one regent professor?

In Section 14 of the requirements Louis had laid it down that the third year curriculum was to comprise ordinances and customs and to explain French law via jurisprudential principles. This vague fiat meant the harried facultyman had to choose between offering in a year a broad summary with no depth or each year teaching a part only in more depth. If this second alternative were chosen, it left students who had only half-time in the third year to get the rest of French law on their own as apprentices. Beyond that there were, annoyingly, no books suitable for either approach. During an academic year running from 12 November to 1 August about three to four hundred matriculants crowded into classes which graduated only about one-third with *licence*. De Launay, first professor of French law at Paris, brought up in his inaugural address the huge compass of the field he was now required to teach. How, he bemoaned, could he handle several hundred students, in a single one-year course, meeting five days a week for one and a half hours each day, the whole taking half of the classroom time of the third year students? Imagine what De Launay would have felt as the twentieth century began and his same subject was given over three whole years with ten times the professors, or had he faced today's classes where one can find one hundred times as many professors for a smaller student body than he ever had.

The result of these academic stresses and the ragged study level meant French law metamorphosed into a more or less complete legal system unto itself. Despite retaining quasi-dependence on both Rome and the canon, particularly on the Roman law of obligations, the French law that now crept into those dual lines tried for its own special niche in the courts. Roman law, taught in the manner of Cujas, was considered "scientific," while French law—short on history, but full of case references—was considered "practical" (De Curzon, *L'enseignement du droit français dans les universités de France aux xviie et xviiie siècles*, 258). However, in addition to its logistical problems the plan was fundamentally unsound. Many French cases could be solved only by considering Roman and canon law as well as French law; and the teaching of French law by itself was necessarily inadequate as preparation for the resolution of actual situations legal problems. The career of the celebrated Pothier will soon serve as a case in point. He could never have written his remarkable treatises on the basis of this kind of patchwork teaching of French law; it took twenty-five years of devoted study just to reorganize the *Digest*. Faced with these dilemmas, De Launay appears to have taken an easy way out: he opted for a condensed summation method, using the little book of 1607 by Antoine Loisel entitled *Institutes coutumières* with which Loisel published also the *Institution au droit français* of Guy Coquille written the same year. Loisel's effort extracted from the customs an underlying "common customary law," that is, for a set of structural principles, it went behind the numerous customary jurisdictions which were deemed closest to the Paris of 1580 (Olivier-Martin, 321). The more Roman of these customs were notably closer to such common customary law than to Roman law.

It was to become the mission of the best of the Royal Professors, with Pothier crowning their work as the best of the best, to promote, in writing, the development of this common customary law; they would end by shaping it for incorporation in the *Napoleonic Civil Code of 1804*, the ultimate achievement of French private law.

But among the Royal Professors there were to be only a few who could publish. Adverse economic circumstances afflicted too great a number, many of whom had to practice simply to augment income. Some took the job with poor health. All found there to be so much local divergence in the compensation system that many sought joint appointment as Royal Professor and as Regent in Roman law simply so the latter title might bring in their income while sidestepping the professorial function (De Curzon, 479). Some faculty were forced to prostitute their standards just in order to keep incoming the fees of their students. At least widespread nepotism of office did not penetrate here, probably because academic posts were not thought to be worth substantial cash. Among 109 professors of French law in twenty-five universities between 1679 and 1792 there were only eight cases of sons succeeding fathers and one of a brother. It was a century so conscious of status that constant quarrels arose stemming from the question of the Royal Professor's precedence, his voting power, his robe, and other such personal details. Since he did not need the doctorate and often did not have it, this academic was looked down upon by his Regent colleagues and never fully integrated into their midst. Even the difference in their language caused friction. Roman and canon law had always been taught in Latin, but the professors of French law were particularly proud that their classes were taught in French.

In other professorial quarrels, Regents did join Royals on the same side as both fought against a 1676 policy which allowed magistrates and practicing lawyers as University of Paris adjunct faculty. The number of this cadre was finally fixed in 1680 at no more than twelve, and in 1682 their function appeared to be clarified as merely substituting when necessary for regular faculty. In fact, however, they actively continued to tutor students privately for fees, an ambitious endeavor which verged on giving classes in competition with the "public lessons" of the professors (Lamasne-Desjobert, *La faculté de droit de Paris aux xviie et xviiie siècles,* 105). By the eighteenth century this ever-growing number of adjuncts outside the box would unfortunately help weaken into vapid and venal formalities both examinations and public thesis presentations (Lamasne-Desjobert, 108). In this slide toward disintegrating standards it became ever more common to find adjuncts pocketing fees from their students for having conveniently arranged with regular faculty that examination be brief and only given on these fragmentary texts adjuncts had required the students to memorize.

If in the competition for students, status, and income this questionable outsider presence caused constant conflict with the staff professors, there remained a unifying point for all: only Catholics were permitted to teach. At Paris none was a Jansenist and all were Gallicans. Ironically, their faith did not keep them from more or less eviscerating the study of canon law by purposefully omitting materials supporting the authority of the pope (Lamasne-Desjobert, vi). However, this textual emasculation actually had a liberating effect, since it produced some positive emphases—on the soul, on moral duty, on equity, and on redemption vs. punishment. As there developed a liberal position against torture, there rapidly grew a keen interest in law reform across the board.

For all the other 1679 steps forward, Louis XIV's refusal to step at all into the domains of academic contention meant a mosaic of failures: failure to provide a sufficient number of professors in French law, failure to provide good organization for them, and failure to provide adequate compensation for university law teachers generally. Moreover, King Louis not only refused reform of the old method of teaching (still followed by faculties that had themselves little interest in reforming it), but he prescribed its very continuance. Classes maintained their one and a half hour length; and topics were still divided among courses, less according to subjects and more according to books, each of which, like Justinian's *Institutes* bulged in embrace of all or many subjects. The crucial *Digest* kept its division according to the old, arbitrary triage of "old" and "new," arrived at about 500 years before.

In the first part of each class the professor, in keeping with medieval practice, could be found dictating his "course" for student copy. After that he gave explanations of the material dictated and concluded the class by interrogating the students. Dictation in an age of printing seems primitive to us and, as might be expected, it led to class attendance by an army of copyists who knew no law; they in turn sold their corrupt *cahiers* to students who lingered back in the cafes—somewhat like today, when the course is often published or found on-line to be read when and where at will. It seems, however, that dictation was deemed more than a means to provide the student with a text; as in the preparatory classes which today train for the *grandes écoles*, writing was the way to fix the material in the memory. No less a person than Nicolas de Lamoignon, Counsellor in the *Parlement of P*aris and member of one of France's prestigious legal families, wrote that it is "'not enough to read, we know nothing but that we have extracted and written in our hand'" (Lamasne-Desjobert, 109). As late as 1770 Chancellor Maupeou in his plan for reform of the judiciary and law teaching pressed for dictation to continue, even though around 1785 there appeared memoranda, probably by magistrates and honorary doctors, in which the practice was described as outmoded.

Surprisingly, even after the 1679 revision, legal education did not end with the *licence*. At the least, the young lawyer needed training, even as today, in office work and in the details of court practice and procedure. But in France in the seventeenth and eighteenth centuries he needed more than that; he needed deeper grounding in that substantive French private law which, as we now know, remained in its state of disorder unremedied by Louis XIV. These needs were filled then as now: partly by various informal association with older lawyers and partly by personal experience with error and defeat. However, concerns of the older men for competence among those who later would be formally listed on the *Tableau des avocats* produced organized efforts which supplemented the work of the universities.

There were in Paris thirty-five courts, nearly all in the center of the city, sixteen at the Palais de Justice on the Ile de la Cité, and more accessed by the Pont au Change, the lawyers' thoroughfare, in the vast medieval Châtelet to the north. As many as 40,000 people spent their days in the Palais de Justice alone. A judge, Louis d'Orléans, wrote in 1607 that Paris, like Caesar's Gaul, had three parts: a "sacred" left bank, home of the University, a "profane" right bank, home of commerce, and the Ile de la Cité with its great Palais de Justice mediating between them. Since the sacred crown of thorns lived as well on the Ile, the men of the law had that higher recourse, as well. Probably some guilty prisoners felt they might be housed in a palace built for justice, but the macabre reminder of a Messiah's wrongful death remained their constant companion. Everything about this home to law was heavily ceremonial. No less a figure than the nation's patron was invoked to open *Parlement* and the University. Beginning the new year on that solemn 12 November of St. Martin, magistrates in brilliant red robes, 240 in number in 1715, would march side by side to a candlelit chapel reverberating with the hymns of the choir. Following the high court came the lawyers in their black and white— "silent, subservient, attentive" (Bell, 24). Such pageantry at the center of judicial power did not mean, of course, that *Parlement* held the center of power of France; and as the lawyers saw it, moving the royal court to Versailles threatened that an "administrative" monarchy would impair the "judicial" rule, thereby cutting back on litigation and reducing liberty.

The comprehensive world of the law was a formidable opponent. It included the magistrates, which meant not just barrister *avocats*, but the solicitor *procureurs*, notaries public, police commissioners, and bailiffs. Every magistrate was required to be an *avocat*, that is, a Catholic university graduate in law who had taken the oath of *avocat*. Until about 1660, one out of twenty *avocats* would at graduation have notified the courts and other *avocats* of an intention to enter practice. He then would have received official listing as such. After 1660, motivated by the venality which closed the magistracy to advancement by merit and out of fear for the future of the judicial monarchy, the practicing *avocats* of Paris formed an informal association called the *Ordre des Avocats*. Without written constitution or rules, it was deliberately not a *corps* or guild of the kind favored by Colbert, that is, a corporation subject to regulation by the state. Nevertheless, it had a leader, the *bâtonnière*, and a committee of seniors who published each year the *Tableau*, a listing of those in practice. Only men listed here could appear in court—an aggregate that between 1700 and 1789 averaged at 549 in number, with a high of 712 and a low of 346. A magistrate in 1735 estimated that a mere seventy-five would be enough to handle ordinary volume of business of the courts. These were called *avocats au parlement*; doing other legal activities were the *avocats en parlement*. Around 1700 two-thirds of those practicing were in families already strong in the law, with ten percent from the great legal dynasties. The others came mostly from families in medicine, finance, and trade. With no maximum number and no venality for men of merit, the law was the easiest road to higher secular social status. *Avocats au parlement* varied widely in wealth, but they all had books. A well-stocked personal library represented close to 17% of the average *avocat*'s fortune, and 33% of all books published in this nation so eager for law were law books. Theological works commanded far less at 14%, while the natural science that was revolutionizing the world affected only 5% of publishers' output.

The *avocat* was engaged for the client by a *procureur* who assembled facts and law, instituted the action by the necessary writings, and handed the papers over to the *avocat* for the trial. The *procureurs* constituted a *corps*; their offices were indeed purchasable, and they were subject to the continual royal exactions made possible by such corruption and made necessary by royal profligacy in finance. Generally *procureurs* had to borrow to buy their offices, and the exactions of the crown kept them in debt; in consequence they squeezed their clients hard and were little liked. *Parlement* regarded their work as mechanical, with little need for knowledge of law or skill in reasoning. Of course, in fact they sorely needed both, and about two-thirds did obtain the *licence.* The required preparation, however, was completely practical rather than philosophical—a long clerkship from about age sixteen to twenty-six. This one-sided practicum increased the temptation of simply going out and buying one of the 400 *procureurs*'s offices that, until 1776 when the number dropped to 300, were required by the city of Paris.

Beyond the *procureur* conduit, *avocats* had as well their own direct relations with clients. Some were on permanent retainer to ecclesiastical prelates or tax collectors. Others worked for princely houses. The staffs of the Princes de Conti and d'Orléans, for example, were full of *avocats* culled from the Jansenist Order, men who did the equivalent work of today's *grandes écoles* in staffing the higher levels of the French government. Some *avocats* decided cases for parties who agreed to arbitrate. Many lived on income from property and devoted time to literature or the arts, while others had jobs in seigneurial organizations, hospitals, the censorship bureau or the royal administration, including diplomacy.

Idealistically concerned for education and no doubt also, as we have suggested, personally piqued by the number of competitors, the Order of *avocats* reacted. They decided to impose upon all wishing to be listed in their *Tableau* a post-graduation requirement of two years (four after 1751) as apprentice *stagiaire*. This highly pragmatic program did not remedy the absence in the university course of natural law school work nor of a good grounding in history. However, too many multiple diploma mills like Reims were using a law faculty to grant the *licence* merely for an attendance of a few days capped by ritual. This kind of examination was devoid of content and even of dignity, and, of course, there was that full payment of fees for the quick package. This threadbare *stagiaire* approach thus became the only defense of the French bar. One at least knew that a *stagiaire* candidate had been obligated to attend court faithfully and study his books, and, as an added guarantee, certificates of such performance from six senior members of the Order were required to reach the *Tableau*. Working for greater excellence, this senior group began to introduce enrichment seminars on selected topics. In addition, about one-third of candidates served as *procureur*'s clerks during their *stage*. This menial task at least could enable a poor man to eat while he tried to reach his goal, and at best it might mean a good source of business afterward.

Beyond technical preparation, this Order of *avocats* strove also to instill among its members a common culture. Theirs was, after all, a serious profession once mainly populated by men of the cloth; and treatises, manuals, and orations by the senior members stressed that each man's gesture should reflect sobriety. Under Jansenist influence new attorneys took themselves so seriously that they often tended to see themselves as priests whose period of training defined a self-sacrificial novitiate for Lady Justice. The comportment and appearance of young law students were strictly regulated until well into the eighteenth century, with immediate expulsion freely meted out for sartorial or social lapses. *Stagiaires* were obliged to wear full length black gowns, with hair to the shoulders—no wigs—until after being *Tableau* listed. Under their arm they carried clean hats, and definitely all were to show a total respect toward magistrate and counsel. As for that counsel he was not to have an impressive emolument; only honoraria were permitted in substantial sums. Contingency fees were not to be entertained, while suits were disallowed for and honoraria failure. In another realm, that of entertainment maintenance, general respectability showed zero tolerance for the keeping of mistresses.

In return for this kind of impeccable behavior, members received a chance to make a respected living worthy, they felt, of nobility itself. We repeat that these lofty standards did decay in the later eighteenth century, but not until a long run of high opinion had given the bar eminent social status. The Edict of 1679 may have had grave weaknesses, but it helped greatly to polish the legal image. The result was a forceful demonstration of an across the board commitment: the vital teaching of law henceforth became not only a task for the universities, but it inevitably included all of society.

Jansenists and Pascal

We have already met briefly two of the best-trained practitioners of this demanding Jansenist legal system: Jean Domat and Henri-François Daguesseau. Before looking at them in detail, it is essential to take into account the special religious and scientific influences that helped form these men. To do that we must now acquaint ourselves with the Jansenists at home and with the philosopher who would bear their standard.

On a low, marshy site called Port-Royal-in-the-Fields in the village of Chevreuse south of Versailles, a Benedictine monastery had been founded in 1204. By 1600 it had been functioning for some time as an abbey for a company of Cistercian nuns, but it was not a particularly attractive venue for their edification. "'A dreadful valley, just the place in which to find salvation'" (Durant, *The Age of Louis XIV*, 50), wrote the cynically observant Madame de Sévigné, who perhaps had heard that the brides of Christ had been seeking that salvation by wide deviation from standard practice. In 1602 the thirteen sisters still in residence lived such a highly relaxed lifestyle that they each had separate property, showed their hair in individualized coiffures, used cosmetics, followed fashion in dress, and had heard no more then thirty sermons in seven years. They were, however, although they did not know it, on the brink of a powerful ascetic movement in French religion.

Their nominal abbess had the propitious name of Angélique Arnauld. She had arrived at Port Royal aged eleven and was by 1608 a seventeen-year-old discontented with religious life in spite of (or perhaps because of) the whalebone corset she had acquired to improve her figure. Then something unexpected happened. In that same year of the trim waist Mère Angélique heard two moving sermons so powerful that discontent with religion turned into a strong wish for complete reform and a truly devout life. Her given name at last had become her

Mother Angélique Arnauld
Courtesy of The Bridgeman Art Library

given lifestyle. Born again, as it were, the young woman threw off the corset, and coiffure time turned into a hair shirt regimen of personal austerities whose severity brought her to illness and depression. When the nuns, who had always been fond of her, asked about her change in mood, she replied that this prayer and sacrifice were struggling to revitalize the full rule of the order. Touched by this confession, they all consented to total change, fired the coiffeur, pooled their property, vowed poverty, and even accepted seclusion. Four biological sisters of Angélique joined her in taking the vows, and even her mother, kneeling at her feet, begged to be admitted. In time five grand-daughters took the veil with their own mother and the others, while Madame Arnauld's son, Robert, and three grandsons were admitted as *solitaires*—celibate, monastic brothers.

In 1622 the nuns moved to a house in Paris to escape the ague at the unhealthy Port-Royal. A vigorous group of men, more Solitaires leading a cloistered life without vows, took over at Port-Royal. They drained the swamps, studied the Bible, produced a manual of logic in use until the twentieth century, and even challenged the Jesuits by opening *petites écoles*, elementary schools for children about ten years old. These pupils may have been youngsters but they studied hard at French, Latin, Greek, and Monsieur Descartes, and prayed severely without the aid of images or any requests allowed to the saints. Unlike Jesuit pupils they neither danced nor gave plays—an ascetic and repressed childhood regimen from which one impressionable boy would emerge as classicism's consummate translator of the tragic vision, playwright Jean Racine.

The Solitaires, who moved to a nearby farmhouse when the nuns, frightened by civil disturbances in Paris, returned to Port-Royal in 1648, took their doctrinal lead from one Cornelis Jansen (1585–1638). A Dutch Catholic professor at the University of Louvain, Jansen had, before taking up his teaching duties, lived for some time in France with a former fellow student from Louvain, Jean Duvergier de Hauranne. In their discussions they concluded, unlike Montaigne who decided on skepticism as the weapon of choice, that the best defense of the Church against Calvinism was doctrinally to follow Augustine's emphasis on grace and predestination and in practice to establish a rigorous piety among the clergy and laity. Here was an almost Protestant Catholicism in which the Jansenist's strong desire to counter the current laxity in court and convent took aim squarely against tolerant secular clergy and the easy-going Jesuits. Jansen began to preach for mystical pietism and against free will, ideas that were put into a treatise he called *Augustinus*. After its 1640 posthumous publication the tract became the doctrinal platform of Port-Royal where Duvergier de Hauranne was spiritual director. For almost a century this book would be at the center of attention in French theology with Port-Royal as its main exemplar.

Cornelius Jansen, Bishop of Ypres
Courtesy of The Bridgeman Art Library

The Jesuits, who believed that the future of the Church demanded domination by their Order, found Jansen's thoughts anathema. Louis XIV always confessed to a Jesuit and felt concerned lest the potential of religious dissent create political disunity to shake his absolute authority. The monarch viewed Jansen as a continuous, nasty problem. However, there would be far more difficulty than he and his heirs could foresee. In this, the final stressful effort of the Catholic Reformation in France, ontological vision of a degraded human race promoted a restive, moralistic ambience which soon would bring encouragement to the revolutionary-minded. From Port-Royal's fervid and prostrate nuns to the Goddess of Reason's stiff eighteenth century opposition to all Christianity, it was just going to be a matter of time.

Yet there was another crucial sociological influence which supplemented Jansen at the origin of Port-Royal reform. This modifying force grew directly from lawyers of the Paris bar, among whom the distinguished *avocat* and father of Angélique, Antoine Arnauld I (1650–1619), started out as a leader. It was he who delivered in 1594 the famous philippic against the Jesuits, an action later called derisively the "original sin" of Jansenism (*Encyclopedia Britannica*, Vol. II, 626a). As the sixteenth century drew to a close Arnauld had already been part of a movement among Parisian *avocats* responding critically to *Parlement's* conquest by monetary corruption. He and his colleagues were bitterly aware that this degrading situation effectively barred ascension both to the bench and to loftier social status or nobility by any *avocat* whose aspiration rested solely on the bases of skill in the law and high character. The decaying standards had been accompanied by a flight of literary and oratorical prestige from the Palais de Justice to the royal court. It was in riposte that Arnauld now gathered around him a group ready for a fight—*avocats*, Gallican legal scholars led by Loisel, du Faur, and Pasquier, old school humanists, and some middle-of-the-road royalist veterans from the wars of religion. *En masse* this motley cohort undertook in letters and treatises to recapture and to redefine an honored place for the legal profession.

The scholars took the lead, stressing how the bar, pure and impartial, was indispensable to the social fabric. For example, Pasquier openly compared *avocats* to preachers whose public work functioned as the visible and audible expression of divine grace. He himself counseled his son, starting out in the law, to support the indigent and speak out for the downtrodden. Lawyers had a summons to battle, he said, and like good Christian soldiers they were recruited, conscience-armed, to fight the amoral. Pasquier was confident that such pious soldiering would surely be worthy of ennoblement.

Along with this legal morality army went a conception of governance in which the divinely ordained king was imbued with supremacy, not because of any Clovian dove, but simply because justice flowed from God through him. The Church refrained from asserting jurisdiction over the Crown in any temporal matter, including status in the realm of the Church itself. But—and it is evident advocacy was behind this caveat—the king was denied interference in the judicial process. Disputes were to be decided by judges advised by *avocats* representing the parties. Clearly, these Jansenist writers were promoting a "judicial monarchy" in which the king's duty to consult called for acceptance of the decisions of his judges. The *avocats* in their turn were enjoined to renounce flamboyant, Ciceronian oratory and to stress legal learning, transmitted after sober judgment, in a careful and restrained statement.

Underlying the new direction was an older, Augustinian attitude toward human nature; heavily tinged with lugubriousness, it spoke for the bleak realization that good works and regular masses were not going to be enough. Since lawyers played the role of a particular chosen few, their duty meant leading others onto moral high ground. Living inside this untraditional anti-Jesuit "judicial monarchy," many lawyers found their new power—even austere—was so congenial that they began making it a family affair. Who can forget the extraordinary Arnauld grouping of parents and twenty children who had come literally to form the Port-Royal core. Jansenist *avocats* as leaders of the Paris bar would remain in place until the latter part of the eighteenth century, when the most prominent jurists—having made intellectual contact with anti-religious thinkers—fully deserted legal learning for flamboyant, even outrageous. When it came to defending clients, these few rogue advocates placed their power over that of the courts.

Bell has carefully studied the Jansenist bar in Paris. He portrays (Bell, 45–49) as its leaders about fifty to sixty *avocats* of the later seventeenth century and the first three quarters of the eighteenth. Most fit the same profile: wealthy nobles of stern and high-minded ideals, strict devotees of legal learning, men standing far apart from the Cicero who stressed oratory aided by only a little law from a jurisconsult. Their goal was justice, and as professionals they regarded the bar as a pillar of French society and not merely a venal institution in advancement of its own special interests. Being Humanists their models were the ancient Roman republican lawyers; but they were loyal to the monarchy and until near 1789 had no thought of a republic, let alone of democracy. Their fear of despotism enhanced an unshakable conviction that decision of cases by the king's judges according to law untrammeled by royal interference was the only way to a well ordered society. They believed legalistic monarchy to be conducive to the salvation of souls in a revitalized Catholic Church; and they raised their voices in national exhortations to that holy end. Not only were they orators who stood to plead cases in court, but they walked amidst a society which had to admit they were among the best educated of their time. Denisart, Camus, de Ferrière, Bayard, Guyot—here were *avocat* authors with prodigious multi-volume capacity for *Collections de décisions nouvelles* or the equally massive *Répertoire universel et raisonné de Jurisprudence civile, criminelle, canonique et bénéficiale*. They were as well effective at writing *mémoires judiciaires* (briefs) in cases involving state and ecclesiastical power, and in speech their eloquence easily encompassed many of the fundamental questions of their time. Because their documents were free from censorship, these became the principal licit outlet under the *ancien régime* for the expression of opinion against encroachments of power, particularly, of course, in the harassment of Jansenist clerks by Jesuit-leaning prelates.

Among the nineteen brothers and sisters of Abbess Angélique Arnauld, the most brilliant was Antoine II, professor of theology at the Sorbonne and admirer of

Descartes. Inspired not only by his father but also by Jansen, he published a treatise in 1643, *De la fréquente communion*, which was no less than an across the board denunciation of the Jesuit system. Fearing reprisal by that Order, Antoine left Paris for Port-Royal. Pope Urban VIII had already in 1642 condemned the general doctrine of Jansen's *Augustinus*. In 1653 affairs reached the point where Innocent X in the bull *Cum Occasione* condemned as heresy five propositions of the Jansen book. When Arnauld, an indefatigable fighter, attacked again in 1655, this time targeting Jesuit methods in confession, a motion was made to expel him outright from the Sorbonne. Arnauld gave an impassioned reading of his defense to friends at Port-Royal, but they were not impressed. One of them, Blaise Pascal, then thirty-two, had joined the religious community in December 1654. Arnauld, sensing no support, threw down a critical historic gauntlet by asking his younger colleague why *he* did not write an appropriate attack. Pascal returned to his room and produced the first of the *Provincial letters*, the beginning of a classic text in literature and philosophy, and a slashing attack on the Jesuits. Voltaire wrote that it was "'the best written book that has yet appeared in France'" (Durant, *The Age of Louis XIV*, 60). A genius with numbers had become a genius with words, and those words were soon to be a bridge to the great natural law treatise of Jean Domat.

Pascal was far more adept than Arnauld at infusing his Jansenism with the Scientific Revolution, for it was in science he had begun and not as a theologian or a literary author. When Blaise's mother died in 1627 he had been only four, and from that time on it would be the remarkable paternal mentor who worked with the young boy's fiercely inquisitive personality. Étienne Pascal was a lawyer as well as a superb student of geometry and physics; he held the important presidency of the Cour des Aides, a sovereign jurisdiction for subsidies. When Blaise was eight a move was made from the stern, volcanic angularity of Clermont-Ferrand in south central France to the vibrant life of Paris. The boy never attended school but instead received gentle yet diligent instruction from his father. Blaise was precocious, one of the few whose precocity was followed by great intellectual achievements in maturity. He was not to become a learned man in the usual sense, for he knew no Greek and would remain rather one-sidedly dependent on Montaigne. However, when Étienne joined the circle of Mersenne, Gassendi, and Descartes, the son, eavesdropping on their conversations, became fascinated by their late night scientific discussions. At eleven he confidently produced his own treatise on the sounds of vibrating bodies. Fearing that such passion for mathematics would lure the boy from other studies, Étienne forbade any more work with figures. But when Blaise wrote on the wall with a piece of coal the proof of angles of a triangle equal to two right angles, the amazed and proud parent relented, and Blaise was permitted to go on to Euclid.

Before age sixteen the youthful genius had written his treatise on conic sections—perhaps a scientific translation of his childhood topography. One theorem, a lasting contribution that still bears his name, caused Descartes, incredulous at these new ideas, erroneously to state it must have been the father who had done the work. It was not the only feat for a mind burning brilliantly before twenty-five. Blaise conceived the idea that mercury in a tube would rise to different heights at different places according to atmospheric pressure. To prove it he sent his brother-in-law in 1648 up the 5,000 foot Puy de Dôme near Clermont with a tube of mercury; at the base it read twenty-six inches, at the top twenty-three, and Europe hailed the experiment. Having been challenged by a gambler, Pascal, still under twenty, developed the calculus of probabilities; inventing an adding machine, he had one sent to the ever-alluring Queen Christina in Stockholm. The royal spider now invited him, too, to visit; he accepted but fortunately found the climate severe and retreated before suffering the fate of Grotius, Descartes, and Pufendorf.

Although it seemed that nothing now could deter Pascal's life from being wholly dedicated to science and reason, his health was not strong. From eighteen he had suffered pain from a nerve problem; at twenty-four he collapsed with a paralytic attack. Recovery was only partial, and with his nervous system permanently damaged, hypochondria possessed him, turning his persona toward the irritable and taciturn. Religious fervor did not accompany his gloom, however. When his sister Jacqueline upon the death of their father in 1651 joined the nuns at Port-Royal, it was contrary to her brother's wishes. He, now a rich heir, took a fine house, hired many servants, bought a coach and four, and joined Parisian society. On trips back home to Clermont he gallantly courted a lady of beauty and learning. Back in the capital he wrote on love, began a deep study of the favored Montaigne, probably for a time was attracted by Pyrrho, and became a member, at least on the fringes, of Parisian libertinage. His devoted Jacqueline frequently reproached him, and for every transgression Blaise could be certain of earnest sisterly prayers for his conversion.

At last the intercessory supplications bore fruit. On 23 November 1654 his horses took fright and plunged into the Seine, nearly taking Pascal with them. It was a libertine who fainted from the shock, but once restored, it was a man of religious fervor who would swear he had had a vision so powerful that God Himself had been manifest. Pascal recorded the ecstatic apparition on a parchment and before sewing it into the lining of his coat, penned concluding thoughts of commitment and eternal devotion. There were more frequent visits to Jacqueline at Port-Royal with now, far more assiduous attention to the sermons. As belief and the ecstatic conviction of the saved grew deeper, Pascal in December 1654 actually joined the Port-Royal community, able to sit respectfully as he heard out those who remonstrated with him for his devotion to science and his fondness for skeptical philosophical probings. Pascal, though not a Jansenist sectarian, capped transformation by henceforth opposing Montaigne and spearheading the Christian faith. This is the time when Jean Domat, friend of his youth in Clermont and younger than Pascal by two years, was exposed to Pascal's Jansenism. An impressed Domat became, in effect, general legal counsel to Port-Royal, aided Pascal by reading pertinent works for him, and at his friend's untimely death in 1662, became the trusted executor of his papers and a beneficiary of income from the Paris "bus" route Blaise had earlier invented.

Pascal was not a philosopher trying to build a system to explain the whole of reality; but he nevertheless did think deeply about ultimate questions and publish his ideas on the philosophy of man. His Christian rebirth had not reduced his faith in science. It did, however, alter his attitude toward the use of the geometrical method in moralistic study; for he perceived, as most who read Descartes do, that

Cartesianism posits a belief in mathematics as a sovereign and universal method. For Pascal that went too far. His interest in geometry—mechanics and arithmetic as well as figures in spatial relationships—could never really leave him, but it was lying now as a kind of altar gift, placed in the context of a life's service to God. He would still accept the geometrical method as indeed supreme, but only in its own field. A beginning with explanations, a symbolic approach, indisputable definition— this he could condone. Nevertheless, propositions using symbols to make statements about the nature of things were not indisputable; they had to be proved unless they were axioms of self-evidence. If self-evident axioms, they would be immune from skeptical attack even by a Pyrrho; reason could make deductions from them and the deductions were certain. The bottom line for the geometrical method, though it is the highest exercise of the mind and the best occupation, extends about the same as that of an able artisan: it only works where it works (Copleston, Vol. IV, 155, 162).

So Pascal held that for theological knowledge neither geometry nor experiment is available. There is only authority. The traditional proofs of God are not proofs, and if they were, they do not prove Christ, who alone is the way to know God. In spite of Aquinas and Descartes there is no natural religion, and philosophers, as distinct from followers of Christ, can neither find the end of man—and here Pascal joined the long legal progression—nor can they find a moral law that all human

Blaise Pascal
Courtesy of The Bridgeman Art Library

beings accept. There are natural laws, but human beings corrupted by the fall cannot find them. Even if they wanted to, they could not follow them, being so arrogant and corrupt that at times and places larceny, incest, infanticide, and parricide have all been deemed virtuous—a legal travesty powerfully summed up by Pascal: "'three degrees of latitude reverse the whole of jurisprudence, a meridian decides about the truth.... A pleasing justice which is bounded by a river! Truth this side of the Pyrenees, error beyond'" (Copleston, Vol. IV, 162).

If what is based only on sound reason is not well founded and justice is only "what is established," (Ourliac and Gazzaniga, 158) Pascal still did not want his reader to take this as a condemnation of the use of reason and the mind. Nor did he want to forget that as the son of the Jansenist's judge he, too, possessed the advocate's brilliance at winning, in this case the embattled trial for the human soul. For people unconvinced either by the Christians or by the skeptics, Pascal, his calculus of probabilities and his close knowledge of worldly high-rollers now placed at God's bidding, proposed his celebrated wager. The tactic had all the panache of a top trial lawyer who knew it was his biggest case: trying to save no less than the souls of humankind.

In today's age of compulsive addiction and hedonistic freedoms, the seventeenth century advocate for salvation strikes a raw nerve as we listen in on the case presented. Wanting to make us believe, Pascal proposes that we might as well bet on Christ. Believe! he urges, it is *not* what you have to lose, but what you have to *gain*. Try abandoning sensual pleasure, he taunts us, (recalling no doubt, the decadent interlude after he inherited his father's money.) Leave luxury and take that leap of faith!

We can imagine that here Pascal, our advocate, actually smiles – enigmatically at first. Is not the possible gain of salvation glorious enough to make the wager? And now the smile broadens as law and Pascal bring the case home to triumphant closure. Acquitted, your honor, and free eternally from the prison of Hell.

Life of Domat

Only exceptionally are distinguished authors distinguished for their modesty. Jean Domat was surely one of the exceptions. Unlike his friend from Clermont, Blaise Pascal, Domat did not have to begin his career with his head in a libertine cloud of self-gratification. All who write about his life bemoan the absence of copious written sources, but in his extreme deprecation it was he who conspired that it should be so. In a famous example, only the intervention of his screaming children saved from consignment to the flames by his own hand copies of the *harangues* (addresses) he had given on ceremonial occasions to Clermont's bench and bar. There is no portrait from life because Domat did not want one; his admiring patron Louis XIV had to be content with ordering a death mask. In what can be seen as the supreme self-effacement Domat asked to be buried with the poor, and his grave is still lost among theirs. Searching for him we even cannot be sure we have the name correctly, since in his will Pascal wrote both "Domat" and "Daumont" (Voeltzel,

Jean Domat (1625–1696): Essai de reconstitution de sa philosophie juridique précédé de la biographie du jurisconsulte, 37, 41). When Domat's parish church of St. Benedict was converted for a theatre, his last editor, Rémy, diligently searched the premises but could find no trace of him.

Following Jansenist preference the great opus of this mysterious dark star was first published without name, even though it had been completed while the young author was a protégé of Louis XIV and had received blessing from the prestigious Henri-François Daguesseau, future Chancellor of France. He was so little known that many people, light in learning, thought the book to be the work of De Launay, one whom we initially met as Paris professor of French law. De Launay was capable but could never have written such a superb piece of work. When Domat was told that in a eulogy the orator had praised the deceased for resembling him, the jurist was horrified. It seems only appropriate that even the biographical eulogy offered him by Prévot de la Jannès, Professor of French law and predecessor at Orléans of Pothier, has perished, being last seen at Orléans in 1777. Only in the middle of the nineteenth century was there found in the Bibliothèque Nationale a *Mémoire* by a Marguerite Périer on the life of Domat which, it is assumed, Jannès used.

The biography and analysis by Voeltzel in 1936 was the only major effort on Domat to that date, but in the latter part of the twentieth century appreciation of Domat's significance rose slightly. Gazzaniga in his 1992 *Introduction historique au droit des obligations* (Gazzaniga, 43; 55) refers more than twenty-five times to this "model jurist of the 17th century" whose "distinguished mind unites a profound sense of justice and equity." Eleven years earlier Carey's *Judicial Reform in France Before the Revolution of 1789* (Carey, *Judicial Reform in France before the Revolution of 1789*, 35) gave Domat the benefit of major historical kudos: "In his work, and in that of others like him, was the foundation of the new state that would emerge during the Revolution...."

The personal impression such biographers create is of a consummate attorney, highly intelligent and energetic who enjoys legal work. Despite being reserved, modest, often even timid, he is regularly challenged by his colleagues to think philosophically in public. Reading widely and thinking deeply, Domat is mainly motivated by a sincere Christianity which sympathizes with Port-Royal; for him the faith-quest has become an effort at reconciliation between the equity of the ancient Roman jurisconsults and the new faith of Rome. But he is also close to the practical day-to-day administration of law and has ample opportunity, which he seizes fully, to observe it in action with all its faults and with all its strengths. He has reached maturity at the bar at a time when its leaders are mainly Jansenist men who have high professional standards and preach an austere morality for lawyers. Domat himself both preaches and personifies their ideal. Wanting to give up his charge as *avocat du roi* some years before he in fact does retire, Domat is prevailed upon to stay by those who, like his bishop, cannot believe a public servant's disinterestedness has actually led him to the unthinkable: he declines fees.

It seems surprising that it took so long for legal scholarship to promote this exceptional mind and his fine books of reference. The reason is perhaps that in his first works it was a completely different foundation that Domat intended to lay. He was that fascinating anomaly: the innovator of a conservative legal horizon who could foresee the new way of the law as an historic amalgam. Legal education could be entirely renewed, he felt, by a revised theoretical and philosophical base, one built from amalgamating the several parts of the current law effective in France into a unified whole. A lot hung in the balance. Success in completing such a challenging task could answer the precise need expressed by royal ministers and royal patron for a single code of French law. The process would be revolutionary, yet because its implementation would involve no equal revolution of government, when Domat reached so boldly, he was proposing it only for his time, not for the future. Nevertheless, because of his powerful talent at synthesis, Domat today is there to help us through well written and accurate analyses developing the theory of contracts. Study of his teaching, bringing together the finest innovations of Christianity, Roman law, and natural law, illuminates an historically determining stage in the entire domain of obligations.

The Domat family had strong bourgeois roots. Jean's father was a notary and alderman in Clermont; his maternal grandfather had served as Clermont's *avocat du roi* (King's counsel) and his great-grandfather was celebrated as author of a commentary on the custom of Auvergne. Domat was born not far from the cathedral and quite near the birthplace two years earlier of Pascal. While still very young the supervision of his education was transferred to his great-uncle, the Jesuit father Sismond, a respected and scholarly man of learning who left among his papers notes on the *Theodosian Code*; Father Sismond's contemporary prominence came from high royal service as confessor to Louis XIII.

The uncle entered the nephew in a preparatory school in Paris, the Collège de Clermont, famous later when renamed for Louis XIV as the Collège de Louis-le-Grand, a part of the University of Paris. Here young Domat, a superb student, learned Latin, Greek, Spanish, and Italian, becoming particularly interested in geometry and theology. He also studied philosophy and sustained to great applause a public thesis in that science with the young Prince de Conti, member of one of the first families of France. The atmosphere was all Jesuit, but Domat showed himself already very conversant with the ideas of Jansenist opponents.

Domat is reputed to have met Molière while at the Collège; however, the theatre obviously was not to be his passion. Instead, in 1642 when about seventeen Domat chose law, the career tradition of his family, and enrolled at Bourges. Under successors of Cujas, the institution had grown into one of France's best. Professor Mérille, a Cujas student and law teacher of the Grand Condé, military hero under Louis XIV, trained Domat to read the works of the Renaissance legal icon "with religious avidity" (Voeltzel, 44). The impact remained, and the Roman law tradition of Cujas replaced the customary law tradition of the Domat family. Mérille approved his protégé for the Doctor's degree after just three years of study. Domat was twenty and likely had already met Pascal. In contrast to his friend, though, the young lawyer elected to resist the Parisian allure and return to Clermont, where he took the oath as *avocat* and began to practice. At the same time, he continued theology studies while filling in some glaring academic gaps. This meant not merely careful study of the procedural and customary law he had not learned at Bourges but also—significantly for his future work—considerable reading of Justinian. Pascal, then twenty-five, was conducting his famous experiment with the barometer about the time that Domat, twenty-three, penned his friend's portrait into his copy of the *Corpus Juris Civilis*. Voeltzel says that Domat would actually participate in Pascal's experiments on the weight of air, and that from his very first conversations with him they had discussed their shared love of mathematics. These exchanges must not only have confirmed Domat's enthusiasm for geometry, but affected his later ideas for the bar about how best to present and argue.

In the meantime, at twenty-two he had dutifully married Antoinette Blondel, daughter of a Clermont *avocat*, the woman chosen for him by his father. Voeltzel speculates (Voeltzel, 47) that even then Domat possessed a clear and strong conception of marriage as society's premiere necessary legal institution—with or without love; he later would anchor it into his legal system and into his personal life, producing thirteen children with a perfect sense of respect, but perhaps not the greatest depth of love. Five young Domats survived: three girls who did not marry, and two sons one of whom died young. The other, a lawyer, proudly fathered a Domat grandson only to see the illustrious line end without issue in 1827.

Although in giving to charity Domat was generous to a fault, he saved enough of the proceeds of his success at the bar by keeping family tradition and purchasing in 1655 at age thirty the office of *avocat du roi* in his home *présidial* court of Clermont. In the sixteenth century, appeals from decisions of the *baillis* (*sénéchaussées* in the South) were still being taken to the *parlements*, but with questions of distance the procedure was slow and expensive. To remedy this problem a royal edict in 1552 had raised some sixty *bailliages* to the status of *présidial* courts. Each possessed final jurisdiction over appeals from the decisions of other courts in matters up to 250 pounds and in appealable jurisdiction up to a limit first of 500 pounds, later raised to 1,000. No doubt the crown was pleased at the proceeds from sales of the new offices. Here would be the arena where for thirty years Domat labored faithfully and successfully, his conclusions overruled only three or four times (Voeltzel, 58).

One of Domat's most important cases brought him squarely to support his now firmly held Jansenistic beliefs. Pascal's conversion to an intense Christianity and then close association with the equally intense group at Port-Royal had come in 1654. It was to be Sainte-Beuve's opinion that Domat's conversion followed immediately that of his friend (Voeltzel, 53); but whether in fact Domat did develop his interest then, or earlier in company with people from his family, or among Clermont friends, or simply on his own, is not definitely known. What is certain is that Domat's character was quite consistent with piety and clerical accents. He was ready, for instance, to espouse the cause of poor litigants denied justice by exorbitant cost. But as a highly successful lawyer Domat already married several years and having begun his large family, had little thought of becoming another *solitaire* at Port-Royal. His closeness to Pascal in religious ideas would increase only as the two men were pushed closer together by the current bitter disputes between the Jansenists and the Jesuits. Some have said that Domat was a counselor of Pascal in the conception and writing of the famous *Provincial Letters*; at least he was among those who aided Pascal by reading for him some of the authors cited.

In the affair of the "formulary" Domat's role is certain. The Innocent X bull of 1653, condemning the five propositions on predestination which Jesuits on the theological faculty had "extracted" from Jansen's book, was buttressed by the French Assembly of the Clergy which in 1659 obliged all French ecclesiastics to sign a prescribed statement, or "formulary," supporting the bull. Jansenism at once became an issue cognizable in the courts: was it lawful to punish those who refused to sign? The issue mobilized the bar. Antoine Arnauld contended that, although the pope was infallible in theology, he was not infallible in matters of fact. Jansen had never intended the interpretation put upon his words by the Paris professors, and thus a Jansenist cleric might sign if he reserved that point of difference. Pascal at first accepted this solution, then changed his mind when he perceived it would imply rejection of Jansen, Augustine, and the efficacy of grace. In a famous scene, Pascal, ill and surrounded by leading men of Port-Royal now split by the question of the reservation, lost his power to respond, leaving Domat, who had followed him on the issue, to carry the argument for him. Apparently pleased with the advocacy, Pascal before his death delivered all his papers on this subject to Domat.

Even after Pascal had left the scene, Domat continued to be close to Port-Royal. He seems, as we have said, to have been their legal counselor, making frequent trips to Paris for them and even receiving consults on matters of theology. Moreover, at Clermont he undertook as *avocat* disputes against the Jesuit side. Once, on request of the deans of the cathedral, he opposed the Jesuit plan to take over the local school; this led him to quarrel with his lawyer son about it, but he went ahead, drafted a brief and presented it to Louis XIV. The cause was lost when he came up against the King's formidable Jesuit confessor, Père Lachaise, who ironically to this day carries the celebrity victory over Domat as tourists flock to the famous Paris cemetery that bears his name. On another occasion Domat, by now regarded as the leader of the Jansenist party in Clermont, dared to defend a local priest against Jesuit charges of heretical sermons. On a later occasion when a Jesuit preached papal infallibility in Clermont Cathedral—a position dangerous for the liberty of the Gallican church—Domat, in the absence of the *procureur du roi*, drafted a brief on the facts with which he included a point-by-point theological refutation of the sermon. The *procureur* at Paris sent Domat's document to the first president of the *Paris Parlement*, and the Jesuits persuaded Louis to exercise his power to "evoke" the matter to himself in his council, an action against which the *procureur* at Clermont strongly remonstrated.

Such bold activities in behalf of the Jansenist party seem not to have imperiled Domat's status as *avocat du roi*. He played, for example, an important role in the *Grands Jours d'Auvergne*, a visit made in 1665 to his native area by a delegation from the *Parlement of Paris* inquiring into and attempting to remedy abuse of power by certain nobles. Although Domat may not have instigated the proceedings, he certainly could be found there in full participation, admired and trusted by the men from Paris. Any such attack on abuse of privilege was in full accord with Domat's legal stand against violation of law. When a local citizen, surprised "in an action contrary to good custom and police" (Voeltzel, 58), was jailed only to be freed by a visiting *Intendant*, Domat promptly returned the accused to prison.

Participation in the geographically distant life of Port-Royal, legal jousts with the Jesuits, and the day to day work of the *présidial*, together with participation in the administration of his household, were not enough to fill all of Domat's energetic days. Interest in tribunal reform led him to work toward reducing the number of courts and their tangle of procedural complexities. In addition, Domat shone in his legal scholarship, regularly studying his books more broadly than required by the legal business he handled. He was able to cite Cicero with ease and retained his youthful passion for the details of Roman jurisprudence. Deepening his qualifications as a legal humanist, his learning is especially well displayed in his final publications. The resolve to produce these superb writings had come relatively late and, commensurate with his self-effacement, appears to have been less his own design than the result of friends who urged him on. The seventeen Clermont *harangues* between 1657 and 1683, stressing the high callings of judge, *avocats*, and *procureurs* and the duties they impose, are vintage Domat "sermons" citing the Bible and Augustine. Taken as a whole such citations are scarce in Domat's work, however, since he did not reveal his modern sources.

This vagueness means that the pressing question for today's scholars remains the influence on Domat of the Protestant school of natural law. Did he study Grotius and the others? There is the historical awareness, especially of French law of customs. Voeltzel after analysis of Domat's work would also say "yes," since some of the ideas one finds in Grotius appear frequently in Domat, sometimes almost in identical words. The same in varying degree can be said for incorporated ideas of Aristotle, Calvin, Cicero, Hobbes, Augustine, and Aquinas. One can at least say with certainty that Domat was a careful if often unimaginative eclectic. When he commenced scholarly work he selected the texts of the *Digest* he considered to be most intelligent and applicable to modern practice, but he carefully put them together in the same order they had occupied in the *Digest* itself. This admittedly rather dull compendium was published four years after Domat's death, and beginning about nine years later it appeared at the end of all editions of his complete works. If not unexpectedly his *Digest* work has attracted scant admiration, there is no lack of interest for the fundamental, elaborative *harangues*. *Digest* selections form the embryo of the *Lois civiles*, Domat's major work, while the *harangues* are the embryo of the *Traité des lois*, its preface.

In this effort at an inclusive rationale of private civil law, Domat understood that such a code would have to be prepared in the first instance by a legal scholar, one who could devote himself fully to it. There are three versions of the events that were to bring Domat himself to that status. According to the dramatic one, Domat, as usual spurred by friends, overcame his natural modesty and went to Paris in 1683 with the beginnings of an *oeuvre*. The judges to whom he first spoke handed his work to Pelletier, Controller-general; the bureaucrat was so impressed he spoke to the monarch, who in his carriage on the way from a supper at Marly to a ballet at Versailles, in typical majestic grandiosity granted Domat a pension of 2,000 pounds which allowed coming to Paris for his writing. One author, Bathie, said that in opening the carriage and intellectual doors for this Jansenist and his natural law Louis was probably making the most decisive blow against his dynasty that his own hand could administer (Voeltzel, 73). The opinion is clever but exaggerated: Enlightenment authors both legal and non-legal leaned on natural law in droves.

According to the second version, Pelletier wanted to continue the law reforms of Colbert and in a cut-and-dried legal hire enlisted Domat and the youthful Henri-François Daguesseau to help out. The royal ministers almost immediately became diverted by the work needed to revoke the Edict of Nantes in 1685, and nothing happened to the efforts of the two legal assistants. According to the third and most flattering version, three counselors of state presented to the King a proposal for a single code. The Council at first thought the job too vast but then decided to try it and appointed a commission which included Pelletier. The latter said only one man in France, Domat, was both sufficiently philosophical and professionally expert in the theory and practice of law to succeed. Louis agreed. Although Domat as a Jansenist probably enjoyed little favor among many at court, in this version he was given a handsome royal pension of 6,000 *écus* (approximately $60,000) to complete the work.

Although these stories vary in detail, it is certain that Domat in 1685 did at last sell his office as *avocat du roi*; after a move to Paris the remaining years of his life were devoted to research and writing. His method was attuned to the group ethos of his time, although it appears eccentric today. Domat could never bear making an outline of the projected work or even a part of it, since at no time was his mind was capable of looking ahead to a whole. Instead, his was a laborious step-by-step progress toward final prose, often with the meditation of an entire night devoted to thinking ahead toward the next section. Awakening, inspiration gushed forth, and he wrote what he had developed in his mind—often a whole chapter in one session—handed the result at once to a copyist, and then distributed copies to his circle. All read, all applauded. Domat revealed that even without the first draft before him, he could rewrite what he had said, word for word (Voeltzel, 83; 74). He seems to have composed easily and wrote with the ubiquitous Cartesian clarity; but in an age of brilliance in French literary style, his prose had its share of critics. His one known attempt at an actual literary output was twelve Latin verses glorifying Louis XIV written on the occasion of the Louvre colonnade. Friends gave Domat their usual hail and applause; but the academician to whom the verses were submitted sourly condemned them, and the King had to be content with architecture minus juristic encomium.

Domat's major works are three books, published by him in two volumes, and by later editors usually as one. We have earlier alluded to the *Traité des lois* (Treatise of Laws) and *Les lois civiles dans leur ordre naturel* (Civil Laws in Their Natural Order); there is also the unfinished *Le droit public* (Public Law). The *Traité* (104 pages in the Boston edition of 1850) contains his fundamental ideas, but *Le droit public* maintains an even stronger reputation. Voeltzel does not tell us whether Domat wrote the *Traité* first, but he does say that at the beginning Domat curiously did not plan to incorporate it into *Les lois civiles*. However, his ever persuasive friends, among whom Daguesseau may have been a leader, pushed the self-effacing author into publication of this, the most important document encompassing the Domat system. Perhaps initial hesitation had flowed from a belief that his work was preparing the foundation of a code and that the code was, therefore, the thing to put into print. *Les lois civiles* (1,530 pages in the Boston edition) branches out from these fundamental ideas into the field of private law. In 1689 the *Traité* and *Les lois civiles* came out anonymously in Paris. *Le droit public* formed a 1697 post mortem; rather than modesty, this time the posthumous route may have been the usual political camouflage for one introducing ground-breaking ideas under the absolute aquiline nose of the paternal monarch.

The 1689 appearance was not an immediate sensation except among the ever faithful friends and a handful of scholars. Most other readers, accustomed to the ponderous tomes of Roman law, thought it far too brief. Explaining the dearth of reaction one biographer surmised, somewhat too ingeniously perhaps, that the text may have been thought so perfect there was no call for discussion. Another felt it probably had been intended only for young people; others complained that to use it one had to be able to make deductions that few could. But Boileau praised Domat as "'the restorer of reason in jurisprudence,'" while Daguesseau, who was apparently tutored by Domat and showed Jansenist sympathies, commented with elegant symmetry that no one "'had better plumbed than Domat the true principles of the laws or explained them in a manner more becoming to a philosopher, a jurisconsult, and a Christian.'" Domat's nineteenth century editor, the faithful Rémy, stated categorically in 1828 that Domat was still the wisest authority of the modern bar (Domat, Joseph Rémy, trans., *Oeuvres complètes de J. Domat,* v), to which Bernardi in 1855 fulsomely added: "'It is the general plan of civil society, the best made and the most finished, which has ever appeared'" (*Biographie Universelle* 166 a, b). In the twentieth century Justice Story of the United States Supreme Court, for whom "'the work...considering the age and the circumstances under which it was written, is a truly wonderful performance'" (Domat, William Strahan, ed., and Luther Stearns Cushing, trans., *The Civil Law in Its Natural Order,* viii), found Domat pertinent enough to star in his Treatise on Bailments.

Louis XIV was the most important potential reader, but Voeltzel does not tell us the royal thoughts, conceivably too filled in 1688 with the disastrous preemptive attack that was about to unite Europe against France, bring her to her knees in 1694–1695, and force his Majesty to seek peace in 1696. Louis did give Domat's son a state appointment. But he realized that the larger vision—to present France the holy grail of a single code of private law—had eluded him. Domat's achievement, though, was great. He had shown that an underlying unity of law did exist. It is true that his sketch of it did not probe deeply into the detail of this tantalizing conclusion, but it had allowed him to play the important leadership part in the natural law current among the pious Jansenists. What is more, Domat had in fact reached an impressive number of readers. There would be two Paris editions of his books in his lifetime; sixty-two others followed thereafter (1696–1838), all issued in Paris except for one in Luxembourg and one in Holland. Many had a scholarly apparatus of notes. Of translations there were two in Dutch (1704, 1713); one in Italian published in five editions between 1790 and 1834; and one in English published in three editions (London 1722 and 1737, and Boston 1850).

Domat's competition and critics came from natural law developing at a fast pace among the anti-Christian intellectuals. Among these, Diderot led in the publication of his *Encyclopedia* (1751–1765); many articles on crucial legal subjects were to be found in the massive compendium, but pointedly none was entitled "Domat." Even the article on natural law gives no mention of Clermont's remarkable native *avocat*. Of course, these omissions of one of Domat's stature could be due to negligence rather than design. Diderot was often guilty of haste and often harassed by his huge undertaking, and these faults were probably fully present in regard to the law entries. However, it does look as if the marked absence of Domat was a fault of commission. After visiting Catherine of Russia in 1773 Diderot published in 1776 his plan for a Russian university. It contained the following: "'Our [French] faculty of law is miserable. They don't read there a work of French law ... nothing of our *Code*...nothing of our law; nothing of our customs ... nothing of ... property, no more of ... contracts.... They occupy themselves with Roman law ... which has almost no relation to ours'" (*Encyclopedia Britannica*, Vol. VIII, 206a). In light of the 1679 Edict of Louis and appointment of a professor of French law at every university, among whom Pothier, the most distinguished, who had recently died (1772) after publishing as Professor of French law his monumental series of treatises, Diderot's remarks can only be viewed with speechless amazement.

Domat continued to work until the end. Still living in his unassuming second floor apartment on a street in the Faubourg Saint-Jacques, he died there on 14 March 1696. He had suffered for some time from asthma and the stone; in life he never shared the skepticism of Montaigne, but at the end he joined with that author in his view of the body's nemesis. A friend saw him once suffering through the violence of an asthmatic attack; Domat assured his visibly dismayed visitor that it was nothing in comparison to the kidney's affliction. He died poor in monies but richly endowed in character, a fit product of the harsh, strong contours of his native Auvergne. He had held fast in his break with the past, and his long labor had so reshaped French jurisprudence that, in Voeltzel's estimation (Voeltzel, 75), it held the cachet of being nearly legislation.

Les Lois Civiles
The Scope of the Work; Roman Law as Natural Law

One would expect that the legal Domat, by regrouping French law into new clarity, was striking out in new paradigmatic territory. Thus it is all the more ironic that in his analysis and outline of Domat's work Voeltzel found it appropriate himself to rearrange the *avocat*'s thoughts. Today we can appreciate Domat for who he is—hewing closely to his quest for control, his legal structures appearing sometimes intrinsically organic rather than extrinsically imposed. Frequently he will state his belief that a subject in the law is easiest to comprehend when it is expressed in its "natural order," that is, in reasoned classifications within which one can take a position flowing naturally from what has been said to what will next be said

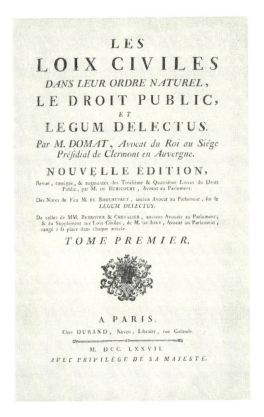

Title page from Jean Domat, *Les Loix Civiles Dans Leur Ordre Naturel, Le Droit Public, et Legum Delectus*, 1777
Courtesy of The Lawbook Exchange

(Voeltzel, 218). Putting the laws in a form easy for study has a pedagogical appeal and marketability, but the non-professorial Domat was nowhere limiting his clarity to a classroom. We may infer from his earlier career and his acceptance of the royal pension that he never lost from view the acute need for a national French law with which many educated people of his time, not just an arcane few, could work. With a bourgeois sensitivity to practical concerns, Domat sought national legal direction which would by its limpidity and accessibility reduce delay, expense, and unjust results.

France was sorely in need of changes in the structure, personnel, and procedure of courts; but these matters, except in areas where a better substantive law code might logically assist, did not engage Domat per se. Obviously, in taking on civil laws in their natural order he held no illusions about the difficulty of a very broad subject. He had to be content that procedure found coverage in the 1679 *Code Louis*, and that his own *Lois civiles*, the only part of his work he completed and published in his lifetime, would itself be limited to private law. It was a perfect choice. Tradition required the king leave this topic to the judges, so it had not previously been reached by ordinance. There it lay, supine in chaotic shambles, stifled by the weight of countless local customs. Because of the entry onto the legal scene of the many new professors of French law, Domat could sense how they were inching toward the production of suitable texts for their students. He knew that their professorial needs increased the pressure toward unification pushed by Du Moulin and others, for they could see multiple aspects of French legal institutions—from advocacy to judgment—which in fact needed development. Nevertheless, because Domat did not propose to follow the technique of earlier erudition—marshalling the customs, aiming at extracting their common principles so as to arrive at a single statement of French customary law as modified by ordinances, canon law, and other sources—he seemed to be proposing France be given what she needed in private law by recognizing the best of a philosophical tradition. By incorporating the tremendous legal innovations of the seventeenth century Domat's redefinition could be channeled into that part of private law which consisted almost entirely of natural law principles. Even though the strong shoulders of the precursors would not be given any expressed credit, it is certain that Humanist Domat had read them in the right compendia—Connan (1508–1551), Coras (1512–1572) his countryman, and Doneau (1527–1591)—and understood rules of property and contract law as reflecting the natural necessities of men (Gazzaniga, 42; 55).

Derivation *ab initio* had been a penchant at least claimed by Grotius and Pufendorf, but interestingly Domat avoided deducing from the basic propositions of natural law all those details of private substantive law obedient to them. Instead, with practicality always tugging at his philosopher's sleeve, the only complete system of private law Domat saw available for his more or less convenient study was the "written reason" (Voeltzel, 71) of Justinian, the hero of his student days. Domat's birthplace happened to lie squarely in the territory of the "written law," where the classical tradition, except when subject to royal ordinances and a few over-riding local customs, was the common law. Domat would actually take some time out to make a book of selections from Roman law which he called just that: *Legum delectus*. It was published after his death. We have seen this Roman tradition of the *Institutes* and *Digest* first studied and integrated into the medieval tradition of the Glossators and Commentators and more recently the historical school of Cujas. In the hands of our *avocat du roi* we now find preference for the latter, probably because of Domat's Cujas orientation at Bourges. The copious citations of the *Legum* are nearly all from the *Institutes* and *Digest*, not Accursius or Bartolus.

Return to Justinian meant Domat faced a large decision: Roman law would not be relevant to his purpose unless it were natural law. On this point he did not at the outset pretend, as did Grotius and Pufendorf, that one arrived at Roman law principles by pure coincidence in the course of deductions from natural law foundations. Domat began by affirming that "as for the laws of nature …we had nowhere the detail of them except in the books of the Roman law," and that "it is in the Roman law that these natural rules of equity have been collected together …" (Domat-Cushing, 58, 96). Domat's direction was not taking him deeply into decipherment of the link between metaphysics and jurisprudence, but instead, was setting him in line with the old medieval tradition of written Roman precepts. He stood before Justinian and beheld law expressed at its most "naturally" cogent.

However, he also sensed a caveat: Roman law captivated as a fantastic prize of natural law, yet there still remained, notwithstanding, Justinian's work and the misfortune of its being marred by infamously great disorder. Thus it was that an incidental but crucial result of the Domat direction came to be a necessary response: he would write a special book, so special that it would become the first general reclassification of Roman law since the time of the great Emperor.

Methodically, Domat explained his attack. Of all the matters regulated in France under its complex legal pattern of ordinances, customs, canon and Roman laws, he would select the following impressive array: contracts (including sales, exchanges, leases, loans, partnerships, and deposits); guardianships, prescriptions, and mortgages; successions, testaments, legacies, substitutions (trusts); proof and presumptions; capacity of persons; distinctions of things; and interpretations of laws. There were two grounds for choosing these topics as well as some lesser but associated areas. First, the century's resort to them was more frequent and necessary than other areas of inquiry. Second, "their principles and their rules are almost all of them natural rules of equity ... even ... such matters as are not known in the Roman law" (Domat-Cushing, 95). Domat's words show that he had discerned the most useful parts of current French legalities and much to his pleasure found them to be natural law. His accentuating contracts, for example, flowed effortlessly from "engagements," the essential element in Domat's philosophical plan of society; the confluence reflected appreciation of a certain unity on this subject (Olivier-Martin, 323), since both in northern France (the area of the customs) and southern France (the area of "written law") contract law was nearly all derived from Rome.

However, Domat did not propose to leave his important questions with no more than such simplistic affirmations. It had to be his beloved philosophical reasoning, presented in his equally beloved easy to comprehend form, which demonstrated legal concurrencies to be true. Thus Domat's rules of private law would descend logically from the Domat philosophy of law and society, a technique similar to the personalized legalisms of Grotius and Pufendorf. Although never expressed explicitly, we can have no doubt that he hoped by this means to give confidence to the legislator whether that legislator were the king making a foray into private law, or *Parlements* making decisions. Unification of French law along the Domat lines was to be, in short, *inévitable*. In fact, he was saying, this was the most extraordinary of inevitabilities, since it already existed. The whole problem was a kind of legal archeology—finding paradigms and grids which had so far escaped detection because neither the rationale of the laws had ever been correctly stated nor had the laws themselves been correctly arranged. For this failure of previous French jurists Domat was gallantly understanding: "... [I]n the books of the Roman law ... [the laws] are placed ... not in the best order, [but] mixed with many other laws which are neither natural nor in use with us .... [T]heir authority is weakened by this mixture.... [M]any persons either are not willing, or are not capable, to discern that which is certainly just and natural from that which reason and our practice do not admit of" (Domat-Cushing, 58; 96).

In spite of all this care in preparation and explanation, the relation in Domat's writing between Roman law and natural law is not entirely clear. Voeltzel, who probably studied Domat as intently as anyone, says (Voeltzel, 10) in his introduction that although *Les lois civiles* constitutes the statement of the fundamental principles and the drawing out of all the consequences, it would be incorrect to say that all the details are directly or indirectly "inspired" by something fundamental like the law of love, or by "some great natural principle." It is a text whose "spirit" is "divine" but whose "letter" is from a fallible human hand. It is a system which left Domat free to make needed positive laws for his day while drawing them from a Roman matrix. Only the "order" of subjects seems to come from a natural law of first principles, even though there is, of course, the possibility that Domat thought maintaining the logical validity of a system necessarily validated its parts (Pound, *Juris,* Vol. III, 215).

Domat's Philosophical Method

Towards showing that the French substantive law as selected by him was natural law, Domat's many words of proof continued to neglect what ancient and modern philosophical and scientific works he may have studied other than the Bible and the Fathers of the Church. His years with Pascal probably led to a familiarity with the work of Copernicus, Galileo, Kepler, and Newton, even, perhaps, with the inductive method of Bacon; and such a familiarity could have encouraged an empirical approach. But although the century's erudite foment was all around him, it seems very unlikely that any such grandiose research ideas occurred to Domat. Rather, sitting meditatively next to his own hot stove it seemed to him Descartes offered the point of light. As Domat did his own cogitating in a quiet study, contemplating man and seeking in that way to find the "first principles" of all laws—principles simple and self-proving like Descartes's *cogito* foundation of *I think, therefore I am*—he could not simply quote language from scripture or authoritative religious writings for his enterprise of winning the natural case. The era's geometric spirit was embraced, not for all endeavor, but for law; and like geometricians and like declarers of independence the Domat method would carefully state the obvious.

There was, however, an important difference between the philosophical jurisconsult and his model. Cartesianism was apolitical, a method not proposed as helpful to social and political institutions (Carey 40; 2) and a method written without the benevolence of any monarch. A sincere Christian, Domat's self-evident truths were tempered by the special piety and awkward ambiguity of a Jansenist working in the heart of Catholic France as a protégé of the "Most Christian" King. He could feel those negative vibrations from Louis's Jesuit confessor as well as from the monarch who, already somewhat disturbed by Jansenism, would in the next fifteen years become so severely disturbed by it, that he would plow under Port-Royal. Domat knew that royal authority, according to king and ministeriat, came from God; he recognized similar descent for the law of his state.

That Domat did not choose to cite the secular natural law work of Grotius, despite Jansenism's proximity to Protestantism, makes one wonder if the special Protestant approach to Christianity really made any difference in the precise selection of rules for the *Lois civiles*. That it may not have had a substantial influence is again suggested by Grotius; his natural law rules, which turned out to be generally consistent with Roman law, were clearly said by him to have been the same whether or not God exists simply because they were based not on Romanism or Christianity but on basic fundamentals engrained in the nature of man. God had created that nature and, whether or not He had power to do it, God had not changed His creation. Domat did affirm at the very outset of his work that one had to be born after Christ with self-knowledge and vision to know the most fundamental principles of natural law; but he also declared that the ancient pagans were in their blindness themselves quite capable of arriving at least at correct subordinate propositions of this natural direction, merely because knowledge of equity and justice had been placed in the human heart by nature. Domat's work, like that of Aquinas, was, it would appear, concerned above all with reconciling the best thought on both the BCE and CE side of the Christian divide.

Still, Domat, however secular the siting of his natural law Mount may have been, had to begin with the existence of God. Unlike the Scholastics and Descartes he saw no need to prove it or even expressly affirm it; he simply assumed it—it was the spirit's Base Camp. Then, when wishing to be scientific and Cartesian, he made moves toward the other mountain of fundamental principles known through reason—axiomatic definition. Domat admitted that such knowledge, being a matter of mind, could not be apprehended by all. The first principles of laws, though, were far more strongly founded; both mind and heart grasped their truth, presumably, we infer, upon their first statement (Domat-Cushing, 3). Moreover, one could reject the axioms of Euclid without rejecting God; conversely, however, to reject the fundamentals of law would imply rejection of God, a state of legal apostasy Domat found impossible (Voeltzel, 94).

The next Domat perception was the end game—the goal of law conditioning rules for the conduct of human beings. If this noble *telos* were reached by good, clear arrangement, Domat knew process would bring the agreeable pleasure of truth (Carey, 39) and therefore grouped first principles by focusing on the roadway of human life. Far from a random walk, had not God created with good purpose a human creature whose soul and body resemble Him? The purpose of the human soul is to know some object and love it; yet that object is nothing on earth, for we easily observe that earth was made for man and not man for earth. Domat carefully chose his motto, *Man is made by God and for God*; and under it he placed the human construct—able to know the Sovereign Good and given a religion by God stating the rules which will lead to that knowledge while encompassed by the fundamental law: seek and love the highest good. This requirement of outreach in turn introduced its corollary: no one can live alone; all of us by our very nature must enter into a human compact in order to be successful in achieving the highest good. Hence, the second law: in societal union men and women must love one another as earthly co-dwellers on a social planet.

Domat's society at the end of the seventeenth century was not obeying these natural laws; yet, as he saw it, law violated did not mean law ceased to exist. Troubles in society—crimes, delicts, litigation, wars—all come because we love the self rather than our compatriots and our God. But right here in this dominion of *amour propre*, that pesky yet powerful given of human nature which dominated *salon* conversation and the day's novels and plays, Domat discovered a legal loophole: God was actually through perversion providing an automatic remedy which could raise post-lapsarian humans to a state even happier than before their transgression (Voeltzel, 161). In a very twenty-first century After-the-Fall ambience of increased needs, self-love actually encouraged the human species to meet these needs through an infinity of useful bondings: read civil laws, read entitlements, read charitable organizations. The Domat comfort factor was that society embraced a multiplicity of such bondings: religion, the authority given by God to princes, God's Providence, and, finally, fallen humankind's natural knowledge of equity. Self-love itself, in requiring some virtue to satisfy need, leaves much to hope for. In this positive, socio-political attitude toward society Domat had met Aristotle, Aquinas, and Grotius and in that meeting broken out of the dark recesses of Augustine and Hobbes. The purpose of a Domat society had become clear: to facilitate through law the work endeavors necessary to sustain physically so each person could function spiritually—a kind of pre-Voltairean cultivating of the soul's victory garden under the rule of law.

Contracts were now right around the corner, and Domat saw them like some elegant classical ballet—detailed statutes moving gracefully from the essential legal methodology of society which enabled each citizen to live the social compact and thereafter, to know the good. In envisaging creation of reciprocities among citizens, Domat allocated the first as the specific linkages resulting from birth and marriage, such as the duty to support children or a spouse. The second occur outside of the home and consist of all other agreements and contracts, gratuitous or commercial, voluntarily entered into or imposed by law. So that a citizenry providentially placed into different social ranks will enter into these exteriorized engagements, God has made each human being with wants that have to be satisfied. And because human nature is mortal and society must continue for the survivors, there must be in the laws provision for succession to such engagements. Although becoming a successor may in itself involve an engagement, it is better to view Succession as a Part II of the law while Engagements form its Part I. Yet be it a question of engagements in Part I or Part II, the essential central principle of all society is the making of them. Engagements are no less than law within whose purview each of us comes—first by birth and marriage, then by making contracts. Engagements are the particular law without which would be no guidance on how to obey succession

Domat, wasting no time in detailing his engagement theory in *Les lois civiles*, dramatically chose Book One, Part One to sound the trumpet: "Voluntary and Mutual Engagements by Covenant." Book Two coped with far more in "Engagements Formed Without a Covenant," —a very large area embracing "Tutors"; "Curators"; "Managers of Others' Affairs"; "Owners in Common"; "Owners of Adjoining Lands"; "Receivers of What is Not Due"; "Damages Occasioned by Faults Which Do Not Amount to a Crime or Offence"; "Engagements Arising from Accidents" (as in finding lost property); and "Acts to Defraud Creditors." The density is prodigious. Even within the seventeen pages of "Damages Occasioned by Faults" one found another basic rule of behavioral etiquette: a person can proportion voluntary engagements to different wants of different people, but no matter in what manner of covenant and diversification of affairs one is entered, there must be no infringement upon the ultimate general rule of respect for laws and good manners (Domat-Cushing, 22–25).

Domat's major thesis of demonstration devolved upon hard evidence: "all the matters of the civil law have…a simple and natural order, which forms them into one body, in which it is easy to see them all"; this order is founded on a "plan of society," which is that the "order of society is preserved in all places by … engagements" which are "perpetuated in all times by successions" (Domat-Cushing, 96). It was a system, or, better, discovery of *the* system, and with it came the very seventeenth century caveat that if a body of rules could not be systematized it was wrong. System proves Rules. Domat believed that in fact within prescription's macro-system lived a micro-systemization of regulation which, as a rigid protocol of preliminaries, had to be followed before proceeding to engagements and successions. "Three sorts of general matters," wrote Domat, are "common to all the others, and necessary for understanding the whole detail of the laws." These were (1) "certain general rules which respect the nature, use, and interpretation of laws," (2) "the ways in which the civil laws consider and distinguish persons by certain qualities which have relation to engagements or successions" (such as whether a person is a major with capacity to contract or a minor lacking such capacity), and (3) "the ways in which the civil laws distinguish the things which are for the use of men, with respect to engagements and succession" (an example being, in successions, whether goods are paternal or maternal) (Domat-Cushing, 96–97).

Domat's system had taken the persons, things, and actions classification of Gaius which embraced all private law; but it had then eliminated consideration of actions, and made the whole antecedent to a single central idea: engagements. And antecedence had large importance. In its first division we find Domat's general description of natural law, a subject to which in the *Traité des lois* he devoted much of Chapter XI (*Of the Nature and Spirit of Laws, and their Different Kinds*) and to which he referred again at the beginning of the next chapter covering the subject matter now to be found in the *Lois civiles* first division:

> All the different ideas which it is possible to conceive of the several sorts of laws that are expressed by the names of divine and human laws, natural and positive, spiritual and temporal, law of nations, civil laws, and by all the other names that can be given them, may be reduced to two kinds, which comprise all laws of what nature soever; <u>one is of the laws which are immutable, and the other, of the laws that are arbitrary</u>" (Domat-Cushing, 49) (underscoring supplied).

Domat was adamant. This distinction as to laws should "precede the other ways of distinguishing them" as "the most essential part in the nature of all laws." The "immutable laws … are natural, and so just at all times, and at all places, that no authority can either change or abolish them." They are "necessary consequences of the two fundamental laws" (love good, love man), and "so essential to the engagements that form the order of society, that it is impossible to alter them without destroying the foundations of the … order."

At this juncture Domat, reverting to Jansenist rigor and putting on his best severe mien, wrote that philosophical generalities had to be buttressed by some strict general rules for each person: (1) engagements are humanity's "proper laws," (2) each should submit to the temporal and ecclesiastical powers which God has established to maintain the societal order, (3) each should stay within rank and make no bad use of the self or of one's belongings, (4) no one should wrong another, but give to each one's due, (5) a citizen should be sincere and honest in making voluntary engagements, (6) and should also faithfully perform the obligations of involuntary engagements, (7) refrain from deceit in all engagements, and (8) perform the duties to maintain order imposed by public office, successory fiduciaryship, eminent domain, taxation, and the like. It is only in item (4) of these "general rules" that Domat embraces the subject of the wrongs that in English law are called "torts" and which in continental law are part of the "law of obligations"; for Domat the subject appeared as a topic supporting the concept of voluntary engagements (Domat-Cushing, 49–50).

By this plethora of stern axioms a single philosopher jurisconsult thus had embraced and brought forward the whole seventeenth century idea of natural law, from its Protestant and secular origins into the Catholic and Jansenist tradition of France's absolute monarchy. The feat was achieved successfully, with, apparently, hardly a political ripple. In the Realist tradition of Aquinas, Grotius, and Pufendorf and against the Nominalist tradition of Ockham, Montaigne, and Hobbes, Domat upheld natural law against its positive counterpart. In doing so he had to separate himself from the philosophy of his friend Pascal, who admitted the ideal but who, like all philosophers opposing natural law, extrapolated from the diversity of legal usage the proof that natural law no longer could be found, or, if found, followed. Pascal and fellow Jansenists, their words a Catholic echo of Augustine via Calvin, were unable to move from man's depravity and God's high and remote omnipotence and, believing in the individual's direct relation to God, lived uneasily with the universal which Catholic tradition required: a divine institution mediating for man. Their point of view clashed with the Domat doctrine that a person *can* find a natural law—a law which has God's authority—simply by having the courage to examine his or her own depraved human nature. The Jesuit confessors of Louis XIV, casuists who worked out morality on a case by case basis, might well indeed have been more comfortable with Grotius and Domat than Calvin would have been. Luther, too, had been driven in the end to their casuistry by trying, as the Jesuit confessors did, to present a morality that an absolute political master could use, even though to lead a nation he was subject to the moral strain of having to attract support from conflicting and shifting blocs of opinion. Not infrequently did that master feel he had to indulge in divorce, misleading statements, hard punishment, and other morally doubtful actions. But natural law?—even a heliocentric monarch of all he surveyed could not change it, and to *that* the man from Clermont would hold fast against God Himself.

Domat and the Law of Contracts

The European tradition of obligation began with the Romans. The root of *obligato* is in the Latin *lig*, something bound, as though by rope or chain. That root today is bifurcated: one party in the procedure has a duty and the other a right. This special legal achievement may have begun when the state first intervened in private vengeance for a wrong, forcing the injured party to abandon revenge and accept instead adjustment or even avoidance of a composition. If the wrong-doer could not pay the composition in money or property at once, he might promise to pay and thereby become "bound"; if he did not perform his promise of mutual agreement, private vengeance would be permitted. The idea was extended to loans and other transactions and gradually the concept of duty and right were recognized. Such right was *in personam*; if one had a relation to a thing which was injured his right was *in rem*. But everything was limited by the old Roman procedure: unless a person's claim fit one of the several kinds of remedies, the state would give no aid. In time came the distinction of Gaius between contract and delict. Then appeared the refinement of Justinian which introduced *quasi* forms of each, giving four categories, a plan which may have satisfied the Emperor's superstition that since in theology three was the occult number, in secular affairs, four was more appropriate. This quadratic division influenced treatises and codes for centuries.

Contracts' fundamental question turned on which promises would be enforced as such. A primary concern was that everyone uses language sometimes seriously and sometimes lightly; it was important that those lightly-tossed-off remarks should not have serious legal consequences. Roman law achieved protection of the loquacious by requiring observance of certain precise verbal formalities to make a contract. Consensus, however, would not always lead to contract. Unless there was a remedy, it was a mere *nudum pactum*—agreement not enforceable by action—thus introducing, in addition to ropes and chains, the idea of the necessity of some "clothing" for the nudity, or something at the end of the rope possessed by the promisor. With an exchange of promises treated like an exchange of property, if there were only "a promise communicated," should it be enforceable? Romans thought not, unless there were proof that it was accepted. But the question persisted: was that enough without more? Should not an equivalent be delivered by the promisee to the promisor? This case of the "simple procedure" seemed like a fundamental starting point in the analysis of the enforceability of promises, yet from the requirement of an equivalent the canon law dissented. Religion, it was held, demanded that serious promises should be kept, and the superiority of such strict procedure of Church courts had for centuries tended to attract plaintiffs. Thus, later medieval writers and others up to the earlier seventeenth century, including Grotius, rejected the idea of "nudum pactum"; by natural law an action arises "from any pact deliberately made," and for a natural lawyer what was morally binding meant it was legally binding as well (Pound, *Juris,* Vol. III, 191; 166; 195; 169).

As the needs of commerce created pressure to depart from formulary contracts and enforce more casual promises seriously made, forms were found by rummaging hard in Roman law closets. Baldus and later medieval jurists, building with certain references to "cause" in Roman statutes (references which, we now know, did not necessarily require such a conclusion [Zimmerman, *The Law of Obligations, Roman Foundations of the Civilian Trades,* 550]), and using as their mortar the scholastic doctrine that every effect, dependent on its reason or "cause," cannot exist without it, laid it down that every contract depended for its validity upon proof of its cause. The doctrine of the invalidity of a contract because the price was unjust—an idea begun by the ecclesiastical courts and later recognized in secular jurisprudence—formed yet another subject (Olivier-Martin, 211). A longstanding alternative approach to substantive requirements for validity of contracts lay in a procedural cloak: require adequate proof before enforcing a simple promise. For instance, back in the sixteenth century the 1566 Ordinance of Moulins, to avoid the complications of lawsuits, imposed something in writing for everything over one hundred *livres* in value (Brissaud, *Manuel d'histoire du droit français,* 511). By 1677 a French lawyer dealing in England would have been aware obligation had been heavily clothed in a new Statute of Frauds.

By needing a structural equivalent, and a tying down of the free-form *causa*, these ideas about *nudum pactum* interfered with what continental law in general came to regard as the essential general approach: that reasonable expectations aroused by promises of advantages should be enforced unless there was some countervailing interest. Lawyers held a strong sense of the social order's resting "upon stability and predictability of conduct" (Pound, *Juris*, Vol. III, 162). True, the history of legal doctrine through the Middle Ages reduced the generality of such a policy, but, by developing their secular natural law, seventeenth century practitioners, beginning with Grotius, had armed themselves with paramount general principles which could enable them intellectually to start anew. Grotius had already led the way in regard to *nudum pactum* and *causa*.

Now in the waning years of the seventeenth century had come Domat, centering law on engagement—that is, law as contract. In this tenacious point of view Domat ignored chronology. The oldest Roman law was family law concerned with property and successions; obligations fell later under this inter-family legality (Zimmerman, 1–2). But Domat's long Part II approached successions only as the necessary provision for survival of contracts against man's incapacities and mortality. He had rejected Jansenist predestination, and his Gaian explications of the nature of laws, of persons, and things were in his view the introductions to contracts In Gaius's plan obligations, relating to things, were put at the end of a tripartite group; things became, in a narrow sense, successions and obligations. Justinian's Eastern Roman counselors saw obligations arising from delict as depending on enforcement for efficacy, and they had placed them at the beginning of Book IV of the *Institutes*, which includes "actions"; Book III had dealt with "things" (as did Book II) as well as obligations other then those arising from delict. Thus neither Justinian nor Gaius gave voluntary contracts—obligations not arising from delict—the place of honor. In Domat's floor plan of society these *are* matters which matter, and therefore they had to dominate in the building of his *Lois civiles*. He still honored Gaius's fundamental distinction (which probably came from Aristotle) as to obligations—those based on contract and those based on delict—but only in a subordinate way, setting those based on delict as a small item he placed under *Engagements Which are Formed Without a Covenant*. From Domat's standpoint in working this way with natural law he was at last creating a new architecture. It differed widely, or perhaps we should say proudly, from those structures raised up by Grotius and Pufendorf, each of whom was more concerned with the state than was the Frenchman postponing public law for another book.

It is not surprising that Domat stressed human freedom in the making of contracts, keeping his interference option of "laws and good manners" as minimal as he could. "Laws," of course, embraced the mercantilism of Colbert, and it is possible that Domat was not satisfied with its restrictiveness. Still it is plain that the centrality Domat imparted to contracts would appeal to the growing commercial and industrial activity of bourgeois who were on the move toward a capitalist society. Only laborers were left standing outside his freshened concept of free contract, their time still awaiting the call to pull down the structure called La Bastile.

In Domat's resolve to restate in better form those current French law rules which were natural law of Roman provenance, his particular scope made it easy to ignore old subtleties like the formulary procedure. As Zimmerman suggests, this should also have made possible an equally facile decision to ignore Roman ideas about *nudum pactum* and alleged Roman considerations about the necessity of *causa* while yet accepting the Roman idea of consensus. What Domat did do was to ignore the Roman language on *nudum pactum*, to accept the idea of consensus, but to accept also the necessity of cause. This decision seems to have influenced Pothier, for we shall find he would soon do the same. His adherence to Domat's view, supplemented by his impressive reputation in England, was destined to help block Lord Mansfield's effort to end the English parallel—the doctrine that there must be a "consideration" (Zimmerman, 567, 570). Pothier's acceptance of his colleague's ideas undoubtedly was going to open up the necessity of cause in Article 1132 of the *French Civil Code*. On the other hand, it was unfortunately going to challenge French lawyers from 1804 on, separating France, at least in analytical language if not importantly in results, from the continental approaches led by the Germans and Dutch. Emancipated from *causa*, they would tend to bear down on the necessity of consensus as well as require proof of "consent."

For Domat, the essence of "covenant"—contracts, treaties, and pacts—was accepting entrance into an engagement. Using modern language, we can ascribe four kinds of covenants to Domat. Under (1) A delivers something (property or money) to B and B delivers something to A, under (2) A does a service for B and B for A, under (3) A does a service for B and B delivers something to A, and under (4) A delivers something to B, or A does a service for B and B does nothing. However, Domat did not accept any covenant as obligatory without a cause. In the first three of the kinds aforestated there is "always (a) cause from something that is either done or to be done by the other party: and the obligation would be null, if it were really without any cause." But, Domat continued, covenants in group (4), which are "donations" or some "other contract where one party alone does or gives something, and where the other neither does nor gives anything," are also enforceable because here "the acceptance … forms the contract"; the donor (as promisor in relation to the "other" contracts) has "some just and reasonable motive," if only "the bare pleasure of doing good to others," and this motive "stands in place of a cause." Here "cause" can be immaterial (Domat-Cushing, 147, 148–149). That the "motive" must be "just and reasonable" should be noted; it was a moral requirement befitting Domat's intense Christian faith.

In the multitude of agreements made by people in their daily lives, these statements hardly suffice as an analytical tool to distinguish which ones are valid as having "cause" and which are not. The old controversies about the enforceability of simple promises continued, shifting from one between canon law and Roman law to one between Romanists inclined to say there is a "cause" and adherents of the "old law" who tended to say that there was none (Brissaud, 516). Still, despite the back and forth, the entire area of "cause," important while at the same time disappointing to a modern reader of Domat's work, never would prevent his writing from having a lasting effect on the attitude of French lawyers toward their law.

As a "to" and "from," Domat definitely owns his place in the history of contractuality. Looking at Gazzaniga's division of European law of obligations into three periods, the Domat name is in two and his influence in the third: (1) beginning at the beginning of Roman law to Domat's determining synthesis of Christian thought, Roman Law, and Natural Law; (2) from Domat and his fruition in the *Civil Code of 1804* to the changes introduced in the period 1880–1900 that nourished the twentieth century; and (3) from 1880–1900 to the end of the twentieth century. Only one other stands in rivalry with Domat for the title of French classicism's greatest lawyer, and we shall meet him now. But Clermont's greatest was to prove unforgettable in his patient and determined analysis of the distinction between natural and positive law. Domat had walked the earth as a modest man, but his giant ambition lived on, finally translated into nothing less than constructing an overall philosophy of law. Not bad for a man without a portrait.

Henri François d'Aguesseau
Courtesy of The Bridgeman Art Library

PART 16

The Second Period of Secular Natural Law
Daguesseau and Pothier

The Progress of Secular Natural Law

Overview

Henri-François Daguesseau

Introduction

Henri-François D'Aguesseau or *Daguesseau* as he and his father wrote it, came into the world with qualifications of mind, character, and circumstances that could hardly have been better for a career in law. Like Grotius, he worked hard throughout his life to make the most of his dispositions, impressing those who knew him by being scholarly, amazingly well read, and gifted with an astounding memory. In contrast to Grotius, he chose not to make literary work the centerpiece of his life. Rather, he would realize another ambition and, occupying high places in government, devote his entire active career to the magistracy of France. For about twenty-eight years he held as Chancellor the highest rank in his country's legal world and in official social position stood as "first gentleman" after the sovereign.

Professional endeavors began at twenty-one. Father Henri (1636–1716) was a distinguished lawyer who, having filled intendancies in Guyenne and Languedoc, had been successfully at work as Intendant for the Limousin when he retired. Henri's own father, many had hoped, was himself on the track for Chancellor, but that honor had to await the grandson. Henri *père* wasted no time: he considered his son ready for higher responsibility after only a few months' experience as an *avocat* in the Châtelet, a Parisian court of first instance. To that end he wrote with confidence to Louis XIV, proposing the young Henri-François as *avocat-général*—one of only three in the *Paris Parlement*. At a meeting of his Council on appointments Louis approved, with the approbative comment that Henri Daguesseau's integrity was such he could never mislead his king even as to a son (Monnier, *Le chancelier D'aguesseau, sa conduite et ses idées politiques, et son influence sur le mouvement des esprits pendant la première moitié du xviiie siècle, avec des documents nouveaux et plusieurs ouvrages inédits du chancelier,* 54). No remark could better confirm the reputation of the Daguesseau family for probity and for posterity.

Throughout his career, the conduct of Henri-François proved high trust to be the central theme of a long life story told between 1668 and 1751. Daguesseau came from a special part of the middle class apex which, during years of nobility's inadequacy, had taken effective political power in France; although the tax collectors and financiers were richer, the *avocats* of the "high robe" dominated in social prestige. The family belonged to the austere Jansenist patriarchate, known politically for a devotion to the monarchy and public service, their passionate belief in state authority maintained without war, and the promotion of *Parlement* as the king's depository of reason in support of all that was legal. Yet these men also stoked the fires of rebellion to come. With the welfare of the people and the fisc as their supreme law, they opposed perpetuation of the ancient privileges of feudalism. Their piety and strong support for the independence of the Gallic Catholic Church made them oppose the Jesuit backers of Roman pretensions. Most importantly, in their tolerance and liberal sympathies for the socially repressed, they stood as a block devoted to reform of the courts and the law. One can have no better example of this high robe intellect applied to liberal legal progress than Henri-François Daguesseau.

He had an extraordinary training, worthy of a ligneage about whose worth he would never harbor the slightest doubt. His ancestors' faith had been saintly, and as one of their own, Henri-François found soul-searching natural and easy. Become a great lawyer, he still never forgot his intense upbringing from a father whose pious gravity (he was suspected as being a preaching Jansenist) gave faith first place. In some years Daguesseau was known to have donated as much as one-third of his income to charity, for he counted the poor as his own children in weighing their claim upon his bounty and concern. When late in life he was named to the Council on Finance, friends lectured him that he must do over his home furnishings to fit his new dignity. At first Daguesseau dutifully handed his wife for the purpose a bag containing 25,000 livres. She replied that, true, their things were old, yet could it not all continue to serve for the couple's few remaining years, given that so many worthy poor in Paris without such option slept on straw and often lacked bread? The old man tearfully admitted that the same idea had occurred to him, too, and Madame was at once told to distribute the money to the indigent as she saw fit (Monnier 122).

As an adult Henri-François said that "'religion serves as the base of all teaching: a half-hour in the morning and a half-hour in the evening must be given to reading the New Testament, to imitation of Jesus Christ, and to the lives of the saints.'" Like his father he cultivated Spartan taste, shunning magnificence and idle amusements for faithful performance of the Catholic cult. Pardessus, publisher of his papers, calls him a "'Christian with the submission of Pascal, the conviction of Bossuet, and the piety of Fénélon'" (Frêche, *Un chancelier gallican: Daguesseau; et un cardinal diplomate,* 7, 18). With this kind of iconoclastic background, contrasting with the luxury of Versailles, the Daguesseau men, despite their loyalty, were fortunate to stay in touch with the royal good graces; like Domat, they appear to have done it by hard work and a complete reliability in an age of backroom intrigue.

Flexibility can mark cleverness in politics and affairs. Henri-François stood prepared to change his mind in the face of better facts, new facts, or, on rare occasions, better reasoning. On fundamentals, though, he could stand even against the King, for which we shall find him twice as Chancellor exiled to his country house. To the second of these exiles (1722–1727) we owe his book in defense of natural law. This significant but fairly unknown text will attract our scrutiny as part of the long skein that from Creon to Antigone to Domat oscillates between realism and nominalism, skepticism and faith, natural law and positive law.

Education of H. F. Daguesseau

Intendant Henri Daguesseau was popular in Limousin territory, and the birth of his son in Limoges, the capital of that province, had meant no less than a Daguesseau fête day for the whole city. People spoke nostalgically of Henri's father, Antoine, regarded as the founder of the family's robe status. He had served both as Intendant in Picardie and First President of the *Parlement of Bordeaux* where the sixteenth century Montaigne served the law and the eighteenth century Montesquieu would elaborate on the tradition. The townsfolk also proclaimed admiration for Henri, who had taken his bachelor's degree at the College of Navarre in the University of Paris and after law study had begun as a Counsellor in the *Parlement* of Metz. He it was who had actively promoted the noble status (although without a title) to which the Daguesseau record in the magistracy entitled them. A courageous, independent thinker, one day he even disputed Colbert, and his colleagues thought him lost. Instead, Colbert appointed him to the next open Intendancy, for he had noticed that although weak and delicate in body, Henri had a perfect bureaucratic soul. The requirements? Being strong as a Roman, dominated by love of *patrie*, devoured by zeal for the public welfare, and more citizen than husband or father.

After father Henri's death Henri-François would write for his own son (164 pages in the Pardessus edition) a *Discourse on the life and death of M. d'Aguesseau, Counsellor of State, by M. d'Aguesseau, Chancellor of France, his son*. In its pages it becomes obvious why Henri-François himself had had no need of a tutor. Taught first to read and then put to the grammar of Greek and Latin as well as modern languages, the child was to study great writers in each category. Work was evidently guided so skillfully, and the boy's talent and taste were so suitable, that his curiosity and appreciation were quickly aroused. The two Henris surely must have appeared an odd couple—the stern parent and malleable child on circuit in the Intendancy, the boy, encouraged to interact with his father's older friends, witnessing and participating in important political events and day-to-day administration until finally leaving the road to return home. There awaited a course of reading and study of books not only planned by the father but followed up by intense one-on-one discussion. The boy would then write his own reports which the father would read, at first accept as satisfactory, then proceed to criticize in detail until nothing was left and the son had to try again. It may have been a severe regimen, but it aroused the interest of a future lawyer, teaching him to observe and to report correctly what he had observed. Equally useful was the impression made on the little traveling companion by his father's habits upon arrival at the hotel: "'to write calmly on the first table he found…in the midst of the necessary noise the servants made in his chamber…. [W]hat he wrote had the same turn, the same exactness and elegance as if he were working in a place with no distraction. Enclosed in the secret of his soul he made it a peaceful retreat where nothing could interrupt him'" (Monnier, 36–37). Such details of autobiography make it clear that while a child Henri-François had been trained to act the man, admiring and imitating Life with Father down to his signature.

A twenty-first century Henri-François might passively have witnessed events as a student among peers or as a digital or computer viewer. But during the active seventeenth century internship on the road, he lived first-hand father Henri's active condemnation of the folly in anti-Huguenot policies and in extravagant royal spending. When Louis listened to his powerful minister Louvois, instead of a weakened Colbert who, when he died, took to the grave any hope of fiscal reform, it was the son who saw his father's counsels to the King now ignored. Both suffered the insult as the Marquis de Saint-Ruth, a tough soldier, was sent to the Daguesseau's own province to suppress rebellion with brutal *dragonnades*. The Protestants, fearing the worst, had prepared as best they could for harsh civil war. One prayer group, led by their minister, fought Saint-Ruth's troops until only twenty men were left alive, whereupon Saint-Ruth burned them in the house to which they had retreated. For five years the boy daily saw such acrimonious, bloody struggle; he was present as the father, so respected that his carriage passed unmolested, often tried to stop the fighting, aiding the wounded and desperate on both sides. But the Edict was revoked, Henri resigned for reasons of health, and his *caritas* was replaced by fanaticism.

The classical poets offered Henri-François a true delight, perhaps because of those frequent business trips and brutal scenes of youth. Being awakened to such esoteric pleasure was to great extent the result of the exceptional Mme. Daguesseau, who usually formed part of the travel team. At the start of a journey, after offering prayer, she would spend time explaining to her son the Greek and Latin authors he was to study and memorize for recitation along the ride. From this formation grew one of the leading Humanists of the century, a lawyer of encyclopedic literary culture whose Latin and Greek learned along countless roads became bolstered by Hebrew, Italian, Spanish, Portuguese, and English. As he grew older, he delved more deeply into Hebrew, began Syriac, Chaldean, and Arabic, and read commentaries on the Old Testament by respected rabbis. His taste for books and study were so strong that while still young he bought the entire library of scholar Claude Chrestien and increased it to nearly 6,000 volumes.

The Daguesseau taste for history became voracious, too, and his bookshelves showed it in the many old manuscripts collected over time. He was a connoisseur of fine bindings, unique copies, and first editions, owning a handsome first printing of Homer in Greek. As a scholar he detected the borrowings of Virgil from old Ionian poets, published an edition of that author, and also a translation of the Crito of Plato. Continuing to build up the legal part of his library as a source of support for studies in jurisprudence, his collection of the printed customs was a nearly complete one. He took special pride in having acquired volumes of the secret registers of the *Paris Parlement*, as well as rare collections of ordinances, treatises, and the like. Known for his prodigious memory, it was said that at age eighty he corrected a friend's rendering of a verse from Martial which he had last read at twelve; in another instance a young poet read him a supposedly new piece only to be astounded when Daguesseau started reciting equivalent lines from work already published by another (Monnier, 276).

Henri Daguesseau had learned logic by study of scholastic models. When he proposed the same approach for his son, though, here the paragon version of Henri-François finally rebelled. After all, this was the period (c. 1670–1678) in which Descartes finally conquered France, and in school at Port-Royal the Jansenist *solitaires* were busily substituting Descartes for the scholastics. Relenting, Henri now gave the works of Descartes to the avid son and, because this was a well-connected family, supplemented them by the conversation of a family friend, the Oratorian genius Father Malebranche, Descartes's disciple. The *cogito* effect was strong on Henri-François, for mathematics and the sciences had long been intellectual predilections, particularly the period's beloved geometry whose mental challenges he continued to juggle as recreation while Chancellor-in-exile. One can see Cartesianism as the main influence in the Daguesseau *Méditations* of 1722–1727.

Exactly when and how the young man had been introduced to jurisprudence is not known, but like the pious Protestant Grotius, whom he much admired, by adolescence Daguesseau was committed to the construction of a philosophical system in support of a secular natural law which, though according a role to God, could be reached without God by reason and experience alone. When he was seventeen, father Henri, having resigned his Intendancy, retired to a small house in Paris. With the "law of justice...a cult in [the] family" (Monnier, [34]), it seemed high time to launch the next *robe* generation into successful magistracy. At about nineteen Henri-François was sent off to learn the Daguesseau profession.

Although Monnier does not say so explicitly, he must have then entered the courses offered by the Paris faculty for obtaining the *licence* without which law practice as an *avocat* was impossible. We infer that up to this time the home-schooled adolescent had never studied at a university or other school; nor is there suggestion that Henri-François resorted for his *licence* to one of those degraded faculties where the *licence* was being bought without study. But imagine the paternal disappointment when the brilliant scion now reacted as negatively to the study of Roman law as he had earlier to scholastic logic. The prestigious texts were airily adjudged to possess no historic or rational relationship either to one another or to daily human life. Henri (and Domat) would have to step in to save the situation. First came Henri, who, having often wished his own career had been in the more intellectual, legal atmosphere of the *Paris Parlement*, rather than in the banal administrative life of an Intendant, indefatigably took his filial avatar in hand again, teaching him the "invariable maxims" that controlled legislation (Monnier, 48). Inspired, Henri went even farther, writing out suggestions for palatable study of the *Digest*: keep in mind the idea of natural law as a background structure; test each text to determine whether it is part of that immutable, universal law; if it is only positive law, decide whether it is necessary and useful, or vicious and deleterious. It was a new game to play, and just as in the travel days the dutiful son, reoriented and refreshed, took up the law books again.

Next, it was time for the second career guide: family friend, Jean Domat. Domat would not begin publication of his ambitious treatise until 1689, but we know that a general scheme of ideas was already being given structure in his mind. He had gone to Paris either in 1683 for assistance in his studies, or at least by 1685 when he moved there permanently. It is said that he and Henri-François were now being solicited by the King himself to develop the single code for France. It is certain that young Daguesseau later did assist Domat and comment on some of his drafts. What is important is that the young law student, having drifted a bit at the very outset of what was to be an extraordinary career, now had the good fortune to come fully under the influence of France's leader in the natural law movement. Domat was a confirmed Cartesian and adept at the method of geometry. Even had the young Daguesseau chosen the unlikely route of not listening to his father's clarifications, there were more than enough shared interests and legal leverage from Domat alone to encourage Henri-François in his lifelong devotion to the study of law. A new Daguesseau was at last headed for the brilliant pinnacle.

Daguesseau on Legal Education

The educative process did not end when success arrived. Instead, Daguesseau's adult learning grew organically from day-to-day study of legal materials in the performance of his work—more or less still the only continuing education for most busy lawyers. He did not keep a diary or provide at the end of life a report on any special career breakthrough, but we know his reading and reflection never ceased. A good guide for the way he approached legal studies comes to us in a different form: Daguesseau Family Education, this time son Henri-François providing Part II for his own five children. In this regimen the father did not neglect his two daughters, but, unfortunately, the period framework of their upbringing would not permit that they break out of approved structure. The older girl was a year younger than the eldest son. When four she entered a convent for her education; at fifteen she returned home to finish studies. She was a bright student, and it is noteworthy that Henri-François showed his pro-feminist inclinations when he told her he hoped she would be so empowered by the quality of her quick responses and mastery of science that she would humiliate her brothers who, he said, too frequently thought themselves excessively clever people (Monnier, 161).

As he began with great earnestness the legal education of the oldest boy, Daguesseau knew that as Chancellor he could not be with him very often, nor, at this exalted level, would he imitate his own father by bringing a child with him to the office or on official royal or parliamentary visits. But again like Henri before him, when it was time for the university Henri-François produced lengthy written instructions for his son's use during any paternal absence, guides which probably helped along the legal tutors also provided to supplement the lectures and exercises of the Paris law faculty. It is posterity's good fortune that all instructions have survived. They are at once not only an index to Daguesseau's perspicacious understanding of the shortcomings of the Paris law faulty, but also illuminate his own studies and ideas on the formal education of a young magistrate-to-be. Here and elsewhere the *Instructions* began with the most general propositions and proceeded to the details—interestingly, the reverse of the "case method" as introduced by Langdell at the Harvard Law School about 140 years later. Carried beyond their methodology, the instructions serve us, together with the history of Daguesseau's own youth already recounted and the events of his career, as an excellent background when considering the *Meditations* on natural law.

The first paternal advisement is dated 27 September 1716 when the son, now eighteen, had just completed his university arts course and was entering law training.

Daguesseau called the series his instructions for higher studies; it is a substantial effort, occupying 156 printed pages in the Pardessus edition. Daguesseau's career was in transformation from his being King's Procureur General, to taking the chancellorship the following February, and there was no time to finish the lengthy advisory until greater leisure during forced exile brought him home to his country estate from January 1718 to June 1720. That the "Instructions" were written and thus could be preserved for us may owe something also to the political situation in 1716, one year after the royal sun had set on Versailles. In the circles of *Parlement*, long repressed, there was finally a burst of freer expression—an atmosphere which may have tended to liberate the pro-Jansenist Daguesseau from political inhibitions.

In these earlier years of the new century Daguesseau could also turn to supplementing his written educational advice with considerable personal supervision. No law student of his should be dreaming of any costly, time-consuming, and temptation-rife grand tours. These were instead the days of chronologies and geography and plain, hard work. In summer, when the family were united at the Chancellor's provincial château, Daguesseau himself took the role of self-styled "country tutor." Even if he happened not to be present, he sent home narratives, letters, and speeches; becoming more and more like his own father, he expected and received back the son's weekly written report, made corrections and annotations, then returned it. When his royal duties did allow him home, he aroused the young man to debate by offering examples of masterful works of opinion. The same instructions and personal assistance served also for the second son and the third. Although by today's standards this sounds like ponderous paternalism, the style of the Instructions generally shows a charm—personal, informal, full of candor, almost as if addressed to an equal, here and there encouraging independent conclusions and at the same time proud of all accomplishments.

Daguesseau began his Instructions by noting that in finishing his dual studies in humanities and philosophy, the son had now to commence the stages of ever greater learning. For the first year of the parental syllabus there were required four major topics: religion, jurisprudence, history, and belles-lettres—areas all supposedly skimped by the law professors. The son was to try in each of these to get as much preparation as was essential for a sophisticated lawyer expecting to be a cultivated magistrate. Religion—the fundamental base of all studies—was presented as a life endeavor involving at least a daily reading of scriptures. In addition young Daguesseau was required to make extracts on the duties of civic and Christian life and to arrange them in perfect order. It was Descartes in two easy steps for study hall: reason and example. Recommended reading—essential for demonstrating the truth of the Christian religion and for definition of the doctrines it teaches—included one of the volumes of Protestant Jacques Abbadie, as well as Grotius, Pascal's *Pensées*, and Bossuet, along with the gospels. Grotius, though Daguesseau found him needful of more order in the arrangement and development of ideas, was to be read only after the son had grasped moral and legal essentials. Calvin's stern summary of Christian principles was not mentioned in this ecumenical adventuring, but as the son's courage grew he was to try Augustine—the backbone of Jansenism—and his defenders: Justin, Origen, Tertullian, and the pronouncements of the Council of Trent. Henri-François was adamant: this metaphysics of jurisprudence was necessary because academic professors were so "bad" they could warp a person's study of positive law. In fact, in addition to such supplementary texts the student had to have the tutoring from an *avocat*, later a doctor of law, as well as enter into extracurricular debates on the *Institutes of Justinian* in company with suitably studious youthful companions.

Daguesseau felt that reading books on first principles of laws would lead directly to asking at the outset of study the knotty question that he, in his *Meditations*, would call the greatest question of life: is there a natural law derived from the nature of man? To answer this, he suggested as the stimulative texts Cicero's *De legibus* for the best style and pagan thoughts more pure and right than those of many Christian thinkers, and Plato's *Laws* and *Republic*, especially the latter for Socratic reflection. Next (skipping as always the medievals) was the seminal work to be read, re-read, *and* meditated: the "Prolegomena" of Grotius's *De jure belli ac pacis*, with its distinctions more exact than those of any Roman jurisconsult. After that, came the book that almost alone would be enough, a text which could never be too much studied and was to be outlined in detail by the son: the *Treatise of Laws* of jurisconsult *extraordinaire* and family friend, Domat. No one had better probed true principles or explained better. This beautifully geometric book would serve as the key, enabling the young mind to grasp the profession's most fundamental distinction: the separation of natural from positive law.

After such introduction to the topic, it was time to prescribe precise steps needed for handling all this general advice. As pro-tem advisor in the informal but obviously very serious "Daguesseau Law School" Henri-François hewed to his own father's line and required the thorny Roman Law for the first year subject. The other great divisions would be canon and French. Counseling that the son should omit public and international law for the present, Domat and grandfather Henri's influence meant advising instead that the fundamental thing was simply to determine, for every "law" encountered, whether it were natural or positive. This well-tried practice inevitably would lead to easier choice when conflicting positive laws presented themselves during professional life. For history and structure Henri-François recommended books from the illustrious Godefroi family and from law professor Jean Doujat. Then came the essential Justinian, still as much the book for students in 1716 as it was intended to be in 533. Advance paternal permission was given to regret that the arrangement of the *Institutes* was by Tribonian rather than Domat; agreeing with Justinian, Henri-François counseled omitting commentaries in the first reading (which was to occupy two months), the better to glean an overview of private Roman Law.

Now came semester two. Beginning on January 1st and continuing until about "la saint Jean" (June 24), the boy was to undertake a second reading of the *Institutes*, this time in far more depth, aided by commentaries, of which those of Cujas were to be read continually as being written in a better law language than any modern could achieve. The in-house Doctor of Law would be there to examine his son on each title, help with difficulties, and present the accepted interpretations. Expected from this second reading—three hours daily—was yet another filial abridgement to be read over from time to time. Still not satisfied, Henri-François, as a special polish to the first year of Rome, requested study again in the manual of Jacques Godefroi for the structural ordering of titles in *Digest* and *Code*, not because the Godefroi order was exceptional but because the study would teach even more legal overview and make it easier to find a given subject. To this would be added an hour and a half a day for those last two titles of the *Digest* which served as a sort of supplement to the *Institutes*: Book 50, title 16, "The Meaning of Expressions"; and title 17, "Various Rules of Early Law."

As adjunctive remarks introducing the son's first Instruction Daguesseau would go on to write a paper for the Châtelet court. This essay, "On the Study and Exercises Which Can Prepare for the Functions of *Avocat du roi*," targeted young *avocats* beginning their careers and repeated publicly the Daguesseau bottom line: a degree like the *licence* should be considered merely a stepping-stone into the deeper waters of Roman jurisprudence. It was not any free-at-last completion for success at the bar. Primary sources, wrote Daguesseau to the graduates, must always be essential; eliminate those Glossators and Commentators—and why not this very book, too. Granted there can be no eliminating a Domat on contracts, obligations, and restitutions—subjects where one best sees the rules of natural law which distinguish Rome. But having read a title in Domat one should read next the laws directly in the *Digest* and *Code*, then Denis Godefroi, followed by the commentaries of Cujas, and those of Jacques Godefroi on the *Theodosian Code*. The *instruction* caveat is clear: rise always toward axiomatic general principles. And read like a machine without an "off" switch.

At this time a first law school year did not, as we know, include the course in French law, but in his Châtelet paper Daguesseau made suggestions for studying it in the customs and the ordinances. For the indispensable Custom of Paris, long since reduced to written form, the Chancellor had his reading list in hand: Le Fleury, Argou, Coquille, Loisel, and de Laurière, along with le Maitre and Duplessis. Peer discussion was still high on the Daguesseau list, and he recommended it revolve around comparison of custom, usage, and especially those specific decisions that had grown from the work by men like Dumoulin, de Lamoignon, Auzanet, and Barthelémi. All this multiplicity of views was intended to gain for an *avocat* a grounding in royal ordinances, as well as an understanding where complete collections were non-existent and where the paper trail might have ended in 1585.

In a remarkably top-heavy conclusion to the first year of jurisprudence came now canon law, although, feared Daguesseau II, at this point the weary Daguesseau III might be getting recalcitrant. Yet the certainty of such procedure was clear (and can we not almost hear the son's deep sigh of dismay): how can the limits of church and state be understood without profound grasp of the papacy and ecclesiastical legal procedure? For a moment Daguesseau paused, wanting so earnestly to convince that self-introspection now faced the reader like a character from a morality play: "Look at me," it said, "I was debauched by literature, by that seductive Descartes, and by all those fools who prattle the history of what men have done instead of what they can do and must do." The drama was quickly over. Henri-François switched gears, hurrying on with yet another flurry of proposed writers—

Le Fleury to Mothe le Vayer, the *Pseudo-Isidore* to Paris's Professor Florent. But even here the goad was padded by the all-important practical carrot: only with such expertise would it be safe to read the paratitles and decretals assigned by the faculty for examinations. Daguesseau also tossed in a required time frame: six months work at one and a half hours daily insured high test marks.

After this merely preliminary panorama, Henri-Francois urged historic accounts of the nations. First the student was to ask scholars which texts to choose, while as an ancillary issue he could start work in genealogy, medals, and inscriptions. If the son again chafed at the burden, Daguesseau held out a carrot once more—perhaps the largest one, called Career. Accepting this way, the family way, was the only approach for one destined for high public service and control of public law. As a help, Daguesseau, admitting the busy world of affairs left little time, began with a boiling down of everything to a how-to method of three essentials: study things divine, things human, things natural, and, he added as a post-script, never waste time on heresy, ritual, or scientific experimentation. Instead (and here Daguesseau felt his *cogito* did need a new page and perhaps a deep breath) one must concentrate on the great object in history: man as citizen and man as public servant. Again remembering Grotius, he counseled one should avoid the usual way humans organize their public law triad of legislation, privileges, and economics. Instead he proposed study of how citizenries divide down the paths of Virtue and Vice, and in analyzing human nature he stressed one be astute and sensitive to effects of milieu and career.

Deep in career tactics, the next instructions were highly practical. Daguesseau, always smitten by *belles-lettres*, knew how important it was to polish linguistic talent. Grasping at globalization and the need of speaking well, he counseled a month's work studying foreign languages like Hebrew, modern Italian, and Spanish. This verbal emphasis carried over into a fourth Instruction Pardessus took from the Châtelet lecture: Rhetorical Skill for Client and Court. This was not pebbles-in-the-mouth advice; Demosthenes was actually to be put off for later years of more sophisticated understanding. Instead, as a virtuoso at speaking cogently, amiably, and persuasively the father came up with another good list of masters as "must reads": Malebranche, Descartes, Pascal, Arnauld. Daguesseau's advice had metacritical self-praise as he spoke of the fine legal proof which always pleased because of its hint of the voluptuous—not a female Eros, but rather the marvelous form and grace translated through antiquity's heroes: Horace, Terence, Cicero. Take out a case transcript and write your own pleading, he suggested. Or give a lecture—no memorization, no reading, and certainly never open the mouth to converse unless clear in object and expression. Do that and a crowded auditorium will be in your hand.

Here, at last at the end of his advice for the young, the Chancellor sat back and reflected. He had urged that France develop method with constant attention to geometry and to that greatest of geometers-in-words, Descartes. But had he demanded more than was necessary? How many *maîtres* sitting in their offices had actually known such preparation? Modestly, he refrained from noting that he, France's Chancellor, had done it all. Yet, in the end he did propose that the many who had not done it would probably admit that they should have. Today's reader can only gape in exhausted and astonished admiration. Daguesseau had certainly transformed himself into a law teacher enthusiastically, boldly, perhaps madly ahead of his time. Instructions for a beloved son had expanded to the most challenging of journey's for an eponymous a*vocat*—a total-immersion plunge into legal education's every nook, cranny, and crevice. These were remarkable lessons from the home front, an extraordinary revelation of the author and the politician, a Humanist deeply devoted to the best of the ancient world, a jurist convinced of the necessity and the beauty of careful study of the finest legal writings generated over the centuries by the best jurisconsults.

As during his own learning journey Daguesseau had stepped over the earlier self-image of an impatient youth who vigorously protested the futility of Roman Law, as Chancellor he had perceived a crucial problem in the modern teaching of law. Uninspired schools were being dragged down by their stolid and confining academicism. While research and new ideas were envisaged for other institutions, the law faculties continued teaching wisdom and techniques fully received and set in stone. Daguesseau, on the other hand, noticed that most of this training left untouched the crucial problem of building one French law out of customs and ordinances. Courageously, he had put forward a different approach, one that began with Domat and that made natural law, the first touchstone, key to the organization of society. He had agreed to situating Justinian's *Institutes* at the beginning of the curriculum. Also, at this, the imperial gateway to knowledge, Daguesseau challenged us all to survey briefly the legendary patrimony—Cicero, Plato, Aristotle, and the whole literature of definitions and maxims. Then might we dare to assimilate Domat's new insights while adding the great sweep of Grotius and even a *soupçon* of Pufendorf—if, that is, we could stay awake long enough.

Above all, he had known enough to emphasize history be put to use in the organization and development of society, in the foundation of public law. Today we call this approach political science and pride ourselves on offering for the first time "innovative" programs in "law and economics." But Daguesseau's steps have preceded ours in all this substance, walking confidently without neglecting the art of communicating in precise yet attractive language—the lawyer's basic tool. If Daguesseau had had time for research, he would have perhaps applied his instructions deeply enough that we "innovators" would be more aware of our roots. Even so, could this extra dimension have insured that his major study, like Montesquieu's, would still be studied today? and could this have led, in the legislative work now to be discussed, to a ground-breaking ordinance on education and studies able to stand the test of time?

Daguesseau's Career in Public Office

The convergence of character, mind, and philosophical convictions on the question of law reform in France was not only a matter of reading and analysis but inextricably part of experience in affairs at the highest level of the French state. A full account of the Daguesseau career would require—and we can just hear him urge us on—first, an account of the history of France in the last years of Louis XIV, say

1690–1715; then on to the regency of the Duc d'Orléans (1715–1723); and finally touching base with the first half (1723–1751) of the reign (1723–1774) of Louis XV. Our shortened account must suffice here, realizing that a fuller presentation could give a more accurate feel for the challenges encountered and met by this giant of the Limousin.

Like the young candidate for whom he wrote his Fourth Instruction, Henri-François had begun as *avocat du roi* at the Châtelet in 1690, progressing in a few months to being *Avocat Général*. In 1693—Bell (Bell, *Lawyers and Citizens: The Making of a Political Elite in Old Regime France,* 63) prefers 1698—he made his rhetorical debut in the *Paris Parlement*. He was only in his twenties, yet here he stood invited to counsel the most august legal body in France. The title he had chosen rang with youth's boldness—*The Independence of the Avocat*—and with confidence and many dramatic staccato sentences, he summoned his colleagues to public service in a moral renewal of the bar. You are accountable to the motherland, he told them, for the talents it admires in you. Do not now deny to your fellow citizens a service as useful to them as it is glorious for you. Think of how in old age, with health weakened by efforts in the public welfare, you will be able to taste a durable repose, an interior peace, the glory of the orator, and the tranquility of a philosopher. You will find then that your independence in wealth has raised you above other men while your dependence on virtue has raised you above yourself (D'Aguesseau, Henri François, J. M. Pardessus and M. Thomas eds., *Oeuvres complètes du chancelier D'aguesseau,* Vol. I, 12).

For a long time France had not heard the like, and from that moment on a Daguesseau speaking engagement was memorable enough that twenty-two of these secular homilies survive. The last preserved, given for the beginning of the term of Saint Martin's day in 1715, was typically entitled "Love of Country." Already in the debut oration Daguesseau had given evidence of recognizing the independence implied in the organization of a bar association; he had appealed to that bar to practice, without embroilment in politics, the virtues of Roman republicanism and to be content with the plaudits of fellow citizens without eating their hearts out in envy of the high robe magistrates. Such farsighted ideals were to bring him the sobriquet of the "eagle of parliament."

In 1694 he picked out, wooed, and won Anne Ormesson, a seventeen-year-old girl from a wealthy bourgeois family. The parvenu middle class often sought out old noble connections, but Daguesseau, whose father offered him freedom of choice, had been the one to pursue and was not a little proud that the Ormessons belonged to the highest parliamentary families. He was very fond of Anne, with her fine features and figure; though she was a little prolix and had a slight stammer, he knew she matched him in a keen wit and strong character. Her friend Mme De Sévigné put aside her usual acerbity to state that she had never seen a marital union more promising. After a fine wedding in the church of St. André des Arts in Paris, the young couple began life together at the beautiful and secluded country seat of the Ormesson family at Amboile on the Marne, a few miles outside the capital. Henry IV had built the château for his mistress Gabrielle D'Estrées; the devout Ormesson parents had made sure to remove all suggestive portraits of the beautiful paramour.

In a variation on "a loaf of bread, a jug of wine, and thou, sitting beside me in the wilderness" the Versailles First Gentleman stepped totally out of type to find his idea of happiness in an escape to solitude with an amiable woman and some books. And there he sat, a man above average height, with a stocky and robust frame, perhaps a bit heavy, his complexion smooth and tanned, his penetrating expression transmitted through deep brown eyes of which the left one, as his portrait shows, had from childhood been held, mysteriously, somewhat closed. It was said he radiated intelligence and good will (Monnier, 88).

As the seventeenth century ended Daguesseau was hoping to inherit the title of First President of the *Parlement*; the current incumbent, de Harlay, was a close friend. However, fate was to push him in another direction, for when *Procureur Général* fell vacant, it was Daguesseau whom de Harlay recommended to Louis XIV in September 1700. The King accepted the advice and informed Daguesseau's father who rushed out to Amboile to inform his son. There he found a reluctant Henri-François who saw the *Procureur Général* as one who spent a rather gloomy life in the midst of the poor, of land charters, and of criminals. But there was *le devoir*, that ever stern duty always compelling service. Graciously accepting, Daguesseau began earnest litigation in defense and in augmentation of the national domain. He also added some celebration to the hard work, by purchasing in 1708 a handsome estate at Fresnes not far from Paris.

As the King's solicitor he became a profound scholar of the royal real estate, of the history of feudalism, and of the customs. His court papers were couched in a simple, hard style loaded with erudition. Points were made by paring back on sentiment and flourishes, for, as he said, a *Procureur Général* stood above such "'magnificent weaknesses'" (Monnier, 93). He turned into an implacable foe of the feudal claims which had clogged royal titles, insisting that history showed the first fiefs as revocable grants or merely life benefices, and that it was by usurpation, not law, that they had become patrimonial and heritable. The old 877 edict of Kierzy-sur-Oise makes clear that Daguesseau's view was correct in downgrading feudalism as disorder and license. These were stands, of course, consistent with a mature political position—the bourgeois position; they advocated kingly supremacy controlled not by the advice of feudal lords but by the advice of ministers and *parlements*. The king was, however, also controlled by law: a royal domain was inalienable and imprescriptable, to be preserved, we can infer, for the benefit of those same citizens of the royal republic whose praise was the chief reward of the *avocats*.

As soon as we see Henri-François in the office of Procureur, we are observing justice in renewal. Gingerly threading his way through the byzantine royal politics at the rather mournful end of the Louis XIV reign, he issued a critical memorandum calling for a council on legal reforms. This memorandum of 1 September 1715—the lay version of the old papally instigated conclaves—recommended judicial officials be chosen by the Regent both for the Council and the place of its sitting; recommended also was that the order of business at each sitting follow that used in the drafting of the ordinances of 1667 and 1670 on civil and communal procedure. Daguesseau knew he was in a strong position. He enjoyed the high regard of *Parlement*, and he claimed the friendship of the Archbishop of Paris, the influential and tolerant Cardinal Noailles who often had one royal ear while Daguesseau had the other. This meant Daguesseau could dare introduce a broad agenda: revision of the ordinances of 1667 and 1670; legislation on costs of criminal cases; rules for lower courts in criminal cases; abatement of the diversity of jurisprudence among the several *parlements* and courts; reduction of the number of offices; and examination of all the abuses in the administration of justice that ought to concern the Regent. He concluded by recommending subcommittees to expedite business and by urging that notice be given to other concerned ministries as matters of interest to them arose. Being the non-academic jurist that he was, he made no mention of the employment of law professors to assist. True, the professors of Roman Law were in a bifurcated world half Bartolist, half Humanist, but even the new (1679) Professors of French Law were not mentioned. Here was an unfortunate oversight. Ill compensated, overwhelmed by the scope of the subject matter to be covered at each university by only one man, nevertheless these were academics who might have contributed much good; moreover, they, no doubt, would have been pleased to be paid for their time.

A second memorandum by Daguesseau refined the details for the composition and procedure of the Council. At this the ultramontane party, including the Jesuits and among them the King's confessor, began trying day by day to wear away the *Procureur*'s credit at Versailles. In whispers or open speech they took Daguesseau's concern for the liberties of the Gallican church and turned it into a subtle mask over pure Jansenism. It was a moment of bitter stress, indicative that the great Sun had begun its final descent. The papal bull "Unigenitus" awaited acceptance by the French bishops and by *Parlement*; the royal Jesuit confessor, had become, as we have seen, a leading political player, but despite approval of the bishops, he faced a recalcitrant *Parlement*. Daguesseau explained to the aging monarch that the draft act of registration appeared to have the King deciding a question of faith for the absent and dissenting bishops, which by law he had no right to do. *Parlement* finally registered the bull but at the same time noted its strong reservations against papal infallibility in France. As Cardinal Noailles seemed to approve of these reservations, the Paris crowds became aroused against the whole idea of "Unigenitus." Additional issues began to arise as the old King made provision for the regency and a council after his death—measures for which Daguesseau succeeded without any disaster in obtaining parliamentary approval. But "Unigenitus" meant that political embroilment for Daguesseau would now be inevitable, as the bar he wished to remain pure began grumbling appeals to the public for political support against the bull. Inextricably a central part of the royal apparatus, Daguesseau, however steadfast his principles, found that he evidently was no longer so eligible to exhort republican virtue.

Finally, Louis called for his First President. Daguesseau ordered that the two of them go ahead and get *Parlement* to approve the bull, there and then, unconditionally. The two hesitated. A little later first minister de Fleury and Daguesseau himself were summoned before the King who informed them that it would be the royal court deciding for the bull with no conditions. Daguesseau made the decision to risk all. He advised that as Chancellor the obligation was his to present the idea to *Parlement*. It was the best he would do. A few days later, after being requested by the King to attend him alone, Daguesseau embraced his wife and children, telling them he might well be in the Bastille before nightfall. Anne, a true Roman, assured him it was better to go in honor to the ominous Bastille than come home in dishonor to the family hearth. Louis, now very weak, made broad hints at punishment and requested the Chancellor have a talk with Daguesseau. Henri-François quietly but firmly repeated that his refusal of blind obedience was simply the best way he knew to serve his king. The whole court was certain that the *Procureur* was lost; his friends no longer called upon him, his house was deserted by staff. Soon the day had been fixed for a *lit de justice*, the final confrontation. But now was also the hour for Providence to intervene: Louis XIV, recorded history's longest reigning European monarch, breathed his last on 1 September 1715, and Henri-François, his humble and disobedient servant, breathed a sigh of relief.

Louis XV, great-grandson of Louis XIV, was a toddler of five years. The King's codicil had made appointment of the duc du Maine, Master of Artillery, as regent. However, the ambitious rival for this powerful position, the duc d'Orléans, counted many followers including the Paris Guard; and he cleverly promised the *Parlement* to restore the right of remonstrance while he vowed to the Jansenists to expel the hated royal Jesuit confessor and release their imprisoned associates. Daguesseau, his hand strengthened, went home to prepare legal papers for the meeting at which this was to be done and at which Orléans was to be approved. With many regiments deployed for Orléans, the King's official codicil was ignored and Orléans was declared regent. Daguesseau and de Fleury in the meantime persuaded *Parlement* to back Orléans, and Louis XIV's Edict of 1673, forbidding remonstrances before registration, was revoked. It was a new political era, when Daguesseau, now playing the role of partisan politician rather than apolitical Roman, pronounced that Saint Martin's day discourse on "Love of Country."

Orléans had a good mind and chose able ministers both from the nobility and the bourgeoisie, but he was tolerant as well of a debauchery that must have pained Daguesseau. Still, there was a surge of new energy for which Daguesseau as *Procureur Général* was a major catalyst. When suddenly on 1 February 1717 the death of Chancellor Voysin was announced, within an hour the duc de Noailles had been to see Orléans where he urged Daguesseau be accepted for the position. Public opinion for a long time had designated Daguesseau as the successor chancellor; his reputation for probity and ability was high, and all knew him to be ready for any challenge. In agreement, Orléans sent for Daguesseau, who was found kneeling in Candlemas prayers at St. André des Arts. Daguesseau, as ever the independent, said he would come to Palais-Royal as soon as the service was over. Then arrived a second messenger brooking no delay; abandoning devotions for duty, Daguesseau was brought at once to a room full of people where Orléans, apologetic for the pressure and giving the cryptic explanation "it's only a matter of a little key," led Daguesseau forward, announcing to the onlookers: "'You see your new and very worthy chancellor'" (Monnier, 68). When the Duc and Chancellor went to see the seven-year-old king, the boy smiled and touched the seals—infant semiotics perhaps, but into which many at once read royal and loyal confirmation for a public servant whose legal work had for so long attracted wide notice for its scholarly base and extraordinary eloquence.

Old Henri Daguesseau had missed by a mere two months seeing the grandiose dream for his beloved son come to realization. It appeared that every one of Henri's lessons and tutorials had been of the utmost pertinence, as everything pointed to an auspicious beginning for thirty years of a Henri-François Daguesseau presiding over the administration of justice in France. As royal solicitor his client had been the most powerful ruler in the world and through him the most powerful nation; now he was legislator, judge, and court administrator all in one. On top of this charge it was time for him to direct the universities, and here, too, the once anti-Romanist had been made ready. When the University of Paris orator greeted France's new chancellor with a speech in Latin, the faculty were astonished to hear Daguesseau reply at once, *ex tempore*, in the same tongue.

Louis XIV had left France so deeply in debt it could be called insolvent; the Orléans government, with the duc de Noailles as Minister of Finance, tried every financial trick and remedy, but without success. France owed 3 billion *livres* offset by an income of only about 150 million against expenses of about the same, without interest. Then Orléans succumbed to the blandishments of John Law, a Scottish adventurer whose trading company centered its activity across the Atlantic, choosing the underdeveloped Louisiana as the prime asset that could save French finances. Law, with a name whose proud sound of probity soon was to ring hollow, was brilliant but amoral, his doubtful genius and faulty judgment expended in raising money by piling issues of paper obligations one upon the other and selling them without adequate real assets.

John Law medal, 1720
Courtesy of Yale University Art Gallery, Transfer from Sterling Memorial Library, Yale University, Bequest of the Charles Wyllys Betts, B.A. 1867, M.A. 1871, Collection

Daguesseau, supported by the *Parlement*, was totally opposed to such paper trading, for he sensed at once that the scheme would turn Versailles into a house of cards. But Orléans yielded to the pressure of the opposing side who accused Daguesseau of asking *Parlement* by day to approve Law's plans and by night whispering for disapproval. When on 26 January 1718 *Parlement* remonstrated against a new edict on finance and Daguesseau in vain told them Orléans wanted approval at once, there was a storm of opposition in the court. The Marquis de la Vallière was sent, as said so elegantly, to "wait upon Daguesseau," which meant a euphemistic "waiting" for the worst: De la Vallière took back the seals and bestowed them forthwith on D'Argenson, opponent of *Parlement*. Daguesseau, still Chancellor but now powerless, wrote bitterly to Orléans: "'I received the seals without meriting them; you have taken them away without my meriting to lose them'" (Monnier, 190).

The abrupt dismissal meant retiring to Fresnes, where in his forced exile Henri-François "showed the firmness of a Christian philosopher" (Monnier, 193). Forbearance only increased his popularity. There was then a cascade of unforeseen complications. While a delighted Law launched his trading company, *Parlement*, itself, was sent off into exile as the price of the Law company's shares soared and with it Law's power. The canny schemer did a quick Henri IV turn: he converted to being a Catholic and was promoted Controller General; the Bank of France itself merged with the trading company whose shares became nearly the only investment available in France. In December 1719 the shares were up by a factor of 40 and the capital of the company reached nominally 12 billion *livres*. To pay 5% on this capital took 600 million *livres* in revenue, but the company, with all the resources of France, could pay 5% on only 1.7 billion. With actual trading undertakings in Louisiana hardly underway, the people, losing confidence daily, began to sell their shares to buy necessities. Share prices crashed, inflation of paper money soared; the bubble had been pricked and gold and silver all but disappeared from circulation. Law fell from power in December 1720 and died in Venice in 1729, poor and forgotten.

Daguesseau, who with almost all other great family heads lost a great part of his fortune in the debacle, had spent his time writing memoranda on the legality of speculation in shares and on the circulation of money, while concentrating on the education of his sons. The government, desperate for a better reputation, recalled him in June 1720, just as the issue of the "Constitution" (as the bull "Unigenitus" was called) arose again. The minister of foreign affairs, Cardinal Dubois, an ambitious intriguer who dreamed extravagantly of the restoration of eleventh century papal government, drafted a compromise doctrine, and Orléans signed it while *Parlement*, still in exile, was ignored. Daguesseau, who had returned fully expecting a resumption of *Parlement's* role, refused to seal the papers and resigned, but Orléans did not dare to recall D'Argenson. He went ahead and sealed the document himself and had Dubois take it to the *Parlement* in exile; they still refused to register. At this point Orléans decided that his Grand Conseil would have to ratify. Daguesseau fought on: he tried to get Archbishop de Noailles to approve the compromise, hoping *Parlement* would then register it. Like a great game of chess, it was now the Archbishop who refused to comply.

At last it was Daguesseau's move. He decided it was perhaps worth participating in the meeting of the Grand Conseil. He would try for their approval, even though he knew that Conseil action would in any event be a nullity in law. For this unexpected backward bend at a moment of compromise, posterity's critics have faulted Daguesseau. Yet although quitting outright would have been a more dramatic show of principle, a statesman on occasion must take some steps left and right in order to remain erect that in due course he may stride again on the true road. Fickle Paris did not see that, thought Daguesseau had become the tool of Dubois, and, now again set against him, singing loudly the many popular songs composed at his expense. Monnier, one who thinks that Daguesseau should have insisted on resigning, manages a positive spin by suggesting (Monnier, 233) that Daguesseau remained for the benefit of the country. The Monnier thesis is that Daguesseau was trying hard to quiet the raging religious dissention and to stop a movement swirling around the Orléans regency that threatened not merely to reduce the power of *Parlement* but to abolish it altogether. Whatever the motives, all the compromises attempted could not at this juncture preserve his influence. Dubois became prime minister, Daguesseau was dismissed, again, and on 1 March 1722 left Paris for a second exile at Fresnes, this one for over five years.

In reliance on his ethic of personal simplicity and reasoned virtue, Daguesseau had once more put on his Roman act when no one cared anymore for that performance. What is worse, he had neglected the courtier's rule: surround yourself with friends who have a stake in your political success. When at last he was re-recalled in 1727, he discovered on arrival back in Paris that this time he was to be chancellor but without those seals. Still, Daguesseau remained a staunch supporter of *Parlement* and a Gallican church, and all knew it; Fleury needed such a reputation to shore up his administration. At the same time the Cardinal favored *Unigenitus* and did not want trouble with this man of strong principles. At a *Te deum* in Notre Dame they said that the seal-less Daguesseau looked at his shoes rather than at the crowd; was he petulant or simply making resolutions to try to stay out of high politics and to concentrate on law reform. It appears the latter, for the seals were finally conferred in 1737, this time to remain in Daguesseau's possession until he resigned them shortly before death in 1751. The ambition of one cardinal had sent him away; the satisfied ambition of another had brought him back.

Fleury, once the tutor of Louis XV, had been governing France with considerable wisdom since 1726. His national care and feeding would end sixteen years after the Daguesseau recall as Louis XV, deciding now under the influence of his mistress to govern by himself as his great-grandfather had done, drew on the army for the ministeriat. The action pleased the nobles but undercut the bourgeoisie—a very grave mistake. It meant that the man with the seals was much in demand as in these difficult times he judiciously tried to recover France's losses while steadying her against social divisiveness. Daguesseau had learned much in exile, and his solution for sanity and justice was to replace the foolhardy Law of Louisiana with the natural law of Heaven. Still, there doubtlessly must have been many days when he felt inadequate as the Bien-Aimé Louis fell under the strong political influence of yet another mistress—Jeanne Antoinette Poisson. The brilliant

"Miss Fish," later transformed into the legendary Marquise de Pompadour, would die by natural causes, fortunate not to accompany the Motherland and another monarch's Antoinette in going over the cataract of Revolution.

Daguesseau and Natural Law; The *Méditations*

The five exile years spent in the political desert of Fresnes had given Daguesseau time to come to a conclusion on an associated duo of compelling legal questions. He had been pondering them more than thirty years, but now was the moment to look at them hard and long for answers. The first question he asked was simple yet profoundly troublesome: can man find in himself natural ideas of what is just and unjust? The second dilemma was no less vexing, especially reminiscent of Pufendorf while linked to the eighteenth century regime: can one know whether it is by these natural ideas that actions are to be judged, or is judgment only conferred by obeying the positive will of a superior? For us, these questions echo back to an absolutist paradise under whose Savonnerie rugs were daily being swept many a petition for rights against wrongs. They were at the heart of a conundrum ready to explode in a scenario where the basic foundations of morality were to create at last that social compact upon which all duties linking one human to another could be declared constitutionally validated.

Daguesseau found his reply to just and unjust almost at once and without a waver in it. Morality would do nothing but float in uncertainly unless there existed a natural, immutable, universal rule of self love—the century's ubiquitous *amour propre*. Anterior to all positive institutions, he saw a special, transcendent rule, one whose universality shone for Daguesseau with an intrinsic beauty of almost religious intensity. He took care to set down these ideas between 1722 and 1727; the manuscript, left unpublished until after death, in the Pardessus edition of 1819 comes to a hefty volume of 636 pages. Daguesseau denied himself any introduction, saying (Daguesseau-Pardessus, xiv, 2): "I speak here only to myself and therefore need no preface." Perhaps denial of publication lay in strategy less humble than politically canny. Obviously, a man who wants to return to public life at the highest level might well wish not to have his actions constantly tested by others against a philosophy presented by himself in such detail. Saying so much about God, he would undoubtedly have had to reckon with surveillance. Were France's Chancellor on the Index—Jansenist heresy giving rise to yet another *Unigenitus*—the scandal provoked could have led to more than a churchly slap on the wrist.

The manuscript was far from a collection written down either for the delectation or mental exercise of one man picking up his quill as ideas occurred. Vague and haphazard are certainly not adjectives that come to mind when speaking of Daguesseau, whose avowed role model—Marcus Aurelius—had also composed his reflective meditations during times when government was in crisis and purity of intellect and personal comportment were a salvation. The Daguesseau text is fully organized, provided with footnotes as well as summaries at the beginning of each *Méditation*, or chapter. Well-formed sentences probe carefully the metaphysical universe that brings them substance, and in that probing Daguesseau reaches for a universal audience of all thinking readers. True, the reflections are an unfinished opus. A tenth and last *Méditation* mentions a following one, but it never came to be. The omission hardly persuades, however, that Daguesseau is not speaking to the world, nor does the fact that world has neglected to study what he wrote, be influenced by it, or publish about it, mean he desired or merited this benign neglect. To examine the book is an act of restitution but it also provides an exciting opportunity. First of all we find ourselves face to face with the general philosophical position held by the prestigious Jansenists and near-Jansenists—Domat, Daguesseau, Pothier. Secondly, we are permitted to see their seminal positions on natural law, beginning its uncheckable expansion into France's landmark 1804 civil code.

Daguesseau's *Méditations* fall into a crucial centenary, between the time soon after 1650 when Descartes began to dominate French thought and the time about 1750 when the new style of thought called the Enlightenment overtook the *cogito*. The work thus reads preliminarily as more appropriate for the seventeenth century than the eighteenth, and this helps us to understand why it set off no major excitement. The form avoids the scorned scholastic style; but born of a method more deductive than inductive, it unabashedly trails old-fashioned trappings. Its Word in the Beginning is structured according to Descartes—"geometric" axioms in the form of "clear and distinct ideas," proceeding in easy prose to detailed conclusions. Certainly the Enlightenment would have preferred a study of social man by the deductive, fact-based method of contemporary natural science, where one could gather the data as Newton did and examine them to detect the general law which they obeyed. Moreover, in Daguesseau's work, there is that all-important role for God, whereas the fundamental position of the Enlightenment, skeptical toward divinity, turns on religious credence being replaced by faith in progress-bound scientific study. Nevertheless, there was much foreshadowing of the late eighteenth century in Daguesseau's Divine One, who brings reason to help us regulate with wisdom our societal relations.

The cornerstone proposition that man's self-love will lead to good is a proposition which could live with Adam Smith's capitalism of the later eighteenth century while taking umbrage at the Hobbes concern for self as being the sure road to chaos. This Hobbesian view happened to be a position which appealed to Daguesseau's friend Valaincourt, a minor philosopher who spent much time at Fresnes during Daguesseau's time of banishment and whose Pyrrhonistic skepticism incited his host to heated argument and vigorous rebuttal from historic precedent. There should be no shock, then, when the Daguesseau debates bring us face to face with the perennial disputation we have followed in so many previous pages: Creon *vs.* Antigone, Platonists *vs.* Pyrrhonians, believers *vs.* skeptics, Realists *vs.* Nominalists, natural law *vs.* positive law, Montaigne *vs.* Raymond Sebond, Hobbes *vs.* Grotius, Pufendorf, and Domat.

In the First *Méditation* (Daguesseau-Pardessus, xiv, 1–16) the author states that his motive is to clarify his own thoughts, and perhaps Valaincourt's as well, in presentation of the book's epic, questing theme: can man find in himself immutable natural ideas of justice without recourse to positive law, religious revelation, or the instinct for self-preservation. (The quest is so Cartesian that one wonders if the

Fresnes exile also ruminated by a stove.) We now know, of course, that Henri-François is being rhetorical, because he has already made up his mind that natural law exists and that man can find it. Still considerable challenge lies within the parameters of the search, and like an ancient hero the writer knows he will have to battle his way through an underbrush of epistemological monsters. Many will be the realms that put the searcher to a test: whether or not these natural ideas are legal justice; whether they are innate; whether they are axioms like those of geometry; whether they really exist at all amidst life's preponderance of injustice; and whether men act fairly as a crass device to get what they want in a ceaseless war of man against man or merely in an equally selfish Platonic effort to enjoy pleasure and avoid pain.

In the Second *Méditation*, Daguesseau considers his method. He will assume the existence of God, although later he seems to think better of that, and like nearly all the philosophical system-builders, states his own "If not God, what else could it be?" Proof. First, he must be blunt: to deny God's existence is so absurd that the very absurdity becomes confirmation. Second, it will be back to axiomatic Cartesianism: nothing happens, exists, or is made without a cause. Daguesseau's *cogito* proclaims its 'therefore' to be supreme cause, necessarily a first cause, necessarily God. The problem then emerges of how to promote the clear and distinct when it is so difficult to know precisely whether an idea possesses either one or the other quality. Daguesseau is convinced he shall know it because, like a proposition in geometry, the idea in his sights will give him such mental repose that he will feel no need to seek more. In this quest Daguesseau the metaphysical displays as well an unexpected modernity which speaks volumes to the space age myths of today. Forged not of metal but from mettle, his sword will be the elucidating power beamed from his own mind. An arrogant tone creeps in here: the idea will be "evident" for no other reason than that Daguesseau is fully competent to judge; it makes no difference if others don't understand—some Pyrrhonians (*pace* house guest Valaincourt) are dense enough to deny even that mathematics exists. Daguesseau easily brushes away any riposte which would argue because some do not know an idea none can; he will not even entertain the thought that if some do have certain thoughts, then by the use of reason all can have them without such rational rigor. His ideas on the psychology of cognition and on epistemology are searching for a bedrock anchorage in the nature of man, and he probably in reading Pascal had been reassured about proof by perception that an idea can be termed "evident" (Daguesseau-Pardessus, xiv, 16–76).

Continuing with the process of cognition, Daguesseau begins with what one might call the surprisingly pre-existential position of his opponents: the human being is necessarily so affected by the impressions made on it, that in this sense we all become trapped into denial of our human liberty. But am I really only a weather-vane? queries the Chancellor. No, he ripostes; I am free to deliberate, I can doubt; and on the other hand, I can know repose. And quickly breaking for such freedom he leaves the Sartre-to-be school as he relies on religion, stating: I say all impressions are not invincible, yet I say also that God does all that happens in me. God sometimes acts immediately, as in miracles, but usually mediately, slowly, in a way that makes it seem one effect causes another. So it is with our minds. But God leaves me free to desire knowledge or not to desire it. If my idea is clear and evident God did that, too, but in consequence of my attentiveness. *I* am the cause. The problem is not that men cannot tell what is just, but that they refuse to make an effort to know it, are not attentive enough, and the object of their passions strikes them too strongly.

The Fourth *Méditation* (Daguesseau-Pardessus, xiv, 76–131) follows this previous pattern of natural revelation, but now the cutting up into cognitive micro-components makes the flow less limpid. Before defining justice, Daguesseau feels he must show what truth is and how it is found, but he will not do this according to the metaphysical subtlety that truth is Being. The useful question is not truth vs. nothing but truth vs. error. As for the origin of truth, it is God who sees instantly, clearly, and perfectly what he created or wishes to create. The essence of truth lies in its two degrees: the idea God has of it that makes it possible, and its actual existence. It is the same in the imperfect human, but the human mind, being weaker, knows less. There are as well two roads to knowledge: clear perception (the definition of a circle) and sensation (the object is red). According to all the philosophers my mind, too, operates in degrees: (1) idea (I am only a mirror); (2) judgment (I witness that I have an idea and this is infallible); (3) reasoning (I compare, and I am free to discern truth or fall into error according to my attentiveness); and (4) method (I follow a progressive order toward discernment).

Now comes a congeries of questions all central in Daguesseau's time and still pertinent to the practice of law: by what means can I discover knowledge of truth? what degree of certainty can I achieve? how can I recognize it? Some knowledge I discover metaphysically by mind alone, some with the help of something outside me, and some in a geometric framework by both. From God I am provided with three sources for discovering truth: (1) an attentive mind uses reason and finds intellectual truth, (2) the senses detect truths that reflect the universal laws of nature, and (3) other men bear witness.

As Daguesseau now posits his very modern—or we should say post-modern—concept of truth, he shows us how close to a new era he was. It is a sentiment in the soul, he tells the reader, which gives repose; usually it is my consciousness of it, not less certain because reason has the least part in it, but often it is a clear idea I can communicate. When reasoning is involved, it remains the force and vivacity of the consciousness that discovers truth. "I exist, I think, I will, I am free, I sense … it is impossible not to acquiesce…." That an idea is truth is determinable only in my self, by my sense of its degree of persuasion. (As if shocked, himself, by the sudden breakdown of his clear and distinct ideas into pre-Romantic intrusion, Daguesseau must here pause for confession.) I realize I cannot define this clearly. It is obviously time to move quickly for a falling back on the faithful guide: I cannot resist, I cannot doubt, I do not know how. I cannot know by what means this happens. God alone does. He gives me, however, repose for my mind when I know the truth. I cannot be misled, for God has not made me that I should seek what I cannot find and need to find.

Carrying this swaying burden of doubt into *Méditation* Five (Daguesseau-Pardessus, xiv, 133–166) Daguesseau's position recalls Grotius: arguments will be now handled on the assumption there is no God, while the implication will arise that geometry does not depend on God. Moreover, God will be presented a limit: he cannot contradict himself. However, after having this strong brush with doubt, Daguesseau quickly knows it is time to turn and fight by facing doubt's despairing champion, Pyrrho, who comes impressively armed with three objections: (1) evidence misleads men and divides them in their conclusions, (2) the argument of men like Daguesseau is circular: they use evidence to prove evidence, and (3) although God does not mislead, man follows what he sees as the most probable opinion; when he errs it is because he wants to. At Pyrrho's first point Daguesseau admits he has always felt men vary in attention and some err. The important thing is that certain truths are agreed upon by all, even the weakest: there *is* a Rome, there *are* true propositions in geometry. Daguesseau is gallantly generous: Pyrrho admittedly does well to begin with doubt—it had been the Descartes stepping stone to the *cogito*. But, concludes *le généreux*, when a proposition is found to be evident, it must be accepted, and even a Pyrrho, when saying only doubt is true, has fallen into line by having to agree there is truth.

As he patronizingly smiles upon Pyrrho's points of circularity and error, Daguesseau begins by repeating his reasoning so far and observing: I see a circle, i.e., I conceive of it. I see that all the radii are equal, it is impossible not to see it, I cannot err. If I am more attentive, I see also that if one erects a perpendicular on a diameter, extending to the circumference, one part of the diameter is to the perpendicular as the perpendicular is to the other part. Yes, it takes a little longer, but I see that too. It all comes down to an interior sensation. And so it is with all truths, which, indeed, are like these propositions: I sense I exist, I sense I think, I sense I will. As to the circularity, I prove that all which is evident is true not by saying that a proposition is evident but by showing the nature of my mind. I know this from an irresistible consciousness of what goes on inside me when I am enlightened; it is what I have in common with all men, so strong and physically dominant it is impossible to doubt it. When asked why a circle is round, I do not reply by saying it is round because it is a circle; I say it is because the radii are equal and that is what round means. The Pyrrhonians say that nothing is certain. Why is that more certain than anything else? Their final stand has to be to deny God's existence and say all is hazard. But if I come from hazard, I still see that the sum of the angles of a triangle equals two right angles.

Moving from triangularity's demolition of Pyrrhonic doubt, the lengthy *Méditation* Six (Daguesseau-Pardessus, xiv, 166–253) begins with Daguesseau's beloved question: is my knowledge acquired, or innate and natural? The lawyer at once reminds himself that, moving as he is toward the quest objective of all law's studies—What is justice?—he must proceed only by way of those clear and evident ideas. Truth is the sight of what is. But what is innate truth? To answer that will take Daguesseau a while, more micro-management, and a bit more personal combat with the enemy camp. He times his attacks to double or triple drumbeats. The latter cadence is the beat for the Triune God who has three routes open to him: (1) all truths He wants us to know could be self-evident and always in the mind, (2) none could be; all knowledge would be acquired, or (3) He could make us capable of perceiving both given and acquired truths. Godhead has chosen the third route.

Daguesseau uses the word "acquired" in the sense adopted by jurisconsults when they distinguish goods acquired from those received by succession. Acquired knowledge is all knowledge not innate; all knowledge is from God, but when God acts subject to laws rather than directly, our knowledge is acquired.

Now close on the heels of natural law, Daguesseau sets up his double beat for an epistemological paradigm: Knowledge is (1) perception of truth, and (2) conviction of truth in the mind. As to (1), God can make it come from operation of my mind, or the speech of another, or the presence of an object (all these are acquired); or (2) He gives it immediately, independently of all interior and exterior causes. The latter is "given" knowledge, and innate knowledge is self-evident truth given by God. I do not have to prove that, adds Daguesseau confidently to his reader's raised eyebrow; it is a definition. "Natural" and "Innate" are the same. Being natural, innate knowledge is a physical necessity, which acts in us by God's will without any will by us; and it is common to all men as a consequence of their being. There is no need for it to be continuously present in the mind, although it may be. After all, some innate ideas are only presented as required. The main point is that all innate ideas are only given, not acquired; they come immediately from God.

Thus having put his foot firmly down, Daguesseau's question had to be: are there any innate ideas? Of course, he concluded, and as examples the well-grounded Daguesseau found no paucity: knowledge of bodies, of thoughts and sensations, of consciousness of consciousness, of desire for self-preservation, of love of happiness, of horror of misery—the list can go on. Daguesseau here joins combat with other philosophers, especially his British predecessor Locke, who would claim an innate idea has to be implicit, always perceived, formally witnessable at every moment. Daguesseau's approach: it is enough that God gives the ideas as needed. Secondly, ripostes Daguesseau, my knowledge of my existence, for example—it seems perfect, but do innate ideas have to be perfect? I, a philosopher know myself better than I do a Caribe native, which means a sensation can be innate and not perfect. Locke was wrong again to say some innate ideas seem new to some men; it is the expression of the sensation, not the sensation, that is new. Why, Locke has asked, if an innate idea is graven in man's being, do men ask the reason for it? Daguesseau reasons that a person's conception of this idea may not be complete (though the person may be fully convinced), and one may ask for proof or an explanation. Do we not see sunlight yet ask for a reason? As for Locke's complaint that innate, natural laws are not universally accessed, no truth is equally recognized by all men. Children and imbeciles have to be excluded. And why not add sleepers? *I* limit innate ideas, suddenly concludes Daguesseau dramatically, to men who can reason. But an innate idea need not be absolutely invincible; there can be contradictions in the use we make of them. For example, an idea innate for some can cease to be there for others due to voluntary blindness of mind. What is innate can be of varying clarity—not always clear, not always obscure. It is like living by the sea and not hearing the surf. Look at Solomon: he had an innate idea of the unity of God and what happened? He forgot it.

Daguesseau appears tired here, plodding toward the crux of his study but becoming less sure, needing recourse both to interrogation of his mind and of his heart. It is a technique that shows law being tugged at by a century in crisis as reason appears on the brink—emotional catharsis, or emotional collapse. It is a dramatic juncture, and Daguesseau is trying hard to define the perimeters of what kind of idea constitutes justice: is it innate, or simply self-evident to all? Is it conformity to an opinion as to self-preservation, or to a positive law on that? Fortunately, he meta-critically finds himself in an area less arid when, beginning the study of the desire for self-preservation and happiness and rounding a mental turn, he finds himself right in front of *amour propre* or self-love. Daguesseau finds this anatomy of the heart deep and full of meaning. Socrates had said self-love was the son of the union of the Goddess Poverty and the God Abundance. But Christian truth dramatically alters the genetics, substituting for Poverty the weakness of our nature and for Abundance our God. Self-love thus goes far beyond the precious boundaries of a *salon* diversion; it is the insatiable search for the Sovereign God.

Méditation Seven (Daguesseau-Pardessus, xiv, 255–372), still looking for the root of justice, starts by the rational, parsing route to law: imitating geometry again, abandoning the dual and triple attack for seven axioms that are "incontestable" and then following up with six "consequences" of these. The axioms: (1) Self-love is not a blind power but a reasonable inclination calling for reflection, deliberation, and choice according to reason. (2) Good use of reason is pursuit of self-evident truth. (3) These first two propositions are innate. (4) The good is a truth I can discover; I can err by using badly my faculties but I will not err always, because God could not have made me that way. (5) As to the Sovereign Good, my faculties of loving good and knowing truth will lead to agreement. (6) Evident truth and sovereign good are invincible in their effect on me. (7) At lower levels I am free to consent and do well or badly. The consequences: (1) self-love is reasonable and its nature will be found by reason, not by passion; (2) I must proceed by the method of clear and distinct ideas and reason, and self-evident truths; (3) and this will lead to conclusions I cannot doubt, and (4) to infallible rules for my conduct, because, (5) if there is conflict, reason and self-evidence will resolve it, and (6) I will use only reason.

At this point of his research, the lawyer readily settles down amidst the *amour-propre* debaters of French classical moralism: Racine, La Rochefoucauld, Pascal, Mme De Lafayette. As they stood elegantly garbed and peered about at the human race they all cynically, realistically, sensed that as axiomatic as the first theorems of geometry inevitably one loves oneself. Metaphorically moving to join their circle, Daguesseau politely but forcefully feels constrained to bring up his discovery of *Méditation* Six: even when self-love finds a convenient mirror in loving others it is really only for the good you can expect—what Daguesseau calls "relative love." When you think of what is good, do you not think of it in relation to your nature? And by trying to rein in on what is appropriate you thereby cut back the good objects of desire to three: durable existence, perfection, and happiness. Mind is weak, and constantly erroneous appearances of good and bad confuse us with real goals and imaginary ones. In turn this means, says the candid jurist, that the desire, the pleasure I experience lies solipsistically in regarding qualities that make for my perfection, in feeling myself as perfect or happy as I may be. The essence of love is this pre-Freudian *complaisance*.

After a complex tracing of ego happiness to the Creator—God created me and therefore loves me, but in fact He can love only Himself, and what He loves in me *is* Himself—Daguesseau has at last come to his choice of a happiness route to satisfy self-love. Hedonists beware, however, for this is no trip to dangerous liaisons. Instead, Daguesseau charts a route to success which leads us, not surprisingly, to *trying* for self-perfection, being reasonable, acting in good faith according to our essence. Well aware there are problems caused by bad use of liberty or from choosing the fecklessness of passion, Daguesseau's Descartes-meets-Sartre conclusion has suddenly revealed that this whole self-love discussion has been, like *Méditation* Six, a road map to the land of natural law and justice. Daguesseau has not tried to prove that humanity ordinarily makes good use of its reason in self-perfecting. Whether happiness is real, whether natural law is real does not depend on whether we can follow them in practice or need help to do it. The only question is: can we find them by use of reason and—by extension here appears the *raison d'être* for Daguesseau's whole exercise—can we find by reason a justice which is just by its nature and independent of the positive will of any legislator? Whether it is going to be hard to conform to the natural principles will be a question of fact, not of the law, and, Daguesseau warns, this is, therefore, a useless, even dangerous question. Better time, he feels, will be spent in concentrating on some motivational guidelines: (1) Humankind desires necessarily, unshakably, perpetually, to be happy; (2) Humans are reasonable beings and can act toward their desires only in a way suitable to their nature following ideas—i.e., natural law—given by reason; (3) Thus happiness comes from our perfection and the contentment of our regard of it; and (4) The only way to be happy is to strive to be perfect.

Daguesseau now thinks he ought to think it out again. Is it natural for us to have relative love for others, or are we basically indifferent and do it only accidentally according to direct self-interest? To answer this, the Eighth *Méditation* (Daguesseau-Pardessus, xiv, 372–460) analyzes the object and nature of love and hate, ascertaining the natural condition of personal relations. It is Daguesseau's Social Psychology 101 in which one distinguishes in love not only a main sentiment but also reflected or accessory sentiments which increase the pleasure. Pure love is the height of well-being; pure hate the extreme of misery. Daguesseau uses the term "love" here to lead the way again to the societal interface with natural law, for it denotes a reasonable inclination to receive from others benefits appropriate to one's nature and to do to others the same out of any motive related to self-perfection and happiness.

No one who had worked for Versailles could avoid realizing the communal can be cruel. There is the power we have over others and they over us, the obstacles that divide us, the goals we can expect and the ills to be feared from one another, the harsh means by which we must achieve these goals by evading the ills. Yet it is in promoting the spirit of the social contract that Daguesseau presents our solitude as weak and miserable when it admits no relation to others. Certainly the advantages given men in society—language and writing, arts and commerce, the power of arms and the protection of laws—far outweigh the disadvantages. If only, he concludes, each individual within the group could show sincere affection rather than the ubiquitous, immoral alternatives of violence and fraud.

Knowing what it is to love and hate alone and within the social unit, Daguesseau comes to his Ninth *Méditation* (Daguesseau-Pardessus, xiv, 464–570), a chiaroscuro descent ever farther into the dark and light of what lies at the heart of the "natural." Pondering whether the word means to love or to hate one's fellow creatures and certain that it definitely does not connote mere vulgar instinct, he arrives at a definition: "natural" is what is comprised in the essence of each being; it is the properties that constitute and make me recognize that essence and at the same time the end to which I judge it is destined. To live naturally is to live this teleological experience according to God's creator intention that each being should arrive at its perfection.

God's love mirrors a Daguesseau judiciary whose natural law of fairness is meant to handle any legal infringement, avoiding cruelty or vengeance in meting out a just severity. All these Enlightenment concepts struggle, however, as Daguesseau faces the equality factor. God loves all beings equally, because all are created with equality as an essential component of their being. The Daguesseau God, however, loves unequally unequal beings, whether unequal by their nature or by unequal use of their equal faculties. As befits godhead's perfect Being, an absolute, arithmetical equality has been superceded by this certainty of a proportional, geometric equality. However, because Daguesseau is loath to abandon either Christ or Enlightenment, he suddenly slips it in that God still preserves a degree of love even for one who has most abused his gifts, because in that evil being there always remains a part of what God gave. God who wishes the good of one does not less wish the good of all.

These metaphysical stumblings alert us that the Daguesseau route to the land of natural law has reached a mythic, ambiguous twilight zone in an amalgam of a search for earthly Paradise, for the Grail, finding itself blocked off by the unexpected trial of a Dante-esque dark forest. It is arrival at the eternal, and for most, unanswerable, problem of Job—the puzzle Romantics of the nineteenth century would handle in a context of grotesque and sublime, communist utopia and capitalist distribution, and that Freud would place at the doorstep of civilization and its discontents. Why, asks the meditator, do I see so much inequality in the external effects of God's love; why do the most perfect of the human race often seem to be unhappy, and prosperity often seems to be the mark of vice and lack of virtue? Why is the common interest so often sacrificed to the interest of one or a few? The clear truth is that if God cannot love unequally equal beings, he cannot love more one with less perfection and less one with more; equal beings are equal only by the equality of God's love. Of course, the obscure but not occlusive caveat is that clear truth has to be reconciled with the unequal distribution of goods and exterior ills. Allotment sadly is never in proportion to perfection. Why? How can this "what we don't know" be offered in contradiction to what we do know? It is impossible for God not to be perfect; is it not equally impossible for the distribution of goods to be inconsistent with equality, absolute or proportional?

Daguesseau comes to our rescue with a way of reconciliation. First of all, only those who merit the treatment they have received by abuse of their liberty are heard to complain of unequal distribution. Secondly, theirs is a useless and arrogant objection, because the goods and ills complained of are not true goods and ills but rather indifferent things, good or bad only in the manner we use them—a matter which certainly does not prove inequality by God. Lastly, any sense of inequality cannot exist longer than a lifetime—only an instant in relation to eternity where we are promised a situation which shall surely be different. Modern day justice cannot but find these answers so offensive to civil rights to be objectionable object lessons; equally difficult for the reader today is Daguesseau's final reflection: the fundamental truth of self-love is that before perversion by passion, reason has been leading one toward the state reason regards as most happy. This stroke is meant to destroy Hobbes whose edifice was built on the assumption a human being enters the world without reason, loves himself, and therefore hates others. But Daguesseau is off on another plane, one where his summation for these ideas on human love is the simple and triumphant "The truth is evident."

In the long Tenth *Méditation* (Daguesseau-Pardessus, xiv, 570–636) Daguesseau, having taken this prophet's stance—perhaps turning his leg out in a Louis XIV pose—comes as close as he ever would to stating in writing the content of the law he has been defending. Ninth *Méditation* disposal of the arch enemy, Hobbes, has fully revealed the unexpected philosophical realization of love: adjudication must consist in an extraordinary feeling of obligation to work for the benefit of the public. Daguesseau is now ready to draw from the three preceding *Méditations* the "general and particular consequences" which are the rules that this self-love must follow in relation to God and others. As usual there are prescient consequences in these far-reaching theorems of the moralist's law, for in them lie strong suggestions for modern principles of pleasure, pain, and ego:

I. Perfection is the use of liberty to learn by reason what is truly useful; this is accomplished by concentrating the will on mind and heart loving God, self, and other human beings.
II. Happiness, the consequence of perfection, can be sought only in the soul.
III. Happiness is personal opinion and can be erroneous; one must judge what is a true value and avoid error from the senses.
IV. The "I" should prefer durable happiness to a transitory form, even if less intense.
V. The "I" should judge pleasures not in themselves but in their results; small pleasures not leading to sadness are better than risky big ones leading who knows where.
VI. Vice versa as to ills.
VII. When comparing pains and pleasures the "I" should recall mere absence of pain is a pleasure; yet, tolerate a passing supportable pain if that is the only way to achieve pleasure.
VIII. Any fear of such tolerable pain should not prevent finding a lasting state which offers both absence of pain and also a degree of pleasure greater than the pain suffered to get it.
IX. Always reasonably tend toward union with God as the final end of self-love. This effort will bring about personal happiness by turning one's attempt at perfection into a beneficial imitation of the sovereign Being. This last rule embraces all the others.

Daguesseau's many soul-searching maxims may have had the occasional questionable ethical direction, but they inspired him toward the two principal characteristics which undergird all law. The first is that law tends to fit the nature and true interests of those subject to it. If such law does not rule me, he calmly proposed, it is not that it lacks authority but that I lack reason. The fault is not in the law but in me. (This may sound like *Julius Caesar*, but Daguesseau was actually readying himself to do an *et tu Brute* job on empire.) The second is that law's power of motivation brings people to it and thus assures the authority of that law graven by our self-love in the base of our soul. <u>Law is not something that is obeyed by beings who cannot understand it</u> (underscoring supplied). Substituting for the word "nature" the term "reason," Daguesseau had come to know natural law as only for the human species. It is the "dictate of right reason," the general duties or fundamental rules which reason teaches to all whose self-love consults humanity's truest interest. To appreciate how advantageous these maxims are, he had realized what the civil state could be if we all lived like members of the same family, with our motives to obey—fear of pain and hope of reward—equally written into society's legal matrix. The pain inevitably delivers certain unhappiness, but the reward promises the greatest gift humans can enjoy on earth: a law-governed social compact. For Daguesseau it is this social agreement which merits the name of natural law far more than the basic behavioral codes applicable to man and beasts to which the Roman jurisconsults gave the name "natural."

But, as we have just noted, the natural law rules he was about to prescribe for the general human society as well as all those already stated regulating self-love conduct toward God, self, or others, brought him to that unexpected anti-imperial stance. Daguesseau had come to see the nation as one moral whole. Studied like a single man, it, like him, was imbued with a self-love which if reasonable would lead to happiness. The "if reasonable" means there are rules to be observed between a nation and its sister states, duties which self-love prescribes to these nations as to all citizens living in them; and there are duties/rules which such inhabitants must observe beyond each other and toward the state. With a clairvoyance that places Daguesseau far in the vanguard of those who would predispose states to become United Nations, Common Markets, or European Unions, he reached what we today would call international law and public law—for him *droit des gens*, law of nations, or the Latin, *ius gentium*. Rules for nation vs. nation he preferred be called *ius inter gentes*, with each nation, as a single human, able to render mutual service and obey the golden rule. Self-defense, including pre-emptive attack, was as well subject to the same rules as for individuals. With treaties more sacred than interior laws, and the good of humanity higher than the good of each nation, the moralistic lawyer portrayed personhood transmuted into that common mother-fatherland where were abolished the distinction of foreigner and citizen whenever the interests involved could be reconciled. Such legal steps, devolved for one nation's relations with other nations and with its subjects within—the *droit des gens*—resemble natural law in being the consequence of reasonable self-love. Daguesseau did not formally call it such because the positive will of men, not nature, had divided the earth into nations. Daguesseau equally placed laws of nations outside civil law, as well as outside any arbitrary positive law. As he ranged them instead under the public law rubric, he stressed they were informally "natural" in being immutable to all those nations once formed by arbitrary action. Fundamental to public law was the perpetual, irrevocable, necessary, and salutary engagement of the founders and their descendants; this pact engaged each to live according to the natural law of being, that is, the *droit des gens*.

The golden rule had thus found that its comfort level lay in lessons wrapped around each nation, each citizen: from the concept of man and state committed to a satisfying reasonableness of self-esteem flowed smoothly the duties of each citizen to the nation and each nation to its citizens. It is the state, wrote Daguesseau, which can save each person's ills and serve each person's needs; but in return one must do it no injury, serve it according to one's power, act toward it as one wants it to act toward oneself, that is to say obeying its laws and commands and refraining not only from revolt but from disturbances of the peace. In placing *patrie* before all other objects we prepare ourselves to die for it. Daguesseau may have been in service to the Versailles avatar of the divine, but obligation to country was in his mind an even greater duty. If national happiness is a by-product of a tolerant self-love, the happiness of Daguesseau's chief of state—even a sun king—depended on the absence of unhappiness among citizens which in turn was caused by an inviolate respect of natural law. A monarch's perfection standard was to set an example, being the first to obey, understanding his self-love meant an attachment to the state stronger than that of any other human simply because he had no private interest to resist.

Having drawn up this idealistic blueprint, Daguesseau was no less demanding of *droit civil*, the civil law appropriate to each nation and prescribed to itself by each people through the ministry of government. We might well think Daguesseau should call this private law, but he did not; for him it was purely positive and arbitrary because it depended on the free will of the legislature. This will, to be truly useful not only to the state but to each legislator himself, had to be animated by the same spirit as natural law and *droit des gens*: our old standby, reasonable self-love.

The *droit civil* should be considered both as to who makes the laws and as to those subject to them. As to the former this can differ following the writer's genius, mores, and diverse interests; but the principle that dictates those laws to the sovereign or his officers remains the same: the rules will not be reasonable or worthy of that sovereign unless founded either on love of humanity in general—forming the natural law—or on love of the sovereign's particular society—that which produces the *droit des gens* for the interior of each society. Hence all the laws of the *droit civil* can have only two principle objects. The first will be explication of natural law, which is accessible to all attentive and reasonable minds but whose consequences, less direct and immediate, often need to be clarified and fixed by the positive authority of the legislator. The second—always on the basis of reasonableness—is elucidation of the *droit des gens* or application of its general principles to the needs and particular interests of each nation, the end of the state's common good. Daguesseau imagined a closely wrought almost sexual, parental nexus in which this same love of man in general or each people in particular would first give birth to natural law, then *droit des gens* would father *droit civil*, which in turn explained or applied these laws in the same spirit that inspired them. He dismissed any argument by two simple caveats: all civil laws which do not conform to the fundamental rules of natural law and *droit des gens* are contrary to human nature; on the other hand each subject will be acting against self-love if he or she does not obey them when they contain nothing against natural law or *droit des gens*.

As if sensing the firestorm to come with the century's end, Daguesseau quickly inserted even more pages on the abuse of authority. Loyal servant of the crown as he had been and wished again to be, he agonized back and forth over this prickly question, setting up arguments which today serve as a fascinating looking glass held up to Versailles, but equally reflective of any current political house of smoke and mirrors. He recalled a reply made by an Englishman (whose name he conveniently forgot) to Charles II: all one can desire is that the people be persuaded the king can do as he wishes while the king be persuaded that he can do what he wishes only according to law. Advantages of submission to a nation's chief are so great, believed Daguesseau, that the question cannot, must not, arise if there is any doubt about whether there has been an abuse of power. The abuse must be clear, evident, certain, and the sentiment of the nation unanimous, because anarchy poses the greatest of all ills, and even bad government is better than none. Daguesseau knew a conflict lay deep in this paradox: a nation destroyed if it were not obeyed; a nation destroyed if its chief unexpectedly turned power against its subjects. He was historian enough to know many cases where heads of state, contrary to right principles, hacked away branches of the body politic. But had there been a case where they destroyed the roots also? Nero wished that the Roman people have only one head so that they could be decapitated by a single blow, but even he had been held to his cruel, stillborn wish.

At first Daguesseau concluded—at least rhetorically—that all this talk of abuse was, really, only a philosophical problem; no nation was going to be obliged to resolve it. Yet, succumbing to the lulling, hypnotic force of meditation, he had then seemed at last to hear his invisible reader, pressing him on with the "but, what if?" And suddenly the man of law found himself going very far into his effort at reply, so far we sense him physically present to us, as his candle burns late into the night. All right, he agrees, you still refuse to leave me alone on this question of *tyrannus rex*, so look, I now offer you three maxims inspired by reasonable self-love.

This is an extraordinary moment of a messianic cleansing in the temple, of law facing its destruction and thinking aloud it might be a far better thing than it has done before. Daguesseau proceeds carefully, holding on for support to his favored one, two, three approach: (1) if the founders of the nation provide a procedure by which subjects *can* demand revocation of a law, nothing in enlightened self-love forbids using it; (2) the rebellion question only arises when the whole nation is essentially or mortally injured by the law; then it is that whole nation, or those who have the right by law to represent it, who may oppose the offending law, for no one individual, or even considerable numbers of citizens, has that right; and (3) even if the body of the nation or those who represent it are convinced the law is repugnant to natural law or the *droit des gens*, when they see that opposition will lead to civil war more hurtful to the people than the law, a reasonable self-love will show that no law against natural law or *droit des gens* is durable over time without correction.

Daguesseau had finally said it. The time bomb of revolution and nationhood had been prepared for the Jeffersons, Dantons, Robespierres, and Napoleons to come. The answer would be unnoticed in the busy prose of the Tenth Meditation as, far less dramatically, Daguesseau wound down drama with detailed maxims which his now rather droning-on principles of self-love prescribed for the more basic, limited kinds of civil law associations: marriage, parenting, other family relations, friendship, and all contracts. But one senses how the rush, the exhilaration of the preceding section had taken hold. In words which have the unmistakable ring of insurrection's political martyrs-to-be—reality's Louis XVI and Nathan Hale, fiction's Sidney Carton, or theatrical heroes from Figaro to Humphrey Bogart—exile Daguesseau has added his personal certainty: my relation to the body of the nation is infinitely more important than the domestic societies of a few, and I must therefore sacrifice to the greater good of the state the advantages of having family and friends. There is even more legal reason if such sacrifice is to the greater good of all humanity: not injuring the whole is in effect a condition of every contract or engagement.

He then would look the "us" of the future straight in the eye. Though I have spoken here only to myself and a small number of friends, one day this work may fall

Daguesseau
Courtesy of The Bridgman Art Library

into the hands of readers who will say: better with Hobbes to take man as he is and concede he is violent. But, explains Daguesseau with wonderful panache reminiscent of the *Instructions*, the problem of these readers will be that they lack a solid and continuous attention; if they had it, they would be convinced: either what I have said suffices or nothing can. My only question is whether each of us can find in the essence of our being the idea of natural duty to be obeyed in order to receive the happiness of which each is capable. As to whether you obey this duty is not part of my concern; my question is law, not fact.

Public Law

The Essai

The great task faced by anyone exhorting people to be responsible citizens and highly moral leaders is how to cope with them as their morality actually is practiced at a given time and place. Daguesseau had faced this challenge of law, and he had thought hard about his philosophical answers as he marched to silent drummers Jesus, Grotius, and Domat. But with the *Méditations* unpublished, the answers France heard were instead imbedded in a lifetime of advising the ruler, exhorting the bar, planning the education of judges, pleading cases, deciding administrative problems, drafting legislation, moving toward a single code of private law for France.

Monnier suggests that the equally unpublished *Essai d'une institution au droit public* found in volume fifteen of Pardessus can be seen as serving the function of a promised terminative eleventh reflection. But the words of the Tenth *Méditation* with their strong accent on learning a moralistic rule for a more formal legal framework, indicate Daguesseau had finished creating the *Méditations*' ambience of proof. The *Essai*'s title, which can be rendered *Draft of an Instruction in Public Law*, refers not to a method of study like the paternal *Instructions*; rather, it is a statement of the theory of public law, useful no doubt for students, but mainly, a presentation in the Montaigne tradition of a personal point of view. It can hardly serve as the eleventh *Méditation*, because it does not proceed, as promised in the tenth, "independently of the orientation of ideas created in me by the desire for happiness from self-love." A guess as to Daguesseau's purport in the *Essai* might be that he wanted to complete what his mentor, Domat, left unfinished—namely, the part on public law in Domat's *Lois Civiles*. If so, the follower did no better than the mentor; the *Essai* of Daguesseau is also unfinished. Perhaps Daguesseau in writing the *Essai* had in mind the possibility of its publication in his lifetime and, therefore, made no reference to the ten *Méditations*. But that it had in Daguesseau's mind a function different from the *Méditations* is also suggested by the fact that in it Daguesseau begins by assuming the existence of natural law without reference to the elaborate proof of it in the ten preceding *Méditations*.

The *Essai*'s main interest lies in its statement that since no one can have rights against Him, God is not bound by natural law. This was no flirtation with Ockham; Daguesseau never doubted that natural law was immutable. Consistent with Grotius, his argument in the *Méditations* as to the content of natural law holds dependency on the nature of man as a reasonable being, a nature for which change is never envisaged. In other words, God, by initial choice, was "stuck" on the seventh day with what he created. In the *Essai* Daguesseau, having said that God is not bound by natural law, hurriedly reassures us by implying that God's perfection will not change, and that man, therefore, treats with God more surely than with any of his fellow men. The *Essai* is notable because of its lengthy Pauline concern to establish that natural law merits the name "law," even though it does not have, unless the legislature accords them, the ordinary sanctions attached to violation of positive statutes. In any case, be it a putative Meditation or freedom for the spirit, the far less dramatic and prophetic *Essai* stands as a theoretical justification of the monarchy, while at the same time it retains part of the *Méditations*' free thinking, enlightened spirit. Daguesseau is still ready for sermonic admonitions to the King, pointing out respectfully, but unequivocally, that monarchy must admit to a higher law. In its benign unpublished form Daguesseau was not put in danger; but it nevertheless clearly shows a man ready to proclaim that being one nation under God's law defines limitation upon all earthly, arbitrary power.

Daguesseau and His English Contemporaries

An original Daguesseau contribution lay in asserting that self-love, the main feature of man's nature, will, when controlled by reason, drive him to seek self-perfection as the only way to happiness. Humankind's fundamental objective had led along the pathways of a reasoning as inevitable as those of geometry. It had been made manifest now to Daguesseau that there was a more flexible, spiritual essence which, being God-sent, could help us to find contentment in life. Self-love in Domat's interpretation had pushed people into engagements in production and commerce to satisfy their needs. Daguesseau though, had amended this economic treatment, giving self-love a higher and central place as a blameless virtue which would impel each one to seek his perfection or, what Joseph Campbell, our modern chronicler of the mythic quest, would reprise under the terminology of "bliss."

Original in his conception, Daguesseau, nevertheless, was participating in the considerable interest the French philosophy of self-love had generated across the Channel during the first part of the eighteenth century. The French Regency (1715–1723) marked a period of remarkable admiration among Frenchmen for English institutions and customs—"*l'anglomanie*" they called it then, and it tended to open up insular French pride in French history and traditions to an intellectual enrichment which went far beyond café philosophizing. It began with Bernard de Mandeville (1670–1733), son of a Dutch physician, educated in Holland for the same profession, who then went to England some time after 1691 to learn the language. His success was such that many Englishmen refused to believe he was a foreigner. He practiced little medicine, living rather on a pension from Dutch merchants and on money which distillers paid him to advocate drinking. Either from this seductive spokesperson role or his charming conversation he ascended in English society. His fame rests on a satire, *Fable of Bees*, published in 1705 as 200 doggerel verses whose popularity had transmitted them in nine editions by 1755. The controversial *Fable* attacked English politics at a time when Tories were saying Marlborough led England to war against the French out of his own personal interest. Mandeville presented, almost like devil's advocate, a philosophy in which humanity's higher life and virtue were merely fictional ideals introduced by hypocritical rulers trying to keep their wretched populace in order. In fact, thought the cynical Mandeville, the rulers erred. An act to benefit others or control passions being unnatural, such benevolent morality actually hindered the intellectual and commercial progress of the state. Vice, not virtue, by leading to the wish for luxurious living, produced inventions, circulated capital, and caused progress; a society possessed of all the virtues would simply fall into apathy and paralysis. For Mandeville absence of vice-prone self-love was the killer of progress; judging civil covenant laws equally harshly, he called them the result of "selfish aggrandizement and protective alliances among the weak" (*Encyclopedia Britannica*, Vol. XVII, 560a). Readying a darkened stage for writers like Laclos, Retif, and de Sade, he denied all moral sense or conscience; in his eyes, social virtues had evolved from the basest instinct for self-preservation, and conduct apparently altruistic and disinterested, was simply the result of that ability by statesmen to play on human vanity and pride. The door shut brutally on natural law, as Mandeville, a skeptical positivist and Nominalist who would reject the existence of universals, played self-love into a barrier against conscience's innate truths.

Bollingbroke sent Daguesseau some English books on philosophy that could well have included Mandeville, although the *Méditations* does not mention the Englishman by name. However, Mandeville was well known among another group of Englishmen, most of them ecclesiastics and theologians; several, in making their primary aim a refutation of the *Fable*'s Hobbesian skepticism, were, in fact, taking care to place themselves in positions of affinity with Daguesseau. Although not lawyers, they had soon constructed a strong oppositional case against Hobbes's idea that man is purely egotistical. They attacked, too, Hobbes's position on a morality legislated either by God or the political power. Hobbes argued that since the policymakers can interpret God, the great national arbiter for all practical purposes is positive law. Hobbes's critics insisted on the power of social nature rather than egoism. Humans possessed a moral sense of conscience to discern moral values independently of the expressed will not only of God but especially of positive law.

The most interesting among these English colleagues is Anthony Ashley Cooper, 3rd Earl of Shaftesbury (1671–1713). Locke had supervised his education, although one could not call Shaftesbury a disciple of any one contemporary. Rather, his main intellectual spring was Humanism. He admired the Greek ideas of harmony, balance, and moderation and was able to appreciate Aristotle's work on the social nature of man in spite of the current distaste for scholastic logic. A shy man, generally not in good health, on his travels abroad he enjoyed most conversing with the abundant corps of tutors accompanying their young gentlemen charges on the Grand Tour. Entering the House of Commons in 1695 he was distinguished for his eloquent support of a controversial procedural bill which granted counsel in treason cases to the accused; Shaftesbury's liberalism also promoted parliamentary independence over slavish obedience to party. When illness forced him to retire in 1698, he spent a year in the exciting Dutch atmosphere of freely discussed philosophy, morals, politics, and religion. After another period of political activity back in England, he returned to Holland in 1703, leaving yet again for England in 1704 to wage a struggle against tuberculosis. Here he devoted himself entirely to study, reflection, and writing. He saw his principal philosophical essays in print between 1709 and 1713; *Letters to a Young Man at the University* were published in 1716. Though his adherence to the details of theology was not orthodox, he was preeminently religious; and belief in an all-wise, just, and merciful God governing providentially pervades all his works. The Shaftesbury character reminded a biographer of Marcus Aurelius, especially in his devotion to ethical speculation. One senses that he and Daguesseau might have become friends had they met, especially keen to exchange their instructional ideas for young lawyers on the rise.

A central concern in Shaftesbury's thought was the ubiquitous natural need for private good. Shaftesbury saw that the human being, by nature a social creature, inevitably existed as part of a natural system. If a person were good, then thought, emotion, and actions would agree with the good of others—in other words, the individual would mesh seamlessly within the collectivity of system. There would be no choice to be made between self-love and altruism, between concern for personal interest and virtue for the public good, as though they were mutually exclusive. True, there could arise an inordinate concern for private good—what we commonly call selfishness—but a measured regard for private good commensurate with public good could not be blameworthy, but rather contributed to the public well-being. Shaftesbury did not accept ideas of virtue as innate, but he did feel that there was naturally in each of us something which enabled recognition of virtue; this, not obedience to divine will and authority, nor the positive law of the state, defined any obligation to be virtuous (Copleston, Vol. V, 172–176).

Shaftesbury's ideas were to have a considerable effect both in Great Britain and abroad. Leibniz, Voltaire, Diderot, and Herder as well as Hume and Adam Smith are all known to have appreciated him. A French translation of his works appeared in Geneva (1769). In England, the Shaftesbury system was both made more precise and questioned by Hutcheson (1694–1746) who, publishing in 1725 and 1728, found less certitude that self-love was necessarily morally virtuous. However, a Bishop Butler (1692–1752) in books published in 1726 and 1736, agreed with Shaftesbury. It is easy to conclude that as a group these English thinkers were not influenced by Daguesseau, for he never published anywhere and did not travel in Holland or England. However, it is less easy to exclude influence upon them by Daguesseau mentor Domat, who published before any. That they in turn influenced Daguesseau remains a high if unproved possibility, the answer being lost in whatever was contained in Bolingbroke's gift box of books or in the undocumented talk of the day.

Whoever influenced whom, it was ultimately, however, in France, where orthodox religion was stronger, that lawyers like Daguesseau and not philosophers like Shaftesbury were doing the speculation that bore directly on the Western European development of the law. The *Méditations* had summarized a philosophical foundation to establish the right direction of active governance. In contrast to the tangled, jumbled, ill-formed, over-crowded legal system of France, here was new unicity of a natural law—whole, homogeneous, immutable, eternal, and universal.

Daguesseau's Final Excursions into Law Reform

Daguesseau's 1713 idea of taking up again the question of a single code and with it reform of court structure came back strongly to mind in 1725. He was at Fresnes and happened to read a new work by the Abbé de Saint-Pierre. Saint-Pierre, not a lawyer but a busy observer of public affairs, had taken as his thesis the need to shorten the time required to get final adjudication in legal proceedings. Daguesseau thought the Abbé generally a fool, but the name was compelling, and being a good Petrinist he nevertheless felt it important to look for truths carefully in what the fool had written. The reading turned out to be worthwhile enough to pen a point-by-point commentary on the Abbé's work. This careful exercise in turn brought a flood of ideas back to Daguesseau—recollection of Domat's 1664 memorandum on court reform, a copy of which he had kept among his papers; hope for recall as Chancellor; and planification strategies for action now that Cardinal Fleury was promising more prudent and stable government.

From this initial groundwork emerged an elucidatory memorandum entitled *General Views on the Possible Reformation of Justice*. It was to prove a highly pragmatic text (thirty printed pages in Volume Thirteen of the Pardessus edition) which, although done in the usual Daguesseau format of personal guide rather than public treatise, now serves as a priceless and fascinating overview both of its time and ours. Here can be found what is faced—and how it is conquered—when swollen bureaucracy clogs the halls of justice. It is first a text of a man, wondering if reform can ever really be possible; then appears the heroic Justinian jurist, forging ahead with his favorite three pivots around which change must come: the rules which constitute jurisprudence, the steps in legal procedure, the discipline of officers who will administer the system.

Daguesseau understands it will be a question of reforming old laws, making new ones, and uniting both in a single body of legislation so that those who want to learn the law, whether as counsel or as judges, will have one code as the fixed and certain object of study. To see the necessity of that unity he urges a look at the multitude and variety of laws; either none of them is studied because of the difficulty of knowing all, or every one is pondered progressively as cases arise, with the result that finding a person who possesses perfectly the entire corpus of French jurisprudence is almost impossible. Knowledgeable of the codes of Spain, Sweden, and Denmark, Daguesseau is willing to propose that, if France cannot lead, at least she can follow in the steps of others. He recalls mentors of codification: Justinian, glorious more because of his *Digest* and *Code* than all his conquests and grandiose titles; Henry III and President Brisson trying valiantly to do the same for France but dying before their codification had reached a state truly useful to the public; Daguesseau especially bows to his master, the *grand* Louis, whose partial structuring of the law has been showing a nation how advantageous it can be to have the whole.

Turning his attention to the secular, civil law—public and private—presents Daguesseau a much greater challenge, and he knows it. Private law has its usual two parts: Roman, observed with the consent of the king as true law in some provinces under royal control, and customs, now drafted in writing and authorized by the king. These latter are not only picturesque in diversity, but annoyingly contrary: what is perfectly just on one side of a stream is totally unjust on the other. To judge customs well, a judge needs to know a text and its true spirit. If one adds, as one must, the royal legislation which decides questions of Roman and French law, then extrapolating from this triple legal layer a general law for all the provinces is a daunting job. Daguesseau faces with *sang froid* and diplomacy the question of project time, assuring his patronate that an antiquated Chronos need not concern a modern monarchy which will live as long as the world. Besides, what are a possible ten years against the eternal utility of the result? And what is time, given the promise of at last putting an end to the annoying habit of jockeying by a party for hearing before any court that happens to offer legal rules favorable to his interest. Yet as to the difficulty of the work, more needs to be said, and so Daguesseau proceeds to outline some of the problems to be encountered. His analysis makes us a fly on the wall to the opening clash of the Revolution's awesome cymbals and of the less bloody 1804 coda.

Daguesseau decides two things have to be included in the new statutes: ordinances deciding certain questions in Roman Law and a coping mechanism for existing conflicts among courts in the decision of those "Roman" questions. The codification is not after all just a matter of simple decisions making the rule for each subject matter. It touches on the fundamental ideas of justice common to all people, ideas embraced in an infinity of reflections and reasonings all of which are grounded on bedrock principles of equity and natural law. The draftsmen of this code will somehow have to penetrate the very minds of the Romans themselves to perceive the concepts and verities which have enabled them to understand their law and make others understand it. Also, since only those parts of Roman law still in use are to be codified, there will be a danger that after promulgation the rest of Roman law may remain unread despite containing the best training for able magistrates.

Daguesseau's long view assumes the continuation of the feudal order. He observes, for example, that when a lord claims one-fifth of something in Paris and only one-thirteenth in Normandy, it will hardly be fair to make either fraction a single rule for all. The old ways will have to continue. (Obviously the draftsmen of the Revolution and of Napoleon, who with a guillotine's assistance could build on the overnight destruction of feudalism, took an easier tack.) Daguesseau, however, notes that other aspects of law controlling private persons in their engagements, dispositions, and successions can be regulated by common rule for the future without altering present fortunes. Any inconvenience caused in expectations as to property will be outweighed by the advantages of improved legal clarity and access to the law. Here, begin with the simplest subjects, counsels the Chancellor—prescriptions, redemptions by an heir against a sale *inter vivos*, security interests, gifts, dowries—since they are a mix of private interests which present no obstacles to the public welfare. Success on this less challenging terrain will allow the draftsmen then to become more bold. They might even gain the confidence to regard opponents as public enemies.

Four centuries after Daguesseau, law makers desirous of new regulation still must make their case against laws already on the books. When it is a matter of improving litigious procedure, Daguesseau admits there are already the general laws of 1667 on civil procedure and those of 1670 on criminal procedure. But, he argues, although the objective then was to abbreviate the length of suits in civil cases—simplifying them, reducing expense—in fact, every day since 1667 the number of suits has grown with no less complexity and difficulty, and with expenses considerably increased. Daguesseau minces no words in a prose litany which, sadly, sounds much like many an angry client today: subtlety and malice always outstrip the foresight of the legislator, making it the science of chicanery, not legal justice, which defines so-called progress. At the same time, the number of judicial officers has increased along with the number of rights to be litigated. All this gives occasion for magistrates to charge fees to try to recover the cost of their offices, and the increase of expense has denied justice to many. The greedy *procureurs*, too, have sharpened their minds; and although one suit may now do what formerly took ten, they avoid loss in their income by offsetting the decline in the quantity of the merchandise by an increase in the price. Lower court judges connive at this, too, because their interest is identical.

Since more laws will hardly help this lamentable state, Daguesseau resorts to his favored trio of answers, one in which there is again that modern echo: (1) reduce the excessive number of officers of judicature—a step which will incidentally push some people into the cultivation of lands, commerce, and other more useful professions; (2) suppress many of the fees for various steps in a proceeding—fees which the *procureurs* are simply passing onto the clients; and finally (3) establish a discipline in the *parlements* and inferior courts so that the conduct of each magistrate is subject to surveillance.

Daguesseau has now reached his finale: discipline for men of the law. This is the most difficult reform because of the large number of officers committed to venality. While Daguesseau cannot hope to correct all the abuses, he does have his usual countdown of steps to start the reform process. First, there is venality—the source of almost all abuses in the administration of justice. Abolish it, he urges, at least as to principal offices. Second, move for the better execution of the laws by annual assizes at which the conduct of enforcement officers is reviewed and the people are heard. Third, for abuses beyond the courage and authority of the *baillis* and others, use annually the *Parlement* oversight of visitation (*grands jours*). And fourth, enforce the existing requirement that the periodic assemblies of the *parlements*, called *mercuriales*, be devoted not merely to a superficial oratorical exhortation but to serious consideration of articles of reform. Once sent to the Chancellor, he can report them to the king and then put them into effect.

No one in power had dared put forth such a powerful legal blueprint for the governance of France. Daguesseau began by giving the explosive memorandum to his friend Joly de Fleury, then Procureur Général. On 12 May 1728 the response came back in the form of another memorandum, and the two documents stood as an elegant diptych describing the low state of justice in the inferior jurisdictions of France. Fleury was emboldened to outline reforms on an even broader scale than his friend's. But Daguesseau needed more than one supporter, and on his own authority as Chancellor he went ahead and formed a Council on Law Reform. Its president was d'Arnouville, Counsellor of State and Lieutenant General of Police. Other members were d'Argenson, another Councillor of State and later Minister of War; several men expert in particular fields; and even that foolish sage the Abbé de Saint Pierre, who, with his usual much to say, submitted many letters.

Paying this committee's staff, to say nothing of funding the much needed reforms they would propose, clearly was going to touch the King's treasury, and when Daguesseau approached the Minister of Finance for his support he was crudely rebuffed. Daguesseau was much put out, and note was taken of the heavy cost for mounted police in the war department and the department of forests and waterways. The royal deer domain alone was costing in excess of 100 million francs, quite a sum for a noble amusement park even if it helped the *miserables* poaching in Anjou and Touraine. Daguesseau and his men knew well how the vivacious Madame du Barry boasted that her kingly lover had just given her five million francs and her brother two; a quarter of the brother's gift might have sufficed for the committee payroll (Monnier, 298). But Daguesseau had a catalytic personality, and the opportunity to work with him attracted enough lawyers that the Council gained several ardent men, including his younger brother and his own two exhaustively trained sons—all pledged to serve voluntarily without pay. Joly induced a few of his personal assistants to work overtime, and Daguesseau's own government office took on double duties.

Having yielded to the political necessity of avoiding changes that involved the King's money, Daguesseau decided to do all he could by way of ordinances whose cost would be measured in the sacrifice of prejudice and tradition. We recall his conclusion in the *Meditations*: natural law imposes duty to apply one's wisdom to improve the lot of humanity. As de Rayes would later write in 1783: "'People, if your civilization improves ... you owe much to Daguesseau. He ... laid the foundations of that philosophy which embellishes thrones and is only concerned with public happiness.'" Another wrote: "'In imitation of the Supreme Being Daguesseau wants the justice in his heart to reign around him'" (Monnier 307–308).

The outcome eventually brought France the following ordinances: Donations (1731), Testaments (1735), Capacity to Donate (1736, not promulgated), Minors (1741), and Trusts (1747). Consensual engagements *inter vivos* between individuals—the law of contracts, primarily important in commerce and industry remained at the time nearly all Roman law; it felt little effect from customs and would seem to have been an appropriate subject for this major codification. However, with only brief mention in Domat's book, the needs of the commercial and industrial economy before the industrial revolution had perhaps not yet produced sufficient cases at this juncture to push Daguesseau in such a direction. He probably also felt he had already covered the territory, for during his first exile Law's paper shares in a joint-stock company had brought the matter to the forefront as many wealthy people in France asked themselves whether it should even be lawful to trade in this strange new form of property. January and February 1720 saw prices on the dizzying way down from 20,000 *livres* in December 1719 to 9,000 in March 1720; by May the plummeting had reached one-half the par value of 500. Daguesseau felt compelled to write an important commercial *mémoire* (Daguesseau-Pardessus, xiii, 513–638) carefully addressing the legality of such economic activity. After some Article One definitions, his Article Two set forth the general principles of natural law on commerce—or at least on sales—then continued by presenting principles of viability one could establish for this new commerce in paper. A useful conclusion reached for and found solutions for many of the legal problems that might arise in the acquisition, possession, and sale of such shares. But his heart was not in the cleverness. A poignant note at the outset avowed that so far he had not been tempted to try and repair the ruins of the Daguesseau fortune by speculation in the shares; now his resolute hope was that if he ever did weaken on this point his memorandum would rise up against him.

For Daguesseau commerce ran on "cause" (consideration, we say), and on "value," "need," "share," and "*agiotage*" (speculation in shares). In defining "need" as the seller's wish for a high price and the buyer's for a low price, he distinguished sharply the seller who wants a low price because in truth he wants to acquire more, and the buyer who wants a high price because in truth he intends to sell more. Daguesseau found the fundamental problem lay in which promises were enforceable. His answer, based on Roman law: all promises that have no cause, or only imaginary cause, or a cause that is false, unjust, or contrary to good morals, or which is not followed by its effect, is null in itself and gives no right. Thus, for instance, taking advantage of the weakness of the poor is not a valid cause. Usually parties can agree on the interest to be paid for a loan, but by natural law one may not extract more from the indigent than the wealthy. A blind, insensate desire to enrich oneself is not a sufficient cause. Admittedly, the cause is the advantage or utility sought in contracting, but this is only the advantage that a reasonable man using his reason can find in a contract by means naturally proportionate to the end he proposes. In fierce remarks against gambling which are as topically astute today as they were in the gaming frenzy of the eighteenth century, Daguesseau decried the excessive proceeds of betting on chance. Their cause is almost never proportionate to effect, or if it is, there remains that wake of human folly. Pascal had used the Game to win souls to the economy of God. Daguesseau on the other hand is a figure of *gravitas* and gravity's pull, constantly bringing the fortune hunter's hand back down to the grindstone of labor and the steady, daily fidelity of natural justice.

How, wondered the jurist, could the self-destruction inherent in all human imprudence be defended as a just means either of enriching or of perfecting oneself? The Daguesseau ruling was tough: any such party unjustly enriched must make restitution even absent a demand for it; there is nothing permissible about retaining an illegitimate gain. But there was a loophole or two from one sophisticated enough for necessary exceptions. If turpitude is only on the side of the deliverer, he cannot recover; but if it is only on the side of the recipient there is no cause and there may be recovery. If the turpitude is equally on both sides, the possession will be upheld according to laws of human justice; but under the laws of conscience the recipient being unworthy must give his gain to the poor. At the end of the day, in very nuanced examples—again whose controversial pertinence speaks to us now—Daguesseau concluded that in casinos, although the games are tolerated by positive law, the gains are themselves illegitimate.

The old Roman moralist in him having been aroused, Daguesseau turned from games to the arts. In painting a nude the painter may have no emotion other than the perfection of his art; yet his gain is shameful (at least to the Jansenistically severe mind). If the picture is exposed in public to people of all ages, sexes, temperaments, and inclinations, it is morally certain that the exhibition will have consequences contrary to good morals. The same reasoning, a pre-Rousseau Daguesseau realized, could be applied to the dramatic stage.

Confident Justinian was still on his side, Daguesseau next approached the concept of just price, that sum dictated by the common and ordinary need of the majority of buyers. This balance of the value of money and goods varies with time, place, and circumstances, but it does not include exigency from special necessity or, indeed, plain ignorance of the buyer. Daguesseau joined Aquinas who recognized that the fair price is not necessarily a precise figure; it is simply a sum not departing considerably from the common price. Diocletian and Maximian seem imperially to have fixed this as to real estate at half the common price: the seller who obtained less than that could recover. Granted, half was hardly always just, but commerce then as now demanded a simple rule. Daguesseau saw natural law as requiring the same rule for the buyer as for the seller, for personal as for real estate, for considerable excess as well as for an excess exceeding one-half. All transactions without cause, or beyond the limits of cause, are, he felt, unjust in view of the effect of the necessity, ignorance, or lack of inspection and reflection by buyer or seller. The better rule, therefore, required inquiry whether the same merchandise has been sold at about the same price to others.

From these principles our contract legalist would now draw two consequences. In the first, any pertinence to Western commerce of our day reaches an abrupt refusal zone: monopoly for Daguesseau was a public crime worthy of civil death. The second, however, having traveled to Daguesseau from Cicero, is still applicable: a dealer may affect price by spreading news about an event such as a flood, fire, bankruptcy, war, peace, etc., but he may not do it falsely, for then his gain will be without cause (if the errors of men are not cause, still less are such errors inspired by the seller). Even these concepts, applicable to all sales, may not suffice when one person intends to be both buyer and seller and on occasion, as noted above in the definitions, may have as seller a motive for a low price because he intends soon to buy. Is this legitimate? Daguesseau here had to revert to his beloved innate principles, the first being that the double role is not impermissible *per se* provided it does not trouble the whole economy—the interest of civil society in a wide commerce demands that attention. However, it is the combat of buyers and sellers that produces the price proportionate to needs, and this struggle must be maintained. The common need of buyers, and, as seller, the common need of sellers' prices set true values. Daguesseau clarified with an example about a man and two guardianships. In one the minors have only something to sell; in the other they have only a need to buy. The duty of the guardian when acting for the former is to concern himself only with the common interest of sellers and sell as dearly as he legitimately can; for the latter, he must comply only with the common interest of buyers.

The second principle, flowing out of the first, is that if both quantities are mixed in one dealer so that he wishes to sell at a low price because he intends mainly later to buy, and *vice versa*, there is a violation of the first rule of human society—the interest of one must not prevail over the interest of all—and the gain will never be legitimized. These private sector legalities Daguesseau made certain to carry over to the state: public relief of misery, folly, or ignorance is no more a reason to enrich national coffers than an individual's. A gain illegitimate for the subject is illegitimate for the sovereign, except for taxes (!) for which there is a cause, but equally an imperative that the sovereign refrain from abuse in imposing them. A cause shameful in itself or in its necessary moral consequences is never purified by state interests: the prince, like any seller, must not induce error in buyers by spreading those false opinions which affect prices. And, importantly, the equilibrium flowing from the combat of buyers and sellers may no more be properly altered by the prince than by his subjects, since that would be against natural law, providence, and the general interest of society. If, however, the prince reserves to himself the sale of certain merchandise, he may fix the price as he pleases, because it is the same thing as a tax on it; as head humanitarian, it is for him alone to decide to moderate the price so that the poor are not excluded.

With generalities and principles for commerce now set up in formulaic structure, Daguesseau was comfortable about choosing Article Three of the *Mémoire* to state principles for commerce in shares; Article Four discussed problems as to the justice of stock acquisition or trading. In Three, although open to the convenience of preferring various forms of paper obligations to coin in conducting business transactions, the risks of paper as compared with coin led Daguesseau to conclude that the same principles stated in Article Two apply to paper. There must be a cause; the usual quartet of misery, necessity, folly, or blindness of one contracting party gives no more right than in contracts generally, and the cause must not be shameful or contrary to good morals. It is more criminal for a dealer artificially to change value by abusing his status as both buyer and seller. For example, a highly involved commercial law like that of the venerated Chancellor de l'Hôpital, which in 1567 forbade sellers of grain and other necessaries to buy in their own localities (or within eight leagues of Paris), would be far too complex ever to work with paper. Daguesseau had noted the unfortunate truth that shares tended to weaken legitimate transactions, even if sponsored by the king.

Fortified with this brave conclusion, Daguesseau moved onward to his Fourth Article for an even bigger explosion of strong caveats: (1) the acquisition or possession of shares as then established was so harmful to the interest of public, state, and families, that even if acquired and possessed with no intention to sell, the practice was contrary to natural justice, (2) *a fortiori* it is not permissible to acquire shares with the intention of selling at a profit, (3) or actually to sell them, and (4) the business of dealing and speculating in them, even indirectly, is likewise forbidden; thus (5) the king, who is bound as to commerce by natural law the same as his subjects, may not validate commerce in shares on the ground of benefit to the state (i.e., to pay the king's debts), (6) none of this is changed because there may be available no other investment, and although (7) gains from this source need not be restored if the turpitude of the cause is equal on both sides, there should otherwise be restitution, as when the seller caused the rise in price. Remember: equality of turpitude does not cure the title of the seller; he should give his gain to the public, represented for this purpose by the poor. In discussion of Point Six Daguesseau had stated what he felt to be the most plausible justification offered by stock speculators when shares rise in price: there is also concomitant inflation in the prices of what one has to buy to live. If one does not own any shares, he suffers loss. The Daguesseau response was that apart from the possibility that the speculators may end up with meaningless paper and be worse off than those who saved their funds, the worst that can happen to the latter is to lose a part—a loss which, in any case, does not affect natural law. It can be considered but one of many accidents of life, none of which authorizes a bad means of restoration. An advantage, however certain, must never be purchased by an action certainly bad.

This excursion by Daguesseau into the law of contracts demonstrates a phenomenon already several times observed: apart from procedures concerning land, which, except in the case of the rare medieval allods, were controlled by customary feudal law, the continental law of contracts, even as late as the first half of the eighteenth century was controlled by Roman concepts rather than custom or royal ordinance. Certainly Roman law was the only authority cited by Daguesseau. But we realize here also that since the advent of Grotius and secularized natural law, the law of contracts had been flexibly opened to respond to modern needs—including a remarkable awareness of the poor—with jurisconsular solutions based on the authority of natural law. Daguesseau's *Mémoire* demonstrates how strongly ethical and non-technical that approach was and how it addressed social ills currently observed. Daguesseau—inimical to the powerful raising of capital by the sale of corporate shares—produced a breathtaking rejection of the fundamental device of the capitalistic theory destined soon to transform the globe's material condition. Such short-sighted rejection was largely the consequence of historical accident which unfortunately had placed the first large-scale use of the share device in Law's reprehensible project rather than in a socially useful program.

The utility of natural law could not be arrested by that misstep. Daguesseau's failure to draft a complete code of contract law was, rather than accident, the result of legal scholarship simply not ready yet. Even Domat was not enough, and codification still awaited the research and writing of one even more attuned to the powerful swell of profound social changes. Daguesseau did make a step forward when he encouraged in 1729 a relatively recent work (1718) by B. J. Bretonnier (d. 1727), *A Collection of the Principle Questions of Law Differently Judged in the Different Courts of the Realm, with Reflections to Conciliate the Diversity of Jurisprudence*. Daguesseau directed his staff to keep consulting the text carefully along with Domat's works and those of others. He would actually insert some borrowings from the *Collection* into his completed ordinances.

Daguesseau's particular responsibility in the drafting work, was, he felt, the need for court reform. As he knew only too well, the fact that Louis would refuse the funds to give his subjects a better court system meant heartbreaking delay. To surmount this problem, Daguesseau even toyed with the idea of channeling almost all cases to the royal courts and making the lords who had seigneurial jurisdiction there pay for the changes rather than the King. In the end, he did draft an Ordinance on the subject which, nearly in final form, went a long way toward the Revolution's plan of 1791: a layer of courts of first instance with appeal to the *parlements* and the Council of State empowered to review their judgments. Comprised in the Ordinance were separate courts of commerce, although without the idea of using a jury for fact finding. But one piece of work by Daguesseau, the new procedural rule of 1738 for litigation before the Council of State, did become powerfully effective. It remained pertinent enough that both the Council and the Court of Cassation used as late as 1860. This inclusive document had an immensely broad scope, for it comprised rules for jurisdictional oversight, as well as the general guidelines for all activities of the Council.

It seems reasonable to presume that the pervasive financial plight deterred Daguesseau as well from presenting innovative reform in education. His papers show clearly his concern for reform of professorial compensation and of the statutes of the University of Paris, but there is no draft legislation. All that is preserved in his files is an unpublished treatise on education by Abbé Saint-Pierre, stressing, as Professor Rollin of the University of Paris had similarly urged in the seventeenth century, that education's objective must always be to teach virtue.

Having with no cost to the nation determined what to study, Daguesseau's next hurdle was how to proceed. Ahead lay more fact-finding, drafting, required approval by the King's Council, and registration needed by the *parlements*. Louis XIV had suspended the latter hurdle in 1673 when he and Colbert proceeded with exquisite partial incorrectness to avoid the legislators altogether. Daguesseau, on the contrary, working about sixty years later and a convinced supporter of the *parlements* at a time when registration had been reinstated, took the opposite approach. He eschewed the idea of positive law made by the king, proposing instead—and Monnier says (Monnier, 355) it is a historic first—that the *parlements* be questioned as to what the rules actually were. As a procedure far more republican than royal, Daguesseau had thought another unthinkable: it would be from the legislative branch, one might idealistically say from the French nation, that new law would henceforth excitingly, dramatically emerge.

Having made the fearless decision to consult the *parlements*, Daguesseau next sent to each a set of carefully prepared questions—sixteen on donations, twenty-seven on wills, forty-five on trusts, and fifty-two on capacity to give and receive. The donations submission was accompanied by a circular letter written personally by the Chancellor in which he introduced his project for uniformity of law by guiding the legislators in what he wanted to know—the jurisprudence of the Companies (as the *parlements* were then called), the changes the topic had undergone in that jurisprudence, the reasons on which current procedure was based, and what one could do to perfect it. Once the replies started to come in, the sons of Daguesseau and Arnouville began their reports to Daguesseau's Council for discussion prior to the drafting. The questions had been challenging enough to daunt even the best scholars, and it is not surprising that Daguesseau by correspondence, had to follow the parliamentary work as closely as he could in order to press for hard results.

The entire Daguesseau reform undertaking with its groundbreaking shift to legislative emphasis has lost none of its excitement or liberalism as we look at it today. Lawyers who at the beginning of the twenty-first century participate in the legislation of democracies can only marvel at the comparative simplicity of a process carried on under the awesome umbrella of nearly absolute power. But there were two fatal weaknesses built in: the legislature and the king. The *parlements* were hardly representative, composed as they were of men who often as a family had embraced the *robe* and who remained overwhelmingly bourgeois. In point of fact, the most representative body in the French system was the Estates General, and it is no accident that most of the great royal ordinances had originated in requests made by this hierarchical body. But the Estates General, since it could only be summoned by the king, had not met since 1614; and Louis XIV and Louis XV seemed determined that they should never meet again. When Count Frontenac became Governor of French Canada in 1672 he had called a meeting of the colonial Estates to take an oath to the king and stir up a little patriotic enthusiasm; Paris told him never to do such a thing again. On the whole, given the commitment of Daguesseau and many others to reason and public service, and their remarkably thorough education and study, one cannot but feel that monarchy should have done better with advisement than it did, even granting that the choice of the recipient of supreme royal power depended on the accidents of one family's biology. Sadly, the basic weakness of monarchy was discouragement of energy below. To royalty, meetings of subjects to consider their condition were generally anathema; had they been able to abolish the *parlements*, they would have done it.

The Last Chapter

Life in the rarefied air of Parliament did not claim all of Daguesseau's time in the closing years of his career. The long wars of Louis XV permitted him the leisure for a diversity of interests: encouraging fellow politicians to study collections of ordinances and to gather more supportive historical materials; inspiring Diderot not only to begin work but to aim for publication of the *Encyclopedia*; and urging Lelong to catalogue bibliography for his *Historical Library*. More symbolic for the future of the law than any of these was that certain encounter in Paris, when Michel Prévôt de la Janès, Professor of French law at the University of Orléans from 1731 to 1749, asked Daguesseau to meet his future successor, Robert Joseph Pothier. Pothier was finishing a book in which he had rearranged the contents of the *Digest* in better order but could not find an editor. It was the gallant Daguesseau who not only found Pothier that editor but in 1749 engineered the appointment of Pothier to the Janès chair in French law at Orléans, a chair which, as we are soon to see, would metamorphose into the cornerstone of the *Civil Code*.

In spite of such volunteer mentoring, the later years of one who had had such great career success and still retained such remarkable intellectual resources to make life interesting and satisfying, were not happy. After Anne lost her battle with cancer in 1735 Daguesseau never remarried nor recovered his good spirits. His determination to seek consolation in work was to be sorely tried as the deaths of close relatives and friends progressively left him bereft of his most pleasant society. In 1749, when his third son passed away, Daguesseau's own health began a serious decline, and in 1750 asthma and other afflictions forced him to stop working on the brilliant schemes for better governance and better laws. To his faithful servant's letter of resignation Louis, in his own royal hand, wrote back a warm letter of appreciation which not only allowed Daguesseau to keep his title as Chancellor but awarded him a pension of 100,000 francs of which a quarter could be bequeathed.

Final thought in the final Meditation had left no doubt about Daguesseau's deep need for religion. Always certain that faith helped hold the scales of Justice, he had composed during his second exile several religious works, among them *Diverse Reflections on Jesus Christ*, 178 printed pages of 307 sections. Now as Daguesseau returned to the world of the Roman poets and the Bible he re-read the text. Similar in form to Pascal's *Pensées*, the work had ended with "The Incredible Success of the Preaching of the Apostles throughout the *Earth*"; perhaps the old man experienced one last twinge of *amour-propre*, convinced that his legal analyses and reforms would soon be granted a wide audience of followers. Despite fever from a bladder infection, he retained to the last his steady, virtuous pace: freeing a condemned criminal who had appealed personally to him for mercy, dictating calmly his last wishes to his two surviving sons and the widow of another. The last words in his hand came in 1751 at eighty-two. Neither they nor the vast writings which preceded them were destined for the apostolic spread.

What does remain is, nevertheless, admirable. Daguesseau was a man who reached government's pinnacle and standing there knew the highest mission of government must be to reform. Through ten, minutely meditative reflections he worked out the stiff yet needed changes for France's legal system. Having proposed them to the most powerful monarch in the world, he then directed the process of their registration by all the *parlements*. Looked at in our large perspective, the Daguesseau effort toward a common law for France in code form was a notable and crucial part of that inexorable progress toward the centralized power that had begun with Hugues Capet in 987. Soon that road forward would culminate in the French Revolution which temporarily exchanged popular control for royal absolutism, while speeding the process of concentrating power in Paris. One can only imagine how amazed the Chancellor would have been when only six years after his passing Adrienne de Noailles, née d'Aguesseau, gave birth to one of the giants of this change, the Marquis de Lafayette.

It is easy to condemn Daguesseau simply because stylistically his elaborate, often tedious argumentation gets in the way. But the ambitious builder was determined to work with nothing less than materials taken from all of legal science's vast store: the Roman Law, the customs, the ordinances, on the one hand, and philosophical natural law of the Ancients, medievals, Humanists, and secular natural law of the eighteenth century enlightenment on the other. The work of significant philosopher, accomplished jurisconsult, and powerful legislator thus formed a mighty bridge, the only important such structure among the many touched on in this study. We cannot fault the powerful ideal of a citizen who, by nature, served his own interest best by obeying a high moral code in which public service was the noblest duty. Regrettably, neither Louis XVI nor Marie Antoinette would be forced to put the stifling court flummery aside and actually read his reasonable propositions for an enlightened chief of state; law professors of his time could only view him in awe at a distance. Only after many heads had rolled would Napoleon's codifiers be eager to reconstruct the social compact by making acquaintance with Henri-François Daguesseau at the closest proximity. As for today's ordering of the legal pantheon, many are certain that, although still denied the apostolicity he may inwardly have sought, this magistrate, reformer, and legal philosopher was the greatest of France's lawyers.

Pothier

Introduction
Pothier and Daguesseau

The hard act to follow must have looked down from Heaven with pride as an admiring follower now moved into prominence. A more social personality standing on the very broad shoulders of the legendary mentor for self-love definitely meant the stage was set for the dreams of Fresnes to become reality. Daguesseau had acted in high public affairs and in the large political issues of his time, yet his remained the unflamboyant persona of the quiet country gentleman who managed also to be an intellectual. Robert Joseph Pothier in contrast tipped the scales the other way. A judge and *pro bono* counselor of truly immense erudition, he lived in close proximity to the affairs of people in ordinary life without ever playing a significant role in politics. Both Pothier and Daguesseau came from long legal traditions in deeply religious families sympathetic to Jansenism. Both had a very considerable effect on the restatement of the law in their time yet neither produced a new legal philosophy to live on in their name. Although both were fully persuaded adherents of natural law, Daguesseau wrote a long, scholarly treatise as if compelled to sustain the very existence of the concept; Pothier, on the other hand, merely accepted natural law while crafting decisions that put it neatly in its place in relation to positive private law. If we compare Pothier's life to Daguesseau's role model Domat, it is their common familiar legal tradition leading to judgeship which links them most. Pothier was also a professor of French law, and while Domat took natural law to construct almost a new metaphysics for private law, Pothier used it and Domat's work as part of a very practical legal summary based on contracts. Born in the last year of the seventeenth century, after his death in 1772, it would be Pothier's intellectual shift which made possible the rapid nineteenth century acceptance of Bonaparte's codification, realizing at last the ambition for unicity which had been part of French royal central power and jurisprudence since the sixteenth century.

The Pothier legal summary, the modern high-water mark of private law achievement in an *ancien régime*, ironically had appeared only a short time before eight centuries of continuous Capetian existence collapsed into 1789. But Themis had been kind to her French progeny, and the progress of legal scholarship had not been interrupted even by the growing corruption under Louis XV. In fact, that decay can be seen as only a sideshow outside the big tent where vied for attention the chaotic French political circus and those trying to set up fair rules of play. When the crown, long the erratic ringleader, became through incredible financial folly, the last obstacle to reformed centralization, its brutal demise left the way wide open for the legal *savants* to achieve homogeneity both in public and private law. If asked, they probably would have said the shoulders they stood on were Pothier's. Self-love often means short memory.

Education and Life of Pothier

Both Pothier's father and grandfather were well-respected, pious judges in the *Présidial* at Orléans. An uncle was Dean of the Cathedral. Such a family possessed the material means to give a scion the education and the leisure for developing intellectual interests. Although the influence of Pothier's father was short-lived—he died in 1707 when his son was eight—Pothier was at that age already a beginning student in the Jesuit college at Orléans, where he was to achieve distinction for his proficiency in Latin and ancient letters as well as in Italian and geometry. Unconcerned for ordinary pleasures and marked by a quiet, contemplative personality, he found diversion with Horace and Juvenal. He must have been present when his Jesuit teachers burned books from Port Royal, but if that affected his leanings toward the *solitaires*, it was only temporarily.

In 1715 at sixteen he again obeyed the paternal tradition by enrolling at the University of Orléans whose law school then numbered about seventy-five students. Quickly he attracted the attention of his teachers: of the excellence and hard work a Goullu-Duplessis noted in the 1717 record, "'*Summa cum assiduitate Diligentia...*'" (Frémont, *Recherches historiques et biographiques sur Pothier, publiées à l'occasion de l'érection de sa statue,* 23). This was the year Pothier began by passing the examination for Bachelor and in August finishing the required public thesis. In April of the following year the young star was examined for the *licence* on a topic in Roman civil procedure and on canon authors as well; by August he was ready to defend both the required public thesis for a degree in those two specialties and another thesis in French law.

The graduate's competence owed little to the faculty who had taught him. His later student and eulogist LeTrosne, says that the professors at Orléans, which had declined from its glory days in the fifteenth and sixteenth centuries, seemed, like the Roman priests of old, more interested that their monopoly be protected by concealing the law rather than by revealing it to their students. They ponderously dictated lessons in the traditional subtle contradictions of the *Digest* with almost complete indifference to the progress of their young audience. Fortunately this did not turn off Pothier who on his own, following a self-taught route that would have made his maecenas Daguesseau proud. From a serious enough study of Justinian's

Institutes, aided by the commentary of Vinnius, he emerged with more than a commendable Roman grounding.

Instructional failings may, nonetheless, still have had some effect, for the graduate was left uncertain about a career in the law. Bereft of any paternal advice, his guides were intellectual—Augustine and Pascal, the Jansenistic fervor for high morality, idealism, and ascetic habits, and Domat's determination that law must be undertaken within clear, organized patterns. So strong were these influences that Robert Joseph actually opted for becoming a monk in the congregation of the Canons Regular. As he learned his prayers, the cause of French private law hung in the balance next to his crucifix. It was time for the dramatic occurrence of yet one more strong and prescient woman who, acting vigorously behind the scenes, now played her role in changing law's course. This time it was Mme Pothier, a determined mother reminding her son of the illustrious legal traditions of the family while adding a more practical argument: she was going to need help in her old age. She prevailed, and for over fifty years Pothier expressed his Christian virtues through equity in well-paid civil jurisprudence, rather than as morality in cloistered poverty. In this, both God and man, if not the pope, were winners. To be accurate, it was never to be a totally either-or choice, for throughout decades of his legal career Pothier did devote time to the study of theology in order to clarify and establish his faith. He would deny the pope all control over French temporal affairs, thereby avoiding fractious public commitment in the lengthy controversy over the bull *Unigenitus*. Then with an exceptionally ecumenical outlook, he would remain always a loyal supporter of the Gallican Roman Church, while at the same time citing Protestant along with the Catholic fathers. He always avoided public controversy about religion, and his tolerant, diplomatic views would later allow him to promulgate without pain judgments of the *Paris Parlement*.

Deciding to aim his main energy at the theory and history of private law, Pothier began his career with some time spent in the chambers of a Monsieur Perche, a distinguished Orléans *avocat*. It was in May 1712, when, only a little over twenty-one, the neophyte *avocat au parlement* was appointed as one of the nine judges on the *Présidial* at the small salary of fifty livres a year. Venality with all its faults propitiously had brought the best Pothier to the bench. Via his father and grandfather who long before purchased the position, Robert Joseph appears to have been able to claim the office as of right.

What he found there was that a *présidial*, set below the *parlement*, gave judges neither noble status nor adequate salaries. The consequence, not surprisingly, was a bench of rather grumpy jurists at a very low state of morale. It became Pothier's lifelong mission, pursued for much of his early career with his link to Daguesseau, Professor Prévôt De la Janès, to lift his colleagues into learning, ability, and the remuneration for it. Although amazingly still under twenty-five, it was Pothier frequently given the job of preparing the judicial reports; in full self-confidence—or was it *amour propre*—he also graciously made available to his fellow magistrates the numerous manuscript treatises he was constantly composing, as topic by topic he pursued on his own expanded research into the law. At hearings Pothier sat silently, saving his views for conference in chambers. He rapidly became highly accomplished in the subtleties of legal procedure, showing himself equally informed in criminal and civil regulation. Soon after taking his seat he evinced interest in the younger lawyers and students and organized with Prévôt de la Janès a weekly conference on Wednesday afternoons to talk about legal questions. The group met in the Janès home until the professor's death, then moved on to be hosted in Pothier's quarters. Under such care and feeding the reputation of the Orléans *Présidial* began to rise dramatically.

Pothier—a kind of Mr. Chips, benevolent and brilliant—commands a biographical portrait which lends itself less to the sharp French acerbity of a Voltaire, Balzac, or Daumier than the more sympathetic Anglo bemusement possible in a Dickens, Austen, or Trollope. Tall and rather ungainly, in walking he leaned to the left and displayed a singular gait. Once seated he seemed terribly embarrassed by his long legs; his well-known personal tic was to cross them and then hook the crossing foot behind the other leg as if to conceal it a little. He lacked manual dexterity and even had difficulty cutting his meat at table; going down on his knobby knees to revive the fire he could often be found there by guests—the frustrated scholar who invariably failed to light the logs properly. So awkward was Pothier at official receptions that he always begged a friend to accompany him and stand close by in case of a mishap or social gaffe.

Pothier's Orléans house, where his entire life he lived as a tenant in the shadow of the Cathedral, was part of a monastery in what is now the Rue Pothier. Every day at five he would arise and walk next door to hear matins. Although his voice was poor, the frustrated monk delighted in the sung psalms and was often deeply moved by the chanting. Returning to his dwelling he breakfasted rapidly at six and then worked in his home office until it was time to go to court or until dinner at twelve. Then he worked again until supper at seven, except after joining the law faculty when he would break for a couple of hours and head out to his daily seminar lesson at one thirty. He never did business after supper or late at night and went to bed promptly at nine; this meant giving up coffee when to his annoyance he realized it meant sleep would not come with the clockwork immediacy he required. Such was the rigid lifelong routine seven days a week, broken only for the conference with young lawyers and students on Wednesdays at five, and going out for visits on Thursday afternoon, Sunday after vespers, and holidays. Pothier had no interest in games or other diversions; but until the 1729 death of his uncle, Pothier did accept the obligation to play at cards with old Canon Pichar every evening. It was said he occasionally would contrive to lose in order to return home earlier. Nevertheless, the avuncular time may to some extent have been well spent; Dunoyer (Dunoyer, *Blackstone et Pothier,* 49) thought that it was Pichar who made pertinent suggestions and advisements which reinforced Pothier's preoccupation with the relation between law and morality. Although a judge, the ethics of his time did not prevent Pothier from giving his own advice; for those who desired such counsel, he would offer occasional public audience between five and nine, helping, it is said, to avoid his clients many an expensive lawsuit. His usual dual role of reporter and judge on cases in his court meant he could share helpful comment with an interested party. Once, however, having assured a young widow that she would win her case, he then neglected a piece of evidence. She lost. Mortified, he indemnified her out of his own pocket, and, according to the record, never again made a judicial error.

As might be imagined, Pothier had no wish to spend time on his clothes or on other personal necessities; nor did the management of his house or building up his inherited investments in real estate hold the slightest fascination for him. He was content to leave at his death no more than he had inherited, except that he did convert a considerable part of his estate into forty loans made in a charitable spirit. He seems to have liked intelligent women and was pleased to include them in his visits or be consulted by them on legal problems. Yet he professed not to be the marrying kind, telling matchmaking friends that he lacked courage for the role. Pothier's real reasons for celibacy were probably contented dependence on his compliant mother and his equally devoted servants.

At Mme Pothier's death in 1728, personal necessities, the house, and finances—but still not his heart—were all placed in the hands of a young housekeeper, Thérèse Javoi. Soon in complete charge of his domestic affairs, Thérèse would preside over them and Pothier for more than forty years, assisted by the faithful manservant César who walked behind on foot when Pothier rode out on his horse to make the Sunday visits. If her master needed a new coat, it was Mlle Javoi who bought it and saw to it that it was worn; friends usually complimented her, not him, on his appearance. For many other mundane matters, such as getting him to sit for his portrait, prudent people found it desirable to approach Thérèse first. She was a veritable bulldog, with control of keys to the Pothier strong box, the better to retard his profligacy in charity. In self-defense, when a tenant occasionally paid the rent directly to Pothier he would quickly secrete the money into a book to avoid her locking it up. His desk was such an appalling confusion the paper trail often could not be understandable even to him; so many books lay strewn on the floor he was forced into a crouch to read them. Once a year, Thérèse, with the help of a young lawyer, reordered his extensive library. It consisted of 1,682 books at his death and included law holdings for his day regarded as "complete." Of all the texts, his copy of the *Corpus Juris of Justinian and the Commentaries of Bartolus* were the most particularly worn.

The regularity and simplicity of weekly routine, aided by almost uninterrupted good health over a long life of enormous dedication and assiduity, enabled Pothier to complete what, by any standards, was an amazing output. He has been called one of the fastest and most methodical workers who ever lived. We shall find him journeying to Paris a few times to talk to Daguesseau about his edition of the *Pandects*, and he did leave Orléans for a trip in 1748 to Rouen and Le Havre to see the ocean. On the way, accompanied by a law student, he talked of nothing but the *Digest*, and that in Latin; his exhausted fellow passengers in the coach concluded he must have been some garrulous traveling Irishman. During the judicial and academic vacations in summer he did vary his regimen, going to Luz in the northern Italian duchy of Monferrat where in 1730 he had purchased a house called La Bigaudière. Here the day's routine broke for an hour's walk after dinner and an hour of conversation after supper, but otherwise Pothier's pursuits continued—legal study and writing in an uninterrupted solitude that he himself admitted was bizarre and comical to behold. Most of his treatises were written at Bigaudière where he must have had notes both voluminous and accurate, given that he could hardly have moved his great library back and forth.

Although inelegant in manners and diffident in address, he was affable, serene, open, and even-tempered. The Pothier sense of justice was acute, both theoretically and in application to his own life. Once, he and Thérèse hired a Savoyard from a labor pool to help in the house. When a silver spoon disappeared, Pothier and Thérèse concluded that the man had taken it and dismissed him without giving a reason. A few months later the spoon was found in the house. Pothier went to the place where at the start of the day the laborers assembled and made there to the man a public apology for this offense of accusation which no one (except perhaps an inchoate Victor Hugo) knew he had even committed. It was events like this that led to his friends talking about him as a "lay Benedictine." Pothier said he felt himself lucky both at Bigaudière and Orléans to have "many" such good friends—a number biographer Dunoyer counts at a fairly stringent ten.

Such, then, was the man who sat on the bench of the Orléans *Présidial* from 1720 until his death in 1772. Not until September 1754 when he was fifty-five did his turn come to be one of the judges designated actually to preside at trials. The records show forty Pothier judgments from 1754–1772 which bore his signature as President. From early in 1720 he had experienced a growing sense of anger with the errors and irrelevancies of counsel far less learned than himself. Admittedly his colleagues, having been told by him that he could not bear to be involved in the "putting of the question" (torture) to an accused in a criminal case, had taken pains to spare him this burden. Authority can erode in some degree even the strongest character. And as an example of this truism Pothier's new and higher duties now transformed placidity into impatience. The gentle, charitable scholar, obviously more than able to grasp quickly and ahead of others the crucial issues, was changed by his talents into a visibly irritable councilor. He henceforth abandoned the equanimious mask of a judge and with it the sage advice of Lamoignon who had said: "'Give them the liberty of saying the necessary things and the consolation of saying the unnecessary. Let us not add to the unhappiness of suits that of being badly received by their judges; we exist to examine their rights and not to test their patience'" (Frémont 61). Fellow lawyers chafed as their President succumbed to that temptation which confronts every judge: to try to push counsel into processing, faster than counsel might wish to do it, the business before the court. The *avocat* for the defense having finished by stating his conclusions, Pothier would turn to the plaintiff's *avocat* and snap: "'This is what they oppose to you, and this is the *only* point to which it is necessary to reply.'" Or he might testily chastise a former pupil: "'That is *not* what I taught you'" (Frémont, 61). Friends, concerned, spoke to him

Robert Joseph Pothier
*Courtesy of Historical & Special Collections,
Harvard Law School Library*

about his change of demeanor. He took their counsel calmly and promised to change, yet it seems he never did.

Pothier also rendered other public services. In 1746 he was elected for a term of three years as *échevin* (alderman) of Orléans. *Échevins* were anathema to the monarchy, but municipalities had long ago won charters that had to be respected in spite of their according certain powers of self-government. The view that Pothier with his lack of practical knowledge of affairs was miscast in the role is incorrect. One cannot sit regularly for many years in a court like the *Présidial* without seeing life as it is, and Pothier's experience of reality must have been useful to the Mayor and the other *échevins*. Pothier also inherited from his father, who had bought it in 1703, a position as *Archer-huissier de robe courte en la lieutenance-criminelle du duché d'Orléans*—a splendid title which translated into the duty of executing criminal sentences at sixty pounds a year, ten more than one earned as judge. But this job being inconsistent with his magistracy, Pothier delegated it to a Louis Asard at twenty pounds and pocketed the rest. In 1747 Pothier began service as one of five commissioners of the local Duke's land council, *Chambre du terrier ou domaine*, a kind of court which decided on the ownership of feudal rights and their tax consequences. The Duke's agents were dissatisfied because Pothier voted for the taxpayer in every doubtful case; but the Duke did not remove him. These, however, were only diversions; Pothier's central effort remained always the written restatement of the law. Such reworking and reframing was soon to have the enormous ripple effect its author could not have imagined; it would begin quietly enough with Pothier himself, but spread ineluctably to his colleagues in the Présidial, back to him again as a Professor of French law, and finally, in eddying, encompassing circles reach the whole French judiciary, professoriat, and bar, before beginning its even farther journey out to lawyers of the Western hemisphere.

The Royal Professor

Although Pothier was a faithful and successful judge and continued to serve the bench with the monarch's permission after his appointment as Royal Professor, it seems that his fondest ambition was for an erudite career teaching Roman law. As Merriman puts it (Merriman, *The Agony of the Republic, The Repression of the Left in Revolutionary France 1848–1851,* 38), the great names in continental civil law have never been judges, but rather legislators like Justinian and Napoleon, and scholars like Gaius, Irnerius, Bartolus, Domat, and Savigny. The French judge, far from being a "culture hero or father figure" as in Anglo-American law, is simply the civil servant who performs important but usually non-creative functions. The judge was often more of a public figure in the absolutist, paternalistic *Ancien Régime* than later, but Merriman's view still has merit.

When vacancies in Roman law did arise on the Orléans faculty after 1720, appointments were made only after public competition—a procedure to which Pothier would not submit. The decision was possibly caused by prudence more than pride. Particularly, as over time his reputation soared, the insecure Pothier may well not have wanted to expose himself to the humiliation of a public lapse of memory. Remaining a Royal Professor of French law meant he could enjoy comfortable royal appointment without the competition.

The routine finally changed when the death of Royal professor Prévôt de la Janès opened an attractive chair .Pothier certainly felt the attraction of the position, as usual but would not solicit it. Guyot, an adjunct Professor, also wanted it; and so well had Pothier concealed his own ambition, that Guyot actually asked Pothier himself to urge the Guyot appointment in a letter to Chancellor Daguesseau. Pothier liked Guyot, but his nineteenth century biographer, Frémont, seems naïve in thinking that Pothier was so modest that he could not have suspected that the Chancellor was thinking of Pothier's name to fill the post. Pothier wrote to Guyot that were it even in his own behalf for the smallest of favors he would never dare to petition the Chancellor by letter. Such an inappropriate plea, he concluded, could only be appropriate when made in person, and he diffidently claimed *he* did not know Daguesseau well enough for that. A less romantic and attractive view is that Pothier wanted the post very much and knew that even if such a letter for Guyot did not convince Daguesseau that he, Pothier, was uninterested in the job, it would probably be seen through as insincere and professionally do him no good with the lofty Chancellor. In the outcome, however, we know Daguesseau did remember

Pothier and was pleased to favor his candidacy when speaking to the King in spite of three other names having been submitted by the *Paris Parlement*. The necessary florid documents were prepared; Pothier's loyal Catholicism was duly noted; and on 20 January 1750, Louis XV made him professor in "'our university of Orléans'" (Frémont, 125).

The next month brought Pothier his colorful installation. The Rector and two regent doctors wore red robes with red hoods while the six adjuncts had black robes with red hoods. The Chancellor, one regent, and Guyot—not surprisingly—were absent. Pothier, brilliant in the red regalia, was admitted to the library room where he took the required oath to live and die a Catholic, after which the Rector led him to the lecture hall where he pronounced the official welcoming discourse and Pothier responded. The students were then notified, and Pothier was put in possession of two chairs, one for lectures and another for meetings of the Faculty. Thence, it was back to the library for final installation and signature of documents attesting the proceedings. The new professor's joy is said to have been marred only by Guyot's frustration; but since Pothier wanted his academic chairs only for the opportunity to teach, he graciously offered Guyot half the emoluments. There ensued *Alphonse and Gaston* exchanges which ended with Guyot's refusal. Some years later, Guyot in competition won the Roman chair which Pothier had so hoped for, but posterity remains more grateful that it was his competitor who had ruled in the French law domain.

From the beginning, Pothier knew much success as an Orléans academic. He had always held that only teaching could arouse interest in law and only lectures would lift the level of the university and the bar. But the cost of preparing such lectures meant, he believed, having absolutely no time left for administration. He not only would decline to attend meetings of the Regents, but when nominated in 1759 as Rector, he firmly refused the post. His heart and purse were always collegial: when the University was in financial difficulty in 1770 he lent it 600 pounds.

We are by now well acquainted with the pedagogical problems of Royal professors; their vast field made it impossible to find enough texts amidst the few suitable published materials. It meant their French law courses took uneven shapes, idiosyncratically broad and shallow, or narrow but deep. Pothier decided to innovate in his third-year course. He abandoned the book-by-book approach for just one which drew on multiple sources. Using the manuscript treatises he had been writing since 1720, he had of each an original and a facsimile borrowed by the students for copying at home. Nearly all the *avocats* of the *Ancien Régime* active in practice wrote treatises for their own use. But the genre was especially common for professors whose necessity of dictating legal philosophy to a class required they write treatises for that purpose at least. Few academics would have elected to read from a printed book, and borrowing from a colleague, even if any would lend, would not generally be satisfactory since nearly all emphasized the customary law of their own province. For example, Jan du Rabot, Royal Professor at Bourges from 1703 to 1742, left sixteen surviving treatises of various lengths which add up to 1,650 closely written manuscript pages. Of these, the first 167 pages in a surviving bound volume—the course taught by Du Rabot in the classroom at Bourges—are a quick survey of customary law entitled *Institutions au Droit François* and arranged roughly in the Gaian order of "Persons, Things, and Actions" including a brief part on Obligations. Bound next are detailed treatises on topics in the "Institution," not including Obligations, a section which Chénon thinks (Chénon, *Les professeurs de droit français de l'université de Bourges et les manuscrits de leurs cours,* 599) the *avocat* copyist who worked after the death of du Rabot could not find. These sixteen treatises may have been used by Du Rabot in the private consultations or the tutoring that he, and others, offered to increase income.

These teaching manuscripts and similar but less impressive writings do not have the breadth and uniform organization that Pothier brought to his class treatises. Densely pertinent study notebooks, the treatises encompassed in convenient form all that the writer, and consequently his students, needed on each subject. They reflected the mind of a universalist who considered all the sources, not just primarily customary law and the Royal Ordinances. Through Pothier's trademark innovation—knitting broad subject matter together by putting each treatise into systematic form—they never failed to ground new concepts within a clear, unified historic frame. Because he completed the basic treatise writing in the years 1720–1750, before he took his Royal Chair, they were more detailed and reflect a content with far greater nuance on doubtful points than most instructional materials.

Delivery of these carefully crafted lectures was the Pothier hallmark, but he devoted much of every class period to questioning students. There remains no syllabus which would show how much he covered in a year, and not even a student's notebook has survived. We do, however, have a fairly good idea of classroom protocol thanks to the 1682 directive issued by Louis XIV. A professor of French law was required to follow the same schedule as the Roman law professor, with each French law class being an hour and a half, held in the third year during the afternoon. The year at Douai began on 5 October and ended 22 July, but at Bordeaux it began on 27 November, and at Paris and probably at Orléans, on 11 November. The settled custom was to dictate for half an hour, to explain what had been dictated for another half-hour, and then to question the students for the rest of the period. Pothier may have reduced the dictation time by the facsimile lending approach. If Pothier's many treatises had first been written only in aid of his teaching, we might well infer that he changed the subject matter of the course year by year; but since they were probably begun as aids on the bench, such a conclusion is not warranted.

The Pothier manner with students could be described as easy, courteous, friendly, and encouraging; the glowing adjectives, however, would tend to stop at his bottom line: be insistent and never yield. He was always the teacher, often leaving his students with problems to solve in study outside of class. But after-hours sessions, often in the Pothier home, would be unforgettable. Loving the young lawyers-to-be like the children he would never have, the professorial host managed to be both mentor and friend, inviting them to dine at his table with smiling promises of old vintage wines and equally good legal questions. Declining to confine himself to the formal written examinations that had long been the only method of testing the competence of students, he revived the practice of public exhibitions in which the students not only responded to his probing, but also challenged each other with queries, on the quality of which they were also judged. These debating occasions aroused immense interest among the doctors of law and the residents of Orléans, and rare was the city father or province dignitary who did not put aside bureaucracy to attend one or all. Development of such public disputation had been Pothier's innovation almost at the start, and by July 1751 he had commenced an annual public award ceremony for gold and silver medals paid at his own expense. He divided his professorial salary between the cost of these medals and the relief of the poor. Once again the University of Orléans found itself celebrated for legal study, as drawing more and more able students, its excellent graduates trained by Pothier began to supply the bar with a truly élite infusion. At the same time the master continued his diligent daily research and impressive written restatements of French private law.

Pothier's Publications

In providing personal statements of legal philosophy Grotius, Pufendorf, Domat, and Daguesseau all obliged us copiously. Pothier left little. It would seem every book offered him a glorious opportunity to expostulate on thoughts in a preface of explanatory character but, maddeningly, never did the otherwise prolific author take advantage of the chance. Even though his edition of the Justinian *Pandects* begins by introducing the history of Roman law, Pothier had requested that his young friend De Guyenne, an advocate in Paris, write it. (The honor, said De Guyenne, with a show of forced modesty, was no less than a task nobly imposed on him by Providence.) In another case Pothier picked De la Janès to do a historical discourse for the 1740 edition of Pothier's custom of Orléans. Nevertheless, the Pothier works, while granting no pride of place for personally introducing the reader to the broad ideas of history, philosophy, or politics remain, for that lack, good faith attempts to demonstrate intricate knowledge. Admittedly gaps occur along the dark paths to Pyrrho, Montaigne, and Hobbes, but proudly displayed in the Pothier library, was the six volume testimony to influence from Daguesseau's published works of 1759. Left at Pothier's death was an epitome on the other model, Grotius. Posthumous, unfinished manuscripts dealt with the rest of land law, successions, gifts, civil and criminal procedure, and other legal matters.

There cannot be any doubt of Pothier's understanding and acceptance of the idea of natural law. His greatest work alone, the treatise of 1761 on Obligations, shows such sympathy on every page. Part of his hesitation toward analytical exposition may have come from an idea that philosophy calls for elevated rhetoric and that his own plain language was not appropriate for it. Or, as he sat at the desk, crossing and recrossing his legs, he may actually have had twinges of intellectual doubt and sensed that basically his mind just was not up to the challenge. In fact and in results, however, Pothier succeeded in a way that erased any skepticism about his attempt to provide right law the right way. What deeper exegetic structure his manuscripts in French law could have revealed around 1760 before he began putting them in shape for a wider audience we cannot say; but when then he did prepare them for publication, his vision was down-to-earth and clear. Accepting Domat's plan and beginning with contracts as law's elegant foundation, he would aid the whole French bench and bar. Influenced by the *Institutes of Justinian*, Pothier brought the topic of contractuality under four clear chapters: I. Kinds of Customary Laws, II. Persons, III. Things, IV. Actions. It was in Chapter IV, delimited to "Personal Actions," where reference to the law of Obligations gave rise to them, and here Pothier provided a definition of the contract concept itself, of bilateral and unilateral forms, quasi-contracts, delicts and quasi-delicts, and engagements arising from natural equity.

It is today impossible to reconstruct the allocation of Pothier's time, as month by month and year by year he gathered together each separate topic of law which extended out from the contractual keystone. We know that for a long time he carried forward several broad subjects simultaneously, including studies in theology which occupied him off and on from about 1718 to 1748. (On such research he left no writing, although at his death was found his synopsis of the juridical institutes of the popes.) During that period he also worked on the *Pandects* (1727–1752), on manuscript treatises for private use (1720–1730), and on the Custom of Orléans (1720?–1740), which, in 1760, reappeared in a new edition. From this later date until his death Pothier was engaged in revising his manuscripts on French law for an ambitious schedule of publication that began with the general treatise on Obligations in 1761, continued with the several kinds of Obligations at the rate of about a volume a year through 1771, and ended with an introduction to land law in 1771–1772. His treatises on "Domaine" and "Possession" are historically interesting but were of short-lived contemporary value. As for the new world upheaval of 1789 which gave immortality to his Obligations work, it destroyed the legal system for land of the *Ancien Régime* and paradoxically replaced it with Roman-style ownership.

It should be remembered that when Pothier published his edition of the Customs of Orléans, the city was not part of the "written law" area in the south of France. Pothier had studied Roman law under the faculty of the University but had taken only the third year course of Lenormant on French law and needed more at the *Présidial*. Assisted with the Customs by De la Janès and Jousse, Pothier provided more than just the text of the official redaction from long ago; he and De la Janès added explanatory notes, with de la Janès providing additional historical discussion. When the printer, having sold out, asked for a new edition twenty years later, Pothier enhanced each title by an introductory summary of French law on that subject. The whole work made for extremely useful scholarship on custom, since the scope was not cramped by the practices of Orléans alone.

Obviously eager to break out from the confinement of hometown custom and with ambition's eye fixed on the elusive Roman professorship, Pothier's famous work with the *Digest* expanded upon Roman Law picked up as a student. Now, however, he was ready to confront the difficulty every serious student of that vast compendium encountered: the disparate, awkwardly arranged structure that the hasty Tribonian commission left unresolved. Pothier's method, honed in French law, lay, at least at first, in those self-oriented private treatises. He did not attempt a restatement of Roman Law and probably never had considered doing so. Rather, he moved in a logical direction appropriate to an effort at the essentials, cutting out useless texts, rearranging his *Digest* quotations in a form that he thought would be more intelligible, and like a master solver of puzzles moving items from one title to another. This, however, was only a partial job; since, unlike Domat, by accepting Tribonian's arrangement of fifty books and the structure of titles under each book, Pothier left intact Tribonian's admittedly defective ordering of those books and titles. Thus, Hadrian's resolve to make perpetual the edict of the praetor—the organization of which controlled the books of the *Digest*—did not to that extent suffer in Pothier's hands, even though Pothier always felt that many of the books showed no relation to the preceding one.

After more than ten years of this work, Pothier noted that his amelioration of Obligations had so far produced enough improvement that he began to think that what had started for his own head could help others, too. Around 1735 he dared submit to De la Janès with much reticent diffidence what he had accomplished up to that time. De la Janès, at once impressed, showed the work to Daguesseau in Paris; and the great man—having long wanted something of this sort to facilitate his own studies as well as those of others—became passionately interested.

Daguesseau and his new protégé now began a serious correspondence. The Pothier letters are lost, but some of Daguesseau's did escape anti-royalist vandalism during the Revolution. Daguesseau's second letter of 16 February 1736, the first surviving, shows that he had recently been sent for his reaction Title 3 of Book 46, "Performances and Releases," a part of the law of Obligations. He promised the younger man he would read it, and in September he wrote again saying that he had seen an order, clarity, and precision that would make Pothier's work as useful as it was praiseworthy. He did feel, however, that it could be brought to greater perfection, and he made some critical notes to that end. He also asked Pothier to come and see him—the celebrated meeting already mentioned at the end of the previous chapter.

The provincial from Orléans, with his plain appearance and lack of all pomp, arrived and presented himself at Daguesseau's elegant Paris office, evidently without an appointment. The staff on their own responsibility told the unprepossessing visitor that the Chancellor of France could not possibly see him. Pothier, modest to a fault, accepted their rebuff and went away, but his friends chided his diffidence and insisted he try again. He did, and this time Daguesseau came hurriedly out of his chambers to greet Pothier with a warmth and distinction that astonished those present. The men had their long talk at the end of which Daguesseau gave Pothier a memorandum, suggesting the Vigilius version of the *Digest* could possibly aid him, but that Pothier's version still was better because he had used only the original language.

Thus began a series of exchanges which would continue until 1748 when with Daguesseau's help, Pothier's Justinian *Pandects* volume was finally published. The Chancellor's perceptive comments on Pothier's version of the Justinian work are based on Daguesseau's view of the inadequacy of the last two titles of Book 50 of the *Digest*: "The Meaning of Expressions," and "Various Rules of Early Law." He begins with kindly prefatory regrets that Pothier received no help with all the research and citations, then cuts quickly to the professorial tone of suggestions. Pothier, his reader feels, must begin every title in the *Digest* with a "'section of laws that define the terms'" and a "'section of the general rules of the title.'" He then is requested to collect all these sections under two general titles called "'significant words'" and "'rules of law,'" putting them into in a more "'natural and perfect order'" than the two somewhat comparable titles have at the end of Justinian's Book 50. Always the instructor, Daguesseau feels this change "'would be good for young people'" (Frémont, 82, 85); and having thus framed "'the elements of all civil jurisprudence,'" Pothier should then be able as well to perfect the rest of the text.

Evidently, Pothier complied with these suggestions, for we find him proposing a separate volume for the two revised titles. In 1745 Daguesseau wrote, at more length this time (as well as more testily), complaining critically of Pothier's title on rules as only a "'residue of rules that don't fit elsewhere.'" The Chancellor found the two volume approach to be inconvenient: the titles in question "'should be the first readers see,'" and it is crucial the reader be aware at once of a whole work. He urged that in aid of this effort at general rules there be consultation of several authors, especially Domat, from whom "'one can get great help on general rules of law,'" Then, too, Pothier in his last letter did not, wrote an annoyed Daguesseau, mention the plan for the title on definitions; surely Pothier was not thinking of a mere dictionary but rather was going to "'include explanations of the words as given by the laws themselves which contain or indicate a principle of law or way to interpret the texts'" (Frémont, 93–94). It is clear that the Chancellor's dream—which would have amounted to a new, complete textbook of the fundamentals of Roman Law—unfortunately was well beyond Pothier's original concept of providing merely a more convenient access to what the *Digest* said on a given topic.

At last, after ten years of faithful proofreading by De Guyenne, the job was done, entirely in Latin and dedicated by the grateful Pothier to Daguesseau. The elevated style, Pothier realized, was not really his forte. He knew he had done his best to be complete: seventy-two folio pages of *Prolegomena*, with prospectus, constituting an ambitious introduction to the study of Roman law. Daguesseau seemed pleased, found the money to support it all, and even announced publication and solicited subscriptions in the *Journal des savants* or Scholar's Journal of 1748. Printing of three folio volumes went along smoothly from 1748–1752, but the beneficent patron ill at Fresnes could not live to see the finish. Surely he must have realized, Frémont wrote, that he had played good shepherd for the protégé, bringing him along until the pride of Orléans had done for the ancient laws of another country what sixty jurisconsults chosen by Justinian could not do with the current laws of their own. The famous syndic of Rotterdam, Meerman, was so impressed with Pothier's brilliant achievement that he hailed him as "*Pandectorum restitutor felicissimus,*" the felicitous restorer of the *Pandects*.

Although the work was received with similar enthusiasm by other legal critics outside of France, its reception at home was on the whole rather calm. It would be Pothier's solutions in the law of Obligations, based heavily as they were on his studies of the *Pandects*, which would arouse adulation. Outside the universities the long sway of Roman law was declining in France, and it awaited Germany of the nineteenth century when the *Digest* could inspire expanded study through renewed erudition. For now the only dissent came from Leipzig where an anonymous journalist crudely dismissed Pothier as nothing new. Pothier did not deign to reply to this blunt misstatement, but de Montromier, a professor at Orléans, vigorously defended the author in the *Journal des savants* by saying the book's goal had been totally misunderstood. A Professor Kellinghausen, also a German, did come to see Pothier and admiringly took home thirty copies (Frémont, 98). There was another edition at Lyons in 1782 and a final twenty-four volumes, octavo from Paris with French translation added in 1818–1821. In 1824 Montalin published in French an analysis of Pothier's *Pandects*, listing subjects—for example, "Purchase and Sale"—in alphabetical order, and introducing under each subject its subheads, gleaned from Pothier's arrangement, with numerical citations to the pertinent paragraphs in the Pothier work.

The text, of course, had been destined from the beginning to have a shelf-life limited to the time when Roman Law would continue to be examined as a guide to current legislation and decisions. It had been back in the sixteenth century when Cujas transformed Roman law into historical artifact, which meant that, although *Pandects* according to an eighteenth century Pothier, might have some value, they could not rival the artifact itself: the great *Pandectae* of Justinian. With the advent of the *Civil Code of 1804* it would cease to be *Pandects* but rather Pothier's treatises on Obligations based on his *Pandects*, which had to be consulted in the first instance for assistance in interpretation. The rediscovery of Gaius in 1813, followed by the German historical approach to law, would leave Pothier's *Pandects* on a very dusty shelf.

Thirty years of hard work gave evidence of having taken their toll. Pothier now was running a constant fever which left him so feeble that for a while he gave up hope of ever walking again. In true Enlightenment fashion he devised a mechanism of pulleys which gave auxiliary support to his body through his arms; it led to his recovering enough to remark contentedly that his regular walk to the Palais de Justice and back home again was more than enough for pleasure and exercise. Later readers have found it is actually these "renascent" years, from 1752 when the publication of the *Pandects* was complete, to 1761 when his treatise on Obligations was published, which are particularly useful in the study of Pothier. His time available for research and writing during the terms of the court and the university may have been reduced—first, by beginning in 1745 his service as a President of the Présidial and second by beginning the professorship in 1750—but neither affected the precious vacations when books were reopened and paper filled with thought.

Pothier and the Philosophy of Law

It is an obvious understatement to say that the academic challenge of communicating during a third year course the whole French legal system to students who had studied only Roman and canon law was one which called for some a tight unity of conception. It was Domat who had understood how to tie everything together in his *Lois civiles* by asserting that the basis of private law is the making and enforcement of voluntary engagements. More than that, he had laid it down that the civil laws selected by him were all natural law, those immutable and universal requirements of the rational and social human beings created by God. Domat certainly understood that what natural law permits can be forbidden by positive law, even if not *vice versa*, and relevant Royal Ordinances received citation by him with not a hint of criticism about their jurisdiction. Joining forces with Domat meant Pothier walked with the mannerisms of Port-Royal: simplicity and clarity of thought and style. It also meant he inevitably stood in the presence of Descartes, whose methodical deduction from axioms weighed so heavily on *Les lois civiles.* It must be admitted that if Pothier did study Descartes directly, even to some extent, he never disclosed the fact explicitly in his writings. Reasonable conjecture would equally suggest that Pothier was influenced in philosophy by his patron Daguesseau, whose six volumes we have already seen shelved with pride in the personal library at Orléans.

When one searches the treatises for Pothier's philosophy, the well-known questions spring to mind: Is he a Realist or is he a Nominalist? Is his legal bedrock a combination of natural law and some positive regulation or is it all positive? Does he present law as the evolving preference of certain people at certain times and places under certain conditions, or is it, at least in part, something for all persons at all times? It is enough for our purpose to study the less than dogmatic answers to such questions in the basic book, the treatise on *Obligations*. The third American edition of the English translation by Evans (Philadelphia 1853) is convenient for readers of English, even though there are some omissions and the translation is imperfect. Pothier had been on earth sixty-two years, had behind him decades of study and reflection, and was ready to write the preface and the book that could guarantee him a permanent place in the history of law. But he instead ignored the opportunity and went at once to quotidian material that would have an immediate utility to judge, student, and practitioner.

At once we see that this utility is not at all limited to positive, that is, currently effective human law. The first obligations he considers are "imperfect" obligations—imperfect in the narrow sense that the courts will not enforce them. To Pothier the faithful churchgoer, however, they were far from mere impractical counsels of perfection, and he chose to present them as charity and gratitude—everyday necessities for which we are accountable to God alone. He writes (Pothier, William David Evans, ed., *A Treatise on the Law of Obligations, or Contracts,* 103), "the giving of alms…is a real obligation, and the neglect of it is a high offence." He then distinguishes the subject of his present treatise: "perfect obligations" which "give…a right to demand their performance." Even here Pothier is not concerned only with obligations enforceable in human courts, because "perfect" obligations include also natural obligations as to which the right to demand performance resides in the courts of conscience rather than in the courts of government. His full title is thus *Treatise on Obligations*, both in the Court of Conscience [*for intérieur*] and in the Civil Court [*for extérieur*]. The rules of the court of conscience are supplied by natural law.

The dual natural-positive method would be followed by Pothier in all his treatise work: state the rules for the conscience then the supplementary rules for enforcement by legal process. Although he offers only one general discussion of "natural" obligations, the partition of obligations into "civil and natural" constitutes the book's first major division. Pothier sees how this distinction existed in Roman law but on a basis that rendered the idea no longer applicable for the French. "Natural" obligations in Rome were the ordinary agreements, infinite in number, made in the common affairs of life. They were unenforceable, since they did not carry enough mandated strength for the patricians who preferred that plebeians come to them for legal matters. Pothier sees this special group of "natural obligations" as now enforceable by specific legal process in eighteenth century France. To comply with his theory he updates the definition to all the ordinary agreements which, though made in good faith, are nevertheless not enforceable 1) for lack of a favored "cause"—for example, expenses in a tavern incurred by one who resides there—or 2) for lack of technical legal capacity in one who in fact has sufficient judgment and discretion—for example, the agreement of a married woman—or 3) for simply being barred by the statute of limitations. These natural, unenforceable obligations, subject to exceptions of course, may not be set off against either enforceable obligations or agreements of suretyship guaranteeing they may not be also enforced. Nevertheless, Pothier admits that voluntary payment of them is generally legally effective—indeed, that is their "only effect" (Pothier-Evans, 197).

Unfortunately, these rather narrowly defined obligations which are only "natural," although their effect may be due to natural law, are of little importance in searching for Pothier's philosophy. More to the point is Pothier's frequent recognition of the general existence of a "natural law" as well as the differences of view as to what that natural law rule is. He will consider that a rule which the courts choose to enforce not only comes from the legal domain of positive law but can also participate in "natural law." Recall that Domat specified that all the rules of private law which he recorded in his treatise were selected from Rome because they were both natural and recognized in France. Pothier, however, took a somewhat different approach. He states that it is of the "essence" of obligations that there shall be (1) a "cause" of them, (not to be confused with the "cause of a contract," discussed below), (2) "persons" subject to them, and (3) an "object" of them.

The "causes" of obligations are: contracts, quasi-contracts, delicts (to which remarkably are devoted only two pages in the treatise), and quasi-delicts. Noting that quasi-delicts are imposed by the law, Pothier is led to observe that generally "Natural law is at least the mediate [i.e. indirect] cause of every obligation, for if contracts and injuries produce any obligation, it is because natural law requires every person to perform his promises, and to repair the injuries which he has wrongfully occasioned" (Pothier-Evans, 166). In the case of quasi-contracts, it is natural law which induces the obligation. There are, moreover, some obligations of which either natural or positive law is the immediate and only cause. For example, the duty to support an indigent parent is founded on natural law. The obligation to restore the money incurred by a married woman who borrowed without consent but had benefit from the loan presents us an example founded only upon the principle of natural law which does not allow one person to gain riches at the expense of another—a *Digest* concept. On the other hand, the obligations of a house-owner in Orléans, selling an interest in his wall to a neighbor who wants to make it a common divider, arises solely from the municipal law of Orléans. Pothier has a broad view on all these obligations; as different as they appear on the surface, all are enforceable by legal process.

Several of the Pothier treatises on the different kinds of contracts begin by a definite pan-naturalism, defining their subject as governed entirely by natural law. In effect, these parts of the law were not touched by custom or Royal ordinances and were left to the jurisconsults who still tended to regard Roman law as "written reason." Among these economic treatises are those which, reminiscent of Daguesseau on shares, discuss sales, partnership, joint venture, gratuitous agency, and insurance. It is evident that Pothier envisaged the idea of natural law as allowing jurisconsults latitude in developing the statutes which control commercial transactions.

Basically, however, the bulk of the rules in the Pothier treatises were in fact considered by him to be natural law specifically engineered into the human setting. Here in this dense positive law allocation come the multiple affiliations with Roman, customary, canon, and municipal law, as well as the realm of royal ordinance. Such thorny problems in public law presented by the idea of natural law—notably the question of the invalidity of a positive law contrary to natural law—were to receive no careful discussion in his treatise. Pothier admitted the gap; and one senses he no doubt realized that had he entered this labyrinth, he would have encountered, if not monsters, then at least powerful difficulties.

He had long recognized as a rule of natural law that in the forum of conscience one side always must retain an obligation to obey positive civil laws. At face value this wipes out natural law, unless the civil laws to be obeyed are limited to those executory of but not inconsistent with natural law. However, writing the treatise on sales Pothier did go as far as to state that the higher standard in natural law as to what a seller need not reveal to a buyer does *not* have to be followed by positive law. He knew well the distinction made by some colleagues that what natural law forbids is not to be permitted by positive law, but that what natural law merely permits need not be permitted by positive law. Thus in his discussion of gambling—a subject that always brought the law classicists to their full Pascalian height—Pothier noted that Roman law, for so many the other side of the equation with natural law, forbade gaming for money. His would be the pliant view: natural law does not invalidate the gaming contract, unless it be made invalid by civil statute.

Growing commerce and industry needed a system for raising capital. We have already considered Daguesseau's natural law argument, born of the scam of John Law, against joint stock paper. In his treatise on "Loans for Consumption" Pothier might have encouraged monetary advances by approving the charging of interest; they lay, he admitted, in a zone not forbidden by natural law, a fact which had permitted Calvin to approve charging commercial interest in Protestant states. But in a sixty page learned discussion of the entire history of the matter, Pothier avoided controversy and remained non-political, comfortably controlled by the Royal ordinances against usury. If there is anything such Pothier accommodations and redefinitions show it is that the great rubbery flexibility of judicial decisions—the 'slippery slope' of natural vs. positive, objectivity vs. subjectivity—was rapidly moving into the modern age of relativism.

Pothier and "Cause" in Contract Law

Domat had failed to extricate French law from the uncertain idea of causal necessity in enforcing contracts. Conditions appeared ripe for another try at this question. If we do not have any law review article from Pothier explaining how his mind grappled—if it did—with the challenge of this issue, we do have the outcome of his investigation and conclusions.

Pothier researched a different generic context from the Roman "cause" of contracts: observance of the required formalities and enforceability if the contractors manifested an intention to that effect. Again, Pothier frames obligations as "caused" by contracts, delicts, and the *quasi* form of each. First considering contract, he finds that it is an agreement consisting of reciprocal promises or a unilateral promise to give a thing or to do or not do an act. If two parties make reciprocal promises, or only one party makes a promise to the other to give/deliver a thing or do or not do some other act, there can be no contract if the promisors by their promises do not also "engage" themselves, i.e. intend to give the other a right legally to demand performance. Thus Pothier has excluded promises made with "light language," one of the problems considered by Domat. There can be no contract if there is only an informal promise, or *pollicitation*; "there must be a "concurrence of intention," i.e. the promise must be "accepted." If there were any doubt about it before, Daguesseau's Ordinance of 1731 on donations has definitely "prohibited all gratuitous dispositions of property, except by actual donation in the lifetime of the donor, or by testament" (Pothier-Evans, 106).

Next Pothier distinguishes things that are of the essence and which a particular contract must have: in a contract of sale one requires both a thing sold and a price. Things not of the essence, yet in the nature of a contract, are included unless the parties agree to exclude them; the sale may do without warranty on the article sold. And finally, things not of the essence or nature of a contract but merely accidental may be included only by express agreement (i.e. the buyer will be home when the object arrives). Pothier can now conclude his affirmative definition of a contract by noting five ways to classify it. These are: (1) as unilateral or bilateral; (2) as consensual or real; (3) as having mutual pecuniary interest or only an interest of beneficence or mixed; (4) as principle and accessory; and (5) as obliged to be in a form prescribed by positive law or regulated only by natural law (Pothier-Evans, 109–112).

Contracts which comply with the foregoing may, Pothier recognizes, not be enforceable because they have "defects." Here he categorizes the presence of mistake, duress, fraud, inequality, or wording—all of which gives a party so much liberty he slips away from obligation and falls into contract's abyss: the lack of a "just cause" (Pothier-Evans, 123). Pothier is no Racine or Corneille, and his dark beclouding of injustice does not cause his prose to attain dramatic power. Yet that a contract may be defective because it is unjust does involve some quiet Cartesian analysis. Pothier states several repugnant cases: a mortgagor in foreclosure who demands payment to give up the paperwork; an officer who promises to pay a soldier to fight in another regiment; a promise to pay for commission of a crime; and the case of a promise for which one forces payment of additional monies to do something which one already is obliged to do. An excellent engagement, and therefore the just contract that includes it, must have a "cause"; it is null if, as in the examples above, "cause" has been unjust.

And what is this "cause"? Pothier says that in "contracts of mutual interest" i.e. onerous, constituting a legal burden, the cause of the engagement of a party is the thing given or done, or engaged to be given or done, or the risk incurred by the other party. In contracts of beneficence (gratuitous, involving no return) the intended liberality of the promisor is the "cause" of the engagement made by him. Here Pothier seems to introduce a new thought: the "cause" must be "sufficient." However, he holds firm that an engagement with "no cause" is null. This carrying forward of the doctrine of Domat without adding any personal analysis, means the Pothier statements are essentially the same as all those almost-but-not-quite pronouncements arrived at by legists and canon lawyers in the Middle Ages. The *Civil Code of 1804* which follows Pothier will also add nothing new, the result being that a central idea in the law of contracts had thus been left on an obscure table for enlightenment in Anglo-American and French law discussions.

A brief parenthetic reflection on all this writing about "cause" in contracts suggests that historical clarity may not be so hard to achieve. The American legal philosopher Pound favored going outside of France. He suggested first the European solution led by Holland: follow the approach of Grotius that anything arousing a reasonable expectation of enforcement will do for cause, with the possible added accompaniment of forms such as seals. Pound's second model came from Germany: contract occurs if the promisor's acts (including words) are sufficient to cause agreement in which the person as promisee reasonably expects to receive the promised performance. Professor Corbin of Yale, the leading contracts scholar of the twentieth century, who agreed with Pound, put a little more emphasis on determining what courts do than on achieving a philosophy of what they ought to do. Aware that at all times in legal history some informal promises have been enforced and some have been rejected, the question for Corbin was: What are the facts that have to be present for enforcement? It is not possible to state an abstract rule from which the answer can be deduced for any given set of data, although the French concept—"the engagement must relate to an objective situation recognized and protected by law" (Dunoyer, 122)—gives it a forthright effort. A lifetime, insisted Corbin, would not be enough for the ablest legal scholar to study all the cases and say conclusively whether any given doctrine bore the "weight of authority." His "condensed" student edition of contract law required 176 pages to describe factors—"considerations"—that cause promises to be enforced. Still, the factors that have resulted in enforcement can be studied; Anglo-American lawyers call them "sufficient consideration," French (and Roman) lawyers call them "*causa*," and beyond semantics the question is the same despite differing court results. Such factors are essential to enforcement, for a line has always been drawn, however impossible or difficult it may be to express it as an abstract rule; and it has been drawn by consideration of motives and inducing causes. Thus from modern perspective it seems, on the basis of legal thought, that Pothier, if he did seek for an abstract rule, was doomed to failure; his method was the axiomatic method of Descartes while his search targeted a rule for the enforceability of a multiplicity of contracts.

The Domat case illustrates how "cause" easily can be made even more elastic in captioning an organized list of factors requiring enforcement. The jurists of the Middle Ages recognized that men's wills are free to make any contract upon which they can reach consensus within the limits juridically fixed—"just cause"—and these contracts become the law of the parties. Admittedly, Pothier was a pioneer when large-scale commercial society was just beginning and experience was limited. In his day it was impossible for him to do what a Corbin would. This weakness in chronological positioning may account for the unsettling ambivalence in his work— its lack of a sense of historical change—while at the same time items like the formalities of Roman contracts do succeed in imparting the feel of the immutability of natural law. His challenge was less to deduce a rule from vast experience than to propose a rule to guide that experience as it developed in the future. Here we may concede with Pound that Pothier does disappoint us a little, and that Grotius still has the edge coming 135 years before. However, the question of "cause" is not the forest, it is the trees. The important achievement of the natural law school was to raise the status of contracts in people's legal thinking. "'The material of contracts,' said Domat, in recognition of the forest-tree syndrome, 'is the infinite diversity of ways in which men regulate among themselves the communications and transactions of their industry and work and all their needs'" (Gazzaniga, 173). The unique sophistication of the enforceable accord enables society to go forward with projects and enterprises, confident that others will do their agreed part. It is by understanding how all civil enterprise rests on contract that such enterprise in the end achieves stability. And that realization one must give Pothier, who did his best to engrain it into the social consciousness.

Pothier and His Age

Common contract doctrine meant independent national economies could begin to flourish through equitable rules which were everywhere the same. When the Pothier school of jurists became known for their axiological goal of freedom of expectations and security in reliance upon those expectations, these themes unexpectedly inspired the music for two new social orchestrations. First, there were the busy libertarian philosophers who with the intense bourgeois money-makers initiated relaxation of the grip of royal regulations. Second, the royal regulators themselves, with an attitude of "one king, one church, one law," reached for ever increased power to bring in line recalcitrant brokers. A very plain man in motley dress had ironically thus become the conductor of a contrapuntal score, providing the formal legal variant of the paradoxical, flamboyant musician allegorized in Diderot's *Le neveu de Rameau*. Like the encyclopedist alert to the natural goodness and catalytic possibilities hidden by the tyranny of power, the jurist's achievement was to evoke an undercutting, revolutionary leitmotif—in Pothier's case freedom of contract—that utterly pulverized the high register of absolutism.

Yet, Pothier had no revisionist publications in his library; he had not met Voltaire, and his treatises offer no clues that he was a contemporary of Rousseau, von Vattel, Wolff, or Burlamaqui. Unlike Diderot, the royal law professor never intended that counterpoint of change whose high-pitch would shatter the monarch's champagne glasses; Pothier spoke of the *Encyclopedia* and Diderot's co-authors with repugnance even though Diderot was helping give France a legal compendium (Dunoyer, 75). The natural law which Pothier brought to Paris from Orléans arrived in old-time travel valises; they contained a baggage of ancient truths from Pufendorf, Grotius, and the Spanish second scholastics which had to be accepted in large part just because of the stellar authority of their sources. The Montesquieus of the world were concurrently dropping this intellectual baggage in favor of observation encouraged by continuing scientific achievements. However, it probably never occurred to Pothier to leave for a while the books in his exquisitely complete library and office in order to learn onsite the fast-changing topics of legal interest for buyers and sellers in the big, noisy marketplace of Paris. Nor would he have wished to invite one of them to advise on the contemporary utility of his system of Obligations. He had resided in the former cloister, and in his way this "Benedictine of the law" was always content to use it as such. He did have volumes on mathematics and physics; and though he used more cases and examples (many of them old and traditional) than Domat, his deductive spirit gave first place to general rules. He was keenly aware of what he felt were the *philosophes*' "unenlightened" attacks upon religion. On 11 January 1767, he wrote (Frémont, 33) to a rising young lawyer friend in Paris, "'I can't congratulate you too much on your connection with M. Gordieu, it will be not only good for your studies to have mutual help but also for your morals through the good example you will give one another which will protect you from the pestilential air of Paris where the Devil is constantly occupied in blowing into conversations the poison of unfaithfulness and libertinage. I pray God to protect you as he saved the three young Israelites from the furnace.'" Nevertheless, as Domat's civil law had ironically undermined his royal master, so Pothier's carefully crafted obligations sounded a knell against those aristocrats who willfully, licentiously, had been neglecting theirs. For too long public law had been by and large closed to French jurists by the top-heavy pyramidal monarchy. When it was emphasized that private law came largely from sources outside royal authority and by tradition free from it, these cracks in uniformity, which could have aided the king, let loose instead the forces which would undermine him in the name of natural law.

Post-Mortem

When he wrote his 1767 letter about the Devil cavorting in Paris, Pothier was sixty-eight, still publishing about one treatise a year on the different kinds of contracts. His beloved treatises did come to an end in 1771, but he had the energy to follow them with two volumes on *Domaine* (real estate) and possession. That would be the end of his work. In July 1771 he made his will. He had an accumulated estate of 167,703 *livres*, (about $210,000 U.S. in 1965 based on French prices of 1750), and from it he provided generously first for Thérèse, for her niece, for César, and for his curé. The public library of Orléans was given those of his law books needed in their collection; his manuscripts went to fellow lawyers. After numerous provisions for charity, the residue remained for surviving relatives. He had bought La Bigaudière from a cousin of a Mme Brochet, and, knowing she wanted it for her family, he specified how she might buy it from his estate. Four days later this giant of legal learning decided that he had not worked it out quite right and quickly drafted a codicil to cover the possibility that Mme Brochet might decide not to buy.

Late in February 1772 he suffered recurrence from his frequent fever. Although on the first of March he felt better and was able to get out of bed, he died the very next day, a seventy-three year old with no obvious physical infirmities and in full possession of his mental power. He had not done for France all he wanted to do, but he had done enough to assure that when the Revolution abolished the land law of the *Ancien Régime* in a few swift strokes, successor governments turned to men trained in the de-absolutized school of private law. More importantly, through his students, a new world was, in effect, choosing Robert Joseph Pothier to put the vision honed in a quiet Orléans apartment into the form of a great French *Civil Code*. It is the Pothier name which precedes the final stage in France's overcoming the destruction of Roman law cohesion, a destruction completed in the fifth century which had required a full thirteen centuries to rebuild.

For all his meticulous work habits, in death Pothier had reverted to simplicity. There were no directions left for the burial of his body, and the executor simply chose a small plot in the city cemetery and organized the most modest of funerals. However, LeTrosne pronounced an eulogy of almost 200 printed pages which were then re-read during two plenary sessions at the *Présidial*. A M. Breton gave another laudation in Latin at the University. In 1810 the famous street which had been Rue l'Ecrivinerie, honoring the monks of the Holy Cross who long ago copied religious works in the old cloister, became Rue Pothier in fitting celebration of a prodigious secular writer who created so much more than he copied. Six years later a part of the Cathedral yard was named Place Pothier. Seven years after that his remains were found and reburied in the Cathedral, although in 1846 they were again moved to a chapel built especially for the purpose: the Cathedral clergy no longer wanted any Jansenist in their precincts. Portraits of Cujas and Dumoulin had reached the new gallery of the Court of Cassation; however, that honor had not yet been accorded Pothier. Then in 1859 biographer Frémont, Commissioner of the Imperial Court of Orléans, went beyond mere portraiture, raising nearly 30,000 francs among members of the bar for an unexpected nine feet of grandiose bronzed likeness to stand tall in the Cathedral yard.

Appraisals of Pothier

Frémont wrote that the events in Pothier's life were his works. It was a just appraisal, one proved by the fact Pothier's books—an extraordinary achievement for one man in one lifetime working almost entirely alone—remained long in demand. Complete editions were published in France in 1805–1810, 1813, 1820, 1821–1824, 1823, 1825, 1845, and the final ten volume set in 1861. These editions include the eight volumes of manuscripts left to Guyot by Pothier at his death and edited and published by Guyot in 1776–1778. Six more treatises in manuscript were considered insufficiently finished for publication. From all this output Pothier, who had no ambition for business and urged for low prices the better to sell his books, obtained little pecuniary profit. Writers on Pothier have not listed foreign editions; however, Pothier would enjoy a high reputation in learned legal circles in England and America, who saw in him the pathfinder cutting a confident, unified way through that forest of ordinances and customs. An edition of Pothier's *Obligations* appeared as early as 1802 in New Bern, North Carolina. Learned Hand's copy of Pothier's treatise on "Maritime Contracts," published by Cushing in Boston in 1821, bears a dedication to Justice Joseph Story and an "advertisement" with the following quote by Chancellor Kent: "'Pothier has treated ... contracts with a clearness of perception, a precision of style, and a fullness of illustration, above all praise and beyond all example.'"

This almost, but appropriately not quite, reaches the exaltation of the Frenchman Dupin: "'Pothier's *Obligations* is the most beautiful book from the hand of a man,'" to which Dupin added, as if to bolster his fulsomeness, that over three-fourths of the *Code Napoleon* were soon to emerge in glory from Pothier's work. The general judgment is only a little less ecstatic. Pothier is regarded as a "true sage, a lay saint, modest, disinterested, obliging, charitable" (*Continental Legal History*, 269), indefatigable in the work to which he devoted his life. He may have shown less ingenuity and originality than Cujas or Dumoulin, but he had no equal in making law readily available to those who wanted to know it, presenting it in a style "simple, methodical, judicious" (Olivier-Martin, 426), as well as "manly, neat, classical, and well adapted to didactic discourse" (Pothier, and Caleb Cushing, ed., *A Treatise on Maritime Contracts of Letting to Hire*"). His was an unpolished clearness, its essence bearing no infusion of personality. Above all, he was careful and thorough, an expert amalgamator of the learning of the ages. His impartiality, not impaired by a fiery zeal for reform, by theological conviction, or by a patriotic resolve to exalt his nation's laws, made him a seeker after middle solutions to contested issues. As late as 1847 a French jurist exclaimed: "'Who today can consider himself equal to Pothier?'" Typographers, apparently already in agreement, were in the habit of merely printing: "By the author of the treatise on Obligations" (Frémont, 2, 150, 161, 166). They knew there was no need to give a name.

Charles Louis de Secondat Montesquieu
Courtesy of National Gallery of Art, Washington

PART 17

Montesquieu
*The Sociological Case for Governance
by Secular Natural Law*

Montesquieu

Introduction

When in 1689 Domat went under anonymous cover to publish his *Lois civiles*, another lawyer-to-be was being born for whom anonymity was also to be a professional accessory. He, too, would write at length about the spirit of laws, but make no substantial contribution in his lifetime to clarifying or developing the practical literature that dealt with French private law. He was neither recommended by Daguesseau nor read by Pothier. Yet, his would be the name to quote when for most academics Domat, Daguesseau, and Pothier had a mere bookshelf life. To read the American Constitution was to find him everywhere. Philosopher-statesman Edmund Burke praised him as "'the greatest genius which has enlightened this age,'" and Horace Walpole, who considered himself equal to any literary titan, felt that he produced "'the best book that ever was written.'" Taine, who knew a thing or two about being a French philosopher, said of him this was "'the best instructed, the most sagacious, and the best balanced of all the spirits of the time'" (Durant, *The Age of Voltaire*, 359). And on a state visit to France in 1996 South Africa's heroic statesman, Nelson Mandela, commenting to his fellow president, Jacques Chirac, chose to summon up this lawyer's name as part of an iconic national triumvirate: "I will return home with the memory of the way I was received in the country of Rousseau, Voltaire, and Montesquieu" (*Paris-Match* 25 July 1996: 42).

Charles-Louis de Secondat, Baron of La Brède and Montesquieu started legal studies at sixteen; three years later he had the degree and began practice. But he did far more than work on the cases of a wealthy clientele. He is the first in the profession since Irnerius—who by his lectures on the *Digest of Justinian* began the revival of legal learning in Europe—to introduce to the learned world a major new intellectual specialization: the discipline we now call sociology. The life of this remarkable luminary in the history of law spanned nearly sixty-five years shared by stellar intellectual company. Although Grotius had died in 1645, Pufendorf lived until Charles-Louis was five, and Domat until he was seven. Daguesseau, twenty-one years older, died at about the same time as Charles-Louis, while Pothier, ten years younger, lived on beyond him until 1772. Voltaire was born in 1694, Diderot in 1713, Condorcet in 1743, d'Alembert in 1717, Rousseau in 1712, and Robespierre in 1758. Descartes had died by 1650, but Newton, born in 1642, lived until 1727. Perhaps the date most important for Montesquieu as a writer on public law was the 1715 day when the heavily conservative Louis XIV died. Charles-Louis was a twenty-six-year old bursting with fresh ideals and ideas and ready to take on a new world order.

Montesquieu appears in these pages and at this place, first of all, because of the enormous assistance and depth brought to legal work by his sociological efforts in transferring to human affairs the same mathematical and scientifically investigative methods which had brought such success when applied to the physical world. Secondly, he fascinates because he was not in the reformist circle of Daguesseau and Pothier but would end helping their message when as a lawyer he actually lost his biggest case: patriotic pleading to convince the French they should change over to a limited monarchy. In a complex dance of death and life it was this position which ironically helped push France into the national constructs of which Montesquieu was so critical. Far more than he ever intended, Montesquieu's parliamentary resistance to reforms were to help bring forth the democratic assemblies eagerly proposed by enlightened royal ministers Condorcet and Turgot in the second half of the eighteenth century. Such changes, had they been passed into law, might have avoided bloodshed and given France a marked gain. But instead of an inviting path to liberty, equality and a constitutional monarchy based on considerable democracy, recalcitrance played a role in the coming of 1789's upheaval. Men would lead who were unable themselves to bring to fruition their wish for a unified French law. These same men were, nonetheless, quite able to push extreme policies that in another *contre-danse* produced a reaction in favor of complex legal rules. It was to be lawyer Montesquieu who unwittingly began the motion which, 800 years after Hugues Capet, would end in the elegant, small hand of an emperor signing up France for legalized centralization and unified law. In yet another irony, it would be because of the continued Roman nostalgia within France's literate population, of whom Montesquieu was a leader, that Bonaparte had become mentally conditioned to make a mythic try at regaining ancient grandeur as he imperially penned his name to civil and legal unity.

Early Life

Montesquieu inherited double empowerment: sword and high robe credentials traced back long enough to create a line of noble respectability. The Secondat de Montesquieu family had been founded by Jacob, born in 1576, whose father, Jean, had bought in 1561 the lonely hilltop lordship of Montesquieu, a name of mixed Latin and Frankish origin meaning wild or barren mountain. It was all very correct. The eminent Renaissance scholar, J. C. Scaliger, was a relative, and Jacob's mother had Plantagenet blood. Jacob's eldest son married a member of the nobility and bought himself a law office with her dowry. His third son, Jacques, the father of Charles-Louis, was a soldier who in 1686 married a descendant of St. Louis, an heiress with vast acres, many debts and lawsuits, but also with the business acumen needed to cope with them all. Among the acres was the château of La Brède, southeast of Bordeaux on the main Roman road to Toulouse, and here Charles-Louis was the couple's firstborn. Fiercely democratized by his family like fellow Gascon, Montaigne, the baby baron had been given as godfather a wandering beggar, commandeered to help baptize the child on the very day of his birth, thereby conveniently imparting, it was hoped, a sense of duty to the world's indigent. It was then off to the miller's wife for nursing and three years of sturdy infancy at the flour mill of La Brède, amidst whose peasants Montesquieu picked up a rustic accent he proudly never abandoned (Shackleton, *Montesquieu: A Critical Biography,* 4). When his mother died in 1696 while giving birth to her fifth child, the boy at seven became the wealthy aristocratic scion of de la Brède.

By early childhood Montesquieu had learned to write in the school of his baptismal parish, but when just eleven his ambitious father sent him for five years to the renowned Collège de Juilly, twenty miles outside of Paris. The school was located in the diocese of Meaux where Bossuet was still serving as France's most celebrated Bishop. Montaigne's Collège de Guyenne could have provided education nearer home, but it had markedly declined. Montesquieu at Juilly shows his liberal family had broken with the traditional Jesuit and Jansenist hold on youth destined for high judicial offices. Juilly was controlled by the Oratory rather than the Jesuits, and if Jesuit-trained boys were more learned, the Oratorians were more rounded, offering an education as liberal as one could get in France. The Fathers lived without vows and were modern in outlook, and it is reasonable to believe their eclecticism had a strong influence on the impressionable and industrious Montesquieu.

The stresses at Juilly were, nevertheless, impressive. The young Baron rose at 5:00, said prayers at 5:15, studied alone until 7:30, then breakfasted half an hour and heard mass at 8:00. With the subject changing every half hour, classes were held from 8:30 to 11:00. Dinner followed, during which the students listened to the reading aloud of the lives of the Saints or the scholarly sixteenth century *Annals* of Baronius, successor of De Neri as Superior of the Oratory. Then after an hour of study, classes began again at 1:30 until tea and recreation at 4:00. Supper at 7:00 led into more study and letters home, with prayers and bed at 8:30. The language of instruction was French, but proficiency in speaking Latin was required along with some Greek. Included were geography, history, and mathematics, plus drawing, music, riding, fencing, and dancing. The Oratorian and Cartesian disciple Bernard Lamy's *Entretiens sur les sciences* served to express the Oratorian ideas on education, and the greatest Oratorian, the philosopher Malebranche—another Cartesian and realistically anti-Skeptic—was revered by Montesquieu.

He had definitely emerged as an ambiguous personality. Consigning his old low-class godfather to sentimental nostalgia, he confirmed his faith in the aristocracy from which came most of his fellow students, developing with that social faith a lifelong sense that he belonged to the Catholic Church, however dispassionately he later was to view it. His intellectual objectivity was putting him on track for precursorship of the Enlightenment; while at the same time his theological confirmation prepared a separation from Enlightenment colleagues— Voltaire, Diderot, d'Alembert, Condorcet, and Rousseau—and, instead, union with politicians anti-constitutional and anti-democratic. When in 1705 time came for the sixteen-year-old Charles-Louis to pick a career, he appeared comfortable that his father, honoring his own paternal scion who had been a lawyer and whose wife also came from a *robe* family, not unexpectedly, chose law for his son. The teenager was sent to the University of Bordeaux and attended the traditional three-year course set in place by Louis XIV. Records of these law student days apparently have not survived. It is evident, though, that the decree of 1679 which marked the Sun King's having warmed to the idea of improvement in legal education, had now begun to grow quite cold at Bordeaux. In 1709 the Dean was ninety-eight, and his son, a professor, was usually marked as absentee. Another faculty member had reached eighty, was totally blind, and had deputized his lectures to dictation by a student.

The first Bordeaux Royal Professor of French law, Blaise Fresquet (who taught from 1681–1711 as only the third Royal Professor in France to have been approved by Louis XIV) appointed as his deputy an Irishman who could not speak a word of French (Shackleton, 8). How effective were the other members of this motley faculty the young Baron's biographers evidently do not know; academic publications, if any, were not noticed by De Curzon in his important overview of the Royal teaching cohort. Yet even assuming that the instructional level was fairly poor does not mean it was so poor as to cause our student to rebel; and he appeared, at least, content to have supplemented the lectures with considerable self-study, especially of the law texts put into his hands when he left Juilly. But by 1708 the nineteen-year-old *licencié*, duly admitted to the bar as yet another of France's superb legal fledglings, began already to veer away from ambitions for a lifelong career as a practicing lawyer or judge. Probably this career path had been lost by the lack of inspiration current at the University; however, in one of irony's felicities, had it not been lost the world might have been denied marvelous scholarship on society and the sources of law, as well as a literary masterpiece, *Les lettres persanes*.

Living in Paris from 1709 until 1713 provided the perfect province-to-town scenario which would create the fame of countless of France's nineteenth century novelists. Side-stepping any legal apprenticeship, Montesquieu frequented instead a learned Oratorian cleric, Pierre Nicolas Desmolets, who encouraged the younger man to begin a scrapbook on science and society rather than one on law. It is in this book that one finds records of Montesquieu's attendance at meetings of the Academies of Science and of Inscriptions, where could be heard daring scholarly forays into science, history, and the Church. Through one of the speakers, Fréret, the impressionable Baron met a young Chinese Christian, Hoange, with whom he had detailed conversations which aroused a lifelong interest in the East (Shackleton, 13). Then, unexpectedly, the broadening intellectual horizon was considerably reduced when in November 1713 Montesquieu's father, Jacques de Secondat, passed away. The twenty-four year old Parisian at once returned to the provinces, his name symbolically shorn of any patronymic for the more dramatic and rebelliously correct Montesquieu.

Home was now his birthplace, the elegant Château de la Brède. Shackleton describes an authentic, working castle, built and fortified not long after 1400, with a moat, three drawbridges, and four turrets with conical roofs. Behind walls of immense thickness were cool chambers including an enormous guard room with a tunnel vault which Montesquieu lined with books and made his study. He knew the hereditary duties of lineage and in 1715 marriage was celebrated to the wealthy Jeanne de Lartigue who brought him 100,000 *livres* and her lifelong loyalty to the Huguenot religion. It is said (Montesquieu, Melvin Richter, trans. *The Political Theory of Montesquieu,* 14) the union had less bliss than inspiration from the De Lartigue dowry; but Jeanne did give Montesquieu a son and two daughters, and during his long absences in Paris and elsewhere she, as an unpaid but completely reliable steward, proved to be, like Mme Montaigne, a highly efficient manager of lands and of the wine business. She is said to have been irritable, but that could well have resulted from her husband's considerable neglect of her. She was never asked to accompany him to Paris on his travels, and there were indications he was not faithful to her when he arrived there. He complained once that, when in a bad humor, she would not talk to him. Could it be she had read his private notebook with its gloomy, introspective query, "Who would marry if concubinage were permitted?" (Shackleton 79).

In 1716 Montesquieu's situation was improved by the inheritance of the estates of his uncle, the current head of the family. Jean-Baptiste de Secondat had been quite a landowner whose domain comprised the entire hamlet of Montesquieu as well as, importantly, an office as *président à mortier* of the *Bordeaux Parlement*. On the eve of the Revolution this body consisted of a *premier président*, nine *présidents à mortier*, and ninety-one *conseillers* (judges). The *présidents à mortier* presided over panels of *conseillers* formed for trials and were so called because with their scarlet robes they wore a cylindrical hat with a flat top reminiscent of a mason's mortarboard. Montesquieu was already a counselor, appointed in 1714, and he now sold that office to accept the more prestigious presidency.

Taking up his new duties, Montesquieu tended, says Shackleton, to sit on the criminal side rather than the civil bench. He did what was necessary but did not glory in the jurisprudence. Some years later, as if to excuse his only average assiduity, he wrote that he had comprehended the questions at issue well enough, except as to their procedure, which he claimed never to have understood well. This strongly suggests that he was not equipped for a distinguished career on the bench, for seldom is an interest in procedure not part of qualities brought by a committed lawyer. His legislative career records giving a formal speech at the opening of the session in 1725, representing the *Paris Parlement* in opposition to a wine tax (probably not a matter of jurisprudence), and making a proposal in 1721 that *présidents à mortier* should not have to attend afternoon sessions. In what appears a kind of self-help library Montesquieu owned a manuscript on how to study legal procedure and left six volumes of notes on Roman law, nearly all in his own hand. There were detailed analyses of Justinian—the *Digest*, *Code*, and some of the *Novels*. There is no marginal commentary by him, but the notebooks do include reports of several cases which he heard and give proof of a mind at serious, faithful work. Montesquieu, some said, was shocked when his son refused to be a lawyer, but Shackleton (12, 84) gives a different slant, revealing that when he offered the boy the choice of being a noble of the sword or of the robe he urged there was far more opportunity in the latter. Evidently the Church, in which many of his family had found their vocations, was not an acceptable alternative; the boy was sent to the Jansenist Collège d'Harcourt, directed by the highly opinionated Abbé Quesnel.

Montesquieu possessed a restless spirit, and even in age he never wearied of long return visits to Paris for intellectual and social stimulation. For these he was granted leave of absence from *Parlement*; but on one occasion at least he was ordered to return. When in residence at La Brède, though, Montesquieu as feudal lord had constant judicial obligations which by all accounts he discharged vigorously and faithfully. Law was a daily preoccupation. He went personally to the houses of his peasants to settle disputes; he defended vigorously in litigation his own titular rights, particularly concerning island holdings in the Garonne; he was a stern collector of debts; and in order to make absolutely certain procedure and practice were in order, he retained in his employ a financial and legal counselor. Having time to accumulate an excellent law library at La Brède, meant he also enjoyed gathering his legal wits and sources together to put in a scholarly appearance here and there. For a polymath of enlightenment this other work held the attraction of sharing with others systems of political philosophy and scientific experiments performed at La Brède. There were regular papers of report for the Bordeaux Academy of Science, as well as clever writing, especially fiction. Inspired by Cicero's *De Officiis* and Pufendorf's short treatise on the same subject, there was a reading before the Bordeaux Academy of a Treatise on Duties, now lost. When the many fine volumes were consulted for his monumental *De l'Esprit des lois* Montesquieu proudly made certain the bookish house productions were cloaked in the greater reflective glory of work by a "French jurisconsult."

Unfortunately, one of his major professional annoyances was that his judicial pay arrived irregularly; gradually the job away from home turf apparently accumulated enough such practical drawbacks that in 1726 he ended his judicial career by selling his office. Colleagues protested that he should stay, but he refused any more paid legal work. Still he would never cease to love his law and its titles, and to the end of his life favored the dignity and the status of being called *Président*. In 1748, not long before he died, he wrote a *Discourse on Possessory Action*, showing that even in age and illness his training remained an indelible marker of his thoughts.

Les lettres persanes

Around 1717 Montesquieu began privately to compose the first book of *Les lettres persanes*. It would be published anonymously in Amsterdam when he was thirty-two and soon put the lawyer as novelist on the map of literary genius. Underneath the prediction made by Desmolets of its success—"It will sell like bread"—looms the Revolution's dangerous contradictory symptoms of dearth and affluence, but Montesquieu's bread for the clamoring public would luckily be an enormous success. Ten editions of the novel came out in the first year.

In form, the book is mainly a collection of 161 letters ostensibly written by two rich Persians, Usbek and Rica, who from about 1711–1720 travel westward to France where they spend ten years in a pre-Voltairean search of wisdom. There are also other letters written by friends at home in Persia and also some by Rhedi, a friend of the two Persians, concurrently also travelling in Europe. The letters present a penetrating, satirical picture of French government, religion, and society, along with an accurate picture of oriental culture, this latter introducing sociologist Montesquieu's definite new tone of relativism into French thought. The orientalism, peppery like Voltaire and foreshadowing another brilliant lawyer *manqué*, Gustave Flaubert, includes suggestive details about the life of Persian women in the harem. These, although never indecent, titillated the reading public who, stimulated, could supply their own lascivious inferences and, thus, further promote the sale of the work. Not only did Montesquieu court the public with his scenes from the seraglio, he had created the unusual in censored France: a clear *roman à clef*, one which dared name names in French politics and religion. The more serious topics in the book showed a philosopher's courageous delve into society, government, economics, religion, philosophy, and history. Such scope revealed a young man already widely and deeply read, able to observe the ways of the people around him with acute penetration and objectivity. Montesquieu, the attorney, had deftly presented the case, while Montesquieu, the judge, had been devastating in deciding the fault.

Several of the letters actually did turn on important legal concerns: the history of French law, international law, penal law, natural law in women's matters, and the connection between law and manners. The comparison of Christianity with other religions, tacitly suggesting that all are entitled to equal consideration, was particularly daring and struck a positive note for enlightenment—topical and needed—then and now. Montesquieu's general tone was negative on the new items of the day—against the bull *Unigenitus*, and, perhaps because of the period under Abbé Quesnel, with no enthusiasm for the Jansenists. Skeptical thoughts toward the Church matched Voltaire in their disrespectful, anti-clericalism. Usbek, for instance, considers God's existence but roundly rejects the arguments of the theologians. He and the other Muslims are fearless in boldly denouncing the Catholic Church: the Pope is a magician, an old idol; celibacy will end the Church in 500 years; the Old Testament story of the flood is a joke; monks are dervishes. Through his sharp satire Montesquieu is pleading an irresistible case in favor of toleration and against prejudice both religious and anti-monarchical. In summation, he again opts for morality, not faith or fanatic liberalism.

Letters 112–122 bring him to a relatively new topic—historical causation—in which he explores the decline of world population. In this case facts and reasoning are for a problem completely opposite to the modern model, but the discussion is highly relevant, since with it he was beginning the new study of society by extensive observation of facts. Already in research Montesquieu had displayed what was to be the keynote of his later "serious" work: augmentation of Daguesseau's solitary *in camera* exploration of universal and inscrutable truths deep in the mind of God. The *Lettres* explored far-flung terrestrial parameters by study of travel reports from all societies. Thus buttressed with personal knowledge of amassed sociological detail, the *Lettres* were then, as a whole, put together to detect unseen, connecting generalities. In an age when men of letters and men of science were not distinct groups, the shift from judicial work to fiction to sociology marked not a desertion of science, but rather its application in innovative ways, foreshadowing nineteenth century naturalism. The witty *esprit* of this fiction may have become a vehicle carrying Montesquieu far from the careful aridity of legal studies, but it proved to be an important staging ground for ideas that were leading straight to law's soul and spirit—*L'Esprit des lois*.

No doubt he had chosen the letter form and anonymous authorship, for both of which there were many precedents, in order to try and escape responsibility for ideas that might anger the monarchy and the Church. Seeking fame as an author of fiction, he could also indulge in many clever thrusts that he might never himself seriously endorse. But no matter how outrageous his personal stand, a traditional laurel wreath was adjudged his, and he was honored by election to the French Academy, the highest public prize of all. The student of society and its governing laws had been transformed by a unique initiation into a great Western legal thinker. And it all had come by sharply pointed satiric barbs sent off to travel through Time on a rug.

Travels, 1721-1731

When the young Montesquieu initiated his many visits to Paris, it was a case of conjugal boredom on a long leash and high ambition with possibilities. Thirsting for facts, he could not be content to sit in a Montaigne tower and wonder what he did not know; it was obvious that the libraries, academies, and salons of Paris, now effervescing in a liberal Regency and feeling release from many of the suffocating intellectual shackles of Louis XIV, offered much more tempting worldliness than Bordeaux. Paris academe was not the venue draw of choice, for the conservative University and its law faculty, bent on teaching the received and approved learning of the day rather than on starting groundbreaking research that alone could augment that learning, had little to satisfy a questioning mind. But by penetration of the high levels of salon society, the young author found Persian harems lived in Parisian mansions, the voluptuous and licentious *fête galante* embarking for painter Watteau's Cytherea with the Duc d'Orléans as an extremely sensuous leader of the revels. For a provincial lawyer from Brède it appeared as the thousand and one nights.

Masquerade did not lead the Montesquieu dance, however. He cared less for wit, wine, and women than for searching out laws which might govern society if only the methods so successful in science could be imitated in the study of human affairs. Soon Montesquieu found welcome where many were asking about society and coming up with multiple answers: the salons of Mme de Tencin on the rue St.-Honoré, Mme Geoffrin at 374 of the same street, and, a top favorite, 27 quai d'Anjou, the home of the remarkable and well-read Anne-Thérèse de Margenot de Courcelles, Marquise de Lambert. Mme La Marquise made certain that the ground rules for her informal meetings and learned discussions had an impeccable Cartesian clarity. Tuesdays were for the nobility (Montesquieu chose that one), Wednesdays for the men of letters. On all days gambling was forbidden, the scandalous excluded, and intrigue permitted, especially if it concerned elections to the Academy. To the endless, well-dressed discussions of duty, taste, love, friendship, and happiness, budding philosopher Montesquieu is said to have contributed a Cartesian materialism which reduced happiness to a certain organic disposition of the body and traced moral effects to physical causes.

Evidence suggests that Montesquieu also could be found giving these and more political opinions as member of an interesting group called the Club de l'Entresol, a group of illustrious citizens who met in a Place Vendôme apartment on Saturdays to read the gazette and to freely discuss topics of the day. Nobles of sword and robe mingled there along with men of the middle class. It was probably a welcome relief for Montesquieu to put aside the abstract and often pastel moral themes of the

Marquise de Lambert and plunge into intensely colored controversies of the time. He participated with presidential fervor as ecclesiastical law was discussed and questioned against the backdrop of Gallican and Jansenist opposition to the chief minister, Fleury. Particularly interesting to Montesquieu were men who dared initiate the great debate on feudal origins and the rights of the nobility in relation to the crown. At first the Entresol's reputation was high, and Fleury kept government hands off; but in 1731 after seven years of indiscretions, Fleury dissolved it. In neither of these circles was Montesquieu likely to have met the influential Jansenist lawyers like Daguesseau who were such a strong force in the *Paris Parlement*. It appears that Montesquieu did not seek them out even though belief in a strong constitutional role for the *parlements* was to be a cornerstone of his political science for France.

Interesting as those days were to Montesquieu, they were marred to some extent by a series of personal problems. In 1724 as he was working on some new literary undertakings his eyes began to fail, and for the rest of his life he would fear blindness. He had borrowed too much in relation to his income, and his finances were in poor shape, although the proceeds of the sale of his presidency somewhat reduce the pressure. It seemed time for personal escapism from life's unpleasantness. In 1728, as if he considered that he had achieved his aims in Paris when he took his seat in the Academy, Montesquieu suddenly revised the agenda of daily activity. Realizing he could not live by Brède alone, he would travel, seizing an overall concept, then achieving a clarity of horizon by making certain always to anchor his thoughts from the new city's highest place—a century later the tactic so beloved of a Hugo or Balzac, before being adopted by Napoleon. Leaving Paris three months after his investiture as an *immortel*, he was off voyaging on his own carpet.

He decided to begin with Vienna. Shackleton (Shackleton, 91) writes of Montesquieu as one who, unlike younger aristocratic travelers relying for *entrée* on birth and inherited rank, was preceded by a literary reputation which easily opened the important doors. After a month's expedition to see the Hungarian mines he chose Venice, Florence, then Rome followed by Naples. It would be an itinerary favored by the nineteenth century, bringing fame to a Flaubert or Stendhal as they copied the Montesquieu chase after happiness and wisdom. The Baron from Brède seemed to have provided their guidebook, as he and they wrote down observations which were societal, climatic, geographical, and political. Strangely, Montesquieu ignored the study of ancient monuments and architecture, even though in a few years he would write on the history of ancient Rome. Florence, however, aroused at once his interest in art. Experts were consulted, and after a serious study of the treasures of Florence and Rome, he wrote what amounts to a *catalogue raisonné* of Florentine art. In Rome he met nearly all the Cardinals and avidly followed papal politics. He talked to few Jesuits but felt close to Roman Jansenism, in its early years more restrained and friendlier to the Enlightenment than the *solitaires* in France. Naples, now an Austrian possession (1707–1734), had an active intellectual life, and here Montesquieu paused gladly to indulge his usual passion: a study of political and social systems.

There were at this time in Naples three major lines of intellectual thought drawn into camps around Giovanni Gravina, Pietro Giannone, and Giovanni Vico. Gravina, who had died in 1718, made important contributions both in *belles lettres* and Roman legal matters, achieving distinction especially as an historian in civil law. In his *Origines iuris civilis* he did not confine himself to texts but related his study to politics and institutions. Montesquieu studied the book seriously and met one of Gravina's pupils, himself an erudite jurisconsult. After Montesquieu's death a French translation of the Gravina opus appeared with the telling title *Esprit des lois romaines*, strongly suggesting a parallel to Montesquieu's principal book. The research Montesquieu devoted to Gravina must be counted for its influence in opening wider the Frenchman's historical eyes.

It would be five years after Gravina's death that Giannone's ambitious four volume *Istoria civile del regno di Napoli* was published. The work was hailed by the Neapolitan government; but Giannone's attack on Papal and Jesuit intrigue and interference aroused implacable opposition in Rome, and he was compelled to take refuge with the Emperor in Vienna. Montesquieu, whose serious study of the book came later, was for now mainly impressed not by the anticlericalism of the author but by his method. History did not mean a guidebook describing battles, natural beauties, and gentle climate; instead Giannone, far ahead of his time, concentrated on Neapolitan government, laws, and customs, while ranging afield into health, buildings, roads, and the University. Montesquieu felt at ease in affiliating himself with Giannone's close linkage of social community and legal fabric.

It was in Naples that the third of these *savants*, Vico, brought out in 1725 the first edition of his important *Principii d'una nova scienza*. Montesquieu happened to be in Venice in 1728 when a second edition was in preparation there. Writers have sought to show that Montesquieu met the well known rhetorician and jurist, but it is only possible that he did. Meeting or no, although Vico's philosophy was both eminent and relevant, it does not appear that his work had much direct influence on Montesquieu, except perhaps to some extent via Gravina. This is a surprise, since Vico's ideas share intellectual space with those of Montesquieu's in *De l'Esprit des lois*. Vico was searching intently for coherence and system which would pattern a unifying common nature to all nations; he felt that it is only when we have established such a tissue of connections that we can obtain sure knowledge. Since humans set forth society, the science of society—human science—can be certain, much like mathematics which also we have made. The natural sciences can yield only approximate truths based on attempts to imitate nature in experiments performed by us. One guesses that Vico began with the idea that mathematics are manmade and yet certain, proceeding onward from there to a fuller conclusion; if so, he overlooked the thought that the degree component of geometric shapes existed long before man noticed the fact, and that mathematics are not made by us, but discovered by us. This posed no problem for the traveling Frenchman, who could have found in Vico's analyses of national and legal cohesiveness greater grist for the intellectual mill at Brède.

In July 1729 Montesquieu left Italy and traveled to England by way of Austria and Hanover, arriving in London in November for what Shackleton calls the "most important period of his life." Unfortunately, it is also one of the least known because Montesquieu's grandson, no Boswell, burned the English journal, conceivably finding there either too much of *Persian Letters* licentiousness or not enough French chauvinism. Montesquieu, well disposed toward a favorable reception of the knowledge England could impart, is said to have commented just before crossing the Channel: "'There are no men of true sense born anywhere but in England.'"

Montesquieu could speak and understood English well enough to comprehend the proceedings at sessions of Parliament. Multiple rich and famous doors opened—Chesterfield, Waldegrove, Townshend, Bolingbroke, and the Duke of Montagu, a practical joker who dunked Montesquieu in a tub of cold water on arrival at his country seat. Montesquieu took it in good humor, praised it as an example of English liberty, and counted his stay with Montagu as one of the happiest times of his life (Shackleton, 117, 121, 125). Viscount Bolingbroke, home from exile, was busily mounting opposition to the Prime Minister, Sir Robert Walpole; and the visiting French baron, with politically active acquaintances among the Tories or dissident Whigs, felt akin to the ideas of this contentious English viscount whose own colorful dossier included impeachment for high treason. London's expatriate community found a stellar newcomer in Montesquieu, who joined a large French community enjoying the English ease of fraternization unfettered by differences of rank and religion. There would be a strong infusion of such liberal thoughts when Montesquieu became initiated into a Masonic lodge. Prestigious membership in the Royal Society brought him the opportunity for intellectual exchange and friendship with the most learned scholars. Pope was the current literary titan, and Montesquieu must undoubtedly have at least been introduced to England's premier wordsmith and master of his own form of *esprit*.

The History of the Romans

By the spring of 1731—Montesquieu's portmanteau now bulging with new ideas as well as confirmation of his enlightened concepts—it was time to go back to work. After a short stop in Paris, return to La Brède brought the traveler enough contentment to spend the next two years at home, reading widely and collecting material on many subjects. But travel may have given him more than expected in those views from the heights, for he now—with another pre-Stendhal link—entertained an ambition to serve France in the diplomatic corps. To show those in authority that the noble author of the *Lettres Persanes* had indeed gained cosmopolitan, statesmanlike qualifications and was available, Montesquieu wrote and printed a small, serious treatise of forty-four pages called *Réflexions sur la monarchie universelle en Europe* (Reflections on a Universal Monarchy in Europe). Almost immediately, though, political ambition awakened the need for honing diplomatic tact; and Montesquieu decided his strong critique of Louis XIV with its reflections on anti-militarism, pacifism, and free trade were politically untimely. The work was tactfully withdrawn before it had been offered for sale, and only a single copy survives at La Brède.

Pursuing the same objective without the topicality, Montesquieu next shifted into a new gear, presenting a carefully researched viewpoint (he called the process "considering") of what had made Rome's greatness and led to her fall. These *Considérations sur les causes de la grandeur des Romains et de leur décadence* of 1734 were informed with similar themes to the *Réflexions* but bore no signature and featured a politically less dangerous, ancient setting. The work had no sooner been printed than ideas for tackling greatness in the spirit of laws themselves began to take shape in his mind. This endeavor would be the Montesquieu masterwork, but it would take fourteen more years for its fruition.

The *Considérations*, rather than narrate Roman rise and fall, concentrated on the causes of both; prominent readers of the day were cool to the diffuse result and accorded the book only moderate approval. The work seemed thin. No significant weight had been given to violation of secular natural law as a cause of Rome's decline. Even Christianity versus Providence found the author unnaturally silent, although we can sense his separation of history into areas of the sacred and the secular. In fact secular Rome *was* inseparable from its ecclesiastical past, a point Gibbon, to whom rises and falls mattered, would carefully show. Montesquieu was determined, as he tried to build a reputation as a serious writer, to be as discreet as possible in the eyes of the Paris authorities without abandoning his intellectual integrity through the escape hatch of Fate. Probably he also considered how little attention the emperors had paid to Christianity. The separation of Church history from national interests was, however, also in accord with the precedents set by several earlier writers of influence such as Bodin, Bossuet, and even Augustine and Jansen. Montesquieu's secular anti-Providentialism put him in the path-forging van of an Enlightenment pioneer. Still, knowing ecclesiastics all thought that Providence was basic, Montesquieu, perhaps to appease them, paid in the book a formal tribute to the dominance of Providence in the history of religion. He also took the diplomatic precaution of asking the fierce Jesuit, Louis-Bertrand Castel, a former tutor to his son at the Collège of Louis le Grand, to make corrections.

What, then, did Montesquieu envisage as the secular causes of greatness and decay? He remembered Giannone: not luck, but general causes rule the world. (Montesquieu did not detail causality's development; he assumed his sophisticated readers knew Roman history.) If a battle is decisive, it is because these general causes determine that it should be so. General causes await an occasion created by man; they do not necessarily operate in spite of man. They lay deep in the ethos of Rome, a society in which many of them fueled establishment of the customs. If appropriate to the situation they led to a rise in social strength; when they were abandoned, the society fell. Montesquieu's Republican Rome, which could enjoy the general spirit necessary to be what it was just because the area of governance was relatively small in size and had stability, confronted the cause of increase, only to find rapid change destroyed the binding spirit.

Conroy (Conroy, *Montesquieu Revisited*, 63) sees a viewpoint like this as showing the influence of Montesquieu's interest in science. It is as though politics were a machine actuated by weights and counterweights, and as though Montesquieu's carefully phrased, economical sentences were themselves pristine equations of the mechanism. No less than the *Lettres persanes*, such ideas all had an allegorical application for Frenchmen who read into them the suggestion that the chieftain of the *cause célèbre*, Louis XIV, had clearly started France down the inevitable slope toward similar ruin. Causality's effect was the brutal moral of the Montesquieu book whose skillful presentation of important ideas should not be eclipsed by Gibbon's more famous tomes of forty-five years later nor by the fact that at its publication the monarchical times were not ready for enthusiasm about societal destruction. Nevertheless, Montesquieu, in writing his book, had offered readers a striking philosophy of history, one which embraced deductive factors while stressing empirical detail. The *Considérations* are a benchmark in Montesquieu's development as a legalist, for he had now paused to assess the causes of the historical development of society and decided to reject accident generally and the accidental emergence of great men in particular.

De l'Esprit des lois

Introduction

With the civilization of Rome digested, Montesquieu had renewed appetite to go back to the analysis of legal philosophy and its complex place in governments. The author would here wear many hats a Justinian had never donned—meteorologist, priest, moralist, businessman, and sociologist. *De l'Esprit des lois* is a methodology volume for understanding the sources of law rather than a treatise for practicing lawyers. Still, it is a law book, and a great one. In his political orientation Montesquieu began being primarily concerned about French constitutional law, but his interest grew in rethinking legal administration and criminal procedures. As an ennobled defender of the *Parlements*, he saw no need for uniformity of French private law, for that would have tended to reduce the influence of the provincial aristocracy. Although a contemporary of Daguesseau, we have no evidence that Montesquieu shared in Daguesseau's actual efforts toward across-the-board law reform for France. It was Roman law that was the main focus of the *Parlement of Bordeaux*, and it was appropriate for his role in that body that Montesquieu hold fast to Rome's legal history and contributions.

Montesquieu's text of the *Esprit*, in type of a generous size, consists of a hefty 1,116 pages. The only English edition is that of Thomas Nugent, approved by Montesquieu and published in the eighteenth century. A current edition of Nugent's translation by Hofner Press, published in 1949 and utilized here, presents the *Esprit* in English in 643 pages. The masterful two volumes on what constitutes law's essence on the spirit of laws are of a significance that really can only be considered by reading them carefully, not reading about them as the current study intends. No summary can do justice to Montesquieu's compact, economical, polished style, employed to present in good literary form a dense nexus of facts and reasoning. The following pages will merely try to suggest the scope of the work and give a preliminary idea of what the author thought he was trying to do, and what posterity thinks he did. Conroy admits (Conroy, vii) that among English-speaking people of learning, the main interest in the work is usually reduced to the literary merits rather than its scientific, legal, or sociological elements. Be that as it may, the book still maintains such wide importance in France that the most recent edition, the French publication of Versini, came out in 1995. The best of the several now available for study in any language, Versini has provided an Introduction, a general Note on the Text, a Bibliography, Chronology, Montesquieu's "*Défense de l'Esprit des lois*" (sixty-six pages), detailed notes on the text, and—a new contribution to the field—a "Table analytique et alphabétique des matières" of both the *Esprit* and the *Défense*. To these 229 pages of useful index Versini adds a meticulous table of contents.

Montesquieu worked hard at carefully organizing his two volumes. Columns of a temple, they lived as it were under law's massive roof and in the metaphysical niche of an impressive architectural entablature. Inspired directly from his years of eye-opening travel, Montesquieu could proudly display over the entrance the grandiose accuracy of his title: *De L'Esprit des lois: ou Du rapport que les lois doivent avoir avec la contribution de chaque gouvernement, les moeurs, le climat, la religion, le commerce, etc*. (The Spirit of Laws, or The Connection Laws Must Have with Every Government's Constitution, Customs, Climate, Religion, Commerce, etc.). Montesquieu had probably been helped to his impressive heading by Domat's Chapter X1 of the *Treatise of Laws*; and there was a Justinian-like feel to volumes divided as six "Parts" and thirty-one "Books," with each Book subsequently divided into one or more "Chapters." The Books and Chapters were numbered with Roman numerals (the Books consecutively without regard for the Parts, and the Chapters consecutively by Book) and a caption was supplied for each Book and Chapter. In prefatory remarks Montesquieu wrote that readers who wanted to know "the design of the author" would find it best by "searching into the design of the work" and discovering it for themselves; but he also confessed that he had "followed [his] object without any fixed plan," and many readers, sensing the "spirit" is unexpectedly floating off into the title's "etc.," find to their chagrin that structure and captions do not sufficiently help. To aid readers several writers have provided their own outlines, which generally follow Montesquieu's order of presentation but break it up into a different outline with different captions. Here is the version of the present writer. (The numbers of the relevant Books are noted at the right of each item.)

Part I. Laws in general   I
    1. Laws as relations
    2. Natural Law
    3. Positive Law
Part II. The principles that control what laws provide.
    1. The principles of the three kinds of government that control laws: republican (democratic or aristocratic), monarchical, and despotic.   II, III
       a. General remarks…   V
       b. As to laws on education   IV
       c. As to civil and criminal laws   VI
       d. As to sumptuary laws and law for women   VII

e. As to defensive forces	IX
f. As to offensive forces	X
g. As to political liberty (and the English constitution)	XI
h. As to the status of the citizen	XII
i. As to taxation	XIII
2. Corruption of the principles of the three kinds of government	VIII
3. Relation of laws and climate	XIV, XV, XVI, XVII
4. Relation of laws and terrain	XVIII
5. Relation of laws to the principles of the general spirit of a nation and its morals and customs	XIX
6. Relation of laws to commerce	XX, XXI
7. Relation of laws to money	XXII
8. Relation of laws to the inhabitants	XXIII
9. Relation of laws to religion	XXIV, XXV
10. Relation of Law to the kinds of laws (natural, divine, canon, laws of nations, political, civil, domestic)	XXVI
11. Relation of Law to the history of laws	
a. Roman law of succession	XXVII
b. French civil law	XXVIII
c. Frankish feudal law	
i. General remarks	XXX, XXXI
ii. Refutation of the theory that the French monarchy in origin was absolute	XXX, XXIII, XXIV
12. The technique of drafting laws	XXIX

A simpler outline is that provided by Lecomte for baccalaureate students in the secondary schools of France:

I. Principles and definitions
II. Connection between laws and the nature and principles of government
III. Connection between laws and citizens
IV. Connection between laws and economic conditions
V. Connection between laws and religion
VI. Appendix   (Conroy, 72).

For the purpose of demonstrating the importance and significance of the book some critics have, after Book One's introduction, brought the complexity down to an informal three parts: political science, politics and geography, politics and legal history. Many have found Book One to stand apart as a Part One statement of deductive secular natural law that has no connection with the rest, and they ignore it in appraising Montesquieu; others defend it and its importance for the whole. The second part (sections 1–10 and 12 of Part II of this writer's outline) is seen by all critics as a new departure, the boldly opened door of Montesquieu's science of sociology leading us out into unexpected brightness. It is law's first attempt to derive legislation for the evolution of society by induction from observed facts. After this sociological bombshell, the more banal third part (section 11 in this writer's outline), consisting of 276 pages in the Versini edition (Montesquieu's books XXVII, XXVIII, XXX, and XXXI), is rejected by many writers as an irrelevant and unduly long appendix; again there are others who defend it and its importance for the whole. Analyzing these differences among readers can clarify the special role *De l'Esprit des lois* plays in the history of legal philosophy.

Writing, Publication and Reception

The *Lettres persanes*, a couple of short novels, the lightly researched *Considérations* on the Romans, as well as the royalist *Réflexions* on a universal monarchy in Europe, had all been rather easy to write. But the reading public had because of them captioned the author facilely as that piquant Persian, a persona both infamous as a libertine courtier and famous as an *habitué* of fashionable drawing rooms. To mention Montesquieu would automatically conjure up details behind these deliciously fascinating rubrics: Madame de Lambert's pet, the notorious member of the Entresol, the provincial landowner, the would-be but rejected diplomat, the magistrate who sold his office (Shackleton, 227).

Yet this was a man restive for more than a pigeonhole. Was it just personal fame, as Shackleton's biography tells us? Or were there not in the curriculum vitae ambitious political plans for a France, made better by a better constitution, with the felicitous result of even better positive law. As for the hero—better, also, in the new life plan—which was nothing less than a fantastic voyage to discover law's soul—he would be Montesquieu the reformer. But he would also be a composite Frenchman drawn wisely from the "intermediary" powers of *parlements*, nobility, Church, and army, all of which lay between king and people and held the solution to ruling well: being and doing the best rather than merely being content with the better.

Montesquieu described the new undertaking as a twenty year project, but he might well have said thirty, because before composition he had been gathering material for quite a long time as he thought seriously about the French constitution. Another head start was provided by Book XI on the English Constitution, already written and first intended, it is thought, for inclusion in the *Considérations*. Massive labor, despite the handicap of visual deficiency, came naturally for a man who believed that "'constant idleness is a torment of hell'" (Shackleton, 234). From the outset, the goal of studying the whole range of man in society was probably fixed and at ease in its constitutional and monarchical grid. However, here was no casual special pleader. Montesquieu the traveler wrote to discover and to extend boundaries of the legal voyage in a very serious attempt to apply his new convenantal cartography to governance. His ambitious plan was thus to go beyond Grotius and Pufendorf country and come back home ready with sound scholarship for the clean blank pages waiting on his writing desk.

The home library was very good, with, if needed, far more books of his own remaining in the capital; libraries of both Paris and Bordeaux were honored to permit him access. Still, he always preferred doing most of the work in the quiet of

La Brède, for after the diligent eight hours of work on the manuscript this allowed him to spend a small part of each day on the administration of his estate. A visitor today to his impressive library and work room can see where his feet abraded the fireplace. He worked alone and talked little about it. Using notebooks, not cards, he began with a fairly large collection of such compendia which had already been completed over the years. Always one or more secretaries were there to assist—nineteen in all according to the surviving handwriting. They often read aloud to him; sometimes he dictated. For facts about foreign countries he used the best available sources, some not very good by modern standards, for their provenance traced back to unreliable writers and travelers from whom a considerable number of inaccuracies crept in. By early 1742 Montesquieu had finished eighteen of twenty-four books and had six in rough draft. In 1744 he began revising the whole, did more research in 1745, and then made another complete revision in 1746. By 1747 he had finished. He was fifty-eight.

Deterred by French censorship, he decided to publish in Switzerland where Burlamaqui was law's big name of the hour. While type was being set, Book XXVI on the applicability of laws was either written or rewritten under the influence of Domat. From the same time came Book XXIX on the drafting of laws. There was now some stress of competition, for the Montesquieu publisher had just put out Burlamaqui's highly successful *Principles of Natural Law*, a book followed in 1751 by the Swiss jurist's equally popular *Principles of the Law of Nations*. Pressed by his agent, Vernet, Montesquieu began three more books for the *Esprit*: XXVIII on the civil laws of the Franks, and XXX and XXXI on the theory of feudal laws. Of all the *Esprit* these three were to be the most arduous to write; Montesquieu confessed, somewhat testily, that readers would breeze through Book XXVIII in three hours, whereas it had taken him three months and his hair turning white in the process to write it. In letter after letter Vernet kept demanding the other two, and Montesquieu, near the end, perhaps a little uncertain and depressed, did confess in a notebook that perhaps all he might have done, when the book was finished, was to have "'built a temple to ennui and to patience'" (Shackleton,241). He realized it was not going to be easy to import any new book from Switzerland into France, but publisher Barillot's French representative in Geneva assisted with the case and the *Esprit des lois* came home. Montesquieu at once sent a copy to Daguesseau, then Chancellor. By October 1748, the work could be purchased in the bookstores, appearing there, like all of Montesquieu's other works, without his name.

Among close friends the first reaction was very favorable, but barely a year after the book appeared, the Jesuits had sprung into action against it. Among other things they accused *L'Esprit* of being based on the free-thinking natural religion systems of Pope and Spinoza. In the Baron they saw no mortar-"bored" president, but a far too clever author for whom religion was only a political device, one of those dangerous minds who believe that man and God are governed by fate and that virtue is not necessary in a monarchy. Montesquieu was publicly undisturbed. But privately, under the insistence of his friend, the Italian writer Ottaviano da Guasco, he wrote and in February 1750 published at Geneva his *Défense de l'Esprit des lois*.

The riposte showed a man who stood his ground. By retracting nothing, courage attracted an irate buzz of attack from the Jansenist camp. This, however, prompted Voltaire to support Montesquieu, peevishly telling a Jansenist pamphleteer that if he were criticizing belief based on reason he had better burn Pope, Locke, and Bayle as well as Montesquieu and, thank God that at least he, the Jansenist, had nothing in common with the rational. Other writers joined the lively fray, until gradually the fracas subsided as Montesquieu's approval abroad increased. *L'Esprit* was hailed in England, and there was no significant dissent in the *Paris Parlement*. Interestingly, Daguesseau was at first hostile and forbade the sale of the work, even though he admired and was pleased to have received the copy. Shackleton says (Shackleton, 363, 367) he was "eventually ... prevailed on not only to permit the sale but to allow a new edition in Paris subject to the usual condition that the name of a foreign town appear on the title page." Many subsequent Paris editions appeared unimpeded. Cabinet philosopher Daguesseau, who never traveled anywhere, must have in the end, found his mind stretched by this Gascon voyager of little piety, for the Chancellor was liberated to become with Montesquieu an ambiguous actor in French politics. Both brought aid and comfort to the Enlightenment and thus the Revolution by permitting publication of innovative ideas—particularly, their doubts as to theology. Yet, paradoxically both men made stout defense of the backward-looking *parlements*.

The ecclesiastical hierarchy was a different matter. The Archbishop of Sens denounced *L'Esprit*, and the General Assembly of the Clergy in 1750 asked Louis XV to take action, upset less with the Montesquieu text than with possible threats to their clerical exemption from taxation. Next, it was the turn of the Sorbonne which drew up a list of eight censurable propositions and then added four more. Fortunately for Montesquieu, with bureaucratic delays added to his increasingly powerful renown, the dozen propositions were never published. In contrast to their French brethren the Italian Jansenists, whom we have noted as remarkable allies of the Enlightenment, were, in general, favorable to *L'Esprit*, even though someone denounced the work, and a revisory deputy was forthwith appointed by Rome's Congregation of the Index. Some elements of *L'Esprit* were unquestionably against Church teaching and deserving of papal censure, but objections of the Holy Office turned out to be mild. Only chapter 11 of Book XXVI received categorical denunciation by the Inquisition. The book went on the Index near the end of 1751, but the European reading world paid little heed and continued to purchase it.

The Nature of *De l'Esprit des lois*

It is difficult at the beginning of the twenty-first century to analyze *L'Esprit* by itself. It has been studied by so many writers whose books, in turn, have also been pored over and commented upon, that the task of anyone who would understand Montesquieu's work must involve at least brief consideration of the points of critique. If there is anything such a review brings out it is that writers on Montesquieu are puzzled by what they have read.

Scholars judging Montesquieu as another scholar find him inadequate to the role. They cannot accept his having tried to explain and augment knowledge, then not following consistently the obligation to make an impersonal, non-subjective and scientific analysis. They fault the work's lack of a neat structure and internal cohesion. There are writers who acknowledge that he read widely and intensively and presented extensive facts, but they are disappointed that the sand has too little cement, and that in trying to be an inductive Baconian, he sometimes calmly rejects or ignores facts if they do not fit the system he is propounding. Others start out happy to find a form of work resembling that of Grotius and Pufendorf only to be denied the comforting overall consistency of those authors. Voltaire, who could never be a supporter without a few rapier strokes at close range, said that in Book I Montesquieu began as both a Realist and a Nominalist, thereby reviving an old dispute better forgotten. Others, doubtful about what they view as the deceptive method of Descartes, have wanted inductive proof, or vice versa; while still others find in Montesquieu no clear difference between the two and a misuse of both.

Particularly distressing is the fact that although Montesquieu sees climate and terrain, for example, as powerful factors determining forms of government, he nevertheless begins by what seems like a deductive statement of the forms of government before proceeding to the physical facts. Jurists who see law, at least positive law, as an exercise of power, have been particularly upset by the very definition upon which, from Book I, Montesquieu seems to base his work: "Laws, in their most general signification, are thence necessary relations arising from the nature of things" (Montesquieu, Thomas Nugent, trans., *Spirit of the Laws,* 1). This is strikingly different from any preceding juristic definition, although, in fact, it does serve well to announce Montesquieu's subject: the relation which must exist between laws and the things they rule.

And so it goes, with many a great mind reading Montesquieu and being unable to agree on what it is that has been read. Rousseau admitted that Montesquieu was the only one brilliant enough to have created a "science of political law," then found failure in work which talked only about the positive law of established governments and avoided the ethical dilemma of what the law ought to be. The distinguished Georges Davy, speaking two hundred years after the publication of *De l'Esprit des lois*, defended the lawyer of Brède, insisting Rousseau had shown a fundamental misunderstanding, and that Montesquieu had specifically studied "'what is'" to get an insight into "'what ought to be and what can be'" (Durkheim, *Montesquieu and Rousseau: Forerunners of Sociology, Foreword by Henri Peyre,* 144–146). These criticisms are all more or less valid, since it is seldom that a competent scholar, studying a subject intensively and in good faith, fails to come to any valid conclusion at all. The issue, therefore, is whether there is an explanation of the Montesquieu work which will take account of these problems while at the same time showing that it does present a coherent argument.

Possibly Versini (Montesquieu, Laurent Versini ed., *De l'espirt des lois,* 38) offers a clue when he defines Montesquieu's book as a political document and not a work on climatology or church history: "*il ecrit un livre de politologue et non de climatologue ou d'historien des Églises....*" Versini has touched on a very important point: one must put Montesquieu *in situ*. He was a French patriot concerned for his country. He was a noble keenly observant of monarchy and its vast, top heavy recrafting by Louis XIV. He was a lawyer who, although he never practiced as an *avocat*, had as a judge wide experience with the management of litigation and had read piles of *mémoires* (briefs) submitted by *avocats*. He was a man who clearly had political ambition and was very familiar with the hazards of coming out in an absolute monarchy with overly frank publications on the sensitive subjects of public law, limits on royal power, and fully crystallized constitutions. But he was a realist and had concluded that France's salvation lay in her renewed recognition of the necessity of inserting into such a constitution the crucial "intermediate powers" between the monarch and the people.

These considerations indicate that the matter foremost in Montesquieu's mind was a legal case—the greatest of his life. It had been, he felt, given to him to persuade his influential countrymen by a major publication that the checks and balances position of the intermediate powers in the constitution must be recognized anew, and, in that apprehending, refined and strengthened. On them lay France's destiny, although Montesquieu could not yet know that right around history's corner was upheaval and terror to preserve and increase the happiness of her people. We have so frequently seen French political history as a slow march, halting at times, but always continuing toward central power, and Montesquieu played the firm dissenter to that process. A Magna Carta man for France, he admired the limitations upon the power of the Frankish kings by those mist-born assemblages of the great, and his strong will was that these constraints be restored.

A publication of such magnitude would obviously be more influential if its conclusion could be seen by readers as possessing two qualities: first, it had been written in good faith after exhaustive scholarship; and second, its very existence lay in the nature of things in those laws comparable to exempla of Newton which now instead of planets controlled men in society. Yet there is deference due this *avocat* who must have comprehended that the presentation needed not be confined to the single prop of hoped-for, philosophically impartial, objective scientific scholarship. Filing a case report in support of a cause may properly offer every relevant argument (even if some are a little inconsistent with others) that will persuade to the desired conclusion. The lawyer whose client is a nation, whose tribunal is the whole of the ruling classes, and who in his preparation and presentation can make a good faith contribution to science, is not to be faulted if his *mémoire* in form looks more like a work of science than of advocacy. In substance, Montesquieu was always the *avocat* who pushed for an outcome known in advance. He aimed for result, and he felt no obligation to be a pure, inductive inquirer who follows the facts wherever they may lead. In his heart his beginning proposition was far from mere hypothesis.

The Three Forms of Government

Montesquieu believed in legislation as a way to happiness, but legislation had to be moderate and the form of government produced had to be moderate, too. Like Grotius and Pufendorf he thought that in the precepts of secular natural law man had norms—always that what "ought to be" as distinguished from the what "is"—which would assure quality. There is no good reason to doubt the Realist here spoke from the mathematical heart:

'Particular intelligent beings may have laws of their own making, but they have some likewise which they never made. Before there were intelligent beings, they [intelligent beings] were possible; they had therefore possible relations, and consequently possible laws. Before laws were made there were relations of possible justice. To say that there is nothing just or unjust but what is commanded or forbidden by positive laws, is the same as saying that before the describing of a circle all the radii were not equal' (Montesquieu-Nugent, 2).

Natural law had been enjoying a good press when it came to Montesquieu's pen. But the Baron regarded natural law as only part of the great puzzle which constituted law's source. Positive law had to conform to natural law, but because Montesquieu observed the actual physical conditions in which men lived, he understood how, unlike natural law, these milieus varied from place to place, and, in addition, how the kinds of government formed to cope with them also reflected enormous differences. So he moved as if from the radii of his circle to these governing forms, launching the second part of his work (the tripartite division defined above) with an *a priori* statement of them.

The first emerged as Montesquieu introduced a Republic which might be either democratic or aristocratic. Even with this dual possibility the Republic held little concern for him—France was just too big. The second form was Monarchy. One would expect that he would find that this also had two forms: limited and absolute. But Montesquieu would have none of that; either Monarchy without boundaries was no Monarchy, and limited monarchy was all one could accept. The alternative and third form, Despotism, was a pejorative which Montesquieu uttered with a curl of the aristocratic lip. He allowed it for a huge empire, but for states of intermediate size the tyrant's curse had no need to be accepted. It is clear that with his avid, sociologist's interest in local color, not one panel of the power triptych was thought of in the abstract. For him, republic meant one of the ancient city states; monarchy began in those fog-bound woods of Germany and was emblematic of contemporary Western European political entities; despotism was the form of oriental powers.

Enlightenment in favor of limited monarchy quickly led to his concluding that the constitution was the most important of any factors. Montesquieu reminded his readers that limited monarchy, is defined not by a head under a crown, but by a crown under moderate positive laws enacted by a form of government resultant of—and here he would shock his readership by what came next—physical conditions like climate. Such considerations of meteorology and geography make Montesquieu excitingly up to date, a trailblazer on the way to modern social historians like Braudel or Lévi-Strauss. Of course we understand that our eighteenth century guide wants us to stay close to the central political axis, but we pause, fascinated, as, while probing northern versus southern areas, he does things like look at sheep tongues, amazed to find how their little pyramids on the surface mysteriously disappear when he freezes them. In Rabelais and Voltaire lessons on four legged ruminants lead to moral and satirical ruminations; with Montesquieu science, determination of human behavioral patterns, and legal statutes are all in a mix which will mean happiness for France.

From sheep tongues, it is not far to human nerves ending in little bundles on the skin and responding more to stimuli if the skin is relaxed, as in warm climates, where these sensations are more numerous. Stimulated himself, this leads Montesquieu ever forward: the fibers of the human frame are contracted by cold and expanded by heat. What this means, he decides, is that men in chill climates need coarse food, get "stout fibers," are slow of penetration and comprehension, are not quick but are cold blooded, constant, more self-confident, courageous, aware of superiority, less prone to vengeance, feel more secure, are more frank, less suspicious in politics, and make fewer mistakes in execution of tasks. They are better as compilers than as insightful observers.

As exhibit A Montesquieu requires the reader look at the originator Franks—those Scandian peoples of a fierce northern chill made from inhospitable rudeness, born in the cradle of pragmatic tenacity and cooperative tenancy. No government on earth was as well-tempered as theirs after their invasion of Gaul. Believing Scandinavia to be the source of liberty in Europe— "'the producer of tools that break the chains forged in the south'" (Conroy, 92)—Montesquieu may well have trusted that some Viking blood ran in his veins, too, a possibility mirrored in the Bibliothèque nationale portrait of his long Nordic face. Men in southern climates, on the other hand, have more imagination, taste, vivacity, and sensitivity. But, after this north/south allocation Montesquieu, diplomatically pushes back from determinism, offering the hopeful caveat that all those who are in danger of disadvantageous characteristics can and should resist giving in to them. Then we learn that this reconsideration is not actually a question of authorial diplomacy, but comes from a professional recognizing the power of his craft— or, to put it another way, of imparting to us human sheep, the benefit of a good shepherd's counsel. For it is law which can aid resistance to personality stereotyping, and it is the knowing the right juristic avenues which can form strong, eclectic citizens capable of writing a sophisticated political compact.

Montesquieu as a Noble

It is remarkable that an aristocratic could become so close to law's spirit—this *e pluribus unum* built on diverse customs and exterior factors winnowed down to the commonality of human beings—and then just as remarkably be led to constitutional legislation. We could have substituted "brilliantly" for "remarkably" had it occurred to Montesquieu that the *unum* of his *pluribus* factors called for majority rule based on a universal suffrage or on an equality of citizenry. Instead he sang the anthem of robe and sword nobility: judicial arbitrator and patriarch for numerous peasants; patronal wine seller; feudal opponent of uniform private substantive law. It had been a quantum leap for him just to prefer being called "Président" rather than "Baron," to learn to take liberal stands against slavery, the Inquisition, torture, religious persecution, and other abuses. However, none of it meant he wanted to be just M. de Secondat, local neighborhood attorney. He supported all that was essential to the robe, particularly the venality of offices that nourished it by bringing in new, vigorous, bourgeois lawyers, and nobles of the sword (like the Secondat family) who wanted offices and could afford to buy them. Joined at the sword hip to the crowned head, he liked to repeat: "'No monarchy, no nobility; no nobility, no monarchy'" (Montesquieu-Versini 56).

In Montesquieu's ideas for the nobility—about one percent of the population in a nation of approximately 20 million—there was progressive thinking indicative of those of the high robe where there was usually more intellect, less debauchery, and some idealism. In the first half of the eighteenth century about 1,250 judges sat in the fifteen *parlements*, and the total of all high robe men in the sovereign courts was about 2,000 to 2,300. Although they still had an exalted position, distinct in many respects from other portions of French society, their status did depend entirely on laws of kingly definition; and for a long time they, like sword aristocrats, conscious of a decline in their importance, had been seeking a new role in state business. As long ago as 1664 they had commissioned an historian to conduct a status study; it was just coming out in 1740. Montesquieu in his satiric Persian phase had become privy to the results, and he did not cringe at frontal viewing of *parlements* lying like ruins trampled under foot, the justice of their paltry governmental role reduced to the parodic act of declining to register a law. In chapter 22 of book XX (Montesquieu-Nugent 328) there is a brutally honest appraisal of the chiaroscuro now coloring aristocratic fortunes:

> In France the dignity of the long robe, which places those who wear it between the great nobility and the people, without having such shining honors as the former, has all their privileges; a dignity which, while this body, the depository of the laws, is encircled with glory, leaves the private members in a mediocrity of fortune; a dignity in which there are no other means of distinction but by a superior capacity and virtue, yet which still leaves in view one much more illustrious, the warlike nobility…

As a conservative, Montesquieu was convinced that France's true constitution, the one with which she began, had relied on the parliamentary, clerical, urban, and military buffer only to have been subverted by royal depredation. As a pre-Romantic he comprehended—long before Victor Hugo, who would love the same Germanic mists painted by Montesquieu—that the time of sword carrier rulers was over. Raising the status of *parlements* with their pedigree, burnished since the ancient councils of old Frankish kings, Montesquieu privileged their co-birth with monarchy forever obliged to consult council and be influenced by it. The Regent had tried after Louis XIV to associate the old nobility with the government by forming seven councils reporting to an eighth: the "Conseil Général de la Régence." Some nobles of the robe and some former bourgeois ministers were included, leading to the expected problem of turf friction. But the inexperienced and bored sword nobility were no longer accepted as natural representatives of the nation, and in about three years the experiment was abandoned. Montesquieu now believed with the greatest intensity that the Robe would have to save France. To do so, becoming truly noble, they would have to comprehend his primary lesson: law formed the soul of national and personal existence. It was, in the end, to build such awareness in this sacred core that the "hard to write" Books of the *Esprit* were imbued with their heroic role. The weighty Word from Brède needed to open eyes, hearts, and minds before it was too late—for France and for an old fighter entering into his sixtieth year.

Montesquieu and the History of French Law

Books XXVIII, XXX, and XXXI, roughly one quarter of the text, can hardly have been an inadvertent gesture on the part of the author. Yet they have been considered by some to be irrelevant, or, at best, something which should have been an appendix a busy reader could more or less ignore in the study of the work. Part of the problem is Montesquieu himself, who did little to aid his readers in grasping his purpose in these particular Books. Like a modern author and, unlike most of his earlier predecessors, he did provide a Preface, but it was designed as a kind of thread to carry in the legal labyrinth, a calmant reassuring any who might have become alarmed by the overpowering ideas they feared to encounter. On the other hand, though, this writing was also innovatively confessional—Montesquieu recounting how he had started the work many times only to give it up; how he had gone forward without any fixed plan; that when he once discovered the initial premises a marvelous concentration of the whole took place. It is hard to resist the end of book XXVIII where Montesquieu refreshingly touches his reader by admitting he should have been more assiduous in following the change lines throughout French jurisprudence and, disarmingly, reveals that, yes, he has offered the reader very little—treating us much like the typical tourist who goes to Egypt, looks quickly at the Pyramids, and departs for home with nothing but the single, reductive image of stony points like so many of those bizarre triangles on a sheep's tongue.

Another difficulty stems from the wording of the explanatory titles provided by Montesquieu for his Books and Chapters. Most readers balk at old words which they know now under newer meanings. For examples, Montesquieu's captions for Books XXVIII and XXX (XXXI has the same caption as XXX) make it reasonably clear that what we will get is legal history: in XXVIII an account of "civil laws" of the French, and in XXX of "feudal laws of the Franks." In Montesquieu's vocabulary "civil law" seems to mean what the continent calls today "private law." But Book XXVIII deals little with substantive private law and much with judicial organization and procedure. It is better understood as a history of the origins of the French constitution, mainly in the period from Clovis in 481 to Hugues Capet in 987. The writing does stretch to lengthy extension at the end of the Book by mentioning the thirteenth century *Code of St. Louis*, the revival of Roman law (put by Montesquieu in the first half of the twelfth century), and the fifteenth century beginning of customal writing under Charles VII.

Although Montesquieu does not help us by saying so, it appears that the purpose of all this history, mainly concerned with public provisions for the settlement of disputes, is to show that France has come through the ages as a kingdom of law and not a kingdom of arbitrary royal power. Montesquieu's depictions can generally stand up well against modern scholarship, although time has rejected some of his interpretations, such as the view of medieval men quite free to choose their law or of early grants of land being accompanied by the right to administer justice.

Some critical students of Montesquieu who do not deny the "history books" as being irrelevant, or see them as relevant but unnecessary appendices, accept them as operating illustrations (Cox, *Montesquieu and the History of French Laws*, 3) set up for the laws of social development, and discovered by him in only the second of the three parts of the work. One does not doubt that Montesquieu did see his chapter books as illustrative, but he must also have seen them as more. "Illustrations" is suggestive of a kind of uncertainty sensed in the work—that perhaps he might have picked a country other than France if he had just been sufficiently informed about it, or that the development outlined in the history books, being the result of his social laws as to, for example, climate, could have been resisted by Frenchmen and taken a different course. Instead, Montesquieu's quest was specific as to nation and to rationale. He was attempting his own personal *coup*: finding just the right key to the Bastille by understanding the constitutional essence of the *ancien régime*. Instead he found that three keys opened the door. The country functioned first under written law whose nature was learned by studying in the books of history the record of the customary practices that comprised it. Second, such law was unwritten, as well, in the sense that it was never reduced to a single official code purporting to be a complete statement of it; and, thirdly, regarded by Frenchmen as a constitution of sorts, royalist France held in its heart a binding customary public law.

Montesquieu's three history books thus stand not only as illustrations, but also as important, judgmental statements of the customary strictures which bound royal power. In this sense the history books were a crucial, unimpeachable part of the whole *Esprit* project. That Montesquieu left them to the end and wrote them in some haste does not detract from the power of their conclusion, while it affords the daring writer some protective camouflage. He was well versed in their subject matter as he started the project. However, it was the discovery and development of laws of society as regards actual law-making which would strengthen his later argument by showing it to be scientifically inevitable; the new material, he had reasonably decided, had to be undertaken before the punch line of the historic example.

Such an interpretation elucidates the post-XXVIII insertion by Montesquieu of a Book XXIX on *The Technique of Drafting Laws*. This particular Book reflects the nucleus of the whole work: a moderate demonstration of the big need for legislative restraint. Any nation which lives by laws needs to make them well, and for the judge from La Brède that meant a concise, plain, simple list of pitfalls to avoid. Among them he listed fixed sums of money (always changing in value); exceptions which crop up just to destroy the law; subversive subtlety; changes not justified by a sufficient reason; laws easy to elude; and procedures in law-making (like Roman prescripts) which lend themselves to arbitrary action.

Montesquieu's history books, it should be said, were also personal responses to other historians, and this element of the debater's riposte served as a special incentive for being as effective as possible. The question of whether royal legislative power was absolute had been around for a long time, but scholarship had been hampered by the poor state of the unedited sources and by political caution. In the 1500s after centuries of smarting over the feeling that monarchy had constantly reduced the status of the nobles, it was those nobles who had found their intellectual comfort in the writings of the Protestant Hotman (1524–1590) the pastor already met in these pages when he succeeded Cujas as professor of law at Bourges. Hotman saw French history as degenerating from the king-counselor society of the triumphant Franks, and he would have been proud of Montesquieu's caption for Book XXX: *Theory of Feudal Laws among the Franks in the Relation They Bear to the Establishment of the Monarchy*. The sovereign courts, of which the *parlements* were the leaders, were for Hotman too Catholic, and themselves too much involved in aggrandizement of royal power, to be true descendants of those free peoples from the North. On the other pro-monarchy side was Jean Bodin (1530–1596), the Parisian advocate who had studied law at Toulouse and lectured there, and who had in his 1576 political science system stressed obedience to a sovereignty which had arisen out of familial recognition. Bodin believed in witchcraft, occult numbers, and astrology, but nevertheless was a clear precursor of Montesquieu in studying money and economics and in stating how the diverse laws and institutions of differing types of humanity corresponded to climatic zones. In the next century Bodin's royal absolutism received a pulpit boost from Bossuet (1627–1704); the Catholic historian of religion and supremely gifted orator pleased his sovereign by biblically demonstrating to Louis how God's hand in Louis's velvet glove permitted total enjoyment of vast power. In the eighteenth century the utilitarian idea of the justification for absolutism had early expression (1718) from Chancellor d'Argenson, Daguesseau's successor, who promoted the King's new laws as the only way to repress abuses caused by the malice of men and the difficulties of the age.

Then, with the death of Louis XIV it became more practical to pursue public law scholarship, and two influential and divergent books were published, both of which were added to Montesquieu's enemies list for response in the *Esprit*. The author of the first was Henri, Comte de Boulainvilliers (1658–1722), a Norman down on his finances but strong in erudition after being educated like Montesquieu at the Collège de Juilly. He had served as a soldier until 1697, when he turned to the history of feudalism to support his extravagant views of the status he and his fellow nobles held in the French state. He attacked both absolute monarchy and popular government. For him feudalism was "'the masterpiece of the human mind'" (Ford 228), and he considered it astonishing that any should find monarchy sitting comfortably founded on the basis of absolute power. The Boulainvilliers works circulated only clandestinely during his lifetime but after his death were published—two in 1727 and one in 1753. Montesquieu is believed to have known Boulainvilliers and may well have been influenced by the count's own *Persian Letters*, a life of Muhammad. However, Montesquieu and others of the *robe*, once passionate for Romanizing their image, had abandoned for serious political purposes the antique romance and were now at one with men of the sword in holding that the monarchy was of Frankish rather than Roman origin. They also joined in admiration of the English, who, with rationalizing help from Locke, had achieved by 1688 a truly aristocratic control of their monarchy. Boulainvilliers, an Estates General man, unfortunately for him lost the *robe* coterie which held that in France it was the *parlements* rather than the Estates which were the institutional successors of the Frankish counselors to the king.

The second scholarly work in public law was written by Jean-Baptiste Dubos (1670–1742). A better scholar than Boulainvilliers, he had studied for the Church but, renouncing theology for public law and politics, had performed diplomatic missions for the government with such success that he was rewarded with a pension and several benefices, including the title Abbé. He wrote on Roman history, on the diplomatic position of England (distinctly predicting, in 1703, the revolt of the American colonies), and enough other subjects that he won the praise of Voltaire and election to the French Academy (1720) where he became its Perpetual Secretary. It was his three volume effort on the establishment of the French monarchy among the Gauls that in 1734 brought him to Montesquieu's attention. Dubos concluded that the Franks entered Gaul not as conquerors but by invitation of the Roman government which delegated *merum imperium* to the Frankish kings. Kings of France, as successors of these Franks, were therefore also absolute rulers exercising Roman imperial power, so that the nobles were now usurpers in declining to register the king's laws. Thus did Dubos refute both Boulainvilliers and aristocratic claims in a book so popular that it put their positions in the shade for a while. Modern scholarship does not fully support Dubos, but his erudition cannot be doubted.

Montesquieu began his Book XXX by showing Europe's feudal laws suddenly appearing full-blown without any connection to former institutions. He likened their handsome creation to an oak, requiring the historical legalist to turn truffle hound and find the root. Although the big question raised by Dubos was whether or not there had been a conquest, Montesquieu began without a doubt: conquerors of the Roman Empire had arrived from Germany. Montesquieu's typical feudal portrait placed the notorious German princes over vassals attached to their service who followed them wherever they went; but atypically he saw no fiefs, since these peoples were pastoral, not agricultural, and did not own lands. In Montesquieu's Gaul the Franks took what land they wanted, and any who opposed them were enslaved. He considered Dubos incorrect in finding that the German princes paid taxes or were only bondmen under their kings. Nor did vassals, after they were granted fiefs, usurp the jurisdictions they exercised in their seignuries; they had them lawfully from "the primitive establishment." Thus strengthened in general convictions, Montesquieu formally turned to a "few strictures on the Abbé Dubos's performance" (Montesquieu-Nugent, 205–207). The Abbé's claim that there was no conquest must have been based on a time after Clovis took and plundered the towns and defeated the Roman commander, a time when the Merovingian leader, master by force of a great part of the territory, was called by the people to sovereignty over the rest. Clovis created his own Roman dignities. And Justinian's renouncing the Empire's rights over Gaul in favor of the issue of Clovis proves nothing; Clovis was already in full control. Nor was Dubos correct in his claim that there was only one order of citizens among the Franks and no nobility.

Having disposed of Dubos, Montesquieu went on to the thesis which was to prove the validity and value of parliamentary status: Frankish tribes made up of a chief and adjunctive men holding high status led groups of wandering hunters and herdsmen, metamorphosing over time into a king and his nobles. In time, the counts were able to purchase the continuance of their offices. These fiefs, rather than handled arbitrarily by kings, sent questions to be debated in legal, pre-*parlement* assemblies. The Mayors of the Palace, taking power, then confirmed the fiefs, since it was by protecting the nobles that they could rule. Montesquieu was now in full flight and next confidently presented the sources of the ancient noble privileges: fiefs decreased royal power; fiefs were heritable and perpetual; the nobles won a law limiting their duty to fight; the kings lost their *demesnes*; the Scandinavians ravaged the kingdom. Facing the gradual dissolution of protective central power, dramatically seeking security of the local magnate, temporal or ecclesiastical, Montesquieu's noble vassalship both irrevocable and hereditary accepted the greatest vassal—for example Hugues Capet—as the transformed maker of royal decisions. The nobles' status and feudal property had thus become protected not only by "political law" (public law) but also by "civil law" (private law). With their role secure, (one can almost hear those trumpets) in triumphal march the aristocratic families gloriously entered into the French constitution via Roman law reborn in the birthing of *parlements*. Dramatic and artful, Montesquieu, knowing he was by now far outdistancing competition of Dubos and his cohorts, first allowed the *parlements* to have their due as excitingly expert law courts for deciding disputes, legal depositories rendering laws effective in their respective territories by "registering" them. No other institution in the Montesquieu century better expressed its role than these custodial, protective *parlements*—vital for law, vital for monarchy. He then rang up the next act: learned men drew charters for towns, an effort which gave them some breathing room for independence vis-à-vis the king. Finally, he again turned to the heroic nobles, this time in war, as they presented themselves loyally to the sovereign in another form of crucial organization: the army.

It had been historic trial drama. Having finished a living theatre testimony for the prosecution, and with the finest of the intermediate powers embodied in the noble parlementarian from La Brède himself, one infers there was nothing more for the *président* to say—at least, to need to say. He had pled a good cause: to restore and to sustain a system of government that he felt would better preserve for Frenchmen those public laws which protect a man's liberty, those private laws between citizen and citizen which protect a man's property, and that judicial organization and procedure which provide for enforcement of both. The moral was, we know, diluted by many sets of ears having each heard its own message, but the counselor felt at ease. Let reactionaries find a cause by refusal to reform, while free-thinkers advocating separation of powers were given the libertarian's role. Such precise definitions of public law were too risky for Montesquieu to present. He would also leave to these opposing factions the contentious working out of private contracts, details of which had long engaged the efforts of Domat, Daguesseau, and Pothier. What the Baron's landmark history books had accomplished for the sociology of law was enough to answer both Dubos and Boulainvilliers while offering important encouragement to all men of the high robe.

Montesquieu and the Sociology of Law

De l'Esprit des lois pushed the study of the sources of law well beyond the point where the secular natural lawyers had left it. Montesquieu accepted the idea that man's essential nature is the same everywhere and at all times and that it implies natural laws which are universal and inevitable. Understanding how these basic concepts needed their positive law reinforcement was enriched and amplified by his close observation of actual human societies. Climate, topography, state constitutions, morals, customs, commerce, population, religion—all were lights Montesquieu held boldly before him to illumine the darkness controlling positive laws and to discover the natural legal matrix behind the whole.

Descartes had considered voluntary communities too varied and uncertain for the methods of exact science, but that had not deterred thinkers from contemplating the problem. Montesquieu made a good beginning, in the method, if not in all the results, yet his ideas remained premature. The empirical work of examining the earth's physical geography and its human societies had in his time not progressed so far as was necessary fully to validate his conclusions. Nevertheless, in the broad view, his groundbreaking attempt to apply to the laws made by human societies those methods of physical science already developed in the course of the seventeenth century's scientific revolution was breathtakingly on target. His was a brave, noble, one-man approach to enlightenment encyclopedism, and in his studying human societies in a positivistic, utilitarian way, he was moving to collect the earth's knowledge and make manifest its order, just as the Diderot group with its seventeen folio volumes of 17,818 articles plus eleven folio volumes of 2,885 engraved illustrations, the work of 272 contributors, writers, and engravers.

It is not surprising that Montesquieu's competition came out of the larger picture of this Diderot team, specifically from the Marquis de Condorcet, who was attempting to elucidate specific social behavior. Although not a lawyer by training, the noted mathematician was seeking to discover the law in science which controlled human groups and permitted human perfectibility. His orientation toward specific applications was especially encouraged by the fact that he was a friend of Anne Robert Jacques Turgot (1721–1781), comptroller general (1774–1776) under Louis XVI. Diverging from Montesquieu's parlementary engine, the Turgot program was radical: the complete abolition of taxation privileges in an enlightened absolutism unimpeded by the *parlements*. They, as under Louis XIV, would be confined to strictly judicial functions. Royal support was to derive from a complex system for local municipal government in which landowners would vote (with no more distinctions among the three social orders) in a four tier system of assemblies, the fourth level being a *grande municipalité* which would administer taxation but not legislate.

Condorcet's connection with Turgot led him into active participation in politics, the only *philosophe* of the Enlightenment to do so. Supporter of republican causes both at home and in the American colonies, he was the draftsman of the liberal Girondin constitution of 1793, and it was his defense of it against the Jacobin constitution that led to his denunciation, imprisonment, and self-inflicted death. A

Marquis de Condorcet
Courtesy of The Bridgeman Art Library

traveler may contemplate him today as the Marquis in bronze standing pensively on the Quai de Conti, near the site of the former Mint of which Turgot had made him director.

Condorcet evidently had studied with care Montesquieu's *De l'Esprit des lois*. He agreed that there are necessary and invariable laws devolving from man's nature. On the other hand, he decided Montesquieu's attempt to find a social science was a failure: although the second part of *Esprit* had traced the historical variation of customs and legislation, there had been no demonstration of their accord with the invariable, reasonable principles derived from human nature. Nor had Montesquieu offered a criterion for distinguishing just from unjust, a failure resulting from his method of collecting examples without an analysis to rationalize them (Baker, *Condorcet, From Natural Philosophy to Social Mathematics*, 222).

Condorcet proposed justice as simply the equality from which flow moral propositions as certain as the truths of mathematics. Trying hard to apply this approach, Condorcet did intensive research in probability theory to show that the voting choices of a majority would be correct. He held that the calculus of probabilities offers the sought after connection between physical science and social science, because all the truths of experience are merely probable. In social science, where there is no laboratory experiment, observation is difficult, and the results are less constant. Yet this probability can be evaluated mathematically by probability theory, and these mathematical evaluations applied even to the degree of probability can be relied upon. Condorcet admitted that the certainty of mathematics was not free from probability. $2 + 2 = 4$ is validated easily, but a right triangle's $a^2 = b^2 + c^2$ requires too much mental accuracy to be more than probable. He did, however, argue that good laws are the same for all men: if it seems there is a necessity for them to differ, for they either deal with matters not fit for legislation or they reflect prejudice and bad habits (Baker, 182; 222). Hence the lesson drawn for lawyers: the grounds and reasons of a law should be separated from text and studied by mathematicians, versed—as was Condorcet—in the calculus of probabilities.

Anti-mathematical Montesquieu along with many an *avocat* would have been loath to accept Condorcet's belief that probability theory held out the only hope of an exact means of bringing laws into accord with the first principles of justice. Baker observes that this legal philosophy actually appears to contradict Condorcet's own general positivism in science, although Condorcet was at pains to show its logic. He insisted that the rights of man can all be deduced from the truth that "man is a sensitive being, capable of reasoning and acquiring moral ideas" (Baker, 222–223). In 1791 the geometer willingly took up the suggestion of his young friend Garat that his work should be called "social science." Yet, in a way, Condorcet was trying, by the application of physical and mathematical science, to return the study to Grotius, while Montesquieu's attempts at the comparative study of human societies were geared to forward motion away from the Dutchman. With important publications during his lifetime and posthumously, Condorcet further perpetuated his name by bequeathing his passion for perfectibility and progress to the open arms of the nineteenth century.

While Montesquieu's pioneering work toward the beginnings of a science of society was not followed up in the rest of his lifetime, he, too, would find in this ensuing century's work of eccentric compatriot, Auguste Comte (1798–1857), a rebirth as innovator and progenitor. Yearning for the reconstruction of a stable social order upon the ruins of the revolutionary scheme of things and accepting Condorcet's philosophy of progress, while totally rejecting the possibility one could mathematize social phenomena, the young Comte as early as 1819 noted down his refusal of any attempts to make social science positive by basing it on some other science. Comte, having proceeded in 1822 to reinterpret Condorcet, made instead his *rapprochement* with predecessor Montesquieu by saying that man in history has been subject to a natural law of development producing a succession of orders each of which in its time prescribed the political action then possible. To distinguish these orders from Condorcet's, Comte called such developmental law "sociology" and is considered the founder of that discipline; his acknowledgement of Montesquieu was merely as a predecessor.

Another Frenchman, Émile Durkheim (1858–1917), allowed Montesquieu center stage when in 1892 he wrote as his thesis a Latin appreciation. Durkheim, successor to Comte, recreated sociology through study according to methods rather than mathematics. Peyre in his introduction wrote (vi) that "Durkheim was an austere and forbidding professor tirelessly addicted to his life work," and went on to praise the "passion in his logic and intense devotion to a moral and even patriotic ideal behind his self-effacing research."

In appraising Montesquieu's work Durkheim began by stating his own rules for studying social science and then going backward to point out how far Montesquieu followed them. Durkheim centers the fundamental premise for such study on laws, customs, religions, and other social phenomena which shall be seen as things—the same "things" as studied scientifically in physics, yet not like the unreal "things" studied in mathematics. To be studied as a science a subject matter must be definite, and the Montesquieu laws, customs, religions, etc., make the cut for qualification. Durkheim obviously is defensive for the status of social science, pointing out that since no one questions any more the possibility of a "natural science" like physics, "there is no reason why social science should not enjoy the same status." Because social phenomena are "governed by the same laws as the rest of the universe" (Durkheim, 10–11), we have to get away from the idea of the old philosophers that this definite subject matter is dependent on human will and that the study is, therefore, only an analysis of what the will should strive for. That is art, not science, and so also, is action based on personal bent. Social science, like any other science, takes out the subjectivity and pushes the limits of knowledge.

Yet if the items of observed data are each unique, there can be no scientific study of a subject; it must be possible to discern types based on a finite number of common characteristics. And if there are types, there are causes that produce the same effects everywhere. These are efficient causes (the factuality of the types engender the laws, etc.) and not final causes (the lawgiver sees that the society needs the laws and makes them for it). Moreover, both the types and the laws engendered have to be perceivable by a method, even though the diversity and fluidity of social phenomena make this hard for social science. Where experiment is not possible, the method is forced to "issue from the science." Social science does, however, offer its substitute for experiment: one can compare many forms of a thing, and "what is constant is a law" (Durkheim 13, 51). We must, urged Durkheim, begin marshalling all the relevant facts and inducing relationships from them; only afterwards should we test our work by interpreting deductively what we have induced. Finally, applying the eighteenth turned nineteenth century idea of progress, we will be able to judge later societies as superior to their predecessors.

Building upon the major blocks of *De l'Esprit des lois*, Durkheim, who ignores the argument about the constitutions in the Baron's thorny "history books," accepts that Montesquieu correctly defined subject matter and purpose as the study of the "laws and customs of all peoples." By not attempting to be a legislator finding fault, he was therefore sensitive to comprehend the causes of social phenomena. In Durkheim's eyes, the Montesquieu fault lay in stooping from time to time into art, though, admittedly, never enough to make art his master. For example, he would show—in his science mode—that democracy is possible only in small states, but then turn about—the artistic mode—and write that a democracy should not overextend.

Montesquieu also confused his case to some extent by positing a group of laws—his "laws of nature"—which had no direct bearing on his subject matter and which only flowed from the nature of man's desire to preserve life, eat, procreate, etc. Approval is given Montesquieu's considering that the "law of nations, civil law, and political law" (what Durkheim calls "the laws relating to society") are the true objects of his inquiry. However, Durkheim, patronizingly excusing Montesquieu for following the vocabulary habits of his age, sharply distinguishing them from his own "laws of nature," preferring (Durkheim, 19) to call such laws of society "natural." Durkheim supports Montesquieu for regarding his law of nations as a "natural" set, derived not from the nature of man but from the nature of the social organism.

Thus, Durkheim accepts Montesquieu as fundamentally correct in beginning with the differentiation of types of societies. He admits there is a peculiarity since Montesquieu, following perhaps the weighty precedent of Aristotle, did differentiation indirectly—literally classifying not societies but the way they are governed. Yet this indirection can work from Durkheim's point of view, because each type of government has its distinction: number, arrangement, and cohesion of parts; size; character of citizens; and customs, religions, families, marriage, rearing of children, crimes, and punishments. To Montesquieu, and to others at first sight, the form of government seemed to be the essential property of a society from which all others flow. Durkheim states (Durkheim, 33) that the truth is that the "form of government does not determine the nature of a society." The variant which clashes severely with twenty-first century approaches to "nation building"—a democratic government promotes a democratic polity—posits social structure which can remain even when the nature of the supreme power changes, and vice versa. But Durkheim quickly reverts to admiration, finding the Montesquieu classification of social life as the most penetrating and true part of his work, even though he overlooked those living by hunting or grazing. In more pro and con Durkheim supports Montesquieu for considering the major cause of the form of society to be its volume, even though he failed to see that the critical volume is the number in a relationship—for instance, a large state can have many relationships so that the size of the overall population of the state may have little effect. Accepting excellent thinking on the part of Montesquieu as regards the lesser importance of topography and climate, Durkheim is critical of a baronial tendency to exaggerate the size of their influence.

Durkheim also faults Montesquieu for incorrectly presenting a lawgiver as indispensable maker of the laws; "Laws are not devices that the lawgiver thinks up because they seem to be in harmony with the nature of the society" retorts Durkheim (Durkheim, 43). Critical of limiting inquiry to philosophical final causes, Durkheim prefers we see laws springing most often from events that engender them by a kind of physical necessity. As society's communal life assumes its particular form, this is expressed by the laws. Montesquieu, in Durkheim's view, erroneously saw the equality and frugality of Republican Rome as imposed by the laws, when, in fact, they were, on the contrary, the result of a way of life consolidated by the laws. Montesquieu failed to see that laws in their nature are the same as customs—created by causes of which men are not conscious—and that laws simply derive from customs in sharper definition.

Durkheim does admire the fact that induction first appeared in Montesquieu's social science, but he is uncomfortable with what he sees as Montesquieu's weak process. In a kind of accusatory 'You, Montesquieu, you're no Condorcet,' Durkheim criticizes the founder's avoidance of beginning with the facts, observing a relation, and then interpreting it. Hence Montesquieu did not follow through on his promise to deal with social science in an almost mathematical way. Although he gathered a large body of data, he proceeded by trying to deduce from the essence of man, society, trade, religions, the same idea he had formed in looking at the facts. Then piling on ever more confirming detail, he ended up giving deduction a greater role than science permits.

At the same time, the Montesquieu achievement was excellent, for he perceived that progress in the study of social science depends on establishing that its laws are, like the other laws of nature, found by the same method, with induction being the primary mover. Fortunately, Montesquieu had the astuteness to understand that neither religion, law, morality, trade, nor administration can be classified separately. They function as a whole, the subject of a definite field of endeavor. Would that our trailblazer had been prescient and confident enough to call his subject a definite science with its own method and name, one embracing all social phenomena. However, Durkheim does the job for him, admitting that although it is always wrong to say that only one particular thinker gave birth to a set of observed data, one must indeed credit Montesquieu with being the first to lay down the fundamental principles of social science (Durkheim, 61). Durkheim cannot resist the parting shot. With unabashed pride in being the honest apologist and hagiographic disciple Montesquieu would have loved, he dispatches Comte as more than a bit of an ingrate, forever professionally weakened by not having fully acknowledged the founding father of a great discipline crucial to any student of the law and its prophets.

Death of Montesquieu

Growing older Montesquieu wrote: "'I have but two things to do: to learn to be ill and to die.'" At home at La Brède from July to December 1754, the sixty-five year old thinker appears to have had an uncanny sense that it was time to start those lessons. Before he returned to Paris he terminated his lease, discharged his housekeeper, and decided that what remained of life would be lived at La Brède. It was too late. On 29 January 1755, still in Paris, he was caught in the midst of an epidemic; overcome by a fever which quickly became serious, he was bled so excessively that he became delirious. In an interval of Roman lucidity he philosophized: "'This is not as frightful as they think.'" He had two doctors, two secretaries, and a throng of visitors, a few in constant attendance. Louis XV made inquiry with both royal pomp and personal sadness. The parish priest called, also, but was excluded on this, his first visit. It was too harsh an exit strategy. Reconsidering, Montesquieu ordered that the man of God be admitted next time and asked as well that his old friend, the Jesuit Cartel, tutor to his son, come with all haste to serve as his confessor.

As news of his condition spread, Europe itself gave full attention. The Pope was intensely interested and asked for a report of this famous battle being fought in the sick room between the Church and the *philosophes*. Cartel, sensing the Roman repercusssions, selected an Irish Jesuit, Routh, a man known to Montesquieu, to receive the confession on 5 February. Routh, going outside of standard procedure, demanded permission to publish the dying man's final sentiments. He questioned Montesquieu closely about his attitude toward the mysteries of religion, about his submission to the decisions of the Church, and about his belief. He would report later to the Pontiff that he received complete satisfaction. Routh now sent for the parish priest to return and administer last rites. Looking keenly into the celebrated face before him the curé told Montesquieu: "'You understand better than others how great God is and...' Montesquieu, quickly interrupting, finished the thought, '...and how small men are'" (Shackleton 392–393, 395). The last rites were administered. Routh stayed on. Witnesses as to the rest differ slightly, but the accounts are persuasive that in Montesquieu's final five days, after the last rites, the Jesuit overstepped his welcome and attempted to both to extract a literary repentance from Montesquieu and to take possession of the Montesquieu papers, including a manuscript of corrections for the *Lettres persanes*. It was too hard a push and remained unsuccessful. At last, on 10 February, all travels upon the oriental carpet and inside the inquiring brain ceased. Montesquieu never went home again and was buried in Paris in the church of Saint Sulpice. The man who is generally regarded as having a tenacity, love of system, and power of organization equal to those of Diderot—part of whose encyclopedic genius lay in recognizing Montesquieu's merit—was attended to his rest by the Encyclopedist himself.

During the Revolution, when, had he lived, he probably would have been welcomed into the salon of Mme la Guillotine, Montesquieu the moderate paid a further price for his views on the French constitution: his tomb was profaned by the mob and the remains lost. One imagines that Mme de Tencin's dear *petit Romain*, his spirit's eyes refreshed by the divine ordinances he had professed at death, might well have seen that the spirit and the law of these angry rebels were also a legacy of a remarkable work in progress to this day.

Prise de la Bastille le 14 Juillet (Storming of the Bastille, July 14)
Courtesy of Yale University Art Gallery, Everett V. Meeks, B.A. 1901, Fund

PART 18

Beliefs and Institutions in Enlightenment, Revolution, and Empire

The Enlightenment

Introduction

Much to Montesquieu's disappointment the French crown differed from its English counterpart in sharing power with nobles who could keep their privileges but not be exclusive. Their ranks were constantly refreshed from the talented and wealthy middle class who for so many centuries had been permitted to thrive and invited to serve their king. Under Louis XIV the monarchy seemed to have achieved the long Capetian quest for the unity required to establish a government of nearly absolute centralization, but in fact the ensuing bureaucratic tangle had rapidly turned the country into a nightmare of red tape. There were multiple provinces and *parlements*; law diverged among canon, Roman, and customary with society's privileged orders based on inequality before it all. As numerous corporations were formed for nearly every function not performed by government, there grew a choking tangle of unequal and overlapping structures—administrative, municipal, judicial, and religious—each with its own internal barriers of restriction. The confusion led to frequent pained outcries from frustrated lawyers trying to cut through the underbrush in order to answer a client's needs with moderate expenditure of time and money. It has been questioned (Delderfield, *Napoleon's Marshals,* 2) whether the Revolution would have gone forward at all had not able professional men in every endeavor, especially the armed forces which had suffered too many defeats, been so thoroughly discouraged by this vast Bourbon inefficiency.

France was a fertile land who could at least feed herself with reasonably good harvests; by adopting the new English technology and rapidly industrializing there were to be several bright years. Louis XV fortuitously left the government mostly to Cardinal Fleury, one of those many bright royal ministers who in reign after reign regularly offset royal incompetence or, admittedly less often, supplemented royal capacity. The nation bustled with clever artisans and dynamic traders; its intellectual life, still more outside than inside the instruction of drone-prone universities, was brilliant and flourishing. Paired with this ideating effervescence the patient, careful scholar-lawyers like Daguesseau, Pothier, and Montesquieu made their clever borrowings from natural law philosophy in order to find common threads in French private law.

How, though, could these public servants cope with the consequences of France's absurd system of royal government finance? There was no overall budget; each of several ministers was empowered to borrow independently; a particularly intermingled confusion of royal personal expenses—especially those of the king's mistresses—joined government outlays in growing rapidly worse. Then arrived several years of bad harvests when the utter misery of famine fell heavily upon the people. What, one can not help but wonder, would have happened to the French monarchy had it practiced after 1750 at least a minimum of financial prudence along with its efforts at administrative and judicial reorganization? Could it have made a

Louis XV, King of France
Courtesy of National Gallery of Art, Washington

peaceful transition to the constitutional government that its people were inevitably and irresistibly going to demand?

When the young Louis XVI ascended the throne in 1774 at age twenty, his ministers decided to punish England for, among other things, French defeat in the French and Indian war. This chance for revenge would ironically forge Franco-American freedoms. The colonists, no longer burdened by violent incursions from the French and their native American allies, had less need for England's army and navy and could indulge in a more independent attitude toward the determination of George III and Lord North to raise revenue across the Atlantic. Of course, when American rebellion frustrated such hopes for any immediate cash influx, England felt compelled to defend to the last the principle of Parliamentary control over the American colonies. But because the French Ministers saw French assistance at a critical juncture might enable the colonies to deal England a mighty blow, they were ready to seize the propitious moment, launching much needed land and sea forces to the struggles on American shores. All schoolchildren who know they accomplished their purpose know as well that the cost in money, especially for a rebuilt navy, broke the French bank. With royal government funds foundering and the French ministers incapable of raising more revenues on the king's own authority, the dreaded

Cardinal Fleury
Courtesy of National Gallery of Art, Washington

call up of Estates General brought forth the 1789 vintage grapes of wrath, fermenting since 1614.

The scene is part of collective memory, wrapped up in thoughts of Tennis Court Oaths and an incorruptible pea-green Robespierre. As the representatives of the clergy and nobles arrived in Paris for the meetings, alongside them came vigorous and intelligent men of the bourgeois Third Estate, a class far more numerous and a cadre which, energized, found ways to dominate the Assembly. There now ensued from 1789 to 1795 one of the world's greatest efforts in positive law. Revolution politicized everything, and everything considered wrong was put out for remedy by central state power expressed in legislation.

Good lawmaking, though, needs careful procedure and in-depth preparation; the revolutionary leaders between 1789 and 1798 were frantically seeking a constitution, and the agenda of public and private law they sought was too ambitious for the means at their disposal. It would be more than the Bastille pulled down: the heights of monarchy, the depths of classes with unequal legal standing, the feudal structure of social engineering, the provinces, the *parlements*, and royal courts—all became the house of cards, destroyed. Since these major societal structures were the well-known pivots on which legal philosophy had been built, and when they were taken down by the women and men wearing their red-white- and blue *cocardes*, down came universities, colleges, regular clergy, church autonomy and property, the *Ordre des avocats*, the trade organizations. When the dust and gore cleared, one could see decapitation even of those serene stone saints' heads which for centuries had on Church structures been so hierarchically emblematic of *ecclesia* leading the law.

The *Philosophes*

Legend has been made of the succession of assemblies, shifts in power from one interest to another, and of the cruel social sanitizing in which often absurd *ad hoc* revolutionary courts, with only a nod toward legal propriety, transformed political dissent or even the possibility of it into treason punished by death. In this, again another of history's ironies, terrorism erroneously seized upon the hard eighteenth century work of legal philosophy. That hard work being our focus, its crucial steps here bear some repetition and clarification.

We know that by taking cues from Montesquieu and his cadre of eighteenth century thinkers had come a kind of unorganized yet highly successful and positive early version of The Manhattan Project. Newton had played Einstein's role in exploding the energetically and excitingly fashioned intellectual bomb of Enlightenment. The fallout idea of reason penetrated French thinking about how society should work and the manner in which humans should discover new knowledge about the world and their place in it. Before it became momentarily warped at the guillotine, this thought of a highly articulate group of thinkers became the lucid and lucent offering of a new and right way. Such light, from broadly ranging speculation to innovative propositions, has turned this time forever into the legendary "*siècle des lumières*," or century of the enlightened.

There were other parallel realities. For some, eating a Nominalist cake meant the life of the mind hardly existed except to prove the power of materialism. Others, kin to the Realists, were strong apostles of natural law. Montesquieu had broken the ground in their movement, along with Bayle and his own encyclopedic dictionary and the centenarian academician Fontenelle (1657–1757). As Descartes and the seventeenth century had sought to apply the method of mathematics to explore the physical world and humanity's place in it, so the disparate yet fraternal order of *philosophes* tried to apply the Newtonian method of empirical science—observation, induction, hypothesis, deduction—to society. Voltaire, Diderot, and Jean LeRond d'Alembert along with their wealthy promoter Baron Paul d'Holbach were all in this crucial discipleship. And, since iconoclasm loves the fringes of any movement, there stood Rousseau (1723–1778), living as a self-fostered image of the "different yet equal" Jean-Jacques.

Rousseau remains a separate type of mind whose difference allowed moving both in and out of the thought world of the *philosophes* while holding even to the iconography on his tomb a torch for natural egalitarians to follow. He violently quarreled with and dissociated himself from the encyclopedists and d'Holbach, stressing the role of passions and the inviolate feelings of the individual human life.

Denis Diderot
*Courtesy of Yale University Art Gallery,
Gift of Mrs. Charles Seymour Jr. in memory of her husband*

Still, his very belief in a subjective, natural man impelled him toward ideas which imparted a powerful group confidence to the revolutionaries. From him they grasped a way to transform government and society, opening a way to the centralized state, even to a democratized *Civil Code*. His peculiar ideas about the General Will—although impractical for France—amounted to something akin to *carte blanche* for natural law.

None of the leading *philosophes* was a university professor. The renunciation of Descartes had not yet captured the academy's interest, and it was still the prestige of an Aristotle born in the fourth century before Christ which remained immense. Thus if we except d'Holbach's 1773 attempt at a social system, these promoters of a new law were not builders of epistemological structures like those of the seventeenth century. Their vehicles were not formal treatises but took shape in an exciting variety—novels and plays, poems and pamphlets, histories and essays. Any more or less systematic "philosophy" therefore could only be gleaned from publications never revised and without aim at controlled consistency. The point of commonality could often only be that these were minds for whom rationality had been co-opted for serving the "science of man." They believed that starting out on their own with the light of Newtonian achievements, which would have dazzled the ancients, could

Portrait of J.J. Rousseau
Courtesy of Yale University Art Gallery, Arts of the Book Collection Transfer

ultimately reveal more truth than any dialogue of Plato. Nor did the gothic, barbarian Middle Ages have anything to teach them. And Augustine, Aquinas, Ockham?

For the eighteenth century thought process they meant nearly nothing, since their approach had been along the road of metaphysics, and the *philosophes* had no doubt that such a road was but a hermeneutic blind alley. *Philosophes* parted company with Cartesianism, too, because, along with the technique of deduction from "self-evident" ideas as started by Descartes and continued by many like Daguesseau, they rejected the concept of "innate ideas." But when it came to institutions of government, education, and human social science it would be Rousseau and the equally difficult to classify Montesquieu who had the exceptional flexibility to transmit their discoveries far into the future, from the succeeding nineteenth century to us in the twenty-first.

To be a card-carrying *philosophe* meant believing in freedom for religious thinking. Some were deists, a few were atheists. Voltaire, who believed in God and in the social benefit of religion, echoed Montesquieu's objective support of religion but was a bit more clever, saying that if God did not exist it would be necessary to invent him. God did not mean Rome, however, and in the seventy volumes of his work Voltaire led the attack on Catholic priests and priestly doctrines with a devastating wit and penetrating lucidity. Rejecting privileged orders, Rousseau also denied the established Church and clergy who alone were permitted administration of revealed religion. This pertinacious attack on the churches, both Catholic and Protestant but more on the former as the established church in France, was a major event, hardly given adequate weight by a few sentences here. The Reformation had come from a devout churchman who intended to lead mankind nearer to what he saw as true Catholic faith rather than away from it. But now Luther's reform was not enough. Brilliant writers with an attitude and an audience wanted to put an end to the immense institution—as well as its Protestant off-shoots—which had dominated European thought for 1,500 years. They could not care less that the cross was a mighty legal fortress which sheltered the private law of marriage, successions, and even pretensions as to contracts.

For every libertarian parry came a thrust from an equally partisan opposition. In addition to the expectable anger of crown, nobles, and clerics, came strong naysayers among the *philosophes*' own Third Estate ranks. From the early days it became obvious that the offer of rationales for a new French society in which the bourgeoisie would control failed to appeal to all these middle class rulers-to-be. On the one hand, there were the *avocats* like Robespierre who not only were ready soon after 1789 for a democratic republic based on law and the suffrage of property owners, but more than that stood prepared to protect against counter-revolution by transforming France into a dictatorship in which the rule of law would be, in effect, suspended. At the other extreme, most bourgeois (with many an *avocat* among them) were, at least in 1789, monarchists and loyal Catholics, too. Like Montesquieu they were ready for a constitution with balances against royal power, for canceling noble *and* clerical privileges, for equality before the law, and for economic freedom based on the protection of property and the efficient enforcement of contracts. Yet despite this prodigious agenda, they certainly did not want either a violent revolution or an answering counter-revolution; nor did many want abolition of professional and trade associations like the *Ordre des avocats* and the guilds, or permanent closing of the doors of academe.

Therefore, as time went on these groups within the middle increased their resistance to the *philosophes*, for in them they discerned responsibility for a disturbing growth of radicalism in the successive assemblies. It would be especially the moderate *avocat* intelligentsia who found themselves more and more directly offended by attacks made on the *parlements*, long held dear as the base of the legal profession. Philosophical critiques of the diversity of existing laws hit a second sore spot; these, after all, although needing some reform, were nevertheless the lawyers' stock in trade, a codified resource they did not want to eliminate in the red flag name of natural law. What is more, once bourgeois colleagues who had won the top *robe* prize as *conseiller au parlement* were, of course, even less enthusiastic, for they had paid dearly for their new noble offices and easeful practice in positive law.

Voltaire
*Courtesy of Yale University Art Gallery,
Gift of Dr. M. J. Sharpe for the Richard Sharpe V (1873s) Collection*

For such reasons it came down to a matter of picking and choosing the provocative new minds to create ideas which might possibly serve self-interest. Montesquieu's learned defense of the *parlements* could be eagerly embraced, while his natural law and his empiricism were generally neglected. Although none of the obvious Enlightenment leaders was a trained lawyer, all attracted attention for their fascination with public law as manifested in the organization of the State. Voltaire and others like him had as well special concern for the reform of criminal law and procedure. Admittedly, none was particularly drawn to private law, and indeed, some who should have been better informed were quite lacking in even rudimentary knowledge. It is worth repeating here those blunt phrases of *philosophe* Diderot when speaking to Catherine the Great. The reader will recall these negative, choleric phrases in which France's global intellect displayed, instead, lamentable ignorance:

> Our [the French] faculty of law is miserable. They don't read there a word of French law; no more of the law of peoples than if there were none; nothing of our Code neither civil nor criminal; nothing of our procedure; nothing of our laws; nothing of our customs; nothing of the constitutions of the state; nothing of the law of Sovereigns; nothing of that of subjects; nothing of liberty, property, no more of

offices and contracts. With what do they occupy themselves then? They occupy themselves with Roman law in all its branches, law which has almost no relation to ours (De Curzon, 322).

However, whatever their allure or their negative vibrations the *philosophes* were to be the semi-official rationalizers of all those social changes sought by the middle class. One *philosophe* group or another dominated the successive assemblies of the Revolution that centralized France. They supported Napoleon's *coup d'état* in 1798 that completed the process, and that drafted the *Civil Code*. In general, the *philosophes* agreed on certain fundamental premises all quickly achieved by the Revolutionary assemblies before final incorporation as bases in the new *Code*. They favored reduction of French society to a single class of citizens, each of whom would have equal status before the law. They supported elimination of the special financial, political, and social privileges enjoyed by nobles and churchmen. They argued to suppress canon law's unique jurisdiction. Likewise, they favored economic liberty protected by enforcing the two basic contracts such liberty permitted them to make: to acquire and own property and to carry on transactions involving it.

The new men of the new thought were not disturbed about excepting inequality of property. They saw it as part and parcel of unequal levels in intelligence and work product. What they wanted above all was an efficient state, a judiciary and bureaucracy manned by paid professionals who did not "own" their jobs and, therefore, could and would give prompt service without legal bribes; such a group effort should, it was believed, be rationally organized so that a citizen would know at the start with what agency he was supposed to deal. Finally, it bears repeating that nearly all the new intellectuals believed in the secular natural law for which this period may well be considered the apogee. They had no doubt this non-institutional *ius gentium* supported their views. In their optimistic opinion the job of government was to discern and put into effect natural law; if rationality were permitted control of the state, the natural law plus rationality then could assure progress. Convinced that as a result of their work France had at last arrived at knowledge of the right way, these *philosophes* literally shot down the Holy chrismatory dove hovering over crowns since Clovis. As it fell with a thud, it brought down with it the idea that kings rule by divine right. Under the Montesquieu shadow *philosophes* instead chose, not democratic voting, but an intermediary power route—kingly action in council—as the best way to put the agenda of enlightened rationality into effect.

If France had in fact been ruled by despots ready for such enlightenment, these ideas might have been transferred into practice without a violent revolution. But the Louis trio were neither enlightened nor despots. The un-illumined Sun XIV had become increasingly devoted to a stiff Jesuit line and an immovable weight of one dour wife plus one insistent Catholic Church. The Well-Beloved XV, except for occasional bursts of energy, preferred idleness with his mistresses and easy tolerance of Catholicism to laboring at government; while XVI, the Citizen Capet, who toward his life's tragic end was actually approving many enlightenment ideas, including

Charles Alexandre de Calonne
Courtesy of The Bridgeman Art Library

reduction of the Church's financial clout, remained committed to a pampered Queen and divine right. These monarchs, like kings for centuries, had grown up hearing many Roman law legists proclaim them successors to the emperors of Rome—a highly gratifying conceit which they each had at once translated into nobly suggestive equestrian statuary. Yet none could in fact play antiquity's despot because the lawyers in the *parlements* and their supporters held fast, as we know, to the old Northern idea that the king could act only with their advice. Except for a long period under Louis XIV, when royal opinion still held influence, and a short term at the end of the reign (1771–1774) under Louis XV, *parlements* doggedly maintained their right to decline to register the king's legislation, whenever, as they said, his advisors had transgressed the "king's religion." This negativism was especially true during the crucial years of Louis XVI (1774–1789), when the King finally became amenable to the very reforms which were going to be made law by the Revolution.

Among the continental powers, there were despots who did have enough power to draft and enact new law. Thus, well before it was the mode, Bavarians completed a criminal code (1751), a code of civil procedure (1753), and a code of private law (1756). Despite Voltaire's popular success while resident sage at Frederick's court, philosophical influences there came instead from two *Christians*—Christian Wolff

(1679–1754), a seventeenth century-style thinker whose natural law ideas had been influenced by Grotius and Pufendorf, and Christian Thomasius (1655–1728), the famous Halle reformer. In Prussia a code prepared in concerted drafting efforts undertaken in 1713, 1738, 1746, and 1780, with publication finally in 1794 (a code of civil procedure was completed in 1793), was made under Wolff's natural law influence. The result was that Rhenish codes included vital features in precedence to the French *philosophes*: the very necessity of a legal code's existence; the duty to publish so all can read it, hence the requirement it should, therefore, be written in German; the proviso that doubtful points should be settled by reason rather than by ancient authority; the right of all agreements to be enforced; and the entitlement that damage would give rise to reparation.

Fredrick II always thought that the law should be clear and simple, yet at the same time with enough comforting detail so that a citizen would never need a lawyer. To help in the clarifying process, a permanent legislative commission was devised to tell the King what amendatory action might be needed from time to time. Frederick knew exactly what he wanted and did not want, and when a draft of the Prussian code was placed in his hands he pronounced it, probably echoing Montesquieu, far too thick. The final form did not correct this amplitude, but retained instead 16,000 detailed provisions while at the same time adding a strong dose of discomfiting paternalism (Merryman, *The Civil Law Tradition: An Introduction to the Legal Systems of Western Europe and Latin America,* 30, 40). On the other hand, the Austrian code of 1811, the result of efforts begun in 1753 and continued in 1772 and 1786, was at last a document both simple and uncluttered, its broad brush strokes easily allowing any future development. It bears repeating that throughout these legal endeavors, neither French nor German philosophers found any of the leaders who appeared willing to sponsor study, groundwork, and codification, to be equally desirous about abolishing their nobilities or accepting the ideas of popular sovereignty and democratic structures. Inside all the crowned heads lay just one request: uniformity of law in the disparate territories each controlled. It was a credo in stone until the day of a crumbling Bastille.

The Physiocrats

Amidst the many new thinkers of the Enlightenment, physiocrats immediately attract a lawyer's attention for their efforts to discover the natural laws of society and then to imbricate them into positive state laws of public policy. The program is the same one which preoccupied Montesquieu, Condorcet, and their followers. Initially calling themselves *les économistes*, the physiocrats' influential early lobbying had a direct link to proposals by royal Controller of Finances Charles de Calonne for serious reforms in French taxation. These visionaries of *laissez-faire* went on to become important enough in inspiring fiery leaders of change that they must be considered as a bona fide wing of the Revolutionary movement. Although in the Revolution itself, when Physiocratic influence proved destructive, their basic tenets spoke to a constructive program in favor of freedom of industry and commerce and encouragement of liberal agricultural reform.

The leader of these thinkers was François Quesnay (1694–1774). A surgeon who after 1744 became the first consulting physician to Louis XV at Versailles, he was esteemed by the King, not only as a man of medicine, but also as a profound intellect. Gradually, Quesnay, ignoring court intrigues, began to hold his own court, as it were, filling his Entresol rooms with those eager to hear more about a fascinating prescription for societal improvement through methods of production. He undertook collaboration with professional economist Jean de Gournay (1712–1759), later to be joined by the elder Mirabeau, Baudeau, LeTrosne, Morellet, Mercier Larivière, and DuPont de Nemours who added his own explosive, charismatic ideas before crossing the Atlantic to found America's Dupont powder mill fortune. Adam Smith would pay high tribute to this talented group, as would France herself when Turgot, Quesnay's protégé, rose to become Controller General. In 1758 Quesnay published a *Tableau économique*, a formulization praised by DuPont de Nemours for its ambitious program and structural clarity "'which serves to calculate...the effect of all operations relative to riches, together with an explication of it, and the General Maxims of Political Economy'" (Baumer, 441). Quesnay's prestige was recognized when he was asked to contribute an article on political economy to the Encyclopedia. Mercier Larivière purportedly was developing Quesnay's ideas when he wrote *The Natural and Essential Order of Political Societies*. As is so often the case in supposedly landmark work, the principles of Quesnay had, in truth, been put forward well before in 1755 by Philip Cantillon, a French merchant banker of Irish extraction. Quesnay and his cohort simply gave them a strong—Einaudi (Einaudi, *The Physiocratic Doctrine of Judicial Control*, 11) calls it "extreme" —systematic form. Nevertheless, it would be given to Quesnay and the Physiocrats to do no less than lay the foundation of economics—not Adam Smith's science of wealth, but political economy which used science in applying natural law to nations.

When Quesnay looked for the natural laws which control society, he did not seek amidst those abstract natural laws of Grotius and Pufendorf with their parallel membrane universe of positive laws. Instead, Quesnay sought governance for the social system comparable to that found by the seventeenth century scientists for the physical universe—laws with which the positive laws must be in accord DuPont de Nemours (1739–1817), whose inventions included coining the actual name "Physiocrats," put it this way in his 1786 work *On the Origin and Progress of a New Science*:

> 'There is, then, a <u>necessary</u> route for achieving the object of association between men, and the formation of political bodies. There is, then, <u>an order</u>, natural, essential and general, which comprises the constitutive and fundamental laws of all societies; <u>an order</u> which could not be entirely abandoned without effecting the dissolution of society and soon the absolute destruction of the human race. This is what Montesquieu did not see...' (Baumer, 440). (underscoring supplied)

Portrait of François Quesnay
Courtesy of Bridgeman Art Library

Life, liberty and the pursuit of physiocratic happiness meant building society to conform to these natural laws by harnessing the force of manmade positive laws for a link important enough to be a matter of life and death. Physiocrats were like *philosophes* in believing the best way to do this was in judiciously exercising the legal despotism of the reigning prince. They, it must be said, did not favor such despotism for its own sake, but finding it set in place they proposed to use it as an efficient way to enact their program. Do nothing, Quesnay counseled the Dauphin, but let the natural laws rule. If the judicial power in reviewing royal acts finds the promulgations to be contrary to natural law, then let these acts immediately be declared null and void. Such a philosophy of judicial review, about which duPont said nothing when he came to America, clearly served as yet another plan to exalt the *parlements*; the Dauphin must have been highly dubious about the advice, knowing full well that these legislative bodies were already bringing royal policy—even when enlightened by the Physiocrats—to a standstill.

Physiocrats conceived France's system of production and consumption as founded on agriculture and regulated by law. Even though in his day agriculture had declined because of the restrictions and tax burdens imposed by the state, Quesnay regarded products of the land, including metals, as the only truly productive power of a nation. Physiocratic thinking could not disregard industry and commerce, but they were felt to be "sterile" and not themselves productive. The argument against was that industry only gives a new form to materials from the earth, while commerce merely transfers wealth from one to another. Adam Smith, when he wrote his *Wealth of Nations* in 1776, would show that this denigration of industry and commerce was wrong; but for any good Physiocrat promoting industry, commerce, and the service occupations, although useful, could create no fund from which to draw. If agriculture created a true "net product"—a return above the cost of production and the owner's profit—capital formation, then, would be essential to stimulate all production which could be done, but only if agriculture were not shackled by the state. To avoid such constraints, taxation, rather than being considered a cost of agricultural production, was levied only on the net product, the "free income of the land owning class" (Einaudi, 11) and not a compensation for service. Quesnay drew a glowing picture of the "new" agriculture, freed from feudal restrictions and from internal and external constraints on the movement of its production. The result would initiate, Quesnay believed, a stunning cycle of capital increases, first reinvested in agriculture, then utilized to augment the national wealth.

In stating the principle truths of the Physiocrats, duPont de Nemours shows how their philosophical structures for private law were to serve as guideposts to the *Code Napoleon*. Consider these excerpts:

I   There is a natural society, anterior to every convention between men, founded on their constitution, physical needs, and obviously common interest.

In this primitive state men have reciprocal rights and duties by an absolute justice... .

The rights of every man...are the <u>liberty</u> to provide for his subsistence and well being, the <u>proprietorship</u> of his person and of the things acquired by the work of his person.

His <u>duties</u> are work in order to provide for his needs, and respect for the liberty, and...movable property of others.

Conventions [contracts] are entered into between men for the sole purpose of...guaranteeing mutually these rights and duties established by God himself.

II   The spontaneous productions of land and sea are not enough to support a numerous population, nor to procure for man all the pleasures of which he is desirous... .

Nature ... prescribes to man the art of increasing production, the cultivation of the land... .

IV   The more...production is increased, the more man can procure pleasures, and [be] happy... .

It is in this way that the prosperity of all humanity is related to the greatest possible <u>net yield</u> ... [of land].

V   It is necessary that there be the greatest possible <u>liberty</u> in the use of all ... movable and landed property, and the greatest possible <u>security</u> in the possession of what one acquired by the use of this property... .

<u>No property without liberty, no liberty without security</u>.

VI   ... [i]t is necessary that men united in society mutually guarantee this property and protect it...by all their physical strength. This...guarantee...is what...constitutes <u>society</u>.

VIII The sovereign authority is not established ... <u>to make laws;</u> for <u>the laws are all made by the hand of the one who created rights and duties</u>.
  The <u>social laws</u> established by the supreme Being prescribe ... the ... right of property, and of the <u>liberty</u> which is inseparable from it.
  The Decrees of Sovereigns which we call <u>positive laws ought to be only declaratory acts of these essential laws of the social order</u>.
  If ... contradictory to the <u>laws of the social order</u> ... they would not be laws... .
  ... [The] Judge of the decrees even of Sovereigns...is the evidence of their conformity or opposition to the natural laws of the social order... .
IX Hereditary Monarchy presents the most perfect form of government, when it is joined to the co-proprietorship of the public in the net yield of all goods, in such proportion that the revenue of the fisc is the largest possible, without the condition of the landed proprietors ceasing to be the best that can be had in society.
  Such is the précis of this doctrine which exposes, according to the nature of man, the <u>necessary</u> laws of a Government made for man and proper to man in all climates and countries. (Baumer, 429–438) (underscoring supplied)

For the aspirations of the ever-rising French bourgeoisie these physiocratic messages proved ideal. Their dual central idea—ownership of property, and liberty for property owners—lived in harmony together under the highly attractive canopy of liberty *as* property. Attractive materiality did not promise a completely rosy outlook for the middle class, though, since a Physiocrat would accept freedom of conscience and political liberty as a given without expressly putting an end to ecclesiastic and aristocratic privileges. What is more, liberty through property rights did not cover the amount of material goods which might be amassed by exercise of this liberty. But for Quesnay and his followers, it seemed enough to have their feet planted on the terra firma of equal property rights. For the 1700s, it was a feat in itself.

The *Avocats*

By the 1750s the *Ordre des avocats*, that self-conscious and disciplined Jansenist bar association coming from the reformed education offered by Louis XIV, had compensated to large extent for the gradual academic lowering of the 1679 reform standards. The *Ordre* had become a formidable organization in Paris as well as a model for the provinces. As the pressures of French politics drew many of the *avocats* away from the austere and aloof Jansenist leadership style toward a considerable politicization and decline of their *Ordre*, they expressed doubt as to whether there should be any of those intermediate bodies favored by Montesquieu. The wishes of the people were moving away from being represented in the form of parliamentary remonstrances toward choosing the conduit of direct expression to the sovereign—soon to be a Republic—as made by talented and educated individuals. The increasingly political *avocats* saw this transmissive role for themselves, untrammeled by the intermediary controls of a professional organization. Well aware of the always seductive pull of legal matters made personal and political by appealing to opinion rather than to law, they were exhilarated at the thought of a different technique, one which had its origins and credentials in the demosthenic style. For these attorneys the goal was not mastery of a jurisprudential group medium, but presentation of the philosophic message spoken in the flamboyant, personally dramatic oratory they knew so well.

Such changes were brought about through two political crises. The first had been the effort made by an aging Louis XIV finally to stamp out the heresy of Jansenism by enforcement of the 1713 bull, *Unigenitus*. The second, which will be discussed below, was the 1770 attempt of Louis XV to break, once and for all, the grip of the *parlements* on royal legislation; for he believed impeding royal efforts could only reduce governmental reforms, cut public revenue, and doom popular happiness. These events were themselves played out, from the point of view of the *avocats*, against a background which closely conditioned their response. Given the steady progress of the royal administration in the first half of the eighteenth century, jurisdiction of the sovereign courts was reduced in scope, and the prestige of the lordly independent *robe* jurisconsults was altered. Yet the *mémoires* (briefs) of the *avocats* in litigation were, by a happy accident of governmental organization, the only form of printed prose in France that was not subject to the royal censoring. Even Montesquieu could not publish in France his *De l'esprit des lois* without the consent of the aging Daguesseau. With the chancellor's office acting as censor, recourse to printing abroad, particularly in Switzerland or Holland, was an open possibility for books to find their way continuously from the frontiers to the French salons. But the lawyers knew this troublesome method involved not only anonymity but annoying delay and expense. There were few in the legal profession who could resist the temptation of setting the political agenda of the bar into printed *mémoires*. They were more than ready to accept this home turf route to personal power, especially since the in-house propaganda came out under their name.

When the *parlements* after 1715 recovered the right of remonstrance, their reaction to *Unigenitus* was singularly and ironically lacking in vigor. However, when the significance of the bull to the bar, and particularly to its Jansenist leaders, began to appear as a direct assault on the core of their religious beliefs—an attack which to them gave every indication of coming from a foreign power outside France—the Jansenist members realized they needed measures without precedent. As the ecclesiastical hierarchy enforced *Unigenitus*, Jansenist clerics found themselves constantly crowded into ironic appeals for protection from the new, draconian discipline being imposed on them.

The big moment came in 1716 when a group of Jansenist clerics from Reims were put on trial. Not confining themselves to appeals based on existing texts of law, the Jansenist counselors Claude-Joseph Prévost and Louis Chevallier addressed their professional speeches and *mémoires* directly to the public. A great number were printed and widely disseminated; three thousand copies of one *mémoire* were not unusual at a time when only 2,000 copies were printed of an average book. The *mémoire* as weapon soon became even more powerful when a handful of *avocats* might prepare one that hundreds of their colleagues had signed. In 1728 even a simple consultation was given hefty weight by the appended signatures of fifty *avocats*. As Bell puts it: "thus began a half-century in which [the *mémoires* of *avocats*], sometimes printed in 10,000 or more copies, became a legal form of opposition journalism, and one of the most effective examples of it yet seen in France." Clearly no longer did the *parlements* keep the old monopoly on the representation of public opinion. As advocacy commanded ever more prestige and influence, political orthodoxy began to be a requirement for membership in an *Ordre* whose leaders were conscious of the need for unity (Bell, 86, 199, 201). When the crown tried in 1730 – 1731 to impose penalties on offending *avocats*, the offenders declined to continue to practice, the courts came to a standstill leaving the ministry pushed to retreat and leaving the *Ordre* in a truly formidable posture.

The parliamentary dissatisfaction of 1770 turned ugly enough to be given a name: the Maupeou crisis, after the first president (1763–1768) of the Paris *parlement*. It all began in Brittany where the Duc d'Aiguillon served as Louis XV's provincial commander-in-chief. D'Aiguillon irately considered that his proper jurisdiction had been invaded when the local *parlement* tried to immerse itself in details of provincial administration beyond its "proper" powers. The Breton *parlement* members for their part felt they, as legislative surrogates for their supporters at the bar, had merely been putting into effect their deeply held conviction that France should be a "judicial monarchy" in which "judges and avocats regulated all important social conflicts" (Bell, 62). Louis XV had for long been exasperated by such an attitude—he always called these men of the *parlements* "the big robes," a derogatory sort of "fat head" expression. But when he met in 1768 René Nicolas Charles Augustin Maupeou (1714–1792), member of an influential legal family, the ruler felt he at last had found a "great robe." Maupeou would prove to be both a loyal supporter of crown authority against *Parlement* and a strong chancellor able to act resolutely because of his familiarity with tactics of parliamentary opposition.

When the *Paris Parlement* involved itself in the Brittany matter, Maupeou decided to act; and Louis XV, gathering uncustomary energy, backed him by forcing the registration on 7 December 1770 of a sweeping disciplinary edict. This document was quite draconian. It condemned strikes, imposed upon *parlement* members views novel enough to include the possibility of their forced resignations and complete disunion. Paradoxically, it also appealed to the interests of the nation against the rights of the king. Maupeou justified presentation of the ambivalent edict as an appeal to monarchical doctrine. In this chess game with feudal France in the balance, both sides were playing for keeps. The *Paris Parlement* accepted *en masse* resignation along with most of their provincial brethren; town and country both hoped that such an unexpected massive suspension of justice would force the royal government to capitulate as it had so often in the past. The judicial strikers misjudged Maupeou, however, who exiled the resigning members and proceeded with royal legislation to reform the judiciary. Olivier-Martin (Olivier-Martin, sec. 505, 664–666) believes Maupeou probably would not have proposed such changes had his hand not been forced and an opportunity offered.

From the outset Maupeou had clearly shown immense audacity. First he set aside the *Paris Parlement* with its enormous geographical jurisdiction over about one-third of France, replacing it with six *conseils superieurs*, each with a roughly equal area and for which were at once recruited entirely new personnel with no power of remonstrance. Their jobs were all appointive. Maupeou would have replaced all of the nation's *parlements* had Louis XV, who usually gave Maupeou steadfast support, not refused to go that far. The King, however, allowed Maupeou to reduce the number of officers, eliminate some exceptional jurisdictions, and cut by over half (naturally concentrating on opponents of the crown) the number of judges in the remaining high courts. The judiciary did retain the right of remonstrance, but Maupeou felt they would no longer dare to use it forcefully. Wanting to institute a new civil procedure he also made changes in criminal law to the applause of Voltaire but to the outrage of conservatives at the bar (Carey, 97). Maupeou, supported as he was by the King, was implacable and impassive, and it was obvious after the tumultuous year of 1771 wound down that he had won his ground. One after another, the angry *avocats* returned to their *cabinets*. By 1774 the people seemed indifferent to the whole business, but as Olivier-Martin (Olivier-Martin, sec. 505, 665) describes the situation: "The king's crowning jump in energy and the skillful tactics of the chancellor had opened everyone's eyes to the superficial character of the parliamentary opposition."

Then, in May 1774, disaster overtook the great effort of Maupeou: the King died suddenly of smallpox. His grandson, only twenty, was suddenly Louis XVI and just as suddenly received the *déluge* in the form of advice from all quarters. One of the first caveats presented him was that the people of France would love him if only he brought back the *parlements*. Turgot, in accord with the *philosophes*, was much opposed to recall but said little, thinking it better tactics to preserve his clout for financial and economic reforms. The result was that the achievement of Louis XV was completely lost. When the new King later declined to have overall budgetary control but still undertook the vast expense of a navy for the American intervention, France gave up her last chance for royal reforms which might have led to a constitutional monarchy without the convulsions of the Revolution.

It is no surprise, then, that Maupeou's measures were regarded by the leaders of the *Ordre des avocats* as a crisis fully as grave as *Unigenitus*. When, using every technique learned in law training, the *avocats* appealed to the public, first in 1730 and then later in the 1770s; it is not astonishing that they mounted the biggest pamphlet campaign yet seen in eighteenth century France. Some of the less affluent, but nevertheless, ambitious lawyers were attracted even more by the promise that in the multiple reforms which clipped the wings of an overly proud magistracy there would be opportunity opening for them to fly up into the high courts.

In another facet of the crisis, suspension of the *Ordre* meant the many men returned to private practice found themselves with time on their hands. Free to indulge literary or political pretensions they enjoyed taking the spotlight in cases they made sensational by filling their arguments with ideas from the *philosophes*. A good example is Metz native Pierre-Louis de Laretelle who found a lot of support when he popularized the new ideal for advocacy by coining the flattering title "*jurisconsulte-philosophe*." Maza records such newly reoriented *avocats* as true successors to the "'heroic first generation of *philosophes*'" (Bell, 207), men who

Louis XVI, Roi de France
Courtesy of National Gallery of Art, Washington

began to yearn for a more simplified law so that it would be easier to concentrate on broad, emotional appeals—a kind of Athenization of French technique.

With the collapse under Louis XVI of Maupeou's changes, leading *avocats* devoted to the old style made their own return to a conservative brand of practice. This more subdued trial protocol, though, had no chance against the new breed. For fifteen years France witnessed dramatically famous and infamous trials in which many a youthful *avocat* made a name for himself by deliberately outrageous courtroom behavior (Bell, 203). One of the most well-known exponents was the advocate-general of *Parlement*, Hérault de Séchelles, who parlayed a precocious talent and good looks into high success in theatrical magistracy. Suddenly critics of the bar were seeing no more need for an *Ordre des avocats* giving privileged access to courtrooms and printing presses; they were joined by more and more *avocats* wanting thorough reforms of the court structure and a simple code of law that any citizen could understand. There was still among many the thought that French justice should let an enlightened sovereign be "guardian of the laws" instead of conferring that honor on those seats of medieval privilege, the old *parlements*. Nevertheless, when in May 1788 the King tried to retrieve his error of 1774 by once again dissolving the high courts, most *avocats* again allied with the magistrates. It was, to be sure, an alliance devoid of trust and only for a moment in time. But that moment was all the lawyers needed. It was obvious now to all that the law problems could no longer remain in-house, and would require a meeting of the Estates General in order fully to represent the French nation.

With politics so much in the forefront, *avocats* were not very busy leading earnest advances in the study of ordinances and customs; nor were they very focused on practical needs, like a national restatement of private law which would reduce the decades of study required for the bar. But other avenues of change remained close to the surface in many a court tirade. When Pierre-Louis-Claude Gin, son of a Jansenist *avocat*, published in 1767 on *Eloquence of the Bar*, he left old fashioned austerity behind for the new, subjective ideal of legal oratory. Technical expertise gave way to an inherent flair for natural law reducible to a different golden rule, one which drew on secular thinkers such as d'Alembert and Rousseau. In prose which foreshadowed pre-Romanticism's emotional release, Gin wrote, "'Feel vividly, [and] you will express yourself vividly as well'" (Bell, 135). Law was definitely turning into hot ammunition fire as musty barristers' offices transformed themselves metaphorically into resistance barricades. It was certainly a lot more exciting than the usual pedestrian run of torts.

The Universities

The Parisian *Ordre des avocats* had made impressive good-faith efforts to supplement the legal education afforded by the declining law faculties. There were stiff requirements—a three-year degree followed after 1751 by a four-year apprenticeship which concluded only after receiving certificates of assiduity from six senior members of the *Ordre*. The system's watchwords of study and oversight had the positive tendency to guarantee each new *avocat* was ready to work hard and long. The system's weakness was that it also depended upon strong and active leadership from the bar; when the *Parlement* struck or was exiled, and law practice was suspended, this internship system necessarily suffered.

To understand better the theoretical foundation of such legal training we must remind ourselves of just what kind of law was being provided by France's ancient universities. For centuries the only admittance to the bar as an *avocat* was the *licence* awarded by a law faculty, and since 1679 the three-year course had been regulated by the Louis XIV edict. We know that after 1750 any young boy intended for such goals began with primary education given at home, either parentally at home or with a tutor, or in a local school. About age seven it was on to a *collège*— an institution often attached to a university—where Jesuits, Oratorians, or some other teaching order provided a simple pre-law course based on humanistic studies. Sixteen year old law students entered a university and matriculated under the law faculty.

Between 1679 and 1789 the young man would have chosen one of the twenty-five French universities in existence; twenty-two were still operating in 1789, and in them served a total of 122 Royal professors. It will be recalled how the distinctive feature of the Louis XIV edict was the creation at each university of a law chair held by one of these special educators who would teach in the third year as much as he could of those polyvalent ordinances, codes, and customs from the Roman law and canon law which comprised the stock in trade of an *avocat*. If we accept that there were about four professors of Roman law and canon law at one time at each university (a reasonable assumption), French law students were in this period served by over 600 professors in all, to which must usually be added at each university several adjuncts from the local bar teaching part-time. In Lyon where there was no university, enterprising local lawyers created their own "chair." Chosen by aldermen and the provost of merchants, this adjunctive star professor would come in for three to five hours a day to teach law. His classes then went to Dijon for their examinations (De Curzon, 250). Even for a nation of about 20,000,000 this is an imposing academic legal cadre, especially in comparison with England with its two universities which taught civil and canon but not the common law.

All law faculties suffered more or less from the same serious handicap: Louis XIV, although determined that there should be "assiduity" in law studies, neglected to provide a decent salary independent of the number of students lured to the classrooms. Law faculties had ancient endowments of productive real estate, but everywhere it was so insufficient that the balance had to come from fees—eighty livres for the baccalaureate, for the *licence* seventy, and for the doctorate one hundred thirty. There were a few scholarships, some cities helped their students, and sons of professors received considerable financial relief. But the costs still kept many aspirants away.

Degenerated faculties decided it was time to call upon their imaginations and set aside old time legal niceties in their eager and enterprising attempts to find the cash. At Angers in 1789 a professor actually supplied answers, at twelve francs each, for the arguments to be put to the candidates responding at the examination. In other cases of egregious abuse the *licence* might be awarded to the young men who had attended only a few days during which they were heavily coached through empty formalities of study and examination; after payment of the fees they were sent away with equally empty diplomas. One faculty even lengthened the required stay by a day simply to please the local innkeeper. Despite many such stories, it nevertheless appears that for most of the century the norm of academic standards was acceptable, only declining sharply as the cataclysm of 1789 approached. Nor were the mediocre institutions all tolerated; the University of Cahors was simply suppressed in 1751.

On the whole, the late seventeenth and early eighteenth century system allowed for considerable academic input from the Royal Professors, some of whom, studied by De Curzon, were indeed very able. Premier among them was Pothier at Orléans, followed by Poullain du Parc of Rennes. There was as well Filleau from Poitiers whose 1777 course in French law survives to this day in manuscript; P. R. Germain was a stalwart on the Paris faculty, as was de Laverne at Avignon and Dumont at Bourges. Also of Bourges, Jan Du Rabot wrote many creditable treatises as did his university colleague Thaumassière. Many others who did not publish offered strong oral teaching. Outstanding here were Davot at Dijon, Mourot at Pau, Prévost de la Jannès (Pothier's Orléans predecessor) and Livonnière from Angers. Besides these Royal Professors of French law, distinction was, of course, earned also by many of their colleagues in Roman and canon law, even though De Curzon thought (De Curzon, 339) that on the whole the French law academics evinced more diligence. That many such academicians held the respect of their provinces was shown in 1789 when, as the universities ceased to function, a number of them made an easy transition into politics, including service in the Estates General and succeeding bodies. Although university lawyers were not to be as strongly represented in France's post-Revolution *Civil Code* drafting as were those professors from Berytus on Tribonian's commission in CE 533, two Roman legalists at least were influential: Simeon from Aix and Jaubert of Bordeaux.

Interestingly, the French academic establishment in law continued to be divided into two schools traceable back to the sixteenth century. The Roman and canon law faculty still espoused the more theoretical "scientific" school; while the Royal Professors represented the more practical French school, attempting to teach the rules needed immediately in the profession. This put the Royal Professors closer to the *philosophes* than the Roman and canon law men; remember how Diderot bellowed to Catherine II against the teaching of law of antiquity. But on the whole, closer to the *philosophes* did not mean very close, because the royals were Christians who did not hide their antipathy to free-thinkers' godlessness. Their Christianity caused them to live like Pothier in deep attachment to the Enlightenment's ideals of equity and humanity in opposition to Roman law rigor and to the stiff criminal law of the *ancien régime*. Moreover, facing as they did the distractive pattern of French customs, the method of these Royal professors—to keep within bounds the amount of material offered to the students—was necessarily comparative, as well, in some cases, historical. France had begun its movement toward the 1804 unification of the law, accomplished in the next *avocat* generation of Bigot du Préamenu, Maleville, Portalis, and Tronchet.

As the eighteenth century unraveled, the decline in the quality of teaching and learning in the university law faculties was well known to Louis XVI. Louis XIV had shown in 1679 that the ancient independence of the universities was no match for his autocratic control, even if he could not always bring them to heel openly. Daguesseau as chancellor settled by correspondence all the university problems submitted to him. Louis XVI, however, had restored the *parlements* in 1774, and a university now tended to lean on its local *parlement* to resist reforms it did not like. Nevertheless, when the King in May 1788 made his ordinance for reform of the administration of justice, he, like his grandfather Louis before him, had, at last been driven to try to curb the *parlements*. His technique was to confine them to judicial duties while creating another body to register laws and taxes.

It was in this strengthened and reformist frame of mind that the King announced he would "'give the most serious attention to surveying the studies in the universities and to improving them by examinations and tests.'" He also promised that "'[t]he reform of our faculties of law is decreed and it will soon be put into effect in all its vigor'" (De Curzon, 330). In fact Miromesnil, guardian of the seals, had already in 1786 directed the intendants to become better acquainted with conditions within their universities by the highly modern approach of answering a twelve-part questionnaire. Hiding at the bottom of the inquiry was a thirteenth question which portentously invited faculties to submit plans for reform. Every university replied, although evidently not very constructively. Strasbourg pointedly saw nothing to change; Douai asked for the drafting of a body of previously approved legal doctrine; and Dijon said that enforcement of the old laws would be enough. The vapid response meant a non-constructive outcome. Versailles continued to weaken, and the Revolution began strengthening its own quest for vast social reform and reorganization. It would not be too long before angry voices would tell Strasbourg, Douai, and Dijon that not only was everything on the table, but that everything had to be attended to yesterday.

Revolution

The Beginning

In Hardman's view (Hardman, *Louis XVI,* 103) the French Revolution began its trip to the Bastille on 20 August 1786, the day a memorandum was presented to the King by Calonne. In it the Treasurer had set forth a striking proposal: a monarchy absolute in form and based on destruction of the *parlements*. Provincial assemblies would take the place of the council format inherited from Viking assembly and the noble constitutionalism of Montesquieu's intermediary powers. Although membership in these bodies came from a newly liberal base—the representation was to be chosen without concern for social status—it was thought no one in the resulting Third Estate caste of non-noble landowners, merchants, guildsmen, and lawyers would lack in traditional loyalty to the crown. These assemblies, Calonne believed and Louis XVI and his foreign minister Vergennes soon concurred, would be able at last to control public opinion in a king's favor.

Money was obviously not forgotten. The always threatening secular independence of the Church would be ended by requiring from both the First and Second Estates a land tax calculated on property held. Government finance would be revolutionized by this replacement of the old levies and generous exemptions. All landowners would contribute now on an equal basis, internal customs barriers would be abolished, and multiple treasuries would be consolidated into one so that budgeting control would be possible. It all amounted to the unthinkable abolition of privilege and the beginning of uniformity. It was confirmation that Maupeou and Louis XV had been right when in the years between 1771 and 1774 they came to accept the acid truth that reform could not be achieved with *parlements* in the way. Calonne intended bypass to begin by seeking approval of his plan directly with an Assembly of Notables appointed by the King, but set up in such a way that the Third Estate would prevail. The last such body had been called by Richelieu in 1625 for the same purpose of outflanking opposition in the *parlements*.

But the *parlements* stood firmly. They would not go away. A magistrate who guards the state seals with all his law training worn as armor is a determined man, and in Armand-Thomas de Miromesnil, the Parisian *Parlement* had a powerful force

Charles Gravier, Count of Vergennes
Courtesy of The Bridgeman Art Library

of refusal to face off against the formidable duo of Calonne, the Comptroller-General of Finances, and Vergennes, the Foreign Minister. Perhaps it was under Miromesnil's influence that in organizing the Assembly of Notables Louis had followed the most traditional path, appointing only a handful of commoners among the 144 members, including all thirty-seven of the first presidents and parliamentary *procureurs-généraux*. On 28 December the *Conseil des Dépêches* rubber stamped the convocation of the notables, and that night, as he told Calonne, Louis XVI could not sleep, so great was his joy (Hardman 109).

On 13 February 1787 Vergennes died, an immense loss to the throne. As Calonne went ahead and presented his plan to the Notables, the *parlementaires* quickly and fully perceived that their right of registration and their privileges were at stake. What they did not grasp was that in a continued deadlock without reform their jobs, their fortunes, their very lives—and yes, their sacred honor—were in jeopardy. However, they did the best limited awareness permitted, making enough loud objections that the Queen turned against Calonne. The King, who adored her, weakened and watered down the plan, not only dismissing Calonne but forcing him to resign from the Order of Saint-Esprit and give back his insignia. Calonne left France and was impeached in absentia by *Parlement*. Louis cancelled the impeachment proceedings, but ministerial responsibility had become a reality. Brienne was now appointed first minister even though the King disliked him a great deal and, from this time on, is said to have sunk into an apathy and depression relieved only by coming to Marie Antoinette's apartments every day to weep over the critical state of his kingdom.

Finally setting some control over his emotional state Louis revived enough to make his last thrust against the *parlements*: dissolution of the high courts in May 1788. When in his turn Brienne fell, Louis recalled Necker and on 5 July, in full collapse after the lost legal struggle, issued a royal declaration for advice on the composition of the Estates General. Calling it had become inevitable. Only nine days later centuries of old authority were successfully confronted in the streets. The people of Paris attacked the Bastille, and the Revolution, with law in the bloody hands of stark mob reality, brandished the first heads on pikes.

The three Estates presented their deputies at Versailles on 2 May 1789. Here was the Nordic Althing now in wigs and taking snuff, gathering together in lace and eighteenth century office coats that law again might bring an alternative to violence. The Third Estate marched in at 598 deputies strong. Such an impressive number was a direct result of the crucial move taken by the King on 27 December 1788. In the hot debate which had followed his general royal declaration of July 5, Louis had agreed in his *Conseil des Dépêches* that the demand of the Third Estate should be honored: the number of its deputies, representing, as they would, the bulk

Mr. Necker
*Courtesy of the Library of Congress,
Prints and Photographs Division, LC-USZ62-99965*

of the population in wealth and numbers, were to equal those of the clergy and nobles combined. Thus, in effect, the basic principles of Calonne's reform were adopted before the meeting began, although the absolute monarchy he had fought to retain was on a most fragile footing. It was apparent that if all three estates met together and found support by the lower clergy the Third Estate would in fact control a majority.

Now it was the King who held his ground. Voting, he decreed, was to be by separate order, as always it had been in the past. The Versailles conclave reached a standstill broken only when the Third Estate, uniting as a separate body, declared itself on 10 June a "Chamber of Commons" and proceeded, with some of the clergy, to verify the credentials of the deputies. Advancing boldly, on 17 June they declared themselves a "National Assembly" with autonomous power and with an authority over the finances to be exercised by the Assembly's own committees regardless of the King's ministers. On 20 June while coming to order in a tennis court, the *Jeu de Paume,* because their own meeting room was closed, and convinced a new Constitution had become an imperative for France, they declared themselves a "Constituent Assembly" and were thereafter in history known as such. After much conflict the King gave in, approved the title "National Assembly," and on 27 June ordered the clergy and nobles to join it.

Lefebvre states unequivocally (Lefebvre, *The Coming of the French Revolution,* Vol. I, 114) that France's cataclysm—a revolution *de jure* as well as *de facto*—was "achieved by the lawyers who borrowed their methods from the *Parlement of Paris*." In sharp contrast of role, however, the National Assembly was not formed to stand like the old *Parlement* in legal advisorship to the king; rather, it had, directly from the people, been promised power to represent the sovereignty of the entire Nation. For the time being it remained an enthusiastic democratization without government or bureaucracy. The King, as usual, lacked energy, but his ministers drove hard to obstruct the committees by which the National Assembly tried to govern.

The *Cahiers*

Following ancient practice, each of the local assemblies along with corporations and other bodies formed now in the parishes to elect deputies to the Estates General. Each received an invitation from Paris to submit a memorandum of complaints, or a *cahier de doléances*. About 50,000 such booklets were submitted, but on the whole they were not particularly revolutionary and often began in conservative tradition by invoking the Holy Trinity. In country parishes it was the *curé* or a man of law who drafted the *cahier*, and, generally, he faithfully captured the spirit of his people. Rather than any fuzzy thoughts about political theory, he stated in blunt, realistic detail the opinions of the peasants and their concerns with local problems like roads, feudal rights, and hunting rights. In the cities the *bourgeois* draftsmen, far more radical and intellectual, generally neglected lower class feelings and were fairly insensitive to any thoughts held by simple artisans and laborers. These radicalized men of the middle already held their own egalitarian ideas which had not yet found resting place in the minds of the masses. Synthesizing many *cahiers*, the *bailliages*, or bailiwick assemblies of taxpayers over twenty-five, enthusiastically added their mix of general points of view to the political proposals. Sometimes generalities would be expanded in an outpouring of lengthy personal opinion. Other groups, being more placid and conservative, merely copied generic, *model cahiers*.

A preponderant number of *cahiers* were written in favor of drafting a highly idealistic Declaration of the Rights of Man, comprising liberty to speak and write; strongly urged as well were regular meetings of the Estates General on taxation matters, and just as strongly refused were any new taxes unless the King granted the written constitution. Many *cahiers* sought maintenance of the Church; none was truly hostile to it. On most other questions opinion was divided.

It is noteworthy that the majority took a middle position in political opinion, with many fairly docile about leaving it to the King to decide on the needed reforms. Nearly all the Third Estate did want an end to feudalism and privilege in fiscal matters. Obviously the last chapter was being drafted to long-historicized societal compartments for those who prayed, those who fought, and those who worked. By implication, a *finis* had also become obligatory for the unequal bearing of governmental burdens. On economic matters there were many opinions, but their united front typified the nobility's resistance to any goal of fiscal equilibration. As for the statutory world, it overflowed the pages of complaint. There were demands for the abolition of the barbarous aspects of the criminal law; for a unification of the customs; an end to the monarch's lifting of cases out of the courts for his own decision in Council (*justice retenue*); the elimination of seigneurial justice; and a reform of commercial law by means of a code legislating bankruptcy and overseeing commercial corporations. At the same time the *cahiers* were so surprisingly silent on questions of private law and civil status that any disinterested reader could truly not have anticipated the extent of the political storm ahead.

The Successive Constitutions

Much of France's bankruptcy could be laid to the large outlay of men and materiel that Vergennes had arranged in helping the Americans progress from royal colony to new nation. The *cahiers* bore witness to a desire that France find intellectual reimbursement, as it were, by herself gaining for her pains the recompense of a written constitution (Ellul, Vol. IV, 270). The revolutionary period would oblige with more than one. Before recounting the fate of the *Ordre des avocats* and their university brethren, it will be convenient to cast a legal eye forward briefly at these constitutions, since it was to be their legal structures through which every seething political, economic, social, and religious pressure would have to be funneled for achieving the new objectives in positive law.

Constitutionalism began between 20 and 26 August 1789 when the National Constituent Assembly drafted and adopted the called-for Declaration of the Rights of Man. Among the documents consulted the writers looked carefully at American bills of rights. Lafayette had made sure to consult Jefferson, then representing the United States in Paris, before structuring in fairly miscellaneous order a final draft of the Declaration's preamble and seventeen articles. Still there was another page, this one turned much farther back to the early concept of power ascending upward from the people rather than inversely descendant from the divine. Lefebvre (Lefebvre, Vol. I, 146) correctly recognized that France's constitutional work embodied this honorable depth of provenance: "In affirming the dignity of the human person and the value of individual initiative, the declarations of both countries carry the imprint that Greek philosophy and Christianity stamped upon European thought." The rights promoted in 1789 were those we have consistently seen as "natural." Their energy of pre-existence, their entelechy that surpassed positive legislation and royal conferment, did cover everything; for the French drafters were not interested in tight focus on specific social and economic problems or in philosophically delving into the unfamiliar potential tyranny of non-monarchical state power. Yet the power of these new rights was unequivocal, protecting abstract legal individuals, all of whom were held identical, and guaranteeing them equality before the law.

A first constitution was crafted piece by piece between the tumultuous days of June 1789 and September 1791. Shockingly, proudly, the National Assembly made its extraordinary departure from the state as king and from power as divine right; instead were established the concepts of a Nation as the state and of a sovereignty flowing into that Nation from the people. Ironically, though, the relentless march over the centuries toward ever increasing state power over a citizenry was not reversed but rather confirmed by the broadest strokes. On 9 December 1789 it was decided to reorganize France in totality, and on 26 February 1790 the country was divided into eighty-three more or less equal departments named for rivers and mountains. Despite bloodshed in the streets there was a steady confidence of Cartesian parsing as these departments were then in turn divided into districts and the districts into cantons—villages grouped under the authority of easily accessible main towns where markets existed (Lefebvre, Vol. I, 154).

For an insurrection that had begun with its combustible *brioche* vs. *pain* statement about comestibles, it was actually the *marché* that had *marché*—walked, or rather trampled on—the customary boundaries of jurisprudence. In just one broad legal swath, the provincial *parlements* as repositories of the high courts, depositories of the statutes, and guardians of the fundamental laws of the *ancien régime* were made geographically irrelevant. Uniformity of private law became entirely possible and non-uniformity based on non-existent provinces entirely unfeasible. Intendants disappeared as the administration of France, completely decentralized, became distributed through wide powers granted to the multiplicity of municipalities.

In the crises soon to follow, this decentralization would itself have to return central power in large measure; but for the time, being non-venal courts with elected, salaried judges were set up for the districts while justices of the peace found their role in the cantons. The result was that a national judiciary had been given new life as an organic state power, not just a service. It still functioned to create law but had been provided a far different roadmap from that followed by the executive and legislative powers (Ellul, Vol. V, 25).

How emotional that night meeting must have been on 4 August 1789, when a surprising surge of patriotism inspired idealistic nobles to lead the way in abolishing feudalism and establishing the shining promise of the new French legal direction in personal liberty and the right to own property. Not unexpectedly, once filtered through the sobering light of dawn, subsequent proceedings did take some steps back, reclassifying feudal rights as "dominant" or "contractual." The former were abolished without compensation; the latter, being property, were set forth as sacred and required payment to retire them. The possessor of land who purchased one of these contractual rights in effect substituted the private law of contracts for a feudal creditor (Ellul, Vol. V, 15, 35).

Yet despite such retractions the legal swath had cut broadly: citizenship was defined; royal monopolies in economic matters were abolished along with privileged manufacture; workmen's associations were impeded; freedom of the market in commerce both internal and foreign and in finance was encouraged. In addition, some private law rules on families were changed, and the validity of marriage was made to depend on state rather than church power, exercised in the same way for Protestants as for Catholics. Not least in importance, 1791 also marked adoption of an extremely needed reform in penal law.

But the Legislative Assembly now had to yield power to a National Convention. Not unexpectedly, this, the longest lived of the Revolution's working bodies, owed its existence to yet another crisis. It was the summer of 1792, and countless pressures of problems foreign and domestic were causing impossible stress and chaotic conditions. Suddenly a dramatic eruption, almost as legendary as the Bastille and certainly more far-reaching, spewed forth innovation and terror that sent the people pouring out into the streets again. Once more France put on the Phrygian cap and readied to tear down again the remaining symbolic structures of oppression. As the rebellious of Paris formed a Commune which angrily stormed the royal palace of the Tuileries, shouts could be heard demanding the end of the monarchy. The Legislative Assembly in shattering response suspended the King on August 10 and called for the election of a national convention to draft a new constitution. All Frenchmen twenty-one years old who had been domiciled in France for a year and were living by the product of their labor were granted voting privileges—the first broad suffrage without class distinction.

The debut session of the Legislative Assembly was held on September 20, and delegates wasted no time in showing the world that their platform had officially begun setting up the new world. Since France henceforth was to live in Time renewed, the old calendar was scrapped and Year I begun on 22 September. Twelve metaphorically renamed months, of thirty days each, were amplified by five "intercalery" days, while holiday fell every ten days instead of on a Sunday every seven—clear proof that Christianity had been dropped in favor of the stern Mother Goddess of Reason, ready to produce more work for the nation.

Although a legislative entity, the National Convention did not hesitate in self-reinvention to take over the government and exercise executive power by its own committees, thus doing profound violence to the separation of powers. With centralization restored, the next step was the codifying of Terror as a means of greater control. It would be this darker Nation which would at last succeed in alarming its *bourgeoisie* base, among whom the uneasy *avocats*—not women crying for bread—began the fateful turnaround against Revolution's fiercer requirements.

By 1794 French policies had achieved victories on the frontiers. The subsequent lessening of international tensions meant the Convention could indulge in the fatal luxury of fast-paced political division at home. Rivals, who coveted the immense power the most perverse of *avocats*, Robespierre, seemed to exercise on the ironically named Committee of Public Safety, started their attack. When the Convention opened its session at noon on 9 Thermidor (27 July 1794) measures Robespierre had defended and the continuance of the Incorruptible himself were placed squarely on the table. Robespierre was forbidden to speak, and by three o'clock he and others had been arraigned for crimes against the State. The Commune failed to aid the accused, cowed as they were by National Guards from the wealthy neighborhoods who arrived under Paul Barras, a former Viscount now surfacing as the new figure of power. Robespierre opted for the drama of an updated Roman suicide and shot himself—an inept bravado which only shattered his jaw. The next evening he and twenty-one others went to the far more efficient guillotine, followed by a "batch" of seventy-one more the next day and twelve the day after that. The worst slaughter had come at the last gasp of the Revolutionary government.

On 22 August 1795 another constitution— "Constitution of the Year III"— established the Directory, this latest governmental turnaround being the achievement of Thermidoreans who had dominated the National Convention after the fall of Robespierre. The moderate upper middle class of the Third Estate, which during the Convention had sustained its victory of 1789 over the aristocracy, now, under the banner of the law, fought vigorously against the social democracy of the Robespierre faction. Wrote Boissy d'Anglas:

> We should be governed by the best. The best are those who are the most educated and the most interested in maintaining the laws. With few exceptions you will find such men only among those who, owning property, are attached to the country in which it is located, to the laws which protect it, to the peace and order which preserve it, and owe to this property and the affluence which it yields, the education which makes them the ones to discuss, with wisdom and accuracy, the advantages and disadvantages of the laws that determine the fate of the land.... A country governed by landowners is in the social order; that which is governed by nonlandowners is in the state of nature.
>
> (Lefebvre, Vol. II, 161)

Not unexpectedly the prefatory Declaration of Rights to this new Constitution omitted the famous article, "Men are born and remain free and equal in rights," specifying instead that "equality means that the law is the same for all men" (Lefebvre, Vol. II, 161). Suffrage ceased to be universal; only about 30,000 electors met the property qualification. The revised executive government was embodied in five Directors and legislation became the purview of a top heavy Council of Five Hundred augmented with a classical Council of Elders. Although departmental and municipal administrations were to be elective, authority was concentrated in a single

Maximilien Robespierre
Courtesy of The Bridgeman Art Library

central departmental administration while the districts completely disappeared. The Directory could both annul any local decision without appeal and remove those who made it. Yet in spite of the patina of antique legalism and stern morality, it was a weak system with neither legislative initiative nor power to dissolve the Councils.

Legal Education

In a unanimous sweep of disintegration the Convention, in close coordination with the committee of Public Instruction and under the "very big stick" of tyrannic virtue wielded by Robespierre (Schama, *Citizens: A Chronicle of the French Revolution,* 828), had totally dismantled the educational system. It was into this maw of destruction that now fell the *ancien régime*'s system of legal education. A fairly large number of post-destruction revolutionaries cheered the loss. They had never wanted this system at all, since legal learning in their view was not only unnecessary, but led to unwanted delay and expense in litigation, to say nothing of promoting injustice. Finding it impossible to agree on establishing a new system, there thus was mounted a strong effort for nothing less than total abolishment of the legal profession.

Shocking as this may sound, it must be remembered that widespread opposition had manifested itself throughout the Revolution. It was an opposition that became a fundamental article of written faith on that extraordinary night of 4 August 1789 when feudalism was abolished and property affirmed. Destruction of the corporate framework of the *ancien régime* is regarded by Fitzsimmons (Fitzsimmons, *The Parisian Order of Barristers and the French Revolution,* 33) as "the most distinctive achievement of the French Revolution." A "corporation" had previously been defined as an assemblage of people who did the same work, and such collectivist associations had come up against the stone wall of Robespierre and hardcore revolutionary theory. The result was that in the new State any legal response was required to be made directly to individual citizens, thus eliminating any political power vested in that group intermediation once so eloquently urged by Montesquieu. Independent associations which could control access to an occupation, the manner of performing it, and even the continuance in it were disapproved because of their selective delegation of power to the few over the many. In part this attitude came from hatred of all privileges and of all special arrangements for particular people. But it also emanated from a deeply held legal belief in natural liberty and natural equality which, if only they could be given free rein, would lead to the greatest happiness for all. Anti-corporatism equaled anti-elitism, a view born of faith in the individual. Exercising self-rights to participate in state business had now become the glory and responsibility of each citizen.

Outside the National Assembly the populace remained slow to grasp such portentous new ideas. The Church and its many organized bodies at once fell afoul of the new Arianism which added to religion's poor reputation among followers of the *philosophes*. Although not specifically requested to do so by the pro-Gallic *cahiers*, the revolutionary state went ahead and appropriated all Church property, adding on special laws of suppression. In the end under Napoleon's 1801 Concordat with the pope, the clergy of the Gallic Catholic Church were to become, in effect, state employees. But the old universities, too, were failing the Revolution's test. The invitation of the King to submit *cahiers* was not lost on the professorial ranks who conferred at length on the massive national shifts. But although paid to think and think well, professors appear to have fallen into a classic trap of history: they were unable to grasp the seriousness of their situation and, what is worse, they regarded themselves as indispensable. Requests from universities that they be represented in the Estates General by deputies chosen by them were curtly refused on 24 January 1789. Although, as we have seen, many law professors did manage to get themselves elected as deputies of the Third Estate, their presence there had no appreciable effect on the fate of the academic enterprises they were representing.

Universities could not remain oblivious to the immensely emotional decision against feudalism, for it resulted in a deleterious reduction of the income from their lands—a cut, in other words, of their precious endowments. The "taking" of Church property on 2 November 1789 to raise money for the bankrupt state, and the suppression of the regular clergy on 13 February 1790 to facilitate the allocation of Church lands as a reserve for new bank notes, were two events which, although cataclysmic, did not directly reach the hallowed precincts. The handwriting would not appear clearly on academe's wall until the Legislative Assembly's law of 18 August 1792 suppressed all secular corporations. Then at last, came a halt to the essential: enrollments. With fewer opportunities for an attractive career at the bar there occurred a shattering change as prospective students were discouraged from entering the field at all.

Law faculties, laid low by the now rapid decline in new students and faculty managed, if barely, to totter on. In 1788, responding to the King's request for information, the general position bears similarities to that experienced by educational bureaucracies everywhere: all is well except for faculty salaries. In this case the complaint was valid, but worse was still to come. With no love lost, the Convention on 14 February 1793 suppressed all teaching corporations, leaving the professors free to instruct as private individuals. The National Assembly had given its own sharp jab at the faltering law faculties by prescribing in September 1791 that their lesson plans should be kept to teaching the new Constitution; morale really fell when the Legislative Assembly in August 1792 then awarded the boxed-in professors insultingly small salaries. By September 1793 the Convention slammed the door when it formally suppressed all establishments of higher learning.

These extraordinary actions reflected the negative thinking about corporations, but they also mirrored an atmosphere of pervasive doubt about the value of the work being done. We know there had been complaints for years about the quality of academic law programs. In the *cahiers* addressing legal reform, all definitely asked for more professors of French law. A few universities added public law on their own initiative, but to make certain the trend became policy, a decree of the National Assembly of September 1791 had mandated this curricular change. At Bourges it was proposed to the Professor of Canon Law that he abandon his field for an immediate switch over to French law, a surly demand to which were added angry voices from the City council. Unfortunately, except for Orléans, Reims, and Poitiers, there was little reaction to the call for change. The realm of Roman jurisprudence may have been losing ground in the courts and law offices, but there were still at each institution three or four Roman law professors to one of French specialization.

The University of Orléans, which had maintained its high standards, demonstrated excellent quality in their Estates' petitioning. The administration felt the time right for a congress of universities to take the large step of proposing a veritable code of national education, and in response the Orléans law faculty had drafted a remarkably far-reaching *cahier* (De Curzon, 334–336). In its well thought-out first part the reader found a learned treatise on constitutional law; in the second surprisingly appeared a plan to pay the national debt; in the third there was a serious proposal for a committee of jurisconsults to unify the customs and reform criminal law; and the last presented an imaginative plan for improving law studies. Of course, even in the heat of revolutionary fervor, reform's flow seemed reined in by the short beat cadence of classical law's clockwork.

It was suggested that first-year students study the parts of Justinian's *Institutes* pertinent for France in one and a half-hour lessons, each divided into a half-hour of dictation and one hour for explanation and what was called "development." After Easter would be two lessons of an hour each. In the second year a course in canon law and another in contracts, successions, and wills would be studied during two one and a half hour lessons each day. In the third year one professor would teach the work of Pothier and the other French law, usually, for one and a half hours each per day. This professor of French law would until Eastertide teach broad principles (the usual persons, things, actions) followed by one of the ordinances on donations, wills, substitutions, or successions. Third year examinations would be scheduled as Easter arrived and at the end of the year. The two hour baccalaureate examination would come at the end of the second year; while at the end of the third year two examinations (French law and Roman law), plus an oral thesis of two hours, were to lead to the *licence*. Gold and silver medals like Pothier's would be awarded at the end of the course. After these details of students' schedules the Orléans *cahier* opened out into a bold and farsighted demand for across-the-board improvement in faculty compensation, distinction, and retirement considerations.

It was a well conceived plan but too much anchored in old ways to get attention in a hot revolutionary time. One may compare it with the Diderot plan of a few years before in which he proposed a law faculty of eight: one each for natural law, history of law, law of peoples, *Institutes*, ecclesiastical law, and procedure, and two for French national law. The Diderot study frame was set at four years with two courses each year. The professors were to have government salaries and no fees, with retirement or a judgeship after only fifteen years. Diderot lavishly avowed that in spite of their "'monstrous vices,' France should recognize her universities for "'the birth of all that has been done of good since their origin to the present'" (De Curzon, 348)—too generous an encomium by far.

The new plans were to have no future. De Curzon believed that the *coup de grace* of university life was the oath required in April 1791 for all who performed a public function. Such a pledge called, among other things, for maintaining with all one's power the Constitution decreed by the National Assembly and accepted by the King. Because this meant upholding the law of the Civil Constitution of the Clergy of 12 July 1790, most of the law professors—whose religion had not been dislodged by the philosophic attacks—felt uncomfortable in swearing allegiance.

Their discomfort was nothing less than another red flag for a defunct system. By 1791–1792 there remained only a few law students. The unthinkable had already occurred when the last examinations in Reims were given in 1792 and in Paris on 7 September 1793. There appeared no substantial defenders to step forward on behalf of the dying universities, either in the National and Legislative Assemblies or in the Convention. Dwindling support was abetted by a feeling that the taking of endowments had naturally turned academics against the Republic. Moreover, most faculty, closely attached to royalty, were very old men rapidly growing older. With higher level teaching establishments having already been forbidden on that grim 15 September 1793, it was left to the Convention finally, *de jure*, to put what appeared to many to be a merciful end to those universities in name only. This last blow took place on 25 February 1795, the day when Central Schools were established. Prestigious university corporations, with their ancient, independent origins which neither pope nor king could wholly extinguish came silently to their end, never to be reestablished. Fit into the general reconstruction that would now build republican, collectivist national schools, universities as later authorized were to live as creatures of government in which political loyalty was the chief concern of those who led them.

The Avocats in the Revolution

Hostility to lawyers is not uncommon in any era in any country. Typically, clients like their own counsel but dislike counsel representing the other side. Broad, literary and political attacks on the profession as a whole, often humorous, often cruelly unfair, find a sympathetic audience. But when trouble comes or an opportunity needs careful organization, that same audience is grateful for effective assistance. So it was in 1789.

The *cahiers* interestingly did not disclose widespread hatred for aristocrats of the legal world who resided but one level under the judges. Many were the *avocats* chosen as Third Estate deputies, and these were men who willingly packed their briefcases with paperwork for the Estates General. Of eight deputies from the suburbs, two would actually come from the *Ordre des avocats*; and of twenty from the city, five were from the *Ordre*. Among the twenty alternates, eight were *Ordre* men. But if the *avocats* as individuals were favored, their group membership made them corporate entities and, therefore, obtrusions between citizens and the state. After a solid consensus on the night of 4 August 1789 they, too, were disapproved by the National Assembly on abstract grounds of legal principle. Their fate was to be determined the next year in connection with business regarded by the delegates as more important: first, a reorganization of the judiciary for a France of departments and districts rather than of old provinces, and second, an in-depth discussion of *parlements* composed of high robe *conseillers*.

This essential judicial reorganization began promptly on 17 August when onto the table was placed the remarkable proposal that the privileged civil case monopoly be broken. Presented as a move forward it, in fact, turned advocacy 360 degrees back to ancient Greece, with each citizen free to plead the case at hand. Regulations for legal practice were now to be the same for all, whether trained in law or not (Fitzsimmons, 57). No *Ordre* was needed; those of formal law background would simply be called *hommes de loi* (men of law). Many proponents argued there was no reason advocates should be restricted to a privileged group rather than know the standards of the highest public authority; their ranks, opened at last, needed to be released from the constraining approval or discipline of any corporate entity. Proof of competence alone remained structured to a required examination.

On 24 August 1790 the new judicial system for civil cases based on departmental districts was approved. Paris was to have six District Courts, each with five judges elected for six years; forty-eight separate adjudicatory sections were each to be served by their own forty-eight Justices of the Peace. This realignment alone was enough to break up the *Ordre*, based as it had been on the easy concentration of one court. With six jurisdictions and very slow transportation, a geographical area almost one-third the size of France was at once the target of swarms of litigants walking or riding considerable distances to present their cases.

Senior *avocats* were adamant in their dislike for this new way but irresolute about what to do. With a show of poor political savvy, they for too long pinned their hopes on younger colleagues in the National Assembly to block the proposals. Many, foreseeing an arid field ahead in the private practice of law, managed to obtain places in municipal government; others left town and went back to their home base. However, *avocats* in some numbers had themselves become convinced the new vision had merit and that argument of cases as a right, not a privilege, should be open to all. It was even suggested that formal training for advocacy was not so important as literary skill. By 1790 some energized *avocats* no doubt saw surrender to these ideas—which for a member of the American bar do not seem inconsistent—as a form of necessary emotional sacrifice to the Revolution, comparable to the long nocturnal purge of 4 August. The *procureurs* defended their solicitor status, unsuccessfully, but the *avocats* did not. Even notarial cadres were dissolved.

Subsequent excesses committed by the progression of revolutionary governments quietly re-transformed the views of the *avocats*; most, no matter how idealistically they had begun, did eventually turn against the Revolution. It would not be until Napoleon decided to permit the Paris *Ordre* in 1810–1811—and that with some reluctance—that regulated advocacy was restored to real life. That life, however, had by then lost much of its old independence. On 2 September 1790 the National Assembly, almost cavalierly referring to the *Ordre* as something already gone, although there had been no such express resolution, effected the all-important vote on the semiotics of being a legal professional: "'the men of law, formerly called *avocats*, not being allowed to form either an order or a corporation, will wear no particular costume in their duties'" (Fitzsimmons, 60). When the new courts opened in Paris over four months later, of six hundred members of the *Ordre* in the *ancien régime*, three hundred of whom were in practice, only about fifty were ready to work as counsel in the new system, and very few became judges. One cannot help wondering how many of this diminished cohort could imagine that even more changes unfavorable from their point of view were in store.

The status of legal practitioners had begun as a secondary matter, and several weeks went by after the vote of 2 September before the National Assembly took it up again. When the legislators began to legislate, however, they did so with a heavy hand. On 15 December the profession of *procureurs* was abolished, taking along with it all venal and hereditary offices. Then came the great sweep when on 29 January 1791 the Assembly, in effect, ended law as a learned profession. Paradoxically, law's abandonment assured it an aura of mythic consecration for much of the collective memory. From Dickens's macabre Lady Justice, Mme Defarge, she of the knitting needle judgments, to his idealistic barrister Sidney Carton doing his far better thing at the guillotine; from the operatic liebestod of *Andrea Chenier,* to the Marquis de Sade as Section judge; from Latude's stringy long rope ladder, to the Widow Capet's stringy long rope hair—the popular remembrance of this time was centered and continues to center on legal injustice and lawcourt martyrdom. And, of course, on what a beauty Marie Antoinette had been.

The *licence* of the old universities which had been the avenue to law practice for centuries, was now an anachronism. Specialized learning being unnecessary, on the first of September the impounded library of the *Ordre des avocats* was consigned to the silence of lock and key. Not surprisingly, all this chilling elimination of books and of the men to interpret them led to a very big problem. How could a person faced with handling his or her own case be expected to observe correct procedure? and how could any Citizen or Citizeness hope for assistance without incurring great expense? François Tronchet, last President of the old *Ordre* and a man sympathetic to the Revolution, answered by making a proposal which was substantially adopted on 29 January 1791. His plan established the new ministerial public office of *avoué*, or attorney, for handling procedural matters for all litigants. If a citizen wished and could pay the attorney's fee, the *avoué* could also, for yet another fee, be engaged further to argue the case on the merits. The latter function could also be performed by an *homme de loi*, or public defender, if the citizen retained him; but here would come the revolutionary alternative already mentioned, permitting any citizen qualified or not, to appear for another's defense. This *défenseur officieux* made oral or written arguments, and it was expected he would generally serve without fee. In the idealistically revolutionary mind—although not, unfortunately, for minds functioning on the Committee of Public Safety—the citizen's right to equality under law was so important that it could not be trammeled in any way.

Herculean labors brought the new civil court system into operation on 25–26 January 1791. Unfortunately, apparent resolution engendered equally mythic travail as different problems and mixed results brought to the Council of the Minister of Justice in that first year alone an overload of 4,774 questions (Fitzsimmons, 81). There were shortages of staff, missed pay days, and no new educated bureaucracy coming from universities. By late 1791 and early 1792 numerous unprincipled men, having entered the courts as *hommes de loi* and *défenseurs officieux*, were in full tilt; their actions went on without restraints, and even when they were challenged, judges did not dare act against this new wild bunch of attorneys. Solicitation of business and excessive fees, including by *avoués*, was not uncommon.

It did not take long for this unsavory situation to prove unbearable for those members of the old Parisian *Ordre* who were still in practice. Mustering what bravura they had left and reacting on the principles of a century and a half, they unofficially organized again. In meeting, working under rules of the *Ordre* they had known from the past, they admitted as colleagues only men who would accept such governance; more pointedly, it was decided that a case was to be entered only with or against *hommes de loi* who would conform to the procedure. No other group needed to apply for consideration. One can understand why many of the new judges were still trying cases according to legalities largely of the *ancien régime*, and that many clients realized how influencing such a judge definitely called for knowledge of the formal law as well as oratorical and literary ability. It was beginning to seem a lot like the wild old days in ancient Greece. Criticisms rained down on the reestablished *Ordre*, but the conservative *avocats* appeared to be standing firm on their strict organizational framework. Then revival of old standards suddenly came to an abrupt end. The National Convention commenced its work on 20 September 1792 and two days later Danton arose and bluntly addressed the members: "'Notice that the men of law belong to a revolting aristocracy'" (Fitzsimmons, 90).

Marie Antoinette
Courtesy of The Bridgeman Art Library

No more *ordre* obtained. Law seemed lost forever. Louis XVI was stripped down to a simple, fearless man telling his rebellious people for the last time how he loved them all. It was as close to the allegorical religion of a morality play that a crowd had seen since medieval time. The difference was that now the Clovis Dove had been demoted to a dead pigeon and God's surrogate was being killed by the crowd to cries of joy. In the fall would fall the lovely head of the Queen, who also showed calm and compassion, begging pardon of her executioner as she inadvertently stepped on his foot. Neither King nor Queen died feeling guilty, Marie writing her sister that her conscience was clear. Their law, after all, was a divine right.

Only two members of the old *Ordre* had been elected to the National Convention, and, conveniently for them, they were no longer loyal to their organization. Legal training being now eliminated as a requirement for administrative and judicial posts, it was confusion's time to reign. One Minister of Justice multiplied into six was emblematic of the growing absurdity. Nearly all the pro-monarch *avocats* conveniently, and in their minds prudently, retired. Three bravely acted as the sovereign's counsel at his trial and many assisted in his defense, but there was again the marked shortage of legal assistance for ordinary litigants. In elections of judges in 1793 the winners included a gardener, a sculptor, a gem cutter, an engraver, a painter, a messenger, a rent collector, a carpenter, a wood merchant, a stone carver, a painter and engraver, and a hairdresser (Fitzsimmons, 97).

When a Revolutionary Tribunal was set up in March 1793 to try citizens for political loyalty, any member or accused with the slightest hint of legal training was immediately suspect. The short-lived office of *avoué* was abolished; those already titled as *hommes de loi* or *avoués* had to prove loyalty to the Convention by grant of a *certificat de civisme*. The impounded library of the *Ordre* was given to the Committee on Legislation of the Convention. Over at the Jacobin Club a committee of twenty-four set themselves up to supervise those of the members who were to serve as an untrained political bar of *défenseurs officieux*. On 6 January 1794 the Committee of Public Safety, central authority of the Terror, was empowered to remove and replace judges. Ten percent of the old *Ordre* were jailed; eleven *avocats* were executed. Many went into hiding, some left Paris, some emigrated. By the middle of 1794 the prestigious old *Ordre* had joined the law profession in ignominious extinction—often literally so.

With history and law being made as precipitately and as rapidly as the drop of a guillotine blade, it was inevitable and fortunate that oppositional change would occur again. On 9 Thermidor (27 July 1794) radicals gave way to a moderate wing which quickly instituted calming changes: the right of an accused to counsel was restored; the Committee of Public Safety lost it powers over the judiciary; rules were adopted for the Revolutionary Tribunal. Loyalty still had to be attested by a *certificat de civisme*, but now once more those surviving members of the old *Ordre* who wanted to practice came to life like so many legal phoenixes, reviving unofficially, yet far from tentatively, their old way. Marking the progress in conservative reforms continued; on 3 January 1795 it was decided there had been enough gardeners and hairdressers on the bench. New Paris judges had to have real juridical ability, and notably fifteen of thirty judges chosen for their expertise and training in the civil courts were actual credential-carrying members of the old *Ordre*. By 5 August 1795 the very unpopular *certificat de civisme* was abolished; already back in May the Revolutionary Tribunal had been terminated, and yet another somberly dressed committee with briefcases was called to sit down to work on another civil code.

We should not view this return to seriousness too euphorically, since legal practice was still scandalously overrun with incompetents. Of 304 men practicing in 1796–1797 only nineteen came from the old *Ordre*. Even that could not guarantee expertise. In a famed example one Leprestre-Boisderville exchanged trial dossiers, as had been *Ordre* custom, with the *homme de loi* on the other side. At the oral argument audience he erroneously returned to this colleague his own client's dossier and kept by error that of the *homme de loi*. Incredibly, with this wrong document in hand Leprestre-Boisderville argued fervently his opponent's case. At this point the *homme de loi* arose to agree wholeheartedly with all his esteemed colleague had just said. Discovering the blunder, Leprestre-Boisderville at once proceeded to plead for his own client, a turnaround utterly contradicting the first presentation. In spite of his appalling mistake, he won the case—and for his man, we should add. Such an absurdist comedy played out with equally ridiculous aplomb was certainly not the stuff which once had made the old *parlement* a legend of probity (Fitzsimmons, 121).

Try as they would, with no trained candidates coming forward, the men of the old *Ordre* could not increase their numbers. It became obvious that their paltry crew could never hope to restore the old standards; that would henceforth have to be a job for the government. The government, however, was not yet ready to do it, even though the establishment of just one civil tribunal for each department might have encouraged the organization of strong bar associations. In December 1797 a bill was offered to allow an unlimited number of *avoués*—that abolished office now to be reestablished—provided all were twenty-one years of age, had passed an examination, and were paid according to a fee schedule to prevent exorbitant charges. Citizens could continue to represent themselves. But even this mild proposal did not win acceptance, for it was attacked on the ground that it created a potential for a privileged corporation: the *avoués* accredited by examination would be different from the ordinary citizen, and *voilà*—France would thus be confronted by another distinct, corporate identity, anathema to the libertarians (Fitzsimmons, 126). It was going to require the *coup d'état* of Napoleon to change these attitudes of naïve obscurantism, and even when imperial plans were put in motion for law's codification Bonaparte would harbor strong doubts about any independence for the bar.

Rousseau and the Changing Conception of Law

The French Revolution can be seen as a great moralistic attempt to lift the quality of life. Turning aside from divine power as a means to that ameliorative end, denying credibility to the time-honored judicial order, this new age placed its faith first in natural law and then in the positive law which could implement it. The shining concept of nation as the transcendent source of achieving equity and unity through the value of the common good dominated the National Assembly from the outset. Then during the Terror, "law was no longer regarded as a collection of imprescriptible rights and formal rules to regulate the behaviors of autonomous individuals seeking their own ends in society; instead, it was considered an expression of the general will, so that justice could be unhampered by the usual rules of law" (Fitzsimmons, 14, 104). Although held through the ages, personal legal rights quickly became viewed as a subterfuge of conspirators to obstruct the general will, which is why at the Revolutionary Tribunal no preliminary examination was necessary, and defense for the accused was prohibited. The *raison d'être* of the tribunal was not as a mediator of differences between the individual and society, but rather as an agency of the broader societal will, punishing those who transgressed it.

The phrase "general will" being waved like a banner over France's bloodletting was itself, however, a perversion. As a code word for termination, it had co-opted the famous idea proposed by the forty-six year old Jean Jacques Rousseau in his *Discourse on Political Economy* (1758), making it work on behalf of Terror's ways, it exploited "legal proceedings as if they were a branch of commerce" (Fitzsimmons, 116). No longer able to explore the facts of man's origin, Rousseau had started out with a hypothetical state of Nature. He knew his tentative proposition to be a necessary beginning of any analysis toward understanding freedom. In this earthly paradise man satisfies his hunger at the first oak, slakes his thirst at the first brook, finds his bed at the foot of the tree which has afforded him its acorns for a repast, and thus supplies his wants. The only goods he recognizes are food, a female companion, and sleep; the only evils he fears are pain and hunger (Copleston, Vol. VI, 65–66). Not being reflective, he makes no distinction between "mine and thine." Not having speech, he makes no comment on such ignorance.

Into this state of Nature now intrudes civil society. To again quote Copleston (Copleston, Vol. VI, 68): "The first man who, having enclosed a piece of ground, bethought himself of saying, 'This is mine,' and found people simple enough to believe him, was the real founder of civil society." Civil society, however, far from being a pristine state of goodness, inevitably sullies the situation by bringing its own governmental ambivalences: moral distinctions between justice and injustice, immoral horrors of war and inequality. Societal control is thereby dangerously rough-hewn; it cannot be established by force since force is neither legitimate nor governance naturally right. What is needed is an association in which each man is as free as before. The answer: a Social Contract. Enter Rousseau.

Rousseau, who tended to be a Realist, found solution to necessity in the idea of the State as a formal being with a determining impetus. That thrust for which he chose the current "buzz word," General Will, tended to the preservation of the whole and all its parts and stood as the source of laws and the rule of the just and unjust. Yet the State could err, expressing then only the "will of all"; since this would include private interest, such a situation could not represent the General Will. Rousseau's idea, in other words, bore the same fruits of ambiguity, for the General Will is not always merely what the assembly votes. Who interprets this comprehensive moral law? conscience? or the yay and nay of the legislator? Is not General Will simply the natural law written in the hearts of men? To posit the action of the National Assembly as in fact General Will meant it could not matter to an individual's freedom that he dissented, for he would be dissenting wrongly. Freedom—acting in accordance with this General Will—paradoxically led to the necessary evil of forcing the individual to be free (Copleston, Vol. VI, 86, 91). However, in actuality, the vote of the Revolutionary Tribunal was raw positivism: it made no appeal to higher law. As the representatives claimed that their decisions were indeed expressing a Rousseauistic "General Will," bitter irony entered the chamber of men smugly holding close the politicized prestige of the writings of an Enlightenment icon while serving the dark interests of the Committee of Public Safety. Although Rousseau did not intend it, the noble savage had become a very useful tool in the often savage drift toward totalitarianism.

Restoration of the Teaching of Law and of Organized Practice

Rebellious attitudes toward law at last gave way to another philosophical shift in 1794. Robespierre fell on 9 Thermidor—27 July—and met his executioner the next day. The new Constitution of the Directory took effect on 22 August. Here was a chance for the younger of the *Ordre avocats* still interested in practice to start reopening their *cabinets* in Paris. Many of the profession privately and quietly hailed the document as favorable once again to the assertion of individual rights by counsel. As October 1795 marked Directory governance and a new judicial year, the resurrected lawyers were infused by a wish to rid the practice of unqualified and unscrupulous men and formally to revive the *Ordre* as the means to this goal. The substitution of one civil court per department for the divisive system of one per district was helpful, as was the attempt by the Directory to reestablish competence in the judiciary. Returning to the attitude of the National Assembly in the idealistic initial stages of rebellion, the Directors chose law rather than a bloody blade as the great leveler against the arrogance of privilege (Fitzsimmons, 114, 118). As legal science regained at last its prestige as the only instrument society could use to end the terrible arbitrariness of blood governance, grievances could from now on again find redress in the regular judicial institutions. Private property, the sacred aim of the bourgeoisie, would be protected.

Despite the balm of this reawakened admiration for fair but comprehensive judicial practices, the new government faced acute financial problems caused by wars both civil and foreign. The latter had brought forward for popular adulation General Napoleon Bonaparte, a young military and political innovator, flawed in character but, nevertheless, one of history's men of exception. Paradoxically, he proved unfit for constitutional democracy and appeared a doubtful factor for the rule of law that had so obsessed yet long evaded the Revolutionary protagonists. As he himself said, he could speak only to command or when he was sure that no one would dare meet his orders with riposte (Lefebvre, Vol. II, 256).

On 4 September 1797, any damaging split between reactionaries and republicans appeared resolved when the three republican directors took power. Yet hardly had a tentative calm seemed established when on 18 Brumaire of the Year VIII (9 November 1799) Napoleon arrived unannounced from his aborted military campaign in Egypt. He wasted no time regretting men and materiel left behind. Forming alliances with two of the ruling directors, one of them being Emmanuel-Joseph Sieyès, the upstart general carried out a *coup d'état* which overthrew the current government. Bonaparte and Sieyès worked out a new constitution establishing a Consulate, and on 16 December 1799, France's most famous little Corporal made the very large proclamation that the Revolution was "finished" (*Continental Legal History*, Vol. I, 289).

He, on the other hand, was just beginning. He would reign as powerful first consul for ten years; carefully appointing two others to share power, he took Machiavellian pains to limit them to a kind of consulting firm. He alone would rule. After all its bloodletting in the struggle for a democratic republic of laws among equals, France thus became a near dictatorship, whose dictator, determined to wear the ancient laurel wreath, promoted himself in 1804 to emperor with succession entrusted to heirs. The centralization process begun by Hugues Capet in 987 had at last been completed, not by a powerful man of royal blood, but by all five feet of this very determined soldier from the minor nobility of Corsica. Fortunately, he was not only ambition in a uniform; his was a remarkably powerful intellect with an interest in everything and a strong desire to make France prosperous. He had a felicitous common touch, ready to lift up from any layer of society one capable of doing good work, although that good work was accepted only as long as the one promoted could support Napoleonic leadership without hesitation.

A "full service" legal offering called for some new, highly trained men. When the Convention on its next to last day (25 October 1795) implemented the establishment of the Central Schools, it planted the seedbeds for such expertise. Starting at the secondary level, one school for each Department was chosen to offer a prescribed curriculum that included an introduction to "legislation." Long-suffering professors who had been former *avocats* saw this course as the exciting initiation vehicle for premier professional instruction. The reality proved less glamorous. Law had suffered too much denigration for faculty to make enthusiasm into a selling point for filling reopened classrooms. After all, the program also had to contend with what awaited after the degree—continuing poor conditions in law practice which still were exerting their negative effect on the choice of law as a career. More crushing for dreams of individual success, Napoleon's monologic stage was perfectly set for uniformity of law, but far less clearly arranged for an independent judiciary.

Nevertheless, given that expertise helped drive the new regime (Fitzsimmons, 134), the growing positive ethos meant educated lawyers were able that very fall to obtain government acquiescence for establishing two private law schools in Paris. Their goal was clear: to remedy the shortage in trained lawyers which, so far, had been only slightly relieved by a few unevenly prepared private tutors. The two new schools opened as the *Université de Jurisprudence* and the *Académie de Législation*. The former, chartered on 27 September 1800, was a unique law school in that it was organized as a for-profit corporation issuing shares of stock; its comprehensive program featured not only the instruction of students and legal publication (*Annales de Législation et de Jurisprudence*), but, functioning like a large national law firm, it offered legal service for all of France. The first classes began in February 1803. Unfortunately, more ambitious than practical, the *Université* closed after the second year—an interesting but unsuccessful experiment.

The non-profit *Académie* which began classes in 1801–1802 was at its zenith in 1803–1804. Its all male membership totalled six hundred twelve; many were important government officials who sat side by side with treatise writers, law faculty, and administrators, each man having paid fifty-four francs as dues. Twelve courses were offered across a three-year degree program attended by over two hundred students, forty of whom had been chosen as departmental scholars by the prefects. In rigor and structure, the curriculum did not disappoint the *Ordre* purists. In its first year *Académie* students learned about natural and international law, logic, morality, eloquence, and French public law. In the second year, attention turned to the Roman codices, to French law both private and criminal, and to the historic fabric of jurisprudence in its broadest outlines. In the third year came public economy, civil procedure, notarial matters, and commercial and maritime law. Practical work was always stressed, since this program was intended to be and was a real advance over

Passage du Mont St. Bernard (Napoleon's Army Crossing the St. Bernard Pass)
Courtesy of National Gallery of Art, Washington

that of the old universities. However, there still must have been risk of confusion for the student who had to be ready to grasp a given subject like obligations the moment it made its comet-like reappearance here and there in each course.

The *Académie*'s considerable success was nothing short of a triumph for its jurisconsult founders, joined to *avocats* either with governmental connections or currently practicing in the courts. While it functioned, this institution was far more than a school. It became a focal point of the effort to raise the level of the bar after the follies of the Revolution, and it acted, to some extent, as Fitzsimmons says (Fitzsimmons, 144), in surrogacy for the old *Ordre*. There was still leftover theoretical opposition to corporations, and Napoleon, too, shared the antipathy to some extent; but the practical start-up problems for a judiciary both efficient and enlightened overrode that opposition. Unbelievable as it seems to us today, it was an incredible step forward for the legal profession when, as of September 1808, admission to the bar once again became limited to those with a law degree. Provision was made for the reestablishment of the old *Ordre* panel of authorized, practicing *avocats*, although threats of future legislation to deny them any powers of final control could always be heard in grumblings from the bureaucratic wings. The important change was that having been condemned in 1790, the judicial *robe* had at last received honor in restoration. *Avoués* became comparable to the old *procureurs*, and *avocats* resumed their former role.

Napoleonic dictatorship initially did not prioritize access to law by each citizen, but the 18 Brumaire coup had definitely given the pendulum a great push in the direction of positive law. Rousseau's General Will was back on the table, molded into a "highest good" —systematized, well organized, and well regulated for a state placed exclusively under centralized control. Yet even though individual legal rights were not part of this highest value, the accession of Napoleon out of the Brumaire mists fortified the new hope felt by all attorneys, relieved and confident once again that at least they might enjoy the more favorable attitude which existed toward professionalism and professional organizations. After nineteen years and more of revolutionary experimentation, most of it foolish, much of it terrifying, the new authoritarian government of Napoleon had raised the colors of the rule of law. Noteworthy breaches by the leader himself had to be accepted as inevitable, but, on the plus side, inevitability also included efficient practice, learning, and integrity in support of law reborn.

Napoleon was never one to waste time, and his legal revisionism took on the gusto of a military campaign. On 18 March 1800 France received a new administrative and judicial structure generally pleasing to the former *avocats*. In August of the same year there was appointed, with much excitement and anticipatory fanfare, a blue ribbon commission of four men whose impressive task was now to draft a uniform civil code which might serve as the magnificently stamped and sealed new living quarters for equality before the law.

The battle for law soon lurched to a temporary standstill, when the leader had to face post-Revolutionary hatreds fuelling yet another of the nation's frequent, politically complex *causes célèbres*. General Moreau, who had aided Bonaparte on 18 Brumaire but since become his rival, was arrested on 15 February 1804, supposedly for royalist plotting but, also, perhaps, for showing his supreme contempt for the supreme First Consul by conferring on his dog the collar of Napoleon's new Legion of Honor. The Paris lawyers sympathized with Moreau, who actually did not favor any royalist reinstatement and had tried to distance himself from the royalist cabal. Two *avocats* even undertook a spirited defense of man and beast. The scene was exacerbated by the blatantly illegal governmental kidnapping and execution in March 1804 of the last scion of the royal Condé family, the Duc d'Enghien. Two weeks later the conspiratorial General Pichegru (Moreau's old commander), who had with the Vendée's George Cadoudal led the Infernal Machine plot to kill First Consul Bonaparte, was found dead in his prison cell. The official report proclaimed the kerchief tied about his neck meant obvious suicide, but many saw Pichegru, Cadoudal, d'Enghien, and Moreau as chilling exhibits for the truth about dictatorships. The public sympathized with the victims and the attorneys who were building a strong anti-governmental case; and the situation was, to say the least, difficult and time-consuming for Napoleon. He became infuriated with the two defense lawyers and soon turned his animosity against the whole profession. The result was that the Emperor never again looked with favor on a strong bar association. He felt great comfort when implementation of the decree of 13 March authorizing ten law schools was delayed until 14 December 1810, misguidedly seeing in it the possibility of more mastery given to the government than to the *Ordre*.

Because of such politicized and authoritarian leadership, these various foundings and reinstatements have been referred to as a "hollow victory" for the legal profession (Fitzsimmons, 181). Yet it was not so hollow, nor did victory lie just on the side of the bureaucracy. The growing reforms in education and the inevitable restoration of an educated bar with some control over its members were important and fulfilling achievements. They would have been of far less significance had they not been braced by equally profound improvements to the private law studied and practiced by all *avocats*. Nor should it be forgotten that imperial bracing still had royal blood in its composition—those strong Versailles mandates of Louis XIV and Colbert who in their time were prescient enough to recommence the work of codification. Finally, the victorious *avocats* and the new ranks of law students could be infinitely proud of legal scholars like Domat, Daguesseau, and Pothier whose contributory efforts now were about to get their chance at reshaping paradigms for republican judicial process. Beliefs and institutions, having been questioned by Enlightenment's reason and tested in Revolution's violence, were now at last hearing the good sounds of rebuilding as yet another Empire tried to emancipate the fulsome promise of *fiat lex*.

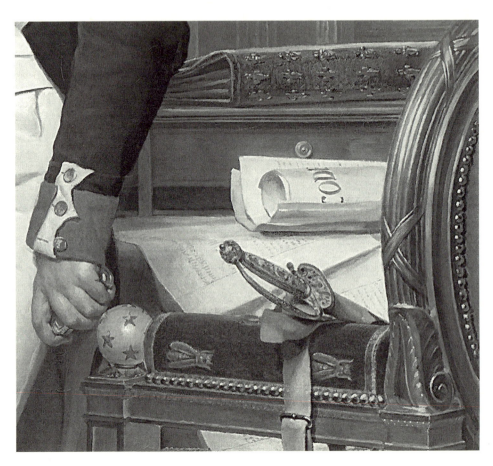

Le Code Civil sur la Table
Courtesy of National Gallery of Art, Washington

PART 19

The Nineteenth Century Intersection of Re-emergence
Antiquity, Empire, and Advocacy

Portalis and the *Code Napoleon*

Introduction

In Revolution's new society the National Assembly based on the Declaration of the Rights of Man presented France a Church-State solution. Under the title, Civil Constitution of the Clergy, it passed on 12 July 1790. Curiously, birth had not been an intellectual process arising from concern to eliminate corporations that shared the emotional outburst of the night of 4 August 1789. Origin, rather, could be traced to the most earthly of commonplaces: the Assembly, no less than the intellectuals, was desperate in its search for cash. Many had come to believe that commerce had been and continued to be impeded by having so much property in a sanctimonious *mortmain*—about one-quarter of France. If only the Church as a corporation might be dissolved, it was argued, its vast real estate wealth would conveniently be positioned without an owner to hold title—in other words, the Catholic fortune could revert to the state.

In the opposition were angry and worried Catholic theologians, who, as to be expected, considered that title to any given Church building was held in perpetuity by its glorious patron saint. Clearly, such reverenced real estate did not hold sway over the revolutionists, and none of these saints in any case was on hand to employ counsel. The new principle of "reversion" was, in truth, a high-handed destruction of the intentions of donors, a far sturdier and more honored principle which had governed centuries of pious giving. And there was a lot packed into the reversion proposal, for it was filled with high hopes that the state, while taking titles, take on as well the Church's functions of religious services, education, poor relief, and vital statistics. It appeared that all the ecclesiastics could hold onto here was a possible loophole allowing any past intentions, as a practical matter, to continue being honored.

On 2 November 1789 the National Assembly voted Church property to be "at the nation's disposal," an attempt at generalized control which would avoid technical arguments about title and get down to the glittering prize: raising a lot of cash by state sale of saintly land and goods. It was decided to do that not by granting title and possession but by selling certificates of state indebtedness, called *assignats*, which paid five percent and were secured by the Church's property as well as some royal lands. When sales were found to be chilled by annoying blocking problems—the clergy might still be in possession, or the property to be sold to satisfy the *assignats* could not be identified—it was voted early in 1790 that, except for teaching and charity orders, the regular clergy was to be suppressed and all its authority stripped away. No longer could religions administer property; nor could they establish budgets for public worship or enter into the particulars of any proposed sale. The old problem of the boundary in secular matters between state and Church power had finally been solved with draconian simplicity: the Catholic religion henceforth functioned as a department of the state.

At first, creditors beholden to the government were ordered to accept payment in *assignats*; but because even this failed to produce the new cash flow needed, the *assignats* were changed to bank notes available to all. Many were purchased by greedy financiers who by removing *assignats* from the market prevented their depreciation in an inflation which would have helped the poor pay their debts and speculators make more money.

Working in the foreground of this chaotic background, the National Assembly, in the Civil Constitution of the Clergy, chose for the newly secularized ecclesiastics a revised structure based on that already being applied to the state. Elected like other local civil servants, one bishop would serve each department, and one or more priests would be placed in each commune. Ancillary to the bishop would be a council for making binding decisions. The pope was deprived of power to draw on the French Church for money or to confirm bishops. Louis XVI glumly accepted this legislation, but many eminent French clergymen, willing to agree with the state but not willing to be its creature, denied validity unless approved by the Church. The Holy Father, not surprisingly, bit his tongue and delayed his response. On 27 November 1790 the National Assembly went ahead and required all priests in office to take an oath to uphold the Constitution of the state, which by then included the Civil Constitution for the Clergy. Expecting easy acceptance by priests, mollified, it was hoped, by now drawing state salaries, the Assembly was astonished when only seven bishops and less than half of the parish priests would comply. The French Church had become split, its divisiveness lying squarely between "juring" and "non-juring" priests.

In March and April 1791 the pope broke silence and spoke out angrily to his wayward French flock. Still wielding much support among the people, he condemned both the clerics' Civil Constitution and the Declaration of the Rights of Man. Effectively, France plummeted into religious strife once again. Peasants who were pro-Church, and workers who were not, divided into angry partisan camps like their curacy. To keep the peace the government found itself compelled to allow non-juring priests to officiate in the same religious structures as their "juring" colleagues. It was a chaotic time for the faith. The "Goddess of Reason" and her *culte décadaire* (worship every ten days) had long since been all but abandoned by the people; now, in the confusion and religious vacuum a push for atheism began to gain ground. Even the constitutional format of Catholicism found itself endangered in the rush for secularism.

Confronting this situation upon taking power as First Consul after the late autumn *coup* of 18 Brumaire, Bonaparte naturally found the confusion unsatisfactory, as it did nothing but destroy the pathway markers of social organization necessary to run a state which would be both disciplined and productive. Napoleon had come to sense France was sick and tired of revolution. The military school student who in jest used to be called *Puss in Boots* had as military leader already put hard wear on the leather and some of his nine lives as he marched into exploits of imaginative daring which far outdistanced the magical range of Perrault's fable. Having seized power, the talking points of his idealistic agenda—restore order, reestablish religion and education, and preserve equality under law—now awaited being turned into everyday practice. Much of the "magic" would come from the bar whose lawyers, like so many Empire officials, stretched across many walks of life but united on the dual recruitment bases of remarkable ability and complete loyalty. To these advocates Napoleon entrusted unifying France with no less than a completely new governmental organization. Their remarkable private law compilation known as the *Code Napoleon* would, in 1804, nearly in a pen stroke, achieve for the continent what post-Hastings Norman England had accomplished in 1066 when it laid the foundation for highly centralized government and judge-made national common law. The French, although ironically soon to know defeat by those English at Waterloo, nevertheless won something so special that it would outlast the battles lost or gained. This was to be the most important effort at legal codification since Justinian.

We cannot doubt that all of Napoleon's draftsmen sensed the ghostly Roman presence of the jurisconsults as they labored to find the right way between royal, customary, Roman, canon, and Revolutionary law. Only one among them, however, would be the reprise-with-improvements of Justinian's master lawyer, Tribonian. This new codifying genius was one of the busiest of the Napoleonic team. Referred to as J. E. M. Portalis, as if even his name were in a hurry to get on with business, Jean Étienne Marie, like his patron Bonaparte, had known how it felt to receive summary sentence and to dwell within the Revolution's prison walls. Now he was a Minister of State serving the century's Great Man, and if his colleagues did not see him yet as this emperor's Tribonian, many must have noticed the striking parallel, closer in time, to Henri-François Daguesseau.

Daguesseau, we already have seen, had also been chosen for ministership by the greatest of the great. Louis XIV and Napoleon readily saw in their star advocates the advantages gained for ambitious youth born into ambitious legal families—Daguesseau from a great one in Paris and Portalis from a modest one in Provence. Matched in their brilliance and precocity, these were students who, educated at home, *collège*, and university, found the university training to be the inadequate phase. In their illustrious careers as *avocats*, timing and personal preference were all that separated these confidants to ultimate power; Daguesseau spent nearly all his professional career in *Parlement* and the monarch's service, while Portalis represented private clients and joined the government late. Both were extraordinary public speakers—Daguesseau generally with a text, Portalis, although sightless in his later years, able, after preparing the text he could not see, to reproduce it extemporaneously from memory. Both knew the bitterness of political exile—Daguesseau for his political opposition; Portalis, forced by the Revolution for no adequate cause to emigrate or risk his life.

In their common ostracism came the shared urge for writing on philosophy. Daguesseau chose to attempt a system supporting the existence of natural law; Portalis opted for a critical commentary on the *philosophes* of the Enlightenment. There is clear evidence that Portalis read at least part of Daguesseau's instructions to his son, but there is none that he had read the *Méditations*. On the whole, the Portalis philosophy seems fairly consistent with the older man's anti-scholastic *Méditations*. Portalis did not adopt Daguesseau's innate ideas, his geometrical frame, and his

Napoleon in His Study
Courtesy of National Gallery of Art, Washington

Cartesianism, but when Daguesseau says his great effort is to show that man can within himself find Natural Law, one can consider this another way of expressing the study of facts observable to Portalis in his inner consciousness. Since these were both men who believed repose of the mind established certainty (Portalis, *De l'usage et de l'abus de l'ésprit philosophique durant le 18e siècle,* 218), they both were stay-at-homes for whom personal observation was not necessary: Rome exists without going there. Because neither finished his work and both withheld publication, both leave us wanting more concrete examples of the application and impact of their ideas, although the Portalis volumes do manage to strike a fairly convincing final chord.

The two men were devout and passionate for religious advocacy, although here the details showed differences in orientation. Daguesseau sympathized with Port Royal; conversely, now that Jansenism no longer was an issue, Portalis the good Catholic and State Minister of Religion began putting the Gallic Church on a new foundation by negotiating the *Concordat* of 1801 with the papal see. Each sought proof of the existence of God but in a different manner. Although Daguesseau declined in his *Méditations* to promote any particular religion, he believed the absence of God would be "absurd." His was the long held argument: nothing happens without need, hence there must be a first cause. Portalis agreed but was compelled to add a post-Revolution chapter in refutation of the atheists who boldly saw material objects but did not see God (Portalis-*De l'usage,* 248).

In political maneuvering while serving their royal and imperial masters, these were men who both had to seem to compromise their principles and consequently suffered some in reputation. For Daguesseau, it will be remembered, this accommodation occurred over the bull *Unigenitus*. Portalis, for his part, found himself obliged to go against his own advice after the Christmas Eve 1800 bomb attack on Napoleon's life led the nervous and angry First Consul to exile without judicial review all suspected anarchists. Both Daguesseau and Portalis would author part of the private law of France—Daguesseau in codes for donations, wills, minors, and trusts; Portalis in major portions of the 1804 *Code*. Finally, both strove mightily that this private law be uniform. Daguesseau's efforts would not be very successful, since in the long run his king lacked the power and the will to succeed. Portalis, on the other hand was to taste success, for he served a First Consul who had a surfeit of both the power and the will.

Young Portalis

When Count Frédéric Portalis published in 1834 the philosophical work of his father's exile, he prefaced the volume with an elder son's affectionate and proud summary of the paternal background. From an independent and modest family had emanated the honorable moral code of private virtue at the service of public good. It already found eloquent expression when an aging Portalis himself placed on the title page of his *Preliminary Discourse on the Code Napoleon* an encomium to the little fatherland of the family which leads inevitably to the great fatherland of the nation. For Portalis as for Daguesseau the kinship unit of good fathers and good sons made up the national patriotic unit of good citizens.

The Portalis family was of Italian origin and had lived in Provence since the sixteenth century. The men had mostly been lawyers working as magistrates or notaries. Portalis *père* served as professor of canon law at the University of Aix-en-Provence, a man highly representative of "nobles without lordship" and so oriented toward law that Portalis *mère*, who married very early and was a second wife, may well have brought him an unusual dowry: a manuscript of a law course carefully copied out in her hand. On 1 April 1746, our Portalis, Étienne, the eldest of eleven children, was born on what is now the rue Portalis in the pretty little village of Le Beausset near Toulon. In a few years his young mother, being overcome with so much maternity, sent Étienne to her parents at nearby La Cadière for care and nurture. Here he found a tender and loving home with a grandfather who favored Montaigne's skepticism and a grandmother who joined deep piety to a surprisingly fine education. The grandson delighted in reading aloud to them his favorite authors, and he evidenced his later penchant for public speaking by, as a little boy, clambering onto a table or a chair and holding forth for a half hour at a time to a captive audience of proud grandparents and amazed little friends.

At seven he was sent to the Oratorian collège at Toulon, but after a serious illness it was felt prudent to shift him to their branch at Marseilles. Here a teacher, struck by the Portalis talent, took a particular interest in him and introduced the precocious child to books presenting the irreligion of the Enlightenment thinkers. Portalis excelled in philosophy and dialectic, absorbing, as Montesquieu had done, the Cartesian point of view of the great Oratorian, Malesherbes. Destined for the bar by his parents, he was sixteen when he started law at the University in Aix. Hardly had he matriculated when he displayed his extraordinary mental gifts by publishing two short pamphlets, one called *On Prejudice*, and the other a critique of Rousseau's book on education, *Émile*. In the first, the better of the two, Portalis expressed a youthful exuberance as he decried the prejudice of always believing past centuries to be superior to the present; also in his sights was the habit of religious enthusiasts to seek in the divine books not what they ought to think but corroboration of what they already believed. In the second, less well written and probably more original text, Portalis objected to Rousseau for trying to reduce non-belief to rules and principles. Portalis was fearless as a devout and opinionated young neophyte. Writing against major free-thinking and opinionated philosophical works of his time, he had not the slightest hesitation in castigating Jean-Jacques whose fault, according to Portalis, lay in wishing less to train the young than to destroy in them the Christian and the sage. These early literary efforts attracted a pamphlet attacking Portalis for plagiarism of foreign writers. In the Portalis critique of theological battles, it would later seem, especially through the lens of Sainte-Beuve's sharp perspicacity, that he had actually been lifting phrases directly from Montesquieu's *Lettres persanes*. In fairness it should be said that, even before Sainte-Beuve's critical remarks there appeared as well an anonymous defense, one probably not by Portalis (Leduc, *Portalis, une grande figure de l'histoire napoléonienne. collection panthéon,* 11–13).

All this complaint of lack of originality became somewhat diffused as Portalis rapidly distinguished himself at Aix. The leading professor was Jean-Joseph Julien; but Sextius Siméon made the greatest impression on his student, probably because Siméon also had an elder daughter, Marguerite, who commanded her own kind of power. The two young people at first saw one another casually while walking around the Aix campus but soon found pretexts for more meaningful encounters. In August 1775 the twenty-nine year old suitor became the happy husband. Marguerite was a capable and intelligent woman whose aid to Portalis in the crisis of the Revolution and throughout his life was going to prove indispensable; the marriage was always harmonious.

Portalis was evidently popular among his fellow students and made some lifelong friends, including the young Marquis d'Albertas. The nobleman invited Portalis home where his mother, who conducted the leading intellectual salon in Aix, presented the young lawyer to a lively culture dominated by the most preeminent men of the robe. Frédéric Portalis records that the youth of Aix were then "'turbulent,'" and that his father, although far from being rambunctious, nevertheless contrived to go along as a "'good comrade'" (Adolphe, *Portalis et son temps, l'homme, le penseur, le législateur,* 14). Leduc assures us (Leduc, 15) that despite this brush with high spirits Portalis passed "brilliantly" all examinations for the *baccalauréat* in the second year as well as the *licence* in the third. In the beginning of 1765 the nineteen year old emerged from the law faculty to be received as *avocat* before the *parlement* of Aix (which also boasted a Court of Accounts and the Office of the *Sénéchaussée*, or Bailiff). He found ready admission to the *cabinet* of a classmate's father, the distinguished *avocat* Colonia, who treated Portalis as though he were another son.

Lavollée, the biographer of 1869, describes (Lavollée, *Portalis, sa vie et ses oeuvres,* 2) the young lawyer as a "Christian humble and sincere, a philosopher by instinct, a born orator," endowed with "good sense, firm principles, literary taste, and love of work," a true example of "our old bourgeoisie, a generous and energetic caste," destined to regenerate France in 1789 and not to lose its influence until "the day when, ceasing to be itself, it has, so to speak, lost its moral nobility." Outside of his work Portalis kept to the religious bent, enjoying membership in the Masonic order which had come to Aix in 1762 and which radiated a strong Catholic character. Lavollée does not mention Jansenism in connection with the committed Christian beliefs of Portalis, conceivably because suppression of the Jesuits by the monarchy in 1764 and by the papacy in 1773 gave the *philosophes* such an opening to fill the vacuum that the Jansenists, stripped of their old power, dealt far less with political affairs. As mentioned above, by the time the Revolution approached there were only a few authentic Jansenist congregations left, and they—buried, as it were, in the provinces—kept a very low profile. Parisian Jansenists especially had lost their power by following an extremism which emphasized emotional excess and the supernatural; at the Paris grave of one Jansenist priest credited with miracles some adepts were found actually eating the dirt above his coffin. Shocked authorities barred access to the grave and an anonymous wit erected a sign: "By order of the king, God is forbidden to do miracles here." (*Encyclopedia of Philosophy*, Vol. II, 5226).

Portalis at the Bar

From 1765 until driven from his law office in 1790 by the Revolution, Portalis remained active as *avocat* before the Aix *Parlement*. There was only one interruption: the 1778 year he would spend as city assessor. From the beginning Portalis aspired to be a leader of the bar and, what is more, a reformer. It was an Aix custom that after one's first oral argument in behalf of a client—usually a fairly anodyne affair—the newly admitted *avocat* received from the presiding judge an avuncular pat on the back with which to begin his career. Portalis, however, had already worked out the more ambitious philosophy that was to stay with him throughout his career. Sustained by his accustomed and, we might add considerable temerity, he had in various conversations previous to his debut performance told the *avocats* of Aix that they were and for a long time had been on the wrong track. Such blows below the professional belt meant that the conclusion of his first oral argument was marked by the most Stygian silence from the bench. An old practitioner, wishing to console him, conceded to Portalis that he had pleaded with spirit but obviously, the older man admonished, *Maître Portalis* would have to change his style to fit with professional compatibility into that of the bar as a whole. Portalis is reported to have shot back the curt reply, "'[It] is the bar that needs to change, not I'" (Lavollée, 7).

Portalis thought a lot about what such needed change should be, and when he presented the eulogy for Antoine-Louis Séguier, *avocat général*, delivered on the ceremonial occasion of Séguier's 1806 entry into the French Academy, it was clear that Portalis felt himself a kind of Southern-style Daguesseau exhorting his colleagues to leave decadence for a higher standard of legal oratory. Every opportunity was used to make trenchant points—lift the bench from its lamentable state of venal debasement and lift the practice from too much private law at the expense of public authority.

Portalis was invariably one who applied law as a science as well as a tool, imploring lawyers to stress good sense and to base their science on the elevated, eternal principles of Cicero and the best Romans; it had been a way recently modeled for all by the brilliance of Domat and by Montesquieu who regularly decided every question by classical application. Pleaders, according to Portalis, should also heed the advice of the great Daguesseau, a man he regarded as not just accomplished in both literature and law, but one who had pushed eloquence beyond a mere "'production of the mind'" into a veritable "'work of the heart.'" Portalis wisdom was sophisticated yet simple: "'For triumph of reason one needs always something more than reason itself.'" Yet this simplicity spoke to a new sensitivity, to feelings which moved away from pure Enlightenment reliance on reason toward a pre-Romantic understanding of the emotional quotient. How could anything less, he would wonder aloud to any who might listen, be considered suitable for a calling as eminent as that of the law? Marveled the enthusiast: "'What treasures of science, what range of erudition, what discerning wisdom, what delicacy of taste must be combined to excel at the bar! Whoever dares to set limits to the science of the *avocat* has never had a correct idea of the vast sweep of that profession'" (Adolphe, 17).

As Portalis looked out over this ambitious scope of legal work, he discovered with the excitement of a laboratory scientist that it entered every nook and cranny of human life. The career lure was clear: servants of the profession—orators at the bar—deservedly could and should be able to enjoy careers no less brilliant than those in academic chairs and even more illustrious than those elevated to the high tribunals.

However, Portalis sadly noted such ambition was blocked by a list of multiple obstacles. Use of Latin in the law faculties and the courts ignored the daily progress of the national language; the condition of the national "legislation," i.e. the rules of the law, consisted only of an unformed mass of incoherent texts collected without choice and distributed without order; the multitude of diverse customs and contradictory decisions were written in popular or superannuated idioms. It all contributed, in short, to a chaos penetrable "'only with the aid of a crowd of commentators whose obscure definitions and interminable discussions fatigue the mind without clarifying it'" (Adolphe, 16). Bitterly, Portalis recognized that these tactics were encouraging many to desert the bar for, of all things (and now you can just hear the Provençal accents as the voice paused then dropped with a scornful accentuation of the rolled "r"), literature.

To this crusade for renewal Portalis brought the strength that came from being able to practice what he preached. Immediately noticed for the elegance and ease of his remarks, he became almost overnight "the oracle of the bar" (Adolphe, 18). His was the fecundity of youth and genius, perhaps, as Adolphe suggested, at first too full of "flowers and ornaments," but that would be but a phase of immaturity which age, experience, and meditation soon cured. To these he added vast knowledge and exact logic. Persuasive dialectic and astonishing memory equally supported these gifts, and his vehemence could be electric even when under pressure in stormy assemblies. Forty volumes of the always noteworthy pleadings survive.

Portalis was not affluent, but he did have some outside income which allowed him to be able to decline cases when he was not persuaded his part would be just; in a contrary situation his strong Christian engagement meant he also accepted work in behalf of the sick and the aged, even taking cases from those with no means to pay. This equable hand defines a man who saw the bar as the premier level of magistracy and a calling whose permanent high responsibility took precedence over frequently mediocre honoraria. The Portalis moral barometer meant an exceptional range in case load, from small litigations between big people, to big problems between little people. One of his most prestigious cases was the defense in 1771 of the Count de la Blache, heir of one Paris-Duverney, against the claim of the writer Beaumarchais, for enforcement of an acknowledgement of indebtedness to the writer made by the deceased. Portalis did his best but in vain; the courts rejected his client's allegation that Beaumarchais himself executed the document.

Although a scholar of the past, Portalis made considerable efforts to keep abreast of all important current legal problems arising outside his office. One of these was the validity of marriages between Protestants, unions which Protestant ministers had continued to perform long after the revocation by Louis XIV of the Edict of Nantes. Magistrates, however, were deciding against such heretical unions, and even the children born of them were being branded illegitimate. This controversy aroused the Portalis sense of justice, and he began to collect relevant materials on the subject. Especially of interest to him was a notorious case in which the undisputed eloquence of the *avocat général* Servan had been insufficient to get a favorable result for his Protestant client. Louis XV had been persuaded by clergy against the ministerial advice of the Duc de Choiseul to hold fast and even abandon some improvements countenanced by Louis XIV. All the *parlements* were discussing the question. Nothing could attest more eloquently to the meteoric rise of Portalis than the act of Choiseul in consulting him for his opinion on the status of Protestant nuptial arrangements. The Portalis response, which, like his *Preliminary Discourse on the Code Napoleon* was a hymn to family and country, courageously affirmed the right of the Protestants to celebrate lawful marriages.

Portalis came to his decision by avoiding history and purely juridical decisions. By building the case on the broadest principles, he found it was easy to deny that the validity of a marriage depended on religious consecration. Foreshadowing work to come on the *Code Napoleon*—to say nothing of casting a light forward on history—

Portalis presented marriage as a natural right, a contract in origin older than the Church, older than society, and one whose deep roots meant positive laws could regulate it only as to form. He cited Augustine who held valid the marriages of infidels as well as bringing in the precedent of other early Church decisions declining to require pagans to remarry. And, as a libertarian, he stressed the separation of the moral power of religion from the coercive power of the throne. Despotism over souls, he wrote, is unknown to the civil law: only God is king of souls, and the State may not shatter the beneficial pattern of the natural order.

As soon as Choiseul finally published the completed consultation, it became an instant success. Said Voltaire: "'This is not a consultation, it is a true treatise of philosophy, of legislation, and of political morality'" (Lavollée, 14–15). Portalis had brilliantly demonstrated the value to an *avocat* of broad intellectual resources, and his stunning moral victory would henceforth be used by all those who espoused the cause. His prophetic words were to be recalled by Malesherbes in the preamble of the royal Edict of 1787 when France at last gave toleration to the Protestants.

There is time for only briefly mentioning here several of those important matters which Portalis handled that did not call for refining expressions of philosophy of law and contractual government but rather were set in the heat of partisan politics. One such was the occasion when the Mayor of Marseilles proceeded against a young Knight of Malta for a public disturbance. The Order quickly voted that the Mayor—a Marquis—and his descendants should forever be barred from membership. Portalis successfully attacked this vote before the *Parlement* of Aix by showing that the history of the Order demonstrated the limits of its power. The Order riposted by asking the King to chastise Portalis. Instead, Louis XVI sent a messenger to Portalis with assurances of his protection. Another case involved the passionate Revolutionary orator, Mirabeau, whose fiery prose and male chauvinism had forced his wife, separated *de facto*, to return to his hearth. Portalis pleaded for the wife and won a separation decree, his brilliant arguments vanquishing the man then esteemed France's greatest in eloquence.

When in 1778 Portalis left the bar to serve as Assessor of Aix and *Procureur* of Provence for two years, he took on the large responsibility of being a chief administrative officer with an immensely active office. His success may be gauged by the many significant public reforms that were carried into practice with no significant public dissent. Among other things Portalis ended the tax exemption of the knights of Malta. Returning to his private practice, he was engaged in 1782 to go to Paris and plead in behalf of his native province on several pending matters. These affairs, far removed from being naïve Provençal shadings of the law, were all settled in fine upstanding form, affording at the same time Portalis's first opportunity to see the excesses of the capital, reported in detailed letters home to Marguerite. In 1787 a Church prelate consulted Portalis on the question of whether there should be a meeting of the Estates General of Provence, and if so whether they should convene in their ancient and long neglected separate form. Portalis in an opinion of 154 folio pages rehearsed the history of the Provençal constitution. With striking prescience in regard to the coming Tennis Court testing ground, he sustained the practical advantages of electing delegates from provincial communities and pointed to the desirability of having a majority for the Third Estate.

As Louis XVI signed his 1788 edicts clipping and even cutting off the wings of the *parlements*, all juridical France became aroused. At Aix the bar decided on a direct appeal to the monarch and engaged Portalis to draft a protest which was signed by every member. This formal complaint dated 17 May 1788 had been framed by Portalis to have the intimate immediacy of a complex, detailed letter to the Keeper of the Seals. With a point of view far different from what might be expected in the hands of an incipient drafter for strongly unified imperial codification, Portalis chose words recalling Montesquieu. He proposed the view of a limited French monarchy, writing that the king did have legislative power but had never yet exercised it without the concurrence of the Estates General or *parlements*. He felt that the proposed plenary court under royal control would be an illusory substitute, and that the alleged inconveniences of the *parlements* for the king were in fact nonexistent. Legislation should be made slowly, counseled Portalis, given that the French national mosaic was made up of so many autonomous provinces, of which Aix clearly was one. Laws prepared in Paris, explained Portalis, came as if from a foreign land and needed careful study; uniformity of law in a monarchy so vast, composed of several peoples with distinct usages, needs, characters, and habits, was, when one really thought about it, not desirable. In fact, he concluded, loyalty to the patchwork quilt of local differences might well be the strongest link uniting the provinces to the warm, blanketing power that protects the whole. (Ironically, not many years later Portalis in presenting the *Code Napoleon* would condemn in blistering terms this line of reasoning.) In so pleading against law-making by an absolute monarch and in favor of a sovereign subject to law Portalis was bravely carrying out views of the great Jansenist lawyers. Through him they entered the fast-moving changes which marked revolutionary triumph and survival under the dictatorship of Napoleon.

Portalis in the Revolution and Its Aftermath

The Leduc description of Portalis shows us a man in his forties, hair prematurely white, forehead bald, found more often than not at his country home in an effort to avoid the public service to which national reputation, talent, and achievements far above his provincial colleagues all inexorably destined him. There is a definite stress factor at work in his intense demeanor as the troubles preceding the Revolution roiled around him, and portents of the future could be read as far from certain. It is not surprising that Portalis for the first time was seen to handle a gun (Leduc, 66, 67). Such was the tension of those about him that when some poor shepherds and their flocks came down the street, concealed in a cloud of dust, a great crowd gathered to oppose what appeared to be an advancing enemy, and each person took as arms whatever could be picked up. On another occasion, a meeting of the municipal council of Aix, the usually orderly proceedings were suddenly broken up by a boisterous, threatening mob. One of the most gripping events occurred in 1790 when Portalis pleaded before the Aix *parlement* as assigned counsel for two royal dragoons who, in repressing a disturbance, had killed a peasant menacing them with a pitchfork. The jurist found that his audience appeared comprised of a horde of onlookers hostile to the dragoons. His tactic, therefore, was to begin by turning and addressing the mob rather than the judges, asking for the calm needed in order for the accused to be accorded the lawful right to a defense, a right, Portalis could point out, which was recently voted by the National Assembly. Sensing the menacing crowd growing restive, the President of the panel offered Portalis at the end of the hearing the safety of his office, but Portalis courageously declined and was permitted to leave without incident. The drama marked his last court appearance in Aix.

Since the fateful spring of 1789 Portalis had been considering retirement. The times were momentous, and Marguerite feared for the safety of the family, now augmented by a son. She wanted Portalis to devote more time to the boy's education, and no doubt was the force behind a move of permanent retreat to their country place, *Les Pradaux*. Here Portalis spent eighteen months—tutoring his son, starting a book on government, entertaining politically proscribed friends. But in February 1792 insurrections burst out in Provence, and the family moved to Lyon where Portalis had many friends and could try to practice law if he exercised scrupulous care to remain apolitical.

It was a general moment of high tension: nobles, clergy, and high *bourgeois* in a pell-mell of desperate exodus, leaving France for safety in exile. Portalis, however, a strong patriot, was determined not to do that, despite being wrongly inscribed on a list of *émigrés*. He at first did try to lie low in Lyon only to renounce that tactic early in 1793 by composing a vigorous plan for the defense of Louis XVI and reading it to numerous Lyonnais groups. In July 1793 the Convention forbade anyone not born in Lyon from living there, and Portalis was again forced to be on the move, this time to Villefranche, where the occupying Revolutionary Army arrested and shot his secretary almost before his eyes. Desperate now, Portalis tried to disappear into Paris itself, only to be arrested on New Year's Eve 1793. Certain death awaited at the hands of the Revolutionary Tribunal. Then came a glimmer of hope when the son of an Aix dancing master who happened to be a friend of Robespierre and an occupant of official place arranged that the official order send Portalis to await trial in hospital rather than a prison. Another glimmer: Portalis *fils* managed to delay the court appearance of his father. As delay and frantic options did finally run out, with the most fortuitous timing, Robespierre fell. This *coup d'état* of 9 Thermidor without doubt saved Portalis's life. He lived on, still confined, until January 1795, when the pleadings of two friends finally succeeded in freeing him.

At last Portalis could settle. He chose Paris and there resumed the practice of his profession. Evidence points to his having found restoration to good standing—except among the minority of the Convention still sympathetic to the Terror—for he received an offer of a judgeship in a projected high court. This he refused. He knew himself too well to think that a quiet role in hushed judicial chambers responded to his intense nature. Early in 1795 he courageously published a pamphlet demanding restoration of the confiscated property of victims put through the anguish of the Revolutionary Tribunal; a little later he wrote against brigandage in Provence and in favor of reparations for seizures of property in Lyon.

As Lavollée says (Lavollée, 43), these acts were daring enough "to push courage to temerity." Portalis began appearing at assembly meetings for his section of Paris (Montmartre) where people appreciated the talent he had to offer. Soon he found himself elected as member from the Department of the Var to the council of Elders, one of the two legislative bodies established by the Directory's constitution. At this point he ceased to practice as an *avocat* and never resumed it, although retirement did not mean he put aside debating performance. Membership on the Council of Elders increased his influence through masterful display of expertise and character; in little time Portalis had risen to be moderator and chief of the constitutional party.

His most celebrated achievement in the Council came near the end of his service. On 14 November 1796 a storm hit the French coast, and fifty-three distinguished French royalist *émigrés* from a large party on board three Danish vessels were cast up on the beach. They had been on the way to India to oppose a revolt against English rule, having stipulated that they should never be required to serve against France. Among them was Portalis's old client for the Consultation of Protestant Marriage, the Duc de Choiseul. All fifty-three were arrested as returning *émigrés*, and a complex litigation ensued. Distinguishing those who returned voluntarily from those who were shipwrecked, Portalis pressed the position that a banished émigré remained a man, and as, such had all the indefeasible rights of natural law which must be respected everywhere. True, the state saw these escaping royalists as enemies, but, he argued, even in war enemies benefit from moral duties which all belligerent nations recognize. Portalis argued with such eloquence that the unfortunate exiles were freed unanimously.

A month later, however, new events ended his illustrious service in the Council. On 4 September (18 Fructidor) 1797 the Directory, with help from the army, roughly put down concilar opposition and in Lefebvre's words (Lefebvre, Vol. II, 197), "returned the Revolution to dictatorship." The Constitution was ignored and the moderate Portalis faction was denounced as royalist. The most eminent of the Council were condemned to deportation, meaning for most death by penal abuse and disease in Guiana. Some who, like Portalis, remained in France proper, were sent to Ouessant near Brest. But an old friend from his first captivity hid Portalis in his house, another friend arranged for flight, the Danish minister gave him a passport, and he left Paris secretly with Frédéric late in September 1797. After a dangerous crossing of the Swiss border, with a pause at Basel and Zurich, Portalis spent the winter in solitude near Fribourg, expecting to journey on in the spring to Venice.

However, a letter from a friend in Germany, fortified by one from the Count Reventlau, former Danish ambassador to Berlin and London, invited father and son to join other refugees from the September *coup* at the Count's castle of Emckendorff. The presence of so many fine minds caused the Reventlau salon to become an important contributor to a distinguished intellectual movement. In Lavollée's melodramatic and chauvinistic words: "Excited by our examples, instructed by our errors, sharpened and made supple by constant contact with *émigrés*, the German genius left its long slumber and paved the way, in creating a great national literature of the foundation still distant of political unity." It was a setting worthy of Rousseau: the Count, aided by the grace, spirit, and incomparable goodness of his Countess Julie who had already suffered twelve years from tuberculosis, received Portalis cordially. The Countess was much traveled, with exquisite taste and a learning as broad as it was modest. Her lively sensibility, tender piety, and affectionate nature made her a living embodiment of Rousseau's fictional Julie, and, as in *La Nouvelle Héloise* her conversation was described (Lavollée, 112, 114) as having an irresistible charm. Portalis and his son were entertained lavishly for nearly two years.

The Philosophy of Portalis

The direct confrontation of philosophy and lawmaking had in the work of Daguesseau taken an interesting route of dual expression: meditations on natural law and precisions for codification. In the mind of Portalis, France had once more been given for its consideration the same subject matter and the bifurcated mode of its expression. The double fascination was a direct outgrowth of authoring those two Emckendorff volumes, a text preceded by an essay of Frédéric Portalis on the origin, history, and progress of French literature. That important work, bearing the rather blunt title of *De l'usage et de l'abus de l'esprit philosophique durant le XVIII Siècle* (On the Use and Abuse of the Philosophical Spirit During the 18th Century) had been carefully and comfortably dedicated to the Count and Countess Reventlau. Undoubtedly the Portalis reticence to write the actual introduction came from being an important actor in the transitional government. He could certainly not afford to give opponents too much insight into his beliefs and aspirations, and thus the only available tactic was simply to refrain from publishing anything himself.

The Portalis book, unlike Daguesseau's, is not a paradigmatic expression of one man's viewpoint, and just in case of comparison he took care to deny that it was. His plan was to review the philosophies of the eighteenth century the better to ascertain their validity by judging them against his method. However, since in so doing Portalis was inevitably expressing his own views, what we have in his work is both a survey of selected writers and an unplanned look at personal philosophy.

Although inspired by the astounding progress in knowledge made by the scientific revolution, Portalis, frankly, was neither mathematician nor experimental scientist, but he was in a manner reminiscent of Descartes or Newton, offering his "Spirit"—a method which must be pursued by all epistemological systems to arrive at truth. Born of the culture of exact science, the "Spirit of Philosophy," as Portalis was to define it, demands of all a behavioral protocol: careful good observation and practice of a sane dialectic founded on the solid principles of an enlightened metaphysics. The requirement of exact observation which permits classifications and generalizations is achieved, Portalis tells us (Portalis-*De l'usage,* Vol. I, 125, 152), by the use of our senses. Knowledge begins with the discovery of objects which are studied first individually, and then, in comparison with others. Ideas thus extrapolated from sensation are not innate, nor do they, as Malebranche had said, come at every instant from Providence. Neither are such thoughts the deductive source of knowledge as once believed; rather they are the byproduct of our senses.

We remain ignorant of what matter is in itself, origin and essence being necessarily inaccessible to us. Except for mathematics, morality, and jurisprudence, we thus are kept from exact definitions.

Portalis throws us, in this drift toward the Unknown, the lifesaving reliance on an innovative metaphysical concept, the Spirit of Philosophy. The materialists—here Portalis mentions quite a lively group of Diderot, d'Argenson, Frederick II, Priestly, Hume, d'Alembert, and Voltaire—all say that everything not based on observation and experiment is foreign to philosophy. But not to be outdone by his blue ribbon panel Portalis asks rather that we open the door wider. *Phenomena*—all facts which are well established—do indeed form the "science of facts," "the science of things." Portalis, however, deciding to go even farther, marches resolutely on, closer to a Proust or a Freud, by explaining what is meant by "fact." It is a remarkable explanation which could have its initial source in his failed eyesight for the physical universe and his resulting heightened awareness of inner consciousness. Do not, he admonishes, limit "fact" to physical phenomena perceived by man's external senses. Allow the world of factual knowledge to include internal ideas in the mind and reasonings from them. Of these extraordinary phenomena known by interior sensation, are we not remarkably as sure as we are of the fact of our own existence? Why then, asks Portalis, should they be foreign to philosophy, given that our certainty of them is more immediate and less contentious than as to physical objects?

In a note Frédéric Portalis would add his own editorial glosses (Portalis-*De l'usage,* Vol. I, 227–228) to his father's sophisticated insight: "...Our author in the whole book establishes with all his force that our interior consciousness, which seizes objects which are impalpable and not visible to the eye, puts us in command of the moral world, and observes phenomena that don't fall under the external senses and can't be seen except with the internal senses." "Our author applies to the study of intellectual and moral phenomena the method of the empirical philosophers and transports observation and experiment into moral and metaphysical science."

It is not with any easy success in view that Portalis then carefully addresses the precise question of how to make these reliable internal observations. There are, he asserts, even for this remarkable progress, rules which guarantee results just as rules guide mathematics. The diversity of data achieved by those who follow Descartes, or Kant, or Locke, or Malebranche and who say that ideas are innate, *a priori* as from God and not sensed, shows that not everyone knows how to interrogate the internal senses. We cannot possibly have a true result every time we think we do. The right approach to the problem, advises Portalis, lies in studying diligently what we sense, avoiding arbitrary suppositions, and carefully ceasing our observations whenever the sullying distraction of passions oppose our study—as when, for instance, we are enmeshed in the prejudices of other people. If then we err it is clearly because we have been dealing without guaranteed faculties.

The Portalis point of insistence had thus brought law to a remarkable new possibility: when deriving true propositions of morality, methodical observation and experiment can be used on facts which are only internal ideas. This stance, while it put Portalis in the camp of the old time realists, set him against the materialists who held that these internal ideas, too, have material (biological or mechanical) causes and therefore no implications as to morality. It is unfortunate for legal posterity that since the form of his book deliberately presented no system, there were to be no forceful applications of his method. We are disappointingly left only with his rather bland assurance (Portalis- *De l'usage*, Vol. I, 222) that the common man has what it takes to make such application.

Portalis took advocacy along the high road of the Golden Rule, playing by an unwritten book of gentleness, humility, disinterest, abrogation of self, control of passions, decency, sobriety, wisdom, and courage. But church-based doing unto others was enforced by a hardheaded advocate's corresponding assertion that the security of person and property must be guaranteed. It is clear that for him righteous complexity did not preclude setting up a juristic wish list: that there be a body of moral doctrine; that morality itself come from a virtuous order whose laws are comparable to those of the physical world rather than derivative from chance. Portalis was standing foursquare on an ethics whose truths to this day have the immutable grandeur of natural law. At the same time he sharply reigned in this grandeur, first by denying our ability to know any rule of explanation for everything, and second, by painting the danger in deducing a system from one predominant idea. Portalis also put in some anti-Cartesian admonitions: geometers are not observers, and the spirit of geometry, right for some sciences, will not do for morality. Pleading principle like a case at the bar, Portalis presented as a cautionary example the physiocrats who by observation concluded that commerce and industry do not create wealth—only land does. This had led the Quesnay *économistes* to deduce that there should be a single tax on land. Portalis, however, saw their observations as insufficient and hoped to prove that weakness by the success of the pre-Revolutionary flexible taxation system in his native Provence. There a Marseille or a Toulon, with only limited *immeubles* (immovable property, that is land and buildings) yet a large amount of *meubles* (movable property, personal property) could not be taxed in the same way as the farms in the rest of Provence.

Because he was a firm backer of religion (and probably a Roman Catholic), the Portalis support for natural law was not so secular as that of some. He turned away from philosophers for whom morality is independent of God, but he did not refute the principle of Grotius that natural law would be the same even if God did not exist. Rather, the famous consultant on marriage stated (Portalis- *De l'usage,* Vol. II, 58) that natural morality antedated Christianity and other positive religions. In other words, before any revelation or positive religion, morality was binding purely by its own force as natural law. Accepting that God exists, Portalis—foreshadowing many a political argument in American presidential elections—thought it a mistake to make the evidence of natural law depend on proving the truth of a positive religion; people weak in religion could then conclude, erroneously, that they were not bound by the rules of morality. Instead—and maybe Portalis wrote with less *angst* than Daguesseau simply because he wanted to concentrate on use rather than abuse—his readership was to understand these rules as eternal, common to all people, and set above all written laws. Neither society, education, politics, nor attorneys have created them; rather, they have been the ageless mortar that made and make society possible.

While he may not have personally rejected many Church dogmas, it is clear that, as outlined by him in his Chapter XXV rules for choosing a religion (Portalis-*De l'usage,* Vol. II, 155), the "necessary" truths of Christianity, confined as they were to the essentials of the four gospels, in a sense represented a return to the simplicity of the early Church. In keeping with his philosophical penchant for internal ideas, Portalis saw choice of religion as a matter for the heart and not the mind. If a belief system is truly divine, its dogmas and ritual will be consistent and function as a supplement to and guarantor of nature as well as a support to morality. In faith Portalis could hardly be called a religious eclectic, since he considered in detail only Christianity, buttressed by its establishment in what he viewed as all "enlightened" countries. His attitude was that a true philosophical spirit is the Christian religion's dominant characteristic; it imposes no limits on reasoning except our reason itself. Portalis had no hesitation in promoting credo in propagandistic terms: where civil morality only oversees actions, Christianity tries for the more ineffable domain of control over affections and thoughts, reigning serenely even in the fury of systems, urging that life be not too contemplative but ordinary. Its rites are not, contrary to what the *philosophes* say, put ahead of virtues; they instead recall its morality and dogmas. Portalis recognized a Church fairly accused of intolerance and furious proselytism and knew well that some of its leaders continued to betray its principles. His goal was meliorative: to define a practical, reformist Christianity on the basis of the central writings, religion that he, as an urbane legal leader and thinker, could support at any time and in any place.

With his keen historicism the lawyer realized that although age alone does not prove the worth of a religion, Christianity must necessarily be granted the pedigree of great antiquity. Even so, while emotionally accepting that God has always existed and that mankind is as old as nature, Portalis held to a high degree of actual proof as necessary for the prophets and miracles. From an advocate's professional point of view these facts of Christianity were more striking in support of faith than any prophets or miracles, for they paved the way to both wide acceptance of the religion and its triumph over secular powers. Despite his visceral quarrel with the Enlightenment over its centerpiece rejection of any organized divine element, Portalis praised wholeheartedly the way the new philosophical and political inquiry had surprised even itself by becoming a felicitous forum of question and answer for faith, eliminating many great errors and abuses while its good maxims spread across the world. Many were the great names and their great views which produced a felicitous sort of "civil sacerdotal" acceptable both to a practitioner of the faith like Portalis and to the new anti-religiosity which had blossomed in the Revolution. The Portalis admiration for Montesquieu frequently and eloquently set his compatriot on a pedestal for being able to achieve a morally hewn legislation and jurisprudence unencumbered by what today would be pigeonholed as faith-based initiative; he willingly compared Montesquieu's legal revolution to the scientific revolutions in natural systems by Newton (Portalis- *De l'usage,* Vol. II, 224–225). Portalis also cited administrative amelioration that had brought most absolute princes to curb their sceptres before the altar of eternal equity; he noted Catherine of Russia giving to her Senate the right of remonstrance, and the reign of Louis XVI permitting all kinds of good things, except, Portalis was forced to admit, intelligent finance.

In recounting some of the history of France to show at what epoch legal philosophy was applied to legislation, the Portalis discernment flagged his country's chaotic misread of ancient wisdom. Feudalism, in his estimation, would simply have to be dismissed as "a monstrous assembly of order and anarchy, servitude and license, tyranny and protection" (Portalis-*De l'usage,* Vol. II, 212). But in framing modernity by the well-known parameters from sixteenth century Jean Bodin to his own age's Montesquieu, Portalis still found little of virtue for the *parlements* to cite in upholding their charge to sustain the rights of the people. Civil law had been so defective and so confused that one could deny it had existed. Even admitting to some fine ordinances promulgated under the glowing rays of Louis XIV, Portalis saw clearly that a sense of social compact and civic principle could certainly have made them better. Though corrective vision had not previously been forthcoming, Portalis sensed now the groundswell of awakening: revolutions of the Swiss, Dutch, French, Americans, and English had all promoted optimistic growth of commerce and comparative knowledge. From them had flourished trends to public discussion and more open governments. Reason—thanks to minds like Gravina and Locke, Domat and Burlamaqui—was now regularly applied to areas before left to fierce ambition or the power of rank. When Portalis decided to place laurels on the brow of Montesquieu as creator of a true science of laws far ahead of his time, it was precisely because this heroic figure had gone far beyond known limits.

Chapter XXXIII (Portalis-*De l'usage,* Vol. II, 341) found Portalis putting on a gown of *gravitas* to explore the question: "By what invisible force did systems of philosophy, true and false, suddenly in our days produce such a commotion in the world?" At the outset he realized that although enlightened men had always had an influence, in the last half of the eighteenth century circumstances caused them to become a corporation, even a party. With strong cohesion promoted by vigorous correspondence and printing, these intellectuals now lived in academies and literary societies, in institutes and assemblies. Emboldened through the ubiquitous presence of "enemies"—principally the clergy—who in uniting them in antipathy reduced the usual philosopher's tendency for internal division, they became defenders of all classes—princes, individuals, and governments. However, warned the juridical *philosophe* in spite of himself, one had to remain cognizant of the darker side. Whereas ancient thinkers tended to withdraw from society and concentrate on morality, modern intellectuals, pushed by politics to question Church virtue, had become inevitably, and excessively drawn into the world of affairs. Here they could find the money needed for their experiments; that same cash could buy publication of the results as well as permit creature comforts. With such expansiveness ethical teaching suffered, paralleling that corruption which for too long had been seeping from the source of power to the masses.

In dismay Portalis joined his age's major preoccupation: forging the elusive, improved Social Compact. He denied any possibility of perfect equality; parity before the law was as far as he could go. Nor could there be perfect liberty, freedom being no more than the ability to live in obedience to law. How, he asked (Portalis-*De l'usage,* Vol. II, 266; 288), could one propose as a property code that the fruits belong to all and the land to none? In a state of nature man, once created, had needs and therefore a natural right to appropriate by work what was necessary; such appropriation must still be a man's own. The right of property comes from the ontological constitution of humankind itself. Its source is Nature, not Society; it does not have to be guaranteed by some kind of positive law. Society may, of course, regulate the use of property and even take it if just compensation is paid; but this eminent domain is an administrative, not a property right. Those who under Louis XV wanted to substitute for the right of taxation a state co-ownership yielding one-third of the net product, were for Portalis as wrong as the land-hungry feudal lords of old.

The *Concordat* of 1801 Between France and the Pope

During the exile in Germany, Portalis had required that Marguerite and his second son, Marcus, stay in France to oversee family interests in Provence. Despite the pleasure of Emckendorff's hostess, Portalis regularly wrote his wife long letters full of affection. His principal activity, he told her, had now become what he called "a little book." In reality it was to be, when finally published in 1834 by Frédéric, the two volumes on philosophy. At the same time he had been following with interest the career of General Bonaparte, and, well aware of 18 Brumaire, had urged Marguerite to ask friends close to the General to have Napoleon authorize a Portalis return. This effort was successful, and early in 1800 philosophical writing and Northern idylls were dropped abruptly when the Portalis men returned to France and a job.

On 3 April Bonaparte, now First Consul, appointed Portalis as Government Commissioner to the new Council of Prizes, a body charged with adjudicating questions arising from vessels seized at sea by the navy and privateers. Installed on 14 May the Council heard an eloquent speech given by Portalis to mark the occasion. He covered so well the work about to begin that his speech was printed, enjoying a considerable multilingual distribution abroad (Leduc, 164). This assignment by Bonaparte had been evidently an evaluative tool, testing the Commissioner's ability and reliability; Portalis obviously had passed impeccably. On 22 September he was appointed to the lofty status of member of the Council of State and attached to the section on legislation. Continuing to rise even more in Bonaparte's estimation, Portalis next became, it is believed, the General's principal advisor in solving the difficult problem of religion's role in a new France. This position fit seamlessly the Portalis persona—informed, able in discussion, eloquent enough to convince but moderate enough not to irritate, of a known piety and an unshakable patriotism. Napoleon kept the appointments coming. Portalis was asked to advise the trio of emissaries charged with negotiating the papal *Concordat*; then, after the signing of that instrument on 15 July 1801, Portalis on 8 October received appointment as Minister of Religion charged with all affairs concerning the several churches of France. The busy enquirer into Protestant marriage vows now bore the heavy responsibility of reorganizing all French faith in accordance with the *Concordat* and the *Organic Articles*.

As a careful legalist with effective ways of expressing his ideas, Portalis had taken stands more reasonable than those of many Realists who preceded him; and that care and that reason meant he had written and thought himself into a position to put these ideas to practical use. It is no surprise that when it came time for proceedings to rethink both *Church* and *Civil Code*, it was he who almost inevitably was chosen for a powerful role far beyond any which an academic thinker, however brilliant, could match. The history of legal philosophy now stood before the door of Provence—the ancient Roman *provincia*—waiting to make French law live for a clientele beyond provinciality, temporality, or geography.

The *porte à lis*, that portal of the lily, would be opened ambitiously by God, as it were, for again, as befitted the Portalis name, some of the symbolic *fleur de lis* of the *Ancien Régime* would stay the course in this updated, scaled-down application of the faith. To solidify organized religion's status, which had been achieved in France at the end of the Revolution, meant settlement officially expressed in the *Concordat of 1801* between the Consular government and Pius VII and in the associated *Organic Articles* made unilaterally by the government. When Portalis presented the first to the Legislative Corps on 5 April 1802 and the latter earlier to the Council of State, it was the occasion for elucidating a landmark—some would have said landmine—philosophical approach: the belief that canon law was a legitimate part of private law. It would be this momentous stamp of Portalis on religion and government which was to last until the *Concordat's* denunciation by the French government of 1905.

Napoleon told Portalis he would need efficiency and power, and Portalis knew that meant establishing religious peace inside a country liberated from fractious Catholic conflict and cleansed of intolerance toward Jews and Protestants. To get that peace France would have to obtain the approval of Rome for a completely new plan aimed directly at the different faiths. Plotting out all these angles toward rebuilding the societal fabric was not so much a case of the Portalis high idealism at work as one more scheme for *real politik*: God manipulated as statecraft. A latter-day Henri IV, Bonaparte was to be required promotion of religion as something which had to be coped with, the eclectic Credo that could be either helpful or unhelpful in politics. As he confided to his supporter, Comte Roederer:

> It was by becoming a Catholic that I ended the war in the Vendée; by becoming a Moslem that I established myself in Egypt; by becoming an ultramontanist ... [pro-papal authority north of the Alps]...that I won over minds in Italy. If I governed a people who were Jews, I would rebuild the Temple of Solomon. (Castelot, *Napoléon Bonaparte*, 115)

Napoleon would always look back at the reestablishment of religion as "'the groundwork and foundation upon which I built'" (Durant, *The Age of Napoleon*,

183). He expected much from his pro-religion policy: legitimation of his upstart rule; peace in the Catholic Vendée; 6,000 non-juring priests enlisted on the Bonaparte side along with the eminence of Pius; denial of the argument that only a king could restore the established religion; reduced hostility from Europe's other, Catholic, states. Not everyone felt as pleased. Opposition came both from shocked old Jacobins in Paris who saw the separation of Church and state as the great achievement of "their" Revolution and, on the other side, from angered and hurt cardinals in Rome who wanted Church property restored and divorce denied. Napoleon pushed ahead, and in November 1800 eight months of negotiations began in the shadow of Notre Dame. Pius VII, who needed an arrangement with France for reasons of his own, made the necessary concessions and in December 1801 ratified the *Concordat* already approved by the First Consul. The French government agreed to recognize Roman Catholicism, not as a state Church, but as the religion of the Consuls and of the majority of the French people; toleration would be granted to Protestants and Jews. The Revolution's confiscation of Catholic property was confirmed, but the state agreed to pay bishops it nominated if they would swear bureaucratic fealty and await their function until approved by the pope. Non-juring bishops had to resign, but the palliative for those who stayed was that the Church could once more accept bequests.

The plan, to be effective, now had to be approved by the legislative bodies of the Consulate. As Napoleon's principle advisor in these matters and also his legal draftsman and presenter of documents to the legislature and the public, Portalis had the role of making the case to Pius on behalf of the *Concordat* and the *Organic Articles*. It would stand out as a fine presentation but also an artificial one, for the government unilaterally controlled positioning vis-à-vis Rome. However, when introducing the *Concordat* to the legislators and, therefore, the French public, Portalis used a different, less blunt approach, delivering a celebrated, heartfelt address on 5 April 1802. After a stirring summary of the history of religion in France in relation to the state, Portalis, who was never one to avoid the broadest sweep in his defense strategy, went right to the deepest and most essential question: is religion even necessary—to a nation? to law? to mankind itself? As we now paraphrase his lengthy answer, we will see it lies at the heart of the fascinating co-existence which religion and republican statecraft were forging for a future, using as materiel both cathedral masonry and Bastille stone.

As he noted the present age's indifference to religion in favor of the arts, sciences, industry, and commerce, Portalis proposed in riposte a great "nevertheless." Since every candid mind concedes that society cannot exist without an ethical system, the necessity of religion arises directly from this need. Laws regulate only some actions; and morals, if they remain "in the lofty regions of science" (5), avail little. In transmitting ethics it is religious institutions that alone can "bring them down" (6) to the people. That there is a diversity of positive religions makes no difference; all have as foundations the "principle articles of natural morals" (7). The essential given is that each cult must connect virtues with rites, for morality lies in action not speculation, and forms are its disciplines. In the opinion of Portalis natural religion, the achievement of cultivated reason, will never become national and popular; there is so little harmony among its votaries, even the redoubtable Plato could not achieve concord.

Gloom also permeated the Portalis opinion on purifying organized religious expression. It was all very well to concentrate on expelling superstition, but in such a cleansing only skeptics and atheists would remain. Even after this power maneuver Portalis recognized that the limited cross-section could not make for a well-run state. He was adamant: it is better sometimes to abuse religion than to have none, for the mind of atheism spells a barbarous independence whose revolt breeds both lack of tolerance and augmentation of egotism's self-love. As a code of laws is necessary to regulate human concerns, so a system of positive religious doctrine is necessary "to give a determination to opinions" (11). For Portalis there had never been a man whose greatness, having formed an institution or liberated a nation, refused in success to call religion to the aid of civil polity.

The truth or falsehood of this or that positive religion was a mere theological question with which Portalis was not concerned. He did, however, distinguish those false philosophies which make the mind contentious and the heart cold. The refreshing candor of Portalis made him admit frankly that even such erroneous belief patterns had their one good point: "false systems of religion have, at least, the effect of rallying mankind around some common principles and to dispose them to the practice of some virtues" (14). After all, although many are the actual crimes religion fails to prevent, we should be aware, cautions Portalis, of the many dark penchants it does check and arrest. As Burke had commented, manners are surely more important than laws (18). While the glories of science remain the lot of the learned few, the many can be well instructed through religion. For attestation, Portalis, always close to his provincial roots, pointed to the countless virtuous citizens in departmental assemblies. Such views are not merely my own, the lawyerly voice confided to his reader, but are consistent with current testimony from prefects, local councils, and visitors. All give witness to the deep love of the country people for their religion and to their equally keen regret for the abolition of Sunday worship.

As a son of revolution, Portalis believed that it is when liberty has been finally accomplished that the question of the utility of religion arises. But the political animal in him knew also that in liberty arise certain stern verities: religion, unlike laws, cannot be made, nor faith commanded. If in the origin of things an extraordinary man made Messiah had been able to speak persuasively of his messianic inspiration to neophytes of the faith, this could no longer be accomplished with experienced, sophisticated nations. Moreover, in religion the novelty that might aid the acceptance of new civil laws bore the character of error and imposture; it was wisdom for government to stop with the religions which existed. Waxing historic, Portalis admitted that at the restoration of learning Christianity sustained a great shock when new thinkers directed attention at its manifold abuses and disorders. From that argumentative discussion had arisen the great schism of faith which Jansenist Portalis recognized as dividing Christian Europe. Nevertheless, on his tree Catholic and Protestant religions grew with equal vitality, viable branches of one Christianity.

Portalis saw it as amazing that in his day it still was a matter of discussion whether a state could or should accommodate itself to such wide embrace of an eclectic Christianity. In the French Revolution it was mistakenly supposed that the only way to eradicate superstition and fanaticism was to lash out against all religious institutions. On the contrary, the correct process, as Portalis saw it, should rather be to compare Christian institutions with manners, philosophy, and changed political institutions. At the establishment of Christianity the world had assumed a new attitude as the precepts of the gospel imparted true morality to the universe. Admittedly, the Christian religion subsequently became a pretext for quarrels, wars, and other ills; but where is that institution which has never been abused? What is that good that has never existed without a mixture of evil? The only question a just and rational man should ask is whether Christianity, to which we are indebted for the inestimable blessing of civilization, can still conduce to our benefit.

Obviously, Portalis was thinking less as a dispassionate, tolerant, and accurate historian than as the fervent Catholic jurist pleading a cause. He depicted Christianity as the ideal—a faith which, in his erroneous, narrow view, had never encroached on the imprescriptible rights of human reason nor bypassed elegance in taste as had, he felt, some religions in Asia and elsewhere. Portalis admired the faith's alliance with letters and the arts, a belief system which had found illustrious men like Descartes, Newton, Pascal, Bossuet, and Fénélon to conceive themselves honored to profess it. And now, was it not the Christian religion—and here the quiet but determined advocate might have raised his voice, looking straight at his surrogate jury audience, pausing for his words to strike home—was not this the very faith which had transmitted to us our entire body of natural law? It does not arbitrarily substitute its doctrines; it does not dethrone reason. It fills instead the void which reason always leaves behind, its priesthood working tirelessly to instruct the mind through the offices of worship. Local neither in place nor time, it is belief transcending national boundaries to encompass the world. Surely—and again the attorney's piercing eye still bores through the printed page—the new government of France should not and could not rationally abjure the ancient source of its brilliant virtues and fervent, charitable habits, a source which had managed to outshine the most heinous outrages of the Revolution.

Turning to the exercise of civil policy, Portalis expressed the view that newfound liberty and enlightened philosophy could not be reconciled to the idea of a predominant religion enjoying special privileges, even less to an exclusive religion like that of the last ages of the monarchy. But as a man of the bar he also advised that the state can only deny exclusivity for tolerance by means of a well devised legal organization that exercises a reasonable superintendence over worship. Persecution is never the right way, but rather—and here listeners to Portalis would have been advised not to be dozing for he had reached a controversial, central tenet of his secularized religion—public congregations can be superintended by civil police. Religious affairs have always been ranked by the codes of different nations as belonging to the high constabulary of the state; men who exercise a great influence over minds and conscience should thus continue to hold ties linking them to structures of state control. Such enlightened state surveillance and protection begs recognition as keeping a vigilant eye over the doctrines of any faith, patrolling and nudging it toward the great objects of public good.

In regards the clerical side of control, the diplomatic Portalis felt it was fortunate that Catholic ecclesiastics continued to acknowledge the pontiff as chief. His intervention in matters French was constantly necessary, and government had to come to an understanding with the Holy See which avoided Roman domination yet was open to hearing and accepting of Roman suggestion. The principle of Lutheranism—that the head of every state can declare himself head of the Church—was, on the contrary, not safe for the cause of French liberty. The challenge, felt Portalis, was for a religious order now to be devised that strengthened national power without menacing national or ethical liberty. Having given a look across the Channel, Portalis decided France need not try to assimilate the revolution of England with her own; a *Concordat* approach far outshone having a political head of the Church.

Under this contract secular clergy were to be enlisted as cooperators in defense of law's codified principles. Those bishops to be nominated by the consul but ordained by the pope would, as formerly, then be allowed appointment privileges to all religious offices in their departments. Financial needs would be supplied by government monies. Some, admitted the humanistically trained Portalis, might well regret that priests had not yet been made free to marry or that the number of rites, ceremonies, and dogmas had not been reduced. However—and now Portalis reprised his famed historic perspective—the objective had to be preservation: Catholics liked their rites, and the civil powers were well advised not to meddle with the beloved ancient dogma. Priests and marriage were inimical; men of the cloth had been purposefully spared the burden of a family in view of the constant dogmatic assiduity demanded of them. As for their flock, Portalis was convinced the people sincerely preferred ecclesiastical austerity and lacked confidence in married clergy subject to the penalties of canon law.

Portalis was hopeful that his legal portfolio thus had been widened to accommodate arguments whose conclusions could enfold both Protestant and Jew in the warm egalitarian cloak of liberty under law. Now he turned to two current critiques of the old Roman rite. First, he examined the frequently held view that Catholicism is the religion of kings and, hence, unsuitable to republics. This idea had recently been supported by Montesquieu who observed that even during the fervor of the Reformation Catholicism survived in absolute monarchies while at the same time the counterpoint of Protestantism won over converts in free governments. Portalis, though, saw the current facts as other: the tenets of Catholicism were prevailing in Switzerland and all the republics of Italy. Admittedly the pontiff executed the law, but it was not he who made that law. Under true Roman principles of faith the sovereign power in spiritual matters resided in the Church, specifically in its councils.

The second reservation concerned ostensible Church intolerance and unsociability in the denial of salvation to all outside her communion. Montesquieu considered that this exclusionary principle worked as a source of attachment to the religion which taught it. Acting as a rather scholastic counselor, Portalis here tried to explain this contradiction by offering a legal parsing of faith's ways. To judge whether a doctrine is useful or pernicious to civil society, he wrote, it is less necessary to examine the doctrine itself than the consequences to be expected from it. Pure and holy doctrines may have bad consequences and false ones admirable consequences; all depends on the conformity of these consequences with the juristic principles of civil society. For example, the very doctrine of the precious immortality of the soul had in some places been so dangerous that it actually induced suicide as a way of rejoining a beloved or respected deceased.

And so, stated Portalis in final flourish, faced with how to organize a religion rent by so many questions as Catholicism meant that vigorous measures were necessary. To the admiration of Europe the resignation of all the titulars, now obtained by the government, could make attainable every belief useful and good: Catholicism avowed as the majority religion, but not the government's, nor the state's; concern for the welfare of Protestants; the eternal Jewish people sharing under a legislative God the liberty of the French legal system. To these ends law, not as defined in the constitution nor "an act of the general will" (Portalis, *"Speech of M. Portalis on the 15th Germinal Year X 5th April, 1802, to the Legislative Body of France, on presenting the convention made between the French Republic and the Holy See,"* 79), allowed to express in a positive declaration what religions believe:

> By the articles of religious organization, all animosities will be appeased, all doubts and differences will be terminated; misery will find consolation; malevolence will be repressed; a rallying point will be established for all hearts; conscience itself will yield, if I may be allowed to use the expression, to the reconciliation of the Revolution with Heaven. (Portalis-*Speech*, 79)

Portalis had now put on the table full legal opinion as requested by his national client. However, the resulting heady handshake between the Almighty and the French nation dancing the Carmagnole in tricolor showed the Portalis Project had been negligent of happenings on the opposite side of the Atlantic. Not for him were the complete religious freedom and separation of religion and state already provided by the still admired civic mentors who authored the American constitution (to which document Portalis pointedly made no reference). *Concordat* meant strongly Gallican and not ultramontane; in other words, being another push forward in the that long march of French government toward centralization, the *Concordat* took pains to reserve to the government, in one powerfully enabling yet innocent appearing clause, authority for making "rules of police."

The appended forum of *Organic Articles* in the 1802 *Loi des cultes*—seventy-seven for Catholics and forty-four for Protestants—turned out to be a unilateral annex inseparable from the seventeen rather general *Articles of the Concordat*. The effort codified all the liberties of the Gallican church that had been disputed by the Vatican for centuries. In true Napoleonic style this annexation had been made without any discussion with the pope or his legate, posing the danger, as Lavollée points out (Lavollée, 285), that Vatican protest against the *Organic Articles* might well have injured the moral authority of the First Consul and troubled French consciences anew. Portalis realized a different approach was needed to persuade Pius VII not to resist.

In the opinion of Portalis the government's course could be defended only if the *Organic Articles* contained nothing contrary to the *Concordat*. It would be desirable, for example, if the content were something like a new setting of ancient maxims from the Gallican church; one could then point out these were made necessary and attractive after ten years of revolutionary confusion. But two provisions in particular did arouse papal ire and objection and were judged by Rome to be unacceptable: (a) no bull or other command of the Holy See could be published in France without the consent of the government, and (b) in case of an appeal against alleged "abuse" by a priest his conduct would be judged by the Council of State. There was great discomfiture over this control of the publication of conciliar decrees added to which came prohibition of clerical assemblies without consent, a requirement that seminaries teach 1682 articles written by Bossuet when Bishop of Meaux, and governmental consent to establishing new *fête* days. None of this Napoleonic fiat was judged acceptable by an irate Vatican.

Portalis, although vigorous in defense of the *Organic Articles*, actually relied on the doctrine of the famous Bossuet. He ferreted out the particulars in two propositions based on the Gospel, confirmed by the constant practice of the primitive Church, and accepted by all the popes up to Gregory VII. The first of these lay in the absolute independence of the temporal power vs. the spiritual power. The second was made manifest in the spiritual primacy of the ecumenical councils of the Church. Lawyer Portalis here had stepped away from his governmental client and instead reflected the teaching of Gregory VII on papal power, later doctrinally codified by Boniface VIII. Lavollée feels (Lavollée, 300) that this Portalis compromise with moderation, his profound delineation of precedents, and the fact that under the *Concordat* the Church was once again permitted its function in France, ultimately persuaded the Pope. His eminence declined to adhere to the *Organic Articles*. He would, however, refrain from further insistence upon their abrogation. Posterity continued to debate the questions, the *Concordat* was at last in place, and the French government had gained the moral foundation upon which to proceed with more reforms.

Portalis and the *Code Napoleon*

Private Law and Codification During the Revolution

As they boldly worked their will on public law, the successive assemblies of the Revolution had also taken care to make extremely important changes in private law. Political feudalism may have already been nearly spent, yet at the same time its bureaucratic miasma of dues, rent charges, quit rents, tithes, rights inalienable and irredeemable, powers of repurchase, and superior and beneficial ownership continued

Count Jean-Etienne-Marie Portalis
Courtesy of The Bridgeman Art Library

to suffocate the land economy. It was this suffocation which had given way to the great collective breath of freedom on that one extraordinary night of 4 August 1789 when the National Assembly abolished feudalism, dovecotes and pigeon houses, and every French man could aspire to any office in the land. Subsequent legislation returned back to the simple agrarian clarity of the Roman allod system. In supplement came the abolition of wills. The requirement that transfers of land be at last publicly recorded ended primogeniture by successions of equal division among children, thus putting more lands into the commercial economy. As to the family, since all persons now had the same status, marriage became a mere civil contract between citizens, and provisions for easy divorce were enacted. For commerce and industry French law henceforth authorized lending at interest as well as adopting provision for patents (*Continental Legal History*, Vol. I, 277–279).

Private law's moment was celebrated on 5 October 1790 when a decree of the Constituent Assembly committed France's leadership to accomplishing a uniform code. In this reach for the fair horizon so long sought, the principal visionary was Second Consul Jean Jacques Régis de Cambacérès (1753–1824), a well-known lawyer from a *robe* family. His first plan, presented in August 1793, appeared in the guise of 695 articles. It reflected the Convention's contempt for Roman and customary law and its new dream that it could make private law a simple, democratic book easily read by every literate citizen (*Continental Legal History,* Vol. I, 280).

The Convention, however, thought the draft too conservative and decided that the job should be transferred from the legal profession to a commission of philosophers. Fortunately, the Convention became distracted and nothing came from their unrealistic plan; it seemed only common sense that any metaphysical coterie might be better employed in influencing lawyers' thoughts than in making law themselves. On 15 September after the 1794 fall of Robespierre Cambacérès tried again, presenting a code shortened to only 297 articles, each of them extremely brief. A few of these articles were actually passed before in its turn the Directory realized it would have to take up the project as its own. The determined Cambacérès offered yet a third draft; but this proposal was never even discussed as successive assemblies began grappling and grumbling over so many other problems including a Constitution that they were unable to undertake birthing a civil code.

The Consular Constitution, Proceedings on the *Civil Code* and Its Preliminary Title

The post 18 Brumaire Constitution was triumphantly enacted by the Consulate on 13 December 1799. Its words of change were to remain in effect with some modifications throughout the Empire. Under it a Council of State (Conseil d'État) of eighty outstanding citizens was appointed by the First Consul; only he could call their general sessions over which he presided. The *Conseil* which drafted all bills divided its work among five sections: legislation, interior, finance, war, and navy. When drafts of their proposals were sent to the First Consul, it was again he alone who introduced them for action. Then came a complex protocol. If the First Consul decided to proceed, he appointed three Councillors of State as presenters to the Tribunate; the one first appointed had the task of drafting a statement of reasons, and it would be frequently Portalis himself who filled this role when France finally reached proceedings on the *Code*. The Tribunate, which consisted of one hundred members appointed by the Senate, could debate a bill and then reject it or accept it, but always without amendment. If it approved, three commissioners were appointed to present the tribunes' view to the Legislative Body (*Corps Législatif*). This group had a membership three times the Tribunate and was composed of notables appointed by the Senate from lists prepared by a special electoral body. The Corps could either enact a bill without amendment or reject it, but it could not debate; members, derisively yet aptly called by some the "Body of Mutes," merely listened to discussions by the three Councillors of State and the three Tribunes. The Senate itself consisted of sixty members. Here the majority were chosen by two active Consuls (other than Bonaparte) who were advised by the two colleagues who had resigned when Bonaparte effectively took over the process of making the new constitution. The rest of the Senators were chosen by co-optation.

It was now time to bring the law into synchrony with France's changing fortunes which, in the remarkable years 1799–1804 began to influence far beyond her borders. Why, one might ask, did law's processes receive attention at this juncture?

Lavollée with his usual euphoria presents (Lavollée, 181) the *Code's* creation as growing in organic harmony from an almost utopian matrix:

> With the voice of Bonaparte, the nation seemed reborn. On the debris of the *ancien régime*, on the ruins of the Revolution, one saw forming a young and vigorous society; a new era began. The enemy armies hesitated and stopped, the Vendée laid down its arms, the bands of looters and assassins ceased to infest the countryside, order in finance was restored, speculation and bureaucratic routine were chased out of administration.
>
> Everyday the *Moniteur* published lists of exiles for whom a wise government opened the frontiers; ties of blood and friendship were renewed, families reconstituted, so to speak, at the same time as society; joy was everywhere and the new century saw opening before it perspectives of infinite peace, greatness, and prosperity. A unique moment in our history! Blessed years the memory of which still charms us and erases the faults of Napoleon committed later.

Planiol, thirty years after Lavollée, had a more clear-eyed focus upon legal innovation:

> The Code ... had the good fortune to be enacted at just the right moment. Had it been made sooner, during the Revolution, it would have yielded too much to Revolutionary passions, to political vagaries. Had it been made later, no doubt it would have felt the rigors of the military rule and of the increasing reactionary spirit.... It is this happy concurrence of circumstances which gave to the Civil Code its dominant merit—that spirit of moderation and wisdom which has secured its permanence..." (*Continental Legal History*, Vol. I, 289)

Leduc (Leduc, 173) gives a darker and more Machiavellian explanation of France's serious turn to strict legal process. He takes the view that it was nothing less—or more—than the assassination attempt on the First Consul, which took everyone by surprise on Christmas Eve 1800 and galvanized Napoleon toward the protections of a strict legal code. Whichever of the two impulses led Bonaparte on—and probably it was a combination of the two—he would now marshal the boundless energy of his thirty-one years and the vast ambition that defined his personality. The resultant vision of extraordinary breadth was to belie less a gift of philosophical genius than an exceptional military mind's tactic for bringing the new social forms, like so many green troops heading into battle, into a state of close order and fighting trim.

Wanting to build a meritocracy, the First Consul was inviting to serve in it all who loved France and would follow him without concern for past politics. An immense majority gave their support. Since Napoleon was never a man to let the grass grow under his feet (unless it was on the damp 18 June 1815 morning of Waterloo), it is said that having mentally constructed the *Civil Code* the very day after the more felicitous battle of Marengo, on 13 August 1800, he wasted no time appointing a blue ribbon Commission to begin its draft (Lavollée, 183). Serving under the nominal control of Joseph Abrial, Minister of Justice, were four leading French jurisconsults. Two were common law experts—François-Denis Tronchet (1726–1806) as chair, and Félix-Julian-Jean Bigot de Préameneu (1750–1825); two were statutory lawyers—the Marquis Jacques de Maleville and Portalis. No doubt Cambacérès would have been included had he not been Second Consul.

Tronchet had been a pupil of Royal Professor Claude Rousseau, a close friend and collaborator of Pothier, and he had trained at Paris in the area of the customs. Afflicted with a poor speaking voice, Tronchet was to retire soon after his first appearance as practicing *avocat*. He having long ago decided he would devote himself full-time to a passionate study of customary law, and could be found working even in his bath—a dangerous Revolutionary pastime as David's portrait of Marat so vividly testifies. Tronchet's forte would be service as a legal consultant, and from it has come to posterity his huge collection of 1,800 written opinions. He was, however, most active in the Constituent Assembly where, as counsel for Louis XVI in the monarch's unsuccessful trial, he escaped arrest by the Committee on Public Safety only by quickly rededicating himself to the neutrality of research. He came back to practice after Robespierre fell, though, and became first President of the Court of Cassation, an appellate body with the highest function for a tribunal after 18 Brumaire. Napoleon, who did not like Tronchet very much but admired the advocate's character and intellect, hailed him as the leading jurisconsult of France. Tronchet was austere to the point of rudeness, scorned life's ordinary pleasures, and not surprisingly channeled his seriousness into a rigorous study of mathematics at the end of his career. In all discussions of the *Civil Code* he was quick to orient debate toward his beloved customs rather than toward Roman law.

Bigot de Préameneu, it is said, was chosen by Napoleon in an unguarded moment of whimsy, not uncommon in a great man often amused by underlings' names. He found it high fun to choose a "Bigot" who, although quite tolerant and religiously broad-gauge enough to have been Minister of *Cultes*, was not the most understanding to his long-suffering spouse. De Préameneu had trained in the law under the reputable Royal Professor Poullain du Parc of the law faculty at Rennes and had been named as a judge in 1790; by 1791 he was deputy to the National Assembly, a body over which he later would serve as President. Having successfully spent the Terror in hiding he was pleased to reappear in public life after 18 Brumaire, an event which he enthusiastically applauded. He would leave a library of 3,000 volumes but no corpus of professional writings. This is a loss for legal scholars, since it was this Commissioner who drafted the general provisions of the *Civil Code* for contracts, the part on sales having been devised by Portalis (*Biographie Universelle,* 249).

The Portalis partner in statutory law, Périgord native Jacques de Maleville, had also served as a judge in the Court of Cassation. Before 1789 his work he been as *avocat* in Bordeaux where he studied under Professor Bacalan of that law faculty. Use of Roman legal structures was at that time highly prevalent in the Bordeaux *Parlement*, and De Curzon (De Curzon, 353) tells of Maleville's becoming one of their warmest admirers.

The four commissioners thus appear to have been equally distributed on each side of the Loire—admirers of customs from the North and proponents of the Roman law South. And, there were other influences; the four called in as collaborators, a kind of *Who's Who* of learned *avocats*, among whom were Favard,

Grenier, Siméon, Chabot de l'Allier, Jaubert, Jacqueminot, Treilhard, and Duveyrier. Favard was a member of the Council of State and had studied in Paris. Siméon had been professor of Roman law at Aix. Jaubert, like de Maleville another Bordeaux man, had been professor of Roman law there before becoming President of the Tribunate in 1804. His assistant Treilhard, deputy to the Estates General and voter for the death of Louis XVI, had done his studies in Paris. Of the remaining four all but Jacqueminot had Paris training under Royal Professor Clément de Malleran. Thus, although the drafting group taken as a whole had more representation of the customs than the Roman law, the Commissioners themselves were equally divided. Their most profound link was the shared past under whose shadow they had all trained, and to that eighteenth century jurisprudence they still remained faithful. Even though Revolution had created the circumstances making a new code possible, in the main, private law was actually writing—or perhaps it would be better to say had not yet ceased churning out—a kind of continuance of the *Ancien Régime* (Ourliac and Gazzaniga, 168).

Looking at the historic gathering of these eminent French lawyers, one inevitably recalls the preparation of the *Institutes* and *Digest of Justinian* 1,267 years in the past. Their existence had come about over a fortunate duet of imperial and academic minds whose brilliant creative project for centuries had been the canon dominant in legal education as practiced in the Western world. Having no legislature with which to contend meant Justinian could rein in or give rein to his professorial drafting committee. In contrast, the nineteenth century variant was worked out against a highly bureaucratic, conciliar structure by commissioners who were not academics. France exhibited a much lessened prestige for teaching—in 1800 her universities had been gone several years—whereas in 533 antiquity's law school at Berytus, that "Roman island in a Greek sea," rode high in the legal waters.

Another point to make is that the *Code Napoleon* came to life in a much larger civilized world than Justinian's. By a curious coincidence, it was born 533 years after antiquity's legal "Bible" of 533 CE. With its emergence there would be set in motion the other current of a vigorous and far-reaching Anglo-American legal tradition. For the most part that tradition would know no Justinian, nor did it want to, standing firmly aloof as well from the recent codes of Denmark (1683), Norway (1688), Sweden (1734), Bavaria (1756), Prussia (1794), and Austria (1811). In 1804 many Frenchmen and their then Emperor sat back for the pleasing spectacle of watching the whole world yield to the intellectual excellence of their code spreading its ethical paradigms so far and wide that today it is still intact after more than 200 years. They had to realize it had no chance of getting the extraordinary dominance achieved by Justinian, whose books offered still in 1800 such formidable sources for the French draftsmen. In ironic comparison one might call this code clash another Waterloo, since the French imperial code would remain dominated by another nation's compilation. The irony of the dominance was that only one great underlying book, the Gaius—a kind of antiquated Blücher to the unexpected rescue of the great Eastern forces—had survived, and it, only by chance.

To return to the drafting Commissioners, they worked well and rapidly, with no sense of inferiority to any ancient models. On 21 January 1801, only four remarkable months after their appointment, they could with confidence present their draft to the Council of State. Now occurred the stunning preliminary discussion of the whole by Portalis, words which were to become almost overnight the classical preface and commentary on the *Code*. Lavollée saw (Lavollée, 192) this Portalis paper of intent as the *chef d'oeuvre* of that great judicial school born in the eighteenth century from the Montesquieu *Esprit* which had in its day at least enlightened jurisprudence with history and philosophy. Draft work finished, the Council of State sent it on to the Court of Cassation and the twenty-eight courts of appeal for comment. Favorable remarks having then been received back with suggestions for some changes, the work was at last referred to the Council's section on legislation, consisting of Portalis as chair, de la Meurthe, Berlier, Emmery, Réal, and Thibaudeau. This group submitted the revised version to the Council of State in July 1801; and in five months, accompanied by three men from the Tribunate, Portalis, de la Meurthe, and Berlier appeared before the Legislative Corps to debate the Preliminary Title.

Politics are seldom smooth. The First Consul had constructed his constitution with care, and the procedural mechanisms were adequate. But there were, nevertheless, in each of the Tribunate and Legislative Corps a group of ultra-republican political opponents resolved to block Bonaparte's every initiative, from the *Concordat* and a peace with Russia, to the *Code*. There were other adversaries no less absolute, basing their dissatisfaction on theological reason and condemning current ideas for the new *Code* as contrary to divine law for the family and society.

Bending before the rough winds of critique, the Tribunate rejected the bill for the Preliminary Title, and the Legislative Corps added its own refusal by voting 'Non' 142 to 139. Bonaparte, outraged, on 3 January 1802 withdrew from the legislature all proposals for a *Code* until there might be a time of "calmness and unity of purpose" (*Continental Legal History,* Vol. I, 283); thus was opposition peremptorily silenced by a complete ending of the proceedings. "'What can you do,' he cried, 'with people who before the discussion said that the Council of State and the Consuls were only asses, and that their work should be thrown back at their heads?'" It came to him he might stage another *coup d'état*, but Cambacérès advised against so brusque a retaliation and suggested instead that the clause of the Constitution calling for the mandatory retirement of one-third of the Tribunate and Legislative Corps and the vague appointment of successors sometime between 1801 and 1802 might easily be interpreted as applicable immediately. It was a view said to be of very doubtful morality and legality; but the Senate went along and Bonapartists were appointed. (Montesquieu's argument for strong intermediate bodies had obviously lost its appeal.) Thereafter, every bill for the *Code* as well as all Bonaparte's other projects was approved without difficulty. The strong arm of the general in dealing with the rebellious will of men of state had been revealed triumphant.

With opposition cowed or eliminated by Bonaparte's rough procedure, the way was now ironically open to a liberal coding of admirable legal paradigms. Napoleon proceeded to submit to the new legislative bodies his thirty-six bills, one by one as they became ready, covering the whole *Code* as well as a reform of the *Corps*

Législatif. Each was approved. The last one received acceptance on 21 March 1804, and on this historic date of final enactment all the bills were united into the massive single code of 2,281 consecutively numbered articles.

Role of Portalis; the Judge

Although he had not chaired the drafting commission, it was Portalis who had played the leading role in preparation and enactment of the *Code*. The Preliminary Title was of his drafting, and he had crafted the articles on the family and on property, by his own estimate the two great bases of the *Code*. Had Portalis drafted also the general articles on contracts, his centrality would have been nearly complete. These were provided by Maleville, but to Portalis was given full responsibility for the articles on Sales, as well as those on Aleatory Contracts. He would furnish in all ten important papers explaining the entire *Code*, including that highly regarded *Preliminary Discourse* for the Council of State. Bonaparte honored this large contribution by allowing Portalis to present the final bill uniting all the previous bills into one ethical system (Leduc, 175–187).

The several parts of the draft of the Preliminary Title were rejected in the final form, however. In his writing Portalis had felt strongly that, just as Justinian had preceded the *Digest* with thought-provoking and metaphysical prose, the French compendium needed his statement of legal philosophy to set the tone of moral guidance. The Council of State and the legislative bodies demurred, however, protesting that such material was doctrine for the the schools and not imperatives for a legislature. One can read these mini-discourses in the Bibliothèque nationale thanks to the gift of the Portalis son, the Vicomte Frédéric. (*Discours, rapports et travaux inédits sur le Code civil de J.E.M. Portalis*).

The refusal would be a great disappointment to the drafter, for taking as his model Domat's famous *Book of Laws*, Portalis had been meticulously careful in his structure. There were six titles: "General Definitions," "Kinds of Laws," "On the Publication of Laws," "On the Effects of Law," "On the Application and Interpretation of Laws," and "On the Abrogation of Laws." From the opening salvo of the first title Portalis was resolute, inspired with the full rationalist faith of the eighteenth century:

> Art. I. There exists a universal and immutable law [*droit*], source of all positive laws, which is only natural reason insofar as it governs all men.

Then, defining *droit extérieur* or international law's *droit des gens*, the draft continued to parse out the sophisticated difference between *droit* and *loi*.

> Art. IV. The interior of particular law [*droit*] of each people is composed in part of the universal law [*droit*], in part of laws [*lois*] particularly appropriate for that people, and in part of its customs or usages which supplement the laws.

In the second title, public (constitutional and political) and private laws (relations of citizens among themselves)—in other words "civil laws"—were carefully distinguished. Portalis envisaged them set apart from regulations for relationships between the citizenry, and the judicial order. He presented, under civil aegis, laws concerning crimes, police, and the control of the public peace and morale. It was these civil rules that guaranteed and sanctioned all law. The remainder of the *lois* concerned public finance, internal and foreign commerce, armed forces, and rural areas—purviews outside the preceding divisions.

The Third Title on "Publication" turned out to be fairly cut and dried as did the Fourth Title on "Effects." However, Article VIII stands out for its liberal, hands-off approach to newly democratized protocols of governance: "Law rules actions, does not scrutinize thoughts and considers licit all not forbidden even though it may not be good."

The Fifth Title on legal application and interpretation brings forward the delicate political problem presented by those revolutionaries who held that the laws should be brief and simple enough to be read by any citizen but also—an impossible added requirement—detailed enough to rule every case. This permitted judges to be mechanical appliers of laws to the facts found; it did not do much for their acting as interpreters, let alone lawmakers. Although they had fiercely rejected the old sovereignty courts the support of which was part of Montesquieu's politics, the revolutionaries had fervently embraced the Jeffersonian idea of the separation of legislative and judicial powers. They almost to a man had vivid mental recall of the independent attitude of those courts toward the application of royal ordinances and at the same time they felt a general disillusionment with the rulings made by judges in the old régime. In their years of work between 1800 and 1804 this cynical realism led Portalis and his colleagues on the Code Commission to be utterly convinced by experience that perfection in governmental lawmaking was impossible. No commissioner hesitated to express his views.

In the famous *Preliminary Discourse for the Council of State*, Portalis wrote that in a society where citizens have property and civil rights to defend, there must obviously be a certain number of laws to provide security. Yet because everything cannot be foreseen—and here he complained that ironically those who whine about the length of codes are loudest in demanding every case be covered and nothing be left to the judge—there is no way to avoid the use of natural reason in the affairs of life. It is inevitable and good that there should arise beside the laws a body of maxims, decisions, and doctrines, growing and being purified incessantly. When there is no guiding law text the judge must go to such old usage, courses of decision, and received common sense; and if they do not guide him, then he must venture as far as the vast space of natural law which covers everything of concern to man.

All this calls for compilations, collections, treatises, many volumes of research, as well as experienced professionals whose calling is good at attracting able men to respond. True, in criminal matters—contests between the public and an individual—if there is no law, the judge can decline to act; but in disputes between private parties there must be a decision. As for the recommended bifurcation in the judgment process which meant in recent years private parties in doubtful cases had been sent on to the legislative power, Portalis believed this procedure could be called, quite simply, a disaster. Decisions between two parties are for a judge, not a legislator, he wrote, seeing in the legislative representative a "minister only of general equity or justice" and of the "universality of things and people." On the other hand, the judge interprets that law by "doctrine" and not by "authority," meaning, not by purporting to make a general rule for all cases. There is definitely one science for legislators and another for judges. If the positive law is clear to the magistrate, let him follow it; but in the silence or obscurity of positive law the judge must apply a usage or, if none, then make his way back for an eternal return to natural law. No judge can peremptorily decline to decide. This is consistent with the true nature of codes which, to speak correctly, are not made by people but make themselves over time.

One may fairly say that this draft and its stirring Portalis argumentation set a high water mark in natural law. Bonaparte approved of the Portalis *Code*; that his government rejected it is not particularly surprising, given, one infers, that revolutionary sentiment against judges was still quite strong. If so, this bureaucratic estimate of opinion turned out to win the day. For decades France, in spite of Portalis, would deal with the new *Code* as if a judge should be the mechanic; any sense that the *Code* alone decided every case was a fiction to be indulged (Merryman, 31). In large part this grew out of the Portalis drafting: consistent with succinct ideas, articles were brief, often a single, very general sentence, and much scope being left with this vague elasticity, a need arose for judicial interpretation.

Lavollée (Lavollée, 216) portrays the duo of Portalis and Tronchet as having dominated all deliberations, the latter by the "breadth of his science and the firmness of his mind," and the former by "the elevation of his ideas, the charm of his style, and the force of his character." Planiol calls Portalis the "philosopher" of the commission, inspirer of the principal doctrines, the best commentator, not a narrow lawyer but an enlightened man of open, moderate mind (*Continental Legal History*, Vol. I, 287). Still, it was Bonaparte whose decisiveness controlled the direction of the Commissioners. It was he who possessed the talent for quickly summarizing a long discussion by a succinct and trenchant statement or two on the governing social and political considerations; so apt were his lay observations that rarely was even his stiffest conclusion—such as legal hostility to foreigners—then resisted. It was he, no doubt with Joséphine's barrenness in mind, who, against the opposition of nearly all the others, carried the decisions for liberal divorce rules and adoption. In attendance at 102 sessions, presiding at fifty-seven, the Emperor hastily read borrowed law books and made speeches with the help of Tronchet and the others. As vigorous a leader in debate as he was in the field, he offered the phrases and jokes of a soldier, fragments of which appear in certain manuscript remains, but which the official minutes, unfortunately, do not preserve. He was not bashful about what he thought of his principal drafters. One day in unguarded conversation he characterized Tronchet and Portalis in the blunt style of the camp: "'Tronchet has great enlightenment and a good head...for his age; Portalis would be the most ornamental and eloquent orator if he knew when to stop'" (Lavollée, 215).

The eminent historian, Sorel, ruminating (Sorel, *Introduction au code civil, livre du centenaire, société d'etudes legistlatives,* xxiv–xxvii) as he waited for the 1904 volumes published to celebrate the centenary of the *Civil Code*, urged we admire Napoleon—and Portalis—for making liberty and property the first article of the legal reform program. Naturally, in Napoleon's mind the whole structure showcased his own genius; his words at St. Helena (later set in stone for his tomb in the Invalides) were unambiguous: "'My glory is not having won forty battles.... What nothing can efface, what will live eternally, is my *Civil Code*, the minutes of the Council of State....'" Sorel decided that in all the drafting deliberations Bonaparte aimed to impart belief and adherence to his comprehensive policy: "'My politics are to govern men as the great number want to be governed.'" One needed not seek in Bonaparte complex explanations of his mind or high philosophy. He assimilated the facts like the facts of war; he saw the end and the means and adopted them.

Using his own central position written into his constitution Napoleon chose to revive the method of Louis XIV in making famous legal ordinances: draft them openly in the Council of State, then tightly confine government's large administrative bodies to approve the work. But the Emperor went farther than the monarch who had attended the sessions of the Council but generally only listened to the discussion and now and then demanded explanations. It was Napoleon, like the bee of his iconography, who took the most active part in the discussions, working, prodding, commanding, stinging. His lack of legal learning actually helped simplify the discussion and compelled evermore lucid explanations by the lawyers, especially Portalis. In Napoleon's panoramic mind stretched the whole of society, and he desired this vast entity be statutorily represented in its entirety, although his penchant for *real politik* taught him such vision when expressed should avoid total candor. The way to getting done what he wanted done highlighted a state rife with secret police, censorship, and domestic life so controlled that women's rights were ignored; as director of this sumptuous French production, he played director to his legal scriptwriters, relying heavily on a mystique of the outsider, born into a lineage where any seaminess was automatically cloaked in the most stage-worthy imperial purple.

The law of Napoleon, rewritten in bold, clean fashion without any drapery of revolutionary romance meant, in a practical way, both Justice and Bonaparte were transformed into exciting theatre—law-in-history as the stirring docudrama of his story. However, despite the Napoleonic name on the playbill, across France's legal landscape there now was walking again the guiding spirit of a backstage facilitator. Where Justinian had relied on his Theodora as muse, her legacy of an unheralded power behind the throne had passed over the boudoir into the bureau of Chief Commissioner. In the end Portalis the prolix had the ennobling, magical function of being the unexpected, powerful hand behind *My Civil Code*. He surprised all by coming up with the challenging words which would live in the innumerable legal dramas of a modern world—the stuff of literary, artistic, political, and religious myth.

Ambition's ladder would carry Portalis no farther upward. Having given his eyes to seeing, then drafting, this extraordinary judicial tour de force, exhausted visual acuity at last deteriorated into blindness. In despair Portalis turned to a certain surgeon, Dr. Forlenze, who from 1799 had enjoyed a high reputation for his work on the human eye, including the removal of cataracts. In 1807 Portalis became an eager patient and accepted the proposal of an operation. For a few days after surgery it seemed that all was successful, and Portalis excitedly gazed upon his two grandchildren for the first time. But the remission was brief, and inability to see returned along with an intolerance for all light. In the following week Portalis' health precipitously declined, his chest swelled with fluid, and on 25 August 1807 the great lawyer lay dead at sixty-one. Portalis had already been named by the Emperor to the Legion of Honor on 1 February 1805, and he had been warmly received into the French Academy on 2 January of the next year. Napoleon was highly moved by the loss of his faithful civil servant and ordered a state funeral. Portalis was ceremonially interred in the Pantheon beside fellow jurist and codifier François Tronchet. The two defenders of both monarchy and empire sleep there to this day.

The Form of the *Code Napoleon*

The following is a brief presentation of the original form of the *Code civil des Français* which the Emperor in 1807 renamed *Code Napoleon* and which is now simply the *Code civil*. Actions (Titles XIII through XVII) could be omitted from the *Civil Code* of 1804 because in continental law, and modern Anglo-American law, with theoretically no effect on substantive rights, they therefore would belong in a separate *Code of Civil Procedure*.

Articles 1–6	Preliminary Title	
Articles 7–515	Book One – *Of Persons*	
Articles 7–33	Title I	Enjoyment and Loss of Civil Rights
Articles 34–101	Title II	Vital Statistics
Articles 102–111	Title III	Domicile
Articles 112–143	Title IV	Absence
Articles 144–228	Title V	Marriage
Articles 229–311	Title VI	Divorce
Articles 312–342	Title VII	Paternity
Articles 343–370	Title VIII	Adoption
Articles 371–387	Title IX	Paternal Powers
Articles 388–487	Title X	Minority
Articles 488–515	Title XI	Majority
Articles 516–710	Book Two – *Of Things, and the Different Kinds of Property*	
Articles 516–543	Title I	Movables and Immovables
Articles 544–577	Title II	Fruits of and Additions to Property
Articles 578–636	Title III	Use of the Property of Another
Articles 637–710	Title IV	Servitudes Imposed on One Property For the Benefit of Another
Articles 711–2281	Book Three – *Of the Different Ways of Acquiring Property*	
Articles 712–892	Title I	Successions
Articles 893–1100	Title II	Donations and Wills
Articles 1101–1369	Title III	Contracts and Obligations by Agreement in General
Articles 1370–1386	Title IV	Quasi-contracts and Wrongs [Torts]
Articles 1387–1581	Title V	The Contract of Marriage
Articles 1582–1685	Title VI	Sales
Articles 1686–1688	Title VII	Exchange

Articles 1689–1831	Title XVIII	Leases
Articles 1832–1873	Title IX	Partnerships
Articles 1874–1914	Title X	Loans
Articles 1915–1963	Title XI	Deposit
Articles 1964–1983	Title XII	Aleatory Contracts
Articles 2092–2203	Title XVIII	Security Transactions
Articles 2204–2218	Title XIX	Execution
Articles 2219–2281	Title XX	Prescription

It is not a useless tautology to restate that along a line which stretched back long before 1500 BCE had come various codes of law. As many writers like Schulz have seen, the use of paradigmatic form in the presentation of knowledge was the essential Hellenistic contribution to the professionalizing of Roman legal science. In Rome's Republican times the admirable "systematic exposition of the whole private law" (Schulz, 38–39, 96), infused the lost *Ius Civile* of Q. Mucius Scaevola, earlier studied here as the first use of the dialectical method in analyzing kinds. System would, we know, follow into the Gaius *Institutiones*. And who can ever forget Justinian's break-through legal vision and then the Domat rearrangement in a "natural order."

The Portalis 1804 civil codification of "Persons, Things, and Acquisition of Things" set the nineteenth century on this same long route. Its quest replicated the past's search for a serviceable dialectic for justice; its careful attempt at legal paradigm reflected these many centuries of organic assemblages. Even its intensely dramatic heart was a genetic throwback to Hellenistic suggestions impinging upon Roman law, when "Person" found its validation from the Latin *persona*, a word whose initial meaning, no matter how complex, was strictly theatrical. First of all it had stood for the most obvious: persona—a "mask" used by a player in a drama or a character represented by an actor. Its purview next expanded to the part or character each person sustains in the world. Finally, it reached broadly to any human being who performs any function or plays any part (Andrews 1125).

In so expanding the "person" definition into law, there came to be foregrounded not an individual but, again, the part law offered an individual. The legal person passed into various phases of role play: contractor, owner, debtor, creditor, husband, wife, father, mother, adult, minor, incapable, guardian, executor, etc. (Bernard, Bernard, *The First Year of Roman Law* 35; Ourliac and Gazzaniga, 171). This was not a new concept, for in the preceding century, England's legal Shakespeare, Blackstone, who was not bound by the basic continental distinction of "public" and "private" law, divided his "Conventories on the Laws of England" into the "acts" of four books: *Of the Rights of Persons*, *Of the Rights of Things*, *Of Private Wrongs*, and *Of Public Wrongs*. The first treated a wide range of roles including "Individuals," "Parliament," "King," "Royal Family," "Councils Belonging to the King," "Subordinate Magistrates," "People, Whether Aliens, Denizens, or Natives," "Clergy," " Military and Maritime States," "Master and Servant," "Husband and Wife," "Parent and Child," "Guardian and Ward," and "Corporations." Thus, the law in essence devolved into drama upon a stage—law as play, presenting first its *dramatis personae*, next their props (things), and then the plot line of their relations *inter sese* (obligations and successions). Because law's drama was an ancient concept,

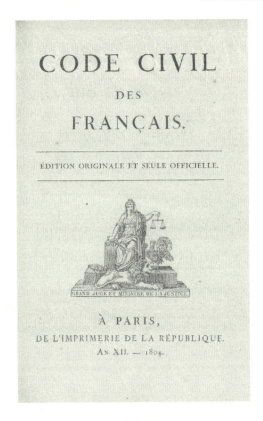

Code Civil des Français
Courtesy of the Rare Book Collection, Lillian Goldman Law Library, Yale Law School

the actors were still masked as types; moreover, there were in fact many individuals in each type, but all had been deemed the same by the law.

The Commissioners of Bonaparte having decided to follow this ancient theatrical tradition of legal classification in drafting their *Civil Code*, Portalis carefully made note of the three act "division of the work." When presenting the draft to the legislative bodies on 25 November 1801, he showed it to have two aspects: the foundation of the matters which were its object and the exterior form in which they were arranged. As to the former the most "natural" arrangement was found to be, like literary efforts still a century away, one in which a subject succeeded another by shadings often unconscious and hard to perceive but which both united and separated. Portalis revealed that in examining the different ways in which jurisconsults had divided the law the commissioners clearly saw arbitrariness in all routes followed. They had therefore refrained either from claiming that their approach was unique or best or from changing the common divisions. Rather, they preserved the order followed in Roman Law (Portalis-*Discours*, 99). In his later analysis Sorel decided (Sorel, xviii) that, although the commissioners were no doubt influenced by the rigorously Cartesian spirit of Domat, Domat's attempt to improve on the form of the Roman books clearly had not succeeded with the Napoleonic cohort. The Portalis team was not aiming at a scientific structure for use in teaching; their *Code* was to be for lawyers who already knew what their field entailed.

Contracts in the *Code Napoleon*

Freedom of the individual person to make legally enforceable contracts forms the foundation of capitalist organization in today's most economically successful societies. At a pace incalculably accelerated by the Internet, an incredible web of agreements, long and short, simple and complex, written and unwritten, constantly being made, unmade, performed and breached, interpreted and enforced, binds us globally together, both within and across multi-national borders. Matters of immense economic consequence progress in reliance upon X's pledged word in a contract to perform an act desired by Y. Parties relying upon the laws made by governments but consulting only their sovereign individual wills without consulting those governments, have in fact gone forward to make for themselves more rules to supplement the general laws. The *Civil Code* with eloquent simplicity proclaimed this principle in a single, short sentence: "Article 1134. Les Conventions légalement formées tiennent lieu de loi à ceux qui les ont faites." (Agreements legally made have the status of law for those who made them.)

This is, in effect, the first Article of Title III, Articles 1101 to 1369, general provisions for contracts. It comes after preliminary Articles (1101–1133) set the stage: definitions of the kinds of contracts and statements of the conditions for their validity (absence of error, violence, and fraud); of the capacity to contract; of the objects and matters which can be the subjects of contracts; and of the necessity that for each there shall be a cause neither false nor illicit. The Article is followed, among other subjects, by provisions for damages, interpretations, third parties, kinds of obligations (among which are conditional, term, alternation, divisible, and indivisible); extinction of obligations (including payment, novation, release); and proof of obligations and payment.

Without, as Gazzaniga points out (Gazzaniga, 183), any revolution in doctrine, Article 1134 may reasonably be seen as the triumphant bourgeois apogee after the Revolution. It put into the hands of individuals and their jurist advisors a document, signed and sealed with all the formal ceremony a civil code entails, one that finally organized legal relationships and laid to rest a thousand uncertainties of the old law. It was a document which elegantly, cogently reflected the principles of natural law—from expression in Roman statutes to the treatises of Pothier. Now the individual businessman bent on wealth had an actual pile of paper telling him, with all the individualized panache which was to characterize the nineteenth century Heroic Quest, that he could be a lawmaker in aid of his goal.

It is not surprising to find a lively contemporary interest in provisions of the *Code* which threatened to invalidate this contract law. One provocation grew from the right of a seller of real property to bring an action voiding the sale if he believed that the price would be found to be less than 5/12 of a just price as determined by experts testifying in the action (Articles 1118, 1674). It was on moral grounds that Portalis, seconded by Bonaparte, pushed into the *Code* this provision of previous law after changing its old 1/2 into 5/12. Although the rule did not imply a general invalidity based on lack of consent intrinsic to an unjust price—it applied only to some contracts made by some persons—it did seem to raise the question whether equality of *quid pro quo* is essential in contracts. It was thus an unsettling "how far might it go?" possibility for aggressive traders functioning in "social disorder" (Gazzaniga 185). Actually, it did not go further, but the ghost was there, and it remained a troublesome specter for the problem of cause. The *Code* also adopted the view of Domat as shared by Pothier that a licit "cause" is necessary for the validity of a contract. However, although it stated what causes were illicit, the articles failed to lay out the defining element of a licit cause. After 1804 this engendered a renewal, with increasing tension, one might add, of the old problem of definition. To take the homely example of a chair for sale, some interpreters were saying that cause is the particular item driving the mercantile contract; to get the chair is the object of the buyer and to sell the chair is the object of the seller. The object in other words, is the causal mechanism of transaction. Others felt cause was something that, for each kind of contract as defined in the law, was always the same. Thus, in a unilateral contract the cause is the fact that the promisor has received something to induce his promise. Nevertheless, no jurist defined cause as the subjective motive of a contracting party—taking a topical example, that X borrows $1,000 from Y to win $50,000 at a casino in order to buy a sports car.

It was in presenting Sales before the legislative bodies that Portalis touched on this peculiar problem of cause in contracts. He stated that it is from "rules of justice anterior to contracts themselves that contracts draw their principal force" (Portalis-*Discours,* 256–257). These rules are not the result of human agreements; they precede them and must control them. Such rules are the gracious structures of natural equity on which the Roman jurisconsults, and after them all civilized nations, based their civil legislation on contracts. Portalis noted that the French legislators had already followed suit in adopting a previous bill in which they "proclaimed the maxim that no obligation can exist without a reasonable and proportionate cause." Thus, according to Portalis, we have here a moral question: assuming that a contract is not "illicit," does it have a "reasonable and proportionate cause"? As to what cause is, he believed that in contracts for private interest (as contrasted with charity) "the cause...according to the jurisconsults ... [is] ... the interest or advantage which is the motive and reason of an engagement." This seems to ignore the distinctions noticed above, but the Portalis formulation does not drain the concept of significance since it validates all agreements entered into for some purpose, whatever that purpose may be.

As judge he knew one must "examine if that interest or that advantage is real or imaginary, if it is proportionate, that is to say, if there is a reasonable equilibrium between what one gives and what one receives." But, Portalis also held that this rule is a rule of morality not of law; its object is virtue, whereas the object of law is more peace than virtue. When the Romans looked into limiting the right of rescision for inadequate equilibrium between the interests or advantages on each side—taking the specific example of cases where the seller received less than one-half of the just price—they considered that the law's object entailed facilitating secure transactions in "the commerce of life." Anticipating the objection that his general language hardly encouraged such security, Portalis carefully noted that in the *Civil Code* the action is limited to immovables and to sellers (Portalis-*Discours,* 263, 267, 272).

Despite his painstaking effort at clarification Portalis added little to the science of "cause" in contracts. No wonder many concluded that these were questions devoid of utility, and that "'the theory of cause is so vague and inexact that one is not astonished that pleaders invoke it at random'" (Gazzaniga, 186). Following Roman law the continental lawyers had turned the subject of cause into a very large hinged tablature; in this legal diptych the contractual form of "obligations" faces the obligation imposed by law to make reparation for wrongs—the torts of Anglo-American law. The *Code* studied squarely both panels of this rather unwieldy topic by paring it down through classic French division into five brief articles dwelling in the minute organization (1382–1386) of Chapter II ("Delicts and Quasi-delicts"), Title IV ("Of Engagements Formed Without Agreement"), Book III ("Different Ways of Acquiring Property"). Article 1382 would present the foundation statement of delicts: "Any act whatever of a man, who causes damage to another, obliges him by the fault from which it came, to repair it." The succeeding two articles enhanced this important doctrine through their complementary material. One is responsible not only for a deliberate act but for negligence or imprudence and for damage caused by things in one's care. As for parents of minors living with their parents, masters of domestics converging through their assigned functions, teachers and artisans interacting with their pupils and apprentices, they are all during their period of surveillance responsible for the acts of these subordinates. The only exception would be if the superior could prove an inability unless they could prove to prevent any incident of an inferior's delinquence.

In spite, then, of the Revolution's preference for statutes, the imposing subject of cause—which was to form a heavy volume when in the first half of the twentieth century professors of the American Law Institute reduced it to abstract statement for United States law in code form—was left by Portalis lying, as it were, on his elegant Empire table. Both he and his colleagues, admittedly, had in this instance missed their chance to reform. Yet paradoxically, leaving that progress to the future meant a day would come when judicial decisions would be at ease in adopting what came to be considered by many a better contract approach: a promise is enforceable if entered into with the intention that it should be enforceable.

The *Code Napoleon* in the Nineteenth and Twentieth Centuries

One can discuss the *Code* pro and con, but two points are certain. The first, on the negative side of the balance sheet, is that for a long time it froze doctrine and congealed legal evolution, just as partisans of judge-made law hoped it would. Despite this show of a strong hand, the work did bring Portalis as writer success in his day. Yet by openly using terms which tended to support strong state power against flexible individual rights, the Portalis victories were won at definite cost to his reputation in history.

In contrast the second point comes down on the side of positive progress: it provided for the nineteenth and twentieth centuries a clear legal statement on such a great range of subjects that it put to rest a myriad of uncertainties in the old statutes and, in this case, just as codifiers said it would, greatly increased the utility of law as an instrument of social advance and unity. For two-thirds of the nineteenth century juridical study in France henceforth came to mean study of the *Code*. Although Napoleon, with views like Justinian's, is said to have exclaimed, when the first commentary appeared, "'My Code is lost'" (*Continental Legal History,* Vol. I, 302), these rapidly appearing expositions and memoranda had begun because of their own talented writers to form an exciting new school of juristic exegesis. Many were written by sophisticated men, mostly *avocats* and judges well informed on their age and its history and often trained in Roman law and the old French law. Their hermeneutic concentration on explicating was not a mistake, for the rigor promoted comprehension and exposed gaps and insufficiencies.

Other critics soon appeared, however, who went well beyond textual critique to call attention to discords between the *Code* and the economic development of the nation. From them came in the last two decades of the nineteenth century a new school reflective of influences from thinkers like Taine, Renan, and Durkheim. Far-reaching advances being made in the exact sciences added to the period's great interest in history, sociology, and philosophy had brought forward young and idealistic minds who regarded law with a keen philosophical spirit matched by an eye as much for what law can be as for what it is. These thinkers now detached themselves from the German historical school of legal study which had dominated Europe during the period of the exegetes and launched their own reform movement. The audience they found for their innovative writing was a French society now lay and republican instead of monarchist and clerical. It proved to be a perfect match as these managers of a prodigious industrial revolution now found themselves being given legal lessons by thinkers of equally impressive training—in Roman law and legal history as well as comparative and international law—whose practical objective was that there be a balance and similarity between life and legality.

Among these law mentors were some revivalists of natural law, but there were, as well, a cohort of verbal opponents whose complaints increased in stridency as social issues continued increasing in importance. Especially to be addressed was the question of the right to employment; and if we look ahead to the eve of the second World War, we see that law would grow to be less normative and general and more obliged to address separately the needs of particular economic groups—farmers, industrial workers, commercial enterprises, tradesmen, tenants, debtors, automobile operators, and a large diversity living under the vast legal umbrella of "*et al.*" Each of these cadres having come to view itself as different, each would clamor for its own code *outside* the Napoleonic paradigm. In Gazzaniga's perspective (Gazzaniga, 62–67) during these times of cold facts' domination over deeply-rooted philosophical structures the "anterior" general principles so important to Portalis found themselves crowded toward the door.

Although many jurists chafed at these circumstantial thrusts, the new forces were not to be resisted. Most legal philosophers of change thought that only they represented the spirit of the Revolution, while in fact, "the abandonment of the guiding principles of the Revolution could not ... [have been] ... more absolute." Destroying the old local independence, with its many bodies, communities, and associations, the eighteenth century Constituent Assembly had established a purely individualistic system; in the next century the provisions of the *Code* for contracts made them law. The central power was to stand alone, relating simply to individual citizens, disarmed but protected. Nevertheless, in the new way local collective forces could not be held back. They sprang up for reestablishment in multiple constituencies, some by individual initiatives but many by the central power itself, overburdened and trying to unload expensive functions (*Continental Legal History*, Vol. I, 297–298), as soon would occur with the monumental divestiture of the Louisiana territory an ocean away.

Amendment of the *Civil Code*: Other Napoleonic *Codes*

It can be no surprise that, not too long after promulgation, arguments against the *Code* from the many whose single alliance was substantial agreement on its defects led these critics to join boldly in pointing out and then demanding adjustments long after Napoleon had left the stage. The severity toward foreigners needed an amendment of 1819 to correct the excesses. The salutory Revolutionary reform requiring publicity for transfers of real estate (immovables) had been rejected, and an amendment had to correct this in 1855. The mortgage system was the weakest part of the *Code*. Better Revolutionary models had been rejected, and Planiol, after several amendments, wrote in 1899 that the conveyance of property was still considered defective. Looking at the large picture, though, this is a remarkably short list. Failure to deal adequately with inadequacies of omission pertinent to matters which arose largely since 1804 can hardly be laid at the door of the Commission and its collaborators. For example, the "error" in lack of sufficient protection for the ownership of personal property (movables) became apparent only with the phenomenal growth of wealth in paper instruments. Other omissions are similar in such post facto exigency: names of persons, attributes of artificial entities, long-term leases, literary and artistic property, bankruptcy for non-traders, bearer negotiable instruments, insurance, syndicates, labor law. There is as well insufficient attention to associations and corporations.

The *Code Napoleon*, of course, dealt only with private law, and not all of that if commercial law is deemed part of the personal domain. Thus, Bonaparte was led ever forward into more codes, as need for them forced emergence in rapid succession: *Civil Procedure* (1806), *Commerce* (1807), *Criminal Procedure* (1808), and the *Penal Code* (1810). On most points the draftsmen confined their efforts to the *Ordinances* promulgated by Louis XIV and Colbert in 1673 and 1681. In his considerations Planiol swept them all under his rug, as it were, deeming them all to be inferior, with the *Commercial Code* especially inadequate to the need. In spite of important nineteenth century legislation on commerce outside the *Code*, the situation was felt by many to be problematic even as the twentieth century began.

The Merits and Spread of the *Code Napoleon*

The argument that a code retards the development of the law by giving it a rigid, statutory form on the day of its promulgation is a criticism of management after adoption rather than an argument that in place of a code there should be miscellaneous statutes and judicial decisions. It always behooves legislators, judges, academics, and the bar—beginning on the very day of promulgation—to be vigilant in studying the continuous evolution of society. Only in this way can they protect the people's laws by detecting the need for interpretation and amendment and by responding prudently and appropriately. That France after 1804 carried on this process with something less than perfection is not persuasive that she would have been better off without this great, comprehensive effort to restate her law. As the post-Portalis years rolled on toward a hundred, most French were delighted to tell the world of the merit of their *Code*. They noted how its moderation and flexibility allowed an admirable accommodation for the most diverse political systems. They were proud of the wisdom which had kept the 1789 spirit of equality while it abandoned chimerical revolutionary suggestions. When the nineteenth century was shaken by powerful social revolutions, the *Code* did not shake; its foundations in civil liberty, family, property in land, and succession were untouched, aiding France, as Sorel saw it (Sorel, Vol. I, xvii), toward that unity which simply fulfilled the natural tendencies of long national evolution.

Celebrations for the centenary of the *Civil Code* were organized by the Society for Legislative Studies, which decided that true French style demanded an ambitious intellectual effort. The result was two volumes totaling 1,108 pages. Volume I weighed in on the *Code* in France with nineteen articles written by as many professors in the now long revived universities. Volume II presented fourteen articles by foreign scholars commenting on *Code* influence in their respective countries; these were followed by five concluding articles which looked into the future, pondering the question of whether there should now be a general revision. But there was no doubt as to the basic grand effort. Sorel in his Introduction to the two volumes proclaimed that the strength of the laws laid down in the *Code* was their "experimental physics" which sustained no less than the "history of French Society." The result, he concluded, was a "book of reason that brings social peace as good hygiene brings health" (Sorel, Vol. I, xxix; xxx). Celebration in Paris of this "health" required four gala days (27–30 October), and we may be sure that in a France bursting with prosperity the four days offered toasts and gastronomy at least equal to the quality of the papers presented.

In addition to admiration of the *Code's* general spirit, praise was given for technical qualities of excellent draftsmanship. Deriving unity from the preponderant implacable will of Bonaparte, the *Code's* systematizing had put down roots in the historic precedents of the ancients without losing precision and clarity in the complex balance between the past's principles and the future's blueprints. It made obsolete the old confusing books upon which lawyers had too long relied, bringing instead a limpidity creditable not only to Portalis and his colleagues but also to Domat, Daguesseau, and Pothier. There was appreciation still for the other echoes, too—the draftsmen of Louis XIV, pushed into clarity by the King himself; Montesquieu's chapter on the crafting of legislation; the quiet conservatism of the acute Cambacérès whose legal manipulations of Bonaparte were especially effective during the sumptuous working dinners at which he was a master.

During these hundred years the influence of the *Code* was not confined to its homeland; its creators were minds inspired by the optimistic idea of universal human nature, and as such they had felt that such an honorable concept allowed, indeed required, legislating for France a work for all humankind. In an extraordinary phenomenon of legal propagation the *Code* came to dwell by fiat not only in the large area conquered by Napoleon—including among other places Belgium, Luxembourg, the Palatinate, provinces on the right bank of the Rhine, Geneva, Savoy, Italy, and the Hanseatics—but knew a voluntary adoption in Westphalia, Hanover, Baden, Frankfurt, Nassau, several Swiss cantons, Danzig, Warsaw, Illyria, and Naples. Germany proper naturally was considered the big prize, and the French of 1804 sat back, confidently awaiting adoption of their *Code* across the Rhine. It was not to be. The historian and legal scholar Karl von Savigny led the intellectual assault, holding up instead law as the chronicle of custom and launching the ambitious and prolific German historical school. When on 1 January 1900 a German *Civil Code* became effective, it reflected this far different spirit of localism and idiosyncratic detail. The *French Civil Code*, however, kept its prestige as it crossed oceans to appear in Louisiana, Haiti, Quebec, Greece, and a long list of South and Central American republics, as well as making inroads across Spain, Romania, and Italy. It thus served as a mother lode, and countless movements of codification knew the Portalis legal influence both from the letter and from the spirit of a work its master draftsman had sought to fill with "more than reason itself." Although that ambition of a lawyer from Aix had been in match as grandiose as any to be held by an emperor from Corsica, it would be Napoleon Bonaparte whose name like Justinian cast its aura over the new *Digest*. That appropriation, too, can now be appreciated as yet but another code, whose Rosetta-like decipherment, reveals Napoleon's fellow participant in exile and trial, in courage become audacity. Next to the greater legend in David's famous portrait, standing stiff and proud with the *Code* at his side, appears this unseen, sightless Other. And Jean-Etienne-Marie Portalis speaks confidently, to all who would listen, of the successful completion of what was his own great vision, too: I have lifted the bench, I have changed the bar, and I have settled for no less than bringing all of human life into the vast mind and heart sweep of the law.

With this zenith in continental legal effort we have reached that point where historians of earlier eras would graciously thank the "faithful reader" for keeping forbearant company throughout the long trek. This author acknowledges no less. The journey taken has yielded no firm caveats nor can it do so, as law's oscillation between realist believers in large natural principles and nominalist adherents to unicity of preference continues to this day its wide pendulum swings. What our inquiry has perhaps awakened as an appreciated given however, is the intricacy and

Codice Napoleone Il Grande 1805 Edition
Courtesy of Dr. Constance C. Ecklund

grandeur of the legal philosophies which have gone into and still inform a profession too often reduced to the butt of angry fee payers. Remembering history, the classicist Lionel Casson recently put on the garb of the disgruntled to ask, "Imagine, if you will," (Casson, 122), "a time without any lawyers at all." (Casson, *Smithsonian* 18.7 (1987): 122–131). He quickly provided his own tongue in cheek answer, colored with a wry touch of the historian's acrimony: "Civilization flourished in Egypt and ancient Greece with little help from lawyering, but then came Rome and our troubles began."

It is to be hoped that with help from these two volumes, the reader, faithful or cursory, has immediately thought of at least a few comments in rebuttal to the Casson "troubles." The goal of our trek has been, after all, to help those interested in law have fewer questions about its origins. Since there has been no need for actual physical displacement, we have had the luxury of the armchair traveler, taking an entire walk of discovery within the transcendent convenience of the mind. Sitting together in a kind of Montaigne tower, asking ourselves the What do I know? question, we have ended up with an extraordinary storyboard of answers. With confidence to rebut the Casson gloom, we can express instead how bleak a time it indeed would be without the legal profession.

Lawyers and judges as well as students and teachers of law should be relieved and proud that Rome, building on the strong rhetorical tradition of Greek legalists like Isocrates, did appear on a long-gone stage and began to address troubles through calming, civilizing edicts. When Sorel took a stand on the same spot of remembrance as we and made his final appraisal of the propagation among other nations of Napoleon's *Civil Code* (Sorel, Vol. I, xvi–xvii), he wrote with an overwhelming sense of pride in the long legal line which now informed Gallic discipline:

> ... [T]he French, in legislating for themselves, found themselves legislating for these peoples. French law was propagated and acclimated among them naturally, here by infiltration, there by direct transplantation. That is all that is possible in the propagation of social laws and it is a lot. It is even, since the diffusion of Roman laws, the only example we have of so large an expansion of the laws of a people. We have the right to find in it some pride and to recognize in it a confirmation of that intellectual and social leadership that France exercised in the 17th and 18th centuries.

In today's admiration of the Napoleonic *Code*, however, one is no longer confined to such an encapsulating contentment in an early nineteenth century accomplishment. We are, rather, liberated to recognize what that achievement meant. It was one more confirmation of the comprehensive intellectual and social leadership of a discipline which transcends Enlightenment's centuries and national boundaries. It is a banality but a marvelous truth as well: there will never cease to be human beings trying to advocate and to codify, with multiple lapses into evil and equally multiple lurches toward good. Beyond any context but with the pride of Sorel, our long look back has shown off legal leadership honed and honored in the torrent of legal words that themselves were the rite of proud passage for so many. From Aristotle to Aquinas, Justinian to Giordano, Mucius to Montaigne, countless advocates have pondered, glossed, commented, and systematized. It is all these children of Themis—that eternal Lady Justice so fond of scales, blindfolds, or just common sense—who made possible the stunning achievement of a Portalis and a Napoleon. More than that, it was they who transmitted those principles and that particular cast of mind which today's legal practitioner, often with ease and insouciance, underscoring an innocence in knowledge of historic precedence, nevertheless still holds as an illuminating, guiding, and confirming torch. It has been to make certain the light from this torch casts its illumination on the personalities and the intellectual guideposts of a legal past too often in shadow that this book's journey has been made.

BIBLIOGRAPHY

ABBREVIATION

Acton   Acton, John Emerich Edward Dalberg, Lord, *Longitude 30 West: A Confidential Report to the Syndics of the Cambridge University Press* (New York: Cambridge University Press, 1969)

Adolphe   Adolphe, Lydie, *Portalis et son temps, l'homme, le penseur, le législateur* (Paris: Les presses modernes, 1936)

Allen   Allen, Carleton Kemp, *Law in the Making* (Oxford: The Clarendon Press, 1927)

Aristotle   Aristotle, Martin Ostwald, ed., *Nicomachean Ethics* (Indianapolis: Bobbs-Merrill, 1962)

Bainton   Bainton, Roland Herbert, *The Reformation of the Sixteenth Century* (Boston: The Beacon Press, 1965)

Baker   Baker, Keith Michael, *Condorcet, From Natural Philosophy to Social Mathematics* (Chicago: University of Chicago Press, 1975)

Balsdon   Balsdon, John P.V.D., *Romans and Aliens* (Chapel Hill: University of North Carolina Press, 1979)

Bartolus-Beale   Bartolo (of Sassoferrato), Joseph Henry Beale, trans., *Bartolus on the Conflict of Laws,* (Cambridge, MA: Harvard University Press, 1914)

Baumer   Baumer, Franklin Le Van, *Main Currents of Western Thought: Readings in Western European Intellectual History from the Middle Ages to the Present,* 4th ed. (New York: Knopf, 1978)

Bell	Bell, David A., *Lawyers and Citizens: The Making of a Political Elite in Old Regime France* (New York: Oxford University Press, 1994)
Benson and Constable	Benson, Robert Louis and Giles Constable, *Renaissance and Renewal in the Twelfth Century* (Cambridge, MA: Harvard University Press, 1982)
Bergin	Bergin, Thomas Goddard, *Petrarch, Twayne's World Authors Series* (New York: Twayne Publishers, 1970)
Berman	Berman, Harold J., *Law and Revolution: The Formation of the Western Legal Tradition* (Cambridge, MA: Harvard University Press, 1983)
Bernard	Bernard, Fernand, and Charles Phineas Sherman, *The First Year of Roman Law* (New York: Oxford University Press, 1906)
Bible *Anchor Bible*	*The Anchor Bible, New Testament, Matthew,* W. F. Albright and C.S. Mann, eds. (Garden City, NY: Doubleday, 1971)
Bible, Revised Standard Version	*The Holy Bible, Revised Standard Version* (New York: Thomas Nelson & Sons, Old Testament, 1952, New Testament 1946)
I Corinthians	*Bible, New Testament, I Corinthians: A New Translation.* With introduction and commentary by William F. Orr and James Arthur Walther (Garden City, NY: Doubleday, 1976)
Black	Black, Donald J., and Maureen Mileski, *The Social Organization of Law* (New York: Seminar Press, 1973)
Bloch	Bloch, Marc Léopold Benjamin, *Feudal Society* (Chicago: University of Chicago Press, 1961)
Brissaud	Brissaud, Jean, and James Wilford Garner, *Manuel d'histoire du droit français* (Boston: Little, Brown, and Co., 1915)
Brown	Brown, R. Allen, *The Normans* (New York: St. Martin's Press, 1984)

Biographie Universelle	*Biographie Universelle, Nouvelle Edition*, (Paris: Firmin Didot frères, 1858)
Burn	Burn, A.R., *The Pelican History of Greece* (Hammondsworth: Pelican Books-Penguin, 1966)
Cairns	Cairns, Huntington, *Legal Philosophy from Plato to Hegel* (Baltimore: Johns Hopkins Press, 1949)
Calhoun	Calhoun, George Miller, and Francis De Zulueta, *Introduction to Greek Legal Science* (Oxford: The Clarendon Press, 1944)
Calisse	Calisse, Carlo, Layton B. Register, trans., *A History of Italian Law* (Boston: Little, Brown, and Company, 1928)
Cambridge Economic History	*The Cambridge Economic History of Europe*, 2nd ed., M.M. Postan and H. J. Habakkuk, eds., (Cambridge: Cambridge University Press, 1966)
Cambridge Medieval History	*Cambridge Medieval History*, H. M. Gwatkin and J. P. Whitney, eds. (New York: Macmillan, 1911–1936)
Cantor	Cantor, Norman F., *Medieval History: The Life and Death of a Civilization*, 2nd ed. (New York: Macmillan, 1969)
Carcopino	Carcopino, Jérôme, Henry Thompson Rowell ed., E. O. Lorimer, trans., *Daily Life in Ancient Rome: The People and the City at the Height of the Empire*, (Aylesbury: Penguin Books, 1956)
Carey	Carey, John A., *Judicial Reform in France before the Revolution of 1789* (Cambridge, MA: Harvard University Press, 1981)
Carlyle	Carlyle, R.W., and A.J. Carlyle. *A History of Mediæval Political Theory in the West* (Edinburgh: Blackwood & Sons Ltd, 1928)
Casson	Casson, Lionel, "Imagine, If You Will, a Time without Any Lawyers at All..." *Smithsonian* 18.7 (1987): 122–131

Castell and Borchert	Castell, Alburey, and Donald M. Borchert, *An Introduction to Modern Philosophy: Examining the Human Condition*, 4th ed. (New York: Macmillan, 1983)
Castelot	Castelot, André, *Napoléon Bonaparte*, (Paris: Librairie Académique Perrin, 1984)
Chénon	Chénon, Émile, *Les professeurs de droit français de l'université de Bourges et les manuscrits de leurs cours* (Paris: Recueil Sirey, 1921)
Clarence Smith	Clarence Smith, J. A., *Medieval Law Teachers and Writers, Civilian and Canonist, Monographies Juridiques No 9* (Ottawa: University of Ottawa Press, 1975)
Clark	Clark, Alan, *Barbarossa: The Russian German Conflict, 1941–1945* (New York: W. Morrow, 1965)
Clarke	Clarke, M. L., *Higher Education in the Ancient World* (London: Routledge & K. Paul, 1971)
Continental Legal History	*Continental Legal History Series*, 11 Vols. (published under the auspices of the Association of American Law Schools, Boston: Little, Brown and Company, 1912–1928)
Collinet	Collinet, Paul, *Études historique sur le droit de Justinien* (Paris: L. Larose & Le Tenin, 1912)
Conroy	Conroy, Peter V., *Montesquieu Revisited. Twayne's World Authors Series* (New York: Macmillan, 1992)
Copleston	Copleston, Frederick C., *A History of Philosophy*, 9 Vols. (New York: Image Books, 1985)
Coulton	Coulton, George Gordon, *Five Centuries of Religion* (Cambridge: The University Press, 1929–1950)
Cox	Cox, Iris, *Montesquieu and the History of French Laws* (Oxford: Voltaire Foundation at the Taylor Institution, 1983)

D'Aguesseau, Henri François,

D'Aguesseau- *Discourses*	—— *Discours de monsieur le chanceller d'Aguesseau* (Paris: Chez les libraires associés, 1783)
D'Aguesseau- *Meditations*	—— *Meditations sur les aires ou les fausses idées de la justice, Oeuvres completes, new edition*, J. M. Pardessus, ed. (Paris: Fantin et compagnie 1829)
D'Aguesseau- Pardessus	—— J. M. Pardessus and M. Thomas eds., *Oeuvres complètes du chancelier D'aguesseau* (Paris: Fantin et compagnie, 1829)
Deanesly	Deanesly, Margaret, *A History of the Medieval Church, 590–1500*, 9th ed. (London: Methuen, 1969)
De Curzon	De Curzon, Alfred, *L'enseignement du droit français dans les universités de France aux xviie et xviiie siècles* (Paris: Société du Receuil Sirey, 1920)
Delderfield	Delderfield, R.F., *Napoleon's Marshals* (Philadelphia: Chilton Books, 1966)
de Zulueta	de Zulueta, Francis, *The Institutes of Gaius* (Oxford: The Clarendon Press, 1951–1953)
Dictionary of the History of Ideas	*Dictionary of the History of Ideas: Studies of Selected Pivotal Ideas*, 4 Vols., Philip P. Wiener, ed. (New York: Scribner, 1974)
D'Irsay	D'Irsay, Stephen, *Histoire des universités françaises et étrangères des origines à nos jours* (Paris: A. Picard, 1933)

Domat, Jean,

Domat-Cushing	—— William Strahan, ed., and Luther Stearns Cushing, trans., *The Civil Law in Its Natural Order* (Boston: C.C. Little and J. Brown, 1850)
Domat-Rémy	—— Joseph Rémy, trans., *Oeuvres complètes de J. Domat, Nouvelle Edition* (Paris: Alex–Gobelet, Libraire, 1835)

Duby	Duby, Georges, *The Chivalrous Society* (Berkeley: University of California Press, 1977)
Dumbauld	Dumbauld, Edward, *The Life and Legal Writings of Hugo Grotius* (Norman: University of Oklahoma Press, 1969)
Dunoyer	Dunoyer, Luc Henry, *Blackstone et Pothier* (Paris: Rousseau & Cie, 1927)
Durant *Story of Civilization*	Durant, Will, and Ariel Durant, *The Story of Civilization*, 11 Vols. (New York: Simon and Schuster, 1965)
Durant *Lessons of History*	Durant, Will, and Ariel Durant, *The Lessons of History* (New York: Simon and Schuster, 1968)
Durkheim	Durkheim, Emile, *Montesquieu and Rousseau: Forerunners of Sociology,* Foreword by Henri Peyre (Ann Arbor: University of Michigan Press, 1970)
Encyclopedia Britannica	*Encyclopedia Britannica*, 11th ed., 19 Vols. (New York: Encyclopedia Britannica, Inc., 1910–1911)
Einaudi	Einaudi, Mario, *The Physiocratic Doctrine of Judicial Control* (Cambridge, MA: Harvard University Press, 1938)
Ellul	Ellul, Jacques, *Histoire des institutions,* 9th ed. (Paris: Presses Universitaires de France, 1987)
Encyclopedia of Philosophy	*Encyclopedia of Philosophy,* 8 Vols., Paul Edwards, ed. (New York: Macmillan, 1967)
Fitzsimmons	Fitzsimmons, Michael P., *The Parisian Order of Barristers and the French Revolution.* Harvard Historical Monographs V. 74. (Cambridge, MA: Harvard University Press, 1987)
Ford	Ford, Franklin L., *Robe and Sword: The Regrouping of the French Aristocracy after Louis XIV.* Harvard Historical Studies, V. 64. (Cambridge, MA: Harvard University Press, 1953)

Frame	Frame, Donald Murdoch, *Montaigne: A Biography* (New York: Harcourt, Brace & World, 1965)
Frêche	Frêche, Georges, and Jean Sudreau, *Un chancelier gallican: Daguesseau; et un cardinal diplomate: François Joachim de Pierre de Bernis. Travaux et recherches de la faculté de droit et des sciences économiques de Paris. Série "Sciences Historiques*, (Paris: Presses universitaires de France, 1969)
Frémont	Frémont, Auguste–Frédéric–Mathilde, *Recherches historiques et biographiques sur Pothier, publiées à l'occasion de l'érection de sa statue* (Orleans: Chez Alph–Gatineau, 1859)
Friedmann	Friedmann, Wolfgang, *Legal Theory* (London: Stevens & Sons, Ltd., 1944)
Friedrich	Friedrich, Carl J., *The Philosophy of Law in Historical Perspective,* 2nd ed. (Chicago: University of Chicago Press, 1963)
Galbraith	Galbraith, V. H., *Domesday Book: Its Place in Administrative History* (Oxford: Clarendon Press, 1974)
Ganshof	Ganshof, François Louis, *Feudalism,* 3rd ed. (New York: Harper, 1964)
Gazzaniga	Gazzaniga, Jean–Louis, *Introduction historique au droit des obligations* (Paris: Presses universitaired de France, 1992)
Gibbon	Gibbon, Edward, *Decline and Fall of the Roman Empire, Modern Library Edition, 1776,* 2 vols. (New York: The Modern Library, Inc., 1932)
Gibson	Gibson, Margaret T., *Lanfranc of Bec* (Oxford: Clarendon Press, 1978)

Gierke, Otto Friedrich von,

Gierke-*Political* — *Political Theories of the Middle Age* (Boston: Beacon Press, 1958)

Gierke-*Natural Law* — and Ernst Troeltsch, *Natural Law and the Theory of Society, 1500 to 1800, with a Lecture on the Ideas of Natural Law and Humanity* (Boston: Beacon Press, 1957)

Gilbert   Gilbert, Sandra M., and Susan Gubar, *Madwoman in the Attic: The Woman Writer and the Nineteenth-Century Literary Imagination* (New Haven: Yale University Press, 1979)

Gilmore   Gilmore, Myron P., *Humanists and Jurists: Six Studies in the Renaissance* (Cambridge, MA: Harvard University Press, 1963)

Glover   Glover, T. R., *The Ancient World: A Beginning* (Baltimore: Penguin Books, 1965)

Great Books   *Great Books of the Western World* (Chicago: Encyclopedia Britannica, 1952)

Great Jurists of the World   *Great Jurists of the World,* Sir John MacDonnell and Edward Manson, eds. (Boston: Little Brown and Company, 1914)

Griswold   Griswold, Alfred Whitney, *Farming and Democracy*, 1st ed., (New York: Harcourt, 1948)

Hamburger   Hamburger, Max, *Morals and Law: The Growth of Aristotle's Legal Theory* (New York: Biblo and Tannen, 1965)

Hardman   Hardman, John, *Louis XVI* (New Haven: Yale University Press, 1993)

Haskins, Charles Homer,

Haskins-Normans
—— *The Normans in European History* (Boston: Houghton Mifflin Company, 1915)

Haskins-Renaissance
—— *The Renaissance of the Twelfth Century* ([n.p.] 1927)

Hazeltine
H. D. Hazeltine, Edwin R. Seligman and Alvin Johnson, eds., "Ancient and Medieval" in "Legal Profession and Legal Education" by Max Radin, A.A. Berle, Jr., and H.D. Hazeltine (324–346) In: *The International Encyclopedia of the Social Sciences Vol. 9*, (New York: Macmillan, 1933)

Heer
Heer, Friedrich, J. Sonheimer, trans., *The Medieval World: Europe, 1100–1350. History of Civilisation*, (London: Weidenfeld and Nicolson, 1962)

Herm
Herm, Gerhard, *The Celts: The People Who Came Out of the Darkness* (London: Weidenfeld and Nicolson, 1976)

Hohfeld
Hohfeld, Wesley Newcomb, W.W. Cook, ed., *Fundamental Legal Concepts as Applied in Judicial Reasoning* (New Haven: Yale University Press, 1964)

Holdsworth
Holdsworth, William Searle, *A History of English Law* (London: Methuen & Co., Ltd., 1932)

Honoré
Honoré, Tony, *Gaius*. (Oxford: Clarendon Press, 1962)

Imbert
Imbert, Jean, *Histoire du droit privé*, 6th ed. (Paris: Presses universitaires de France, 1985)

Jolowicz and Nicholas
Jolowicz, H. F., and Barry Nicholas, *Historical Introduction to the Study of Roman Law*, 3rd ed. (Cambridge: University Press, 1972)

G. Jones
Jones, Gwyn, *A History of the Vikings* (London: Oxford University Press, 1968)

J. Jones
Jones, J. Walter, *The Law and Legal Theory of the Greeks: An Introduction* (Oxford: Clarendon Press, 1956)

Jourdain	Charles Jourdain, *Histoire de l'université de Paris au XVII e et au XVIII e siècle* (Firmin–Didot: Hachette, 1888)
	Justinian,
Justinian–*Digest*	—— Theodor Mommsen and Alan Kreuger, eds., Alan Watson trans., *The Digest of Justinian* (Philadelphia: University of Pennsylvania Press, 1985)
Justinian–*Institutes*	—— J.B. Moyle, trans., *The Institutes of Justinian* (Oxford: Clarendon Press, 1913)
Kantorowicz	Kantorowicz, Hermann, W. W. Buckland, and British Museum Department of Manuscripts, *Studies in the Glossators of the Roman Law. Newly Discovered Writings of the 12th Century* (Aalen: Scientia–Verl, 1969)
Keeton	Keeton, George Williams, *The Norman Conquest and the Common Law*, (New York: Barnes & Noble, 1966)
Kennedy	Kennedy, George Alexander, *The Art of Rhetoric in the Roman World, 300 B.C.–A.D. 300* (Princeton: Princeton University Press, 1972)
Kitto	Kitto, H.D.F., *The Greeks* (Baltimore: Penguin Books, 1954)
Knight	Knight, William, and Stanley Macbean, *The Life and Works of Hugo Grotius* (London: Sweet & Maxwell, Ltd., 1925)
	Knowles, David,
Knowles–*Thought*	——*The Evolution of Medieval Thought* (Baltimore: Helicon Press, 1962)
Knowle–*Monastic*	——*The Monastic Order in England; a History of Its Development from the Times of St. Dunstan to the Fourth Lateran Council, 940–1216.* 2nd ed. (Cambridge: Cambridge University Press, 1963)
Krieger	Krieger, Leonard, *The Politics of Discretion: Pufendorf and the Acceptance of Natural Law* (Chicago: University of Chicago Press, 1965)

Kunkel	Kunkel, Wolfgang, *An Introduction to Roman Legal and Constitutional History,* 2nd ed. (Oxford: Clarendon Press, 1973)
Kuttner	Kuttner, Stephan G., *The History of Ideas and Doctrines of Canon Law in the Middle Ages, Collected Studies Series* (London: Variorum Reprints, 1980)
Kuttner *Harmony*	—— *Harmony from Dissonance; an Interpretation of Medieval Canon Law. Wimmer Lecture,* (Latrobe, PA: Archabbey Press, 1960)
Kuttner *Jurist*	—— "The Father of the Science of Canon Law" *The Jurist,* 1941, Vol. 1:1–19 (Washington, DC: Catholic University School of Canon Law, 1941)
Lamasne–Desjobert	Lamasne–Desjobert, Marie–Antoinette Laurance, *La faculté de droit de Paris aux xviie et xviiie siècles* (Paris: Chez Cujas, 1966)
Langer	Langer, William L., *An Encyclopedia of World History; Ancient, Medieval, and Modern, Chronologically Arranged,* 4th ed. (Boston: Houghton Mifflin, 1972)
Lavine	Lavine, T. Z., *From Socrates to Sartre: The Philosophic Quest* (New York: Bantam Books, 1984)
Lavollée	Lavollée, Rene, *Portalis, sa vie et ses oeuvres* (Paris: Didier et Cie., 1869)
Leake	Leake, Roy E. and Alice Elder Leake, preparé par Roy E. Leake, Indiana University, David B. Leake et Alice Elder Leake, *Concordance des essais de Montaigne,* 2 vols. (Genève: Droz, 1981)
Leduc	Leduc, Edouard, *Portalis, une grande figure de l'histoire napoléonienne. collection panthéon* (Paris: E. Leduc, 1991)
Lee	Lee, Robert Warden, *Hugo Grotius* (London: H. Milford, 1931)

Lefebvre	Lefebvre, Georges, R.R. Palmer, trans., *The Coming of the French Revolution* (Princeton: Princeton University Press, 1947)
Lévy-Ullmann	Lévy–Ullmann, Henri, M., and Frederic Maurice Goadby, *The English Legal Tradition, Its Sources and History* (London: Macmillan, 1935)
E. Lewis	Lewis, Ewart, *Medieval Political Ideas* (New York: Knopf, 1954)
N. Lewis	Lewis, Naphtali, *Life in Egypt under Roman Rule* (Oxford: Clarendon Press, 1983)
Lloyd-Jones	Lloyd–Jones, Hugh, *The Greek World* (Baltimore: Penguin, 1962)
Llull	Llull, Raimon, William Caxton, trans., *Book of the Order of Chivalry*, (London: Kegan Paul 2004)
Louis XIV	Louis XIV, King of France, 1638–1715, Paul Sonnino, trans., *Mémoires for the Instruction of the Dauphin* (New York: Free Press, 1970)
Lysen	Lysen, Arnoldus, *Hugo Grotius: Essays on His Life and Works, Selected for the Occasion of the Tercentenary of his De Iure Belli ac Pacis* (Leyden: A.W. Sythoff's Publishing Co, 1925)
Lyte	Lyte, H.C. Maxwell, *A History of the University of Oxford from the Earliest Times to the Year 1530* (New York: Macmillan, 1886)
MacKenzie	MacKenzie, Thomas, *Studies in Roman Law with Comparative Views of the Laws of France, England, and Scotland.* 7th ed. (Edinburgh: William Blackwood, 1898)
MacMullen	MacMullen, Ramsay, *Roman Government's Response to Crisis, A.D. 235–337* (New Haven: Yale University Press, 1976)

Maine	Maine, Henry Sumner, *Ancient Law: Its Connection with the Early History of Society and Its Relation to Modern Ideas* (London: Oxford University Press, 1931)
Maitland	Maitland, Frederick William, *Legal Theory Lexicon, A Prologue to a History of English Law* (London: 14 L. *Quarterly Review* 13, 1898)
Mango	Mango, Cyril A., *Byzantium, the Empire of New Rome, History of Civilization* (New York: Scribner, 1980)
Marrou	Marrou, Henri Irénée, *A History of Education in Antiquity* (New York: Sheed and Ward, 1956)
McDougal	McDougal, Myres S., *International Law and the Grotian Heritage: A Colloquium at the Hague, 8 April 1983 at Hugo Grotius's 400th* (The Hague: Netherlands, 1985)
Merriman	Merriman, John M., *The Agony of the Republic, The Repression of the Left in Revolutionary France 1848–1851* (New Haven: Yale University Press, 1978)
Merryman	Merryman, John Henry, *The Civil Law Tradition: An Introduction to the Legal Systems of Western Europe and Latin America* (Stanford: Stanford University Press, 1969)
Monnier	Monnier, Francis, *Le chancelier D'aguesseau, sa conduite et ses idées politiques, et son influence sur le mouvement des esprits pendant la première moitié du xviiie siècle, avec des documents nouveaux et plusieurs ouvrages inédits du chancelier* (Paris: Didier, 1860)
	Montaigne, Michel de,
Montaigne-Screech	—— Montaigne, Michel d', M. A. Screech, trans., *The complete essays.* (London: England, Penguin Books 1991)
Montaigne -P. Villey	—— Montaigne, Michel d', Pierre Villey ed., *Les essais de Michel de Montaigne, 3 volumes* (Paris: F. Alcan, 1930–1931)

Montesquieu, Charles de Secondat,

Montesquieu-Versini	—— *De l'espirt des lois,* Laurent Versini ed. (Paris: Gallimard 1995)
Montesquieu-Nugent	—— *Lettres persanes,* Laurent Versini ed. (Paris: Flammarion, 1995)
	—— *Spirit of the Laws,* Thomas Nugent, trans. (New York: Hafner, 1949)
Montesquieu-Richter	—— Melvin Richter, trans. *The Political Theory of Montesquieu* (Cambridge: Cambridge University Press, 1977)
Morrall	Morrall, John B., *Political Thought in Medieval Times* (London: Hutchinson, 1958)
Morris	Morris, Clarence, *The Great Legal Philosophers; Selected Readings in Jurisprudence* (Philadelphia: University of Pennsylvania Press, 1959)
Murray	Murray, Alexander, *Reason and Society in the Middle Ages* (New York: Oxford University Press, 1978)
New Cambridge Modern History	*The New Cambridge Modern History,* 14 Vols. (Cambridge: University Press, 1957–1979)
Njal	Njal, *Njal's Saga,* Magnus Magnusson and Hermann Palsson, trans. (Baltimore: Penguin Books, 1960)
Norwich	Norwich, John Julius, *The Kingdom in the Sun, 1130–1194* (London: Longman, 1970)
Olivier-Martin	Olivier-Martin, François, *Histoire du droit français des origines à la révolution* (Paris: Domat Montchrestien, 1951)
Ourliac and Gazzaniga	Ourliac, Paul and Jean–Louis Gazzaniga, *Histoire du droit privé français de l'an mil an code civil* (Paris: Editions Albin Michel, 1985)
Pagels	Pagels, Elaine H., *The Gnostic Gospels* (New York: Random House, 1979)

Paris Match	Nelson Mandela's reply to Jacques Chirac, *Paris Match,* 25 July 1966, 42
Parks	Parks, E. Patrick, *The Roman Rhetorical Schools as a Preparation for the Courts under the Early Empire* (Baltimore: The Johns Hopkins Press, Johns Hopkins University, 1945)
Pegues	Pegues, Franklin J., *The Lawyers of the Last Capetians* (Princeton: Princeton University Press, 1962)
Pelikan	Pelikan, Jaroslav, *Jesus through the Centuries: His Place in the History of Culture* (New Haven: Yale University Press, 1985)
	Plato,
Plato	—— Benjamin Jowett, trans., *The Dialogues of Plato,* 5 vols. (London: Oxford University Press, 1892)
Dialogues *Republic*	—— H. D. P. Lee, trans., *The Republic,* (Baltimore: Penguin Books, 1955)
Plucknett	Plucknett, Theodore Frank Thomas, *A Concise History of the Common Law,* 4th ed. (London: Butterworth, 1948)
	Portalis, Jean–Etienne–Marie,
Portalis–*l'usage*	—— *De l'usage et de l'abus de l'ésprit philosophique durant le 18e siècle* (Paris: Moutardier, 1834)
Portalis–*Discours*	—— *Discours, rapports et travaux inédits sur le Code civil de J.E.M. Portalis, publiés par le vicomte Frédéric Portalis,* BN F41.881 (N.P.: Joubert, 1844)
Portalis *(Speech)*	—— "Speech of M. Portalis on the 15th Germinal Year X 5th April, 1802, to the Legislative Body of France, on presenting the convention made between the French Republic and the Holy See" Translated from original French (New York: Robert Wilson, 1802)

Pothier, Robert Joseph,

Pothier–Cushing —— Caleb Cushing, ed., *A Treatise on Maritime Contracts of Letting to Hire* (Boston: Cummings and Hilliard, 1821)

Pothier–Evans —— William David Evans, ed., *A Treatise on the Law of Obligations, or Contracts,* 3rd ed. (Philadelphia: R.H. Small, 1853)

Pound, Roscoe,

Pound–*Intro Phil* —— *An Introduction to the Philosophy of Law* (New Haven: Yale University Press, 1954)

Pound–*Juris* —— *Jurisprudence* 5 vols. (St. Paul: West Publishing, 1959)

Previté–Orton Previté–Orton, Charles William, *The Shorter Cambridge Medieval History* (Cambridge: University Press, 1952)

Pufendorf, Samuel Freiherr von,

Pufendorf-Oldfather —— Introduction by Walter Simons, C.H. and W. A. Oldfather, trans., *De Jure Naturae Et Gentium Libri Octo. Classics of International Law* (Oxford: The Clarendon Press; H. Milford, 1934)

Pufendorf-Seidler —— Michael Seidler, ed., *Samuel Pufendorf's on the Natural State of Men: The 1678 Latin Edition and English Translation. Studies in the History of Philosophy* (Lewiston, NY: E. Mellen Press, 1990)

Pufendorf-Tully —— James Tully ed., Michael Silverthorne, trans., *On the Duty of Man and Citizen According to Natural Law (Epitome). Cambridge Texts in the History of Political Thought* (Cambridge: Cambridge University Press, 1991)

Radding Radding, Charles, *The Origins of Medieval Jurisprudence: Pavia and Bologna, 850–1150* (New Haven: Yale University Press, 1988)

Rashdall Rashdall, Hastings, F. M. Powicke, and Alfred Brotherston Emden, *The Universities of Europe in the Middle Ages* (Oxford: The Clarendon Press, 1936)

Rawson	Rawson, Elizabeth, *Cicero: A Portrait* (London: Allen Lane, 1975)
Readings in Western Civilization	*Readings in Western Civilization*, 9 vols., John W. Boyer & Julius Kirshner, eds. (Chicago: University of Chicago Press, 1986)
Reese	Reese, William L., *Dictionary of Philosophy and Religion: Eastern and Western Thought* (Atlantic Highlands, NJ: Humanities Press, 1980)
C.E. Robinson	Robinson, Cyril Edward, *A History of Greece,* 9th ed. (London: Methuen & Co. Ltd., 1957)
J.H. Robinson	Robinson, James Harvey, *Petrarch, the First Modern Scholar and Man of Letters* (New York: Greenwood Press, 1969)
O.F. Robinson	Robinson, O. F., T. D. Fergus, and William M. Gordon, *An Introduction to European Legal History* (Abingdon: Professional Books, 1985)
Rodes	Rodes, Robert E., *Ecclesiastical Administration in Medieval England: The Anglo–Saxons to the Reformation, This House I Have Built.* (South Bend, IN: University of Notre Dame Press, 1977)
Rudy	Rudy, Willis, *The Universities of Europe, 1100–1914: A History* (Rutherford, NJ: Fairleigh Dickinson University Press, 1984)
Russell	Russell, Bertrand, *A History of Western Philosophy, and Its Connection with Political and Social Circumstances from the Earliest Times to the Present Day* (New York: Simon and Schuster, 1945)
Schama	Schama, Simon, *Citizens: A Chronicle of the French Revolution* (New York: Knopf, 1989)
Schulz	Schulz, Fritz, *History of Roman Legal Science* (Oxford: Oxford University Press, 1946)
Schweinburg	Schweinburg, Eric F., *Law Training in Continental Europe*, (New York: Russell Sage Foundation, 1945)

Sellery	Sellery, George C., *The Renaissance, Its Nature and Origins* (Madison: University of Wisconsin Press, 1950)
Shackleton	Shackleton, Robert, *Montesquieu: A Critical Biography*, (London: Oxford University Press, 1961)
Shepherd	Shepherd, William Robert, *Shepherd's Historical Atlas* (Totowa, NJ: Barnes & Noble, 1980)
Sophocles	Sophocles, E.F. Watling, trans., *The Theban Plays: King Oedipus, Oedipus at Colonus, Antigone* (Baltimore: Penguin Books, 1947)
Sorel	Sorel, Albert, *Introduction au code civil, livre du centenaire, société d'études législatives* (Paris: Arthur Rousseau, 1904)
Southern	Southern, R.W., *Western Society and the Church in the Middle Ages. The Pelican History of the Church* (Hammondsworth: Penguin Books, 1970)
Symonds	Symonds, John Addington, *The Revival of Learning* (Gloucester, MA: P. Smith, 1967)
Thompson	Thompson, James Westfall, *The Middle Ages, 300–1500*, (New York: Knopf, 1931)
Tomkeieff	Tomkeieff, O.G., *Life in Norman England. English Life Series* (New York: Putnam, 1966)
	Ullmann, Walter,
Ullmann-Renaissance	—— *The Carolingian Renaissance and the Idea of Kingship. The Birkbeck Lectures, 1968–9* (London: Methuen, 1969)
Ullmann-Government	—— *The Growth of Papal Government in the Middle Ages; a Study in the Ideological Relation of Clerical to Lay Power*, 2nd ed. (London: Methuen, 1962)
Ullmann-Thought	—— *A History of Political Thought; the Middle Ages* (Baltimore: Penguin Books, 1965)
Ullmann-Law	—— *Law and Politics in the Middle Ages: An Introduction to the Sources of Medieval Political Ideas. The Sources of*

	History: Studies in the Uses of Historical Evidence. (Ithaca: Cornell University Press, 1975)
Ullmann-DePenna	—— *The Medieval Idea of Law, as Represented by Lucas De Penna; a Study in Fourteenth–Century Legal Scholarship* (London: Methuen, 1946)
Ullmann-Papalism	—— *Medieval Papalism: The Political Theories of the Medieval Canonists. The Maitland Memorial Lectures, 1948* (London: Methuen, 1949)
Ullmann-History	—— *A Short History of the Papacy in the Middle Ages* (London: Methuen, 1972)
Verger	Verger, Jacques, *Les universités au moyen age* (Paris: Presses universitaires de France, 1973)
	Villey, Michel,
M. Villey-Philosophie	—— *Définitions et fins du droit. Philosophie du droit* (Paris: Dalloz, 1982)
M. Villey-Leçons	—— *Leçons d'histoire de la philosophie du droit. Annales de la faculté de droit et des sciences politiques de Stasbourg*, (Paris: Dalloz, 1957)
P. Villey	Villey, Pierre, *Les sources & l'évolution des essais de Montaigne.* (Paris: Hachette & Cie, 1908)
Vinogradoff	Vinogradoff, Paul, *Roman Law in Medieval Europe. Speculum Historiale.* (New York: Barnes & Noble, 1968)
Voeltzel	Voeltzel, Rene, *Jean Domat (1625–1696): Essai de reconstitution de sa philosophie juridique précédé de la biographie du jurisconsulte* (Paris: Librairie du Recueil Sirey, 1936)
Vreeland	Vreeland, Hamliton, *Hugo Grotius, the Father of the Modern Science of International Law* (New York: University Press, American Branch, 1917)
Watson	Watson, Alan, *Law Making in the Later Roman Republic* (Oxford: Clarendon Press, 1974)

Weinberg	Weinberg, Julius R., *A Short History of Medieval Philosophy* (Princeton: Princeton University Press, 1964)
Wieruszowski	Wieruszowski, Helene, *The Medieval University: Masters, Students, Learning. An Anvil Original, 90.* (Princeton: Van Nostrand, 1966)
Wigmore	Wigmore, John Henry, *A General Survey of Events, Sources, Persons and Movements in Continental Legal History. The Continental Legal History Series, Pub. Under the Auspices of the Association of American Law Schools.* [*V. 1*]. (Boston: Little, Brown and Co., 1912)
Wigmore-World's Legal Systems	—— *A Panorama of the World's Legal Systems* (St. Paul: West Publishing Company, 1928)
Woolf	Woolf, Cecil Nathan Sidney, *Bartolus of Sasoferrato* (Cambridge: Cambridge University Press, 1913)
Zimmerman	Zimmerman, Reinhard, *The Law of Obligations, Roman Foundations of the Civilian Trades* (Capetown: Juta and Co, Ltd., 1998)

INDEX

Note: Page references in *italic* refer to illustrations.

A

abacus, 281
abbots, 148, 175, 179, 181, 198, 222–223, 260, 264, 269, 281, 287, 391, 402
Abelard, Astrolabe, 332
Abelard, Peter, 300, *331,* 331–332, *332*
    Aquinas and, 414
    Aristotle and, 405
    and canon law, 330–340
    on education, 486
    Gratian and, 342, 343, 346
    at University of Paris, 366
    William of Ockham and, 488
Ableiges, Jacques d', 459
Abrial, Joseph, 954–955
Académie de Législation, 920–921
Academy (of Plato), *12,* 29, 32, 38–39
Academy, Calvin's, 590
Accursius, Francisco, 314, *324*
    as glossator, 322–324, 439
    on Roman Empire, 448
    as teacher, 443
Adelaide, 221
Adelboro of Laon, Bishop, 254
Adeodotus, 160
Ad Herrenium (Cicero), 237
Admiralty Courts, 437
Adolphe, L., 931, 933, 934
Adrian I, Pope, 202
Adrian V, Pope, 309
advocacy, 437–438, 467–471
Afer, Domitius, 73
Africa (Petrarch), 509
Agobard of Lyon, 205, 213
agreements, 254
agriculture, 248–251
Aicelin, Gilles, 469, 472

Aidan, Saint, 231
Aiguillon, Duc d', 894
Aitherius of Lisieux, Bishop, 169
Alamanni, 187
Alaric I, Visigoth king, 161
Alaric II, Visigoth king, 206–207
Albericus, 321
Albertas, Marquis d', 931
Albert of Brandenburg, 581–582
Albertus Magnus (Albert the Great), 410, 414, 420
Albright, W. F., 134–135
Alciato, Andrea (Alciat), 370, 527–530, *528, 530,* 541–542
Alcuin, 195–196, 201, 231, 237
Alembert, Jean LeRond d', 840, 881
Alexander III, Pope, 307, 350, 368
Alexander III the Great, King of Macdeonia, 32, 37, 185
Alexander IV, Pope, 394
Alexander V, Pope, 477
Alexander VI, Pope (Rodrigo Lanzal y Borgia), 515
Alexander of Aphrodisias, 400
Alexander of Hales, 581
Alfonso VIII, King of Castile, 465
Alfred, King of Wessex, 218, 231, 269
allod, 249
Alphonso, King of Naples, 516
Althing, 233–234, 243, 902
Althusius, Joannes, 662
Ambrose, Saint, 166–167, 508
American rebellion, French involvement in, 879
Amsterdam, 617, 618, 619
Anabaptists, 650

Anastasius, 101
Anatolius, 104
Andronicus of Rhodes, 115, 399–400
Angelico, 411
Angles, 225–227
Anglo-Saxons, 226
Annals (Boronius), 842
Annals (Grotius), 648, 842
Ansegius of Fontanelle, 210
Anselm of Bec, 292–300, *295*
    Abelard and, 331
    Aquinas and, 415
    at Bec, 239
    Descartes and, 670
    Humbert and, 288
    and law as principle, 7–8
    on philosophy, 145
Anselm of Laon, 331, 332
Anselm of Lucca, 341
Antigone (Sophocles), 25–26
Antiphon, 22
Antoinette, Marie, 813, 902, 913, 915, *915*
Antwerp, 618, 619, 655
Apellicon of Teos, 399
Apology for Raymond Sebond (Montaigne), 563, 569
a priori knowledge (*a priori* principles), 629
Aquinas, Thomas, *396,* 408–432
    Anselm and, 296
    Augustine and, 164
    on church and state, 418–422
    and Council of Trent, 594
    Cujas and, 541
    Domat and, 759
    Galileo and, 697
    Grotius and, 651, 657, 658
    Hobbes and, 681
    influence of, 431–432
    and law as principle, 8
    life of, 408–412
    Luther and, 577, 578
    and natural law, 422–431
    Petrarch and, 505, 512
    politics during time of, 416–418
    and realism, 413–416
    on Roman Empire, 448
    and royal national states, 436
    and Scientific Revolution, 621, 622, 623
    Suarez and, 603–605
    William of Ockham and, 492
    writings of, 412–413
Arabic numerals, 280
Arcesilaus, 29, 41, 561
Aretinus, Gratian, 364
Argenson, Marc-Pierre d', 782, 805
Arian Christians, 188
Arians, 140
Aristarchus of Samos, 624
Aristophanes, 19
Aristotelianism, 153, 347, 628, 632
Aristotle, *34*
    Abelard and, 336
    Aquinas and, 412, 415, 420
    Augustine and, 164
    Bartolus and, 448
    and forms, 280
    Galileo and, 697
    Grotius and, 657–658
    Hobbes and, 673, 681
    and law as principle, 7
    logic of, 151–152
    Luther and, 578
    medieval rediscovery of, 398–408
    Montaigne and, 558
    and natural law, 424
    Petrarch and, 505, 508, 512
    as philosopher, 32–37
    and *philosophes,* 882
    and philosophy of law, 115–120
    Pufendorf and, 694
    and Scientific Revolution, 621–623
    and Skepticism, 560
    on Sophists, 21
    on study of law, 16
    Suarez and, 602–604
    and Talmud, 151
    Theophrastus and, 38
    William of Ockham and, 492, 499–500
    works of, after death, 398
Arius, 140
Arletta, 240
Arminians, 650–654
Arminius, 650

Arnauld, Angélique, 735, *736*
Arnauld, Antoine, I, 670, 738, 747
Arnauld, Antoine, II, 739–740
Arnouville, Jean-Baptiste d', 810
Arthur, King, 226
Asard, Louis, 819
Assembly of Notables, 900, 901
Assizes of Ariano, 245, 309
Association of American Law Schools, 126
astronomy, 566–567
Athanasians, 140
Athanasius, 140
Athelstan, 218
Athens, 13–41
    Aristotle and, 32–37
    constitution of, 398
    democracy in, 14–21
    Epicurians/Stoics/Skeptics, 38–41
    Hellenism, 37
    Plato and, 29–31
    Socrates and, 26–29
    Sophists, 21–25
    Theophrastus and, 37–38
Attica, 17, 18
Auerbach, Boniface, 528–529
Augur, Quintus Mucius Scaevola, 60, 64–67, 112
Augustine, 159–166, *166*
    ages of time defined by, 129
    Aquinas and, 418–419
    and Benedictines, 173
    and Calvinism, 586
    and canonical hours, 169
    Charlemagne and, 194, 195, 202
    Charles the Bald and, 203
    creation dated by, 128
    Descartes and, 668
    double faith theory of, 155
    in England, 227
    on farm work, 248
    on God and mind, 211
    Gratian and, 348
    Hincmar and, 213
    Hobbes and, 681
    on knowledge, 478
    Petrarch and, 508, 512
    Portalis and, 935
    as Roman, 504
    and Scientific Revolution, 623
    Suarez and, 603
    William of Ockham and, 492
Augustinians, 431–432
Augustinus (Jansen), 737, 740
Augustus Gaius Julius Caesar Octavianus, *69,* 69–71, 79, 82
Aumelas, Pons d', 472
Ausculta fili, 470
Austin Canons, 389
Austria, 188
Austrian code, 888
Authenticum, 314
Averroes (Ibn Rushd), 401–402, *402,* 486
Avicenna (Ibn Sina), 401
Avignon, *476,* 506, 507, 511, 523, 527–529, 535, 542, 727
avocats
    in Enlightenment, 892–897
    in French Revolution, 912–917
    Portalis as, 932–936
Avril, 691
Azo of Bologna, 320, 322, 442

B

baccalaureate, 362
Bacon, Francis, 563, 599, 623, 629, 645, 674
Bacon, Roger, 159, 294, 296, 338, 498
Bainton, R. H. (*Reformation*), 578–579, 582
Baker, K. M., 869, 870
Baldus, 450–452, *452,* 565
Baldwin II, Emperor of Constantinople, *465*
Balsdon, J. P. V. D., 49
Bandenelli, Rolandus, 350
bankers and banking, 281, 618–619
bannum, 258
baptism, 127, 146, 152, 160, 167–168, 191, 194, 199, 298–300, 345, 383–384, 393, 527, 582
Barbarossa. *See* Frederick I, Holy Roman Emperor
Barbeyrac, Jean, 710
Barnardone, John, 387

Barras, Paul, 907
Barry, Madame du, 805
Bartolus, *434,* 443–453, 500
    Alciato and, 529, 531
    Bodin and, 539
    Cujas and, 538
    Montaigne and, 565
    Petrarch and, 504, 505, 507, 513
    Valla and, 516
Bassanianus, Johannes, 321
Battle of Hastings, 149, *242,* 243, 268, 462, 928
Baudouin, François, 541
Baumer, F. L. V., 129, 889, 891–892
Bautillier, Jehan, 461
Bavarelli, Pellina, 445
Bavarians, 887
Bayle, Pierre, 857, 881
Beaumanoir, Philippe de Rémy, Sire de, 267, 432, 457–460, 723
Beaumarchais, Pierre, 934
Beaupère, Jean, 487
Bec (monastery), 236–240, 275
Becker, C., 628
Beckmann, Nicholas, 689
bedels, 357, 363–364
Bede the Venerable, 195, 227, 268
Bell, D. A., 727–728, 733, 739, 777, 894, 895, 897
Bellarmine, Cardinal, 518
Belleperche, Pierre de, 472
Benedict, Saint, 169, 171, *172*
Benedict IX, Pope, 343
Benedict XI, Pope, 474
Benedict XIII, Antipope, 477
Benedictines
    contributions to society by, 389
    and early Roman Catholic Church, 171–174
    government service, 179–181
    land gifts to, 170
    land management, 175–179
    and manual labor, 175
benefices, land, 263
Benson, R. L., 345, 348, 405
Bentham, Jeremy, 500
Béranger of Tours, 293–294
Bergin, T. G., 505, 507, 511, 512
Béri, Duchesse de, 535

Berman, H. J., 124, 125, 200, 207, 245, 334, 336–339, 341, 345, 346, 349
Bernard, F., 963
Bernard of Chartres, 150, 406
Bernard of Clairvaux, 333, 344, 374
Bernard of Fontaines, 284
Bertrand de Got, 474–475
Berytus, law school at, 78–79, 82, 96–98, 106, 244, 360
Bible, 574, 583, 651, 661. *See also* New Testament; Old Testament
    Gratian and, 348
    Grotius and, 651
    Hobbes and, 682–683
    as legal document, 202
    and natural law, 425–426, 429
Bibliotheca Universalis (Gesner), 520
Bigot de Préameneu, Félix-Julian-Jean, 954–955
bishops
    and early Roman Catholic Church, 169–171
    as law-makers, 211
    as temporal governors, 148
    University of Paris controlled by, 366
    as vassals of the king, 264
Blache, Count de la, 934
Black, D. J., 190
Blackstone, William, 85, 438
Blanche, Queen of France, 465
Bloch, M. L. B., 171, 233
Blondel, Antoinette, 746
Bluhme, Prof., 105
Bodin, Jean, 446, 539, 682, 865
Boethius, 151, 336, *400,* 400–401, 623
Boileau, Étienne, 456, 750
Boissy d'Anglas, François Antoine de, 907
Bollingbroke, 800
Bologna, 275. *See also* University of Bologna
    and birth of universities, 305–309
    during Carolingian Renaissance, 301–327
    glossators in, 319–327
    Gratian teaching in, 346
    Irnerius and, 303–305, 310–319
    notaries and dictamen in, 309–310

and rediscovery of *Digest,* 301–303
study of Roman law in, 342
Bonaparte, Napoleon, 716, 919, 922, *929*
and Charlemagne, 199
and *Civil Code,* 953–958, 960, 971
crowning of, 10
as First Consul, 927–928
and legislative process, 961
Portalis and, 944–946
and Roman nostalgia, 841
Bonaventure, Saint, 393, 410, 414–415
Boniface, Saint, 195, 269, 393
Boniface VIII, Pope, 309, 351, 394, 421, 467, 474, 572, 951
Book of Creatures (Montaigne), 554
Book of Laws (Domat), 958
Book of the Order of Chivalry (Lull), 255
Borchert, D. M., 673, 679, 680
Bordeaux, 544
Bordeaux Parlement, 768, 844, 852
Bossuet, J.-B., 772, 842, 851, 865, 951
Boulainvilliers, Henri, Comte de, 865–866
bourgeoisie
  in eighteenth-century France, 783, 884, 892, 907, 919, 932
  and Humanism, 514
  offices bought by, 548–549
  Orléans and, 780
  Pufendorf and, 709
  rise of, 612
  in seventeenth century, 642
  and study of law, 607
Bourges, 529, 541
bourses, 619
Boussuet, Bishop, 842
Brabant, Siger de, 431
Brach, Pierre de, 569
Bracton, Henry de, 432, 438
Bradwardine, Thomas, 496
Brahe, Tycho, 566–567, 624, 630
Brand, Gustav A., 2
bread colonies, 613, 616
Breton, A. M., 835
Bretonnier, B. J., 809
Breuil, Guillaume du, 459
Breviarium Alricianum, 206–207

Brienne, 901
brigands, 250
Brissaud, J., 126, 128, 129, 438, 457–459, 761, 763
Brisson, 802
British Empiricism, 645
Brochet, Madame, 835
Brown, R. A., 226
Bruno, Bishop of Toul, 285. *See also* Leo IX, Pope
Bruno, Giordano, 626–627
Bucer, Martin, 585
Budé, Guillaume, 524–527, *525*
Buisnes, Prof., 728
Bulgarus, 320–323, 327
Bunel, Pierre, 554
Burchard, Bishop of Worms, 341, 345
Burgundians, 126, 187, 480, 482
Buridan, Jean, 497, 498
Burke, Edmund, 840, 947
Burlamaqui, Jean Jacques, 710–711
Burn, A. R., 29, 30
Butler, Bishop, 801
Butterfield, H., 575
Byron, Lord, 185

C

Caccia report, 593
Cadoudal, George, 922
Caesar, Gaius Julius, 54, 69, 184
cahier de doléances, 903
cahiers, 903–904, 910, 912
Cairns, H., 30, 33, 35, 36, 60, 113, 348, 407, 408, 414, 429, 495, 668
Cajetan, Cardinal, 582, 602
Caleo, 622
Calhoun, G. M., 15, 16
Calisse, C., 126, 128, 129, 441
Calonne, Charles Alexandre de, *887,* 888, 900, 901
Calvin, Gérard, 584, 830
Calvin, Jeanne, 584
Calvin, John, 583–591, *587*
  Alciato and, 529
  Augustinian predestination and, 163
  Copernicus and, 626

and French Protestantism, 608
    Grotius and, 650, 651
    Montaigne and, 546
    and Protestant Reformation, 6, 573
Calvinists and Calvinism, 615, 650–652
Cambacérès, Jean Jacques Régis de,
    952–953
Cambridge University, 367, 485, 504,
    635, 637, 638
Campbell, Joseph, 799
canon law, 330–394
    Abelard and, 330–340
    Gratian and, 340–352
    Innocent III and, 375–386
    at medieval universities, 370–375
    and Mendicant orders, 387–394
    and professors at University of
        Bologna, 356–365
    Reformation and, 605–608
    and students at University of
        Bologna, 352–356
    at University of Paris, 365–370
    used by clergy, 454
Cantillon, Philip, 889
Cantor, N. F., 124–125, 129, 131, 138,
    139, 151, 155–157, 162, 163, 166,
    188–191, 194, 195, 222–225, 230,
    234, 276, 287, 333, 339, 343, 349,
    377, 383–385, 387, 389, 390, 392,
    402, 403, 411, 413, 416–419, 423,
    497, 498
Canzoniere (Petrarch), 507
Capella, Martianus, 143, 201, 647
Capet, Hugh, 212, *212,* 268, 812, 919
Capetian kings, 463–466
capitalism, 617, 619
Capito, 79
capitularies, 208–210
Caracalla, Antoninus, Emperor of
    Rome, 87, 110
Carcopino, J., 53
Carey, J. A., 744, 755, 756, 895
Carloman, 192
Carlyle, R. W., 422, 460
Carmichael, Gershom, 711
Carneades, 41, 561
Carolingian Renaissance, 218–221,
    273–327
    Bologna during, 301–327

economic conditions during, 276
legislation, 149
manors, 250, 253
mathematics during, 280–282
money during, 278–279
population during, 276–277
Roman Catholic Church during,
    282–300
towns during, 277–278
Carpentras, 506
Carrara, Francesco di, 511
Cartel (Jesuit), 873, 874
Cartesianism, 755, 770, 883
Carthusians, 284
Cassius, 79
Casson, Lionel, 972
Castell, A., 673, 679, 680
Castelot, A., 945
casuists, 759
Categories (Aristotle), 400, 401
Cathar heresy, 573
Catharina (Portuguese ship), 649, 650
Cathars, 383–384
Catherine II, Empress of Russia, 751
Catholic Reformation, 591–605
    and Council of Trent, 593–595
    in Italy, 592–593
    Loyola and, 595–600, *598*
    in Spain, 591–592
    Suarez and, 600–605, *601*
"cause," in contract law, 831–833
Cavendish, William, Earl of
    Devonshire, 674
Celestine III, Pope, 375
Celestine V, Pope, 309
Celestine VI, Pope, 468
Celsus *filius,* 79
Celsus *pater,* 79
Celtic Iron Age, 186–187
Celts, 184–187
Central Schools, 911
certificat de civisme, 916
Cerularius, Michael, Patriarch, 287
César, 817, 835
Cestius Pius, 54
chancellors, 722–723, 766
Chancery, 269
Charlemagne, 193–195, *209,* 260, 264,
    275, 280, 652

Alcuin and, 195–196
and education of clerks, 147
education program of, 201–208
Franks after, 210–212
legal reforms of, 196–201
lineage of, 192
records of, 179–180
Charles I, 378
Charles I of Anjou, King of Naples and Sicily, 417, 463–464
Charles II, King of England, 674, 677
Charles II the Bald, King of France, 203, 210, 213, 217
Charles III the Simple, King of France, 232
Charles IV, Holy Roman Emperor, 481, 510
Charles V, Emperor, 572, 573, 594
Charles V, King of France, 479
Charles VI, King of France, 480
Charles VII, King of France, 461, 480, 481
Charles VIII, King of France, 524
Charles XI, King of Sweden, 688, 689
Charles the Bold, Duke of Burgundy, 479
Charron, Pierre, 569
Chénon, E., 822
Chevallier, Louis, 893
China, 4–5, 518
Ch'in Shih Huang Ti, 4
Chirac, Jacques, 840
Choiseul, Duc de, 934, 938
Chrestien, Claude, 769
Chretien, Jean, 691
Christian III, King of Denmark, 583
Christina, Queen of Sweden, 666, 667, 741
Chrysippus, 424–425, 560
Church Code, 945
Church of England, 615, 650
Cicero, Marcus Tullius, 111–115, *114*
as advocate, 53
approach of, to rhetoric, 55
Aristotle and, 118
Cujas and, 530
Daguesseau and, 773
Latin translations by, 50
and law as principle, 7

Montaigne and, 542
in Pavian education, 237
Petrarch and, 506, 508, 510, 512–514
and philosophy of law, 111–115
Portalis and, 933
Quintus Mucius Scaevola Augur and, 60
and systemization of Roman law, 337
Valla and, 517
works as part of Charlemagne's educational reforms, 201
Cimbri, 186, 187
Cino Simbuldi of Pistoia, 441, 444, 450
Cisneros, 596
Cistercian order, 175, 284, 389, 469, 572
City of God [*Civitas dei*] (Saint Augustine), 161, 162, 194
Civil Code, 763, 827, 832, 835, 886, *924,* 945, 953–958, *964,* 971. *See also Code Napoleon*
Civil Constitution of the Clergy, 926
civil law
Bartolus and, 446
Pufendorf on, 697, 698
teaching of, outlawed in Paris, 369
The Civil Law in Its Natural Order (Domat), 750
Civil Procedure (1806), 969
Clark, A., 201
Clarke, M. L., 33, 50, 74
classics, and Petrarch, 508
Claudius, Emperor of Rome, 70, 133, 226
Clement III, Pope, 375
Clement V, Pope, 351, 450, 475
Clement VII, Pope, 373
Clement VII, rival pope, 476
Clement XIV, Pope, 600
Clementines, 351, 361, 606
Clericis laicos, 469
clerks, 147, 168–169
Clermont, Robert de, 457
Clisthenes, 16, 18
Clotilda, 191
The Clouds (Aristophanes), 19

Clovis I, King of the Salian Franks, 191–192, 199, 214, 866
Club de l'Entresol, 847–848
Cluniac order, 572
Cluny, 173, 282–284
Code (Justinian), 359, 360, 527, 774, 844
    Irnerius' glosses of, 314
    Peter of Belleperche and, 441
Code (Theodosius), 537
Code Louis, 725, 752
Code Napoleon, 951–973. *See also* Civil Code
    in 19th and 20th centuries, 967–969
    amendments to, 969–973
    and consular constitution, 953–958
    contracts in, 965–967
    form of, 962–965
    and *Ius Civile,* 66
    Portalis and, 951–973
    and private law, 951–953
    role of Portalis in, 958–962
Code of 529 (Justinian), 106–107
Code of 534 (Justinian), 106–107
Code of Henry III, 724
Code of St. Louis, 863
Codex Gregorianus (Gregorius), 94
Codice Napoleon II, 972
coffee (and other vegetable and animal imports), 615
coinage, shortage of, 267
Coke, Edward, 674, 679
Cola di Rienzo, 510
Colbert, Jean Baptiste, *720,* 762, 768, 769, 810
    and legal education reform, 729
    Louis XIV and, 717–721
    and *Ordinances,* 969
    and special councils of justice, 724
Colet, John, 576
Collège de Clermont, 745
Collège de Guyenne, 842
Collège de Juilly, 842, 865
Collège de Louis-le-Grand, 745
Collège d'Harcourt, 844
College of Navarre, 485, 768
colleges, 372, 485
Collège sexviral, 728

Collinet, P., 97, 99, 100
Cologne, 410
coloni, 250
Colonna, Cardinal, 474, 477, 510
Columbus, Christopher, 613
Comentarii in Digesta (Alciato), 529
comitia centuriata, 46
comitia curiata, 46
comitia tributa, 46
commendations, 261
Commentators, 439–453
    Bartolus, 443–453
    and royal national states, 439–453
Commerce (1807), 969
commercial law, 462
Committee of Public Safety, 907, 916, 918
Committee on Legislation of the Convention, 916
Commodus, 77
common law, 459, 615
commons, land held in, 251
Comte, Auguste, 870
Concordat of Boulogne, 608
Concordat of Worms, 1122, 307, 311
Concordia discordantium canonum (Gratian), 345, 350, *351,* 361
Condé, Prince de, 648, 656
Condorcet, 620, 840
Condorcet, Marquis de, 868–870, *869*
Condordat of 1801, 944–951
Confessions (Saint Augustine), 161
Confucius, 5
Connan, 753
Conrad II, Holy Roman Emperor, 221, 224–225
Conrad III, Holy Roman Emperor, 307–308
Conrad IV, Holy Roman Emperor, 417
Conroy (historian), 852, 853, 854, 861
Conseil des Dépêches, 902–903
consideration, 265
Considérations sur les causes de la grandeur des Romains et de leur décadence (Montesquieu), 851
Constable, G., 345, 348, 405
Constance, Queen, 244
Constance of Sicily, 308

Constantine I, Roman Emperor, 6, 96, *122,* 652
 and Donation of Constantine, 141–142
 and early Roman Catholic Church, 137–141
Constantinople, 78, 79, 139
Constantinus, 104
Constituent Assembly, 903
constitution
 consular, 953–958
 of Dominate, 90–92
 of French Revolution, 904–908
 of Rome, 45–48
constitutionalism, 904
Constitutione Omnem (Justinian), 99
Constitution of Melfi, 309
Constitution of the Year III, 907
consular constitution, 953–958
Continental Legal History, 126, 836, 919
Continental Realism, 645
Contorini, Cardinal, 593
contract law, 831–833
 in *Code Napoleon,* 965–967
 Domat and, 760–763
conventus, 363
conversi, 276
Cop, Nicholas, 585
Copernicus, Nicholas, 498, 566, 567, 623–628, *625,* 632, 656
Copleston, F. C., 398, 401, 403, 405–407, 410, 412, 414, 415, 422, 427, 428, 489, 491, 492, 494–497, 572, 602, 663, 665–668, 670, 676, 679, 681–683, 705, 742, 743, 801, 918
copyhold, 257
copyists, 520
Coquille, Guy, 533, 549, 730
Coras, 753
Corbin, 832
Corpus Juris, 107, 307
Corpus Juris Canonici, 351, 361, 606
Corpus Juris Civilis, 251, 266, 351, 360, 746
Corpus Juris Naturae, 691
Coulton, G. G., 176, 381
Council at Constance, 477
Council of Elders, 938

Council of Nicea, 140, 202
Council of Paris 829, 210–211
Council of Sixty, 588
Council of Soissons, 8
Council of State, 810
Council of State (France), 953
Council of Trent, 375, 572, 577, 593–595, 671
Council of Tyre, 141
Council on Law Reform, 805
councilors, to Louis XIV, 722
Counter-Reformation. *See* Catholic Reformation
Courcelles, Anne-Thérèse de Margenot de, 847
Court of Arches at St. Mary-le-Bow, 437
Court of Cassation, 810
courts records, 461–462
Coutume de Paris (d'Ableiges), 459
Coutume du comté de Clermont et Beauvaisis (de Rémi), 267
Coûtumes de Clermont et Beauvoisis (Beaumanoir), 457
Cox, I., 864
Coyet, Peter Julius, 687
Crassus, Lucius, 111
Crassus Severus, 54
Cratinus, 104
crime, in manorial systems, 256
Criminal Procedure (1808), 969
Critique of Pure Reason (Kant), 711
Crusades, 260, 282–283, 344, 384, 469
Cujas, Jacques, 370, 443, 453, 515, 531–541, *532,* 543, 606–607, 727, 745, 827
Cumberland, Richard, 697
Cum Occasione, 740
Cur Deus homo? (Anselm of Bec), 294, 298–300
curia regis, 269
Cushing, Luther Stearns, 750, 753, 754, 756, 758, 759, 763
customary law, 289, 455, 459
customary local law, 248–270
 and ancient agriculture, 248–251
 and feudalism, 259–270
 and manorial system, 251–258
 policital unit in, 256–258

Custom of Orléans, 824
customs
    Pufendorf on, 698
    recording, 455–456
    royal law vs., 460–461
    written law vs., 453–454
Cyprian, 155

D

Da Gama, Vasco, 613
Daguesseau, Antoine, 768
Daguesseau, Henri, 766, 768–770, 773, 778, 781
Daguesseau, Henri-François, 744, 749, 750, *764,* 766–813, *797,* 840, 857, 883
    education of, 768–771
    and English contemporaries, 799–802
    Essai, 798–799
    in late life, 811–813
    and law as principle, 8
    in law reform, 802–811
    on legal education, 771–776
    Méditations, 784–798
    Portalis and, 928–930, 941
    Pothier and, 813–814, 820–821, 823, 825–826, 830
    in public office, 776–784
    Pufendorf and, 691
Damiani, Peter, 286–288
Dante, 406, 506, 631
Danton, Georges, 914
Datzelaer (merchant), 653, 654
Datzelaer, Mme, 654
David, King of Israel, 136
Davot, Gabriel, 898
Davy, Georges, 858
Deanesly, M., 143, 145, 147, 148, 168–171, 173, 220, 341, 346, 350, 393
De Anima, 412
decima collatio novellorum, 251
De Cive (Hobbes), 677, 678
Declaration of the Rights of Man, 904
Decline and Fall of the Roman Empire (Gibbon), 10, 44, 76–77, 130, 131

De contemptu mundi (Innocent III), 376, 379
De Corpore (Hobbes), 677, 678
decretalists, 352, 605
decretists, 605
Decretum (Gratian), 605
Decretum Gratiani (Gratian), 350, *351*
De Curzon, A., 380, 730, 731, 898, 899, 911, 955
De Dominis, 622
De Elegantiis Latinae Linguae (Valla), 516
De Esse (Budé), 526
De falso credita et ementita Constantini donatione declamatio (Valla), 517
Défense de l'Esprit des lois (Montesquieu), 853, 856
Defense of the Lawful Government of Holland (Grotius), 657
De Guyenne, 823, 826
De Homine (Hobbes), 677, 678
De imperio summarum potestatem circa sacra (Grotius), 651–652
De institutione oratoria (Quintilian), 74
De inventione (Cicero), 237
De jure belli ac pacis (Grotius), 649, 655, *655,* 658, 660, 773
De jure naturae et gentium (Pufendorf), 689
De jure praedae (Grotius), 649, 695, 699
De la fréquente communion (Antoine Arnauld II), 740
De Launay, 730, 744
Delderfield, R. F., 878
De legibus (Cicero), 773
De l'Esprit des lois (Montesquieu), 846, 852–873
    and history of French law, 863–867
    and nobility of Montesquieu, 861–863
    organization of, 853–855
    publication of, 856
    reception of, 856–859
    and sociology of law, 868–873

three forms of government
described in, 859–861
writing of, 855–856
De l'Hôpital, 535
Del Magno, Jason, 527
Del Maino, Giasone, 523
De Marleberge, Thomas, 381–383
demesne, 252
Demosthenes, 16, 22, *22,* 23, 24
Denis, Saint, 192
Denmark, 583
De Nogaret, Guillaume, 469, 471, 474, 475
De officio hominis et civis juxta legem naturalem (Pufendorf), 689, 699
De Oratore (Cicero), 201
Descartes, René, 663–673, *665*
    Cujas and, 536
    Daguesseau and, 769–770, 785-
    Domat and, 755
    Galileo and, 629
    Grotius and, 656
    Hobbes and, 676
    and individualism, 707
    and Jesuits, 600
    life of, 664–668
    Montaigne and, 564, 727
    Montesquieu and, 840, 868, 881
    Newton and, 635
    Pascal and, 740
    philosophy, 668–673
    Pothier and, 828
    Pufendorf and, 692, 699, 711
    and Scientific Revolution, 620, 622, 623
    Suarez and, 601
De Secretis Secretorum, 405
Desmolets, Pierre Nicolas, 842
Despotism, 860
de Thou (lawyer and historian), 533, 647
De veritates religionis Christianae (Grotius), 653
De viris illustribus (Petrarch), 509
De Voluptate (Valla), 517
Dialectica (Abelard), 337
dialectics
    Aristotle and, 118–120
    and Sophists, 21

Dialogue between a Philosopher and a Student of the Common Laws of England (Hobbes), 679
Dialogus (Ockham), 493
dicasts, 19
Dickens, Charles, 439
dictamen, 309–310
Dictatus Papae, 288, 290, 340, 379, 471
Diderot, Denis, 710, 811, *882*
    Domat and, 751
    educational reforms, 911
    Montesquieu and, 868, 874, 881, 885–886
    Pothier and, 833, 834
    Shaftesbury and, 801
Diet of Roncaglia, 308, 320
Digest (Justinian), 300–303, 505, 840, 844
    Alciato and, 527
    Aquinas and, 428
    Bartolus on, 444
    and Bolognese lectures, 359, 360
    Budé's annotation of, 525
    and Catholic Church, 127
    and *Civil Code,* 956
    and Commentators, 441
    compiling of, 104–108
    Cujas and, 532, 535, 537
    Daguesseau and, 770, 774
    Domat's study of, 748, 753
    and feudalism, 538
    and feudal law, 266
    Gratian and, 345, 347
    and Humanism, 532
    Irnerius' glosses of, 314
    Louis XIV and, 732
    Loyseau and, 539
    Norman disregard of, 245
    in Odofredus's lectures, 359
    in Parisian curriculum circa 1600, 730
    Peter of Belleperche and, 441
    Poliziano's critical study of, 522, 523
    and Pope Urban II's theology, 152
    Pothier and, 814, 824–826, 830
    and Reformation, 574
    Tertullian and, 155

Tribonian and, 337
and University of Paris, 367
and Valla's philological research, 516
Digestum Novum, 313
Digestum vetus, 313
Diocletian, 88–92, *89,* 227, 250, 807
Diodatus, 112
Diodorus, 184, 185
Dionisio-Hadriana, 204
Dionysius Exiguus, 134
Dionysius the Elder, King of Syracuse, 29
D'Irsay, S., 688
Discours de la Méthode (Descartes), 668
Discourse on Political Economy (Rousseau), 917
Discourse on Possessory Action (Montequieu), 845
Discourse on the life and death of M. d'Aguesseau, Counsellor of State, 768
Discourse on Voluntary Servitude (La Boétie), 553
di Segni, Lotario de Conti, 375
disputatio, 360–361
Disputationes metaphysicae (Suarez), 602–603
Dissensiones Dominorum, 320, 327
Diverse Reflections on Jesus Christ (Daguesseau), 812
Divine Principle, 560
doctorate, 362–363
Doctore decretorum, 605
Doctors' Commons, 437–438
Dogmatica (Grotius), 649
Domasus, Pope, 157
Domat, Jean, 717, 743–763, 840
    biography of, 743–751
    and *Civil Code,* 964
    and Daguesseau, 773
    Daguesseau and, 770–771, 798, 799, 801, 802
    and law as principle, 8
    and law of contracts, 760–763
    Les Lois Civiles, 751–755
    and Pascal, 741
    philosophy of, 755–759
    Portalis and, 958

    Pothier and, 813, 827–828, 829, 831, 834
Domesday Book, 177, 178, 277
domina, 264
Dominate (Rome), 88–101
    constitution of, 90–92
    jurisconsults in, 92–95
    law school at Berytus, 96–101
    rhetoric in, 95–96
Dominic, Saint, 387, 388, *389*
Dominicans, 572, 601–602
    Aquinas as, 410
    founding of, 387–391
    Franciscans vs., 393
Domitius, Emperor of Rome, 74
Donation of Constantine, 289, 379
    Bartolus on, 447–448
    and early Roman Catholic Church, 141–144
donatism, 288, 387
Doneau, Hugues, 541, 753
Dorotheus, 104, 106
Douaren, François, 541
Dracon, 16
Le droit public (Domat), 749–750
dry farming, 248
Duaren, 535
Dubois, Pierre, 473, 782, 783
Dubos, Jean-Baptiste, 866
Duby, G., 124, 170, 173, 178, 196, 218–221, 228, 274
Dukes of Savoy, 588
Dumbauld, E., 649–650
Dumont, 898
Du Moulin, 753
Dumoulin, Charles, 515, 526–527, 533–534, 606, 726
Dunoyer, L. H., 816, 832
Dunstan, 218
Dupin, 836
DuPont de Nemours, Pierre, 889, 891
Du Rabot, Jan, 821, 898
Durant, W., 14, 18, 26, 29, 31, 44, 51, 87, 157, 159–162, 177, 411, 412, 414, 469, 518, 583, 584, 590, 591, 719, 735, 740, 939, 942, 943, 945–946
Durkheim, Émile, 858, 870–873
Dutch East India Company, 648–649
Dutch Republic, 650

E

Easter, 280
East Goths, 187. *See also* Ostrogoths
East India Company, 619
East Indies, 646
ecclesiastics
    Gratian and, 361
    in Ottonian revival, 221–222
    in reign of Charlemagne, 195–196
    and royal authority, 215
    at University of Bologna, 353
échevins, 819
economic classes, 483–484
les économistes, 888
Edict of 1673, 780
Edict of 1679, 726, 729
Edict of Kierzy-sur-Oise, 778
Edict of Louis, 751
Edict of Milan, 138
Edict of Nantes, 609, 720, 749, 934
Edict of Theodoric, 206
Edmund Ironside, 235
education
    and Dominicans, 390–391, 393–394
    and early Roman Catholic Church, 154–159
    and Franciscans, 391, 393–394
    and Franks, 201–208
    Innocent III and, 380
    in Rome, 48–52
Edward I, King of England, 378, 418, 468, 469
Edward the Confessor, 235, 240, 241
Einaudi, M., 889, 891
Elementa jurisprudentiae universalis (Pufendorf), 687, 691, 699
Elements (Euclid), 636
Elements of Law, Natural and Politic (Hobbes), 676
Ellenborough, Lord, 452
Ellul, J., 191, 457, 458, 722, 904–906
Émile (Portalis), 931
Encyclopedia (Diderot), 751, 811, 834
Enghien, Duc d', 922
England, 279, 573
    black monk houses in, 177
    Daguesseau and, 799–802
    feudalism in, 268–270
    Innocent III and, 377
    Montesquieu in, 849–850
    and New World, 614–617
    Roman influence in, 226–227
    as royal national state, 436–439
    universities in, 367
English Chancellors, 574
English common law, 438
English Domesday Book of 1087, 265
Enlightenment, 642, 878–923
    avocats in, 892–897
    Daguesseau and, 785
    and French Revolution, 900–923
    Montesquieu and, 842
    philosophes in, 881–888
    physiocrats in, 888–892
    universities in, 897–900
Enneads (Plotinus), 405
Entretiens sure les sciences (Lamy), 842
Ephialtes, 19
Epicureanism, 38–41, 560–561
Epicurus, 38–39, *39,* 560
Epistle to the Genevese (Sadoleto), 588
Epitome (Pufendorf), 689, 694–695, 697, 701, 702, 704
equality, 707–710
Erasmus, Desiderius (Erasmus of Rotterdam), 515, 526, 536, 575–577, *576,* 584, 642, 651
Erigena, Johannes Scotus, 203
eristics, 21
Esprit des lois romaines (Gravina), 849
Essai d'une institution au droit public (Daguesseau), 798–799
Essais (Montaigne), 546, 556, 558, 559, 568
Establissements de Saint Louis, 457
Estates General, 470, 480, 723, 811, 897, 902
Estienne, Henri, 562
Estoutville, Guillaume d', 482
Estrées, Gabrielle d', 647–648, 777
Eternal Law, 658
Ethelred the Unready, 235
Ethelstan, King of England, 269
Ethics (Abelard), 339, 412
Etymologies (Isidore), 207

Euclid, 636, 645
    Descartes and, 668
    Hobbes and, 675
    Pufendorf and, 699
Europe, unification of, 659–660
Eusebius Hieronymous Sophronius.
    See Jerome, Saint
Eusebius of Caesarea, 129, 138, 158, 419
Evans, William David, 828, 829, 831
Evesham (monastery), 381–383
Exposistiones, 237
Extravagantes, 361
Eyquem, Pierre, 550

F

Fabius Quintilianus, M., 72
Fable of Bees (Mandeville), 799–800
Faculty of Decrees, 727
Farel, William, 588
farmers, 45, 49, 149, 186, 233, 236, 250, 255, 276, 544, 968
Fathers of the Early Church, 512
Fause, John, 317
Favard, 955–956
fealty, 262
Ferdinand I, King of Castile, 279
Ferdinand II, King of Sicily and Aragon, 591
Ferrara, Princess of, 592
Ferrier, Arnauld de, 534–535
feudalism, *246*, 259–270, 538
    and the Church, 264
    contract, feudal, 261–262
    and customary law, 265–267
    in England, 268–270
    fief in, 262–264
    manoralism vs., 260–261
    scope of, as term, 260–261
    weakness of, 267–268
feudal law, 454, 499
Ficino, Marsilio, 515
fiefs, 259, 265, 267
Filleau, 898
Fitting, Hermann, 302
Fitzsimmons, M. P., 909, 913, 914, 916, 917, 919–923
Flanders, 277

Fleury, Cardinal, 779, 783, 802, 804, 878, *880*
Florence, 281, 521, 525, 848
Florida, 614
florilegia, 505
Flote, Pierre, 468–471
Fonseca, de, 602
Fontaines, Pierre de, 457
Fontenelle, 881
Ford, F. L., 865
forests (Norman), 276
Forlenze, 961–962
four-year plan (Norman), 277
France, 523–524
    advocacy vs. papacy in, 467–471
    Capetian kings in, 463–466
    Grotius in, 655–656
    medieval universities in, 370
    and New World, 614
    periods in Middle Ages in, 126
    Petrarch and, 514
    under Philip IV, 466–467
    Reformation in, 587, 608–609
    royal lawyers in, 471–473
    as royal national state, 462–501
    secular control of universities in, 478–487
    temporal power of papacy in, 474–478
    William of Ockham and, 487–501
Francis I, King of France, 529, 548, 550, 594, 728
Franciscans, 572
    Dominicans vs., 393
    founding of, 391–394
    William of Ockham as, 489
Francis of Assisi, St., 287, 387, *392*
Francis of Victoria, 602
Frankfurt Council of 794, 200, 202
Franks, 189–212
    after Charlemagne, 210–212
    Alcuin, 195–196
    Charlemagne, 193–195
    and educational reforms, 201–208
    Bishop Hincmar, 213–217
    and king as source of law, 208–210
    and legal reforms, 196–201
Frêche, G., 767

INDEX

Frederick I, Holy Roman Emperor (Barbarossa), 308, 314, 322, 356, 409
Frederick II, Holy Roman Emperor, 308–309, 370, 376, 377, 386, 409, 410, 416–417
Frederick II, King of Prussia, 888
Frederick III the Wise, Elector of Saxony, 579, 581, 582
Frederick III, Elector of Brandenburg, 690
Frederick William, Elector of Brandenburg, 690
Frémont, A. F. M., 814, 818, 820, 826, 827, 834–836
French Civil Code, 762, 971
French monarchy (Frankish beginnings), 191
French Revolution, 268, 900–923
    avocats in, 912–917
    cahiers in, 903–904
    customary law and, 266
    and legal education, 908–912
    Portalis in, 936–939
    and restoration of legal practices, 918–923
    Rousseau and, 917–918
    successive constitutions of, 904–908
Fresquet, Blaise, 843
Friedmann, W., 681
Friedrich, C. J., 7, 14, 15, 30, 32–33, 37, 159, 163
Frisians, 225–226
Frogerius, 322
Frontenac, 811
Fulbert of Chartres, 238, 266, 332
furlong, 252

G

Gaetani, Benedetto, 394, 467–468
Gaguin, Robert, 524
Gaius, 6, 761, 827
    in Berytus law school, 99
    birthplace of, 78
    in *Institutes* (Justinian), 106
    in later Roman law, 93
    and philosophy of law, 110–111

    and Principate, 80–87
Galba, 73
Galbraith, G. H., 229, 240
Galileo Galilei, 567, 612, 620, 627–634, 631, *633,* 656, 658
    Aquinas and, 697
    Aristotle and, 697
    Descartes and, 667
    Grotius and, 658
    Hobbes and, 675
    Pufendorf and, 699
    William of Ockham and, 498
Gallicanisme, 608
Gallo-Romans, 191
Gallus, Aelius, 104
Ganshof, F. L., 458
Ganvill (Walter), 266–267
Ganvill, Ranulph de, 266
Gassendi, 622, 657, 677
Gaul, 184–213
Gazzaniga, J. L., 723–725, 743, 744, 753, 763, 833, 956, 963, 965–968
Geirlan Adelis, 231
Gelasius I, Pope, 167, 198, 200, 289
Gelasius II, Pope, 311
general causes (concept), 851
General Views on the Possible Reformation of Justice (Daguesseau), 802
General Will, 917–918
Geneva, 588–589
geometry
    in ancient Greece, 21, 30
    in ancient Rome, 143
    in Carolingian period, 201
    Realists and, 8
    and Scientific Revolution, 567, 621–622, 631, 635
    and secular natural law, 644
Gerard of Cremona, 405
Gerbert of Aurillac, 223–224, 237, 238, 280
Germanic Iron Age, 187
Germanii, 186–187
German states (Reformation), 573
German universities, 504
Germany, 177, 534
Gerson, Jean, 486, 487

Gesner (*Biblioteca Universalis 1545*), 520
Geta, 87
Giannone, Pietro, 849
Gibbon, E., 10, 44, 76–77, 130, 131, 137, 189–190, 192, 193
Gibson, M. T., 176, 236–239
Gide, André, 555
Gierke, O. F. v., 163, 422, 430–431, 451, 489, 660–662
Gilbert (magnetism), 622
Gilmore, M. P., 442, 443, 505
Gin, Pierre-Louis-Claude, 897
Girondin constitution, 868
Glanvill, 281
Glanville, Ranulph de, 456
Glasgow University, 711
Glossa (Accursius), 314
Glossators
    Commentators vs., 439–440
    on Roman Empire, 448
Glosses on Porphyry (Abelard), 335
Glover, T. R., 62, 68–69
God, existence of, 603
Godefroi, Denis, 323, 774
Godefroi, Jacques, 774
Godfrey of Bouillon, *209*
gold, 613–614, 616, 618
Gosia, Martinus, 320–321
Goths, 187–188
Gottschalk, 213
Goullu-Duplessis, 814
Gournay, Jean de, 889
Gournay, Mlle de, 569
Grand Coutumier de Normandie, 267
Grand Coutumier de pays et de duché de Normandie, 457
Grands Jours d'Auvergne, 747
Gratian, 605
    and Canon law, 340–352
    on customs vs. law, 460
    and natural law, 426
Gravier, Charles, *901*
Gravina, Giovanni, 849
Great books of the Western World (Augustine), 160
Great Schism, 523
Greek language, 545
Greek philosophy
    in Ancient Rome, 5, 64, 68
    Epicureans, Stoics, and Skeptics, 38
    and French Revolution, 905
    in Jewish thought, 402
    and medieval Christianity, 150, 157
    Sophists, 21
Gregorius, 94
Gregory (scientist), 635
Gregory I the Great, Pope, 143–144, *144,* 204, 419
Gregory VII, Pope (Hildebrand), *272,* 284–286, 288–291
    and *"artes litteratum,"* 365
    Augustine and, 195
    and Benedictine land management, 177
    and Bologna, 307
    Boniface VIII and, 470, 471
    and canon law, 340, 341
    and *Digest,* 302
    and feudalism, 265
    Grotius and, 651
    Innocent III and, 379
    Lanfranc and, 238
    Matilda of Canossa and, 304
Gregory IX, Pope, 306, 309, 350, 369–370, 384, 416, 605–606
Gregory X, Pope, 309, 468
Gregory XI, Pope, 476
Gregory XII, Pope, 477
Gregory of Nyasa, 140
Gregory of Rimini, 496
Gregory of Tours, 169, 189, 192
Gregory the Great, Saint, *190*
Groot, Jan de, 628, 646, 657
Grosseteste, 498
Grotius, Hugo, *640,* 643–662, *655*
    Aquinas and, 409, 428
    Daguesseau and, 691, 770, 773, 787
    Descartes and, 663
    Domat's study of, 748, 753, 754, 755
    Gaius and, 85
    Hobbes and, 674, 681
    and individualism, 707
    Jesuits and, 600, 759
    and law as principle, 8

legacy of, 656–662
life of, 645–650
Montesquieu and, 840
and natural law, 612, 620–621, 623
natural law treatises of, 655–656
and *nudum pactum,* 761
Parisian exile, 655
political career, 650–652
Pothier and, 823, 833
prison and escape, 652–655
Pufendorf and, 688, 692, 699, 711
on role of government, 682
and scientific method, 628
on source of law, 694–697
Gualfrido, Bishop of Siena, 304
Guanerius. *See* Irnerius
Guanilo of Marmoutier, 296
Guidubaldo, Marchese, 632
guild(s)
   in Ancient Rome, 91
   anonymity of, 340
   bankers', 281
   in Bologna, 305
   and early capitalism, 618–619
   educational, 362–363, 365–367, 487
   growth of, 500
   of judges, 322
   legal, 437
   of notaries, 310
   philosophes and, 884
   and rise of towns, 277, 455–456
   student, 354
   theological, 394
Guiscard, Robert, 290
Gunpowder Plot, 600
Gustavus Vasa, King, 583
Gutenberg, Johann, 518–521, *519*
Guyenne, 550, 551
Guy of Brionne, 240
Guyot, 820, 821, 836
Guzman, Dominic de, 387, 388

H

Habita, 356
Hadrian, 76–77, 82, 825
Hadrian's Wall, 226
Hale, Nathan, 797
Hamburg, 618
Hamburger, M., 35
Hardman, J., 900, 901
Harlay, de, 778
Harold, Earl, 241
Haskins, C. H., 235, 244, 245, 274, 359, 401
Hauranne, Jean Devergier de, 737
Heer, F., 145, 153, 330, 333, 368, 369, 375, 376, 379, 394, 406
Heliaea, 19
heliocentric model, 626–627, 630, 632–633
Hellenism, 37
Heloise, *332,* 332–333
Henry I, King of England, 292
Henry I, King of France, 240
Henry II, Count of Champagne, 466
Henry II, Holy Roman Emperor, 221, 224, 238
Henry II, King of England, 465
Henry III, Holy Roman Emperor, 221, 225, 285
Henry III, King of England, 378, 417–418
Henry III, King of France, 802
Henry IV, Holy Roman Emperor, 290, 302
Henry IV of Navarre, King of France
   Grotius and, 647–648, 651
   Louis XIV and, 718, 728
   Montaigne and, 552, 557, 563
   and Reformation, 606, 609
Henry V, Holy Roman Emperor, 311
Henry VI, Holy Roman Emperor, 376, 442
Henry VI, King of England, 480
Henry VII, Holy Roman Emperor, 450
Henry the Navigator, Prince, 613
Herder, 801
Herluin, 236, 238
Herm, G., 185, 186
Hermann, Bishop of Metz, 289
Hermogenes, 75
Hermogenianus, 94
Hervé de Chatelier, Gabrielle, 535
Hicetas of Syracuse, 624

hide (land measurement), 251
Hildebrand. *See* Gregory VII, Pope
Hilduin, 213
Hincmar, Bishop, 210, 213–217
Historia Animalium (Aristotle), 398
Historia Ecclesiastica (Tolomeo), 409
Hobbes, Thomas, 656, 673–685, *676*
    Daguesseau and, 785, 793, 800
    Descartes and, 663
    Grotius and, 650, 662
    and individualism, 707
    and law as principle, 8
    life of, 674–679
    and natural law, 623, 679–685, 759
    as Nominalist, 500
    Pufendorf and, 692, 711
    and rise of middle class, 612
    on source of law, 694–696
Holbach, Paul d', 881, 882
Holdsworth, W. S., 170, 190, 438
Holkot, Robert, 496
Holland, 648–649, 650–652
homage, 243, 245, 262, 264, 377, 468
Honoré, T., 78, 79, 81–84, 97, 105
Honorius III, Pope, 364, 368–369, 388
Hôpital, de l', Chancellor, 808
Horace, 72
horses
    at Battle of Hastings, 242
    in medieval agriculture, 277
    in medieval ploughing, 252
    and monastic guest-master, 175
    in New World, 615
Hotman, François, 541, 727–728, 865
House of Commons (England), 437
Houvaningen, Elsje van, 654
Hrolf the Walker, 231–233, 245
Hugh of Fleury, 419
Hugh of St. Victor, 428
Hugo, "Doctor," 308, 320–321, 518, 818, 862
Hugo, Victor, 518
Huguenots, 608–609, 614, 843
Humanism, 574, 575–577, 586
    Alciato and, 527–530, *528, 530*
    Budé and, 524–527, *525*
    Cujas and, 531–541, *532*
    Daguesseau and, 769

    Gutenberg and, 518–521, *519*
    Montaigne and, 543–547, 549–569, *559*
    Petrarch and, *502,* 504–515
    Poliziano and, 521–523, *522*
    Shaftesbury and, 800
    as term, 530–531
    in universities, 897
    Valla and, 515–518
Humbert I, dauphin of Venice, 468
Hume, David, 623, 645, 801
    as Nominalist, 500
    Pufendorf and, 711
Hundred Years' War, 617
Hus, John, 481
Hyperdes, 20

I

Ibn Rushd (Averroes), 401
Ibn Sina (Avicenna), 401
Iceland, 233
Ihering, Rudolph von, 82
Imbert, 459
individualism
    in *Civil Code,* 963
    Descartes and, 672
    Grotius and, 661
    Hobbes and, 679–680
    Pufendorf and, 707
    and terrorism, 662
indulgences, 581, *581*
Ineffibilis amor, 469
Inferno (Dante), 631
inflation, 255
Infortiatum, 313
Innocent II, Pope, 244
    Gratian and, 342, 343
    official letters by, 343
Innocent III, Pope, 149, 284, 317, *376,* 416, 421, 463, 572, 659
    and canon law, 362–363, 375–386
    Francis and, 391–392
    and middle class, 387
    and University of Paris, 366
Innocent IV, Pope, 307, 309, 370, 386, 394, 410, 416–417
Innocent X, Pope, 740, 747

Inns of Court, 437
inquests, 219
inquests (*turba*), 461
inquests (villeins), 254
Inquiry Concerning Human Understanding (Hume), 711
Inquisition, 633, 634
    Cathars and, 384
    Maimonides and, 403
Institutes (Gaius), 345, 346, 963
Institutes (Justinian)
    and Alciato's pedagogy, 527
    and Bolognese lectures, 360
    and *Civil Code*, 956
    Daguesseau and, 773, 774, 776
    Domat's study of, 753
    and emperors' power, 88
    and "extraordinary" lectures, 359
    Grotius and, 657
    Irnerius' glosses of, 311–314
    Louis XIV and, 732
    in Middle Ages, 303
    and obligations, 761
    in Parisian curriculum circa 1600, 728
    Pothier and, 814–815, 824
    structural arrangement of, 106
    structure of, 699
    and universities during Enlightenment, 910
Institutes coutumières (Loisel), 730
Institutes of Dutch Law (Grotius), 699
Institutes of Gaius (Gaius), 80–81, *81*
Institution au droit français (Coquille), 730
Institutiones (Gaius), 83
Institutions au Droit Français (Du Rabot), 822
Institution Theologica (Proclus), 405
Institutio Oratorio (Quintilian), 201
Instructions (Daguesseau), 771
interest, 275
interest (thirteenth century towns), 278
Introduction historique au droit des obligations (Gazzaniga), 724, 744
Introduction to the Jurisprudence of Holland (Grotius), 653, 657, 658
Irnerius, 301, 303–305, 311–313, *315*, 448, 620, 840

Iron Ages, 186–187
Isabella, Queen, 591–592, 596, 613
Isagoge (Porphyry), 400
Isidore of Seville, 207, 216
Isidorus Mercator, 216
Isocrates, 23–25, *24*, 56
Israel, ancient, 5–7
Istoria civile del regno di Napoli (Giannone), 849
Italian Inquisition, 593
Italian universities, 504
Italy
    Catholic Reformation in, 592–593
    Lombards in, 188
    medieval universities in, 370
    Normans in, 244
    periods in Middle Ages in, 126
    Petrarch and, 514
    universities in, 482
Iulianus, Salvius, 79
ius civile
    ius gentium vs., 109–110
    and Twelve Tables, 57
Ius Civile (Q. Mucius, Pontifex), 64–67, 83, 85, 963
ius gentium
    and *ius civile*, 57–58
    and natural law, 347–348
    and philosophy of law, 109–110
ius honorarium, 57
ius respondendi, 82, 104
Ivo of Chartres, 239, 338, 341

J

Jacobian Club, 916
James I, King of England, 602
James II, King of England, 637
Jansen, Cornelis, 737, *737*, 738, 740
Jansenists and Jansenism, 734, 735–743, 746, 747, 755, 766, 769–770, 813, 842, 844, 846, 848, 857, 893
Jars de Gournay, Marie le, 558
Jaubert, 899, 956
Javoi, Thérèse, 817, 835
Jefferson, Thomas, 904
Jerome, Saint, 71, 139, 157–159, *158*, 508

Jesuits, 592, 597–600, 602, 607, 633, 642, 738, 740, 747, 842, 856, 897
Jesus, 5–6, *133, 135*
    and early Roman Catholic Church, 132–137
    and government, 138
Jews
    and Ancient Greece, 154
    Calvin and, 587
    in Carolingian period, 200, 205
    in England, 6–7
    Gibbon on, 137
    intellectualism of, 151
    Jesus and, 132, 139
    in Napoleonic France, 945–946
    in Spain, 403, 545, 592
Joachim of Fiore, 129
Joanna, Queen of Champagne, 466
Joan of Arc, 461, 480–481
Johannes, Archbishop, 404
John I, King of England, 261, 263, 377, 378, *379*, 382
John I, King of Portugal, 613
John XXII, Pope, 344, 373, 490, 491
John XXIII, Pope, 477
John Law medal, *781*
John of Mirecourt, 496
John of Monte Corvino, 393
John of Salisbury, 150, 281, 369, 374, 406
John the Deacon, 142
Joinville, Jean, Sire de, 465–466
Jolowicz, H. F., 78, 81, 87, 91, 93, 94, 97, 100, 102–106, 109, 110
Jones, G., 186, 187, 226, 228, 229, 231, 232
Jones, J., 15, 30, 31
Jonson, Ben, 675
Jordanes, 187
Josephus, 508
Jourdain, C., 729
Journal des savants, 826, 827
Jousse, 824
Judaism
    Aristotle and, 402–403
    Plato and, 151
Julian (jurist), 82
Julian "The Apostate," Roman Emperor, 139

Julien, Jean-Joseph, 931
Julius III, Pope, 594
Jumièges, 235
Juris (Pound), 755, 760, 761
jurisconsults
    in Dominate, 92–95
    in Principate, 75–78
    in Rome, 56–68
jurisdiction
    of Church, 291
    in manorial systems, 256
jurisprudence, 146, 266
jurists
    popes as, 344
    in Roman legal system, 60–64
Justin I, Emperor of Rome, 101
Justinian, *42,* 101, *102*
    and Alciato's pedagogy, 527
    and alterations to classical texts, 94
    Cujas and, 537
    Daguesseau and, 773, 802, 807
    dilution of influence on contemporary law, 96–97
    Domat's study of, 746, 753
    on emperors' power, 88
    Grotius and, 657
    Irnerius and, 301
    legal education reform by, 97
    Louis XIV and, 732
    and medieval classical scholarship, 505
    medieval revival of interest in, 303–304
    Montesquieu and, 866
    and obligation, 760
    and obligations, 761
    in Parisian curriculum circa 1600, 728
    Poliziano's critical study of, 522
    Pothier and, 814–815, 824, 826, 827
    Rome under, 101–108
Justinianus, Flavius Anicius, 101
Jutes, 225–227
Juvenal, 72, 814

K

Kant, Immanuel, 297, 500, 711
Kantorowicz, H., 321, 350
Keeton, G. W., 243
Kellinghausen, 827
Kennedy, G. A., 52, 54, 68, 70–72, 74, 75
Kepler, Johann, 566, 567, 630–631, 656
Kern, 266
king, as source of law, 208–210
Kircher (scientist), 622
Kitto, H. D. F., 14
Knight, W., 647, 656
Knights Hospitaler, 390
Knights Templar, 390, 459, 475, 600
Knowles, D., 150, 153, 159–161, 164, 174–180, 218, 235, 240, 241, 292–293, 330, 333, 338, 346, 353, 355, 357, 362, 366, 380, 381, 405, 406, 488, 491, 497, 498
Knut Sveinsson, 235
Krieger, L., 685, 686, 688, 689, 691, 693, 697–701
Kunkel, W., 47–48, 56, 57, 59, 60, 74, 78, 82, 87
Kuttner, S. G., 331, 342, 343, 345, 346, 348, 350

L

Labeo, Antistius, 79
Labienus, 71
La Boétie, Étienne de, 550–554, 551, 553–554, 556, 558–560, 559, 560, 563
La Brède, 844, 845, 850, 873
Lachaise, Père, 747
La Chassaigne, Françoise de, 555–556
Lactantius, 113
La faculté de droit de Paris aux xviie et xviiie siècles (Lamasne-Desjobert), 731
Lafayette, Madame De, 790
Lafayette, Marquis de, 812, 904
La Flèche college, 664
Lamasne-Desjobert, M. A. L., 731, 732
Lambertzoon, Jan, 654
Lamoignon, Nicolas de, 732, 818
Lamy, Bernard, 842
land, division of, Vikings and, 230
Landulf, Count, 409
Lanfranc, 236, 237–240, 241
Lange, 459
Langer, W. L., 188, 191, 193, 210, 615, 679
Langton, Archbishop of Canterbury, 382, 383
Laon, 279
Laretelle, Pierre-Louis de, 895
Larivière, Mercier, 889
La Rochefoucauld, 790
Lartigue, Jeanne de, 843–844
Lateran IV (council), 385
Lateran Council of 1059, 287
Latin language
  Montaigne and, 545
  Petrarch and, 513
  Valla and, 516
Laverne, 898
Lavine, T. Z., 145, 153, 666, 667
Lavollée, R., 932, 933, 935, 938, 939, 950, 951, 954, 957, 960
law
  Daguesseau and reform of, 802–811
  Franks and reform of, 196–201
  as principle, 7–10
  purpose of, 116–117
  Roman vs. tribal, 204–205
Law, John, 781, 782, 830
law of contracts, 760–763
Laws (Plato), 773
law schools, 78–80, 96–101
lawyers, 453–462, *643*
Leçons d'histoire de la philosophie du droit (Villey), 7
lectura, 319
Leduc, E., 931–932, 936, 944, 954, 958
Lee, R. W., 648
Lefebvre, G., 903, 905, 907, 919, 938
Lefèvre d'Étaples, Jacques, 523
legal education
  in Athens, 14–21
  in China, 4–5
  and French Revolution, 908–912

Louis XIV and, 726–735
in Rome, 44–68
Legal Philosophy from Plato to Hegel (Cairns), 30
legal science
in Ancient Greece, 4, 15
in Ancient Rome, 44, 68, 87–88, 92, 118, 963
Calvinism and, 590
Christianity and, 608
in France, 463, 524, 725–726, 812, 919
in Middle Ages, 124–125, 128–130, 225, 245, 266, 291, 301–302, 310, 316, 318, 321, 346, 437
Petrarch and, 513
printing press and, 518
Pufendorf and, 685
Legislative Assembly, 906, 910
Legum delectus (Domat), 753
Leibniz, Gottfried Wilhelm von, 297, 601, 635, 801
Leif Eriksson, 228
Lelong, 811
Lenormant, 824
L'enseignement du droit français dans les universités de France aux xviie et xviiie siècles (De Curzon), 730
Leo I, Emperor of Rome, 96
Leo III, Pope, 199
Leo IX, Pope, 285–287, 340, 343. *See also* Bruno, Bishop of Toul
Leo X, Pope, 521, 577, 582, 626
Leo XIII, Pope, 412
Leprestre-Boisderville, 916
Le Roy, Louis, 568
Le Tellier (Chancellor), 726
Le Tellier, Michel, 720
Le Trosne, 814, 835
Letters to a Young Man at the University (Shaftesbury), 801
Letters to Posterity (Petrarch), 506, 507
Les lettres persanes (Montesquieu), 843, 845–847
Leviathan (Hobbes), 673, 678, *678,* 679
Lewis, E., 420, 422, 423, 426–430, 450, 489–490, 493
Lewis, N., 61
Lex Dei, 537
Lex Romana Burgundiorum, 537
Lex Romana Curiensis, 207
"Lex Salica," 204–205
Libanius, 96
Liber De Causis, 405
Liber Sextus, 351, 361, 606
Libri Carolini, 202
Libri feodorum, 266, 359–360
Libri tres iuris civilis (Sabinus), 83
Liege, Bishop of, 171
Lindisfarne, 231
Lippershey (optician), 632
Littera Bononiensis, 313
Little Commentary (Copernicus), 626
Livonnière, Claude Pocquet de, 898
Livre de justice et de plet, 457
Livre des métiers (Boileau), 456
Livy, 72, 184, 513
Lizet, 533
Lloyd-Jones, H., 18
local custom. *See* customary local law
Locke, John, 500, 710, 789, 800
Loevestein Castle, 652
Loi des cultes, 950
Les lois civiles dans leur ordre naturel (Domat), 749–755, 798, 828, 840
Loisel, Antoine, 730
Lombard, Peter, 414
Lombard League of 1167, 308
Lombards
in Celtic Iron Age, 187
invasion of, 143
and Scandinavian influences, 188–189
Lombard Sentences, 489
London, 617, 618, 619
Lothair, 442
Lothair I, Holy Roman Emperor, 211
Lothair II, Holy Roman Emperor, 217, 302, 307
Louis, Emperor of Bavaria, 491
Louis II the German, 317
Louis IV, Holy Roman Emperor, 491
Louis V, King of France, 212
Louis VI, King of France, 464
Louis VII, King of France, 464
Louis VIII, King of France, 465

Louis IX, King of France, 283, 411, 417, *458,* 463, 465–466
Louis XI, King of France, 479, 482, 540
Louis XII, King, 592
Louis XII, King of France, 482, 526, 548
Louis XIII, King of France, 655, 719, 727, 728, 745
Louis XIV, King of France, 717–735
    and chancellors, 722–723
    and Colbert, 717–721
    and colonialism in the Americas, 614
    Daguesseau and, 778, 779–780, 810
    Diocletian and, 90
    and Domat, 743, 744, 750
    Domat and, 755
    and Edict of Nantes, 609
    and Enlightenment, 878, 886, 887
    and famine in seventeenth century, 642
    Grotius and, 656
    and "high robe" lawyers, 550
    Montesquieu and, 840, 842
    Paris as center of learning under, 656
    and *parlements,* 716
    and private law, 723–724
    reform of law teaching by, 726–735
    and seventeenth century codes, 724–725
    standardization of legal education by, 822
    and universities during Enlightenment, 898, 899
Louis XV, King of France, 780, 783, 802, 814, 821, 878, *879,* 886, 887, 894
Louis XVI (Hardman), 900
Louis XVI, King of France, 797, 813, 879, 886, 887, 890, 895, 896, *896,* 899, 900, 901, 915
Louisiana, 614, 781–782
Louis the Pious, 199, 210, 211, 213, 267
Louvois, Marquis de, 720, 769
Loyola, Ignatius de, 515, 573, 584, 595–600, *598*
Loyseau, Charles, 442, 539–540
Ludwig, Karl, 687, 688
Luke, Saint, 137
Luther, Hans, 578, 579
Luther, Martin, 349, 515, 519–520, *570,* 572, 574–575, 577–583, 585, 586, 626, 650, 884
Lutheranism, 650
Lutterell, John, 490
Lyceum, 33, 38

M

Machiavelli, Niccolò, 682
MacMullen, R., 63, 90
Magna Carta, 377–378, 417
Maimonides (Moses Ben Maimon), 151, 403, *404*
Maine, Duc du, 780
Maine, H. S., 57, 58, 62, 63
Maine, Henry, 120
Maintenon, Madame de, 721, *721*
Maitland, 124, 260, 301, 407
Malacca, 649
Malebranche, 770, 842, 939
Malesherbes, 931, 935
Maleville, Jacques de, 955, 958
Malherbe, 727
Mandela, Nelson, 840
Mandeville, Bernard de, 799–800
Manfred, 417
Mango, C. A., 98–99, 102
Manlius, 64
Mann, C. S., 134–135
manoir, 251
manorial court, 256–257
manorial system, 251–258
    anatomy of, 251–252
    economics of, 254–255
    political unit in, 256–258
    unit of production in, 251–254
manse, 251
Mantegna, Andrea, *10*
Manuel d'histoire du droit français (Brissaud), 761
manufacturing, 617–618

Manutius, Aldus, 518, 519
Map, Walter, 374
Marcus Aurelius, 75, 77, 87, 784
Mare Liberum (Grotius), 649
Marguerite of Valois, 563
maritime law, 462, 920
Marrou, H. I., 18, 21, 25, 29–30, 49, 72, 95, 237
Marsilius of Padua, 477, 491, 572
Martel, Charles, 192, 197
Martin V, Pope, 477
Martinus, 350–351, 370
Massachusetts, 615
Masuer, 459
materialists, 940
mathematics, 644
    Descartes and, 664–665, 667–668
    Grotius and, 662
Matilda, Countess of Canossa, 240–241, 304–305, 311, 315
Maupeou, René Nicolas Charles Augustin, 732, 894
Maupeou crisis, 894
Maurice of Nassau, Prince, 650, 652, 664
Maurice of Orange, Prince, 628
Maxentius, 138
Maximian, 90, 807
Mazarin, 718
McDougal, M. S., 661
Medici, Giuliano de', 521
Medici, Lorenzo de', 521
medicine, 626
medieval history, 124–130
Meditations (Descartes), 676
Méditations (Daguesseau), 784–798, 928, 929
Mémoire (Daguesseau), 806–809
mémoires, 893–894
Mémoires for the Instruction of the Dauphin (Louis XIV), 718, 721
Mendicant orders, 387–394
mercantilism, 616–619
Mercenne circle, 657
Mérille, Edmond, 535, 745
Merovingian dynasty, 191–192, 261
Merriman, J. M., 820
Merryman, J. H., 888, 960
Mersenne, 635, 656

Descartes and, 666, 670
Hobbes and, 675, 676
Montaigne and, 657
Merton College (Oxford), 486
merum imperium, 538, 540
    Bartolus on, 444, 449
    and Commentators, 442–443
Mesmes, Henri de, 546
Messala, 72
Metaphysics (Aristotle), 399, 412
Michael of Cesena, 490–491
Middle Ages
    Abelard and, 331, 340
    Alaric II and, 206
    Aristotle and, 399, 405
    Augustine and, 159
    and Benedictines, 175
    Boethius and, 401
    Carolingian law, 208, 274
    and contract law, 833
    contrast with secular natural law, 761
    and customary law, 265, 456–457
    definition of, 124, 127
    end of, 487–488, 498–499, 504, 519
    and the Franks, 189
    Geneva, 588
    high water mark, 471
    influence on Descartes, 672
    influence on Pothier, 832
    influence on Pufendorf, 690, 707
    intellectual reach, 150–151
    and Irnerian glosses, 312
    Jerome and, 158
    job acquisition in, 479
    Joinville history of, 466
    Justinian in, 303, 322
    and late Roman Empire, 129, 226
    legal training, 317
    and litigation, 138
    and money scarcity, 260
    and natural law, 431
    in northern Alps, 249
    papal litigation, 139, 142
    and the poor, 136
    record keeping in, 309–310
    regarded as barbaric, 883
    religious jurisdiction, 148

and scholasticism, 292–293
and Thomist influences, 422
universities in, 170, 370, 372–373
waning of, 436
middle class
    in Ancient Rome, 131
    Aristotle as member of, 32
    and concept of equality, 709
    Daguesseau as member of, 766, 777
    Descartes and, 663
    in France, 533, 566, 878, 884, 886, 892, 907
    Grotius as member of, 643, 646
    in Middle Ages, 387, 437, 467
    Montesquieu and, 847
    and rise of capitalism, 612, 615, 617
Milan, 90, 138, 160, 166–167, 290, 359, 477, 511, 516, 521, 523, 527, 529, 592
Mirabeau, 935
Mirabeau the Elder, 889
Miromesnil, Armand-Thomas, 899–901
Miscellany (Poliziano), 522
mixtum imperium, 538
Modestinus, 93
Moerbeke, 420
Mommsen, T., 78, 107
monarchy, 10
    Aquinas and, 422
    and bailiffs, 465
    Carolingian, 192
    and Chancellors, 722
    and Christianity, 139
    Cicero and, 113
    in *Code Napoleon,* 892
    Daguesseau and, 766, 799, 803
    in *Digest* (Justinian), 318
    and Dominicans, 391
    Dumoulin and, 533–534
    and *échevins,* 819
    and Estates General, 811
    and French revolution, 880, 900, 903, 906
    and Glossators, 448
    Greek, 16
    Grotius and, 646
    Hincmar and, 215
    and Jansenists, 738–739, 932
    and Jesuits, 759
    Louis XIV, 717–718, 720, 725, 729, 733, 878
    and Maupeou, 894–895
    Montesquieu and, 841, 846, 850, 854–856, 862
    in Montesquieu's *De l'esprit des lois,* 859
    and Normans, 233
    and papacy, 467, 469, 475, 865–867
    papal, 341
    Portalis and, 936, 948, 962
    Pothier and, 834
    Roman, 45, 68, 70, 90
    and Roman Catholic Church, 606, 609
    Roman law on, 438
    and Romans Catholic Church, 282
    Suarez and, 602
    William of Ockham and, 488
monasticism
    under Archbishop Dunstan, 180
    of Augustinian canons, 284
    Benedictine, 171
    of Franciscans and Dominicans, 375
    Gratian and, 343
    and territorial acquisitions, 176
monastic law, 235–240
money
    Alciato and, 527, 529
    Aquinas and, 423
    and *assignats,* 927
    and bailiffs/seneschals, 465
    Benedictine management of, 176, 179
    and capitalism, 617–618
    in Carolingian Renaissance, 278–288
    Charlemagne and, 194
    clerks' pay, 170
    and contract law, 760, 762
    Cujas and, 536
    Daguesseau and, 767, 799, 807, 826
    Domat and, 743

and eminence, in Rome, 67
and exploration, 613
in feudal system, 260, 263–264, 267, 270
and France, 781–782, 878–879
in French Revolution, 900, 909
and Gresham's law, 626
Grotius and, 646, 653
Henry III and, 417
and indulgences, 582
Justinian and, 101
and Knights Templar, 390
and law reform, 805
and legal representation, 565
and legal studies, 374
Louis XIV and, 719, 721–722
making, for Roman advocates, 52
in manorial system, 254
Marleberge and, 381–382
and Mendicant orders, 387
Montaigne and, 544, 556
Montesquieu and, 854, 864–865
and Ottonian revival, 225–226
and papal litigation, 344
Petrarch and, 508
and philosophy, 943
Pothier and, 817, 829–830, 833
Pufendorf and, 692, 703, 709
Quintilian's wealth, 73
required by empires, 90
and Roman Catholic Church, 575–576
for royal wedding, 591
and tenants, 250
and tribal law, 204
and venality of office, 547–550
and war, 642
wergild, 233–234
Monnier, F., 766–771, 778, 780–783, 798, 805, 810
Monologion (Anselm of Bec), 294–296
Montagu, Duke of, 850
Montaigne, Michel de, 543–547, 549–569, *559*
  and classicism, 727
  Cujas and, 536
  Descartes and, 665
  Domat and, 751
  education of, 544–547
  Essais, 558, 559, *568*
  Hobbes and, 677
  judicial career, 550–554
  La Boétie and, 550–554, 556, 558–560, 563
  and law as principle, 8
  marriage and retirement, 555–557
  Mersenne and, 657
  and natural law, 563–564, 759
  Pascal and, 740–741
  and positive law, 565–566
  Pufendorf and, 711
  and Scientific Revolution, 566–568
  and Skepticism, 41, 559–563, 600
  translation of Sebond's *Theologia Naturalis,* 554–555
  and venality of office, 549–550
Montaigne, Pierre de, 544, 545, 556
Monte Cassino, 171, 409
Montesquieu, Charles-Louis de Secondat, *838,* 840–874, 883
  death of, 873–874
  De l'Esprit des lois, 852–873
  early life, 841–845
  and Enlightenment, 881
  and history of French law, 863–867
  history of Romans, 850–852
  and law as principle, 8
  Les lettres persanes, 845–847
  Napoleon and, 957
  as noble, 861–863
  Portalis and, 942
  Pufendorf and, 710
  on religion, 949–950
  and sociology of law, 868–873
  travels of, 847–850
Montesquieu, Jacob Secondat de, 841
Montesquieu, Jacques Secondat de, 841, 843
Montfort, Simon de, 384
Montreal, 642
Montromier, de, 827
Monzambano, Severinus de, 688
moral concepts
  Portalis on, 941
  Pufendorf on, 693–694, 696
More, Thomas, 576

INDEX 1021

Moreau, General, 922
Mornay, Pierre de, 469
Morrall, J. B., 342, 343, 379, 422
Morris, C., 659–661, 675
Mourot, Jean-François-Regis, 898
Murray, A., 136, 233, 243, 370, 374, 383, 386, 391, 457, 458
Muslims
    Dominican conversions by, 413
    and Greek philosophers, 154
    Henry the Navigator and, 613
    invasions in North Africa and Spain by, 401–402
    learned princes, 403
    medieval influence, 125
    in ninth century raids, 217
    at Poitiers 732, 192
    as religious heresy, 145
    in seventh century invasion, 151
    toleration of Luther, 596
    Usbek (Montesquieu) denunciation of Catholic Church, 846
    in Western Europe 700-1050, 128

N

Nagera, Duke of, 595
Naples, 510, 848–849
Napoleonic Civil Code of 1804, 730
National Assembly, 903, 905, 910, 913, 926–927
National Convention, 906
The Natural and Essential Order of Political Societies (Larivière), 889
natural law, 644–645, 715–836
    Aquinas and, 422–431
    Aristotle and, 117–120
    Daguesseau and, 766–813, 789, 798–799
    Domat and, 743–763
    in Enlightenment, 886
    Grotius and, 655–659, 661–662
    Hobbes and, 679–685
    and *ius gentium*, 347–348
    Louis XIV and, 717–735
    Montaigne and, 563–564
    Pascal and, 735–743
    Portalis and, 941, 960
    Pothier and, 813–836
    Pufendorf and, 685, 690–691, 697–698
    and succession, 705–706
    William of Ockham and, 493
natural motion, 675
natural right(s)
    Hobbes and, 680–681
    marriage as, 934–935
Necker, Jacques, 902, *902*
Neleus of Scepsis, 399
Nennius, 226
Nero, 70
Nerva *pater*, 79
Netherlands, 628, 646, 647
Le neveu de Rameau (Diderot), 833
New College, 486
New France, 614
New Testament
    and Bec curriculum, 239
    caritas and, 287
    Cathars and, 383
    Daguesseau and, 767
    Grotius and, 651, 654
    Jerome's translation of, 157
    and Jewish bible, 6
    Justinianism and, 317
    as redemption, 146
    and Roman law, 136, 139, 141
    and Scrolls, 134
Newton, Isaac, *610*, 612, 634–638, 840
    Descartes and, 672
    and Enlightenment, 881
    Portalis and, 942
    William of Ockham and, 498
New World, 613–619, 646
Nicene Creed, 140
Nicholas, B., 78, 81, 87, 91, 93, 94, 97, 100, 102–106, 109, 110
Nicholas I, Pope, 217, 289
Nicholas II, Pope, 239
Nicholas V, Pope, 517–518
Nicholas of Autrcourt, 496–497
Nicholas of Oresme, 498
Nicholas of Tusculum, 382
Nichomachus, 33
Nicomachean Ethics (Aristotle), 32, 33, 116
Niebuhr, Barthold Georg, 80

Njal's Saga, 233, 234
Noailles, Adrienne de, 812
Noailles, Archbishop de, 782
Noailles, Cardinal, 779
Noailles, Duc de, 780–781
Nominalism, 504, 560, 573, 759
    Abelard and, 339
    and Enlightenment, 881
    Gratian and, 351
    Grotius and, 662
    Hobbes and, 674
    and law as principle, 8
    Pufendorf and, 696
    Realism vs., 9, 153
    William of Ockham and, 488, 500
Norman Conquest, 241–245, *242*
Normans, 231–245
    monastic law under, 235–240
    origins of, 231–234
    in Ottonian revival, 231–245
    politics of, 234–235, 240–241
Northwestern University, 126
Notre Dame, 330–331, 345, 364–365
Notre Dame de Paris (Hugo), 518
Novels (Justinian), 359, 360, 844
Nugent, Thomas, 852, 860, 866

O

obedentiary system, 178–179
obligation, fief as cause of, 265
Obligations (Pothier), 828, 836
Observationes et emendationes (Cujas), 538
Ockham. *See* William of Ockham
Ockhamism, 576, 657
Ockham's Razor, 491–492
Odo, 170, 222
Odofredus, 302, 304, 310, 323, 358–359, 442, 443
Odovakar, 143
Oeuvres complètes de J. Domat, 750
Oeuvres complètes du chancelier D'aguesseau, 777
Of Private Wrongs (Blackstone), 963
Of Public Wrongs (Blackstone), 963
Of the Rights of Persons (Blackstone), 963
Of the Rights of Things (Blackstone), 963
Of Wisdom (Charron), 569
Olaf, King of Norway, 235
Oldenbarneveldt, Johan, 647, 648, 650–652
Old Testament, 6, 132, 136, 139, 146, 155, 158, 200, 208, 215, 287, 391, 574, 583, 590, 683, 769, 846
Olivier-Martin, F., 718, 725, 730, 754, 761, 836, 894, 895
On His Own Ignorance and That of Many (Petrarch), 512
On Interpretation (Aristotle), 400, 401
On Prejudice (Portalis), 931
On Sophistical Refutations (Aristotle), 400
On the Duty of Man and Citizen according to Natural Law in Two Books (Pufendorf), 691, 699, 708
On the Heavens (Aristotle), 399
On the Law of Nature and Nations in Eight Books (Pufendorf), 691, 693, 699, *702,* 708, 712
On the Origin and Progress of a New Science (Nemours), 889
On the Rights of Man and Citizen, 708
On the Structure of the Human Body (Vesalius), 626
Opus Majus (Bacon), 296
Oratorian collège, 931
Oratorians, 842, 897
Ordinance of Moulins, 761
Ordinances, 969
Ordonnances écclesiastiques, 589
Ordre des avocats, 733, 884, 892, 912–914
Organic Articles, 944–945, 946, 950, 951
Organon (Aristotle), 400, 401
Origines iuris civilis (Gravina), 849
Orléans, Duc d', 780–781, 782, 783
Orléans, Louis d', 732–733
Ormesson, Anne, 777, 780, 811–812
Orr, William F., 138
Orto, Obertus de, 359
Osiander, Andreas, 626
Osler, William, 626
Ostrogoths, 187–189

INDEX

Otto I, Holy Roman Emperor, 221,
223, *224,* 279, 280
Otto II, Holy Roman Emperor, 221,
223
Otto III, Holy Roman Emperor, 142,
221, 223–224
Otto IV, Pope, 385
Ottonian revival, 221–245
    Angles/Saxons/Jutes, 225–227
    Normans, 231–245
    Vikings, 227–231
Otto of Brunswick, 377
Otto of Friesing, 405
Ourliac, P., 723, 725, 743, 956, 963
Ovid, 72
ownership
    Portalis on, 943–944
    Pufendorf on, 703
Oxford University, 367, 504–505
    colleges at, 485, 486
    Hobbes at, 674
    and Mendicant Orders, 394
    William of Ockham at, 489

P

Padua, 505, 632
paganism, 139
Pagels, E. H., 134
Palais de Justice, 726
Palais des Papes, 476, *476*
Pandectae (Justinian), 827
Pandects (Pothier), 301–302, 824, 825, 827
Pantaléon, Jacques, 386, 463–464
papacy
    advocacy vs., in France, 467–471
    Charlemagne and, 199–200
    and French monarchs, 463
    temporal power of, in France, 474–478
Papal Index, 554
papal infallibility, 217, 747, 799
Papianus, Aemilius, 87
Papinian, *77,* 93
    in Berytus law school, 99
    birthplace of, 78
    and Principate, 87–88

Paradoxa (Alciato), 528
Paraphrasis (Poliziano), 522
Parc, Poullain du, 898
Pardessus, 767
Paris, 617. *See also* University of Paris
    as capital, 192
    Grotius in, 655–657
    Montesquieu in, 847–848
    William of Ockham and, 496
Paris Parlement, 724, 747, 769, 815, 894
Parks, E. P., 53, 55
parlements, 543, 549–551, 553
    in exile, 782
    in the French Revolution, 900
    Louis XIV and, 722
    and Maupeou, 894–895
    and universities, 371
Parma, 510
Pascal, Blaise, 564, 600, 627, 717, *742,* 790
    Daguesseau and, 786, 806
    and Domat, 745–747
    and Jansenists, 735–743
    and natural law, 759
Pascal, Étienne, 740
Pascal, Jacqueline, 741
Paschal II, Pope, 286–288, 311
Pasquier, Étienne, 552, 568, 738
Passage du Mont St. Bernard, *921*
Pater, Walter, 39
Paul, Saint, 93, 100, 133, 137, 138, 166, 426, 580
Paul III, Pope, 593–594, 626
Pavia, 275
Peace of Augsburg (1555), 583
Peace of God movement, 149, 260
Peace of Westphalia (1648), 690
peasants
    in France, 903, 927
    Frankish, 192
    and legal learning, 374
    in Middle Ages, *246,* 455, 464, 481
    Montaigne and, 565
    Montesquieu and, 841, 844, 861
    in New France, 614
    Pufendorf on, 709
    and Reformation, 583, 608

and rise of middle class, 617
and rise of towns, 277
in Roman Empire, 227
Saint Gregory and, 144
Pecock, Reginald, 517
Pegasus, 79
Pegues, F. J., 467, 469, 472–474
Peletier, 567
Pelikan, J., 134, 158, 334
Pelletier, 748, 749
Penal Code (1810), 969
penance(s)
    abbeys founded with, 241
    in Church paradigm, 127
    of Henry IV (at Canossa), 290
    and legal absolution, 299
    life science of, 146
    of Louis (son of Charlemagne), 211
    Luther and, 579
    and science, 622
    war, 149, 175
Penna, Lucas de, 441
Pepin I, ruler of the Franks, 192
Pepin II, ruler of the Franks, 192
Pepin III The Short, ruler of the Franks, 148, 192
Pepo, 304, 310, 315
Perche, 815
Pericles, 18, 19, 25
Périer, Marguerite, 744
peripatetics, 32
Peter, Saint, 127, 135, 136–137, 582
Peter of Belleperche, 440–441
Peter of Corbeil, 375, 383
Peters, Ellen, 8
Peter the Lombard, 159, 342
Petrarch, *502,* 504–515
    Budé and, 523
    Cujas and, 531
    Grotius and, 651
    as historian and legal scholar, 513–514
    and Humanism, 574
    as Italy's poet laureate, 509–510
    life, 506–509
    Montaigne and, 543
    politics of, 509–511
    and Reformation, 593

    religion and scholasticism of, 511–513
    and Scientific Revolution, 620
    works, 509
Philip II, King of Macedon, 32
Philip II Augustus, King of France, 366, 464–465
Philip III, King of France, 462, 466
Philip IV the Fair, King of France, 448, 457, 459, 466–467
    Boniface VIII and, 468–471, 474
    Clement V and, 475
    de Villepreux and, 472–473
Philip of Macedon, 32
Philo, 402
Philolaus the Pythagorean, 624
Philosophers (Athens)
    Aristotle, 32–37
    Epicurians/Stoics/Skeptics, 38–41
    Hellenism, 37
    Plato, 29–31
    Socrates, 26–29
    Sophists, 21–25
    on study of law, 15–16
    Theophrastus, 37–38
philosophers, of early Roman Catholic Church, 159–168
philosophes, 881–888
Philosophiae Naturalis Principia Mathematica (Newton), 636, 637
philosophy of law
    Aristotle and, 115–120
    Cicero and, 111–115
    Gaius and, 110–111
    ius gentium, 109–110
    Pothier and, 827–831
    and Rome, 108–120
    in Rome, 108–121
    and stoicism, 111–115
    Ulpian and, 110–111
physics, 567, 629, 634–635
Physics (Aristotle), 399, 412
physiocrats, 888–892
Pichar, 816
Pichegru, General, 922
Pilo, 112
Pisa, 506, 628, 632
Pisana, 302
Pius, Antonius, 77

Pius IV, Pope, 591, 594, 595
Pius VII, Pope, 946, 951
Placentinus, 322
plague, 510
Plaisians, Guillaume de, 474
Plan for a Russian University (Diderot, De Curzon), 885–886
Planiol, M., 954, 960, 969
Plato, 280, 508, 542, 560, 561, 603–604, 623, 773
    Abelard and, 336
    Augustine and, 160, 164
    on democracy, 14
    and education, 20
    in Judaism, 151
    and law as principle, 7
    in Middle Ages, 406
    and natural law, 424
    as philosopher, 29–31
    and rhetoric, 25
    and Socrates, 26–27, 164
    on Socrates, 26
    on study of law, 16
    William of Ockham and, 492
Platonism, 153
Pliny the Elder, 187
Pliny the Younger, 70–71, 72, 79, 133
Plotinus, 164, 280–281
Plucknett, T. F. T., 229, 230, 438
Plutarch, 111–112
Podesta of Bologna, 320
Poisson, Jeanne Antoinette, 783–784
Politics (Aristotle), 116, 412, 430
Poliziano, Angelo, 521–523, *522*
Pollio, C. Asinius, 52, 72
Polybius, 184
Pomponius, 66, 79, 82
Pontifex, Quintus Mucius Scaevola, 83, 85, 120
pope(s)
    authority of, 127
    as legislator, 290
    as temporal governors, 148
Porphyry, 281, 335, 400–401
Portalis, Frédéric, 930, 931, 938, 939, 940, 958
Portalis, Jean Étienne Marie, 926–973, *952*
    as *avocat*, 932–936
    and *Civil Code,* 971
    and *Code Napoleon,* 951–973
    and *Concordat* of 1801, 944–951
    early life of, 930–932
    in the French Revolution, 936–939
    philosophy of, 939–944
Port-Royal, 736, 737, 738, 747
Portugal, 613, 614
positive law
    Aquinas and, 430
    Grotius and, 659
    Hobbes and, 680, 684–685
    Montaigne and, 565–566
    Portalis and, 960
    and succession, 705–706
post-Glossators, 439
Pothier, Madame, 815
Pothier, Robert Joseph, 730, 762, 813–836, *819,* 840, 898
    appraisals of, 836
    biography of, 814–820
    and "cause" in contract law, 831–833
    Daguesseau and, 811
    education of, 814–820
    in late life, 831–835
    and law as principle, 8
    and philosophy of law, 827–831
    publications of, 823–827
    as Royal Professor, 820–823
Pound, R., 409, 416, 425, 427, 431, 592, 712, 755, 760, 761, 832, 833
praetorian edict, 61, 84, 103, 825
praetor(s), 47, 58–59, 82–83, 541
Pragmatic Sanction of Bourges (1438), 608
The Praise of Folly (Erasmus), 577
precarium, 176, 194, 252
Preliminary Discourse for the Council of the State (Portalis), 958–959
Premonstratensians, 389
Previt, C. W., 197, 199, 222, 224, 225, 417, 469
Previté-Orton, 290, 470, 471
Prévost, Claude-Joseph, 893
Prévôst de la Jannès, Michel, 744, 811, 815, 816, 820, 823–825, 898
price edicts, 264
Principate (Rome), 68–88

Gaius and, 80–87
jurisconsults in, 75–78
law schools under, 78–80
Papinian and, 87–88
Quintilian and, 72–75
rhetoric in, 68–72
Ulpian and, 87–88
Principes du droit naturel (Barbeyrac), 711
Principes du droit politique (Barbeyrac), 711
Principii d'una nova scienza (Vico), 849
principle, law as, 7–10
Principle of Parsimony, 491–492
printing press, 518–521
Prior and Posterior Analytics (Aristotle), 400
Priscus, Iavolenus, 79
Priscus, Neratius, 79
private law
    and *Code Napoleon*, 951–953
    and French Revolution, 951–953
    Louis XIV and, 723–724
    by Portalis and Daguesseau, 930
    Pufendorf on, 692
Problems (Aristotle), 398
Proculus, 79–80, 97
Procureur Général, 778–779
Les professeurs de droit français de l'université de Bourges et les manuscrits de leurs cours (Chénon), 822
professors
    American, 25, 270, 486
    in England, 437–438
    in Germany, 437
    of other medieval universities, 370–375
    of University of Bologna, 356–365
    of University of Paris, 365–370
Proslogion (Anselm of Bec), 294, 296–298
Protagoras, 21
Protestants
    and Bible, 630
    and Catholic Reformation, 591
    Charles V and, 572
    and Council of Trent, 593–594
    Daguesseau and, 769
    and Edict of Nantes, 609
    and French Revolution, 945–946, 950
    Grotius and, 651
    Hobbes and, 683
    La Boétie and, 553
    and marriage, 906
    Montaigne and, 563
    and Old Testament, 574
    Portalis and, 934–935, 945, 950
    Pufendorf and, 710
    and secular natural law, 716
Provence, 510
Providentialism, 851
Provincial letters (Pascal), 740, 747
Prussia (West Prussia), 625, 690, 701, 888, 956
Pseudo-Isidore, 213, 216, 239, 341, 345
Ptolemy, Claudius, 624, 626, 627, 632
public law, Daguesseau on, 798–799
Pufendorf, Esias, 686, 688–689
Pufendorf, Samuel Baron von, 685–712, *702*
    arrangement of topics by, 699–700
    complete jurisprudence attempted by, 701–704
    Descartes and, 663
    Domat and, 753, 754, 759
    on equality, 707–710
    Grotius and, 660
    on human nature, 700–701
    influences on, 692–693
    and law as principle, 8
    legacy of, 710–712
    life of, 686–690
    Montesquieu and, 840
    and natural law, 697–698
    philosophical characteristics, 693–694
    and rise of middle class, 612
    and Scientific Revolution, 623
    on source of law, 694–697
    on the State, 704–705
    on succession and family, 705–707
    works and style of, 690–692
Pupillorum patrocinium, 539
Purgatory, 298

INDEX

Puritans, 622, 685
Pyrrho, 37, 41, 561, 563, 564, 567, 788
Pyrrhonians, 562, 786
Pythagoras, 9, 280

Q

Quebec, 614, 642
Quesnay, François, 889, 890, *890,* 890–891
Questiones Disputatae, 319
Quintilian, 72–75, 201, 517
Quispel, 134
Qur'an, 401–402

R

Rabelais, 446, 529
Racine, Jean, 737, 790
Radding, 302, 310–311
Raimon Lull, Blessed, 255
Rashdall, H., 170, 189, 342–343, 349, 353–355, 357–361, 363, 364, 369–371, 394, 431
Rationalism, 560
rationality, 886
Rawson, E., 50–52, 111–113
Rayes, de, 805
Raymond, Archbishop, 404
Raymond VIII, Count of Toulouse, 465
Raymond of Penaforte, 350, 390
Realism, 629, 645, 759
    Abelard and, 337
    Aquinas and, 413–416
    Descartes and, 663
    and Enlightenment, 881
    Gratian and, 351
    Grotius and, 658
    and law as principle, 8
    Nominalism vs., 9, 153
    Pufendorf and, 696
    William of Ockham and, 488
Realism–Nominalism controversy, 504, 505, 524
real property, 251
Reason and Society in the Middle Ages (Murray), 136

Recceswinth, Visigoth king, 206
Recherches historiques et biographiques sur Pothier, publiées à l'occasion de l'érection de sa statue (Frémont), 814
rectorships, 355
Red Book of the Exchequer, 179
Reese, W. L., 41
Reeve, Tapping, 83, 270
Réflexions sur la monarchie universelle in Europe (Montesquieu), 850
Reformation, 572–591, 607, 650. *See also* Catholic Reformation
    Calvin and, 583–591, *587*
    and canon law, 605–608
    Church in period preceding, 575
    and Enlightenment, 884
    Erasmus and, 575–577, *576*
    Luther and, 577–583
    overview, 572–575
    and universities, 375
    and the universities, 606–608
    William of Ockham and, 497
Reformed Churches, 6, 585, 650
Refussus, 370
Regents, 731
Reigersberg, Maria van, 652–653, 652–655
religion
    Montesquieu, 949–950
    Napoleon on, 945–946
    Portalis and, 942, 946–949
religious politics, Grotius and, 650–651
Rembrandt, 651
Rémy, Joseph, 750
Republic (Plato), 31, 773, 860
Rerum memorandarum (Petrarch), 509
Res cottidianae (Gaius), 83
Reventlau, Count, 938, 939
Reventlau, Countess, 939
Révigny, Jacques de, 440, 441
Revolutionary Tribunal, 918
Rhenish codes, 888
Rheticus, Georg, 626
rhetoric
    in Carolingian education, 201
    in Dominate, 95–96
    Gratian and, 347
    and Isocrates, 24–25

in Principate, 68–72
in Rome, 52–56
and Sophists, 22
Rhetorics (Alcuin), 237
Ricci, Ostilio, 631
Richard I, King of England, 308
Richard II, Duke, 235
Richelieu, Cardinal, 656, 719, 900
Richter, Melvin, 843
Rights of Man, 500
Robert, abbot of Molême, 283
Robert, Duke of Normandy, 240
Robert, King of Naples, 450, 510
Robespierre, Maximilian, 840, 884, 907, *908,* 918, 937
Robin Hood, 250
Robinson, C. E., 28
Robinson, J. H., 506, 507
Robinson, O. F., 650, 660
Rodes, R. E., 344, 350, 380
Roederer, Comte, 945
Roger II de Hauteville, 244, 245
Rogerius, 321, 322
Rollin, Prof., 810
Rollo, 231, 233, 240
Roman Catholic Church. *See also* Catholic Reformation; Reformation
    and abbots, 174–175
    Anselm and, 291–300
    Benedictine government service, 179–181
    Benedictine land management, 175–179
    and Benedictines, 171–174
    and bishops, 169–171
    during Carolingian Renaissance, 282–300
    Charlemagne and, 194, 199–200
    Constantine I and, 137–141
    in development of law, 6
    and Donation of Constantine, 141–144
    early, 132–181
    and education, 154–159
    feudalism and, 260
    and Franks, 191–192
    and French Revolution, 909, 926–927
    Gratian and, 348
    Hobbes and, 683
    and indulgences, 581, *581*
    and its people, 168–169
    Jesus and, 132–137
    and Lateran IV, 385
    and law, 146–150
    and *Les lettres persanes* (Montesquieu), 846
    and medieval intellect, 150–154
    Montesquieu and, 842
    in Napoleonic France, 949
    and natural law, 716
    and Norman Conquest, 243
    papal "revolution" in, 284–291
    in period preceding Reformation, 575
    philosophers of, 159–168
    and *philosophes,* 883–884
    philosophy of, 144–146
    Portalis and, 942
    royal power vs., 418–422
    and university students, 373
    William of Ockham and, 499
Roman Iron Age, 187
Roman juridical system, fall of, 130–132
Roman law, 505, 522, 608
    Beaumanoir and, 459
    coloni in, 250
    as custom, 454
    in France, 533–534
    perception of, in England, 270
    tribal law vs., 204–205
Roman numerals, 280
Romanus, Aedgidius, 448
Romauld, 342
Rome and Romans, 43–121
    agriculture, 248–249
    constitution of, 45–48
    decline of, 130–132
    Dominate, 88–101
    education, 48–52
    jurisconsults, 56–68
    Justinian, 101–108
    legal legacy, 120–121
    legal science, 44
    Montesquieu and history of, 850–852

INDEX

Petrarch's view of, 507, 510, 513
and philosophy of law, 108–120
Principate, 68–88
rhetoric, 52–56
Romulus Augustus, 142
Roscelin, 8, 330, 488, 623
Rotterdam, 650
Rousseau, Jean-Jacques, *883,* 884
and French Revolution, 917–918
Montaigne and, 555, 564
Montesquieu and, 840
in order of *philosophes,* 881
Portalis and, 931
Pufendorf and, 710
Routh (Jesuit), 874
royal law, customs vs., 460–461
royal lawyers, 471–473
royal national states, 435–501
and the Commentators, 439–453
England as, 436–439
France as, 462–501
practicing lawyers in, 453–462
royal power, Roman Catholic Church and, 418–422
Royal Professors, 730, 731, 820–823
Royal Society, 636, 637
Rudolf I of Hapsburg, Holy Roman Emperor, 417
Rudolf II, Holy Roman Emperor, 630
Rule of Augustine, 284
Runnymede, 261
Russell, Bertrand, 388, 491, 572, 586–587, 593

S

Sabinian law school, 79, 81, 97
Sabinius, Caelius, 79
Sabinius, Massurius, 79, 83
Sabunde, Raymund de. *See* Sebond, Raymond
Sadoleto, 588
St. Amour, Guillaume de, 410
St. Bartholomew's massacre, 544, 609
St. Genevieve college, 365
St. Giulia of Brescia (manor), 255
St. Victor abbey, 365
Sainte-Beuve, C. A., 719, 746, 931

Saint Etienne (monastery), 176
Saint-Martin, Jean de, 569
Saint-Pierre, Abbé de, 802, 805, 810
Saint-Ruth, Marquis de, 769
Saisset, Bernard, 470
salons, 847
Salvator mundi, 470
Satyricon (Capella), 201
Savigny, Friedrich Karl von, 80, 515, 971
Saxons, 225–227
Scaevola, Q. Cervidius, 87
Scaliger, Joseph Justus, 647
Scandinavia and Scandinavian influences, 184–245, 573, 583
Carolingian heritage, 218–221
Celts, 184–186
Cimbri, 186
early migrations, 187–212
Franks, 189–217
Iron Ages, 186–187
Lombards, 188–189
Ottonian revival, 221–245
Schama, S., 908
Scholasticism, 512, 602
Schulz, F., 44, 52, 53, 60, 62–64, 66, 67, 78, 79, 83, 84, 88, 92–94, 96, 104–105, 107, 109, 542, 963
Schwartz, Joshua, 689
Schweinburg, E. F., 661
scientific method, 622, 637
Scientific Revolution, 620–623, 645
Kepler and, 631
Montaigne and, 566–568
Scipio Africanus, 509
Scotists, 576
Scotus, Duns, 495
scutage, 270
Sebond, Raymond, 554–555, 563
Séchelles, Hérault de, 896
"second scholastics," 651
Secret (Petrarch), 512
Séguier, Antoine-Louis, 933
Seidler, M., 658, 674, 687–690, 701, 711
seigneur, 251
Selden, John, 677, 697
Sellery, G. C., 471, 517
Senate, Roman, 47–48

Seneca, 72, 542, 560, 585, 653
serfdom, 16, 192, 617
Servan, 934
Severinus, Anicius Manlius, 400
Severus, Alexander, 87, 88
Severus, patriarch of Antioch, 98
Severus, Septimius, 70, 77, 87
Sévigné, Madame de, 735, 777
Sextus Empiricus, 561–563, 564
Shackleton, R., 843, 844, 848–850, 855–857, 874
Shaftesbury, Anthony Ashley Cooper, 3rd Earl of, 800–801
share cropping, 255
Shelley, Percy Bysshe, 14
Shepherd, W. R., 226
Sic et Non (Abelard), 333, 337–338
Sieyès, Emmanuel-Joseph, 919
Silvester, Pope, 141–142
Simeon, 899
Siméon, Marguerite, 931
Siméon, Sextius, 931
Simonides, 18
Sismond, Father, 745
Skepticism, 38–41, 559–563
slavery, 249, 252, 613, 709
Smith, Adam, 801, 889, 891
Smith, Clarence, 441, 457
Snell (laws of refraction), 622
Social Contract, 500, 662
social status, 252–253
Society for Legislative Studies, 970
sociology of law, 868–873
Socrates, *27,* 790
    on Athenian democracy, 18
    and education, 20
    Gratian and, 347
    and litigation, 20
    methods of, used by Plato, 30
    as philosopher, 26–29
    Plato and, 164
    and rhetoric, 25
Socratic approach, 28
soils, light vs. strong, 249
Solitaires, 736, 737
Solon, 16, 17, *17,* 18
Somme rural (Bautillier), 461
Sonnino, Paul, 718
Sophists, 561

Aristotle and, 32
in Athens, 21–25
and education, 20–21
Gratian and, 347
and law as principle, 7
on study of law, 15–16
Sophocles, 25–26
Sorbonne, *328,* 485, 739, 740
Sorbonne, Robert de, 485
Sorel, A., 961, 964, 970, 972–973
Soto, Dominic, 602
Southern, R. W., 126–129, 150, 180, 341, 343, 377
sovereigns, Hobbes on authority of, 684
Sozzini, Bartolommeo, 523
Spain
    Catholic Reformation in, 591–592
    medieval universities in, 370
    and New World, 613–614
Spanish Netherlands, 647
Spinoza, Baruch, 297
Spiritual Exercises (Loyola), 596–597, 599
stagiaire, 734–735
Stagira, 32
Stalin, Joseph, 201
Staples, John, 585
Staples, Seth Perkins, 25, 270, 585
The State, Hugo Grotius on, 659–660
Steinbach, Gustave, 689
Stephen II, Pope, 141
Stevinus (Simon Stevin), 567, 628–629, 632, 656, 657
stock companies, 618
Stockholm, 618
Stoicism, 560, 561
    in Athens, 38–41
    Gratian and, 347
    and natural law, 424–425
    and philosophy of law, 111–115
Story, Joseph, 750, 836
Strasbourg, 588
student organizations, 354–355
studia, 319
studia humanitas, 505–506, 530–531
Suarez, Francisco, 600–605, *601,* 651
Suetonius, 72, 133
Suger, Abbot of St. Denis, 464

Sulla, 399
Sumatra, 649
Summa Contra Gentilis (Aquinas), 412
Summa manuscript, 320, 322
Summa Theologica (Aquinas), 411, 412, 415, 428
summulae, 320
Svein Forkbeard Haraldsson, 234
Sweden, 583, 656
Switzerland, 856
Sylvester II, Pope, 224
Symonds, J. A., 531
Syracuse, 29

T

tabelliones, 309
Tableau économique (Quesnay), 889
Table des matières de la Géometrie (Descartes), 668
Tacitus, 70, 72, 187
Taine, H., 840
tallage tax, 253
Talmud, 151
Tancred of Hauteville, 244
taxation
    in ancient Rome, 91, 250
    Charlemagne and, 180, 194
    Church and, 575
    Council at Constance and, 478
    Domat and, 759
    and French Revolution, 904
    Gratian and, 344
    Louis XII and, 482
    Montesquieu and, 854, 857, 868
    Norman Conquest and, 244
    in North America, 615, 617
    Philip the Fair and, 467–469, 473
    physiocrats and, 888, 891
    Portalis and, 941, 944
Tempier, Bishop, 478, 505
tenant(s)
    and *Code Napoleon,* 968
    in England, 269
    French landlords, 617
    in late Roman era, 250, 442
    and manorial system, 178, 251–257

    under Scandinavians, 230
tenants' assembly, 256–257
Tennis Court Oaths, 880
tenure, ownership vs., 253
Teodora, 409
terrorism, 662
Tertullian (Quintus Septimius Florens Tertullianus), 155–157, *156,* 227, 407, 414
testimony, 256
Tetzel, John, 582
Teutones, 187
Teutonic Knights, 390
Thaumassière, 898
Thaumaturgus, Gregory, 95
thegnage, 268
Themis, *9,* 16, 814, 973
Theodius I, Roman Emperor, 139, 166
Theodius II, Roman Emperor, 94, 97
Theodora, Empress of Byzantium, 303
Theodora, Empress regnant of Rome, 101, *102*
Theodoric the Great, 143, 188, 206, 400, 401
Theodosian Code, 745
Theodosius, 537
Theologia Naturalis (Montaigne), 554
Theologica Aristotelis, 405
Theophano, 221, 223
Theophilus, 104, 106, 522
Theophrastus, 37–38, *38,* 399
Theutberga, Queen, 217
Third Estate, 902–903
Thirty Years' War, 630, 642, 655, 656, 659, 686
Thomas, Saint, 153, 296, *396*
Thomasin of Zirclaria, 374
Thomasius, Christian, 710, 888
Thomas of Chartres, 330
Thomists, 576
Thompson, J. W., 138, 140, 143, 193
Thorgeir, 234
The Three Books Against the Simoniacs (Humbert), 287
Tillet, Louis de, 585
Timon, 41, 561
tithe(s)
    bishops and, 170
    and *Code Napoleon,* 951

Gregory VII and, 290
and monasteries/abbacies, 264
parishes and, 198
Toletus, 602
Tolomeo of Lucca, 409
Tomkeieff, O. G., 168, *172,* 179, 233
Tonelli, Georgio, 711–712
Topics (Aristotle), 237, 400
Torricelli, Evangelista, 622
Toulouse, 535
Toulouse, Count of, 384
town charters, 455
trade, 615–616
Traité des lois (Domat), 749–750, 758, 773
Traité du monde (Descartes), 667
A Treatise on Maritime Contracts of Letting to Hire (Pothier), 836
A Treatise on the Law of Obligations, or Contracts (Pothier), 828
Treaty of Westphalia, 656
Treilhard, 956
Très ancien coutumier de Normandie, 267, 456
trials
    in ancient Rome, 46, 55, 91
    Curia Regis and, 466
    in England, 384
    Louis XIV and, 721
    Louis XVI and, 896
    and manorial system, 256
    Montesquieu and, 844
    Pothier and, 818
tribal law, Roman law vs., 204–205
Tribonian, 103, *103,* 337, 537, 565, 825, 928
Trinity College, 635
"The Triumph of Julius Caesar" (Mantegna), *10*
Tronchet, François-Denis, 914, 954–955, 960
Truce of God, 149, 260
Tully, J., 689–692, 694–698, 701–703, 705–709, 712
Turgot, Anne Robert Jacques, 868, 889, 895
Tuscianus, 79
Twain, Mark, 518, 519
Twelve Tables, 56–57

Tyler, Wat, 572
Tyranion, 399–400

U

Uguccio of Pisa, 375
Ulfjot of Lon, 233
Ullmann, W., 139, 141–143, 152, 159, 168, 189, 193–195, 198–200, 202–204, 211, 214, 216, 344, 361, 413, 443, 451
Ulpian (Domitius Ulpianus), 87, 92, 93
    in Berytus law school, 99
    birthplace of, 78
    and command, 538
    in *Digest,* 104
    Grotius and, 657
    Montaigne and, 565
    and philosophy of law, 110–111
    and Principate, 87–88
    Pufendorf and, 694
Unam Sanctam, 471
Unigenitus, 779, 783, 815, 893
United Provinces, 650, 652
United States Bill of Rights, 904
United States Constitution, 840, 950
universalia, 8
universalism
    Abelard and, 333–336
    Boethius and, 401
    William of Ockham and, 488
Université de Jurisprudence, 920
universities
    canon law at medieval, 370, 372–375, 381
    and Dominicans, 393–394
    in Enlightenment, 897–900
    and Franciscans, 393–394
    in French Revolution, 909–910
    Innocent III and, 380
    in Italy, 482
    and mendicant orders, 388
    papal control of, 478
    rectorship in, 355
    and Reformation, 606–608
    secular control of, in France, 478–487

INDEX   1033

University of Aix-en-Provence, 370, 930, 931
University of Angers, 370, 371
University of Avignon, 370, 371, 535, 727
University of Basel, 590
University of Berlin, 80
University of Bologna, 153, 370, 506, 508, 527, 535, 625
    Bartolus at, 444
    canon law and professors at, 356–365
    canon law and students at, 352–356
    Cino at, 441
    Gratian and, 347
    University of Paris vs., 366–367
University of Bordeaux, 370, 842
University of Bourges, 370, 727, 745, 821–822, 910
University of Caen, 370
University of Cahors, 898
University of Dijon, 900
University of Douai, 900
University of Ferrara, 370, 625
University of Heidelberg, 687
University of Holy Roman Court, 370, 372
University of Jena, 686
University of Leipzig, 686
University of Lerida, 370
University of Leyden (Leiden), 647, 687–688
University of Louvain, 737
University of Lund, 688–689
University of Montpellier, 370, 371, 471, 506–508
University of Nantes, 370
University of Naples, 370, 409–410
University of Orléans, 369, 371, 648, 811, 814, 820–821, 823, 910
    Commentators in, 440
    customary law at, 457
    de Belleperche at, 472
    de Villepreux at, 472
    Grotius and, 648
University of Padua, 370
University of Paris
    Aquinas and, 408, 410–411
    Aristotle and, 406, 407
    Calvin and, 584
    canon law at, 365–370
    colleges at, 485
    colleges for poor students at, 479
    Cujas at, 535
    Daguesseau and, 768
    Domat and, 745
    Erasmus and, 576
    and Estates General, 480
    Glossators and, 327
    Gratian and, 350–351
    and Humanism, 524
    Innocent III and, 380
    Innocent III at, 375
    Loyola and, 597
    and Mendicant Orders, 394
    Petrarch and, 510, 523
    role of, in politics, 480
    teaching reforms in late 17th century, 727–729, 731
University of Pavia, 370, 527
University of Perugia, 370, 447
University of Piacenza, 370
University of Pisa, 523, 631, 632
University of Poitiers, 192, 732, 910
University of Prague, 481
University of Reims, 910
University of Salamanca, 370, 597
University of Siena, 370, 523
University of Strasbourg, 900
University of Toulouse, 370, 431
University of Valence, 370, 727
University of Vienna, 496
University of Wittenberg, 580
Uprauda. *See* Justinian
Urban II, Pope, 152, 156, 282, *283*
Urban IV, Pope, 386, 394, 417
Urban VI, Pope, 476
Urban VIII, Pope, 633, 634, 740

V

Valaincourt, 785, 786
Valens, 79
Valentinan, 96
Valla, Lorenzo, 515–518
Vallière, Marquis de la, 782

Varro, 201
Vasquez, 602
vassals, 262–269
Veer, Kornelis van der, 654
venality of offices, 547–550
Venice, 508–509, 632
Vergennes, 901
Verger, J., 352, 355, 360, 371–374, 380, 432, 479–487, 498
Vernet, J., 856
Verona, 80
Verona codex, 508
Versini, Laurent, 858, 862
Vesalius, Andreas, 626
via moderna, 590
Vico, Giovanni, 704–705, 849
Vienna, 848
Vikings, 227–231
village assembly, 256
villages, self-governing, 255, 257
villas, 248–249
villeins, 254
Villepreux, Phillipe de, 472–473
Villey, M., 7, 85, 111, 114–119, 413, 420, 425, 431, 487, 495, 498, 499, 500, 673
Villey, P., 558, 559, 562–563, 644
Vinogradoff, P., 94, 130, 205–207, 457, 459
violence, 659, 660
vir de plebe, 285
Virgil, 72, 769
Virginia, 615
Visconti, Giovanni, 511
Visigoths
    origins of, 187–188
    Roman laws of, 126
    sack of Rome by, 128, 161, 418
Vitalis, Odericus, 236, 237
Voeltzel, R., 743–752, 754–757
Voltaire, 600, 635, 740, 801, 840, 881, 883–884, *885,* 935
Voysin, Chancellor, 780
Vreeland, H., 648, 652–654
Vulgate Bible, 139, 157–159, 313, 517

W

Waldrada, 217
Walpole, Horace, 840
Walter, Hubert, 266
war and warfare, 189, 277, 308, 642, 660
Warnerius. *See* Irnerius
Watson, A., 44, 66
Watzelrode, Lucus, 625
Wealth of Nations (Smith), 891
Wehberg, H., 691–692
Weigel, Erhard, 686, 687, 692, 699
Weinberg, J. R., 334–338, 408, 415, 491, 492, 494, 495
West Goths, 187. *See also* Visigoths
Wieruszowski, H., 338, 343, 366, 369
Wigmore, John H., 7, 27, 126
William of Champeaux, 330–331, 335
William of Dijon, 240
William of Moerbeke, 410
William of Normandy (William the Conqueror), 108, 176, *182, 183,* 233, 235, 240–244, *242,* 260, 262, 269, 285–286
William of Ockham, 8, 487–501
    Aquinas and, 432
    and end of Middle Ages, 504
    Grotius and, 657
    and natural law, 759
    Pufendorf and, 696
    and rise of Humanism, 504–506, 572, 578, 580, 586
    and rise of middle class, 612
    and Scientific Revolution, 620, 623, 629
    and sovereignty, 477
    Suarez and, 604
William of Orange, 650
William of Volpiano, 235, 240
William Rufus, King of England, 292
William "the Pious" of Aquitaine, 173
William the Silent, 647
Willielmus de Cabriano, 321
Wittenberg, 579–580
Wodham, Adam, 496
Wolff, Christian, 601, 710, 711–712, 887–888

Woolf, C. N. S., 417, 422, 446–449, 451
world state, Hugo Grotius on, 660
World War II, 968
written law, customs vs., 453–454
Wyclif, John, 481
Wytenbogaert, Johannes, 651

X

Xenophon, 26–27

Y

Yale Law School, 25
Yale University, 8, 270

Ynerius. *See* Irnerius
"youths," 220, 259–260

Z

Zacharias, Pope, 309
Zacharias the Rhetor, 98
Zasius, 528, 542
Zeno, 39–41, *40,* 560
zero, 280–281, 283
Zimmerman, R., 761–762
Zulueta, F. de, 81, 83–86, 110, 111
Zwingli, Ulrich, 585